Las Vegas

timeout.com/las-vegas

Time Out Guides Ltd
Universal House
251 Tottenham Court Road
London W1T 7AB
United Kingdom
Tel: +44 (0)20 7813 3000
Fax: +44 (0)20 7813 6001
Email: guides@timeout.com
www.timeout.com

Published by Time Out Guides Ltd, a wholly owned subsidiary of Time Out Group Ltd.
Time Out and the Time Out logo are trademarks of Time Out Group Ltd.

© Time Out Group Ltd 2012
Previous editions 1998, 2000, 2001, 2003, 2005, 2007.

10 9 8 7 6 5 4 3 2 1

This edition first published in Great Britain in 2012 by Ebury Publishing.
A Random House Group Company
20 Vauxhall Bridge Road, London SW1V 2SA

Random House Australia Pty Ltd 20 Alfred Street, Milsons Point, Sydney, New South Wales 2061, Australia

Random House New Zealand Ltd 18 Poland Road, Glenfield, Auckland 10, New Zealand

Random House South Africa (Pty) Ltd Isle of Houghton, Corner Boundary Road & Carse O'Gowrie, Houghton 2198, South Africa

Random House UK Limited Reg. No. 954009

Distributed in the US and Latin America by Publishers Group West (1-510-809-3700)
Distributed in Canada by Publishers Group Canada (1-800-747-8147)

For further distribution details, see www.timeout.com.

ISBN: 978-1-84670-196-2

A CIP catalogue record for this book is available from the British Library.

Printed and bound in Great Britain by Butler Tanner & Dennis, Frome, Somerset.

The Random House Group Limited supports The Forest Stewardship Council (FSC®), the leading international forest certification organisation. Our books carrying the FSC label are printed on FSC® certified paper. FSC is the only forest certification scheme endorsed by the leading environmental organisations, including Greenpeace. Our paper procurement policy can be found at www.randomhouse.co.uk/environment

Time Out carbon-offsets its flights with Trees for Cities (www.treesforcities.org).

MIX
Paper from
responsible sources
FSC® C023561

Contents

WHENEVER, WHEREVER YOU NEED MONEY...

WE GET IT THERE IN 10 MINUTES*

WELCOME TO Fabulous LAS VEGAS NEVADA

CHOICE IS IN YOUR HANDS℠

1. Arrange for the person sending the money to visit a MoneyGram agent near them. After sending the money, they will give you a reference number.

2. Find your nearest MoneyGram agent at **www.moneygram.com** or anywhere you see the MoneyGram sign.

3. Give the reference number and your ID** to the MoneyGram agent.

4. Fill out the simple form or pick up the MoneyGram phone to receive your money.

1-800-MONEYGRAM® MONEYGRAM.COM

Introduction

'The World's Playground,' they call it. 'What happens here, stays here,' runs the famous ad. However they try to sell it, the one constant in Las Vegas is change. But while the landscape goes through endless metamorphoses, the core Vegas concept – bring your money and go nuts – stays the same. Slot machine exposure still starts in the baggage claim area at McCarran Airport. Hookers still flourish under the thinnest of 'escort service' veils. And in the majority of bars, there's still no such thing as last call.

What's changed most about today's Vegas is a matter of scope. No longer fully satisfied with its 'adult Disneyland' identity, this century-old frontier town now wants to grow up into a world-class city. It's an aspiration reflected not only in what's rushing to fill the vacuum left by vanishing buildings, but in the new images sported by a number of the ones that are still standing. The concerted revamping projects on the Strip are made a good deal easier by the fact that most of the big hotels are now owned by the same corporation. On the Strip's four-mile Monopoly board, the MGM Mirage group is in the lead, with a portfolio of properties comprising the MGM Grand, the Bellagio, the Mirage, Mandalay Bay, the Luxor, New York New York, the Excalibur, the Monte Carlo and Circus Circus. It also developed and owns the new crown jewel, the CityCenter complex, as well. In other words, about half the Strip, and roughly 50 per cent of its 80,000+ hotel rooms. Harrah's controls around half the remainder in the shapes of Caesars Palace, Paris Las Vegas, the Imperial Palace, the Flamingo, Bally's and its namesake resort. The dizzying number of deals that have lit up the Vegas business pages are all part of a tightening food chain that closely follows a national trend toward dry, megacorporate entities. It seems a particularly heartbreaking compromise for a town built on a foundation of libertarianism that bordered, at times, on anarchy.

There has been no bigger swing in Vegas's image than in the changing demographic face of its visitors – which is reflected most visibly in its nightlife (and in the attendant new pool-party concept dubbed 'daylife'). See-and-be-seen dance clubs and so-called ultralounges have become screamingly popular over the last few years, ever since someone realised that 20,000 square feet of space without slots could still yield big profits if it was tricked out with state-of-the-art lighting effects, sturdy cover charges and wallet-draining bottle-service policies. As such, casinos now market ethereal, monosyllabically named bars and clubs as aggressively as they hawk their poker rooms. And – more than anywhere else in the world – celebrities, particularly reality stars – reign supreme. *Joe Brown, Editor*

Get the local experience

Over 50 of the world's top destinations available.

Las Vegas in Brief

IN CONTEXT

Our In Context section examines the development of Las Vegas from the open land used by Paleo-Indians, through the impact of Mormon missionaries, to the 24/7 international playground it is today, catering to visitors drawn by the headliners and big-budget shows, the swanky hotels, the increasingly excellent food, the fashionably nightlife and, of course, the possibility of instant riches.
▶ *For more, see pp15-66.*

SIGHTS

The Strip is newly hip, beckoning twentysomethings who couldn't care less about Wayne Newton or prime-rib buffets with an explosion of all-night dance clubs and swanky lounges. The latest pre-crash wave of construction reshaped the skyline with casino-resorts, high-rise condos and mixed-use properties that are virtual cities of their own – such as the new CityCenter complex.
▶ *For more, see pp67-96.*

CONSUME

For years, the choice of cuisine didn't extend far beyond all-you-can-eat buffets, 24-hour coffeeshops and swanky steakhouses. But in the past decade or two, casino moguls have spent millions luring the world's best chefs to the city. Meanwhile, shopping opportunities have multiplied with glamorous new malls like Crystals, while hip hotels like Cosmopolitan have joined the city's ranks of megahotels.
▶ *For more, see pp97-214.*

ARTS & ENTERTAINMENT

Las Vegas calls itself 'the entertainment capital of the world,' and arguably it is, although here the new is almost inevitably the old, recycled, remixed, repackaged. The musical headliners are won't frighten your parents (Celine Dion, Donny & Marie, Barry Manilow). And there are no fewer than seven Cirque productions in town, with at least one more – a Michael Jackson tribute – on the way.
▶ *For more, see pp216-275.*

ESCAPES & EXCURSIONS

Believe it or not, there's life – and even nature! – beyond the manmade neon skyscape. Daytrip options include the Hoover Dam, one of the world's modern marvels; the fiery escarpments of Red Rock Canyon and Valley of Fire State Park; the snowscapes (and skiing) of Mount Charleston; and, of course, the jawdropping grandeur of the Grand Canyon.
▶ *For more, see pp277-306.*

Las Vegas in 48 Hrs

Day 1 Walk the Walk

9AM It's longer than it looks, and often hotter than Hades, but every visitor should stroll the length of the Strip at least once, to get the measure of its absurdity. Start with the **Fabulous Las Vegas sign**, in the middle of Las Vegas Boulevard, near Mandalay Bay (*see p109*). Have an indoor and outdoor look at the oddest and somehow most fabulous of the Vegas casino buildings, the sci-fi-looking black glass pyramid that is the **Luxor** (*see p118*).

11AM Continuing north on the Strip, **New York New York** (*see p121*) is worth a peek, for its simulacrum of Manhattan's streetscapes and shops – make time for the rollercoaster, which goes careening skyward, offering an upside down view of the Strip. Push on north, to the magnificent heart of the Strip. The new **CityCenter** complex (*see p33*), is vast, but its main points of interest are the gorgeous **Aria** casino-hotel (*see p102*) and the high-end **Crystals** shopping centre (*see p194*). Go next door to the **Cosmopolitan** (*see p107*), the hippest hotel on the Strip. Head upwards to third floor, a people-watching haven ringed with restaurants; its time for lunch.

3PM Catch the monorail that connects CityCenter and the Bellagio; and make sure you're in a good viewing spot for one of the on-the-half-hour performances of the famous, fabulous fountains; also have a look at the scrumptious chocolate fountain – the world's largest – inside, at **Jean-Phillippe Patisserie** (*see p103*). By now you may be ready for a rest.

7PM It's dinner time and you've got options. Head for the **Venetian** (*see p112*) and have an Italianesque bite by the famous faux canal, with its singing gondoliers, perhaps.

9PM Nighttime is the right time for exploring Old Las Vegas, which predates the Strip and is still buzzing with its own seedy grandeur. Poke around the **Golden Nugget** (*see p140*), **Binions** (*see p141*), the **El Cortez** (*see p142*), and some of the other legendary redoubts that still carry more than a bit of the old-school swagger and style.

NAVIGATING THE CITY

Once you've made it to the fabled Las Vegas Strip – and to your casino-connected hotel room, the sparkling city is at your feet, made for enjoying by foot, by cab or hired car, bus or monorail.

A useful bus for tourists is the Deuce: the double-decker travels the length of Las Vegas Boulevard from the BTC in the north to just by I-215 in the south, stopping in front of all major casinos. Deuces are often busy, especially at night.

The Las Vegas Monorail is now running a reliable service along Paradise Road and then behind the Strip. However, it hasn't displaced the numerous hotel buses and monorails.

A car is recommended if you're staying away from the Strip or are keen to visit off-Strip attractions, and essential if you're planning to visit any out-of-town destinations. Most car-hire agencies are at or near the airport. Call around for the best rate, booking well in advance if

Day 2 Away From the Strip

9AM You'll need a cab to explore these off-Strip highlights. Start the day with an only-in-Las Vegas experience that doesn't involve gambling – well, at least not with money. At **Vegas Indoor Skydiving** (*see p81*), you can free-fall in an indoor 21ft vertical wind tunnel that generates air speeds of up to 130mph. After an hour of instruction, you get 15 minutes of flying time. This is best experienced before lunch...

11AM Another only-in-Vegas attraction – the **Atomic Testing Museum** (*see p80*). Relatively few know how near Vegas was to the Nevada Test Site, the US's principal on-continent nuclear weapons testing facility from 1951 to 1992. The story the museum tells is fascinating: how nuclear power came to represent the future, how it came to be something approaching a tourist attraction in this most carefully blasé of states and – most crucially, and in layman's terms – how it actually works.

12.30PM A quick spin to the west side of town, to visit **Las Vegas Springs Preserve** (*see p92*), an experiential ecological museum, and a huge site given over to botanical gardens, nature trails and a number of conservation-oriented exhibits. While you're there, why not take time for lunch at the sustainability minded, on-site café by celebrity chef Wolfgang Puck. It offers picnic-style dining with wonderful vistas of the desert and the city.

6PM Here's a more eccentric and entirely more urban jaunt: the gritty, quirkily fascinating **Commercial Center** (*see p80*), a nondescript enclosure surrounding a 28-acre parking lot. Diverse tenants include an underground theatre company (Insurgo Theater Movement), at least two sex clubs and a swingers' lounge, an ice-hockey rink, a cluster of jovial (and very different) gay bars, and shops specialising in wigs and other showgirl accessories, karaoke joints, nail spas and more. While you're at the Commercial Center, you'll want to visit its chief attraction – and chief anomaly – the internationally recognised Thai restaurant, **Lotus of Siam** (*see p170*), perhaps followed by a nightcap in one of the Center's one-of-a-kind bars.

you're planning to visit over a holiday weekend or for a major convention.

There are taxi ranks outside most hotels, and restaurants and bars will be happy to call a cab for you. Technically you're not allowed to hail a cab from the street and most won't stop if you try but it's usually OK to approach an empty cab with its light on.

Limousines are a flashy and popular way to get around, and are available for hire outside hotels and at the airport.

SEEING THE SIGHTS
Many of Las Vegas's attractions – the majority of them on or near the Strip – are free or close-to-free for visitors and open seven days a week.

PACKAGE DEALS
Las Vegas is big on package deals for hotels, flights, dining and entertainment – see visitlasvegas.com or the Las Vegas Convention & Visitors Authority's business-related website, lvcva.com, for more.

Las Vegas in Profile

THE STRIP

The most preposterous four-mile stretch in America. The Strip begins begins around Russell Road, where the classic **Welcome to Fabulous Las Vegas** sign reminds visitors of old Vegas. To the east is the **Little Church of the West** wedding chapel; dating from 1942, it's old in Vegas terms. Just north, the South Seas-themed **Mandalay Bay** effectively marks the beginning of the 21st-century Strip. Next to Mandalay Bay is the onyx

pyramid of the **Luxor**, with other huge resorts lining the Strip as it heads north: **MGM Grand**; **New York New York**, with its **Manhattan Express** rollercoaster; **Paris Las Vegas**; the **Bellagio**, the **Venetian**, with its gondola rides, and **Caesars Palace** among them. The key new development is the architecturally cutting-edge hotel-casino-condo-retail-dining complex **CityCenter**, home to **Crystals** shopping centre and the **Aria** hotel. Next door is the even more hip **Cosmopolitan**. North of Sands Avenue, the top-end **Wynn Las Vegas** has an artificial mountain as its star attraction. North of Convention Center Drive, the Strip quickly peters out into disrepair, with a few highlights: it's back to blazing neon at the 50-year-old **Riviera**, where life-size bronze statues promote the Crazy Girls; ageing **Circus Circus** features the Adventuredome indoor amusement park. Further north, across Sahara Avenue, is the **Stratosphere** resort, the tallest building in Nevada, featuring three thrill rides.
▶ *For more, see pp68-78.*

OFF-STRIP: EAST OF THE STRIP

Running parallel to the Strip, **Paradise Road** has been a site of major development since the 1960s. The showroom at the **Las Vegas Hilton** stages Elvis Presley's iconic shows, while the **Las Vegas Convention Center** is more responsible than any hotel for bringing visitors to Vegas. The **Atomic Testing Museum** tells the fascinating story of the role played by nuclear power in the US psyche, as well as how it actually works, while **Commercial Center** is a gritty, quirky Strip Mall.
▶ *For more, see pp79-81.*

OFF STRIP: WEST OF THE STRIP

The I-15 runs to the West of the Strip. Wedged next to it, **Frank Sinatra** drive offers a back-door access to many Strip hotels. On the northern side of Flamingo Road sits the Brazilian-themed **Rio**, with its tired but free *Masquerade Show in the Sky*, staged seven ties daily. Just past the Rio are the **Gold Coast** and the **Orleans**, a pair of locals' casinos with bowling alleys and other attractions. **Palms**, meanwhile, is a landmark resort, popular with a younger, more sophisticated clientele, attracted by nightclub **Moon** and music venue **Pearl**. Beyond here, Valley View Boulevard continues north; an easterly turn at Sahara Avenue leads past endless strip malls to the train-themed casino **Palace Station**.
▶ *For more, see pp81-82.*

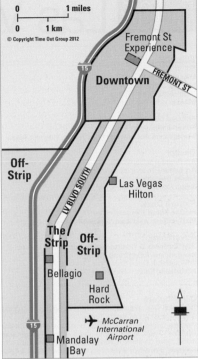

DOWNTOWN

Once the centre of Las Vegas, then a shadow of its former self, **Fremont Street** is the focus of a regenerated Downtown. The **Fremont Street Experience** mall is dominated by an LED-studded canopy, flickering into action on the hour each night with sound and light shows. There's a kitsch compendium of street performers and retail kiosks, but the casinos are the main draw, **Binion's**, the **Golden Nugget** and the **Plaza** among them. Also here, the open-air **Neon Museum** is a small collection of classic Vegas signs. Across Las Vegas Boulevard, Fremont Street has a seedier feel, but some chic venues, like the **Beauty Bar**, have found their way here. To the north, along Las Vegas Boulevard, sits the **Neon Boneyard**, a park full of historic signs, along with a series of low-key attractions: the **City of Las Vegas Galleries** in the Reed Whipple Cultural Center, the **Las Vegas Natural History Museum** and the **Lied Discovery Children's Museum**. Also nearby is the **Old Las Vegas Mormon Fort Historic Park**. The **Arts District** is bordered by Charleston, Las Vegas Boulevard, Wyoming Avenue and the railroad; its focal point is the **Arts Factory**, filled with galleries.

▶ For more, see pp83-89.

REST OF THE CITY

In north-west Las Vegas, **Charleston Boulevard** defines the southern edge of the 'planned community' of **Summerlin**. Further west, the **Red Rock** is the first billion-dollar off-Strip casino-hotel, while **Bonnie Springs Old Nevada** is a kitsch reconstruction of an old mining town. **Rancho Drive** leads also north-west out of town, past affluent neighbourhoods such as

the **Scotch 80s** and **Rancho Circle**. On its route, the **Southern Nevada Zoological National Park** has an interesting collection of of birds and reptiles indigenous to Nevada. Nearby is **Las Vegas Springs Preserve**, a desert-ecology themed attraction. The **University District** is an enclave of normality not far from the Strip. The stunning **Leid Library** and a beautiful desert garden compete for attention here, along with the **Marjorie Barrick Museum**, with displays on ancient and modern Vegas. South-east of the city centre, **Henderson** was founded as a company town, but now is home to **Ethel M Chocolates**. North-west of Henderson, across US95, **Green Valley** is technically part of Henderson.

▶ For more, see pp90-96.

Time Out Las Vegas

Editorial
Editor Joe Brown
Deputy Editor Ros Sales
Listings Editor Stacy Martin
Proofreader John Watson
Indexer Holly Pick

Editorial Director Ruth Jarvis
Editorial Manager Holly Pick
Management Accountants Clare Turner, Margaret Wright

Design
Art Director Scott Moore
Art Editor Pinelope Kourmouzoglou
Senior Designer Kei Ishimaru
Group Commercial Designer Jodi Sher

Picture Desk
Picture Editor Jael Marschner
Picture Desk Assistant/Researcher Ben Rowe

Advertising
New Business & Commercial Director Mark Phillips
International Advertising Manager Kasimir Berger
International Sales Executive Charlie Sokol
Advertising Sales (Las Vegas) Dorie Leo

Marketing
Senior Publishing Brand Manager Luthfa Begum
Guides Marketing Manager Colette Whitehouse
Group Commercial Art Director Anthony Huggins

Production
Group Production Manager Brendan McKeown
Production Controller Katie Mulhern

Time Out Group
Chairman & Founder Tony Elliott
Chief Executive Officer David King
Chief Operating Officer Aksel Van der Wal
Chief Technical Officer Remo Gettini
Group Financial Director Paul Rakkar
Group General Manager/Director Nichola Coulthard
Time Out Communications Ltd MD David Pepper
Time Out International Ltd MD Cathy Runciman
Time Out Cultural Development Director Mark Elliott
Group Marketing Director Andrew Booth

Contributors
This guide was updated, with additional writing throughout, by Joe Brown. **History** Will-Fulford Jones; Deke Castleman; Gregory Crosby. **Las Vegas Today** Joe Brown, David Surratt. **Architecture** Phil Hagen. **The Juice** Dayvid Figler. **Land of the Free** James Reza. **Gambling** Deke Castleman. **Casinos & Hotels** Will Fulford-Jones, Phil Hagen, Amy Schmidt (*Lavish Loos, Water, Water Everywhere* Joe Brown). **Sightseeing** Will Fulford-Jones, CM Buford, Dayvid Figler, Emily Richmond, Deke Castleman. **Restaurants & Buffets** Will Fulford-Jones, Al Mancini, James P Reza, Amy Schmidt. (*Sin City's Sweet Tooth* Joe Brown). **Bars & Lounges** Kate Silver. **Shopping** Amy Schmidt (*Tattoo You* Joe Brown). Calendar Beverly Bryan. Adult Entertainment James Reza. **Casino Entertainment** Joe Brown, Will Fulford-Jones, Julie Seabaugh. **Children** Phil Hagen. **Film** Mike Prevatt. **Galleries** Erika Pope. **Gay & Lesbian** Mike Prevatt. **Music** PJ Perez (*We Love the Daylife* Joe Brown). **Nightclubs** PJ Perez. **Sports & Fitness** Kate Silver. **Theatre & Dance** David Surratt, PJ Perez. **Weddings** Beverly Bryan, Renée Battle. **Escapes & Excursions** Will Fulford-Jones.

Maps john@jsgraphics.co.uk

Cover photography by Mitchell Funk.
Back cover photography by Jonathan Perugia, Luxor, Tom Donoghue.

Photography by Jonathan Perugia, except pages 3, 75, 76, 77 Songquan Deng/Shutterstock.com; page 7 (top) Tory Kooyman; page 7 (top left) Chee-Onn Leong/Shutterstock.com; pages 7 (middle right), 10 (middle), 28, 81, 97 167, 200, 201, 254 Mona Shield Payne; pages 7 (bottom left), 234 Tomasz Rossa; page 11 (top) Inggita Notosusanto/Shutterstock.com; page 16 Gamma-Rapho via Getty Images; page 20 Charles Zachritz/Shutterstock.com; page 24 Kevin Tietz/Shutterstock.com; page 32 Matt Carbone Photography; page 33 Tory Kooyman; page 34 Las Vegas News Bureau; page 39 Alamy; page 69 Helen & Vlad Filatov/Shutterstock.com; page 70 James Mattil/Shutterstock.com; page 72 Lowe Llaguno/Shutterstock.com; page 73 Las Vegas Convention and Visitors Authority; page 85 Golden Nugget; page 87 Tomas Muscionico; page 107 Thomas Hart Shelby; pages 53, 67, 112 (bottom), 116, 124, 128, 293, 296, 297, 299, 301, 302 Shutterstock.com; page 115 (top) Jose Gil/Shutterstock.com; page 126 (top) Reed Kaestner Photography; page 130 O'Gara/Bissell Photography; page 135 Erik Kabik; page 146 The Big Tom Project; page 213 Gary Krieg/Shutterstock.com; page 217 Feld Motor Sports Inc; page 231 Denise Truscello; page 232 RD/Kabik; page 247 (left) courtesy of Mark Moore Gallery, California; page 247 (right) Joan Adams; page 263 Walter G Arce/Shutterstock.com; page 264 Eric Broder Van Dyke/Shutterstock.com; page 268 Bill Hughes; page 270 JeffSpeer.com; page 277 Nickolay Stanev/Shutterstock.com; page 278 James M Phelps, Jr/Shutterstock.com; page 279 Alexey Kamenskiy/Shutterstock.com; page 280 Nagel Photography/Shutterstock.com; page 286 Brett Mulcahy/Shutterstock.com; page 290 Chris Geszvain/Shutterstock.com; pages 291, 305 (left) Tom Grundy/Shutterstock.com; page 292 William Silver/Shutterstock.com; page 295 Jorg Hackemann/Shutterstock.com; page 304 Mariia Sats/Shutterstock.com; page 305 (right) Peter Weber/Shutterstock.com; page 306 Krzysztof Wiktor/Shutterstock.com.

The following images were supplied by the featured establishment/artist: pages 10 (top), 15, 89, 102, 108, 111 (left and bottom), 123, 131, 132, 134, 137, 153, 154, 177, 192, 193, 196, 199, 220, 223, 224, 226, 227, 230, 233, 237, 246, 256, 257, 258.

About the Guide

GETTING AROUND
The back of the book contains street maps of Las Vegas, as well as overview maps of the city and its surroundings. The maps start on page 328; on them are marked the locations of hotels (❶), restaurants and cafés (❶), and pubs and bars (❶). The majority of businesses listed in this guide are located in the areas we've mapped; the grid-square references in the listings refer to these maps.

THE ESSENTIALS
For practical information, including visas, disabled access, emergency numbers, lost property, useful websites and local transport, please see the Directory. It begins on page 308.

THE LISTINGS
Addresses, phone numbers, websites, transport information, hours and prices are all included in our listings, as are selected other facilities. All were checked and correct at press time. However, business owners can alter their arrangements at any time, and fluctuating economic conditions can cause prices to change rapidly.

The very best venues in the city, the must-sees and must-dos in every category, have been marked with a red star (★). In the Sightseeing chapters, we've also marked venues with free admission with a FREE symbol.

PHONE NUMBERS
The area code for Las Vegas is 702. You don't need to use the code when calling from within Vegas: simply dial the seven-digit number as listed in this guide.

From outside the US, dial your country's international access code or a plus symbol, followed by the US country code (1), 702 for Las Vegas and the seven-digit number as listed in the guide. So, to reach the Bellagio, dial + 1 702 693 7111. For more on phones, including information on calling abroad from the UK and details of local mobile-phone access, *see p315*.

FEEDBACK
We welcome feedback on this guide, both on the venues we've included and on any other locations that you'd like to see featured in future editions. Please email us at guides@timeout.com.

Time Out Guides

Founded in 1968, Time Out has grown from humble beginnings into the leading resource for anyone wanting to know what's happening in the world's greatest cities. Alongside our influential weeklies in London, New York and Chicago, we publish more than 20 magazines in cities as varied as Beijing and Beirut; a range of travel books, with the City Guides now joined by the newer Shortlist series; and an information-packed website. The company remains proudly independent, still owned by Tony Elliott four decades after he launched *Time Out London*.

Written by local experts and illustrated with original photography, our books also retain their independence. No business has been featured because it has advertised, and all restaurants and bars are visited and reviewed anonymously.

ABOUT THE EDITOR
Joe Brown worked at the *Washington Post* and *San Francisco Chronicle*, before taking a gamble and moving to Las Vegas to work at the *Las Vegas Sun* newspaper and *Las Vegas Weekly* magazine. After three fascinating and infernal years in Vegas – during which he saw every show – he's back in the Bay Area, where he works as an editor at tech news website AllThingsD.com.

Your City Break doesn't have to cost the earth

Trees for Cities

Reduce the impact of your flight by donating to Trees for Cities

To donate, text 'TREE37' to 70070 or visit www.treesforcities.org

Trees for Cities, Prince Consort Lodge, Kennington Park, Kennington Park Place, London SE11 4AS
Tel. +44 (0)20 7587 1320; Charity registration 1032154

In Context

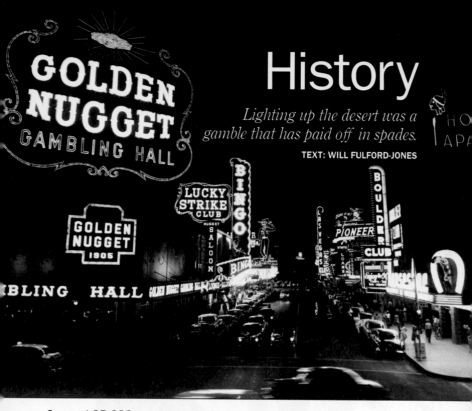

History

Lighting up the desert was a gamble that has paid off in spades.

TEXT: WILL FULFORD-JONES

Around 25,000 years ago, at the tail end of the last ice age, the large valley in which Las Vegas now sits was partly under water. Glaciers were retreating from the mountains that ring the Las Vegas Valley; the glacial run-off fed a vast lake, 20 miles wide and thousands of feet deep.

The Strip was built at what was once the deepest part of the lake. The lake's outlet was a river known now as the Las Vegas Wash; it flowed for only 40 miles, but was larger than any other river in the western United States. At its mouth, the Wash was swallowed by the monster waterway that had been carving the Grand Canyon for a couple of hundred million years, later named the Colorado River.

Palaeo-Indians lived in caves near the lake's shoreline, which receded as the climate changed gradually from cold and wet to warm and dry. The first Las Vegans shared the tule marsh at the edge of the lake with prehistoric horses, giant ground sloths, American camels and massive condors, and hunted big Pleistocene mammals (woolly mammoth, bison, mastodon and caribou) as early as 13,000 BC. Little is known about these early inhabitants. However, from 5,000 years ago, a clearer picture of the local prehistoric people begins to emerge.

'In 1830, Rafael Rivera named the area "Las Vegas" meaning "the Meadows".'

FROM HUNTER GATHERERS TO FARMERS

Hunter-gatherers known as Archaic Indians introduced a culture that evolved over four millennia. The area they occupied was by then desert, although spring water bubbled to the surface and flowed down the Las Vegas Wash (now a creek) to the canyon-carving Colorado River. Even so, it wasn't until the first centuries AD that signs of civilisation sprang up in and around Nevada's southern desert. By AD 500, they had evolved into an organised people: hunting with bows and arrows, making pottery, mining salt and trading with their neighbours.

Three centuries later, the Anasazi tribe was cultivating beans and corn in irrigated fields, living in 100-room pueblos, fashioning artistic pots and mining turquoise. Mysteriously, they disappeared from the area around 1150: perhaps due to disease, drought, overpopulation or war, though no one really knows for sure. A large Anasazi village was discovered in 1924; parts of it are now preserved at the Lost City Museum in Overton, north-east of Las Vegas.

Southern Paiutes, hunter-gatherers more like Archaic Indians than the Anasazi, claimed the abandoned territory, but they never achieved the advanced elements of their predecessors' society. For the next 700 years, the Paiutes remained semi-nomadic, establishing base camps of movable 'wickiups' (similar to tepees), cultivating squash and corn at the springs and creeks, and travelling seasonally to hunt and harvest wild foods. A frequent stopover on their travels was the Big Spring, the centre of a lush riparian habitat. Now known as the Las Vegas Springs Preserve, it opened as a park, visitor attraction and educational facility in 2007.

MEXICANS AND MORMONS

The first white men to enter the region, arriving in the early 19th century, were Mexican traders, who travelled along the Old Spanish Trail blazed by Franciscan friars to connect Spanish-Catholic missions scattered between New Mexico and the California coast. In 1830, three decades before the Civil War, Antonio Armijo set out from Santa Fe to trade goods along the trail. An experienced scout in his party by the name of Rafael Rivera found a short cut via the Big Spring, and became the first non-native to set foot on the land. He named the area Las Vegas, or 'the Meadows'.

By the time John C Fremont, a surveyor and cartographer for the Army Topographical Corps, passed through the Las Vegas Valley in 1845, the Old Spanish Trail had become the most travelled route through the Southwest. With Big Spring providing the only fresh water within a day's march, the area had become a popular camping spot. Having settled at the shore of the Great Salt Lake a few hundred miles further north-east, Latter-Day Saints also regularly passed through Las Vegas on their way to Los Angeles. Indeed, by the early 1850s, Mormon pioneer parties, wagon trains and mail carriers travelling between central Utah and southern California stopped at Big Spring with such frequency that Church elders decided to colonise the area.

In 1855, a party of Mormon missionaries was dispatched from Salt Lake City to establish a community at Las Vegas that would serve the travellers on the trail and convert the Paiute people. The missionaries erected a fort, dug irrigation ditches, cultivated crops and even managed to befriend some Indians. But the rigours of domesticating a vast desert proved beyond them. Crops failed and rations were meagre. Timber had to be hauled from the nearest mountainsides, 20 miles away.

Even so, the mission might have succeeded had the colonists not located deposits of lead nearby. The discovery attracted miners from Salt Lake City, whose need for food, lumber and shelter taxed the colonists' already inadequate supplies to breaking point. Despite the miners' vociferous objections, the colonists petitioned Salt Lake City to be recalled, and the mission was abandoned in 1858. A small remnant of the Mormon fort survives as the oldest standing structure in Las Vegas.

OD GASS AND HELEN STEWART

Soon after the Mormons abandoned Las Vegas, prospectors picked up where the lead miners left off and discovered that the ore averaged a rich $650 per ton in silver. A small mining boomtown mushroomed in the desert around Big Spring. Miners who arrived too late to get in on the action fanned out from the settlement and found gold along the Colorado River, about 50 miles south-east of Las Vegas.

One of the gold-seekers, Octavius Decatur Gass, saw a more enticing opportunity: homesteading the well-watered valley. Craftily, Gass appropriated the Mormon fort in 1865, using the lumber to build a ranch house and utility shop. He dug irrigation canals, planted grain, vegetables and fruit trees, and ran cattle on a chunk of land known as Las Vegas Ranch. Over the next ten years, Gass expanded his land and water holdings, assumed civic duties and helped other homesteaders get established.

However, Gass's ambition eventually got the better of him. In financial trouble by the 1870s, he took a loan from Archibald Stewart, a rich rancher from the mining boomtown of Pioche. When, in 1881, Gass couldn't repay the loan, Stewart foreclosed on it and took over the Las Vegas Ranch, expanding the property until he was shot dead in 1884 after an argument with a ranch hand from a neighbouring spread. Stewart's wife Helen ran the ranch for the next 20 years, buying up more acreage, making a living in the livestock business, and running a resort for nearby ranchers and a campground for travellers on the Mormon Trail.

The San Pedro, Los Angeles & Salt Lake Railroad arrived in 1903, its planned route running through the heart of the ranch. Thanks to its strategic location and plentiful water, Las Vegas had been designated a division point for crew changes, a service stop for through trains and, eventually, a site for maintenance shops. Ready to retire, Mrs Stewart sold most of her 2,000-acre site for $55,000, but deeded ten acres to the Paiutes, who'd been reduced to living on the edge of town through government largesse. For this and other civic-minded deeds, Stewart is considered the First Lady of Las Vegas.

In preparation for the land sale, Stewart hired JT McWilliams to survey her property. The canny McWilliams discovered and immediately claimed 80 untitled acres just west of the big ranch, planned a town site and began selling lots to a steadfast group of Las Vegas 'sooners' (the earliest speculators on the scene). In late 1904, two railroad construction crews, one from the north-east and one from the south-west, converged on Las Vegas Valley. And then, in January 1905, a golden spike was driven into a tie near Jean, Nevada, 23 miles south of Las Vegas, ceremonially completing the railroad.

GAMBLING ON PROSPERITY

McWilliams's settlement, known as Ragtown, was one of a long line of boomtowns that had been erupting across Nevada over the preceding 50 years. On the day the first train travelled through Big Spring on its route between Salt Lake City and Los Angeles, Ragtown's saloons, banks and tent hotels teemed with settlers, speculators, tradesmen and itinerants. But the San Pedro, Los Angeles & Salt Lake Railroad had other plans for the settlement. It organised a subsidiary, Las Vegas Land & Water, to build its own town.

Officials laid out the town site, scraped the scrub from 40 square blocks and staked 1,200 lots. The new town site of Las Vegas received national publicity, and demand for the land was high, with prospective buyers coming by train from Los Angeles ($16 return) and Salt Lake City ($20). Competition for locations proved so overwhelming that the railroad scheduled an auction, pitting eager settlers against Los Angeles real-estate speculators and East Coast investors. All were gambling on the prosperity of yet another western railroad boomtown.

Take Me to the Moon

The best-laid plans can fail to come to fruition.

If you hadn't noticed, Las Vegas is all about excess. You won't be able to move in the city without bumping into the world's largest this, the world's most luxurious that or the world's most expensive other thing. But for all the visions of grandeur that come to fruition, there are twice as many delusions that never make it past the planning stage.

Some of these plans are good ideas that, for whatever reason, can't find the financing or the favours required for lift-off. Some are heavy on hype yet light on logic, tossed out by hucksters hoping to make a quick buck. Others are so absurd that they don't stand a chance. And still others are such hopeless pipe dreams that even normally respectful TV reporters can't help sniggering between the lines.

Perhaps the biggest and most symbolically foolish of these fantasies was Moon, a 250-acre, $5-billion, 10,000-room lunar-themed mega-resort announced with much fanfare in 2002. Michael Henderson, the pitchman for this lunacy, poured every imaginable amenity into his plans, probably figuring he might as well throw it all against the wall and see what stuck. But despite the promise of a zero-gravity simulator and a 'crater wave pool', Moon disappeared almost immediately from the local radar screen. From the start, it had as much chance of being built in Las Vegas as it did of opening on the moon itself.

Following behind Moon in terms of unrealised scope are the various figments of the imagination that have dogged the old El Rancho property. After plans for the $1-billion Starship Orion hotel-casino were lost in space in 1996, several ill-conceived incarnations of Countryland USA (1997-99) came and went. The lot was subsequently slated for casinos modelled on London, one of three such proposals down the years, and San Francisco, a theme favoured at various times by no fewer than four teams of Vegas developers. Both fell by the wayside, and plans for the 4,000-room, Miami Beach-themed Fontainebleau on the site are still on hold.

Some developers simply don't seem to have done their research. Desert Kingdom (1994) was the name of a proposed hotel planned for 34 vacant acres next to the Desert Inn and aimed purely at high rollers. The plans called for 3,500 rooms, which was only about 3,000 rooms in excess of the number of high rollers around at the time; the project was quietly but quickly cancelled. Just up the Strip in 1999, promoter extraordinaire Bob Stupak floated a proposal for the Boat, a 1,200-cabin, *Titanic*-themed hotel and time-share complex complete with an iceberg-shaped mall. Naturally, it sank without a trace.

Other failed adventures have come with celebrity endorsements. The World Wrestling Federation bought Debbie Reynolds' hotel-casino (originally the Paddlewheel, now the Greek Isles) for $10.6 million in 1998 and pinned its hopes on a $100-million, 1,000-room resort with a wrestling theme. They sold it a year later. The site now occupied by the Palms was once tagged as the home of Desert Winds (1993), an $87-million, 400-room fantasy themed after the ill-starred musical Jackson family, and for Sound Stage, a 1,000-room project launched by Black Entertainment Television in 1997. Other off-the-wall plans that never left the drawing board included casinos themed after Bugsy Siegel (1998), Elvis Presley (1999 and 2006) and even Gen X (2000). But none were quite as absurd as Winter Wonderland, a chilly casino centred around a climate-controlled dome where it snowed every day. Only in Vegas? Happily not.

Vegas Vic Says Howdy

'Still a Frontier Town!'

The tag line dreamed up in the 1940s by the J Walter Thompson Agency in Los Angeles, in order to promote a dusty little gambling town halfway between the City of Angels and the City of Saints (Salt Lake City), was an appealing one. The fact that Las Vegas had never actually been a frontier town – watering hole and railroad stop would be more accurate – was no bar to the creation of a quintessential cowpoke to go along with the Chamber of Commerce's PR campaign. Thus was born Vegas Vic, a long and lanky cartoon with a strong chin and a welcoming glint in his squinty eye. Decked out in dude-ranch finery, a cigarette dangling from his lips, Vic beckoned the weary traveller to fun and sun in the desert.

However, Vic would likely be forgotten if not for his incarnation as that most powerful of Vegas icons: the neon sign. Translated by the Young Electric Sign Company into 48 feet (15 metres) of metal and glass, Vegas Vic became the unofficial mayor of Fremont Street when he was installed on the façade of the Pioneer Club in 1947 (the current version dates from 1951). Motors moved Vic's arm, his thumb out like some sort of demented hitchhiker, while a hidden loudspeaker boomed out, every few minutes or so, a welcome to the rubes: 'Howdy, Podner!'

Vic's monotonous greeting got on everyone's nerves after a few years, most famously actor Lee Marvin's. While in town working on a Western, Marvin leaned out of his hotel window, across the street at the Mint, and shot poor Vic full of arrows. It seems Vic's voice was interfering with a particularly heavy hangover. Vic was soon silenced; a few years later, when the mechanism in his arm gave out, the Pioneer Club's owners didn't bother to fix it.

They didn't need to. By then, Vic, in his gaudy wide-brimmed hat, yellow-checked shirt, red kerchief and blue jeans, was a signature part of Downtown. It's a measure of his fame that when the Fremont Street Experience canopy was built in 1995, he wasn't removed but merely lowered a few feet, giving him the appearance of a giant stuck in a low-ceilinged room. Long before then, though, he'd been joined on Glitter Gulch by Vegas Vicky, a neon cowgirl with entirely different assets.

Sadly, Vic and Vicky were doomed to enjoy each other only from afar: they literally work different sides of the street. Vic now presides over the Pioneer Club in name only, the casino having long since been replaced by a souvenir shop, while Vicky crowns the Girls of Glitter Gulch strip joint. Vic and Vicky might not be remnants of an 'Old West' Vegas that never was, but they're cherished relics of the honky-tonk town of the last century, at the moment when the final frontier of glitz, glamour and gambling was about to be crossed forever.

The auction was held on 15 May 1905 at the intersection of Main and Fremont streets. The bidding quickly inflated the price of choice lots to more than double their listed values. The locals over in Ragtown grumbled about the railroad tactic of encouraging out of town investors to heat up the prices. But when it was over, nearly 1,000 lots had been sold for the grand total of $265,000, which was $195,000 more than the railroad had paid for the entire Las Vegas Ranch only three years earlier.

The proud new property owners immediately searched out the stakes marking the boundaries of their lots and erected makeshift shelters on them. Ragtowners rolled their possessions over to the new Las Vegas on horse- and ox-drawn wagons. What remained of the first town site burned to the ground four months later, and the first Las Vegas building boom followed.

SETTLING IN

In stereotypical western fashion, the first structures to go up were saloons and brothels, built in the designated nightlife and red light district on Block 16 between Ogden and Stewart streets, and 1st and 2nd streets (now the parking lot at Binion's). Hotels, restaurants, banks and shops were erected along Fremont Street; railroad and town administrative offices, a school, a post office and two churches surrounded the core. The railroad company built the infrastructure: gravel streets and plank sidewalks, water service and sporadic electricity. Houses went up along the residential streets of the eight-block-long and five-block-wide town; supplies arrived daily by train. By New Year's Day 1906, some 1,500 pioneers were calling Las Vegas home. However, the initial boom was short-lived. Barely a year passed before the railroad town managers showed their true colours, concerned first with operating the main line and last with servicing the town. Their refusal to extend pipes beyond the town site stunted growth, forcing the rural dwellers to dig wells and tap into the aquifer. Fires, conflicts and the usual growing pains of a young settlement slowed the influx of new residents, reducing both property values and optimism. The heat, dust and isolation contributed to the consensus of discomfort.

A rare bit of good news arrived in 1909, when the Nevada Legislature created Clark County in the south of the state (it was named after William Clark, the chairman of the San Pedro, Los Angeles & Salt Lake Railroad) and named Las Vegas as its seat of government. Two years later, the railroad gave the town a boost when it opened a shop designed to help maintain the steam locomotives, passenger coaches and freight cars along the line. Hundreds of jobs were created at a single stroke; by the time the shop was fully staffed, the population of Las Vegas had doubled to 3,000. Telephone service arrived, with the first phone (taking, of course, the number '1') installed at the cigar counter in the lobby of the Hotel Nevada (now the Golden Gate). And in 1915, big town generators began supplying electricity to residents 24 hours a day.

But for the next 15 years, everything went downhill. The railroad found itself losing business to car and truck traffic, and workers were laid off. Union Pacific bought up the San Pedro, Los Angeles & Salt Lake Railroad, relegating it to the status of a small siding on a vast nationwide network. Measures brought in by Union Pacific severely inhibited the town's growth; when it then closed the railroad maintenance shops, locals were driven to leave town in search of work. Las Vegas would have disappeared by the late 1920s if it hadn't been for a monumental federal dam-building project gearing up nearby.

THE HOOVER DAM

The 1,450-mile Colorado River had been gouging great canyons and watering lush valleys for aeons, when the US government became determined to harness its flow in the service of irrigation, electricity, flood control and recreation. The Bureau of Reclamation began to consider damming the Colorado in 1907, eventually narrowing down the choice of locations for the dam to two canyons east of Las Vegas. In 1930, six years after the site for it had been selected, Congress appropriated the $165 million necessary to build the Boulder Dam.

IN CONTEXT

Anticipation of the dam project began to fuel noticeable growth in the railroad town. By the time construction began in 1931 (the name change, from the Boulder Dam to the Hoover Dam, was announced at the inauguration ceremony), a long-distance phone service, a federal highway linking Salt Lake City to Los Angeles and regular air-passenger services had arrived. The population soared to 5,000, with thousands more passing through Las Vegas en route to the soon-to-be-tamed river.

Even today, the building of the Hoover Dam is mind-boggling in its immensity. The nearest power plant was 200 miles away in southern California; wires had to be strung all the way from it in order to supply electricity. Some 5,000 workers had to be hired, and an entire town (Boulder City) was built to house them and their families. Most dauntingly of all, the mighty Colorado River itself had to be diverted simply for the project to begin. It took 16 months to hack four diversion tunnels through the canyon walls before the river could be routed around the construction site. Only then could work begin on what would eventually become one of the man-made wonders of the world.

Some five million buckets of concrete were poured into the dam over a two-year period. When it was completed in 1935, Hoover Dam stood 656 feet (200 metres) wide at its base, 49 feet (15 metres) thick at its crest, 1,358 feet (414 metres) across and 794 feet (242 metres) tall. After the diversion tunnels were closed, it took a further three years to fill Lake Mead. At 109 miles long, reaching a depth of 545 feet (166 metres), it's the largest man-made lake in North America. The legacy of the dam has been monumental, endowing Las Vegas with the power and the water it needed to fulfil its early promise.

THE NEW BOOM

In 1931, another event occurred that was to have long-lasting implications for Las Vegas: the statewide legalisation of wide-open casino gambling. Backroom illegal gambling had long been the norm for the libertine frontier state of Nevada. But when legislators gave gambling their blessing (along with easy divorces, no-wait marriages, prostitution and championship boxing matches), the transformation of Las Vegas from a railroad company town into a casino company town began in earnest.

Casino operators migrated in droves to the only state in the union where they could ply their trade without risking arrest; vice-starved visitors followed. The bars and casinos moved a block, from the shadows of Ogden Street to the more inviting Fremont Street. The ladies of the night stayed behind at Block 16, but lights began to brighten the gambling joints along Fremont, soon nicknamed 'Glitter Gulch'.

Las Vegas also enjoyed widespread publicity from the building of the dam. By 1935, when 20,000 people saw Franklin D Roosevelt preside over the Hoover Dam dedication ceremony, word was beginning to get around that this little town by the dam was a slice of the authentic Wild West, with legal casinos, legal prostitution and legal everything else. Temptation led to prosperity, which in turn led to construction. Three new casinos were built at the start of the 1940s: the El Cortez in Downtown, and the Last Frontier and El Rancho on the Los Angeles Highway, a stretch of road that would eventually come to be known as the Strip.

With the nation preparing for World War II, the federal government took over a million acres north of Las Vegas for use as a training school for military pilots and gunners. Between 1940 and 1945, the Las Vegas Aerial Gunnery School trained thousands of pilots, navigators, bombers and gunners, then shipped them to the fronts in Europe or the Pacific. The school eventually expanded to three million acres. And in 1942, Basic Magnesium, one of the largest metal-processing factories in the country, was built halfway between Las Vegas and Boulder City. At the peak of production, 10,000 workers were processing millions of tons of magnesium, a newly exploited metal used in the manufacture of bomb casings, aeroplane components and flares. To house them, an entire town was built: Henderson, Las Vegas's first next-door neighbour. During the war years, its population doubled from 8,500 to 17,000.

Hoover Dam.

THE MOB AND THE BOMB

As much as the war brought economic benefits to Las Vegas, it also gave a boost to organised crime throughout the US, as the black market in scarce consumer goods resulted in handsome profits for those savvy enough to sell them. But while the masters of the underworld were making a decent wage all over the US, they looked upon Las Vegas as the Promised Land. Flush with cash from bootlegging during Prohibition and black-market trading during the war, gangsters from all over the country stood poised to invade Nevada with money, management and muscle. All they needed was someone to raise a torch and show them the way. Enter Benjamin 'Bugsy' Siegel: tall, handsome and fearless, and partnered by the most powerful criminal bosses in the country.

Siegel elbowed into and bowed out of several casinos during the early 1940s, until he finally settled on the Flamingo. He insinuated himself into the management (which, contrary to popular myth, already existed), then so terrorised the team that they fled for their lives and left him with the unfinished joint. Siegel knew nothing about building a casino; construction ran $4 million over budget. What's more, he wasn't around long enough to enjoy its spoils: less than six months after the doors opened in December 1946, Siegel was assassinated in his girlfriend's Beverly Hills mansion.

Thus began 20 years of the Italian-Jewish crime syndicate's presence in Las Vegas, and ten years of the biggest hotel-building boom the country had ever seen. Black money from top Mob bosses, along with their fronts, pawns, soldiers and workers, poured in from the underworld power centres of New York, New England, Cleveland, Chicago, Kansas City, New Orleans, Miami and Havana. Between 1951 and 1958, 11 major hotel-casinos opened in Las Vegas, nine on the Strip and two Downtown. All but one was financed by dirty cash.

Eventually, a full 25 years after gambling was legalised in Nevada, the state and federal governments woke up to the questionable histories of the people who were in charge of the largest industry in Las Vegas. In every other state in the country, they were considered criminals; in Vegas, they'd successfully bought power, influence and respectability. The war between the police and the gangsters began, but it was overshadowed by an event that cast the town in a very strange light.

When the federal government went looking for a vast tract of uninhabited land on which to perfect its nuclear weapons, it found one at the Las Vegas Aerial Gunnery School. Just 70 miles north-west of the city, the Nevada Test Site went on to host roughly 120 above-ground nuclear test explosions, about one a month for a decade. Thousands of guinea-pig soldiers were deployed near the explosions, purposefully exposed to the shockwaves so medical teams could measure the effects of the radiation.

A few locals worried about which way the wind blew. However, most of the 65,000 Las Vegans seemed to revel in the notoriety that radiated from the tests. The boosters

IN CONTEXT

Wynn Las Vegas. See p26.

had a ball, marketing everything from 'atom burgers' to pictures of Miss Atomic Blast, and the openings of several casinos were scheduled to coincide with blasts. People had picnics atop the tallest buildings in town, looking across at the mushroom clouds. The Nuclear Test Ban treaty in 1962 drove the explosions underground, where 600 tests were held in the following three decades. But the reputation remained.

THE DIATRIBE

The Mob, the bombs, the gambling and the general naughtiness of Las Vegas attracted plenty of heat from the rest of the United States, most of it magnified by the media. A steamroller of criticism levelled the town's reputation, turning it into a national scandal. Known as 'the Diatribe', this systematic attack remains the greatest ever public castigation of an American city. The assault coloured Las Vegas's image for 30 years.

At the same time, though, people flocked to the town, proving the old rule about all publicity being good publicity. These pilgrims found that a strange thing happened at the Nevada state line: criminals who crossed it were suddenly accorded the status of legitimate businessmen, while the good citizens of the rest of the country suddenly became naughty boys and girls. These were the glamour years, when you didn't go out in Las Vegas after dark if you weren't wearing a suit or a cocktail dress. Crap shooters rolled the bones elbow-to-elbow with hit men. Mafia pit bosses had the 'power of the pencil' to hand out free rooms, food and beverages at their discretion, and the comps flowed as easily as the champagne.

During this period, Frank Sinatra, Dean Martin and Sammy Davis Jr performed in the Copa Room at the Sands, then invaded lounges around town. Joining the likes of Shecky Greene, Buddy Hackett and Louis Prima on stage, the Rat Pack became iconic fixtures of the new, high-rollin' Vegas. Many locals and visitors who were around from the early 1950s to the mid '60s still pine for these lost years.

The end of the Diatribe can be traced back to the arrival of multi-millionaire Howard Hughes. Smuggled under cover into town in November 1966, the tycoon settled into the ninth floor of the Desert Inn, from where he cultivated his eccentricities and planned his assault on the city. When the management at the Desert Inn threatened him with eviction, reputedly because they wanted to reserve his penthouse for high rollers, he dug $13 million from his bank account and bought the hotel. Over the next few years, Hughes went on to spend $300 million in the city, buying five casinos (including the Sands), an airport, an airline and the KLAS TV station, the latter purely so he could control the all-night programming he obsessively watched.

The publicity generated by his spending spree turned around the town's reputation: no longer was the town run by the Mob. Between 1968 and 1973, another dozen casinos opened, many of them run by respected companies that had previously been careful not to touch the crime-riddled town with a bargepole. It took a little while for various task forces to hound the old gangsters into oblivion; one scandal after another erupted at the older casinos at which the Mob was still entrenched. But eventually, in the mid 1980s, the city's casinos were free of any discernible Mob involvement.

THE NEW LAS VEGAS

In November 1989, a maverick 47-year-old businessman by the name of Steve Wynn opened a $650-million pleasure palace in the heart of the Strip. The size, elegance and price tag of the Mirage stunned the old guard in Las Vegas. But the enthusiasm with which the public greeted it, and the $1-million-a-day profits that resulted, galvanised the industry, and changed both the look and the culture of Las Vegas. The old casinos, with their scruffy buffets and lounges, were soon replaced by sophisticated resorts, complete with impressive restaurants, high-budget shows and plush lounges. A new breed of vacationer, more moneyed than at any point since the 1960s, came to see them.

Casino Heists

In this crazy city, crime sometimes pays.

For a large chunk of Las Vegas's colourful history, even the most accomplished thieves and robbers shied away from stealing from the casinos. Security surrounding the cashier's cage was thought to be virtually impenetrable; on the few occasions that a robber did make it out with the money, the police were usually close behind. And if the thieves somehow managed to elude the cops, a few heavies quietly employed by the casino would track them down and turn them into coyote bait.

Over the last couple of decades, however, the city's casinos have been the target of thieves pulling a variety of jobs. On average, the Las Vegas police deal with between 15 and 20 casino robberies a year; it may not sound like many, but the yields can be huge.

In the mid 1990s, Vegas casinos were subjected to a rash of armed robberies by LA gangs. Talk about audacious: the robbers entered the casinos in great numbers, submachine pistols clearly visible, and vaulted the counter into the cashiers' cages. As they fled, they sprayed a few rounds of ammo for good measure. However, most of the gang-bangers were caught.

Inside jobs aren't quite as public and messy, and the well-planned ones can be lucrative. One of the best known and most successful of all inside heists took place in 1992 at the now-defunct Stardust. A cashier in the sports book managed to stuff $500,000 of cash and chips into a duffel bag while the other employees were busy taking bets on a big game; he then walked out of the casino with the loot, never to be seen or heard from again. How did he do it? The strongest theory is that he worked with a confederate to whom he surreptitiously passed the money. But no one knows for sure.

The most lucrative casino theft in recent Vegas history amounted to the perfect crime. On the morning of 1 October 1993, an armoured truck operated by the Loomis security firm pulled into Circus Circus, the first stop of the day for guards dispatched to fill the city's ATMs. But as two of the guards went into the casino to load the machines, the truck's driver sped away.

Heather Tallchief, a 21-year-old with no prior criminal record, had driven the truck to a garage; here, she met her lover, a career criminal named Roberto Solis who is believed to have planned the heist. The duo emptied the truck of $3 million in cash and boarded a chartered Learjet to Denver, later travelling to Miami and the Cayman Islands. At all times, the duo remained one step ahead of their pursuers, and eventually vanished. It came as some surprise when, after 12 years on the run, Tallchief returned to the US from her new home of Amsterdam and turned herself in, whereupon she was sentenced to five years in prison. Solis remains at large – currently one of America's Most Wanted.

'Las Vegas developed from a desolate railroad town to the glamour capital of the world.'

There was plenty to see. The Excalibur, a family-friendly, medieval-themed casino-resort, opened in June 1990, followed in 1993 by the pyramidal Luxor, the pirate-technic Treasure Island and the 5,005-room MGM Grand. The Hard Rock Hotel brought some glamour back to the town when it opened in 1995; the 1,257-foot (383-metre) Stratosphere Tower, the opulent Monte Carlo and the pop art New York New York all opened between April 1996 and January 1997. Another wave of construction crested in October 1998 with the opening of the $1.6-billion Bellagio, then the most expensive hotel ever built. The $1-billion Mandalay Bay, all hipness and whimsy, followed six months later, with the $1.5-billion Venetian and the $760-million Paris Las Vegas making their debuts in September 1999, and a year later, came the Aladdin.

The biggest thing – literally – ever to hit Las Vegas is the CityCenter complex, a $10-billion city within a city, and a high-style confluence of casinos, resort hotels, condos and time-share units, and high-end shopping, dining and entertainment. Owned by MGM Mirage and located between the Monte Carlo and Bellagio (its own internal monorail links the properties), it is the largest and most expensive private construction project in history. Eight world-class 'starchitects' designed the components of the project, which include Aria Resort & Casino, Vdara Hotel & Spa, Mandarin Oriental Las Vegas, Veer Towers and the Crystals retail and entertainment district. Adjacent to CityCenter is the Cosmopolitan, which opened in 2011 and quickly became the liveliest place in town.

While these major casinos went up, others came tumbling down. The building boom of the 1990s was accompanied by the spectacular implosion of a number of key casinos. Between October 1993 and April 1998, the Dunes, the Landmark, the Sands, the Hacienda and the old Aladdin were all levelled, to be replaced by the Bellagio, a parking lot, the Venetian, Mandalay Bay and the new Aladdin (now Planet Hollywood) respectively. Implosions in 2001 and 2004 finally levelled the Desert Inn; on its site now stands Wynn Las Vegas, which in 2005 became the first major casino to arrive on the Strip in a half-decade. And in 2007, nearly 50 years after it opened, the Stardust was blown up. The beloved Sahara is next – it closed in 2011 and is expected to be replaced with a new complex by 2014.

21ST-CENTURY VEGAS

Despite the fact that the town already has more than 150,000 hotel rooms and 19 of the 30 largest hotels on earth, Las Vegas continues to grow – this despite a global economic crisis that nearly brought new construction to a standstill and left several large casino projects (Echelon, Fontainebleau, New York Plaza Las Vegas) waiting to fill their concrete-and-steel foundations. After a slight blip post-9/11, visitor numbers in Las Vegas have now reached record levels. An astonishing 37 million people, around ten per cent of them from abroad, visited the city in 2009, spending billions in the process. Many people check out Sin City once just to see what all the fuss is about, but millions more become regulars, attracted by the agreeable climate, the big-budget shows, the swanky hotels, the increasingly excellent food, the fashionable nightlife and, of course, the chance of instant riches.

Indeed, many have relocated to the world's greatest boomtown. Las Vegas is the largest American city to have been founded in the 20th century, and has also been its fastest growing major metropolitan area for more than a decade. The city celebrated its 100th birthday in 2005, marking a century during which it developed from a desolate railroad town to the glamour capital of the world. Heaven only knows what the next ten decades will bring.

Key Events

c800 Anasazi civilisation begins to develop in the southern Nevada desert.
c1150 The semi-nomadic southern Paiute tribe claim territory abandoned by the Anasazi.
1830 Rafael Rivera discovers a short cut via Big Spring while on the trading route from Santa Fe. He names the area Las Vegas.
1845 The surveyor John C Fremont visits the Las Vegas Valley.
1855-58 Mormon missionaries from Salt Lake City establish a short-lived community at Las Vegas. Lead is discovered in the area.
c1858 Silver ore and gold are discovered, prompting the growth of a mining boomtown.
1865 The old Mormon fort is appropriated by OD Gass and redeveloped as the Las Vegas Ranch.
1881 The Las Vegas Ranch is taken over by Archibald Stewart.
1903 Helen Stewart sells most of the Las Vegas Ranch to the San Pedro, Los Angeles & Salt Lake Railroad. JT McWilliams claims 80 acres of land west of the Las Vegas Ranch and subdivides it as lots for a planned town site, known as Ragtown.
1905 The Salt Lake City to Los Angeles railroad is completed at Jean, Nevada. A subsidiary of the railroad company auctions 1,000 lots for a new town site across the tracks from Ragtown. Four months later, Ragtown burns down.
1905 The new town of Las Vegas begins to develop with a nightlife district on Block 16 (today's Downtown).
1924 Two canyons east of Las Vegas are chosen as the site of an ambitious new project to dam the Colorado River.
1931 Gambling is legalised in Nevada, prompting an influx of casino operators into Las Vegas. Construction begins on the Hoover Dam, with Boulder City established to house the workers.
1935 President Roosevelt and 20,000 others attend the Hoover Dam dedication ceremony.

early 1940s Three major casinos are built: El Cortez, El Rancho and the Last Frontier.
1946 Construction of Benjamin 'Bugsy' Siegel's Flamingo casino.
1947 Bugsy Siegel is shot dead in Beverly Hills. For the next 20 years, the Mob dominates gambling in Las Vegas.
1951-58 Eleven hotel-casinos open in Vegas; ten are funded by the Mob.
1951-62 Around 120 nuclear bombs are detonated over the Nevada Test Site.
1960-61 The Rat Pack perform in the Copa Room at the Sands casino.
1962 First Limited Nuclear Test Ban Treaty prohibits atmospheric nuclear explosions.
1962-92 800 nuclear devices are detonated underground at the Nevada Test Site.
1966 Millionaire Howard Hughes takes up residence at the Desert Inn, buying up six casinos and stimulating a boom.
1990-2000 Myriad new resorts are built on the Strip and beyond it. The town undergoes a new lease of life and the population of Clark County soars.
2003 Celine Dion opens '...A New Day' at the custom-built Colosseum at Caesar's Palace. The show changes the face of entertainment in Las Vegas.
2004 Hard Rock Hotel launches its Sunday pool party called Rehab, launching the 'daylife' craze.
2005 Ultimate Fighting becomes a major draw, along with NASCAR and televised poker championships.
2005 As the town celebrates its centenary, Steve Wynn opens Wynn Las Vegas.
2007 The Stardust is demolished.
2010 MGM Mirage's 67-acre CityCenter complex opens. Two beloved off-Strip cultural institutions – the Las Vegas Art Museum and the Liberace Museum – close their doors.
2011 The Cosmopolitan opens next door to CityCenter. The Sahara closes. Carolyn Goodman, wife of Oscar, is elected mayor.

IN CONTEXT

Las Vegas Today

All eyes on the video screens.

TEXT: JOE BROWN & DAVID SURRATT

Video screens are everywhere in Las Vega today. And, being Vegas, these screens are supersized and hyper-high-definition, and inescapable. Video screens long ago supplanted the spinning wheels on slot machines, of course. Vegas is nothing if not an innovation-happy, tech-savvy town, and digital video screens are ubiquitous indoors and out, displaying restaurant menus, casino revue and movie showtimes, hotel and resort directions. Most notably – and emotionally for many – this brighter-than-bright digital signage has pushed out neon, so long an integral part of the Strip's identity. The last century's fanciful, animated neon signs are all but obsolete today (some finding a home in the so-called Neon Boneyard), replaced by towering, colossal, playing-field-scaled screens that blare and blast enormous moving images over the traffic, making night for day down on the street. Las Vegas may be superficially sentimental about the past – echoes of the Rat Pack and the mob heyday still linger, and will continue to do so as long as there's money to be made from nostalgia shows and souvenirs – but the place is notorious for blowing up its landmarks and building bigger, better, newer.

THE THRILL OF THE NEW

By the time you finish reading this chapter, something new will have been born in the city – a casino game, a shiny revue, a restaurant headed by a newly crowned celebrity chef. It's a sad irony that the main news about this novelty obsessed town for the past five years has been about not what is beginning, but what is ending. And because of the worldwide financial crisis – which rocked Vegas to its admittedly shallow core and has left it still reeling – there have been so many endings, so many losses. Beloved landmarks, from casinos and restaurants to mom-and-pop cornershops, have closed. And many projects, including such developments with sky-high aspirations as the star-crossed Fontainebleau and Echelon casino-resort complexes, were stopped in their tracks, leaving their foundations and structural shells as sad monuments to a time when the party seemed like it would never end.

Built by hustlers, opportunists and big dreamers, Vegas is a bounce-back city, and it's not about to let a little thing like a worldwide recession keep it down. Even while long-time shows, stores and restaurants are closing, and even while residents are leaving town with their possessions tied to the roofs of their cars, new shows, stores and restaurants are opening – and new Las Vegans are moving in. The dream is alive. The place is changing, no doubt about it. A younger generation is taking its rightful place as ruler of the Strip's sense and sensibility, and the sights, sounds, textures and tastes of 21st-century Las Vegas are evolving in front of our eyes. Case in point: the arrival of the massive CityCenter casino-resort-shopping-dining-entertainment complex, a startling, futuristic city-within-a-city that has emerged at the heart of the Strip, changing the centre of gravity of the entire city. It may be a few years before growth regains momentum here, but the impact of this development, and the more sophisticated crowd it was designed to attract, is going to be felt for a long time.

Some other manifestations of the new, now Vegas include the 'daylife' trend, almost surpassing nightlife now. And rather than blowing themselves up, casinos are lining up for facelifts: the façades of ageing properties like the Tropicana and the Cortez – even the not-so-old Bellagio – are getting a superficial 'reskin' at street level, and a more extensive renovation inside.

Like almost nowhere else, celebrities are used as crowd magnets here, and reign at the Strip's clubs and parties. And speaking of celebs, the now-ubiquitous red carpet events that pop up daily and nightly all around the Strip have become a siege and syndrome. Crooners such as Celine Dion and Garth Brooks are still a consistent entertainment draw, but the big ticket at most of the casino clubs is now the DJs, and the devoted dancers who follow them, who have made Vegas a crucial stop on the international party circuit. Meanwhile, ultimate fighting and mixed martial arts have all but replaced boxing as the city's most iconic sporting event.

It may be broke on paper, but Vegas still insists on looking effortlessly extravagant and excessive: one of the most amusing, enjoyable (and free) manifestations is the appearance of luxe loos – more opulent than your home, certainly, and often more decadently opulent than the casino or club encasing them – that have popped up all over town. Whatever happens in the local and international economy, it's certain that Las Vegas will remain defiant. People will always need a place to play, and Vegas will always be one of the world's playgrounds.

ALTERED STATES

In the wee small hours of 13 March 2007, a crowd of tourists and locals gathered just west of Las Vegas Boulevard, a safe distance from the evacuated and spotlit Stardust hotel. After several minutes' worth of fireworks had exploded above them, a further pyrotechnical display attached to the hotel's 32-storey west tower traced the enormous digits of a ten-second countdown. And then, at 2.33am, a formerly indispensable piece of the Las Vegas skyline slouched and sank to an upsurge of dust, cheers and cries. 'Bye-bye, Stardust: thanks for the memories!' It was a memorable moment, but hardly

IN CONTEXT

a unique one. The 16-storey Boardwalk fell in 2006, as did Bourbon Street and Castaways. Two years earlier, the Desert Inn's St Andrews Tower came down; as, for that matter, did its Palms Tower, just seven years after it went up.

What's changed most about today's Vegas is a matter of scope. No longer fully satisfied with its 'adult Disneyland' identity, this century-old frontier town now wants to grow up into a world-class city. It's an aspiration reflected not only in what's rushing to fill the vacuum left by all these vanishing buildings, but in the new images sported by a number of the ones that are still standing. The de-theming of the Strip is well under way.

When Treasure Island got a makeover back in 2003, its owners reasoned that too much yo-ho-ho and Jolly Roger might not be the most sophisticated way to draw an adult market that, they now realised, was a better bet than the family crowd they'd been courting. The strategy worked; and, like any casino-led innovation that works here, it got adopted by its originator's rivals. In 2007, after a long time in limbo, the Aladdin became Planet Hollywood, but a more sophisticated Planet Hollywood than its siblings across the world.

In fact, there's been no bigger swing in Vegas's image than in its nightlife. See-and-be-seen dance clubs and so-called ultralounges have become screamingly popular over the last few years, ever since someone realised that 20,000 square feet of casino space without slots could still yield big profits if it was tricked out with state-of-the-art lighting effects, sturdy cover charges and wallet-draining bottle-service policies that bring with them the kind of air of exclusivity that only money or celebrity can buy.

ONE FOR ALL

The concerted revamping projects on the Strip are made a good deal easier by the fact that all the hotels just mentioned, with the exception of Planet Hollywood, are now owned by the same corporation. On the Strip's four-mile Monopoly board, the MGM Mirage group is in the lead. After buying the Mandalay Resort Group in 2005, the MGM Mirage group expanded their portfolio of properties to encompass the MGM Grand, the Bellagio, the Mirage, Mandalay Bay, the Luxor, New York New York, the Excalibur, the Monte Carlo and Circus Circus – it developed and owns the new crown jewel, the CityCenter complex, as well. The $9 billion, 68-acre complex – a city within the city, featuring a 60-storey resort and casino, two additional boutique hotels, multiple condo and condo-hotel towers, vast amounts of retail space, theatres, restaurants, spas and a parking garage with room for 7,500 vehicles. While MGM Mirage is now responsible for roughly 50 per cent of the Strip's 75,000 hotel rooms, Harrah's controls around half the remainder in the shapes of Caesars Palace, Paris Las Vegas, the Imperial Palace, the Flamingo, Bally's and its namesake resort.

If it appears over the top, it's really just a reflection of changes in the country at large. The dizzying number of deals that have lit up the Vegas business pages are all part of a tightening food chain that closely follows a national trend toward dry, megacorporate entities. It seems a heartbreaking compromise for a town built on a foundation of libertarianism that bordered, at times, on anarchy. Bugsy Siegel at least had a face.

TROUBLE AT HOME

In the last two decades, before the worldwide catastrophe made its dire mark on even this most optimistic (and opportunistic) of cities, population numbers and property values were booming in Las Vegas. So, simultaneously, are the city's problems with substandard education, pollution, homelessness, addiction and even suicide: although still-high visitor numbers may skew the statistics a little, all are issues in which this tourist-distracted city ranks among the worst in the nation.

New residents arriving from all over the world eventually become deeply familiar with a key truth that isn't so visible from hotel balconies: Sin City is less about sin than it is about moral lack of interest. To those who visit with plenty of cash and a sense of when to give the debauchery a rest, good luck. To all others... well, good luck.

IN CONTEXT

'21st-century Las Vegas is very different to the showgirls-and-steaks scene of days past.'

WHERE ALL THE LIGHTS ARE BRIGHT

With the arrival of high-budget stage shows fronted by international stars, and celebrity-helmed world-class dining options, 21st-century Las Vegas is very different to the showgirls-and-steaks scene of days past. The streets just off the Strip are also morphing constantly and dramatically. But it's Downtown where the real changes are being set in motion, or so waggish former mayor Oscar Goodman would have you believe. Goodman – who was succeeded in 2011 by his wife, Carolyn, who promised to pick up right where Oscar left off – made the revitalisation of Downtown one of his top priorities. For years, Downtown was something of a shambles, a cluster of seen-better-days casinos frequented by seen-better-days gamblers that was overshadowed in every way by the mega-resorts on the Strip. After several false dawns, the collaborative efforts of local business owners and Goodman's Office of Business Development are at long last starting to reap rewards. One of the first real harbingers of this change is the arrival of internet shoes-and-accessories giant Zappos, which imported several hundred San Francisco employees and set them loose Downtown.

The light-show canopy above casino-lined Fremont Street now regularly attracts tourists. To the south, in a square roughly bounded by Charleston Avenue, Las Vegas Boulevard, Wyoming Avenue and the railroad tracks, an arts district is gradually emerging, brought to life once a month by the increasingly popular First Friday block party. North-east of here (just south-west of the Fremont Street Experience), construction on the Union Park development is under way; already among its additions is the Lou Ruvo Brain Institute, the city's first Frank Gehry-designed building.

There are further changes just across Las Vegas Boulevard from the Fremont Street Experience, where the rather stolidly named Fremont East Entertainment District is coalescing around the retro-chic Beauty Bar. Since opening in 2004, it's been joined by similar nightspots such as the upscale Downtown Cocktail Room. Comedy clubs, music venues and art galleries are also in the plans for what the city hopes will be a Strip-alternative haven. As Fremont East takes shape, out-of-towners may well find what a growing number of locals want them to find: a relatively authentic urban entertainment nook where their presence is welcome but not desperately needed. Las Vegas is a service economy town full of bartenders, cocktail servers, dancers, pit bosses and other workers whose job it is to keep visitors from so-called real cities happy. The trouble is that it doesn't offer much in the way of real-city decompression areas where that workforce can retreat at quitting time – the Strip is 'the office' to most who work there. Most simply punch out and head back to a suburban sea of stuccoed, monochrome housing that, while fast and functional, doesn't do much for a strange young town's social development. The new Downtown aims for a way to feel 'real' in a city where, on the whole, the word itself tends to lose meaning.

The problems faced by Las Vegas are the kind felt by any city faced with challenges of recession, planning, corruption control, and the building of an infrastructure that can support what's coming as it comes. The question seems to be whether Las Vegans can overcome a peculiar and ironic handicap in the process. How does a town like this learn to take care of itself while putting the tourists first at all costs? Building and revitalisation efforts in any city are typically high-risk, especially without the insurance of another thousand video-poker screens to fund it. But until the gambling capital of the US can bring itself to make that bet, the world-class reputation it craves might remain a mirage.

IN CONTEXT

Architecture

It's easy come, easy go in the neon oasis.

TEXT: PHIL HAGEN, JOE BROWN

The Las Vegas Strip has always been a movie set of sorts. With each new era, relics of the greatest hits in oasis-style hospitality make way for a fresh backdrop and new stars. Just as the mid-century modernist Dunes was imploded for the sake of the opulent Bellagio, so the Treasure Island that helped launch the theme-happy family era in Vegas was repackaged into the younger, sexier TI. The trend in Las Vegas has always been for disposable or mutable architecture; this is a city more likely to tear down its laurels than rest on them. Along the Strip, it's survival not so much of the fittest but of the tallest, the biggest and the boldest.

But times are changing. The next era in Vegas architecture seems set to throw things off cycle. While some of the town's history will inevitably vanish, what's going up – high up – are attractions that are more dense, more metropolitan and even a little more green. For a change, they're also being built to last.

CITYCENTER

The most significant new exponent of the new era in Vegas construction, and the most expensive privately funded development in the US, is MGM Mirage's $11-billion **CityCenter** complex of buildings, which sprang up on the 76 acres between the Bellagio and the Monte Carlo. A city within a city rising from the middle of the Strip, CityCenter suddenly dominated the skyline. The addition of 'starchitect'-designed Aria, Vdara, Mandarin Oriental, Veers Towers – and the star-crossed Harmon, which is in danger of being demolished without ever opening, because of faulty construction – changed the gravitational centre of Las Vegas.

CityCenter opened in stages, beginning in December 2009 with Pelli Clarke Pelli's 60-storey, 4,004-room hotel-casino **Aria** (*see p102*). A striking addition to the new skyline is Helmut Jahn's two 37-storey **Veer Towers**, twin oblongs that lean a startling five degrees in opposite directions. Other world-class architects contributed buildings to the complex, including Rafael Vinoly (the condo-hotel **Vdara**, *see p132*); London's Foster & Partners (the star-crossed Harmon Hotel & Spa, which was never completed); Kohn Pederson Fox (**Mandarin Oriental** hotel and residences, *see p131*); and Daniel Libeskind (the strikingly spiky, museum-like **Crystals** high-end shopping centre, *see p194*). A unifying theme is conspicuous by its absence; instead, CityCenter is a model of large-scale contemporary urban architecture, with a number of sleek towers and eco-friendly credentials. Next door to CityCenter, there's the even newer **Cosmopolitan** (*see p107*), which opened in 2011 and attracts a younger, more urbane crowd. It was designed by Arquitectonica with an unusual vertical orientation – the casino, clubs, entertainment venues, restaurants and retail are played out on three floors rather than the usual single-story sprawl.

ECONOMIC WOES HIT DEVELOPMENTS

There were big plans for more of this mini-metropolitan movement at the northern end of the Strip, where Echelon Place started going up on the old Stardust casino lot. Boyd Gaming president Robert Boughner summed up the project and the new Vegas attitude. 'Echelon, in terms of architecture, is more about designing a building that will evoke an emotion. A theme doesn't evoke an emotion; it evokes a cheap thrill.' But construction on that massive project, which called for four hotels – among them the Asian-glam Shangri-La and the Hollywood-chic Mondrian, both unthemed, boutique-style resorts – came to a sudden halt in 2010, leaving a half-finished framework as a dire symbol of the economic collapse that affected Las Vegas more than perhaps any other US city.

Another dream deferred is a casino-resort project called the Fontainebleau. Former Mandalay Resorts boss Glenn Schaeffer proposed what would have been one of the most architecturally significant resorts in modern Vegas; its 25-acre, 68-storey, 3,889-room design was inspired by the style of Morris Lapidus (who designed the original in

IN CONTEXT

Crystals.

Miami Beach in the 1950s). Construction ceased due to bankruptcy in 2009; the casino-hotel's furnishings were sold to Downtown's Plaza Hotel & Casino for its refurbishment.

Las Vegas is unsentimental about getting rid of what's not working – in other words, not making as much money as it once did – and that means literally blowing up old buildings to make way for new, potentially more lucrative structures. The latest landmark to meet this fate is the venerable Rat Pack roost, the Sahara casino and hotel, which closed its doors in 2010, just shy of its 60th birthday. Casino demolitions are a major entertainment event in Las Vegas; keep an eye on the news for the date of the Sahara demolition for a once-in-a-lifetime spectacle.

BRIGHT SPOTS

Some bright spots have emerged despite the money crunch: the City of Las Vegas (with help from Newland Communities) has been developing its own urban core on a long-barren Downtown railroad lot formerly known as the 61 Acres but now renamed **Union Park**. Marquee projects here include the Frank Gehry-designed **Lou Ruvo Center for Brain Health**, which opened in 2009 – the typically twisty steel-clad structure appears to be melting in the Vegas heat — and David Schwarz's more conservatively styled **Smith Center for the Performing Arts**, which will provide a home for non-casino culture in the Vegas valley when it opens in May 2012. They'll eventually be joined by a new City Hall, a couple of boutique hotels and the 57-storey World Jewelry Center. On adjacent land, the vast **World Market Center** continues to change shape and dominates its corner of the cityscape, with seven buildings devoted to hospitality and the home-furnishings trade, including the **Las Vegas Design Center**, which is open to the public.

The old **Las Vegas City Hall** has been taken over by the giant internet shoes-and-accessories website Zappos.com, which has imported hundreds of energetic young hipsters to Las Vegas – their presence is already having an influence on the culture of Downtown Las Vegas. Known for its sense of fun in its corporate culture, Zappos is considering installing an aerial 'zipline' – akin to a thrill ride – to connect the company's office to Downtown bars and clubs.

The cityscape isn't only developing aesthetically: Las Vegas has also finally got out of the starting blocks in the green movement. Around 20 projects in the area have been approved for the US Green Building Council's LEED certification, among them a sustainable TV campus (Vegas PBS) and a neighbourhood of luxury holiday

The implosion of the Landmark Hotel in 1995.

'Modern Vegas has upped the scale and sophistication of its resorts.'

homes (Enchantment Way). Even CityCenter is getting in on the act, the largest project to be LEED-certified. But the granddaddy of all green projects is the **Las Vegas Springs Preserve** (see p92), a central park with seven LEED Platinum structures that are both built to be sustainable and designed to teach sustainability to visitors.

With such high-profile urban and urbane projects in the pipeline, Vegas is adopting a more refined appearance. But those who hanker after the decadent ol' days will still find plenty to dazzle. The 64-storey gold-and-white **Trump International Hotel & Tower** (see p132) opened in 2008 – notably without a casino – across the Boulevard from Steve Wynn's bronze-and-tan **Wynn Las Vegas** (see p114), standing taller, gaudier and somehow even shinier than its neighbour. Wynn named his building's sibling **Encore**; the adjacent 2,000-room tower opened in 2008 and featured even more lavish decor, with a butterfly motif. Meanwhile, Wynn's competitive neighbour Sheldon Adelson played his **Palazzo** (see p113) card in the same year, opening a 3,000-room tower resort to complement his Venetian casino-resort.

THE EARLY DAYS

Although Las Vegas has been a popular resort town for more than half a century, the way in which its hotels are designed has altered hugely down the years, as much thanks to social change as by any direct design imperative. The old Vegas was a Mafia-controlled demi-monde, where men gambled wearing jackets and ties, watched by women clad in diamonds and ballgowns. Back then, gambling was illegal in much of the US. But now that it's permitted in 48 of the 50 states, and now that the industry is controlled not by the Mob but by big business, the town has reinvented itself.

From World War II onwards, when the town's expansion began to take hold, Las Vegas developed its own distinctive style, a dazzlingly vulgar cocktail of expressionist modern architecture and monumental neon signs that illuminated stretches of desert on Las Vegas Boulevard. A key figure in this development was Wayne McAllister, a pioneering southern Californian architect whose influence over modern Vegas is perhaps greater than that of any other designer. It was McAllister who built the cowboy-flavoured **El Rancho**, the first themed resort on what's known as the Strip, back in 1941. A decade later, he constructed the original **Sands**, the Rat Pack's casino of choice, and also had a hand in the Desert Inn.

The town's smaller hotels were, if anything, even more exotic, and in some cases positively space-age. Many were products of the automotive age, built to dazzle and attract passing drivers. At the original **Mirage**, built in 1952, swimmers could be seen through portholes on the street-front side of the pool; indeed, the motel became better known as the **Glass Pool Inn**, as it was rechristened more than three decades after it opened. In 1961, Paul Revere Williams' **La Concha Motel** drew attention for its zinging concrete lobby, the design of which aped the form of a shell.

Modern Vegas has upped the scale and sophistication of its resorts, adding shops and amusements to create vast complexes replicating the kind of walk-through fantasies popularised by Disney. The kaleidoscope of neon that was once the city's trademark has been dwarfed by themed resorts approximating all kinds of cities, countries and (the key word here) experiences. As a result, little remains from the 1950s and '60s. As the town unsentimentally continues to cut ties with its past, most of the properties mentioned in the preceding pair of paragraphs have been destroyed in the name of progress. The sole survivor is the old La Concha lobby, salvaged in 2007 and scheduled to be rebuilt Downtown by the Neon Museum (see p86 **A Paean to Neon**).

IN CONTEXT

ENTERTAINMENT ARCHITECTURE

The earliest gambling joints on what became the Strip had a western flavour. The **El Rancho**, which opened in 1941, and the **Last Frontier**, which followed a year later, took as their themes nostalgia for the Old West. A few years down the line, Benjamin 'Bugsy' Siegel helped create the **Flamingo** (*see p116*) in 1946, an LA Moderne-style tropical paradise. With variations, this style reigned during the adults-only, post-war years. But when Jay Sarno built his instantly sensational, pseudo-Roman **Caesars Palace** (*see p104*) in 1966, and followed it two years later with the camp **Circus Circus** (*see p126*), the die was cast.

After a relatively quiet few years, the stakes in the theming game escalated with the work of Steve Wynn, without whom Vegas would look very different. In 1989, Wynn opened the South Seas-themed **Mirage** (*see p110*), which melded the upmarket stylings of Siegel's Flamingo with the fantasy of Caesars and the mass appeal of Circus Circus, and became the Strip's first mega-resort. Then, four years later, the entrepreneur delivered the Caribbean-inspired **Treasure Island** (*see p124*) just next door. The same period saw the construction of the riotous, candy-coloured **Excalibur** (1990; *see p127*), the agreeably preposterous **Luxor** (1993; *see p118*) and the ugly but enormous **MGM Grand** (1993; *see p119*). However, it was Wynn's duo that really reversed the downward spiral of Las Vegas during the early 1980s.

Casino bosses have since gone in for even more extravagant design. Where once the properties were signed by fizzing neon, the theming is now so wild that the casinos introduce themselves. The Egyptian-themed Luxor is, from street level, a vast black glass pyramid guarded by a squatting sphinx; the hotel, casino and sign are integrated into one structure, so the building itself is the sign. **New York New York** (*see p122*) represented theming at its most fully realised when it opened four years later with a mini-Grand Central Station, a half-size Statue of Liberty and 12 jaunty, 1:3-scale skyscrapers mimicking the Manhattan skyline. And in 1999, **Paris Las Vegas** (*see p111*) dropped a half-size replica of the Eiffel Tower on to the Strip. It looks tongue-in-cheek – and it is – but the attempts at authenticity are touching; although the tower is welded together, cosmetic rivets have been positioned in the appropriate places.

Paris Las Vegas is one of several resorts that have taken their cues from across the Atlantic. For casino moguls – and, arguably, for middle Americans who make up the greater part of Vegas's custom – Europe equals sophistication. With that in mind, it's no surprise that two of the Strip's most luxurious and expensive resorts have carefully realised European themes.

The first to open was the $1.4-billion **Bellagio** (*see p102*), an Italianate theme park for high-rolling grown-ups built by Wynn in 1998. The property is fronted by an eight-acre imitation of Lake Como; inside, marble is conspicuous in both the lobbies and the rooms. The basic trefoil tower structure is hardly innovative, but there are imaginative moments within, among them the glass anemones by sculptor Dale Chihuly on the lobby ceiling, the extravagant conservatory and the lake's dancing fountains. The Sands, meanwhile, was replaced in 1999 by the **Venetian** (*see p113*), which links the Rialto bridge to the Doge's Palace and piazza San Marco.

Other developments in Vegas's casinos have come with the expansion of its shopping scene from negligible to extensive. One of Las Vegas's most stunning themed environments, the **Forum Shops** (1993; *see p194*) at Caesars Palace, set a trend that's since been emulated at Paris Las Vegas, the Venetian and Planet Hollywood. This cod-Roman shopping street, complete with trompe l'oeil sky (and lighting that simulates the transition from dawn to dusk), showed casino moguls that malls could be money-spinners, and also introduced convincing aged walls and styrofoam sculptures to a city that had previously been quite happy with cheerfully silly evocation. The mall's expansion in 2004 brought another only-in-Vegas innovation: spiral escalators.

New York New York.

AFTER DARK

Aiming for younger, more upscale and more urbane customers, the gaming kings of Las Vegas have hired some of the world's top architects and designers to create swanky new restaurants, nightclubs and lounges inside their casinos. It's here that you'll find some of the city's more exciting design touches. Not all are original, granted; some restaurants have been described as 'New York-style', while a few nightclubs are keen to play up their European origins or their retro fittings. But there's vibrancy here, not to mention excess.

The **Palms** resort (*see p135*), which opened in 2001, has been at the forefront of the movement towards a cooler kind of ostentation. Three of its venues deliver it in spades: **Rain** (*see p260*), a nightclub and concert venue with a lounge, an elevated dancefloor and (the Vegas touch) light fixtures that shoot fire; **Ghostbar** (*see p184*), where the similarly retro edge would make Austin Powers feel at home; and the **N9ne** steakhouse (*see p172*), where coloured lights wash the ceiling. Other casinos have been getting in on the act, most recently the Beatles-themed, Cirque du Soleil-created **Revolution** lounge (*see p182*) at the Mirage.

Not every ode to modernity sits on the Strip. At 3rd and Ogden streets in Downtown, the owners of the currently-closed Lady Luck casino have opened a handsome locals' favourite called **Triple George** (*see p173*), complete with an adjoining, brick-walled piano bar. Next door is George's little brother **Sidebar** (*see p185*), a quaint, stylish hangout that wouldn't look out of place in San Francisco. Completed in 2007, the **Fremont East Entertainment District** benefitted from wider, more pedestrian-friendly sidewalks and retro signage, with smartly designed venues such as the **Downtown Cocktail Room** (*see p184*) and the **Griffin** (*see p185*) teasing a hip, metropolitan vibe out of some gritty old structures. And all without a single slot machine in sight.

NON-RESORT ARCHITECTURE

Attention was first drawn to the city's public architecture in the late 1980s with Charles Hunsberger's ambitious and controversial library-building programme. Using a range of architects with a view to making each of the nine libraries adventurous and unique, the programme was an attempt to create, without precedent, a Las Vegas 'high' architectural style. Characterised by earthen forms, variegated concrete and sandy stone, pyramids, cones and dry desert landscaping, the libraries can be seen as an effort to reflect and adapt to the harsh environment of the Mojave desert; the **Sahara West Library & Las Vegas Arts Museum**, the **West Charleston Library** and the **Summerlin Library & Performing Arts Center** are perhaps the best examples. This trend reached its extreme with the **Clark County Government Center** (600 S

IN CONTEXT

Grand Central Parkway). Other lively buildings also welcome visitors, and perhaps even inspire them. The tech-savvy **Lied Library** (see p313) at UNLV, for example, is a concrete, steel and glass structure with towering east windows and a massive, inviting lobby. And the first structure visitors are likely to notice is the sleek Terminal D at **McCarran International Airport**. Having announced its authority with steel and glass, the terminal incorporates both past (Googie-style graphics, vintage passenger planes) and contemporary (exposed steel trusses, hangar-high ceilings, large glass windows). While you're here, look out for the airport's award-winning new control tower, a robot-like structure crowned with what (intentionally) looks like a policeman's cap.

One of the most visible additions is Downtown's **Lloyd D George Federal Courthouse** (333 Las Vegas Boulevard South). Designed by Dwarsky & Associates of LA, with a keen emphasis on security in the wake of the 1995 Oklahoma City bombing, the plaza is raised above street level, and the building itself has a blast-resistant wall of windows facing Las Vegas Boulevard. Nearby is the **Regional Justice Center**, an award-winning complex designed by Tate Snyder Kimsey that consolidated the operations of the municipal, justice and state supreme courts into 'one user-friendly courthouse'. One of these more friendly uses is the Marriage License Bureau, which has its own entrance, as well as a small courtyard and canopy of trees for happy snappers.

Yet despite growing aspirations, these public buildings represent only a few bright points in an architectural desert. Non-resort Las Vegas is still defined by endless one- and two-storey stucco-and-Spanish-tile tract houses and monotonous shopping centres, convenience stores and fast-food restaurants. There's little evidence of planning, just an ugly chequerboard of 'leapfrog' development spreading in all directions.

Downtown is re-emerging as a residential district, especially within the historic 160-home **John S Park neighbourhood**, east of Las Vegas Boulevard South and north of Charleston Boulevard. However, on the whole, living close to the centre is still seen as undesirable in a city where roads have not yet become permanently gridlocked. Affluent and middle-class families prefer residential enclaves built around golf courses and artificial lakes on the edge of the valley; on the Strip, high-rise condos such as **Turnberry Place** at the north end, and **Park Towers** at the south, appeal largely to jet-setters here for six weeks a year. One of the latest such statements comes in the shape of the two sleek **Panorama Towers**, perched near the Strip alongside Interstate 15.

Supplementing its gated neighbourhoods, Las Vegas has gone one step further – as usual – with 'master-planned' communities, town-sized swathes of privately owned land on which management companies create entire societies (housing in several price brackets, business and commercial districts, retirement complexes, schools, parks – even hospitals). Residents sign up to the community's rules and, in theory, settle back to enjoy their suburban utopia.

The most carefully planned of such communities was **Summerlin** (see p91). With its abundance of parks, sports fields, tennis courts and trails, not to mention its proximity to Red Rock Canyon, it's favoured by outdoorsy urbanites and disdained by those who thrive on an independent lifestyle. (You want to paint your house green? Forget it.) People have continued to buy into what has become the new American Dream; similar planned communities include **Seven Hills** and **Anthem**, both in Henderson, and **Aliante** in north Las Vegas. However, the latest breed, among them **Inspirada** near Anthem and **Kyle Canyon** in the north-west, have at least attempted to incorporate 'new urbanism' to counteract ills such as the lack of pedestrian destinations.

Of all the structures here, there's one you absolutely can't miss. The quirk? It's not a building, not in Las Vegas and not designed by an architect. Conceived by engineer John Savage and built as part of Roosevelt's public-works programme, the monumental **Hoover Dam** (see p278) on the Colorado River is a marvel of human ingenuity. Utterly utilitarian, with art deco touches, it has the grandeur and permanence missing from most buildings in Vegas. What's more, completed in 1935, it's older than almost anywhere else in the city.

The Juice

One man's comps is another man's corruption.

TEXT: DAYVID FIGLER

80351
4-12-28

Early in the campaign for the national mid-term elections in 2006, Harry Reid – then Senate Minority leader, now Senate Majority leader – found himself under the spotlight in DC. One morning, the Democratic senator for Nevada awoke to find himself the subject of an accusatory story in the *Washington Post*; 'Reid Accepted Free Boxing Tickets While a Related Bill was Pending,' read the report. Yet Reid's constituents at home, especially those in southern Nevada where he was born and raised, merely shrugged. Out here, one person's bribe is merely another's 'comp', and all the nuance in between is part of the vocabulary of corruption endemic throughout the development of Las Vegas as a modern city.

So when Reid accepted ringside seats from the state agency that regulates the sport, despite the fact the agency had a bill pending before the Senate at the time, locals were quick to dismiss any allegations of impropriety. This was clearly just a courtesy comp to someone with power; or, in Vegas parlance, 'juice'. (As it later turned out, Reid voted squarely against the agency that gave him the tickets.) Comps? Juice? Allowable bribes? Is this proof of a lower standard of morality in Las Vegas government? Throughout history, the answer has been as jumpy as a roulette ball during a particularly lively spin around the wheel.

BUILDING ON QUICKSAND

Even the creation of the state of Nevada in 1864 was a bit of a spirited horse trade. Aware that this great land mass was rich in minerals and speculative investment potential, powerful people lobbied to shape the state from the territory in which it rested. Capitalising on Abraham Lincoln's desire to add another non-slave state to the union, Nevada's forefathers aligned themselves with the president. In so doing, they cannily gave themselves a head start in the race to wield power in the new state.

By the beginning of the 20th century, the doors were open for all sorts of outsiders to reinvent themselves in Nevada and help shape the future of Las Vegas. None was more successful than Montana native William Clark, considered by many to be the

Dirty Dealings at the Crazy Horse Too

Was this strip club Vegas's own Bada Bing?

Once upon a time, the Crazy Horse Too strip club in Las Vegas was famous less for its notorious alumni, among them future porn diva Jenna Jameson, than for its Teflon-like resistance to law enforcement. For more than a decade, cops struggled to lay a finger (easy now) on the joint, despite long-standing rumours that it was tied to organised crime. The club was dogged by allegations of disreputable business practices; one customer received a $10-million settlement in a plea deal after he was left paralysed from the chest down, reputedly following an argument about the accuracy of his bar tab.

Still, the Crazy Horse Too continued to strut its stuff until a fateful day in 2003, when strapping FBI agents, clad in blue windbreakers and armed with semi-automatic weapons, stormed the joint during business hours. The sight of high-heeled dancers clutching their sweaty dollars to cover their naked breasts is indelibly etched in the minds of anyone who caught the seemingly endless replays on the evening news in the weeks following the raid.

Upon raiding the Crazy Horse Too, local government officials were shocked to learn that lap dancing, liquor sales and the exchange of untaxed money took place within these allegedly regulated businesses. In the end, a complicated plea bargain plucked the property from owner Rick Rizzolo, who was convicted on the relatively trifling charge of tax evasion. With the plea bargain, all parties avoided a trial at which the issue of the influence of organised crime over Las Vegas strip clubs, or at least over this one Las Vegas strip club, might once and for all have been settled.

Rizzolo lay low in 2007, having apparently sold the club to local businessman Mike Signorelli. However, his name was never far from the headlines, and a cloud continued to hang over the operation. When Signorelli and his lawyer Jay Brown applied for the reinstatement of the liquor licence that had been removed from the club in the wake of Rizzolo's conviction, the local police strongly objected. 'A reasonable person,' sighed a police-issued statement that was reported by the *Las Vegas Review-Journal*, 'could draw the conclusion that Signorelli is simply running the business for Rizzolo, who is forbidden to do so.' The council unanimously approved the alcohol licence regardless. The club reopened for just eight months, but was shut down by the city following Signorelli's failure to obtain the necessary finance to go through with the purchase. It was shut down in July 2007 and later seized by the government. The US Marshals Service has had little luck trying to sell the club; there were no bids when the building was put up for auction in July 2011.

IN CONTEXT

founding father of Vegas. Clark was no stranger to allegations of corruption, having been caught red-handed trying to buy a seat on the Montana legislature in 1899. But such behaviour didn't stop voters from electing him to the Senate in Montana two years later. And nor, in 1905, did it prevent Clark from manoeuvring himself and his family into control over the San Pedro, Los Angeles & Salt Lake Railroad, which was set to run through Las Vegas, and then over the city's water supply and its plum plots of land. Clark's power enabled him to extract or extort huge fees from anyone who wanted to venture into the uncharted future of Las Vegas.

Four decades later, another corrupt force controlled the ways and means of Las Vegas in the form of the shadow government known as the Mob. This period has long been romanticised by popular culture. It's also remembered fondly by old-timers who long for 'the days when the Mob ran things', forgetting the killings and the thefts associated with what was, in reality, one of the darkest chapters in the town's past.

At the time, the growth of Las Vegas was linked to the interests of 'businessmen' with nefarious pasts. Benjamin 'Bugsy' Siegel didn't come up with the idea for the Flamingo hotel, stealing the concept and the property from a fellow named Billy Wilkerson, but he saw it through in such a way as to lay the foundations for what Las Vegas later became. And when the mobster met the wrong end of a .30-caliber bullet in 1947, Siegel also inadvertently set in place the rules for how such power and influence was won and lost.

It's a moot point whether the mafia actually ran the town. However, it's certain that there was at least a tortured co-existence between the bad guys and the government, necessary to ensure that the Bugsy-styled resorts would keep on earning. To those ends, the Mob eventually became respectable in Las Vegas high society and in local philanthropic circles. At the same time, the scandals, continued profit-skimming and ceaseless brutality fuelled a spectre of corruption that lasted until the last identifiable organised-crime boss was ostensibly driven from power over any local entity.

Originally known in Las Vegas as the man behind the Desert Inn, Morris 'Moe' Dalitz was long tagged as a gangster and racketeer. Tied in many accounts to the Cleveland Mob, Dalitz was also rumoured to be tight with the likes of corrupt union leader Jimmy Hoffa and Nevada senator Pat McCarran. Several hotels, not to mention one of the first major hospitals in Las Vegas, were built with Teamster pension money secured through Dalitz's connections. But if there was corruption afoot, no one seems to have cared in the wake of Las Vegas's emergence as a major city. And after selling the Desert Inn to Howard Hughes in the 1960s, Dalitz successfully reinvented himself as a beloved benefactor to many local charities and religious organisations.

ALL 'GOOD' THINGS COME TO AN END

Ralph Lamb, the town's tough-as-nails sheriff from 1962 until 1980, had a reputation for literally slapping around the good fellas if they stepped out of line. But the kind of violence depicted in popular books of the time such as *The Green Felt Jungle*, and in later movies such as Martin Scorsese's *Casino*, escalated to eye-catching levels, and federal intervention soon loomed on the horizon.

By the 1970s, corruption had established a chokehold on Las Vegas. Even good ol' Sheriff Lamb was the subject of an investigation after allegations of financial wrongdoings. Absolved of all charges but bruised to such a degree that he lost his bid for re-election, Lamb was far from the last public official accused of exchanging favours for cold hard cash. But as Roger Foley, the US District Court judge who acquitted Lamb, put it, 'Many fringe benefits come to a public official which may be accepted along with the honest discharge of duty.'

Since the 1980s, innumerable allegations of public corruption have been made, mostly involving the development of land or other business opportunities. In 1991, for example, Las Vegas mayor Ron Lurie didn't stand for re-election amid accusations (which he denied) that he had profited from insider information regarding land development when he was a city councillor. Similar controversies have been

IN CONTEXT

caused by what's been termed the 'revolving-door principle', with private-sector jobs provided by businesses to the politicians who once regulated them.

ASK AND THOU SHALT RECEIVE

Former county commissioner Yvonne Atkinson Gates resigned in 2007 to spend more time with her family and her business, at roughly the same time that police were investigating whether she misused campaign funds to the benefit of her family. The allegations, which she refuted, were just the latest in a long line of complaints about her ethical behaviour during her long tenure as one of the gatekeepers of areas that included the Strip. Gates's most notorious escapade involved her plan to open her own businesses in casinos that, at the time, she was responsible for regulating. At the 1997 hearings, it was learned that the embattled Gates had placed her reputation on the line for a string of frozen daiquiri concessions. Of *course*.

Consider also the case of retired Las Vegas mayor Jan Jones. During her two terms in office, Jones was accused by her detractors of being too friendly to the casino industry. After stepping down from the rigours of government in June 1999, Jones stepped up four months later into a vice-president position with Harrah's, one of the major players in Nevada gaming. Still, at least Jones waited a while before mailing her résumé to the private sector: county commissioner Lynette Boggs McDonald briefly served in a paid capacity on the board of directors of a local casino chain while she was serving the public on the Las Vegas City Council. Boggs McDonald, incidentally, lost her bid for re-election in 2006 amid allegations, which she denied, that she received favourable treatment from a developer whose interests she had previously supported on the council.

Of course, there are gifts, and there are *gifts*. In 2005, ten lawmakers (affiliated to both parties) accepted comped tickets to a sold-out Rolling Stones concert from former attorney general and latterday lobbyist Frankie Sue del Papa. The freebies were granted on behalf of Del Papa's client, the now-defunct Ameriquest, a national mortgage-lending firm that at the time was dogged by allegations of financial irregularities and has since been accused of the kind of predatory lending that contributed to the recent global financial crisis. When the propriety of such largesse was questioned, the concertgoers maintained that in Las Vegas, there's a difference between freebies and bribes.

The distinction baffles the outside world, but it's nonetheless one that the local populace is happy to make. Comps in Las Vegas are dispensed for many reasons: as a sign of respect, as a gesture of friendship, as a motivational tool to ensure a full house or as a way to unload something that might otherwise go unused. 'Influencing the recipient' hardly makes the list, although comps are also often distributed with the hope that good karma payback will someday land the giver a similar comp. That said, it's telling that none of the Rolling Stoners were ousted from office in the next election.

NAKED CITY

Not everyone was as lucky. Take the four former Clark County commissioners who were stung in what may be the granddaddy of all corruption probes, dubbed 'Operation G-Sting' because of its strip-club connections. Although one of the commissioners had retired by the time the investigation moved into full swing, two were seeking higher office; only they lost their respective races were indictments pinned on them.

With favours, cash and even sex proffered in exchange for votes, Operation G-Sting is a textbook tale of political corruption. In this case, bribes bought an easing of regulations hampering 'free speech' (lap dances) in clubs, and a limiting of competition for one well-heeled strip-club owner. The bottom fell out for the accused only after years of surveillance, with the realisation that key witnesses would be prepared to testify for the prosecution in exchange for favourable treatment at trial. The FBI came down with a vengeance on the former officials, resulting in a corruption trial hitherto unseen in Las Vegas' history. After months of testimony and cross-examination, the Department of Justice was able to secure convictions on its targets, resulting in prison time and fines.

IN CONTEXT

Land of the Free

FRANKIE'S
Cocktails

SMOKING AND GAMBLING FRIENDLY

Does what happens in Vegas still stay in Vegas?

TEXT: JAMES REZA

Long before the Disneyfication of excess became the city's calling card, Las Vegas packaged and sold an atmosphere of freewheeling libertarianism. From its mid-1800s mining and Mormon settlement years through until the end of the 20th century, it prided itself on being a true Western city, one that went beyond a basic American sense of liberty and extended to extreme notions of freedom, individual rights and, especially, personal privacy. Las Vegas was the quintessential Western outpost. The town was watered by natural springs, yet socially and physically isolated by hundreds of dusty miles of desert; surrounded by mountains ripe with minerals yet challenged by efforts to extract them; populated by a small but hardy group of Native Americans but willing to displace them for financial gain. It was every man for himself, and that's how the settlers liked it... as long as the money and the liquor were flowing.

DRAWING THE BOUNDARIES

Having been settled by Mormon missionaries in the 1850s, Las Vegas was a different roll of the dice from other Wild West towns. By design (and sometimes, incongruously, by government intervention), Las Vegas neither dried up and blew away like nearby Goldfield, nor grew into an international cosmopolitan crossroads like San Francisco. Instead, it became the longest-standing, largest example of old-school Western freedom, one that would hold dear its libertine roots until the turn of its own centennial.

As in other frontier towns planted far from what pioneers saw as the overreaching shadow of the federal government, gambling and prostitution were an accepted (if not officially endorsed) part of daily life in Vegas. Alongside legal prostitution, gambling was unregulated and openly tolerated until 1909, when it was briefly criminalised to appease a national movement that all but swept it away. But in the face of declining mining revenues, the law was short-lived. In a direct effort to boost the struggling state's bottom line, the Nevada legislature officially legalised gambling in 1931.

And herein lies a clue. If one can point to any reason as to how and why Nevada evolved as such an unharnessed state, it's the cycles of boom and bust. Discover valuable minerals within a day's trot of Big Spring? *Boom.* Suffer the harsh realities of life in the Mojave Desert? *Bust.* Here comes the railroad: *boom!* There goes the railroad and here comes the Depression: *bust!* So let's build a dam, legalise gambling, make it easier to get married (and divorced), pour liquor 24 hours a day; hell, let's put the favourite vices of the American frontiersmen on a pedestal and celebrate a lifestyle built around them. *Boom boom boom!*

As the East Coast struggled to balance the spirit that spawned it with the needs of its ever-growing, ever-challenging urban populations, Las Vegas fashioned itself as the nation's last bastion of freedom. Come as you please, leave your past behind and embrace the vices of greed, gluttony and sex in a town that not only was built upon them but upholds them as virtues.

TAKE IT TO THE LIMIT

It wasn't all boosterism. For those who lived here in its early days, which one can count as lasting until the late 1970s, Las Vegas offered a unique combination. In 1970, a mere 273,000 people called the city home, while 6.8 million visitors streamed through it, making Vegas an energetic phantasmagoria at the weekends and a small desert town during the week. Those who lived here reaped more than mere financial rewards: they came to live within and embody its spirit of freedom and privacy. In a nutshell, it was a kind of conservative libertarianism: you have the right to do what you want as long as it doesn't hurt me, but I also have the right to not have to hear about it.

Out of such an attitude came some of the unusual realities of life in Las Vegas: gambling in grocery stores, liquor on tap around the clock, and unavoidable sex. Speeds were posted as 'unlimited' on roads to Reno, minors drank in casino bars, and respectable civic figures bought gasoline with casino chips. Relatively unskilled workers made barrels of money in the service industries; at the other end of the scale, corporations were formed with anonymous owners and money was shielded and transferred with no outside knowledge of where it came from and where it was going.

Aware that their neighbours might be showgirls or stickmen (or, more nefariously, mobsters or corrupt politicians), Las Vegans lived under a frontier philosophy that combined live-and-let-live with don't-ask, don't-tell. The philosophy is illustrated by the Mormons, who wielded (and continue to wield) great power in law offices, banks and local government, yet did daily business with the city's purveyors of sin.

This era spawned the longtime local's lament, part reality and part romanticism: 'Things were better when the Mob ran the place'. Underworld figures reputed to be behind the casino operations were reinventing themselves as good Samaritans with deep pockets, and were also credited with keeping crimes against the average citizen at a low rate. Just as crucially, they sat at the top of the food chain at a time when most Las Vegans, straight and crooked, were never more than one step removed from a casino job. Fortunately, there was more than enough money to go around.

MOVING DAY

As time marched on, the Mob was vanquished, once-glorious casinos fell into disrepair and the city became a caricature of itself. But Las Vegas rebounded and reinvented itself again, and again. Shiny new resorts, high-class shopping, star chefs? *Boom boom boom*! Las Vegas was reawakened not as a shady little outpost of freedom and sin but as a relatively respectable world-renowned resort town. Something had to give.

Perhaps most responsible for the change in the city's character was the unimaginable success of Las Vegas as a place to live. With more hotels and casinos came more visitors, and the need for more workers to serve them. As labourers with little or no skill flocked to the city, eager to capitalise on the cash flow of what had by now morphed in name from the 'casino industry' to the 'service industry', cultural commentator Kurt Andersen tagged Las Vegas as 'the Detroit of the 21st century'.

In 2003, the ratio of annual visitors to permanent residents remained steady at the 1970 figure of 25-to-1. The difference? There were 35.5 million visitors that year, and they required 1.65 million residents to serve them. Las Vegas was no longer capable of behaving like a small town with too much money. The cash was no longer as easy to get as before, and neither were the jobs. And amid the growth, the infrastructure – roadways, social services and so on – started to buckle.

As the now-infamous 'What happens here, stays here' ad campaign was launched around the dawn of the 21st century, some new arrivals in the city started to cry foul. 'What kind of image is this for my family?' Many of these folks, often transplants from California, were accustomed to what some would call a more socially responsible government culture. And yet longtime Las Vegans looked on in disbelief as expats who moved to suburban enclaves such as Summerlin and Green Valley did so without realising just how pervasive the so-called culture of Las Vegas was. The uproars – about neighbourhood casinos, about naughty billboards, about taxicabs carrying ads for strip clubs – got louder, and the jaws of old-timers dropped ever lower.

During this time, state gaming regulators started cracking down on casinos for a variety of offences, most notably the behaviour of their nightclub patrons and the portrayal of those clubs in ads. The most famous incident occured in 2004: two years after the Hard Rock agreed to pay a fine of $100,000 to the Gaming Control Board after officials investigated allegations of 'overt sexual activity' in its nightclub, the casino forked over further fines totalling $300,000 to the GCB following a racy billboard advertising campaign.

NO SMOKE WITHOUT FIRE

The shift in the city's social culture manifested itself dramatically in 2006. Gambling, drinking and smoking have long existed symbiotically here. But, spearheaded by anti-smoking groups and lobbyists, a battle over smoking in Las Vegas eventually went to a ballot, hung on the idea of protecting children from second-hand smoke.

The regulations squeaked by, eliminating smoking from grocery stores and anywhere – restaurants, cafés, bars – that served prepared food. The hitch? Casinos with full gaming licences and strip clubs were exempt from the law. By the middle of 2007, challengers from the old guard had won a small victory: as the inherent difficulties of enforcing the anti-smoking law made headlines, so they were stripped of their criminal penalties.

Las Vegas is definitely undergoing a shift in its culture, but is it much different from the wholesale reinventions it has undertaken in the past? All had one goal in mind: to protect the cashflow. Perhaps selling a watered-down, packaged version of the libertarian ideal that built Las Vegas is the answer; perhaps it's not. Meanwhile, the 'real' city changes its own course, demanding ever more cosmopolitan experiences, as well as a government far more responsive (some would say invasive) than ever before.

IN CONTEXT

Gambling

Place your bets.

TEXT: DEKE CASTLEMAN

The old and oft-told joke runs that no one in Las Vegas ever got rich through gambling except the owners of the casinos. For many people, it's a gag that's a lot funnier at the start of their trip than it is at the end. Gambling built Las Vegas, and the fact that the city is still expanding at record speed is proof enough that the novelty of the pastime is as bright as it's ever been. This may open your eyes to just how bright: in 2010, Nevada casinos took in $10.4 billion in gaming revenues.

Sorry to shatter your dreams, then, but if you're thinking that you'll walk away from Las Vegas set up for life, you'd best think again. However, if all you're after is a little fun, having filed your gambling budget under 'entertainment' and prepared yourself for manageable losses, you're in the right place. And you'll certainly have more fun if you know a little about the games you're playing. While the games staged by the casinos aren't especially complicated, a little knowledge will help your money last a good deal longer than it otherwise might. Indeed, play your cards right and you may even end up ahead. But don't bet on it.

HOW CASINOS MAKE MONEY

Before learning how to play the games, it's wise to get acquainted with the casinos' angles on them. There are four ways for the casinos to generate gaming revenue: the house edge, favourable rules, commissions and dumb players.

● The house edge is the difference between the true odds of an event occurring and the odds used for payouts. For example, in double-zero roulette, there are 38 possible winning numbers. If the casino paid true odds, it would pay off a winning number at 37:1 (for a total of $38, including your $1 bet). Instead, the casino pays off a winning number at 35:1. Calculating the house edge from this scenario is simple.

First, imagine placing a $1 bet on every possible number in double-zero roulette, a total wager of $38. No matter which number wins, you'll receive a payout of $36: winnings of $35 at the 35:1 payoff, plus your original $1 bet. The difference between the true-odds payout and the actual payout is $2, money that goes directly into the house's coffers. To calculate the house edge, simply divide the money kept by the house (2) by the money that the house would have paid on true odds (38). This calculation shows a house edge of 5.26 per cent, which means that the house expects to keep 5.26¢ of each dollar bet at a roulette table.

The house edge varies from game to game, and even within each game. Casinos love it when gamblers keep playing for hour after hour, because the house edge grinds its little takes from every dollar wagered. The law of averages favours the casino.

● The rules for casino games are structured to favour the house. The best example is blackjack, where the dealer gets to play his hand last. Should a player bust beforehand, the dealer wins by default. Even if the dealer ends up busting later, the player loses and the house wins.

● Commissions are collected by the house in a few table games. In poker, the house serves as dealer but doesn't play a hand. Instead, the house takes a percentage of every pot (a sum of money that's called the 'rake') or charges players a flat fee of $5 to $7 per half-hour of play. In baccarat, the house takes five per cent of all winnings from bank bets.

● Be they drunk, superstitious, careless or ill-informed, dumb gamblers are a boundless source of funds for the smart house. Why else do casinos offer gamblers free drinks? Alcohol is wonderful for loosening inhibitions, such as the inhibition against losing next month's rent, but it also causes sensible players to make stupid mistakes. An example: although the house edge in blackjack has been calculated at around two per cent, casinos expect a win (or 'hold') of 15 to 20 per cent of the total amount of money brought to the table (the drop), due entirely to the incompetence of the players.

BETTING LIMITS AND MINIMUMS

At every table game, there's a sign detailing the minimum (and often maximum) allowable bet. At blackjack, it might be $5 to $500. Casinos expect players to bet towards the low end of the limit. This separates players by class, so a big player seeking a speedy $500-a-hand game doesn't have to endure poky play from a piker betting five bucks each time. High rollers can bet at higher-than-posted limits if the house is willing to 'fade' (cover) them. In roulette, the minimum means the sum total of all bets that an individual gambler can place in one round; in other words, if the table has a $5 minimum, you can cover it with five $1 bets. But in blackjack, if you play two hands at once, you must bet the minimum on each.

ETIQUETTE

Before you lay down your money, always note the minimum-bet requirement, usually posted on a sign in the far left corner. If you don't want to embarrass yourself, don't toss out a red ($5) chip on a $100-minimum table. Similarly, don't put a quarter into a dollar slot or video poker machine; the coin will pass through the thing and clank into the hopper, alerting the other players that you're a novice. That said, most machines no longer accept coins; only bills and cashout tickets will pass muster.

Table games have strict rules about when players can touch chips or cards, rules that exist to discourage cheats. Many blackjack games are dealt face up and players never touch the cards. Once you make a bet, never touch the chips you've laid down; if you're 'splitting' or doubling down in blackjack, push out a new pile of chips but don't touch the original bet. This rule is to discourage 'past posting', a scam by which cheats sneak more chips on to their bet after peeking at their cards.

Only handle dice with one hand. The pit bosses, the dealers and the other players will all get very nervous if you touch the dice with two hands, or make a fist around them with one hand so they can't be seen. Blow on them, shake them and

The Gambler's Lexicon

Speak the language of Las Vegas.

IN CONTEXT

ante a small bet that players must place into the pot before a hand of poker is dealt.

bankroll your total gambling budget.

Black Book a list, kept by the State Gaming Control Board, of people barred from casinos due to cheating or a link to organised crime.

boxman casino executive who acts as the umpire in a game of craps.

bust a blackjack hand exceeding 21.

buy in exchange cash for casino chips.

cage the cashier, where chips and tokens are converted into cash and credit is established.

carousel a group of slots that are often connected to a joint progressive jackpot.

change colour swapping chips for ones of a higher or lower denomination.

checks another word for chips.

chips tokens issued by casinos and used, instead of cash, for table games.

colour up exchange small denomination chips for larger denomination chips.

comps 'complimentaries'; anything from free cocktails to 'RFB' (room, food and beverage). Their value is calculated by the gambler's average bet, multiplied by the time spent playing, multiplied by the house edge. To qualify, you must be a rated player or belong to a players club.

credit line amount of credit a gambler is allowed.

croupier casino employee who controls the action in baccarat and roulette.

drop total funds, including chips, cash and markers, gambled at a table or a machine.

edge see *house edge*.

European wheel a roulette wheel with a single '0' position, which gives players better odds. Most wheels in Vegas have '0' and '00'.

even money a bet that pays back an amount equal to the bet itself. In other words, if you win on a $5 bet, you receive your $5 stake plus a $5 win.

eye in the sky casino surveillance systems.

face cards jacks, queens and kings; also known as 'pictures' or 'paint'.

funbook a booklet of vouchers (meal deals and the like) or match-play coupons (valid in conjunction with cash).

George dealer-speak for a good tipper.

grind joint a casino with low table minimums and low-denomination slot machines.

high roller gambler who bets at least $100 per hand on a table game, and plays $5 slots.

hit in blackjack, to take another card.

hole card blackjack dealer's face-down card.

house edge the percentage difference (retained by the casino) between the true odds and the actual payout.

inside bet in roulette, betting on a single number or small combination of numbers.

juice power and influence; who you know.

turn them so your favourite numbers are up, but don't hide them for a second. That's how dice cheats use sleight of hand to get loaded dice into a game of craps.

All told, it's best for novice gamblers to stand back at first and watch the action; after a few minutes, you'll get the hang of the procedures. If you need to be corrected, the dealer will do so gently and unobtrusively. And don't worry if it happens: the other players at the tables have all been corrected at one time or another. They didn't step up to a crap table for the first time knowing everything about the game.

You must be 21 to gamble. If you're under 21 and start winning (or hit a jackpot that requires you to sign tax forms), your chips or jackpot will be confiscated and you'll be tossed out of the casino faster than you can say, 'But...'. You may even

layout diagram on the playing table that marks the area of the game.

loose a term used to describe a slot machine that pays out frequently. Casinos compete in claiming that their slots are the loosest.

low roller gambler who bets at low-minimum slot machines, usually in grind joints.

marker IOU signed by a rated player to obtain chips and paid off with chips or cash.

natural in blackjack, a two-card total of 21; in baccarat, a two-card total of eight or nine.

outside bet in roulette, betting outside the single-number layout: on black or red; on odds or evens; on the first, second or third 12 numbers as a group etc.

pit area behind the gaming tables reserved for casino employees.

pit boss casino executive who oversees the gambling action from inside the pit.

players club clubs for slots and video-poker players by which members accrue points as they play; these can then later be redeemed against meals, gifts, cash and other perks.

pot the bets accumulated while playing a hand of poker.

progressive a slot or video-poker machine on which the jackpot increases as more coins are played. A linked progressive is a group of machines networked to share their jackpot.

push in blackjack, where the dealer and player(s) have the same un-busted hand. No money changes hands.

rated player player whose gambling is assessed by the casino and is thus eligible for comps.

shill casino employee who plays at empty tables (with house money) to encourage visitors to join the action.

shoe container for decks of cards from which card games are often dealt.

shooter the player who throws the dice in a game of craps.

stand in blackjack, to refuse another card.

stiff someone who doesn't tip, one of the worst insults in Las Vegas; also refers to blackjack hands totalling 12-16.

tight used to describe a slot machine that is perceived to pay out infrequently.

toke a tip for a casino employee, often given in the form of a bet on their behalf.

true odds real chances of winning on any game as opposed to the money actually paid out by the casino.

underlay a bet that's higher than strict probability suggests is wise.

up card the blackjack dealer's face-up card.

vigorish also 'vig'; *see house edge*.

whale big-money gambler prepared to wager at least $5,000 a hand at high-stakes games.

IN CONTEXT

be turned over to a Gaming Control Board agent. The lower your age and the higher your bet, the bigger the trouble.

Most casinos subscribe to the old tradition that cameras are unwelcome, and it's wise to leave your SLRs and camcorders in your room, your car or your backpack. If you're discreet, or even if you ask permission, you can sometimes get away with taking photographs in casinos, particularly at the Excalibur and Harrah's. On the other hand, wherever you go in a casino (except the toilets), you'll be watched by eye-in-the-sky cameras and taped for posterity. Nowhere on earth is Big Brother busier than in a casino; make sure you behave accordingly.

MONEY, MONEY, MONEY

To play table games, you'll need chips. However, in some games, you can throw down a bill for your first plays; in blackjack, for example, it's usually fine to play with cash, though any winnings will be paid as chips. You can buy chips at the table in a process called a buy in; you can also buy chips at the cage. Chips can only be redeemed at the cage.

Chips are like currency in the casino within which they're issued. However, due to problems with counterfeiting, casinos rarely honour each others' chips for gambling unless, as is the case with the MGM-operated Mirage and TI (for example), they're under the same ownership. It's sometimes possible to exchange sub-$100 denominations from other casinos for house chips at the cage.

Most modern slot and video-poker machines have bill slots that change greenbacks into credits. If you don't want to use it, or if you only have bills in denominations not accepted by the machine, press the 'Change' button. This activates a light on top of the machine, which summons a roving cashier.

Most casinos are converting to cashless machines (also known as 'ticket in/ ticket out', or TITO). You play the machines by putting a regular bill in the slot; however, when you're ready to cash out, the machine dispenses not cash but a ticket detailing your total credits. You can either take the ticket and feed it into another machine, or redeem it for cash at the cage. Be very careful with the tickets, and be sure to redeem them before leaving the casino: some expire in 30 days. And don't leave a TITO machine for even a moment: someone will almost certainly press the 'Cash Out' button, grab the ticket and run.

LEARNING TO GAMBLE

If you want to study before arriving, you'll find hundreds of books on everything from baccarat to video poker. For recommendations, see pp318-319, though you're generally safe with anything published by Huntington Press (3665 S Procyon Avenue, Las Vegas, NV 89103, 1-800 244 2224, www.shoplva.com). There are lots of software programmes available, as well as a slew of instructive websites (see p319). The **Gamblers Book Club** and the **Gamblers General Store** are both excellent resources.

Many of the large casinos offer free hands-on lessons at table games. The instructors, usually informative and personable sorts, will take you through the playing procedures and etiquette one step at a time, but they almost certainly won't warn you about sucker games and bets: after all, they're paid by the casino. Lessons are usually held in the late morning during the week, when the casino is at its quietest; some are followed by open low-minimum 'live' games for punters who want to celebrate their new-found skills under casino conditions.

When you're ready to join a game, first stand back and watch the action for a while in order to pick up the rhythms and routines. (However, don't stand too long behind blackjack tables, as most bosses will suspect you of 'back counting' the deck in order to slip in a bet at the most advantageous time.) Choose a table with the lowest possible minimum, so that you're not risking $100, $25 or even $10 a hand at a game you're playing for the first time. Downtown casinos and locals' casinos tend to have lower minimums than the casinos on the Strip.

MAKING THE MOST OF IT

There are plenty of ways to make the most of your money, many of them set up by casinos in an attempt to draw customers. Most popular among them are the casinos' players clubs: they cost nothing to join, and the points you accrue on them can be redeemed for rooms, food and even cash.

Always ask for 'comps' when you play table games. As soon as you make a bet, call over a floorman and ask: 'How long do I have to play to get a buffet comp?' He or she will look at your bet and tell you. Play for as long as he or she indicates, then head off and eat yourself silly. And look for coupons in 'funbooks', free coupon booklets handed out in front of many casinos. Two-for-one, three-for-two and seven-for-five coupons on even-money bets give gamblers a huge edge over the house at blackjack, craps and the like.

While the casinos can help you make your money last, you can also help yourself. Play slowly, for one thing: you're better off exposing your bankroll to the house edge for 50 hands an hour at a busy table than 100 hands an hour playing one-on-one against the dealer, or pulling the handle on a slot machine for 400 spins an hour rather than running at double-time by hitting the spin button like a lunatic.

To ensure you have gambling funds for your whole trip, it's a good idea to divide your money into 'session' portions. Lost an entire portion quickly? End of session. Don't dig into your remaining bankroll until it's time for the next session. Always keep an eye on your coins, cash, tickets and chips; watch for 'rail thieves' when you're at the crap table; and ensure back-to-back slot machines have a plastic or metal guard between them to prevent 'reach through' thievery.

TIP TALK

Las Vegas is a town that runs on tips. This goes particularly for casino dealers, who are paid little more than the minimum wage. Every shift of dealers combines and divides their tips, which make up the bulk of their pay. Giving tips (or 'tokes', as dealers call them, short for tokens of appreciation) is smart, as a happy dealer is your friend. Dealers can assist players in a number of ways: they can slow down the pace of the game (extremely useful when you're playing for comps), create a sociable atmosphere, and even deal a little deeper in the deck, critical for card counters.

You can toke the dealer as you leave the table. However, while they appreciate the tip, it won't gain you any help while you're playing. A better method is to toke immediately after a big win; this way, the dealer knows you're thinking of him or her and could start to help you. Don't bother toking if the dealer is rude, creepy or unco-operative. In fact, don't even play there: just get up and move on to another table.

The best way to show your appreciation is to place a bet for the dealer alongside your own wager. If you win, the toke is paid off at regular odds and the dealer takes the winnings. If you lose, the house wins the toke, but the dealer will still appreciate the gesture. In blackjack, you can place a chip outside the line surrounding your wager circle, but if this toke bet wins, it has to be scooped up by the dealer right away. Alternatively, if you're riding a hot streak, place the dealer's toke next to your bet within your wager circle. If you win, you can let the toke ride (continue to the next deal): it's yours until you give it to the dealer. Just tell the dealer the extra bet is a toke. Note, though, that some dealers resent it if you let their tokes ride, and have a take-the-money-and-run attitude.

Baccarat

Long viewed as an obscure, weirdly ritualised game for high rollers, baccarat ('ba-cuh-rah') is a table game with a small house edge. It is currently the hottest trending game in town. In 2010, gamblers bet nearly $11 billion on baccarat – more than a third of the total wagered on table games that year.

Up to 15 players sit around the layout and bet on BANK, PLAYER or TIE. Dealers lay out two hands of two cards each, titled PLAYER and BANK. The object is for each hand to total as close to nine as possible. Face cards and tens count as zero and any total over nine is reduced by eliminating the first digit (for instance, 15 is valued as five). Players have no control over whether to 'draw' or 'stand'. Dealers follow a strict set of rules to determine if they must 'hit' either hand with a third card.

If PLAYER or BANK bets win, the house pays at even money. Since the rules determine that BANK wins slightly more often, the house retains a five per cent commission on all BANK winnings. Even with the commission, the house holds only a 1.17 per cent edge on BANK bets and 1.36 per cent on PLAYER bets. (The TIE bet should be avoided. It pays off at eight to one, but since the true odds are about 9.5:1, the house edge equates to a whopping 14 per cent.)

The rhythm of baccarat is leisurely and the mood subdued. In fact, it's rarely necessary for players to speak. Baccarat pits are usually secluded behind velvet ropes or in high-limit rooms, which often come complete with small buffets that lend an air of exclusivity. However, if you can handle the minimum (often $100), you're welcome to join the action. Casinos catering to low-end gamblers tend to ignore baccarat, but high-end casinos hold it dear for good reason: it's very profitable. The Mirage has estimated that as much as ten per cent of its annual revenue comes from baccarat.

MINI BACCARAT
Mini baccarat is a low-stakes version of the game played in the main pit, usually near the blackjack tables. It's a good introduction: the rules are the same but the bets are lower. As it attracts fewer players, the pace of the game is faster.

Bingo

It might not be posh, but bingo is a gambling stalwart in Vegas, especially in neighbourhood casinos: the game is played in the same way as it is all over the world. The house edge is slightly better than the similar keno, though it's hard to pin it down to a precise figure since so much depends on the variety of the game and its payout. The one advantage bingo has over keno is that bingo numbers are called until a player wins. By contrast, a million keno games can go by without anyone hitting the big jackpot.

Blackjack (21)

Blackjack is by far the most popular table game in the casinos. The reasons are obvious: it's easy to play, the basic strategy slims the house edge to nearly zero, and dozens of books claim the house can be beaten with card counting.

THE BASICS
After placing their bets, everyone at the table is dealt two cards. Single- and double-deck blackjack (games played with either one deck, or two decks shuffled together) are dealt from the dealer's hand; for multiple-deck blackjack, the decks are combined and placed in a 'shoe', from which the dealer pulls cards. Face cards count as ten; aces can count as one or 11. (A hand in which an ace is counted as 11 is known as a 'soft' hand; for example, an ace and a six is called 'soft 17'.) Each player competes against the dealer's hand by trying to get as close as possible to a total of 21 without exceeding it (or 'busting'). The game moves clockwise around the table; the player sitting on the right as he or she faces the dealer is the first to play. The first of the dealer's cards is dealt face up (the 'up card'), with the second dealt face down (the 'hole card').

First, check your cards. If you want an extra card, ask to 'hit'; when satisfied with your total, you 'stand'. After all players have stood or busted, the dealer reveals his or her hole card and plays the hand according to fixed rules: he or she must hit totals of 16 or less and must stand on 17 or above. (The rules vary if the dealer has soft 17, with some casinos requiring dealers to hit and others to stand; the players' edge is increased by 0.2 per cent for the latter.)

Once the dealer has stood or busted, the hands are compared; players who beat the dealer are paid off at even money. Ties between the house and player are a 'push' and no money changes hands; dealers indicate a push by knocking gently on the layout. If a player is dealt an ace and a ten-value card, it's considered a natural blackjack (also known as a 'snapper'); unless the dealer's up card is an ace or a ten, indicating a possible blackjack, the player is immediately paid at 3:2. Watch out for games (often single-deck or low-limit) where naturals pay only 6:5; *see p63* **Sucker Bets**.

Blackjack Strategy

H=hit; **S**=stand; **D**=double down; **Sp**=split

Dealer's up card

If you have a total of

	2	3	4	5	6	7	8	9	10	A
2-8	H	H	H	H	H	H	H	H	H	H
9	H	D	D	D	D	H	H	H	H	H
10	D	D	D	D	D	D	D	D	H	H
11	D	D	D	D	D	D	D	D	D	D
12	H	H	S	S	S	H	H	H	H	H
13-16	S	S	S	S	S	H	H	H	H	H
17-20	S	S	S	S	S	S	S	S	S	S

Dealer's up card

If you have an ace

	2	3	4	5	6	7	8	9	10	A
A+2	H	H	D	D	D	H	H	H	H	H
A+3	H	H	D	D	D	H	H	H	H	H
A+4	H	H	D	D	D	H	H	H	H	H
A+5	H	H	D	D	D	H	H	H	H	H
A+6	D	D	D	D	D	H	H	H	H	H
A+7	S	D	D	D	D	S	S	H	H	S
A+8	S	S	S	S	S	S	S	S	S	S
A+9	S	S	S	S	S	S	S	S	S	S

Dealer's up card

If you have a pair

	2	3	4	5	6	7	8	9	10	A
2s	Sp	Sp	Sp	Sp	Sp	Sp	H	H	H	H
3s	Sp	Sp	Sp	Sp	Sp	Sp	H	H	H	H
4s	H	H	H	H	H	H	H	H	H	H
5s	D	D	D	D	D	D	D	D	H	H
6s	Sp	Sp	Sp	Sp	Sp	H	H	H	H	H
7s	Sp	Sp	Sp	Sp	Sp	Sp	H	H	H	H
8s	Sp	Sp	Sp	Sp	Sp	Sp	Sp	Sp	Sp	Sp
9s	Sp	Sp	Sp	Sp	Sp	S	Sp	Sp	S	S
10s	S	S	S	S	S	S	S	S	S	S
As	Sp	Sp	Sp	Sp	Sp	Sp	Sp	Sp	Sp	Sp

Players should consider 'surrendering':
• with hard 13-16 against dealer's A
• with hard 14-16 against dealer's 10
• with hard 15-16 against dealer's 9
But if all that's too much to memorise, at least remember the following five golden rules:
• stand on 17-21, but always hit soft 17
• stand on 12-16 against dealer's 2 to 6, but hit on 12-16 against dealer's 7 to A
• always split 8s and aces, but never split the 'F's, (4s, 5s and face cards)
• double down on 10s and 11s against the dealer's 2 to 9
• never take insurance

ETIQUETTE

With the crucial exception of the dealer's hole card, almost all multi-deck blackjack games are dealt with the cards face up. In these games, players never touch the cards, but instead indicate hit or stand with hand motions. This reduces the potential for misunderstandings, and also makes it easier for disputed plays to be reviewed on security videos. For a hit, players hold one hand palm down above the felt and brush their fingers toward them. To stand, players hold their hand the same way, but with the fingers straight outward, and move it right and left.

Single- and double-deck games are almost always dealt face down, and players hold their own cards. Always hold them with one hand; it makes the dealer and the eye nervous if you use both. Hitting is indicated by scratching the cards towards you on the layout, while standing is indicated by sliding the cards face down under the chips.

Though blackjack sets each player's hand against the dealer's, most players view the game as everyone against the dealer. Their goal is to make the dealer bust, which means payoffs for all players still in the game. These folks don't take kindly to people playing stupidly ('splitting' tens or hitting a 14, say, against a dealer's six), especially if the offending party sits in the last seat on the left (known as 'third base'), since they feel those cards should have gone to the dealer. In truth, it doesn't really matter, since on average, a player's good decisions cancel the bad decisions. However, many gamers focus only on the bad decisions, which is why novices shouldn't sit at third base.

BETTING

There are four ways in which players can alter their bets after the cards have been dealt: 'doubling down', 'splitting', 'insurance' and 'surrender'. Splitting and doubling down aggressively are the secrets to winning at basic strategy blackjack, as they give players the chance to press their bets when they're holding a strong starting hand.

● When a player 'doubles down', he or she makes another bet equal to the original and receives one (only one) more card. It's the choice move when you've got a total of nine, ten or 11 and the dealer shows a weak card such as a six. You can double down only if you haven't already taken a hit.

● 'Splitting' is an option when players are dealt two cards of the same value. An additional bet equal to the original bet is put out and the cards are split, with each played as a separate hand. It's to the player's advantage to double down or split each of the post-split hands, though some casinos limit what you can do. Check the strategy chart (p53) for more advice.

● 'Insurance' is a side bet offered when the dealer has a possible blackjack (in other words, when the dealer is showing an ace or ten-value card). An insurance bet is limited to 50 per cent of the original bet and is lost if the dealer doesn't have a blackjack. If he or she does have a blackjack, insurance pays at 2:1, making the whole bet into a push.

Despite the word's connotations, insurance is a sucker bet. Unless you're a card counter and can calculate the odds of a blackjack, there's no reason to take insurance, even if you're holding a natural 21. If you're holding a natural and the dealer is calling for insurance bets, you can take even money on your bet. If you don't take even money and the dealer has a two-card 21, it's a push. If the dealer doesn't have 21, your natural is paid at 3:2 (again, don't play 6:5 games; *see p63* **Sucker Bets**).

● 'Surrender' is an obscure but useful rule that's not in effect everywhere. It permits players to fold and sacrifice half their bet as long as they haven't played their hand. This is an excellent way to drop out and minimise losses when dealt weak cards. If used correctly, it increases the player's edge by 0.2 per cent.

CARD COUNTING

Card counting is a technique whereby a player visually tracks exposed cards and mentally keeps a running total to determine if the deck is positive or negative. In the simplest count, the ten-value cards and aces are valued at −1, while cards numbered two to seven take a value of +1; the eights and nines have no value. If the running total is positive, players have an advantage and should raise their bets.

Does it work? Yes, but only if you devote weeks of practice, are cool under the pressures of casino play, and develop camouflage skills so that the house doesn't know you're counting. Although card counting isn't against the law, casinos frown upon it, and 'back off' (forbid card counters from playing blackjack) or 'bar' (kick them out of the casino) any player that they suspect of using the practice. Counting cards is a gruelling discipline at which most fail. However, successful card counters, especially high-stakes players, are among the few gamblers who beat the casinos at their own game.

If you're not among the handful of people who have perfected this dark art, it's best to stick to basic strategy. At its simplest level, this entails memorising a chart that contains the answer to every decision in blackjack, based on your first two cards and the dealer's up card. You can usually bring the chart to the table and check it as you play, as long as you don't slow down the game. For the chart, *see p53*.

Craps

Fast, furious and enormously confusing, craps is an action-filled dice game that terrifies most novices. It can also be hugely exciting: if you hear a roar of excitement while wandering through a casino, it's probably coming from a craps table. The players cheer, curse and scream; dice and chips fly across the table; and everybody roots for different numbers. Fortunes can be won and lost in minutes, which is why craps is worshipped by a subculture. It's confounding, but by sticking to a few smart bets, players can enjoy a boisterous game with a house edge as low as one per cent, and occasionally lower.

THE BASICS

Craps is played on a large table surrounded by a low, padded wall, with a rail for chips on top and, outside, a shelf for the ever-present drinks. The game is staffed by between one and four casino employees, and there's room for 12 to 14 players to belly up to the table.

The layout is divided into three sections. The two at each end are identical, but in the centre is an area reserved for special wagers known as 'proposition bets'. A game starts with dice being offered to a new shooter by the 'stickman', the dealer located mid-table who's holding the stick. This first roll of the dice is known as the 'come out roll'. (Each player will be offered the dice at some point, though it's common to refuse.) The shooter must throw two dice in such a way that they bounce off the table's far wall.

Basically, players bet on which numbers the shooters will throw, and in what order they will appear. The shooter must place a bet before his or her first throw, and traditionally chooses PASS (*see below*). Those betting with the shooter are known as 'right bettors' while those betting against the shooter are called 'wrong bettors'.

BETTING

There are four basic wagers known as 'line bets' marked on the layout: PASS, DON'T PASS, COME and DON'T COME (the DON'T bets are for wrong bettors). Players bet on the PASS or DON'T PASS lines. If the dice show seven (statistically the most likely roll) or 11 on the come out roll, PASS bettors win at even odds and DON'T PASS bettors lose. If the shooter throws a total of two or three, DON'T PASS wins and PASS loses. If the dice show 12, PASS bettors lose and it's a 'push' (or tie) for DON'T PASS bettors. Rolling two, three or 12 is known as 'crapping out'. If any other number is thrown (four, five, six, eight, nine or ten), that number becomes the 'point'.

Once a point is established, the shooter keeps rolling, attempting to repeat the point before rolling a seven (known as 'sevening out'). In this context, the point and seven are the only numbers that count: all PASS and DON'T PASS bets ride until the 'point'

IN CONTEXT

is hit or the shooter sevens out. If the shooter hits the point, PASS bettors win and DON'T PASS bettors lose. If the shooter tosses a seven, DON'T PASS bettors win, PASS bettors lose and the shooter relinquishes control of the dice. The shortest roll a shooter can have is two throws, hitting a point on the come out roll followed by a seven; in this situation, wrong bettors win. But if he or she avoids 'sevening out', the shooter can roll forever, and right bettors can rack up big bucks. Every time the 'point' is hit, the whole game is reset and the next throw is a fresh 'come out roll'. However, all the side bets, such as COME bets, remain in play.

COME and DON'T COME bets represent an optional second layer of betting that runs concurrently to the original layer. They're similar to PASS and DON'T PASS bets, with the same set of outcomes (an immediate win, lose or 'push', or the establishment of a 'point'), but they can only be made on throws subsequent to the come out roll. For instance, say the shooter establishes a point of four; on the next roll, you make a COME bet. (If you want, you can enter the game with a COME/DON'T COME bet at any time during a hand without having previously made a PASS or DON'T PASS bet.) The next roll is nine, so nine becomes your 'point'. If that throw had yielded seven or 11, you would have won, and the DON'T COME bets would have lost. If the dice had totalled two, three or 12, your COME bet would have lost. And if the shooter had hit his number, the COME bets would have ridden, awaiting a seven or a repeat of the come point.

TAKING THE ODDS

If a player sticks to the four 'line' bets outlined above, the house edge is only about 1.4 per cent. But even that tiny amount can be further reduced with the use of the 'odds' bet, a wager where the house holds an edge of, believe it or not, zero. Unsurprisingly, these are the only such wagers in the casino, which is doubtless the reason why the layout of a crap table doesn't mention them at all.

Once a point is established, any player with a line bet can back up that wager with an 'odds' bet, placing the bet behind the original 'line' bet on the craps layout. This allows players to increase their bet midstream. In a game with single odds, the maximum odds bet equals the line bet. That alone slashes the house edge from about 1.4 per cent to 0.85 per cent. Some casinos offer double odds, triple odds, 10x or even 100x odds, all of which reduce the house edge even further. A few offer different odds on specified points. Anyone making line bets in craps should take, at the very least, single odds on every bet made. It's worth attending a lesson to learn how to make the most of this tactic.

THE REST OF THE TABLE

Smart players stick to line and odds bets, but action junkies need more. For them, the table offers another world of wagers, none of which is worthwhile. Granted, some bets offer an edge only slightly worse than line bets. But most of the one-roll proposition bets are simply horrific.

For instance, the ANY 7 proposition bet has a stunning house edge of 16.67 per cent, the worst edge of any game wager apart from keno and the Money Wheel. Don't waste time on it. Instead, stick to right and wrong betting with line bets pressed with odds and you'll get more than enough action. A straightforward odds-effective play is to bet the minimum stake on PASS and bet the same amount on two COME bets, taking odds on both (double or triple, if they're offered and you can afford it).

Keno

This lottery offshoot is the worst bet in the casino, with an appalling house edge of 25 to 40 per cent. You might as well climb to the top of the Stratosphere and throw your money into the wind. At least you'll have a nice view.

As with an old-style lottery or bingo, keno involves a ticket (or 'blank') containing 80 numbers, on which players circle as many as 15 or 20 numbers. When the game starts, 20 numbers are selected at random (ping-pong balls are blown from a 'goose' into a pair of 'arms') and displayed on screens around the casino. If your numbers are picked, you win. If not, you lose. (Get used to the second option.) The greater the proportion of your numbers picked, the higher the payback. Remember that, if by some remote chance you win at keno, you must claim your money before the next game begins or you will forfeit your winnings.

There are many variations of keno, but none makes the edge even remotely acceptable. Worst of all, payouts for keno in no way reflect the true odds of your bet, since they're capped at an arbitrary figure. For instance, your chances of selecting nine numbers and hitting all of them are 1,380,700:1. Your payout for such a feat? Usually no more than $250,000 on a $2 bet. Here's another fun fact: if two players hit the big jackpot at the same time, they have to split the cash. The only way to win at keno is never to play it.

Money Wheel (or Big Six)

It makes sense to be wary of a game that's been imported to casinos from the morally challenged world of carnivals. That's the case with the Money Wheel (aka Big Six), the grandchild of spin-the-wheel games loved by carnies everywhere.

The game is simple. A large, ornate wheel is mounted vertically a few feet above the floor. On it are 54 evenly spaced slots. Two show joker or house symbols; the other 52 are divided into $1, $2, $5, $10 and $20 denominations. There are usually 24 $1 slots and only two $20 slots. A layout in front of the wheel has squares matching those denominations. Players put cash or chips on the squares of their choice, and the wheel spins. When it stops, bettors who selected the correct denomination win, with the payoff determined by the dollar value of the winning slot. A $20 symbol pays off at 20:1; a $1 symbol pays off at even money. House or joker symbols pay off at 40:1, sometimes 45:1. As you might guess, the casino holds a serious edge, ranging from 11 per cent for a bet on the $1 symbol to 25.9 per cent on the joker. Don't be a sucker.

Poker

From the casino's point of view, poker isn't a good bet. In poker, gamblers bet against each other, not the house. A casino employee merely deals, acting as the cashier. The

IN CONTEXT

house's income is limited to a percentage taken from each pot, or a seat rental of $5 or $7 per half-hour. This small take is the main reason why many casinos opted out of the game in the 1990s.

However, thanks to the explosion in the popularity of poker over the past few years, many casinos have got right back into it. The entire state of Nevada had 701 poker tables in 2005; in 2010, Las Vegas alone had a total of 920 tables. Another telling statistic: in 2002, 631 players competed in the $10,000-buy-in World Series of Poker, the granddaddy of all gambling tournaments, with the winner taking home a first-place prize of $1.1 million. In 2010, the main event drew a record 7,319 entrants. And it's a younger crowd too: in the 2010 WSOP, only one player at the final table was older than 30; the 2011 winner, Canadian Jonathan Duhamel, was just 22 when he beat his 24-year-old competitor and took home the $8.9 million kitty. Blame television, which has cottoned on to the camera-friendliness of the game to dramatic effect. TV networks such as ESPN, Fox and even NBC now televise poker tournaments, celebrity matches, one-on-one showdowns and even dramas based on the game. Online poker is also growing at an amazing rate: a whole new generation of poker players are training on their computers for the big games and tournaments. However, while poker has arrived as a national pastime, it still has a way to go before overtaking blackjack as the biggest-grossing table game in town. Whereas poker netted casinos $161 million in 2006, the same year saw blackjack yield an astonishing $1.38 billion.

PLAYING IN VEGAS

To join a poker game in a Las Vegas casino, just sit in an empty seat and buy in (which usually costs ten times the minimum or maximum bet, depending on the game) with chips or cash. If there's no space at any of the tables, put your name on a waiting list. The traditional rules that everyone knows are in effect for poker in Las Vegas: the most popular games are Texas hold 'em and seven-card stud, but many casinos in town have recently been experimenting with variations.

In Texas hold 'em, each player is dealt two cards face down, before five common cards are pitched face up on to the layout for the table. The first three common cards appear together (this is called the 'flop'), followed by the fourth card (the 'turn') and the fifth card (the 'river'). Players determine their best five-card hand from the seven cards available to them.

In seven-card stud, players get two cards face down and one face up, followed by three cards face up and a final card face down. Again, players then put together the best hand from their own seven cards.

Both of the above games have numerous rounds of betting and raising, so for all but the lowest-stakes games, a hefty bankroll is crucial. For games with betting limits, posted signs indicate the smallest and largest bet allowable (usually in the form '$5/$10'). In a limit game, you'll need a bankroll of at least 20 times the maximum bet. There are also pot-limit games, which means raises can go as high as the pot, and no-limit games, in which raises can go as high as the largest bankroll on the table. In all games, no matter the stakes, players are not allowed to bring more money to the table once a hand is dealt. If a player goes 'all in', betting all his or her money, and he or she can't match another player's raise, a side pot is formed for those who wish to continue betting. The all-in player is limited to playing for the main pot.

Explaining poker strategy here is impossible. Besides the complexities of the game itself, much of poker is psychological. Reading other players and bluffing are a huge part of the process; if you didn't know this already, you'll learn the first time you sit down in a card room. If you're not a seasoned poker player, be very careful of high-stakes games, which can be populated by sharks (sometimes operating in teams). They've learned the main casino secret: it's easy to take money from amateur gamblers. If you're a novice, stick to low-stakes games, which are usually straightforward and friendly.

CARIBBEAN STUD

Caribbean stud is a rather dumb game with a house edge of 5.27 per cent, just a hair worse than double-zero roulette. Sitting around a table with a layout similar to blackjack, players put out a single ante and receive five cards face down. The dealer also gets five cards, though one is dealt face up. At this point, players either fold (and lose their ante) or 'call' by adding a bet that's twice their ante. All players then reveal their cards. If the dealer doesn't 'qualify' with at least an ace and king in his or her hand, all players win even money for their ante and the call bets are returned. Should the dealer's hand qualify, each player's hand is compared against the dealer's. If the player wins, the ante is paid at even money and the call bet qualifies for a 'bonus' payout based on the hand. Bonus payouts range from even money for a pair to 100:1 for a royal flush (most of the payouts are lower than those found in Let it Ride).

The maximum bonus payout in Caribbean stud is usually capped somewhere between $5,000 and $60,000, so make sure your bet is no higher than it needs to be to win that amount. For example, if the bonus payout is capped at $5,000, your ante should never be above $25: this would make your call bet $50 and so a 100:1 payout would hit the $5,000 ceiling exactly. The simple math? Divide the maximum bonus payout by 200. Your ante should never exceed that figure.

For a side bet of a dollar per hand, Caribbean stud poker also offers players the chance to hit a progressive jackpot, with payoffs based on the quality of their hand. A royal flush wins 100 per cent of the jackpot, while a flush gets a mere $50. The fact that jackpots have been known to go up to $5 million tells you something about how often a royal flush occurs.

LET IT RIDE

Let it Ride offers the unusual feature of allowing players to take back two thirds of their wager. Players bet three equal amounts and are dealt three cards face down. Two common cards are then dealt, also face down. At this point, players can pull back one of their bets by signalling to the dealer (don't touch your chips). When the first common card is turned over, players can withdraw their second bet. The final common card is then shown and payouts are made according to a fixed schedule, ranging from even money for a pair of tens or better to 1,000:1 for a royal flush. As you might guess, the payouts are way below true odds. For instance, the odds against drawing a flush are 508:1, but the payout is eight to one. Overall, the house holds about a four per cent edge, if players make all the right decisions.

The biggest lure of Let it Ride is that players compete against the cards, not each other, so it's more appealing to amateurs. Also, the option to withdraw two thirds of the bet gives players the illusion that their money is lasting longer than it might in other games. However, don't be fooled: the house edge grinds down almost everyone in the end. And since it's basically five-card stud, it can be a long time between winning hands.

PAI GOW POKER

Pai gow poker – not to be confused with pai gow, a Chinese game that utilises tiles – is played with a 53-card deck, a standard deck plus a wild joker. Players get seven cards, which they assemble into a five-card hand and a two-card hand. The five-card hand must score higher than the two-card hand. The object is to beat both the banker's hands. The banker wins all hands that tie; if a player wins only one hand, it's a push. The house or any player can be the banker. Winning hands are paid at even money, minus a five per cent commission.

If it sounds intimidating, don't worry; the dealer will help you arrange your cards in such a way as to maximise your two hands. Once you've watched a few hands, it's easy to get the hang of it. Pai gow poker is a lot slower – and friendlier – than blackjack or mini baccarat, so it's a good game to play if you want to relax, socialise, or play as few hands as possible in a given period of time (more comps, less risk).

IN CONTEXT

How to Win Friends at Poker

The lowdown on poker table etiquette.

DO...

Know the rules If you don't know how to play, attend a poker class at a casino and learn the basics, or learn at one of the many free poker websites. When in doubt at a game, ask the dealer, not the other players.

Be ready Pay attention. When it's your turn to act, do so with alacrity. A surefire way to raise the hackles of other players is to drag down the game with long deliberations. But don't jump the gun, either. Always wait until it's your turn before acting.

Handle your chips properly Stack your chips in such a way that other players and the dealer can tell what you're betting. 'Splashing' chips into the pot is rude and disruptive. Also, push your chips out in one move; 'stringing' your bets a few at a time is a bad move.

Ask for comps All players get free drinks. You can swipe your player's card to track your time; you usually get about a dollar in comp value for every hour. However, not all casinos use this system; be sure to ask how to get food comps and room discounts for your play.

DON'T...

Be an asshole Most of the problems that crop up at a poker table are due to bad or uncouth behaviour. Don't use foul language. Don't abuse other players. Don't hit on other players. Don't throw temper tantrums. Lose graciously and win graciously.

Blurt Don't be the peanut gallery at the table. Speculating on hand possibilities or, worse, talking about cards you just mucked can lead to all kinds of unfair advantages and recriminations. Likewise, after you've mucked your hand, stay out of it. You can inadvertently provide too much information to players still in the hand by reacting to the community cards.

Eat at the table or smoke at a non-smoking table The main problem with bringing food to a poker table is that the cards get greasy. And lighting up in a non-smoking area is one of the easiest ways to get beaten up in a poker game, either verbally or physically. Even at smoking tables, there's no smoking at the seat on either side of the dealer.

Roulette

Roulette doesn't have much of a fan club in the US. That's partly due to the calm nature of the game: Americans want action and speed when they gamble, and roulette gives them neither. Another reason is a subtle but crucial change in the US version. In Europe, roulette wheels typically have 36 numbered slots and one zero slot. On most American wheels, there are two zero slots (marked as zero and double zero). That change alone nearly doubles the house edge to 5.26 per cent, as compared to 2.7 per cent on single-zero wheels.

Roulette is simple to play. The wheel is mounted horizontally and a matching table layout serves as the betting area. All numbers are coloured red or black except for the zero and double zero, which are green. Players place their chips on the layout, before a ball is launched on to a spinning wheel. The ball comes to rest in a slot, and the winners are paid off at set odds. To minimise confusion about who made which bet, each player receives individually coloured 'wheel' chips when they buy in; these chips can only be used at the roulette table.

The easiest wager is a straight-up bet, where the player drops a chip on a single number. (Apparently, 17 is the most popular, due both to its central location and to the fact that James Bond bets it in the movies.) If the ball settles on your number, the bet will be paid off at 35:1. You can also make bets on groups of numbers: on lines separating numbers, on rows of numbers, or in special areas denoting odd or even, red or black and so on. In this way, a single bet covers anywhere from two to 18 numbers. Needless to say, the more numbers covered by the wager, the lower the payoff. For instance, betting odd or even pays even money.

The variety of wagers makes roulette an interesting game, especially if you like the languid pace. However, the odds are tough. Your best bet is to find a casino with a single-zero wheel – these come and go on occasion – and try to look elegant while losing.

Slot Machines

Slot machines were once shunned by 'real' gamblers, patronised only by their bored wives and girlfriends or first-time casino-goers who knew nothing more about gambling than how to drop coins into a slot. How times have changed. These days, they're the most popular and profitable part of the entire casino industry, so much so that some smaller casinos offer nothing but slots and video poker (see p65). Slot machines on the Strip collected $3.5 billion in 2010.

Novice gamblers prefer slots because there's little to learn and no pressure from dealers or other players. Put in money, pull the handle (or, more often nowadays, press the spin button) and in a few seconds, you're either a winner or a loser. Simple. What's more, jackpots can reach millions of dollars. But there is a downside, and a big one. Slots give the house an edge varying from two to 25 per cent, often making them one of the worst bets in the casino. And your chance of hitting a million-dollar jackpot is... well, what's the tiniest unit of measurement you can imagine? Smaller than that. Way smaller.

The basic slot machine in Las Vegas accepts a maximum of either two or three coins; however, some take four or five, some just one, and a new breed of slot machines is now able to take hundreds of coins, including pennies. Each coin beyond the minimum increases the payout proportionally (twice as much for two coins, triple for three) should a winning combination appear. In most cases, the winnings on betting the maximum number of coins are exponentially higher; almost always, the posted jackpot can only be won by betting the maximum number of coins on the winning pull/spin. What's more, many machines have multiple pay lines; on these machines, an added pay line is activated each time another coin is wagered. Always check the pay tables at the top of the machine.

Modern slots usually have a coin counter that displays your credits. Instead of coins crashing into the stainless-steel bin, wins are registered as credits. There's usually a bill changer on the machine: players can simply slide in a $20 bill, for example, and $20 worth of credits appear on the counter. Bets are made by pulling a handle or pressing a 'Spin' button. When you're done, hit the 'Cash Out' button and one of two things will happen. In older machines, coins equal to the unused credits will drop into the bin; the casino provides plastic cups to carry coins to other machines or the cashier. However, most slots these days are 'coinless'; when you hit 'Cash Out', you'll receive a voucher that can be redeemed at a ticket machine, a change booth or the cage, or fed into another slot machine and used as credits.

Slots fall into two categories: non-progressive (aka regular) and progressive. Regular slots have fixed payouts, which are posted on the front of the machine. Progressive slots offer a fixed payout schedule, but also offer the chance to hit a huge jackpot. This jackpot, funded by a percentage of every coin wagered, grows continuously until somebody wins it. A meter above the machines displays a running total of the current jackpot.

Many progressive slots are linked to form a system that feeds the jackpot. These machines might be from one carousel in a single casino, with a jackpot that resets at

IN CONTEXT

$1,000 and grows from there, or spread across casinos state-wide, yielding multi-million-dollar jackpots. With literally hundreds of machines in the system, jackpots can reach astronomical levels. The Megabucks linked progressive, for example, consists of more than 700 machines; the world record slot jackpot of nearly $40 million was hit in March 2003 at the Excalibur by a 25-year-old computer programmer. Though rare, these payouts are well publicised, not least because they make excellent bait.

NEW SLOTS
A few years ago, video machines with oversized screens, multiple games and other gimmicks were all the rage. Today, a new generation of slots is being developed. New machines are more interactive and look a lot like video poker; on these slots, you'll be able to make choices about which symbols to hold or discard, based on a certain internal and intuitive logic. Pop culture themes are still big: some of the most popular slots in town are based on hit movies and TV shows such as *The Hangover* and *Sex and the City*. Enhanced by digital bonus features and video pop-ups, slots are more fun to play today than they were even ten years ago, when they were still primarily 'one-armed bandits'; table-game players derisively referred to them as the 'idiot pull'.

However, these machines still won't line your pockets. Slot (and video poker) machines now account for upwards of 65 per cent of total casino revenues, which means that they take in twice as much revenue as all other casino games combined. Of the $12.6 billion won by Nevada casinos in 2006, $8.3 billion – just under 66 per cent – came from slots and video poker.

HOW SLOTS WORK
Modern slots are controlled by a random number generator, a computer chip that churns out strings of numbers regardless of whether the game is being played. Pulling the handle (or pressing the spin button) on a machine releases the reels and selects one of these numbers. Each number corresponds to a certain set of symbols on the reels, which determines the outcome. The force of the pull has nothing to do with the point at which the reels stop rotating.

Regulating the payout amounts to computer science. By adjusting the random number generator, a slot technician can make a machine tighter or looser. In the old days, slots often had a built-in edge of 20 to 30 per cent, but the players flocked to the machines with the higher returns. Casinos did the sums and realised it was better to get five per cent of a lot than 30 per cent of nothing; hence, most Vegas slots now return between 92 and 95 per cent of the drop (less on nickel machines), leaving the house edge at between five and eight per cent. In 2006, $138 billion was bet on slots and video poker in Nevada; the casinos' win of $8.3 billion equates to an overall hold of six per cent.

Certain casinos boldly advertise 98 or 99 per cent payouts, but the small print is crucial. In such circumstances, the payout is usually 'up to 99 per cent', which could mean that a single machine on the floor might be set at 98 or 99 per cent, if that. Short of running 2,000 to 5,000 plays through similar machines and comparing payouts, there's no way to find out which slots are set tight or loose. Payout percentages are supposedly verified by the state Gaming Control Board, but it rarely checks unless a casino advertises something truly absurd.

The real advantage for the house comes with the constant repetition of slot plays. For instance, say that a player with $50 starts betting $1 per pull on a quarter machine, via four 25¢ bets per pull. Sometimes the player wins and those winnings are reinvested: the drop might only be $50, but if they're playing at a reasonable speed, they could end up giving the casino $240 of action every hour. The six per cent edge is enough for a slot machine to retain about $14 an hour (six per cent of $240), a hold equal to more than a quarter of the original bankroll. With a little less luck, that money could vanish even faster. And over time, even an edge of half of one per cent grinds down players, which is why so many of them stumble away from machines empty-handed. That and the fact that the payout percentage factors in the big and seldom-won jackpots.

SLOT TIPS

Slot jockeys say non-progressive machines are looser (the technical term for this is 'hit frequency') than progressive machines, though payouts are smaller (again, the technical term is 'average payback'). Non-progressive machines that give smaller top payouts are reportedly looser than those that give large top payouts. Similarly, among progressive machines, those with smaller jackpots hit more often. In fact, the amount of your bet that goes to the progressive jackpot is an indication of payout frequency. According to one executive, if the amount is less than one per cent, the progressive machine is likely to have more non-jackpot winners. If three to five per cent of every bet goes towards the progressive jackpot, the game is seriously weighted towards fewer large payouts.

It gets more complicated. Machines with high hit frequencies pay out small amounts. Those with low hit frequencies pay out less frequently overall, but when they do pay out, each return is higher. And there's no correlation between hit frequency and average payback: hit frequency can be high while average payback is low and vice versa, or both can be low or high. Of course, none of this information is posted in a casino, so players are mostly flying blind. Some believe that slots placed near doorways and aisles are looser than others. And one casino executive has said

Sucker Bets

You gotta know when to hold...

Just when you think you know the rules, Las Vegas changes the games. Take blackjack, for example. Many gamblers know that a blackjack game dealt from a single deck offers savvy players the best chance to win. Now, however, many casinos have made a seemingly minor change to the single-deck rules, hoping players won't notice that it's no longer the best version of 21, but quite easily the worst.

A few years ago, single-deck blackjack was only available in the high-roller salons, with most of the low-limit games dealt from four or even six decks. In the last few years, however, single-deck tables have become more common than fake breasts at Mandalay Bay. This should be good news for gamblers. However, in the process, the payoff for natural 21s has been lowered in many casinos from 3:2 to 6:5; in other words, hitting a blackjack on a $10 bet will win you only $12 where it used to net $15. Doesn't

sound like much of a difference? Think again. The rule change is so bad that the casino's profit is several times higher than at the city's worst six-deck shoe game, and up to eight times more than at a regular single-deck game.

Keen-eyed Europeans will also notice that the odds have been shifted out of their favour on the roulette wheel. In many European casinos, the wheel has only a single green '0'. However, in the US, there's also a double zero ('00') on the wheel; that one extra green spot tips the house edge from 2.7 per cent to 5.26 per cent. Check before you play.

Finally, avoid almost anything called a 'side bet', extra bets beyond the basic wager at table games. They include jackpots for making certain hands at Let it Ride and three-card poker, or being dealt your first two cards of the same suit at blackjack. Don't waste your money: the casinos aren't charities, so there's no reason to give until it hurts.

that house machines, those with the casino's name and logo on them, are more generous than non-house-brand slots.

The only recommendation that makes any sense is that if you're going to play the slots for big money, bet the maximum number of coins on each pull. That way, if lightning strikes and you're a winner, you'll get the biggest payout possible. Avoid pumping cash into slots in non-casino locations such as convenience stores, which have a house edge one step below thievery. And, of course, never put a nickel into a slot machine without first having inserted your players club card into the reader. As long as you're playing the house's favourite game, you might as well get a bit of your play returned in the form of cashback or comps.

Slots can only pay out so many coins at any one time, so if you hit a monster jackpot, stay put and wait for an attendant to arrive. If you walk away, someone might claim your prize. The attendant will inform you of your tax obligations. US citizens need to fill out IRS paperwork on slot wins of more than $1,200; the tax situation varies for non-nationals.

PLAYERS CLUBS

Virtually every casino has a players club, the main aims of which are to keep track of a customer's slot and video poker play, and to retain customer loyalty by providing rewards in the form of points that can be redeemed for hard cash or merchandise. Many clubs offer introductory gifts such as free buffets, bonus points, rebates on losses or other perks to get your name on the dotted line.

All players clubs issue their members with an ID card, which should be inserted into the slot or video poker machine to allow the machine's computer to track the amount of play. Points awarded by the computer are then redeemable for cash or for comps in the casino's restaurants and at the shows. Members also qualify for discounts in the resort's shops, for reduced room rates, and for tickets to parties, barbecues and special tournaments.

Players club benefits change frequently. You can get an idea of what the various clubs are offering by checking out the *Las Vegas Advisor*, or the 'Best Bets' section of the Friday edition of the *Las Vegas Review-Journal* newspaper. All it takes to join a players club are a picture ID and a few minutes at the slot booth. Some casinos even have roving recruiters who'll sign you up at the machine. Membership is always free.

Sports betting

Thanks in no small part to Frank 'Lefty' Rosenthal, the casino executive whose life was dramatised in the movie *Casino*, betting on sports in Vegas is now a cult all of its own. Almost every casino has a sports book, at which money is gambled on countless aspects of the outcomes of pro sports and college games. They're lively and passionate places on big game days; even if you're not betting, they're often good places to watch the action. Whatever sports wagers you make and wherever you make them, remember that cellphones and two-way communicators are prohibited in or near the sports books, a policy that's strictly and universally enforced.

Glance up at the vast boards and you might think that sports betting here is tough to understand. It's not, but it is hard to beat the system and come away rich.

THE MONEY LINE

Most of the sports on which you can bet (baseball, boxing, football, hockey, basketball) offer 'money lines', which lay the odds on the favourite or take the odds on the underdog. Take the following baseball-related example:

Boston Red Sox	+	145
New York Yankees	–	160

This means that you must bet $16 on the Yankees to win $10 (plus your stake back). However, you need bet only $10 on the Red Sox to win $14.50. The favourite team is always the one with the '−' prefix, with the underdog denoted by '+'. (Unlike in European sports, the home team is always listed second.)

OTHER BETS

There's a large variety of bets in the Vegas sports books. Here, though, are examples of two of the more common ones. Both of them even the odds so that punters can make a 'straight bet', which here means putting up $11 to win $10 (plus your $11 stake back). In team games, one popular bet is on the margin of victory, or the 'point spread'. Take, for example, these odds for the 2007 Super Bowl.

Indianapolis Colts −7
Chicago Bears

This means that the Colts were favoured to beat the Bears by seven points. Everyone favouring the Colts on the point spread was betting on them to win by more than seven points, while everyone favouring the Bears was betting on either a Bears victory or a Colts win by fewer than seven points. The game ended Colts 29, Bears 17. The Colts won the game and also covered the point spread, meaning that everyone who bet on them won. If the Colts had beaten the Bears by exactly seven points, it would have been a push, and all money would have been refunded.

Another popular bet is to gamble on the total number of points scored in any given game. The casino advertises the total number of points they think will be scored in the game, and gamblers decide if they think the actual number will be higher or lower. This is known as the 'over/under'; like the point spread, this pays off at 10:11 odds. As above, if the outcome matches the casino's prediction, it's a push, and all bets are refunded.

Video Poker

This electronic cousin of live poker enjoys a huge following in Las Vegas. Although a video-poker machine resembles a slot machine and is typically located on the slot floor, it is an entirely different beast. Make no mistake about it: video poker is a game not of chance but of skill. If played perfectly, the house edge can often be flattened to zero or even pushed into the negative, which means a return to players of more than 100 per cent. Casinos can only afford to operate their machines in this way because perfect play is the province of the merest handful of experts, those people who use powerful computer programmes to work out strategies that are accurate to within ten thousandths of a percentage point.

A video-poker screen displays a five-card hand of draw poker, with every deal coming from a freshly shuffled 52-card deck. Buttons allow the player to hold or replace the dealt cards. After the draw, the game pays off according to a payout schedule listed on the screen. A pair of aces might pay even money, while a royal flush usually pays out at a rate of 4,000:1. Most basic poker rules are in effect as far as hand rankings go (minus 'kickers', or unpaired or unsuited high cards, on all but one or two variations), but the psychological angle is jettisoned. You're playing against a machine that doesn't respond to bluffing, so the quality of your hand is everything.

There's no way to summarise basic strategy for video poker, partly because it's extremely complex and partly because the game comes in so many different varieties. Each variety of video poker has its own unique characteristics such as wild cards and bonus options, giving rise to different pay tables and different strategies. You can buy video-poker strategy cards (Huntington Press produces

IN CONTEXT

a good set), which allow you to make the right decision on every hand; in essence, you'll be playing computer-perfect strategy.

The most basic variation of video poker is 'Jacks or Better' (JoB), which plays most like five-card stud (no wild cards) and pays out on pairs of jacks or better. The strategies for JoB are pretty much intuitive for anyone who already knows how to play poker, but some rules have to be learned: for example, you never hold a kicker (a high-value card to be held along with a pair); you never draw to a four-card inside straight (for example, you're holding 3, 4, 6, 7 and you're looking for a 5); and you always go for a royal flush if you hold four of the cards required for it, even if it means sacrificing a flush, a pair or a straight in the process.

As with slots, it's wise to play the maximum number of coins, as this greatly increases the top payout for a royal flush. Another tip: be sure to play 'full-pay' games as opposed to their 'short-pay' brethren. For instance, in JoB, the full-pay version returns 9:1 on a full house and 6:1 on a flush; it's called a '9/6' machine. On the short-pay version, it's sliced to 8/5, 7/5 or even 6/5. The only reason to play a short-pay version of JoB would be if it was connected to a progressive jackpot or paid off on a pair of tens or better. However, 8/5 Bonus, with extra payouts for four-of-a-kind, is a different animal, as are Double Bonus, Double Double Bonus, Triple Bonus and Double Triple Bonus variations. Then there's Joker Poker, plus many different varieties of Deuces Wild.

Video-poker players should consult the books and reports on the market that detail proper play for sample video-poker hands. There are excellent computer programmes available that tutor players in strategies. Casinos don't mind if you refer to strategy charts while playing, but they draw the line at laptops. Since it's impossible to absorb the tactics for all the possible variations at once, we recommend you study and master strategy for JoB, then, as you feel more comfortable, move on to more complex and rewarding games such as the full-pay Deuces Wild and Double Bonus varieties.

The latest varieties of machine to become all the rage in Las Vegas are multi-play machines, such as Triple-Play, Five-Play, Ten-Play, 50-Play and even 100-Play. Here, three, five, ten, 50 or 100 hands of video poker are dealt at the same time from the equivalent number of decks, requiring three, five, ten, 50, or 100 times the bet. The twist is that only the cards in the bottom hand are displayed on the deal. When you hold cards from the hand, the held cards appear in all the upper hands; when you draw, all the hands' cards are filled in around the held cards.

In Spin Poker, when you discard cards, the open spots spin like slot reels. Heads Up Poker, meanwhile, combines live poker with video poker. You're dealt five cards and you bet the hand. The machine responds by calling, raising or folding (and sometimes bluffing). You play out the video-poker hand, but you still have the live hand to be resolved.

Sights

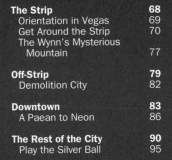

Bellagio Fountains. *See p73.*

The Strip

This is it: Vegas incarnate.

When he built the tropical-themed, volcano-fronted Mirage in 1989, Steve Wynn lit the fuse on a renaissance that would see Las Vegas Boulevard virtually rebuilt within 15 years. The city awoke from a long dormancy – the years when it was popular with those slightly embarrassing friends of your parents – and began to deal in high-volume density. At first, families were the target. As Wynn followed the volcano-fuelled Mirage with the pirate ships of Treasure Island, populist attractions began to spring up all along the Strip, effectively the stretch of Las Vegas Boulevard South between the 'Welcome' sign and Sahara Avenue.

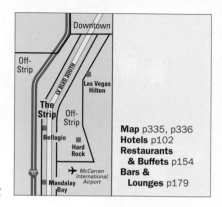

Map p335, p336
Hotels p102
Restaurants
& Buffets p154
Bars &
Lounges p179

Map p335, p336
Hotels p102
Restaurants
& Buffets p154
Bars &
Lounges p179

SIGHTS

THE STRIP'S NEW LOOK

This new flashy style saw hotels fashioned after pyramids, castles and there was even a Disney-esque version of New York. In 1998, Wynn steered the race in another direction, defining a new era of quality with the Bellagio. High-end travellers who previously had cared little about either gambling or rollercoasters discovered a city that now offered celebrity chefs and one-of-a-kind shows. By the time Wynn finished Wynn Las Vegas in 2005, resorts such as Mandalay Bay, the Venetian and Caesars Palace had already added boutique environs or were getting ready to do so, further upping the upmarket ante.

On the eve of the city's centennial in 2005, a new phase dawned. The Strip was now hip, beckoning twentysomethings who couldn't care less about Wayne Newton or prime-rib buffets with an explosion of all-night dance clubs and swanky lounges. The latest wave of construction is reshaping the skyline with high-rise condos and mixed-use properties that will be virtual cities of their own. Will Trump towers and glitzy high-rises erase the neon legend of the old Vegas? Watch this space.

RUSSELL ROAD TO TROPICANA AVENUE

As the tiny, neon-lit motor courts of the 1950s and '60s near Russell Road continue to perish under the wrecking ball, only the classic **Welcome to Fabulous Las Vegas** sign reminds visitors of the old California highway that once beckoned hot, thirsty drivers to get out of the heat. First-timers still brave the traffic to get a snap under this iconic landmark; you can purchase a miniature version, complete with flashing lights, at various gift shops along Las Vegas Boulevard. Facing the sign, the old Howard Hughes air terminal is behind you to the east (right), while the **Panevino** restaurant (*see p163*) lies beyond the runways on Sunset Road, offering gorgeous views of the Strip and aircraft in transit. At your back, 300 miles away, is Los Angeles; in front of you lies the Strip, Las Vegas's raison d'être.

To the east is the **Little Church of the West** wedding chapel (*see p274*). Dating from 1942, it's the oldest building on the Strip,

INSIDE TRACK
HOTELS & CASINOS

For full details of the city's hotel-casino resorts, see pp98-152. The chapter covers every major casino in Vegas, detailing everything from its entertainment to its eating options, its guestrooms to its golf courses.

though with the caveat that it's been moved several times, most recently from the front lawn of the old Hacienda casino (imploded in 1996) to its current site. Across the Boulevard is the **Bali Hai Golf Club** (*see p265*), one of only two golf courses on the Strip (the other is the guests-only facility at Wynn Las Vegas).

Just north, where the Hacienda once stood, is the South Seas-themed **Mandalay Bay** (*see p109*), effectively the beginning of the

21st-century Strip. The hotel's **Shark Reef** aquarium (*see p239*) is the best of the many animal-focused attractions in the city, but the resort is also home to a broad range of excellent eateries, the folk-art decorated **House of Blues** (*see p252*), the **Mandalay Place** mini-mall (*see p195*) and two other hotels, the tranquil **Four Seasons** (*see p131*) and the chic **Thehotel at Mandalay Bay** (*see p131*).

Orientation in Vegas

Find yourself.

The Las Vegas Valley is split into quarters by two intersecting freeways: I-15, coursing north–south through the centre of town on its way from Salt Lake City to LA, and US 95 (aka I-515), a north–south freeway that makes an east–west jink across the city. On a map, these roads approximate a twisted pinwheel shape, with a pivot just north-west of Downtown.

In street numbering terms, ground zero is at the junction of Fremont and Main streets, in Downtown. From the Plaza at 1 S Main Street, numbers increase as you travel in any direction. Main Street ends at its intersection with Las Vegas Boulevard South; street addresses either east or west of the Main Street/Las Vegas Boulevard artery are tagged accordingly with 'E' or 'W'. North/south street delineations are based on an imaginary line from the eastern end of Charleston Boulevard, along Fremont Street in Downtown as far as Main Street, and then on to US 95 to the west.

Metropolitan Las Vegas is made up of four jurisdictions: Las Vegas, North

Las Vegas, Henderson and unincorporated Clark County. Within and over-lapping these jurisdictions are a number of areas and neighbourhoods, only some of which have widely recognised names. The Sights section of this guidebook has been divided into four chapters: **The Strip** (*see p68-78*), the nickname for the stretch of Las Vegas Boulevard South between Russell Road in the south and Sahara Avenue in the north; **Off-Strip** (*see p79-82*), loosely covering the streets immediately surrounding the Strip; **Downtown** (*see p83-89*, centred around the junction of Fremont Street and Las Vegas Boulevard; and **The Rest of the City** (*see p90-96*), covering everywhere else.

The one mistake made by many visitors is not leaving the Strip; understandable, given the hypnotic, wow-inducing glitz of the place. But there is a whole city beyond it, relatively low on sights and arts but with plenty of restaurants, bars and points of local interest worthy of your attention. Try to get out and see a couple.

SIGHTS

The Strip.

Next to Mandalay Bay is the unmistakable onyx pyramid of the **Luxor** (*see p118*), lights racing up its angles and exploding in a dramatic sky-bound beacon. An exhibition devoted to the *Titanic* proved popular enough to earn permanent residency at Luxor. If it sounds a bit soft, head for **Bodies** (*see below*), which offers a peek at the human anatomy beneath the skin.

Just north of the Luxor lies the intersection of the Strip and Tropicana Avenue, home to more hotel rooms than you'll find in the whole of San Francisco. All around, crowds spill on to street corners and squeeze through pedestrian overpasses.

On the south-east corner of this ever-crazed junction are the white towers of the **Tropicana** (*see p130*: it was built in 1957 and was looking its age, until 2011, when the new owners gave it a makeover with a South Beach vibe.

Across Tropicana Avenue to the north is the forever-expanding **MGM Grand** (*see p119*). The signature lion guarding the entrance is the nation's largest bronze sculpture; there are more felines inside the resort, lurking in the **Lion Habitat** (*see below*), the **Crazy Horse Paris** cabaret (*see p228*) and sprawling nightclub **Studio 54** (*see p261*).

Opposite the MGM Grand (and connected by an overhead skywalk) is the gloriously preposterous **New York New York** (*see p122*). Overhead runs the **Manhattan Express** rollercoaster (*see right*); inside, kids will enjoy the **Coney Island Emporium** (*see below*), while adults sweat at Cirque du Soleil's sexy **Zumanity** (*see p227*). Across a walkway to the south, completing the circle of casinos, looms the medieval-themed **Excalibur** (*see p235*). It's still family-friendly but, in perhaps the most blatant symbol of the Strip's recent drift, has replaced its puppet show with a motorcycle-themed bar called Chrome.

Get Around the Strip

Get out of your car.

In an effort to eliminate – or at least reduce – the Strip's gridlock of rental cars, Hummers and limos, the city offers two competing systems of public transport. Part of the city's public transit network, the **Deuce** is a fleet of pimped-out double-decker buses that trawl the Strip, dropping passengers in front of hotel-casinos, timeshares and restaurants. The **Las Vegas Monorail**, meanwhile, travels on an overhead concrete platform east of the Strip, with seven stops at the back of hotels and at the Convention Center; it's privately owned and operated by the Las Vegas Monorail Company.

Las Vegas Monorail.

Bodies

Luxor *3801 Las Vegas Boulevard South, at W Hacienda Avenue (262 4450, www.luxor.com).* Bus Deuce, 201. **Open** 10am-10pm daily (last entry 9pm). **Admission** $24-$32. **Map** p336 A8.
In the unlikely event that you've ever fancied dropping the best part of $30 in order to peek underneath the skin of dead strangers, this is the show for you. Having donated their remains to science, around 20 altruistic souls have been dissected, preserved and put on display for the edification of visitors to the Luxor (the exhibition used to be at the Tropicana). All things considered, the merchandise is in surprisingly good taste.

FREE Coney Island Emporium

New York New York *3790 Las Vegas Boulevard South, at W Tropicana Avenue (740 6414, www.nynyhotelcasino.com).* Bus Deuce, 201. **Open** 9am-midnight Mon-Thur, Sun; 9am-1am Fri, Sat. **Admission** free. **Map** p336 A8.
This arcade and family amusement centre attempts to recreate the atmosphere of the original Coney Island with more than 200 video and midway games, Bumper Cabs, a prize counter and lots of sticky candyfloss (but, sadly, no freak show).

FREE Lion Habitat

MGM Grand *3799 Las Vegas Boulevard South, at E Tropicana Avenue (891 7777, www.mgmgrand.com).* Bus Deuce, 201. **Open** 11am-10pm daily. **Admission** free. **Map** p336 A8.

SIGHTS

Lion Habitat.

Not to be outdone by the Mirage's tigers, the MGM has its own pride of 'display' lions. The habitat is pretty small, but the glass walls mean you can get a close-up view of cubs and adult lions.

Manhattan Express
New York New York *3790 Las Vegas Boulevard South, at W Tropicana Avenue (740 6969, www. nynyhotelcasino.com). Bus Deuce, 201.* **Open** 11am-11pm Mon-Thur, Sun; 10am-midnight Fri, Sat. **Tickets** $12.50. *Re-rides* $6. *All-day pass* $25. **Map** p336 A8.
Gotham never saw anything like it: a rollercoaster soaring around skyscrapers and Lady Liberty. The Express twists, loops and dives at breakneck speeds, and features the first ever 'heartline roll', which creates the sensation a pilot feels when going through a barrel roll in an aeroplane. Try hard to smile in the last section: this is where the photos are taken.

Shark Reef
Mandalay Bay *3950 Las Vegas Boulevard South, at W Hacienda Avenue (632 4555, www.mandalaybay.com). Bus Deuce, 104, 105.* **Open** 10am-11pm daily (last entry 10pm). **Admission** $15.95; $12.95 reductions; free under-4s. **Map** p336 A9.
A 'walk-through' aquarium, the AZA-accredited Shark Reef is filled with 100 species of underwater life, including rays, jellyfish, eels and, of course, 11 varieties of shark. A perfect complement to the South Seas-themed Mandalay Bay, the Shark Reef is an unexpected gem in a city lacking in the educational entertainment department.

Titanic: The Exhibition
Luxor *3801 Las Vegas Boulevard South, at W Hacienda Avenue (262 4450, www.luxor.com). Bus Deuce, 201.* **Open** 10am-10pm daily (last entry 9pm), **Admission** $21-$28. **Map** p336 A8.
More than 3,000 bits and pieces recovered from the mother of all seafaring disasters are now on permanent display at the Luxor in this diverting show, which also affords visitors the chance to experience a simulation of the kind of weather experienced by the poor unfortunates on the night in question.

TROPICANA AVENUE TO HARMON AVENUE

A pleasant pedestrian boardwalk that morphs into a replica Brooklyn Bridge leads north on the eastern side of New York New York as far as the **ESPN Zone** sports bar (*see p122*). As you stroll, note the classic 'Pepsi and Pete' sign on the wall of a replica brownstone building, challenging the Times Square-style giant neon Coke bottle on the Showcase Mall across the street. The mall houses the Strip's only cinema (the **UA Showcase 8**; *see p244*), **M&M's World** (*see p72*), and a huge arcade with the world's tallest indoor climbing wall.

Further on, past the **Empire Ballroom** (*see p258*) and fronting the **Polo Towers** timeshare, sits the **Hawaiian Marketplace**. It's surprising that this jumble of shops, restaurants and a bird show has survived the wrecking ball, especially when you see what's going on across the road. The fountains and arches of the middle-market **Monte Carlo** (*see p121*) still draw the crowds, but it's the activity directly north of it that has observers excited.

Right now, the Las Vegas skyline is lined with cranes, as Strip casinos add new towers, and vacant lots are filled with condo towers. However, no one stretch defines the future of Vegas more dramatically than the vast plot of land between the Monte Carlo and the Bellagio on the west side of the Strip.

The key development on the Strip – and, for that matter, in the city – is MGM Mirage's vast, ambitious hotel-casino-condo-retail-dining complex, **CityCenter**. The $9 billion, 68-acre complex – a city within the city, designed by eight international architects – features a 60-storey resort and casino, two additional boutique hotels, multiple condo and condo-hotel towers, vast amounts of retail space, theatres, restaurants, spas and a parking garage with room for 7,500 vehicles. It even has its own power station and fire station, making CityCenter a semi-autonomous community in an unincorporated township (the Strip) within a larger, sprawling desert outpost that's struggling to address some far less flashy concerns of its own. But that's Vegas for you.

SIGHTS

SIGHTS

INSIDE TRACK
ART AT CRYSTALS

In addition to its upmarket shopping facilities, Crystals is home to engaging art, including frozen sculptures, dramatic oversized popsicles and dynamic obelisks that emerge then melt into patterns.

Right next door, there's the even newer **Cosmopolitan**. The choice of stylish international visitors (and locals, who took to the place immediately), Cosmo attracts a younger, more urbane crowd, who like to look at each other as much as they like to gamble – maybe more – and are well-catered for by the resort's chic boutiques.

★ Crystals
CityCenter *3720 Las Vegas Boulevard South, at E Harmon Avenue (1-866 754 2489, 590 9299, www.crystalsatcitycenter.com). Bus Deuce, 202.* **Open** 10am-11pm daily. **Map** p336 A7.
Outsparkling everything around it is Crystals, the ultraluxe shopping complex that fronts the new CityCenter complex on the Strip, with its elegant angles designed by architect Daniel Libeskind. With its vast ceilings and pristine all-white settings, Crystals looks like a museum of shopping designed by a sci-fi art director, and it features boutiques by Balenciaga, Dior, Pucci, Gucci and Fendi, Stella McCartney, Paul Smith and Tom Ford.
▶ *For more about the art at Crystals, see above Inside Track.*

FREE GameWorks
Showcase Mall, 3785 Las Vegas Boulevard South, between E Tropicana & E Harmon avenues (432 4263, www.gameworks.com). Bus Deuce, 201. **Open** 10am-midnight Mon-Thur, Sun; 10am-1am Fri, Sat. **Admission** free. **Map** p336 A8.
If you'd rather shove quarters into a video game than a slot machine, this place is for you. This huge madhouse is a great place in which to try out the latest games: you can save money if you pay by the hour, though none of it's cheap. There are more than 250 games, a billiards lounge, two restaurants, a coffee bar and a 75ft (23m) indoor climbing wall.

FREE M&M's World
Showcase Mall, 3785 Las Vegas Boulevard South, between E Tropicana & E Harmon avenues (736 7611, www.m-ms.com). Bus Deuce, 201. **Open** 9am-11pm Mon-Thur, Sun; 9am-midnight Fri, Sat. **Admission** free. **Map** p336 A8.
This is a four-level chocolate-lover's paradise. Check out M&M Academy, an interactive entertainment attraction showing visitors how these chocolate candies earn their trademark. The attraction includes a 3-D movie, and 'graduates' get a diploma. Yes, it's a bit overmarketed. But at least it's free.

HARMON AVENUE TO FLAMINGO ROAD

Planet Hollywood (*see p123*), which opened as the Aladdin in 2000, sits on the east side of the Strip at Harmon Avenue. The Aladdin was never one of the Strip's more popular casinos; the new owners judged that by getting rid of the ill-timed Baghdad motif, things would turn

Manhattan Express. *See p71.*

Bellagio Fountains.

around. Alas, you won't find the Terminator dealing cards: unlike at the Planet Hollywood restaurants, the movie bric-a-brac is confined to the guestrooms, and the neutrally decorated casino lacks a specific theme. The hotel connects to the **Miracle Mile** mall (*see p195*), itself subjected to a facelift in 2007.

To the north of Planet Hollywood is the spectacular (but small, in Vegas terms) **Paris Las Vegas** (*see p111*), complete with half-scale Eiffel Tower, grand fountains and sidewalk café (**Mon Ami Gabi**; *see p161*). From here, it's a skip north to the original 'Four Corners', where the Strip meets Flamingo Road. On the south-west corner of the street, at **Bally's** (*see p115*), a video screen competes with the bizarre tunnel entrance. To its north sits **Bill's Gamblin' Hall & Saloon**, recently bought and renamed (it was the Barbary Coast until 2007; *see p125*) by Harrah's amid rumours that it's not long for this world. Either way, both Bally's and Bill's are overshadowed by their neighbours right across the Strip.

At the south-west corner of the Strip's intersection with Flamingo is the **Bellagio** (*see p102*), the most renowned property in the city since it opened in October 1998. The fountains that dance upon the large replica of Lake Como are one of the best-loved attractions in Las Vegas, but there's plenty of note inside: the **Gallery of Fine Art** (*see p246*), Cirque du Soleil's **O** (*see p235*) and the glass-domed **Conservatory & Botanical Gardens**, which lie beyond the lobby and are home to thousands of exotic plants and flowers.

With its striking blue-white lighting and huge fountains, the opulent and ever-expanding

Caesars Palace (*see p104*) commands attention as the sole Strip casino to successfully mate the past with 21st-century Vegas. Little of Jay Sarno's Roman kitsch remains; the resort has successfully reinvented itself as an altogether more chic property. Just to the north of the main fountain is a small Brahma shrine, where visitors worship and leave offerings of fruit and flowers in exchange for good luck.

Near where Caesars meets the Mirage is the entrance to the Roman-themed **Forum Shops** (*see p194*), a vast atrium served by a spiral escalator and filled with luxury boutiques. The high-end shopping is conducted under an ever-changing 'sky' that's spelled by a Disney-like robot show. Animated statues come to life for a bizarre and very loud seven-minute revel with dancing water and laser lights.

★ FREE Bellagio Fountains

Bellagio *3600 Las Vegas Boulevard South, at W Flamingo Road (693 7111, www.bellagio. com). Bus Deuce, 202.* **Shows** 3pm-midnight Mon-Fri (every 30mins 3-8pm; every 15mins 8pm-midnight); noon-midnight Sat, Sun (every 30mins noon-8pm; every 15mins 8pm-midnight). **Admission** free. **Map** p336 A7.

The Bellagio's lake throws up entrancing fountain displays choreographed to music from Pavarotti to Sinatra (and, less appealingly, Lee Greenwood). The 1,200 water cannons, arranged in lines and circles, shoot water that dances and sways to the music, reaching as high as 240ft (73m). The best seats are in the Bellagio restaurants, but you get a good view from the pavements out front, and from the top of the Eiffel Tower at Paris Las Vegas.

Eiffel Tower Experience.

Eiffel Tower Experience

Paris Las Vegas *3655 Las Vegas Boulevard South, at E Flamingo Road (946 7000, www. harrahs.com). Bus Deuce, 202.* **Open** 9.30am-12.30am daily. **Tickets** $9-$12; $7-$10 reductions; free under-5s. **Map** p336 A7.

OK, so it's only half the size of the original, but the Vegas Eiffel Tower gives visitors a great view of the Strip and the surrounding mountains, something you won't find in Paris. Take a lift to the 46th-floor observation deck; go at dusk to watch the Strip suddenly light up as if someone's flicked a switch.

FLAMINGO ROAD TO SPRING MOUNTAIN ROAD

Wedged against Bill's Gamblin' Hall & Saloon, the **Flamingo** (*see p116*) is one of the Strip's most storied properties, although nothing remains of Bugsy Siegel's 1941 original. In its place is a lush pool area and winding pathways that take you past penguins, Chilean flamingos, Mandarin ducks and koi fish swimming in ponds under three-storey-high waterfalls. If it weren't for the tennis courts, pool and spa, it could be a wildlife habitat, albeit the only one in the world with a plaque honouring a mobster.

This stretch of the Strip, covering Bill's Gamblin' Hall, the Flamingo, the low-priced, casino-only **O'Sheas** (no.3355, 697 2711), the faded **Imperial Palace** (*see p118*) and the altogether unremarkable **Harrah's** (*see p117*), is owned by Harrah's Entertainment, a mid-market corporation that's second only to MGM Mirage in terms of its influence on the city. It's been widely speculated that the firm will demolish the

Imperial Palace and build a new property that allows for an uninterrupted flow of gamblers along this stretch. While the Palace remains, the chief reason for non-guests to visit is the **Auto Collections Museum** (*see right*), behind the hotel on top of the parking garage. And just past Harrah's, a 24-hour parade of hungry characters scoff food at Denny's, inside the small and still independently owned **Casino Royale** (*see p125*), a worthwhile stop if you're slumming for Hunter S Thompson's Vegas.

Back across the street, north of Caesars is a block-long tropical paradise that begins with the **Mirage** (*see p110*), which in 1989 became the Strip's first modern mega-resort. When it opened, the Mirage introduced the first large-scale free spectacle to Las Vegas: a 54-foot (16-metre) volcano right on the Strip. The revamped volcano is small, lacks a cinder dome and looks more like a granite wall than Mount Etna. However, the brief spectacle (every 15 minutes, 7pm-midnight daily), spewing fire and a piña colada scent into the palm trees, waterfalls and lagoon, is worth a look.

Inside the resort, pygmy sharks swim in a large aquarium behind the registration desk. After looking tired for years, the Mirage got a much-needed shine in advance of **Love** (*see p234*), Cirque du Soleil's much-heralded Beatles show. After the show, fans can huddle at the **Revolution** lounge (*see p182*) to decide if they liked it; if, that is, they don't fancy hitting any of the Light Group-operated hotspots elsewhere: in-the-moment nightclub **Jet** (*see p259*), and eateries **Stack** (*see p165*) and **Japonais** (*see p159*).

Just up from the Mirage sits **Treasure Island** (*see p124*), now marketing itself as **TI** in an attempt to shake off its family image. The resort fronts the Strip with a replica of an 18th-century sea village set on a lagoon, surrounded by cliffs, palm trees and nautical artifacts. The focus of attention, however, is the two fully rigged ships on which the Sirens of TI clash with a band of renegade pirates (every 90 minutes, 7-11.30pm daily). Formerly a family-friendly pantomime, the show received a crass revamp that tries to rebrand the property as a more adult resort. Regardless, it fills the pavement to capacity, as onlookers stare slack-jawed at the blazing cannons, toppling masts, exploding powder kegs and – key to the whole thing – heaving bosoms.

Opposite TI and the Mirage on the eastern side of the Strip, just north of Casino Royale, sits the **Venetian** (*see p113*), Sheldon Adelson's hugely successful reinterpretation of the city of canals. Attractions include super-fashionable restaurant-club **Tao** (*see p261*, **Madame Tussaud's** (*see below*), the highfalutin' **Grand Canal Shoppes** (*see p195*) and **singing gondoliers** (*see below*), who drag embarrassed tourists along the resort's canals.

Gondola Rides

Venetian *Grand Canal Shoppes, 3355 Las Vegas Boulevard South, between Sands Avenue & E Flamingo Road (414 1000, www.venetian.com). Bus Deuce, 105, 203.* **Open** 10am-11pm Mon-Thur, Sun; 10am-midnight Fri, Sat. **Tickets** *Indoor ride* $15; $7.50 reductions; $60 2-passenger gondola. *Outdoor ride* $12.50; $5 reductions; $50 2-passenger gondola. **Map** p335, p336 A6.
Purchase your tickets at St Mark's Square, then take a ride along canals that weave through replica Venetian architecture. The wooden boats are authentic and the singing gondoliers are tuneful. However, despite the number of newly married couples that take the ride, the backdrop of gawking tourists will dampen any hopes of a romantic moment. *Photo p76.*

Imperial Palace Auto Collections

Imperial Palace *3535 Las Vegas Boulevard South, between Sands Avenue & E Flamingo Road (731 3311, www.imperialpalace.com). Bus Deuce, 105, 203.* **Open** 9.30am-9.30pm daily. **Admission** $6.95; $3.50 reductions. **Map** p336 A6.
Tucked away in the parking garage are 200 rare and speciality cars (part of a rotating collection of 750, all for sale). Among them are Hitler's 1936 Mercedes, JFK's 1962 Lincoln, vehicles that once belonged to Al Capone, WC Fields and Howard Hughes, and a room full of Duesenbergs. This latter room was where former casino owner Ralph Engelstad held secretive 'Hitler birthday parties', before being fined by the Nevada Gaming Control Board for the activity.

Madame Tussaud's

3377 Las Vegas Boulevard South, between Sands Avenue & E Flamingo Road 866 841 3739, www. madametussauds.com/lasvegasMC). Bus Deuce, 105, 203. **Open** 10am-10pm daily. **Admission** $24; $14-$18 reductions; free under-6s. **Map** p335, p336 A6.
The first US incarnation of London's all-conquering attraction contains more than 100 wax celebs in various settings and rendered with various degrees of

SIGHTS

Treasure Island.

accuracy (Johnny Depp good, Shaquille O'Neal less impressive). The comparatively small attraction tones down the British history in favour of celebrity culture 'encounters': a photo opportunity to don a wedding dress and 'marry' George Clooney, for example, or a chance to sing in front of Simon Cowell. Hokey but fun.

Secret Garden & Dolphin Habitat

Mirage *3400 Las Vegas Boulevard South, between Spring Mountain & W Flamingo roads (791 7188, www.miragehabitat.com). Bus Deuce, 105, 202, 203.* **Open** *Summer* 11am-7pm Mon-Fri; 10am-7pm Sat, Sun. *Autumn-spring* 11am-5.30pm Mon-Fri; 10am-5.30pm Sat, Sun. **Admission** $15; $10 reductions; free under-3s. **Map** p335, p336 A6.

Marine mammals in the desert? Nothing's impossible in fabulous Las Vegas. Here, bottle-nosed dolphins frolic in a special habitat behind the Mirage. Adjacent to their home is the Secret Garden, a small but attractive zoo with Asian-themed architecture and some big-ticket animals: white tigers, white lions, Bengal tigers, an Indian elephant, a panther and a snow leopard.

SPRING MOUNTAIN ROAD TO CONVENTION CENTER DRIVE

For 15 years, the stretch of the Strip north of Spring Mountain Road was old Vegas through and through, a parade of forgotten resorts and empty plots of land. A few of the old casinos remain, but it's mostly all-change around here,

Gondola Rides. *See p75.*

and has been since about 2005. In a nutshell, the difference between then and now is the difference between Sinatra's *Ocean's 11* and Clooney's *Ocean's Eleven*.

Naturally, Steve Wynn is at the centre of it all. It was Wynn who kickstarted the Vegas renaissance by building the Mirage in 1989. Then, 16 years later and just a couple of stone's throws from its front door, he opened the $2.7-billion **Wynn Las Vegas** (*see p114*), a hyperreal return to the 'intimacy' of old Las Vegas. The resort sits on land formerly occupied by the Desert Inn, a Vegas classic that bit the dust just a few years earlier.

In a reversal of the philosophy of streetside spectacle pioneered at the Mirage, Wynn Las Vegas is hidden from the Strip by a mountain. Behind it is a golf course, a lavish spa, top-end shops and even a Ferrari dealership; Wynn has never done things by halves. Right next to the resort, Wynn built a second building in a similar style to the first, though with even more lavish decor. Encore opened in 2008 and stands apart as a separate resort.

Directly across the road, the **Fashion Show Mall** (*see p197*) is further accelerating the redefinition of Vegas. The two 13-storey towers would dominate the landscape were it not for the **Cloud**, a 479-foot (150-metre) metal oval suspended between them. The Cloud serves as an outdoor projection screen, but it also provides much-needed shade for the de facto piazza and four rare (for Vegas) restaurants featuring outdoor seating facing the Wynn, including **Ra Sushi**, serving rock 'n' roll Japanese food. In coincidental but purposeful synergy with Wynn Las Vegas, the Fashion Show is a theme-free shopping centre (except for the runway shows every 30 minutes); before long, themed resorts will seem as dated as the old casinos did in 1989.

North of the Fashion Show sits what is the most expensive piece of land in Las Vegas. For decades, the south-west corner of the Strip and Desert Inn Road was home to the **New Frontier**, built in 1942 (as the Last Frontier) and one of the first resorts on what became the Strip. The resort trod water for years, as rumours came and went about owner Phil Ruffin's plans for redevelopment. But then, after mapping out his ambition to build a Montreux-themed resort on the site, Ruffin abruptly sold up to New York-based developers El Ad in May 2007.

Across the Desert Inn Arterial, an east–west expressway that avoids both the Strip (by tunnelling under) and I-15 (by flying over), further changes are afoot. The plot of land on the western side of the street was home to the Stardust for nearly 50 years. Proving that nothing is sacred, the iconic resort was demolished in 2007 to make room for **Echelon Place**, a 90-acre, multi-hotel complex that

SIGHTS

The Wynn's Mysterious Mountain

This resort's star attraction isn't out front: you'll have to come in to discover it.

The Mirage volcano, the Treasure Island pirate show and the Bellagio's dancing waters are the most popular free attractions on the Strip. All three were conceived by Steve Wynn, and were designed to lure passing visitors inside each resort. A decade later, though, Wynn reversed his previous policy of visibility. The volcano, the siren show and the fountains all front directly on to the Strip. But at **Wynn Las Vegas** (*see p114*), visitors have to go inside the casino to find the signature attraction.

From outside the resort, visitors can see a small hill covered in trees: nearly 500 of them, some 65 feet (20 metres) tall and 60 years old (transplanted from the old Desert Inn golf course). Mount Wynn, however, isn't immediately obvious, either from here or from inside the resort. To get the full effect, you'll need to take the spiral staircase down to the terraces at the SW Steakhouse or Daniel Boulud; there's also a small outdoor bar and a tiny free-viewing platform.

The mountain consists of four environments that provide the backdrop for the row of restaurants and bars, each with its own distinct alfresco view. Eight waterfalls descend into the three-acre Lake of Dreams, with its 4,000-plus individually controlled and submerged LEDs. A freestanding 70-foot (21-metre) wall serves as the projection screen

for a free light-and-sound show that plays every half-hour starting at 9pm.

The mountain serves a second and perhaps equally important purpose. It blocks the lights and drowns out the sounds of the Strip, cocooning Wynn Las Vegas and providing the visual centrepiece for the whole property. Once, that is, you've figured out where to look.

SIGHTS

---

was due to open in 2010 but now sits sadly unfinished on the Strip like a broken tooth, a monument to the worldwide economic crisis.

The opposite side of the Strip is an altogether more sedate sight. Development here has yet to really take hold, leaving the Catholic **Guardian Angel Cathedral** (336 Guardian Angel Way, 735 5241) to go about its business in relative peace. The themed stained-glass windows here are one of the few places where you can still see old Vegas icons such as the Landmark Hotel. Rumour has it that the church accepts casino chips in its collection plate.

CONVENTION CENTER DRIVE TO SAHARA AVENUE

North of Convention Center Drive, the Strip quickly peters out into disrepair. A couple of scruffy strip malls sit adjacent to and opposite some creaking old casinos, though the most

eye-catching features are the acres of empty lots and the clusters of construction work. The north Strip may be on the rise, but it's got a little way to travel before it reaches lift-off.

A fun little ode to the '70s stubbornly survives in the shape of **Peppermill's Fireside Lounge** (*see p181*), though the lounge recently ruined its cosy, Playboy-like atmosphere by bolting flat-panel TVs on to every surface. The site next door was once home to the delightfully Googie-style La Concha Motel. But after innumerable plans for redevelopment fell by the wayside, the land is currently, stubbornly vacant, while the motel's old lobby has been moved Downtown by the Neon Museum (*see p86* **A Paean to Neon**).

It's back to blazing neon at the 50-year-old **Riviera** (*see p128*), where the façade and sign very nearly constitute overkill even by Vegas standards. You can skip the actual show, but don't miss the life-sized bronze statues

SIGHTS

INSIDE TRACK FRIGHTDOME

Prepared to be scared: in October, the **Adventuredome** (*see below*) transforms into the pleasantly creepy FrightDome, in time for Halloween.

promoting the **Crazy Girls** (*see p228*) just in front of the casino; punters rub their butts for a boozy photo-op. However, the Riv seems to be marking time while it awaits extinction, a refuge for the cost-conscious traveller but easily skipped by those not staying there.

Lucky the Clown still leers cheerfully over the Strip from the front of **Circus Circus** (*see p126*) across the road, though the original family fun palace is now showing its age. The casino under the pink concrete big top stages free circus acts (11am-midnight daily) above the casino floor, while what was **Horse-a-Round Bar**, now a family friendly gelato stand, was immortalised in Hunter S Thompson's *Fear and Loathing in Las Vegas*. The cramped space and shabby decor lessen the spectacle; it's an odd experience watching a spangly trapeze artist fly overhead. While mom and pop gamble away the rent, kids whoop it up at **Adventuredome**, a popular indoor amusement park (*see below*).

North of here, there's much promise but, at least for now, little tangible excitement. Much of the land between here and Sahara Avenue was purchased by Circus Circus owners MGM Mirage in 2007, though no development plans have yet been announced for the largely vacant site. Across the road, construction has stopped on a Las Vegas version of Miami's famous **Fontainebleau**, another forlorn, unfinished monument to the financial crash.

For many, the Strip begins and ends right here at Sahara Avenue, although the Stratosphere's looming tower has pushed the unofficial boundary another half-mile north.

Adventuredome

Circus Circus *2880 Las Vegas Boulevard South, between W Sahara Avenue & Desert Inn Road (794 3939, www.adventuredome.com). Bus Deuce.* **Open** 10am-6pm Mon-Thur; 10am-midnight Fri, Sat; 10am-8pm Sun. **Admission** *Unlimited rides* $22.95; $14.95 reductions. *Individual rides* $4-$7. **Map** p335 B5.

The five-acre park, climate-controlled under a pink plastic dome, is a scene Fred Flintstone would love: waterfalls, faux mountains and animated spitting dinosaurs stuck in fake tar pits. The rides here are good, though hardly white-knuckle; the best is the double-loop, double-corkscrew rollercoaster ($5), but it lasts a disappointingly brief 90 seconds. Tots will like the bumper cars, Ferris wheel and

other small rides, as well as an obstacle course for creative crawling. *See also left* **Inside Track**.

STRATOSPHERE AREA

The lot at the south-western corner of Sahara and the Strip is eye-catchingly vacant, while the much-rumoured redevelopment of the north-eastern plot has yet to occur. Diagonally opposite the Sahara, **Bonanza Gifts** (*see p208*) holds the fort at the intersection's north-western corner; claiming to be the world's largest gift shop, it sells a vast array of souvenirs, in a pleasantly kitschy time-travel to the Route 66 era. Just west is the rising pricey condo tower of Allure overlooking the Strip, and the classic **Golden Steer Steak House** (*see p172*).

Standing outside Bonanza, you'll be able to hear screams. Glance north, and you'll see why. At the top of the **Stratosphere** (*see p129*), the tallest building in Nevada, is a trio of thrill rides: the **Big Shot**, which propels passengers vertically; **X Scream**, which dangles them over the edge of the tower; and **Insanity: The Ride**, an inverted centrifuge that spins over the edge of the observation deck at a 70-degree angle. It's enough to make anyone scream… including Bob Stupak, the Stratosphere's former owner, who suffered a series of financial and construction setbacks when trying to complete the tower.

The Stratosphere sits where Main Street and Paradise Road cross Las Vegas Boulevard and turn into each other by way of St Louis Avenue. As you approach it from the south, you'll see a string of downmarket motels, though the old **Holiday House Motel** (no.2211, 732 2468) is notable for its animated neon sign and Palm Springs-like motor court design. At the intersection with Oakey Boulevard is the **White Cross Drugstore**; in it is Tiffany's, one of the few drugstore food counters left in town.

Big Shot, X Scream & Insanity: the Ride

Stratosphere *2000 Las Vegas Boulevard South, at St Louis Avenue (380 7777, www.stratospherehotel.com). Bus Deuce, 108.* **Open** 10am-1am Mon-Thur, Sun; 10am-2am Fri, Sat. **Tickets** $12-$13 each. *All 3 rides* $31. *All-day pass* $34. **Map** p335 C4.

If you're afraid of heights, stay away from the 1,150ft (350m) Stratosphere Tower. And even if you don't suffer from vertigo, you might want to steer clear of the resort's thrill rides. The Big Shot will rocket you 160ft (49m) up the tower's spindle under a force of four Gs; at the top, you'll experience a moment of weightlessness before free-falling back to the launch pad. X Scream will propel you headfirst 27ft (8m) over the edge of the Tower and then leave you there to dangle. And during Insanity, an arm will extend 64ft (20m) over the edge of the tower and spin you around at a terrifying rate. Best save dinner for later.

Off-Strip

Guess what? More casinos…

You wouldn't expect to confuse **Paradise Road** for the Strip. Lined with an erratic hotchpotch of posh hotels and scruffy apartment blocks, convention facilities and adult clubs, strip malls and, er, more strip malls, Paradise is a low-key thoroughfare. However, as the Las Vegas Convention Center draws ever-increasing numbers of conventioneers, and the Strip attracts even more tourists, so the traffic along it gets fiercer. Paradise Road now resembles Las Vegas Boulevard in one crucial regard: if you're foolish enough to try driving down it in rush hour, you'll be waiting a while. During off-peak hours, though, locals swear by it as a time-saving way to avoid stop-start Strip-stalled traffic.

Map p335, p336
Hotels p132
Restaurants &
Buffets p168
Bars & Lounges
p183

SIGHTS

EAST OF THE STRIP

Running parallel to the Strip, Paradise Road has been the site of major development since 1969, when the Landmark and International casinos opened south of Sahara Avenue. The Landmark was erased a while ago (see *Mars Attacks!* to witness its real-life destruction), while the International was renamed the **Las Vegas Hilton** (*see p134*) in 1971, the same year that it starred as the **Whyte House** in *Diamonds Are Forever*. The Hilton's showroom staged Elvis Presley's record-breaking run of 837 sell-outs in the 1970s; prosaically, it now hosts a nightly array of comedians, impressionists and golden-oldies acts; directly behind it is the exclusive **Las Vegas Country Club**.

Sprawling out from the south end of the Hilton and across Desert Inn Road, the **Las Vegas Convention Center** (*see p311*) has been more responsible than any one hotel for the huge growth in visitor numbers over the last decade. Seven million travellers arrive in the city for conventions each year, and many of them pass through this site to do business. The assortment of uncharismatic chain hotels nearby stands testament to its influence. At the intersection with Desert Inn Road, **Envy** steakhouse (*see p169*) serves hungry conventioneers; across the street is a shuttle to whisk patrons to the

Wynn Las Vegas resort. Paradise Road, in fact, might aptly be renamed Steakhouse Alley, as it hosts, in addition to Envy, at least half a dozen steak purveyors, including Morton's, Del Frisco's Double Eagle and AJ's.

Further south, the road widens and the traffic eases. At Twain Avenue begins a collection of eateries known as 'restaurant row'. However, the stretch of Paradise between Flamingo and Tropicana holds more points of interest. On the eastern side lies a succession of strip malls that house a slew of excellent restaurants (try **Origin India**; *see p170*), bars (the boisterous and authentically German **Hofbrauhaus**; *see p169*), dive bars (such as the **Double Down Saloon**; *see p183*) and gay hangouts (in the **Fruit Loop**; *see pp248-251*). East of all these businesses sits the campus of UNLV, which more or less backs on to Paradise Road.

And on the western side of Paradise, at the junction with Harmon Avenue, is the **Hard Rock** hotel-casino (*see p132*), crammed with memorabilia, suntanned hipsters and cash-happy baby boomers. Despite competition from Palms, the Hard Rock is holding its own as a favoured resort for the young and restless, thanks to the renovated, state-of-the-art concert hall called the Joint, which opened with a pair of concerts by Vegas natives the Killers and none other than Sir Paul McCartney; and the weekly

Atomic Testing Museum.

SIGHTS

flesh-feast that is the Rehab pool party (Sundays in season; see p260). See if you can find the one-of-a-kind Sex Pistols-themed slot machine on the Hard Rock gaming floor.

A bit further east and to the south (about six miles) is a locals' casino called the **Silverton** (3333 Blue Diamond Road, 1-866 722 4608, 263 7777, www.silvertoncasino.com), which has a few unique rustic Americana-themed amenities that make it worth the trip. Chief among these is the Mermaid Restaurant & Lounge, encrusted with undersea kitsch and featuring live mermaid performances in the colossal barside aquarium – you can pull up a chair and have a drink while pantomiming conversation with one of these underwater entertainers. There's also a micro-bowling alley in a vintage mobile home, and a vast Bass Pro Shop – complete with onsite fishing river, archery and rifle ranges – catering to outdoorsmen and those who merely fancy themselves as rugged outdoor types.

South of Tropicana sits the vast **McCarran International Airport** (see p308) – the gleaming rows of slot machines in its lobby never cease to amaze the waves of fresh arrivals. McCarran is one of the world's most fascinating people-watching spots, as its population changes by the hour: it's variably and visibly overrun by black-clad retrobilly bikers, NASCAR fans, NBA stars, rodeo cowboys and, occasionally, hovering hordes of hookers waiting for their baggage.

East on Tropicana is the **Atomic Testing Museum**, located on the Desert Research Institute campus. And to the west of Paradise, between Flamingo and Tropicana, sits a maze of small streets and empty lots, awaiting the inevitable redevelopment but content for now to serve as a rat run for those savvy drivers smart enough to avoid both Paradise and the Strip.

★ Atomic Testing Museum

755 E Flamingo Road, between Swenson Street & Paradise Road (794 5151, www.atomictesting museum.org). Bus 202. **Open** 10am-5pm Mon-Sat; noon-5pm Sun. **Admission** $12; $9 reductions; free under-6s. **Map** p333 Y3.

From the city that once trotted out atomic pin-up girls in mushroom-cloud swimsuits for cheesy publicity stills comes a one-of-a-kind insight into the Nevada Test Site, the US's principal on-continent nuclear weapons testing facility from 1951 to 1992. The story it tells is fascinating: how nuclear power came to represent the future in the USA, how it came to be something approaching a tourist attraction in this most carefully blasé of states, and – most crucially, and in layman's terms – how it actually works.

An affiliate of the Smithsonian Institution, its headline exhibit is the motion-simulator that endeavours to give visitors a taste of what it must have been like to sit in on one of the several hundred tests carried out at the site between 1951 and 1992. But the real keys to the museum's success are the clarity with which it tells its tale (chronologically, through a succession of themed rooms), and the eye-popping quality of the exhibits (some kitsch, some terrifying). The last two or three rooms essentially comprise an advertorial for nuclear power, which doesn't sit well after what's gone before. But this is still comfortably the most interesting and enlightening museum in the city.

Commercial Center

943 E Sahara Ave, between S Maryland Parkway & Paradise Road (737 3478, www.commercial centerdistrict.com). **Open** times vary. **Map** p333 Y2.

If you absolutely must visit one strip mall in a city of strip malls (it might be argued that the fabled Strip itself is nothing more than a strip mall with an overdose of self-esteem), you may as well make it to the gritty, quirkily fascinating Commercial Center, a nondescript enclosure surrounding a 28-acre parking lot. Just a mile east of the Strip, within sight of the Stratosphere tower, tenants of Commercial Center include a five-star Thai restaurant (Lotus of Siam) and other well-regarded Asian venues, an adventurous underground theatre company (Insurgo Theater Movement), at least two sex clubs and a swingers' lounge, an ice-hockey rink, a cluster of jovial (and very different) gay bars and the city's gay and lesbian community centre, shops specialising in wigs and other showgirl accessories, and a constantly changing constellation of storefronts that host accountants, acupuncturists, karaoke joints, nail spas, prayer revivals, 12-step meetings and children's birthday parties. Commercial Center is a reality show begging to be made.

Town Square

6605 Las Vegas Boulevard South, between 15 & 215 (269 5000, www.mytownsquarelasvegas.com). Bus SDX. **Open** 9am-10pm daily.

This upscale outdoor mall – an appealing aggregation of shopping, dining and entertainment, with its own home-design district – has become the go-to place for locals who can't be bothered with the Strip. Major outlets include a Whole Foods grocer, Hollister, Apple, H&M, a *churrascaria*, a Yard House ale house/sports bar/restaurant, and a digital movie multiplex called Rave. It's a planned environment focused on walkability, though it's certainly no substitute for a real urban experience – Town Square's streets are kept eerily pristine, with piped-in music burbling merrily from the flowerbeds, and spray-misters keeping the would-be spenders cool on hot days. The place has quickly developed its own nightlife district, though, with singles mingling between the sprinkling of restaurants and saloons, centred around Blue Martini.

Vegas Indoor Skydiving

200 Convention Center Drive, between Las Vegas Boulevard South & Paradise Road (1-877 545 8093, 731 4768, www.vegasindoorsky diving.com). Bus Deuce, 108. **Open** 9.45am-8pm daily. **Rates** $75. **Map** p335 B5.
Skydiving without an airplane? Well, sort of: you can free-fall in one of only three skydiving simulators in the world, an indoor 21ft vertical wind tunnel that generates air speeds of up to 130mph. After an hour of instruction, you get 15 minutes of flying time shared with five others.

WEST OF THE STRIP

The area between busy Las Vegas Boulevard and unremarkable Valley View Boulevard is bisected by I-15, which carves a rift into a section of land that didn't offer much resistance to it. Wedged next to it and running parallel, Frank Sinatra Drive offers quicker, back-door access to many Strip hotels. Continuing north, Industrial Road itself is just as speedy, but is otherwise notable only for the parade of strip clubs that lines its western edge.

Overpasses at Tropicana, Flamingo or Sahara take drivers across I-15 to Valley View Boulevard (which, incidentally, isn't continuous between Tropicana Boulevard and Flamingo Road). If you're heading this way from the Strip, Flamingo is the road to take: it's lined with a quartet of very different hotel-casinos, each with something to offer the visitor.

On the northern side of Flamingo sits the **Rio** (*see p135*), still touting its Brazilian tropics theme with its tired but free *Masquerade Show in the Sky*; staged seven times daily, it's a kind of floating Mardi Gras parade, but without the topless girls or free tequila. Wickedly funny magicians Penn & Teller have been holding court since 2001 in their own dedicated theatre at the Rio (*see p231*). Just past the Rio are the **Gold Coast** (*see p150*) and the **Orleans** (*see*

Commercial Center.

p148), a pair of locals' casinos with bowling alleys, movie theatres and other attractions – the Orleans has been successfully attracting lovers of country music and 1970s pop culture with its near-nightly concerts; you'll also find such down-home American events as tractor pulls, rodeos and barbecue competitions at its Events Center.

More likely, though, you'll end up at the **Palms** (*see p135*), the closest competitor to the Hard Rock in terms of attracting the beautiful people – it was made world-famous and began attracting a younger crowd to Vegas when 'seven strangers' settled into a custom-built penthouse suite for a season of MTV's *The Real World*. The nightlife here is energising, with nightclubs such as **Moon** (*see p259*) competing with the **Pearl** music venue

(*see p254*) and a whole slew of restaurants for the attentions of visitors. The nightclub-esque **Brenden Las Vegas 14** (*see p242*), one of the top cinema multiplexes in town, adds to the fun; it even has a disco ball spinning in the lobby. Vegas isn't really known as a movie town – the casinos would rather have you out on the gambling floor for those two hours – but when a film does get a première here, it's often at the Brenden, which is also the home of the Las Vegas International Film Festival.

Beyond the Rio, the Gold Coast and the Palms, Valley View Boulevard continues north through a semi-residential, semi-industrial district. An easterly turn at Sahara leads past small strip malls ad infinitum until the train-themed casino **Palace Station** (*see p150*) just before I-15.

Demolition City

Here today, gone tomorrow.

Will Self once compared the constant, inevitable and yet barely tangible regeneration of urban landscapes to an intruder entering one's house in the middle of the night and moving all the furniture by a couple of inches. You know something's changed, but you can't quite tell what, or how, or even when.

In Las Vegas, things are different: progress happens instantaneously yet takes forever. Structures are erased without ceremony or sentiment, the swing of a wrecking ball bouncing from building to building like dice cascading backwards from the wall of a craps table. And then begins the inexorably tedious yet painfully visible process of regenerating the space. What takes five minutes to destroy can take five years to rebuild, by which time everyone has lost interest.

The streets surrounding the Strip are filled with casualties that time hasn't managed to erase. The Bourbon Street casino (formerly at 120 E Flamingo Road) was levelled by Harrah's in 2006, but its sidewalk remains lined with stars that together comprise a cheap-as-chips jazz walk of fame. South of the Strip and closed since 2006, the crumbling Klondike (5191 Las Vegas Boulevard South) is the first casino most visitors see as they drive from the airport into the city. And then there are the high-profile casualties on the Strip itself: the Stardust, erased in 2007; the Algiers, a memory since 2004; even the El Rancho, built in 1941 as the first resort on what became the Strip but closed since 1960.

The one thing these casinos have in common is that the land they once occupied remains empty. Their demise was brought about by real-estate moguls with the grandest of plans for their lots. Eight-figure sums were spent, but on nothing more than a crash, a bang and an 'And finally' item on the nightly news. After all, they eventually figured, why build on the land if we can make as much cash by leaving it empty?

Harrah's has been slow to announce plans for the Bourbon Street's plum site. For a change, though, there's still something in its way: the land surrounding the scruffy, unassuming Stage Door casino at the corner of Flamingo Road and Audrie Street, across from the Bourbon Street lot, is empty; the single-storey building is in the shadow both of its skyscraping neighbours and the monorail that runs above it. But the owners have bucked a citywide trend and refused to sell to Harrah's, who own the vacant lots around it.

Inside, the Stage Door is like any blue-collar local bar late in the evening. Outside, the world wanders by, looking on with amusement at this mutinous holdout. The owners would make far more by selling up than they are by staying open, but pride is keeping them rooted to the spot. Usually used to advertise some putatively terrific gambling schedule or food special, the building's frontage now reads, with insouciant defiance, 'We have 20 years left on our lease'. The furniture, for now, remains unmoved.

Downtown

Old Las Vegas has got its groove back.

North of the Strip, Downtown Las Vegas is another world. Sure, there's been a splash of paint here and an outrageously uninteresting electronic canopy there, but Downtown hadn't changed much in spirit for as long as anyone can remember. After years in the shadow of the Strip, it has slowly and painfully been becoming the graveyard of dreams, a place where plans for revitalisation were long articulated but never realised. Cheerleaders were waiting for years for *something* to happen, only to see their hopes fleeing further with each passing year.

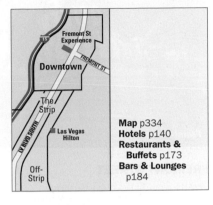

Map p334
Hotels p140
**Restaurants &
Buffets** p173
Bars & Lounges
p184

Imagine the local surprise, then, when a 21st-century Downtown began to sprout in 2006. Huge cranes and land-movers arrived, bringing steel beams, glass panes and concrete. With them came speculators armed with small-scale business plans and modest amounts of capital, who soon began seeing uncharacteristically swift fruition of their notions. Whatever next?

ONE HUNDRED YEARS OF HISTORY

Las Vegas began at what is now the core of Downtown. In May 1905, settlers and speculators gathered in front of a wooden railroad platform, land now occupied by the Plaza hotel, in order to bid on the 1,200 lots that constituted the original town site. In the 1930s and '40s, hotels and casinos dotted Fremont Street, the area's main commercial drag for decades. But the rise of the Strip saw trade drain from Downtown, where there was no space for expansion. In time, the area grew dowdy.

The construction of the Fremont Street Experience in 1995, which turned a five-block section of the road into a pedestrian-friendly gambling mall and covered it with a canopy that screens light and sound shows, succeeded in luring some tourists back to Glitter Gulch. Despite the later addition of some restored neon signs, some locals complained that it destroyed much of Fremont Street's character. But the march of progress is irresistible; not as irresistible as it is on the Strip, granted, but still inevitable.

In implosion-friendly Las Vegas, where experiments are sometimes shelved before

their natural expiration date, don't be too upset or surprised if today's guidebook treasure is tomorrow's empty lot. Even so, there's never been a better time to discover Downtown, an amorphous amalgamation of things gone right and wrong. By turns sleazy and chic, downcast and upmarket, desperate and enthusiastic, it's a section of town in which constant and concerted efforts to make something incredible have failed only in specificity. Something wonderful *is* emerging, just not quite as originally intended.

GETTING THERE

If you're using public transport, you can reach Downtown from the Strip by catching the double-deckered Deuce bus. If you're driving, head north on I-15 and then east on US 93/95, taking the Casino Center exit (the faster route); alternatively, drive north on the Strip and 4th Street (the more interesting route). The parking garages off Fremont Street are all safe places to park, though you may need to get your parking ticket validated inside one of the casinos or other local businesses to get free parking.

SIGHTS

Fremont Street.

FREMONT STREET

Once the centre of Las Vegas and then a scruffy shadow of its former self, **Fremont Street** has been officially tabbed as the focus of efforts to save Downtown. The old casinos remain, lining the stretch of Fremont west of Las Vegas Boulevard much as they have done for decades. But as proved by the 2007 arrival of the Las Vegas Grand Prix, an open-wheel race around the streets of Downtown, things are changing around here.

The Fremont Street Experience

Many tourists think that Downtown begins and ends under the electronic canopy that covers Fremont Street between Las Vegas Boulevard and Main Street. It doesn't, but on the grounds both of safety and of convenience, this stretch is the best starting and finishing point for an exploration of the area.

Inaugurated in 1995 and modified several times since, the five-block **Fremont Street Experience** was Downtown's attempt to drag a formerly desolate road into the 21st century. It's been a qualified success, but it's never quite drawn the crowds it was intended to muster. Sure, tourists come to this pedestrianised mall and in great numbers, especially for the special free weekend events (concerts, car shows and the like). Still, the demographic hasn't changed much in decades; this remains a blue-collar corner of Vegas's sprawling network of resorts.

The pedestrianised mall is dominated by a huge LED-studded canopy that flows 90 feet (27 metres) above it, flickering into action on the hour each night with intermittently entertaining sound and light shows. More

interesting is **Vegas Vic**, the 75-foot (23-metre) neon cowboy who's been waving to visitors since 1951; sadly, he no longer calls out 'Howdy, pod'ner!' from a hidden speaker. Across the street, Vic's female counterpart Vegas Vicky kicks up her heels over the recently renovated **Girls of Glitter Gulch** strip club, a long-standing embarrassment to a city desperate to make seedy Downtown into a respectable destination. A strip club ringed by casinos beneath a vintage neon sign that itself sits under a vainglorious 21st-century bibelot; it is at this corner that Downtown's attractions and distractions congeal into one.

At night, the FSE is littered with crazy-eyed desperados, too-tanked hoochies and wide-mouthed tourists craning their necks to see every pixel of the jet fighter images soaring above them to some-or-other patriotic song. Keep your eyes at eye level: the street is a vital gathering spot for the keen people-watcher. Vitality seeps from the schlock and kitsch compendium of street performers and retail kiosks: witness the souvenir beads flow from the giant mermaids, the speed-painting airbrush artist, the deep-fried Twinkies. And don't miss – how could you? – the only two-time winner of the International Liberace Pianist Competition, tickling the ivories into a frenzied rendition of 'Chariots of Fire' on a piano mounted upon a giant flatbed truck in the middle of the street. But for all the flash and filigree, the casinos remain the main draw: partly for the gambling rules, more generous here than on the Strip, but mostly due to the low accommodation prices.

Once upon a time, the former Binion's Horseshoe was the Wild West home of outlaw gaming, the World Series of Poker and true no-frills, no-nonsense gambling. Scandal and debt gave rise to a sequence of ownership shuffles that resulted in it losing its family ownership, its name (it's now just **Binion's**; *see p142*) and its magic. Across the street, the **Golden Nugget** (*see p140*) has changed hands a few times in recent years, but with a more attractive outcome. After a renovation brought swanky lounges, upscale restaurants and, most eye-catchingly, shark tanks in the swanky new pool, the Nugget continues to bring a little glamour back to far-from-fancy Fremont.

Happily unchanged down the years is the **Golden Gate** (*see p144*), the city's oldest hotel. Built in 1906 as the Hotel Nevada, the Golden Gate was known for decades as the Sal Sagev (try reading it backwards). The hotel may be the only property in town where the smiling casino owner can be seen enjoying a cup of chicken soup in the booth next to yours.

Further nods to old Vegas can be found with the throwback elegance and overwrought decor of Hugo's Cellar at the **Four Queens** (*see p143*), and with the utterly basic interior of the **Fremont** (*see p144*), the archetypal Downtown grind joint. However, they're both topped by the **Plaza** (*see p145*), sitting at the end of Fremont like the old man at the head of the table but trying harder than any Downtown property to reinvent itself as hip. *Shag With a Twist*, the hotel's new signature show, is a musical murder mystery set at a Tupperware party in the 1960s. It's touted in press materials as cool and campy; based in a hotel adjacent to the Greyhound bus depot, how could it be anything but?

Golden Nugget.

Neon Road

At the opposite end of the Fremont Street Experience to the Plaza, closer to Las Vegas Boulevard, the attractions are a little patchier. There's the open-air **Neon Museum**, a small but growing collection of classic Vegas signs that have been restored and placed on poles between the what was formerly the Neonopolis shopping and entertainment complex and the FSE parking garage. For more on the signs, *see p86* **A Paean to Neon**.

Several such signs can be found on North 3rd Street between Fremont and Ogden Streets, a stretch that both complements and anticipates the changes further east (*see below*). The western side of 3rd has been taken over by a slew of businesses that pay homage of sorts to old Downtown: witness the steakhouse swank of **Triple George** (*see p173*), the cultured **Sidebar** (*see p185*) and the often-raucous **Hogs & Heifers** (*see p185*). And back across from the former Neonopolis on Fremont are **Hennesseys**, **Mickie Finnz** (*see p173*) and **Brass**, three spots that are trying to draw a mix of tourists and locals with upscale bar food, local bands and gambling.

Downtown is home to a number of public artworks in the 'City of 100 Murals' series, commissioned to celebrate the city's centennial in 2005. Most have some sort of gaming theme, but an abstract stand-out is the five-panelled light sculpture located by the elevators of the Fremont Street parking garage. Designed by Las Vegas artists Mary Warner and Rayann Figler, it refashioned the discarded bulbs of the FSE when it converted to LED technology.

The area's newest landmark is a pair of 45-foot paintbrushes by artist Dennis Oppenheim – imaginatively called *Paintbrushes*, they are a can't-miss-it indicator of the city's still-struggling arts district.

East of Las Vegas Boulevard

Across Las Vegas Boulevard, Fremont Street is an almost unrecognisably different place. This stretch is protected not by a vast, LED-studded canopy but by shady security staff, protecting the interests of their employers by keeping the drunks, drug dealers and down-and-outs away. The **El Cortez** (*see p142*) and **Western** (*see p145*) supplement the seamy feel with a portion of Vegas charm at its most reliably basic.

Things, though, are changing, thanks to the city's official plan to install an 'entertainment overlay'. The Fremont East Entertainment District, it's putatively called, a soon-to-flourish (hopefully) string of bars and restaurants that will have to make it on charm and liquor alone:

SIGHTS

A Paean to Neon

This city's all lit up.

If there's one piece of the past that lovers of Las Vegas miss above all others, it's the old-time signs. Just listen to Alan Hess, author of *Viva Las Vegas: After-Hours Architecture*, wax nostalgic about one of his favourites: the 15-storey, 40,000-bulb Aladdin sign from the 1960s. 'It was a full-blown fantasia, a dreamy mirage made real. The artistry that requires – to put that much steel and neon up in the desert sky and make it convincing, otherworldly, floating – is tremendous. It represented the ultimate achievement of that era of Las Vegas design. And it's an art that has not been recaptured in recent years.'

Discarding the past is itself a key part of Vegas history. The giant movie set known as the Strip constantly moves on to the next big idea without so much as a glance behind it. These days, though, the town's two-million-strong permanent community of non-tourists carries enough influence to preserve some of the neon left in the wake of the economic machine. The main voice of this movement is a non-profit project called the **Neon Museum**, set up 'to collect, preserve, study and exhibit neon signs and associated artefacts to inspire educational and cultural enrichment.' Its collection consists of three components: the Boneyard, the Fremont Street Gallery, and the Neon Signs Project.

One of the museum's first achievements was to refurbish the genie's lamp that once crowned the old Aladdin sign and install it at the corner of Fremont Street and Las Vegas Boulevard in 1996, 40 years after its original debut. Since then, the collection has expanded apace, and now includes everything from 1940s pieces to the decommissioned Stardust sign. Piece by piece, each sign is moved from its location to the Neon Boneyard on Las Vegas Boulevard, where it undergoes enough work to spruce it up without washing away its patina.

There are 11 old signs dotting Downtown, in the so-called 'outdoor galleries' on or just off Fremont Street. The old Hacienda horseman is riding high again, and the long-defunct Nevada Hotel continues to help light up the night, alongside smaller signs devoted to the Flame Restaurant, the Chief Hotel Court and the Anderson Dairy. The museum has also put several signs on display at the Old Las Vegas Mormon Fort Historic Park (*see p88*), including the shapely Arabic 'A' from the Sahara.

The best, though, is yet to come. The Neon Boneyard is a three-acre park full of historic Vegas signage, which at the time of writing was open for viewing by appointment only, but is making incremental moves to becoming a full-scale museum. The landmark lobby from the old La Concha hotel, one of the city's great Googie structures, has been rescued and moved up the boulevard to serve as the visitor centre, gallery and gift shop for the museum. Keep track of progress and book a tour by visiting www.neonmuseum.org.

gambling will be conspicuous by its absence, as Vegas aims to construct an urban core that bears comparison with the likes of San Diego. Local authorities have widened the streets, shuffled the urban blight down the way and given decent tax incentives to new businesses.

A few pioneering daddios have taken the bait already. The Vegas version of the tiny but mighty **Beauty Bar** was followed by the swanky **Downtown Cocktail Room** (*for both, see p184*) and the more pubby **Griffin** (*see p185*). These bars, now supplemented by tasty fast-food joints such as **Kabob Korner** (*see p173*), look set to be joined by coffeehouses (the **Beat Coffeehouse**, which sells beer and vinyl records, is the new favourite among Vegas's small but tenacious literati and hipoisie), stores and perhaps even a music venue. In time, the redevelopment may pay off for those who have invested so much in reinvigorating the famous Glitter Gulch of yore. For now, though, it's the up-and-coming part of town, and local hipsters are already dreading the day when the tourists discover it.

Trying in their own way to compete with the Strip, in the hope of attracting a younger generation of ironic appreciators of classic Vegas, several Downtown casino-hotels have recently submitted to extensive facelifts. The **El Cortez** (*see p142*), once owned by Bugsy Siegel, has hip-ified its tower and cabana rooms, and even held a contest inviting local designers to remodel its suites (the winner: a Mob-inspired remake). The old **Gold Spike** (*see p145*) has also had a bit of work done, and the **Plaza Hotel & Casino** (*see p145*) snapped up the furnishings and accoutrements of the dead-in-its-tracks Fontainebleau resort project, which gave it more than a bit of a glam injection.

Further down Fremont Street, shabby old Downtown returns, a wonderworld of decrepitude and danger. Walking around here after dark isn't advisable, but if you lock your car doors, it makes a great night drive. The road is lined with vintage neon motel signs, giving a glimpse of the era when east Fremont resembled the Strip. The 1960s-mod City Center Motel that stood at the corner of Fremont and 7th Streets is now a Super 8 motel; further down Fremont are **Fergusons Motel** (between 10th & 11th streets) and the kitschy red-and-yellow-trimmed motor court of the **Gables** (at 13th Street).

NORTH TO WASHINGTON AVENUE

Parallel to Fremont Street a couple of blocks north, **Stewart Avenue** is where Downtown winds down. The corner with Las Vegas

El Cortez.

Boulevard was home to the old City Hall, and is now the home of Zappos, the internet shoe and accessories merchant, which has already brought an influx of San Francisco start-up energy. The old City Hall has an interesting art gallery and (until recently) near-constant sightings of the happiest mayor/movie star/gin spokesman in the world: Oscar B Goodman, who will gladly autograph your martini olives if you ask nicely. (Now that his wife, Carolyn, has been elected mayor, Goodman is in negotiations to open his own saloon Downtown: keep an eye open for that.) Also on Stewart is **Squires Park**, the site of sporadic free concerts, and the original federal courthouse building, which formerly housed a post office. It's an interesting example of neo-classical architecture.

To the north along Las Vegas Boulevard sit more remnants of the city's past. Beyond the **Neon Boneyard** (*see p86* **A Paean to Neon**) are a series of low-key attractions that have been designated, slightly optimistically, as the Cultural Corridor: the **City of Las Vegas Galleries** (*see p246*) in the Reed Whipple Cultural Center, the **Las Vegas Natural History Museum** and the **Lied Discovery Children's Museum** (for both, *see p88*).

Just to the east is **Cashman Field**, where the Las Vegas 51s, the Los Angeles Dodgers' AAA team, play baseball through the heat of summer (*see p263*). Also in the general area is the fascinating **Old Las Vegas Mormon Fort Historic Park** (*see below*). And those into old architecture should check the Biltmore Bungalows, which aren't bungalows at all. Located a block west of Las Vegas Boulevard on Bonanza Road, they were built to house all the civilian workers stationed in Las Vegas to aid in the war effort, and remain a great representation of a mid-century, master-planned community.

Las Vegas Natural History Museum

900 Las Vegas Boulevard North, at E Washington Avenue (384 3466, www.lvnhm.org). Bus 113, 208. **Open** 9am-4pm daily. **Admission** $10; $5-$8 reductions. **Map** p334 E1.
This small, enthusiastically run museum doesn't offer much in the way of bells and whistles. The Marine Life Room features small sharks in a large tank, the Wild Nevada Room has exhibits on the flora and fauna of Nevada, and the Young Scientist Center has some interactive displays. However, the big draw is five roaring, robotic dinosaurs, among them a vast T-Rex.
▶ *Combine a visit with a trip to the nearby Lied Discovery Children's Museum (see below).*

Lied Discovery Children's Museum

Las Vegas Library, 833 Las Vegas Boulevard North, between W Washington Avenue & Bonanza Road (382 5437, www.ldcm.org). Bus 113, 208. **Open** *Summer* 10am-5pm Mon-Sat; noon-5pm Sun. *Autumn-spring* 9am-4pm Tue-Fri; 10am-5pm Sat; noon-5pm Sun. **Admission** $9.50; $8.50 reductions. **Map** p334 D1.
A stimulating museum similar to (though smaller than) the Exploratorium in San Francisco, the Lied features dozens of scientific exhibits that involve the viewer as a part of the demonstration. Don't be put off by the name: this is the sort of place that many adults would visit by themselves if they thought they could. Creative exhibits include a tin-can telephone, which should entertain the kids for hours. Rumour has it that the museum will soon be moving to a new location, leaving behind the public library that surrounds it. Check before making a special trip.

Old Las Vegas Mormon Fort Historic Park

500 E Washington Avenue, at Las Vegas Boulevard North (486 3511, www.parks.nv.gov/olvmf.htm). Bus 113, 208. **Open** 8am-4.30pm Mon-Sat. **Admission** $1; free under-12s. **No credit cards. Map** p333 Y2.
Built by a group of Mormon missionaries in 1855 and then left to become part of the Las Vegas Ranch, this is Vegas's pioneer settlement site, the oldest Euro-American structure in the state and an example of what Vegas was like before the railroad. Though only remnants of the original structure remain, restoration and reconstruction have brought the compound back to life, and guides are on hand to answer questions.

SOUTH TO OAKEY BOULEVARD

Las Vegas Boulevard grows less pleasant the further south of Fremont you travel, but the stroll does at least begin with several points of interest. The **Lloyd George Federal Courthouse** is a handsome steel-and-glass building that hosts occasional cultural events during lunchtimes and less official protests on the streets outside. Across the street is the under-renovation Fifth Street School, due to house an arts and design campus.

Nearby on Lewis Avenue stand two very singular attractions: **André's** (*see p173*), the best French restaurant in Nevada, and the **Poets Bridge**, done out with a curious water feature, a sidewalk engraved with quotes from 20 Nevadan poets. The bridge's main feature is a brass plaque on which is inscribed 'The Long Shot'; written by New York writer (and former Las Vegas resident) Gregory Crosby, it's perhaps the best poem ever written about Las Vegas.

There's ancient history around these parts; though in Las Vegas, that means the 1930s at the earliest. Although most of residential Las Vegas is unimaginatively cast in the same faux-Mediterranean stucco, the area bounded by 6th Street, Bridger Avenue, 9th Street and Oakey Boulevard is a rare example of architectural diversity and small-town comfort: well-kept single-storey homes with large yards and wide driveways are typical. The list of 1940s and '50s buildings in the area is headed by the **Las Vegas Academy of International Studies & Performing Arts** (*see p269*), the only piece of 1930s art deco architecture in the city.

On South 7th Street, just before Charleston Boulevard, sits a cluster of attractive, early 20th-century bungalows with plaster walls and wooden floors; it's now known as 'Lawyer's Row', after the punk attorneys who've taken over the locale. South of Charleston, meanwhile, is the **John S Park** neighbourhood. Filled with 1940s bungalows and swankier dwellings from the '50s and '60s, it was the city's first official Historic District. Self-guided tours created by the City Historical Preservation Division are available from City Hall.

Back on Las Vegas Boulevard, the scene soon degenerates; the street lined with shady-looking storefronts and vintage motels that do most of their business either by the hour or by the month. Among the various buildings offering quickie marriages, the angels-on-crack painted ceiling of the 24-hour drive-through **Little White Wedding Chapel** (*see p274*) is worth a look. For the most part, the street isn't as dangerous as it looks, but nor is it an especially salubrious or attractive part of town.

Things spruce up a little just before Oakey Boulevard, near the point at which Main Street meets Las Vegas Boulevard. Chow on an omelette with a side of trout

SIGHTS

at **Tiffany's**; (1700 Las Vegas Boulevard South), a classic 24-hour counter-service joint inside the White Cross Drugstore (and one of the main settings for Drew Barrymore vehicle *Lucky You*); follow it with the city's greatest dessert at **Luv-It Frozen Custard** (*see p169*); and wash it all down with a beer at **Dino's** (*see p184*).

When you're sufficiently lubricated, two nearby adult businesses are waiting to take the dollars you didn't donate to Dino's video-poker machines: the relatively smart **Olympic Garden** (*see p224*) and the more down-at-heel **Talk of the Town** (1238 Las Vegas Boulevard South), home of the ten-dollar lap dance. The latter sits opposite the **Aruba Hotel** (*see p139*), where the vast **Thunderbird Lounge** (*see p286*) hosts everything from swing dance lessons to alternative theatre.

The Arts District & around

Walk south of Fremont Street along Main Street, and the pickings are slimmer than on Las Vegas Boulevard. Here you'll find old-fashioned eaterie **El Sombrero** (*see p173*), high-end retro duds at the **Attic** (*see p203*) and the card-playing, chip-tossing paraphernalia of the **Gamblers General Store** (*see p208*).

When you reach Charleston Boulevard, you'll be on the edge of the **Arts District**, loosely bordered by Charleston, Las Vegas Boulevard, Wyoming Avenue and the

railroad. The focal point of the area is the **Arts Factory**, a block-long, two-storey 1940s building filled with an ever-changing line-up of galleries (such as **Emergency Arts**, *see 247*), studios and other creative businesses. But the district also holds an array of shops (among them the **Funk House**; *see p212*) and bars (including **Beauty Bar**, *see p184*), all of which bring culture and edge to a once-downtrodden part of town. The Arts District is at its best on **First Friday** (*see p219*), a monthly block party when the streets come alive with festive cheer.

East along Charleston are a number of other new Downtown landmarks. At the corner of Charleston and Grand Central Parkway stands the **Holsum Lofts**, a long-time commercial bakery that's lately been regenerated into a little cultural centre of sorts, with a decent grill (*see p173*), galleries, artists' studios and shops.

North up Grand Central, the open-air **Las Vegas Premium Outlets** (*see p198*) yields cut-price goodies from the likes of Kenneth Cole and Banana Republic. And nearby stand two landmark buildings: the ever-expanding **World Market Center**, a hulking slab on the horizon, and the **Clark County Government Amphitheatre**, which hosts First Friday concerts. Nearby is where **Union Park** will eventually reshape Downtown, with a performing arts centre, medical campus, condos, retail operations and other enterprises.

SIGHTS

The Beat Coffeehouse. *See p87*.

The Rest of the City

Vegas is a real town too.

Like Los Angeles, off-Strip Las Vegas is a sprawling, unwalkable suburb made up of still-mushrooming residential developments, with the institutions and infrastructure that any large city requires scattered within their midst. Until the global economic collapse – it hit Las Vegas harder than just about anywhere else in the US – new estates seemed to spring up overnight, barely keeping pace with the 8,000 people who migrated to Clark County every month (those numbers have since decreased).

Its interest lies not in great beauty or a wealth of visitor attractions (it has neither), but as a reassuringly benign refuge of normality, far from the neon overload. For most Vegas residents, the Strip is 'the office', a glittering cubicle farm, 'the place Mommy and Daddy work'. Yet despite Vegas's well-earned reputation as a town devoid of coherent town planning, you will find glimpses of a rich history, pockets of character and a defiant civic identity, with surprisingly old and deep religious – mostly Mormon – roots.

THIS CITY IS FOR DRIVING

When you set out, keep in mind that this is not just your average sprawling, unwalkable suburb: it can be downright hostile to pedestrians. (And this is without mentioning the often glaring sun and melting desert heat.) The bus system is reliable and will get you to most places of note, but a car is necessary to explore the city properly. Leave plenty of time for delays caused by the new construction work. But fear not: it's hard to get lost in a flat city that's built on a network and that has, at its centre, the tallest observation tower west of the Mississippi.

The neighbourhoods in this chapter are arranged clockwise, starting in the south-west corner of town and finishing in the south-east.

SOUTH-WEST LAS VEGAS

Much of south-west Las Vegas is unremarkable in that, like much of the town, it consists largely of middle-class suburban homes surrounded by strip malls. Past the **Orleans** (*see p148*), a locals' joint, Tropicana Avenue and its adjoining streets offer little more than bland private tract homes and apartment blocks. Further west, halfway to the mountains, are the ultra-posh and guardedly private residential developments of **Spanish Trail** and **Spanish Hills**, home to many of Las Vegas's notable figures. Go north at Rainbow and you'll head through **Spring Valley**, one of the older Vegas locales. Taking the new beltway (I-215) south unveils an area of town that until recently was, like the north-west before it, scattered with ranch homes on large lots. Now, it's covered by ever more indistinct sprawl, including new yuppie enclave **Southern Highlands**.

NORTH-WEST LAS VEGAS
Sahara Avenue

Like the majority of Las Vegas's east–west streets, Sahara Avenue yields little of interest to the travelling motorist. National chains and big-box warehouse stores dominate the landscape; there are few better examples than the four-cornered **Sahara-Decatur Pavilions** at the junction of Sahara and… well, you know. Chains make up most of the tenants, though there's fine Persian food at independent eaterie and market **Habib's** (no.4750, 870 0860). Continuing on, you'll pass countless car dealerships and chain eateries before reaching Rainbow Boulevard, surrounded by residential properties and heavy commercial development.

Further west is Durango Drive, the beginning of the **Lakes** neighbourhood, where the waterside homes afford residents the chance to go boating and fishing. Lake East Drive features a walking trail through the surrounding parks, eventually dumping you out at Twain Avenue.

Sahara's western reaches are home to the beautiful **Sahara West Library**. The cinema at neighbouring **Village Square** (*see p244*) is known for the indie film selections it regularly screens – pretty much the only venue in town that reliably shows anything other than the blockbusters of the week (though blockbusters take up most of the space). At the far-western end of Sahara Avenue, nestled at the base of the mountains, lies the **Red Rock Country Club** (2466 Grassy Spring Place, 360 3100), a desert golf community that gives new meaning to the word 'exclusive'.

Charleston Boulevard

Flat, wide and seemingly endless, Charleston cuts a broad swathe through the city, extending westwards right out to the foothills of the mountain from which it takes its name. It's more residential than Sahara, though not much more attractive. Still, there are occasional diversions, including, close to the Strip, the Charleston Heights Arts Center, home to a theatre and one of the **City of Las Vegas Galleries** (*see p246*).

Along the way, Charleston defines the southern edge of **Summerlin**. This 'Westside' planned community incorporates homes ($100,000 condos to multi-million-dollar mansions), parks, schools and businesses to create a regular prefab life; the infrastructure is magnificent, but the *Truman Show* effect is disconcerting. European visitors won't have trouble navigating the numerous roundabouts, but the wayward local motorists, unaccustomed to such complexity, seem to have more trouble.

At Rampart Boulevard, development has transformed what were once empty acres into a commercial area. The **Boca Park Fashion Village**, an upscale 'lifestyle centre' of shops (Ligne Roset, Talulah G) and restaurants (Kona Grill, Melting Pot), sits close to **Rampart Commons**, home to the likes of Banana Republic and Pottery Barn. A skip north are two resorts: the so-so **Suncoast** (*see p151*) and the smarter **JW Marriott Summerlin** (*see p147*), surrounded by the green, manicured fairways of several major golf courses.

Further west, across from the **Summerlin Town Center** mall at Charleston's intersection with Town Center Drive, sits the **Red Rock** resort (*see p147*), the first billion-dollar off-Strip casino-hotel. If you head still further west across the Beltway, you'll enter open country, and the gorgeous canyon from which the casino takes its name (*see p282*). Just past it, you'll find an agreeable taste of the Wild West at **Bonnie Springs Old Nevada** (*see p282*), an honest-to-goodness mining town back in the 1800s. Now it's an adorable tourist trap, with pony rides, a comically eclectic petting zoo, a tiny railroad train – and, of course, a saloon. Don't miss the general store, if only for the fun of spotting the 'Made in China' stickers on the bottom of nearly every souvenir.

SIGHTS

Sahara Avenue.

Rancho Drive

Bordered by Oakey and Charleston boulevards, Rancho Drive and I-15, the **Scotch 80s** offers a different taste of old Vegas. Las Vegas Mayor Carolyn Goodman and her husband, former mayor Oscar Goodman – are among those who live within this swanky neighbourhood of large-lot homes built mostly in the 1950s and '60s, an 80-acre enclave just a dice roll from Downtown. The quiet labyrinth of tree-lined streets hides ranch-style estates and one-acre home sites, along with surprisingly lush gardens: underground water meant the area was once almost swampy. To the south of here are the **Glen Heather Estates**, smallish homes with a modernist bent; west lie the 1950s-vintage **McNeil Estates**, where young professionals are joining more established residents in a bid to restore the charming ranch-style homes.

If you continue north, you'll reach the corner of Rancho and Alta drives. Just north is **Rancho Circle**; perhaps the city's most exclusive old district, it's home to Bob Stupak and Phyllis McGuire. Slightly west of here, loosely bordered by US 95, Valley View Boulevard and Alta Drive, is the historic 180-acre **Las Vegas Springs Preserve**, recently reopened as a desert ecology-themed visitor attraction (*see below*). And east of Rancho Drive at Tonopah Drive is **Binion Ranch**, the home of the legendary gambling family who launched – and, until recently, owned – Binion's. Family patriarch Benny Binion once lived in this long-boarded-up block-and-timber ranch house; as recently as the 1990s, horses and cattle were still kept on the property.

The primarily African American area of **West Las Vegas** spreads north-east from Bonanza Road, home to the long-closed **Moulin Rouge** (900 W Bonanza Road, *see right* **Inside Track**).

To the west of Rancho Drive sits **Lorenzi Park**, home of the **Nevada State Museum & Historical Society**. Further north leads you past the **Southern Nevada Zoological Park** (*see p93*); a turn west at Vegas Drive passes the palatial home of the elusive master illusionists Siegfried & Roy, who can still stir up the town when one or the other makes an appearance at a show opening on the Strip. It's on the north side; look for the white adobe walls and the wrought-iron gate bearing the initials S and R. Tiger Woods wannabes can try out their skills (golf only, please) at the **Las Vegas Golf Club** (*see p265*) across the road; budding Schumachers might prefer the **Las Vegas Mini Gran Prix** (*see p240*).

Rancho Drive continues in a north-westerly direction past the **Texas Station** (*see p152*),

Las Vegas Springs Preserve.

Fiesta Rancho (*see p149*) and **Santa Fe Station** casinos (*see p151*) en route to the outdoor attractions of **Floyd Lamb State Park** and **Mount Charleston** (*see p283*). Five years ago, much of this area was empty desert. Today, though, stucco has engulfed everything and shows no sign of abating.

★ Las Vegas Springs Preserve

333 S Valley View Boulevard, at Meadows Lane (822 7700, www.springspreserve.org). Bus 104, 207. **Open** 10am-6pm daily. **Admission** $18.95; $9.95 reductions; free under-5s. **Map** p333 X1.
Also known as Big Spring, this is where legendary Old West explorers Kit Carson and John Fremont parked their horses in the mid 1800s. Huge cotton-woods and natural scrub fill the area, surrounding an early 19th-century well house. The land has survived both fire and the threat of being paved over in the name of freeway expansion; it was restored as the Central Park of Las Vegas for the city's centennial in 2005 and opened to the public two years later as the Las Vegas Springs Preserve, a huge site given over to botanical gardens, nature trails and a number of museum exhibits. All in all, a very laudable endeavour, if heavy on the videogame-style educational exhibits aimed at youngsters. The sustainability minded Springs Café, by celebrity chef Wolfgang Puck, offers picnic-style dining with wonderful vistas.

SIGHTS

▶ *For more on facilities for children at Springs Preserve, see p240.*

Southern Nevada Zoological Park

1775 N Rancho Drive, between Vegas Drive & Lake Mead Boulevard (647 4685, www.las vegaszoo.org). Bus 106. **Open** *9am-5pm daily.* **Admission** *$9; $7 reductions; free under-2s.* **Map** *p333 X1.*

It'll never be confused with the similar operations in the Bronx or San Diego, but Vegas's zoological park contains an interesting collection of reptiles and birds indigenous to the state of Nevada, as well as a variety of endangered cats and the last family of Barbary apes in the US. The park also has a coati exhibit, botanical displays of endangered palms and rare bamboos, plus a children's petting zoo.

NORTH LAS VEGAS

A working-class city that grew from the Nellis Air Force Base to the north-east, the officially incorporated city of North Las Vegas has experienced a limited renaissance of late, a result of the growth in the valley as a whole. African-American, Asian and Hispanic residents have moved in as Anglos have moved out, turning the area into a melting pot of ethnicities; new homes and shops have sprung up to fill land north of Craig Road (between Rancho Drive and I-15) in a pricey new development known informally as the **Golden Triangle**. The shiny new locale seems somewhat removed from its surroundings, but that's the price of progress.

Largely untouched by redevelopment, the older sections of North Las Vegas carry more urban flavour than does Las Vegas itself. To reach it, turn off either US 95 or Rancho Drive and head east along Craig Road, then turn north back towards Downtown along Las Vegas Boulevard North. En route, you'll pass **Jerry's Nugget** casino (No.1821, 399 3000), numerous ethnic eateries, the historic public **Forest Lawn Cemetery** and the **Las Vegas Paiute Indian Reservation** (1 Paiute Drive, 386 3926), which represents the original ten acres deeded to the Paiute by Helen Stewart back in the 1900s.

Planetarium

Community College of Southern Nevada, 3200 E Cheyenne Avenue, between Las Vegas Boulevard North & Van Der Meer Street (651 4759, www.csn.edu/planetarium). Bus 110. **Shows** *6pm, 7.30pm Fri; 3.30pm, 6pm, 7.30pm Sat.* **Admission** *$6; $4 reductions.*

The small cinema here has a 360° screen. After the day's last performance, you also get the opportunity to scan the sky through the planetarium's telescopes (weather permitting).

EAST LAS VEGAS

Once characterised by ugly quick-build housing tracts and trailer parks, East Las Vegas has been unable to avoid the incursion of new development. Still, the once-posh **Commercial Center** (953 E Sahara Avenue, between S 6th Street & S Maryland Parkway) has resisted change. One of the city's older malls, it's a scruffy spot that's home to the city's best ethnic restaurant (**Lotus of Siam**; *see p170*), various gay bars and, incongruously, a trio of swingers' clubs (*see p225*). South on Maryland is the smarter (and swinger-free) **Boulevard Mall** (*see p197*); behind it is the modernist **Paradise Palms**, another old 'hood at the earliest stages of revival. Further down Maryland is the University District (*see p94*).

The casinos at Fremont Street's western extremity grab the headlines, and with good reason. But the road has a life further east, well away from the bright lights of Downtown. What it doesn't have is much tangible and engaging history, at least not since the Green Shack bit the dust. In continuous operation from the 1920s until 1999, the restaurant evoked decades of memories: construction workers building the Hoover Dam stopped here, as did politicos and gangsters. But despite protests from preservationists, the building was demolished in 2005 to make way for a banqueting hall that's yet to be built.

South of Sahara, Fremont becomes the **Boulder Highway**, along which sit several locals' casinos. Catch a movie at **Boulder Station** (*see p149*); if you're here in December, don't miss the Christmas lights at **Sam's Town** (*see p150*). A turn east down Tropicana Avenue (or an interstate ride from town) takes you to the **Acacia Demonstration Gardens** (50 Casa Del Fuego Street, 267 4000,

INSIDE TRACK
SEGREGATED VEGAS AND
THE MOULIN ROUGE

In the bad old days, when Vegas was called 'the Mississippi of the West', hotels forced African-American entertainers to flee the Strip after showtime. Performers such as Nat King Cole and Sammy Davis Jr sought refuge at the **Moulin Rouge** (*see left*) and generated a legendary stint of after-hours shows. In 1960, five years after the Moulin Rouge opened, casino bosses signed an agreement here that ended the city's racial segregation. However, plans to revive the casino ground to a halt when it was gutted by a suspicious fire in 2003.

SIGHTS

www.snwa.com), where you can explore gardens and wetlands dedicated to animal habitats. West along Tropicana, at the northeast corner with Pecos Avenue, is the **Pinball Hall of Fame**.

At the far eastern end of the valley is Frenchman's Mountain, commonly known as **Sunrise Mountain**. Here, in the 1960s and '70s, the independently minded rich who had declined spots in the Scotch 80s built modern desert homes with pools and panoramic views of the city. Following their lead, there has been a lot more new housing developement in this part of town.

FREE Pinball Hall of Fame

1610 E Tropicana Avenue, between S Maryland Parkway & S Eastern Avenue (no phone, www. pinballmuseum.org). Bus 201. **Open** 11am-11pm daily. **Admission** free.
See right **Play the Silver Ball**.

THE UNIVERSITY DISTRICT

Bounded roughly by Flamingo Road, Paradise Road, Tropicana Avenue and Eastern Avenue, the University District is an enclave of normality and casual sophistication a mere skip from the Strip. Most businesses of note are on Maryland Parkway, with the rest of the area given over to apartments.

The University of Las Vegas, aka **UNLV** (4505 S Maryland Parkway, 895 3011), runs along S Maryland Parkway, where the stunning **Lied Library** (*see p313*) and a beautiful desert garden compete for visitors' attention. The university also has many walking paths and trees, a tranquil refuge from the summer sun. The **UNLV Barrick Museum** (*see below*) and the **Donna Beam Fine Arts Gallery** (*see p246*), both on campus, stage shows by student and professional artists; the former also houses a permanent natural history exhibition.

Local businesses reflect the presence of the university, which is to say that prices are keen. **Paymon's Mediterranean Café & Market** (*see p176*), a local lunch favourite, is adjoined at the corner of Maryland and Flamingo by the restaurant's **Hookah Lounge** (*see p188*), a Bedouin-styled cocktail bar. Across the way is the used-clothing superstore **Buffalo Exchange** (*see p203*); further up Maryland are two shopping centres filled with pizza joints, coffee-houses such as the **Coffee Bean & Tea Leaf** (which offers free Wi-Fi; No.4550, 944 5029), bars including the **Freakin' Frog** (*see p187*), the new **University Theatre** (*see p256*), and even a tattoo studios: the **Pussykat Tattoo Parlor** (*see p212*) is one of the best in town, in a town with more tattoo shops than most.

FREE Marjorie Barrick Museum

4505 S Maryland Parkway, at E Tropicana Avenue (895 3381, http://barrickmuseum. unlv.edu). Bus 109, 201. **Open** 10am-6pm Tue, Wed, Fri; 10am-8pm Thur; 10am-4pm Sat, Sun. **Admission** free; suggested contribution $5; $2 reductions. **No credit cards**. **Map** p333 Y3.
Technically UNLV's natural history museum, the Barrick has fine permanent displays on ancient and modern Vegas, including a wonderful collection of folk-art masks. It's also one of the city's finest exhibition spaces: a number of excellent shows have graced its front rooms, drawing from UNLV's art faculty and regional sources. It's a must for any gallery crawl; call for details of current shows.

GREEN VALLEY & HENDERSON

The history of Henderson and Green Valley is a tale of a city within a city. Henderson itself was founded in 1941 as a company town for workers at the then-new Basic Magnesium Plant. North-west of Henderson across US 95, Green Valley is technically a part of the city of Henderson, and contains the vast majority of its visitor attractions. If you've time, a few hours spent down here makes an engaging diversion, especially if you're en route to Boulder City and the Hoover Dam.

Henderson

Thanks to its origins, Henderson garnered a reputation as an industrial city, one that it retains to some extent, even though it was, for a time in the booming early 2000s, the fastest growing suburban area in America. The city has kept its original downtown, centred on Water Street. It's currently undergoing a revitalisation spearheaded by the city government, which is making an active effort to attract galleries and pedestrian-friendly shops. The purchase of land by loft developers is a sign that the area may soon soar skywards. The **City of Lights Gallery** (No.26, 3 E Army Street, 260 0300, www.citylightsart.com), is attempting to lead the way in the creation of the arts district.

Elsewhere, less sophisticated pockets of original tract houses, mobile home parks and low-rent apartments survive, and are unkindly referred to as 'Hendertucky'. Even so, the area's not without appeal. Manufacturing continues at **Ethel M Chocolates** (*see p96*), which offers tours to the public – the chocolate factory's Christmas display, which lights up an acre of ground containing 300 species of cactus and other desert plants – is not to be missed. And not far from here, the **Clark County Heritage Museum** (*see p96*) is also worth a look.

Play the Silver Ball

A place for pinball wizards.

For the most part, a pinball machine is just a pinball machine. To some folks, though, it's a kinetic monument to a simpler time when mindless entertainment didn't necessarily involve sex, hyper-violence or the pixellated undead – a perfectly designed blend of challenge, workmanship and skill. In Tim Arnold's world, it's all these things and more. How else to explain his **Pinball Hall of Fame** (*see left*), a functioning museum of sorts where more than 100 operational pinball machines spanning seven decades are on show? The Pinball Hall of Fame is a true attraction in a city of replicated ones.

Over the years, Arnold has assembled a vast array of machines from Gottlieb, Bally, Williams and other oddball manufacturers, from gear-and-magnet models to modern digital wonders. Descriptions of each machine's attributed and historic values have been attached to them, most handwritten on index cards. And then, best of all, Arnold invites all comers to play his machines. All you need is quarters; and if you don't have them, he can exchange your bills for them.

Arnold has re-cast some of these machines so visitors can best appreciate their inherent beauty. Take, for example, his painstaking public refurbishment of a 1978 Bally machine devoted to the band Kiss. Paying attention to the smallest detail (excepting, perhaps, an actual drop of Ace Frehley's blood in the back glass), Arnold is like an Italian restoration specialist working on the Sistine Chapel. But while both share a certain reverence in their respective circles, only at the PHoF can you both touch the art and shake it around.

In possession of all 384 Gottlieb pinball machines, Arnold claims to have the only complete set of one manufacturer in the world. Sadly, not all of them are on display, thanks to lack of cash, staff and, right now, visitors. When asked to name his favourite machine, he deadpans, 'the one with the box full of coins.' It's a straight response from somebody who owned his first pinball machine at age 14 but who always seemed more interested in the collecting and tinkering than the playing. 'It's all I've ever done. It's all I know,' says the man who refers to himself as the simple ringmaster of this peculiar and beautiful show. 'Someone's got to wear the top hat.'

SIGHTS

Pinball Hall of Fame.

Clark County Heritage Museum
1830 S Boulder Highway, between Horizon Drive & Wagon Wheel Avenue (455 7955, www.co. clark.nv.us). Bus 107. **Open** 9am-4.30pm daily. **Admission** $2; $1 reductions.

Long before Las Vegas was a resort destination, it was just another western railroad town. Here you'll find an assortment of exhibits relating to southern Nevada's past: a recreated city street featuring historic area homes with period furnishings, a 'timeline' mural and a 1918 Union Pacific steam engine.

FREE Ethel M Chocolates
2 Cactus Garden Drive, at Sunset Way & Mountain Vista Street (435 2655, www.ethelm.com). Bus 217. **Open** 8.30am-6pm daily. **Admission** free.

Chocolate producer Ethel M offers self-guided factory tours complete with samples. To offset any feelings of overindulgence, it also has an environmentally aware cactus garden and a fascinating 'living machine', showing how plants can recycle wastewater. Here during the holidays? Check out the gardens, bedecked in millions of lights.
▶ *For more on Christmas/winter holiday celebrations in Vegas, see p221.*

Green Valley

Green Valley was established in the late 1970s as the valley's first master-planned community. Its design, and its eventual success, proved massively influential across the whole region; developments such as Summerlin wouldn't have happened without it.

The presence of homes in all price ranges has drawn all kinds of people: ethnic eateries, creative businesses and cultural events thrive here, creating a sense of community synergy of which others in the metropolis are envious. Take the **Biosphere** at Vanderburg Elementary School, for example, a large rainforest habitat complete with a waterfall, plants, fish and even free-roaming lizards. The $1.2 million cost of building it was covered by private donations and proceeds from campus fundraisers.

The high-tone **Green Valley Ranch** casino resort *(see p146)* is the subdivision's best accomplishment, its fine restaurants (especially Hank's steakhouse, named after Green Valley founder and local legend Hank Greenspun), bars, day spa, comfortable casino, concert venue and multiplex cinema all drawing visitors and locals. In summer, the resort's outdoor pool area, which flaunts bocce courts and a design by Michael Czyz, hosts shows at its amphitheatre.

Virtually next door is the **District**, an open-air esplanade of upscale restaurants and shops; among the latter is the **Flea Bags Barkery & Bowtique** (2225 Village Walk Drive, Ste 173, 914 8805, http://fleabag sonline.com), selling gourmet pet biscuits (named after favourite customers) and Juicy Couture pet carriers. Across from here is the **Henderson Pavilion**, an outdoor performing arts facility that hosts an annual Shakespeare in the Park event. And south on Green Valley Parkway is **Anthem**, an over-the-top country clubthat introduces the absurdist notion of gated communities within gated communities.

In the older section of Green Valley, the **Green Valley Town Center** reveals the area's community focus. This area is home to **Barley's Casino & Brewing Company** (4500 E. Sunset Road, 458 2739), a microbrewery and casino. Further attractions lie along Sunset Road: to the east is **Sunset Station** *(see p151)*, a neighbourhood casino with a fabulous, Gaudi-inspired bar, while a spin westbound will lead you past the **Ambiance Bistro** *(see p174)*, Wayne Newton's home (at the south-west corner of Russell Road) and the huge **Sunset Park** (at 2601 Eastern Avenue, 455 8200), which contains picnic sites, grills and games courts and hosts **Age of Chivalry**, with medieval guilds practising their jousts in public most weekend evenings.

Lake Las Vegas

While Las Vegas grew, failed, grew, stagnated and grew again during the last century, the land that now holds **Lake Las Vegas** remained isolated and undeveloped. Eventually, it was settled not by Spanish traders, indomitable frontiersmen or stop-at-nothing prospectors, but by 'Ronald F Boeddeker, President and Chairman of Transcontinental Properties, Inc, [who] envisioned a body of cool water surrounded by an unparalleled Mediterranean resort destination showcasing mountains, homes, golf courses, hotels, gaming, restaurants and boutiques' (the quote is from the official Lake Las Vegas website). Under the supervision of Mr Boeddeker, construction began here 20 years ago.

Lake Las Vegas is now a resort community with hotels, homes and golf courses surrounding a vast man-made lake that empties into Lake Mead. Set in a desert environment, the opulent homes start at $750,000, but the prices aren't any deterrent to those with the cash. The **Ravella Lake Las Vegas** *(see p152)* offers the Strip's Four Seasons serious competition in the ultra-luxe, casino-free lodgings sector; adjoining it is the **MonteLago Village**, a twee lakeside spot with tiny boutiques, restaurants and a wine bar. In the summer, bring a blanket and watch as musicians take to the marina.

SIGHTS

Consume

Cosmopolitan. *See p107.*

The smart way of giving

Give the perfect getaway

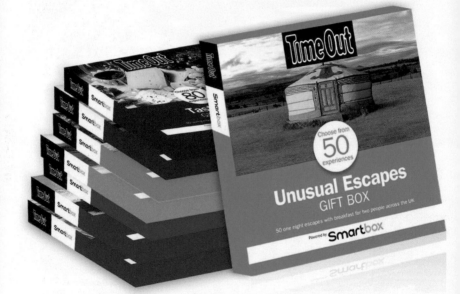

Browse the full range of gift boxes from Time Out
timeout.com/smartbox

Casinos & Hotels

Eat, drink, sleep, gamble and be merry.

Six decades ago, Vegas was framed around Downtown, a raffish cluster of buildings that provided little more than lairy gaming arenas and a few scruffy bedrooms. In the 1940s, a number of large resorts opened several miles away on deserted highway, spurring a boom that saw the city reinvent itself as a swanky resort town. After a decade of the doldrums, in 1989, Steve Wynn opened the **Mirage** (*see p110*) and inspired a regeneration of Las Vegas Boulevard. In 2005, Wynn returned with **Wynn Las Vegas** (*see p113*), raising the bar once again for aspiring casino operators and prompting yet more improvement works among his rivals. Fast-forward another five years, and the Strip is transformed again, with the appearance of **CityCenter**, a city within a city rising from the middle of the Strip, dominating the skyline and changing the gravitational centre of the city. Not as colossal, but perhaps as important in what it means for how the 'next Vegas' will play out is the **Cosmopolitan** casino-resort (*see p107*), squeezed in next to CityCenter, with an unusual vertical, rather than horizontal, orientation – the main people-watching action is on the third floor.

CONSUME

The industry is always building something new: a 1,000-room tower, a 4,000-seat theatre, a 100-unit shopping mall (the penultimate trend). The latest Strip trend is the construction or expansion of already existing resort pools, taking off from the success of the Hard Rock's scandalous Rehab pool parties. The casino moguls have cannily capitalised on the daylight hours with a concept called 'daylife' turning the de rigueur pools into money fountains with spa-like accoutrements and massive pool parties and poolside concerts.

Hotel-casinos that don't expand are quick to change; it's a case of adapt or die. If you've not been to Vegas for four or five years, the changes will be noticeable. But even if you were here six months ago, you'll still see something new.

STAYING IN LAS VEGAS
Though you could plump for an alternative – a motel, a hostel, even an RV park – the majority of visitors to Las Vegas stay where the action is: a hotel-casino. These often-vast complexes, which line the Strip and clutter Downtown, are where most tourists spend upwards of 90 per cent of their time. All have casinos, restaurants, bars and assorted entertainments, alongside other amenities that range from the predictable (pools, malls) to the truly exceptional (zoos, rollercoasters). And all, of course, have guestrooms, from the 100 or so offered at the **Golden Gate** (*see p144*) to the 6,000-plus at the **MGM Grand** (*see p119*).

Visitors to Las Vegas once spent very little time in their gaming-subsidised guestrooms, which is why rooms in hotel-casinos built before 1989 are smallish. But during the 1990s, casino moguls realised the value of providing guests with a nice place to sleep: rooms in newer hotel-casinos are brighter and more capacious. Wireless internet, phones – and at many places, use of an iPad or other tablet device – TVs (with cable) and air-conditioning are standard in rooms within Las Vegas hotel-casinos, which all offer free parking. Beyond that, it's a crapshoot.

❶ Red numbers given in this chapter correspond to hotels as marked on the street maps. See pp333-336.

Bellagio. *See p103.*

WHERE TO STAY

The vast majority of visitors stay on the three-mile stretch of Las Vegas Boulevard South that runs from the Mandalay Bay resort north to the Sahara, aka the Strip. Most never leave it. The Strip is where you'll find almost all the city's most glamorous, upscale and eye-catching resorts, as well as a number of its best bargains. If you want to stay on the Strip, remember it's a long (and, in summer, debilitating) hike from one end to the other. It's not enough simply to stay at a property with a Las Vegas Boulevard South address; the street number is also crucial.

The range of properties on the Strip is not as huge as it was a half-decade ago: most historic mid-century hotels and motels have been levelled in the name of progress. However, there's still variety. Note that while some hotel amenities are off-limits to non-guests, many others are open to everyone (bars, restaurants, clubs, shows). Access to spas (*see p211*), varies by hotel; most are open to the public, but a few limit access to their own guests.

There are, of course, hotels in other parts of town. A handful of big resorts are located just off the Strip, chief among them the **Hard Rock** (*see p133*) and the **Palms** (*see p135*). Downtown, the hub of Las Vegas until the 1950s, can't compete with the Strip in the glamour stakes, but you'll find bargains galore. Near the Convention Center sit hotels aimed squarely at the business traveller. And although the Station casinos are chiefly frequented by locals, a few of them – principally **Sunset Station** (*see p151*), **Red Rock Resort** (*see p147*) and **Green Valley Ranch** (*see p145*) – are well worth investigating.

RATES AND RESERVATIONS

Las Vegas has more rooms than anywhere in the world: roughly 130,000 in total, with the numbers still rising. And eight out of ten of the world's largest hotels are here. However, with up to 40 million visitors a year, it needs them. Some weeks, bargains abound in even the poshest properties; at other times, you'll need to book way ahead if you want to avoid sleeping in your car.

Rates fluctuate wildly depending on the date and what convention or event happens to be in town: the same room can quadruple in price from one night to the next. You'll often find exceptional deals midweek and/or during off-season, when $200 rooms can go for a quarter of their rack rate, even at the ritziest places – it's worth asking (and asking again) if there are any special rates or discounts that

---

INSIDE TRACK FIND A DEAL

Due to the dip – OK, dive — in the economy, and international competition from casinos in and out of the US, Vegas room rates have accordingly adjusted, you can find extraordinary deals with a bit of research online.

can be applied. There's no consistency, though: at weekends, prices skyrocket, and a two-night minimum is in effect almost everywhere. Steer clear of major conventions, too; for a full list, see www.lvcva.com.

For one night in a double room, expect to pay $40-$100 in a budget hotel-casino, $70-$200 in a mid-range operation, and $150 and up in a first-class property. In addition to these basic rates, rooms are subject to hotel tax (12 per cent on the Strip, 13 per cent elsewhere). You can book either by phone or online with almost every property in the city.

PLAYING IN LAS VEGAS

Depending on the time and location, the action on Vegas's casino floors can be fast and furious, as slot players hammer 'spin' buttons, blackjack players celebrate 21s and crap players whoop it up in the dice pit. The scene is played out to the soundtrack of clinking glasses, rattling chips and the electronic arpeggios of slot machines. It's overwhelming.

Still, with the nationwide spread of gambling, the experience has been dumbed down from the high-rolling James Bond image, and there's little required etiquette: common sense and common courtesy should see you through. Any outfit will do, from shorts to a dinner jacket, though you may want to carry a watch (clocks are conspicuous by their absence) and a sweater (the air-con is always cranked to the max).

Playing in Las Vegas is no longer just about gambling: casino attractions have evolved with the times. The circus acts at **Circus Circus** (*see p125*) and the dancing fountains at the **Bellagio** (*see p103*) remain, but resorts have also embraced adulthood. Nightclubs are all the rage, though you'll need to win big at the tables if you want to really enjoy yourself within their swanky confines.

ABOUT THIS CHAPTER

This section is divided geographically, with each area subdivided into hotel-casinos and non-casino properties. The majority of the hotels are either right on the **Strip** or very close to it (a loose area that we call **Off-Strip**), and range from the incomparably luxurious to the hopelessly dissolute. In **Downtown** Las Vegas, the properties are smaller, less Disneyfied and cheaper. Casinos in the **Rest of the City** appeal more to locals than visitors, but compensate for their lack of frills with a full array of gambling and good-value eating options.

LISTINGS INFORMATION

The address we've given for each casino is its main entrance. This is the place to arrive whether you're on foot or in a car. Here, you'll find the valet parking (for hotels that offer it) and directions to self-parking: some casinos have extra entrances at the side and/or around the back. These can be essential if you don't want to spend hours stuck in traffic driving along the choked up Strip.

Most hotel-casino reviews have four headings: **Accommodation**, a survey of the guestrooms;

Eating & drinking, where you'll find details on each hotel's bars and restaurants (many of these are also reviewed elsewhere; follow the cross-references for fuller critiques); **Entertainment**, detailing the main shows and lounges (again, follow the cross-references for more information); and **Games**, which provides an overview of the gambling facilities. Reviews of non-casino hotels are shorter for one key reason: there's less to review.

At the end of each review, we have detailed the property's key Amenities and the specific range of Gambling it offers. Bear in mind that table minimums are subject to change and can rise at night.

For reviews of restaurants mentioned here, *see p153-178* **Restaurants**. For shows, *see p226-237* **Casino Entertainment**. For clubs, *see p257-261* **Nightclubs**. For bars and lounges, *see p179-189*.

The Strip

Almost two thirds of the hotel rooms in Las Vegas are on the Strip, the stretch of Las Vegas Boulevard between the 'Welcome to Fabulous Las Vegas' sign and Sahara Avenue. Furthest south are **Mandalay Bay** (plus the **Four Seasons Las Vegas** and **Thehotel at Mandalay Bay**) and the **Luxor**. A little north, at the junction of Tropicana Avenue, sit four large casinos: the **Tropicana**, the **Excalibur**, **New York New York** and the **MGM Grand**. The **Monte Carlo** is

just north of NYNY, just by the massive resort complex that is **CityCenter** (*see p33*).

The centre of the Strip has the biggest cluster of hotel-casinos: **Planet Hollywood** and **Paris Las Vegas** are followed to the north by **Bally's**, the **Bellagio**, **Barbary Coast** and **Caesars Palace**, all at the junction with Flamingo Road; it's the liveliest corner of the city. Slightly further north, past the **Flamingo**, the **Imperial Palace**, **Harrah's**, **Casino Royale** and the **Venetian**, is the intersection with Spring Mountain/Sands Avenue, home to **Treasure Island**, the Fashion Show Mall and **Wynn Las Vegas**. North of here is **Trump International**, **Circus Circus** and the **Riviera**.

HOTEL-CASINOS
Expensive

★ Aria
CityCenter, 3730 Las Vegas Boulevard South, at East Harmon Avenue, Las Vegas, NV 89158 (reservations 1-866 359 7757, front desk & casino 590 7757, www.arialasvegas.com). Bus Deuce, 202/self-parking Las Vegas Boulevard South/ valet parking Las Vegas Boulevard South or W Flamingo Road. **Rooms** 4,004. **Rates** $159-$859 double. **Map** p336 A8 ❶
One of the newest and most strikingly beautiful buildings in Las Vegas, Aria is also the tallest and largest structure in the CityCenter complex. Its other attributes are equally high-flown: Aria is an AAA five-diamond hotel, with 4,004 guest rooms and

Aria.

suites, and a scale and level of amenities that makes it a destination on its own. The casino-hotel-resort, which opened in December 2009 as a joint venture between MGM Resorts International and Dubai's Infinity World Development, is a pair of 61-storey curved glass-and-steel towers joined at the centre.

Sustainability is on everyone's minds, and particularly in resource-challenged Las Vegas. Described as perhaps 'the most technologically advanced hotel ever built', Aria exemplifies the trend, with its efficient, and gorgeous, incorporation of energy-saving ingenuity into the design of the hotel, including smart rooms that 'automatically turn off lights, regulate temperature and even shut curtains when a guest leaves the room'.

Aside from its height and techno-superiority, another element that makes Aria is its dedication to artwork, from the parking garage and exterior fountains to the lobby and interior spaces. Spanning the vast windows above the lobby check-in stations is a sculpture of the Colorado River, made of (reclaimed) silver by world-renowned designer Maya Lin, who conceived of the Vietnam Veterans Memorial in Washington DC. Look past Lin's sculpture and you'll see a giant, curvy Henry Moore bronze; the parking area features an illuminated art piece featuring illuminating aphorisms by Jenny Holzer.

Along with the scores of entertainment options, including restaurants, bars, clubs, shops and a candy store and a Cirque du Soleil theatre and show devoted to Elvis (*see p235*), Aria also offers a state-of-the-art convention centre, 38 meeting rooms, four ballrooms with theatrical stages – and, when your mind wanders away from the convention at hand, is a three-storey, 400ft window – a glass curtain – overlooking the pool.

Accommodation

In the top ten of the largest hotels in the world, Aria has 4,004 rooms, more than 500 of which are suites – and some of those are Sky Suites or rooftop Sky Villas, accessed by private elevator. The rooms are scaled from 520 to 2,000sq ft; the Sky Villas soar up to 7,000sq ft. Every room features flat-panel TV screens and a central-console touchscreen automation system that automatically opens and closes curtains, adjusts or turns off lights and electronics, and regulates the temperature when a guest enters or leaves the room. Bathrooms are stylish and spacious, with double sinks and enough counter space to comfortably suit two preparing for a night (or day) out; with a separate WC and enclosed shower and sunken tub.

Eating & drinking

Aria offers a startling array of restaurant choices, many of which joined the ranks of the city's best upon opening. Fine dining options include Barmasa, Shaboo, Julian Serrano, Sage, Jean Georges Steakhouse, Sirio Ristorante, Michael Mina's American Fish, Blossom, and Union Restaurant and Lounge. More casual options include Lemongrass, Skybox Sports Bar & Grill, Cafe Vettro and, of course, a (surprisingly stylish) buffet with international flavours.

Entertainment

One of the central features of Aria – well, it's on the second floor – is Cirque du Soleil's seventh permanent Las Vegas show, a spectacular if spotty homage to the life and legacy of Elvis Presley. Entitled *Viva Elvis*, the show opened in February 2010 and offers the usual array of aerialists, acrobats, singers and dancers, all performing to a pumped-up remix of the King's greatest hits. Just outside the theatredoors is the Presleyiana-filled Gold Boutique Nightclub & Lounge, themed around Graceland, and a lavish gift shop, which is not to be missed by Presley devotees.

Gambling

Aria contains the only gambing space within the CityCenter complex, and its casino is a contemporary beauty, with 150,000sq ft of gambling space. The expected table games and slots are surrounded at the fringes by restaurants, shops and cafés – and natural light makes its way into the floor via windows and skylights, an unheard-of development in Vegas.
Amenities *Bars (10). Business centre. Concierge. Disabled-adapted rooms. Gym. Internet (Wi-Fi, $15). No-smoking floors. Pool (outdoor). Restaurants (16). Room service. Spa. TV: pay movies.*
Games *Baccarat ($100-$15,000); Big Six; blackjack ($10-$10,000); Caribbean stud; craps (3x, 4x, 5x; from $5); casino war; Let it Ride; mini baccarat ($25-$15,000); pai gow poker; pai gow tiles; poker (39 tables); roulette (single & double zero); three-card poker.*

★ Bellagio

3600 Las Vegas Boulevard South, at W Flamingo Road, Las Vegas, NV 89109 (reservations 1-888 987 6667, front desk & casino 693 7111, www. bellagio.com). Bus Deuce, 202/self-parking Las Vegas Boulevard South/valet parking Las Vegas Boulevard South or W Flamingo Road. **Rooms** 3,933. **Rates** $159-$859 double. **Map** p336 A7 ❷
Since the Spa Tower opened at the Bellagio in 2005, the property seems to have paused for a breather. Sure, it's added the Adam Tihany-designed Club Prive, a high-limit gambling lounge that spotlights unbelievably rare spirits and world-class cigars. Granted, it's redone the poker room, and all 2,500 rooms in the main tower received a $70-million makeover in 2011. Otherwise, though, why tamper with a winning formula?

The Bellagio continues to evoke a supersized, all-American Italian villa, complete with an eight-acre lake fronting the Strip, a lush garden conservatory that changes with the holidays and an elegant pool area that's been reimagined as a formal Italian garden. And it remains the archetypal playground for

CONSUME

CONSUME

the well-heeled adult, with high-minded, grown-up entertainment in the form of posh restaurants, a tiny but tony promenade of boutiques, and Cirque du Soleil's most sophisticated show. The expanded spa in the Spa Tower features a salon, a fitness centre and even a one-chair barbershop; it's a lavish perk available only to guests, as is access to the renowned Shadow Creek golf course. But the most eye-catching attraction is the signature fountain, which, in the afternoons and evenings, shoots water into the air, synchronized to a variety of different soundtracks. The sidewalk on the Strip in front of the hotel offers superb views, as do the Bellagio's lakefront restaurants and bars. *Photos p100.*

Accommodation

Bellagio's 3,933 rooms are large and beautifully furnished. The beds all have Serta mattresses, and the spacious, marble-floored bathrooms come with deep-soaking tubs and private-label amenities. Wireless internet, flatscreen TVs (27-inchers), electronic drapes and well-stocked minibars are standard. The Presidential suites atop the Spa Tower are ultra-modern; and the nine luxury villas, outfitted with gold fixtures, Lalique crystal accents, butler service, gyms, steam rooms, kitchens and private pools, are open to anyone willing to fork out $6,000 a night. The hotel's TV network simulcasts the fountain show music, so you can listen in your room as you watch the water.

Eating & drinking

The Bellagio has Vegas's best collection of superstar chefs under one roof. The roster starts with Julian Serrano's French/Mediterranean Picasso, decorated with paintings by the eponymous artist. Lovers of steak head for Prime, Jean-Georges Vongerichten's superior chophouse, while those after seafood seek out Michael Mina. For Italian, try Todd English's Olives, with its splendid view of the fountain show, or the circus-themed Circo; the latter is overseen by Manhattan restauranteur Sirio Maccioni, who also owns the more formal Le Cirque next door. In the Spa Tower, you'll find the serene Sensi, in which Martin Heierling serves Asian, Italian, grilled and seafood delicacies, and Pâtisserie Jean-Philippe, where a towering tri-coloured chocolate fountain (milk, white and dark) hints at the sweet sensations held within. The glitterati enjoy the upscale comfort food at Fix, while those looking for casual fare can check out the 24-hour Café Bellagio. The best drinks are served at Petrossian, named several times as one of America's best hotel bars by the hospitality industry's *Santé* magazine.

Entertainment

A cast of dancers, musicians, clowns, acrobats, divers, swimmers and aerialists takes to the watery stage in *O*, a breathtaking spectacle from Cirque du Soleil. Catch cover bands at the Fontana Bar, a lounge with great cocktails and superb fountain views. For

late-night fun, check out the pretty crowds sipping pricey martinis at Caramel or gyrating at Light.

Gambling

The Bellagio's casino draws celebs such as Ben Affleck and Drew Barrymore, but its ostentatious luxury verges on vulgar: the upholstery, carpets and striped canopies are a clash of colours and patterns. As you might expect, table limits are higher than at most Strip properties: minimums are often $25-$50 and it's difficult to find even $10 blackjack. Still, the race and sports book is one of the most comfortable in town, and the poker room has replaced Binion's as the mecca for pros, sharks and big-time players. **Amenities** *Bars (7). Business centre. Concierge. Disabled-adapted rooms. Gym. Internet (Wi-Fi). No-smoking floors. Pools (outdoor, 5). Restaurants (19). Room service. Spa. TV: pay movies.* **Games** *Baccarat ($100-$15,000); Big Six; blackjack ($10-$10,000); Caribbean stud; craps (3x, 4x, 5x; from $5); casino war; Let it Ride; mini baccarat ($25-$15,000); pai gow poker; pai gow tiles; poker (39 tables); roulette (single & double zero); three-card poker; slots.*

★ Caesars Palace

3570 Las Vegas Boulevard South, at W Flamingo Road, Las Vegas, NV 89109 (reservations 1-866 227 5938, front desk & casino 731 7110, www.harrahs.com). Bus Deuce, 202/self-parking & valet parking Las Vegas Boulevard South or S Industrial Road. **Rooms** 3,349. **Rates** $140-$920 double. **Map** p336 A7 **❸**

When it was announced in 2005 that the powerful Harrah's group was set to take over Caesars Palace, many Vegas observers feared that the chain would denude the place of all of its sass and turn it into Just Another Strip Resort. It didn't happen. While the Bellagio is perhaps the epitome of new Vegas luxury, Caesars remains an icon of classic Sin City decadence, a meld of affluence, kitsch and glamour that continues to be a compelling sight more than four decades after its 1966 opening.

The resort remains a monument of sorts to ancient Greece and Rome, with miles of gold decor, marble columns, arches and colonnades, manicured gardens and copies of Greek and Roman statuary. These days, though, it's more about elegance than the kind of camp instilled in it by legendary founder Jay Sarno, at least in theory. It's an enormous place, spread over a bewildering, labyrinthine casino floor and up into a variety of different towers.

Key to Caesars' continuing allure is the 4.5-acre Garden of the Gods pool area, a San Simeon-like peach with four mosaic pools, marble statuary, fountains and mini-throne lifeguard stands. A section of it, by the Venus pool, is set aside for topless sunbathing. While the pool draws a crowd only in summer, the ever-expanding Forum Shops (*see p194*) pulls visitors year-round. Fashioned, in true Vegas style, after an ancient Roman streetscape, the mall

Water, Water Everywhere

And it's all for your entertainment.

Vegas, as pointed out elsewhere in this guide, is all about extravagance and spectacle, the ostentatious display of the pricey and precious.

And in this sun-dazed desert redoubt, what could be more precious than water? The humble element is priceless for its very scarcity, and Las Vegas revels in the perversity of its presence amid the heat and glare. From the famous choreographed fountains of the **Bellagio** (*see p103*) to the long-running aquatic-themed spectacles *O* and *Le Rêve*, water has become one of the Strip's most phenomenally popular attractions. Vegas's moguls have ingeniously contrived to make water *work*, squeezing the cash from every splash, making the humblest liquid into liquidity. They've taken humble H20, something most people don't spare a second thought about, and made it into a destination, a spectacle.

Somehow, water is the most unpredictable element – it sprinkles, it sprays, it floods, it evaporates. And here it has attained the glamour and discipline of a Vegas showgirl, performing for our pleasure on a precise hourly or half-hourly schedule.

Aside from the Bellagio, the water features at the new CityCenter have made a splash recently. The **Crystals** shopping centre (*see p194*) is filled with opulent shops, but what draws the punters and casual passersby are the mesmerising waterworks: colourful liquid vortexes that swirl in plexiglass cylinders; and towering ice totems that emerge and then dwindle, unique sculptures shaped by heat, breezes and the touch of visitors' hands.

At CityCenter's **Aria** (*see p102*), meanwhile, visitors come to a standstill at the first glimpse of the playful sprays and squirts of the central courtyard fountain, which holds its neon colours even in bright daylight. One of the most dynamic features of Aria is a sweeping, all-embracing waterwall that creates a waterfall hush.

There are many other manifestations of water turned wonder, from steam to ice; shark reefs and aquariums; thunderstorms in shopping malls; scented steam and snow flurries; the mermaid tank at the **Silverton** (*see p148*); and the Minus5 ice bar at **Mandalay Bay** (*see p109*).

And then there are the splashy pool parties – the casinos took something that was an expected, somewhat mundane, hotel amenity and turned it into a money fountain, creating a concept called 'daylife' and making the sunlit hours and previously untapped poolside real estate into a high-style (and high-paying) natural resource.

CONSUME

Bellagio.

Caesars Palace. *See p104.*

contains an unmatched range of shops, many of them not found anywhere else in the city. Other selling points include the luxurious Qua Baths & Spa and the Venus salon; guests also get access to Cascata, the resort's golf course in Boulder City.

Accommodation

You'd expect a certain level of variety in a hotel this huge, and so it proves. The standard rooms (billed as 'Classic') are expansive and well maintained, but they aren't decorated in an especially inspiring fashion. If you've got a little cash, it's worth splashing for the 'Deluxe' rooms in the Augustus and Palace Towers, upgraded with high-tech facilities and stylishly modern design. The suites are fancier still: some have circular beds, in-room saunas, wet bars, living/dining rooms, home theatres, wine grottoes, and even steam and workout rooms.

Eating & drinking

Top of the tree are Bradley Ogden's chic regional American eaterie, high-end French spot Restaurant Guy Savoy, and 808, Jean-Marie Josselin's Euro-Asian-Pacific Rim restaurant. The Vegas edition of Bobby Flay's Manhattan-based, Southwestern-slanted hotspot Mesa Grill looks great but promises more than it delivers; you're better off visiting Rao's, another New York import. Other options include the Japanese-oriented Hyakumi; the Empress Court, for upscale Chinese; Café Lago, the prettiest coffeeshop on the Strip; and the 24-hour Augustus Café.

There are also a number of excellent eateries in the Forum Shops, among them Florida's Joe's Seafood, Prime Steak & Stone Crab, Santa Monica's Boa Prime Grill and Manhattan's ridiculously pricey Il Mulino. Alternatives include Sushi Roku, straightforward Italian eaterie Trevi, and two Wolfgang Puck spots, Asian restaurant Chinois and trend-setting Spago. For casual fare, try Stage Deli, where portions and prices are both huge.

Entertainment

Elton John makes an appearance with his hits-packed Red Piano show 50 times a year; other semi-regular headliners include comic Jerry Seinfeld. The acrocabaret of Absinthe is another popular attraction.

The most notable nightlife option, and one of the most fashionable in the entire city, is the perpetually celeb-packed Pure, a South Beachian spot part-owned by Dion, Shaquille O'Neal, Andre Agassi and Steffi Graf; included in it is the burlesque-oriented Pussycat Dolls Lounge, which does pretty much what you might expect. The Shadow Bar offers bartenders with flair and silhouetted beauties bumping and grinding behind backlit scrims; for old-time Caesars Palace kitsch, there's the enduring Cleopatra's Barge. In summer, there's the Venus Pool Club. Also on site are the Seahorse Lounge, serving high-end cocktails in a room dominated by a giant aquarium, and the 24-hour Galleria Bar. And in the Forum Shops, there's OPM.

CONSUME

Gambling

Few casinos offer the limits or the atmosphere of Caesars; when there's a big fight in town, limits on the main floor can go through the roof. The sports book is one of the liveliest spots to watch the action, and accepts some of the biggest bets. You get a good view of the baccarat pit, an intimate nook where huge wagers are common. And for the boldest of slot players, the $500 machine, with a $1 million jackpot, uses gold-plated tokens. (Caveat: it pays a winning spin of only two $500 coins; for every other payback, the machine locks and an attendant hand-pays, for tax-paperwork purposes.) The high-limit slots are in the Palace Casino near the main entrance; blackjack pits and slots in the Forum Casino offer slightly lower limits. There's also a Pussycat Dolls themed area.

Amenities *Bars (7). Business centre. Concierge. Disabled-adapted rooms. Gym. Internet (Wi-Fi, $11.99). No-smoking floors. Pools (outdoor). Restaurants (10). Room service. Spa. TV: pay movies.*

Games *Baccarat ($100-$15,000); Big Six; blackjack ($5-$10,000); Caribbean stud; casino war; craps (3x, 4x, 5x; from $10); keno; Let it Ride; mini baccarat ($25-$5,000); pai gow poker; pai gow tiles; poker (40 tables); roulette (single zero & double zero); Spanish 21; three-card poker.*

★ Cosmopolitan

3708 Las Vegas Boulevard South, between W Harmon Ave & W Flamingo Road, Las Vegas, NV 89109 (reservations 1-855 435 1055, front desk & casino 698 7000, www.cosmopolitan lasvegas.com). Bus Deuce, 202/self-parking Las Vegas Boulevard South/valet parking Las Vegas Boulevard South or W Flamingo Road. **Rooms** 2,995. **Rates** $220-$2,000 double. **Map** p336 A7 ❹

Like Aria, its similarly new next-door neighbour on the Strip, the Cosmopolitan is a luxury resort hotel and casino made up of two high-rise towers. But perhaps because of its unusual vertical orientation – the action plays out on three floors, instead of the usual sprawling single floor – the Cosmopolitan almost instantly became the new favourite of hip visitors and, most unusually, Vegas locals, who typically shun the Strip in favour of closer-to-home casinos and entertainment. Its third floor, which is also atypical in that it doesn't have any gaming or cocktail waitressing, has become the place to see dressed-up cosmopolitans, observed from a comfy perch on the witty assortment of mid-mod furnishings positioned mid-floor.

Built on what used to be the parking lot for the tiny Jockey Club timeshare, the $3.9 billion Cosmopolitan, designed by Arquitectonica, has

Cosmopolitan.

CONSUME

Mandalay Bay.

CONSUME

2,995 rooms and 300,000sq ft of stylish retail and restaurant space. The emphasis on high design and contemporary style makes the gambling action seem almost secondary – which may end up posing a bit of a problem for the Cosmo's owners. But for the moment, they're enjoying the buzz and the kudos of owning the most electrically current of the city's casinos.

Accommodation
Rooms at the Cosmopolitan are outfitted to make you feel as if you were at home – if home was within the pages of a high-end shelter magazine. Stylish and stylised, yes, but comfort was a guiding principal of designing Cosmos rooms and suites, which come standard-equipped with HD plasma screen TVs, high speed internet, minibar, and unusually luxurious bathrooms with marble floors. A big plus: most of the property's 2,995 rooms have sliding glass doors that open on to individual patios – this is highly unusual for Vegas, where the windows customarily do not open, for a variety of reasons.

Eating & drinking
Cosmopolitan has an internationally spiced collection of restaurants, including two by chef José Andrés – his signature tapas restaurant Jaleo, and China Poblano, which combines Mexican and Chinese cuisine. Other big food-world names with stakes in Cosmo include Blue Ribbon by Bruce and Eric Bromberg; Esitatorio Milos from Costas Spililadis; Scott Conant's Scarpetta (he also opened a wine bar called DOGC); and Comme Ça from David Myers. Other likely spots for a good meal include

Todd Mark Miller's self-explanatory STK, and high-end burger joint Holsteins.

Entertainment
Upon opening, Cosmopolitan's 62,000sq ft Marquee club became the most buzzed-about new space in Las Vegas. The indoor-outdoor venue, which accommodates the increasingly popular 'daylife' concept of clubbing and concerts by the pool, features a multimillion-dollar sound stage and coliseum-style seating surrounding a focal dance floor, which itself is decorated with four-story LED screens and projection walls that display light and image shows customised for each performance. The club is now solidly on the circuit of visiting international house music DJs, and the Marquee stage attracts an unusual array of up-to-the-moment artists – often of the sort that usually don't deign to play Vegas, including Foster the People, and, startlingly, Morrissey. All this in addition to some serious stylish shopping and spas.

Gambling
As mentioned before, the glitter and glam of the constantly moving crowd can distract from the action and attraction of the casino floor, but that doesn't mean it's not equipped to be a serious player on the Strip. In addition to its relatively intimate race and sports book, the 100,000sq ft casino (featuring cabanas!) offers nearly 1,500 state-of-the-art slot machines, plus baccarat, blackjack, roulette, and several varieties of poker and pai gow.
Amenities *Bars (5). Business centre. Concierge. Disabled-adapted rooms. Gym. Internet (Wi-Fi).*

No-smoking floors. Pools (outdoor). Restaurants (19). Room service. Spa. TV: pay movies.
Games *Baccarat ($100-$15,000); blackjack ($10-$10,000); craps (3x, 4x, 5x; from $5); Let it Ride; Crazy 4 poker; fortune pai gow poker; three-card poker; Ultimate Texas poker, roulette); slots.*

Mandalay Bay

3950 Las Vegas Boulevard South, at W Hacienda Avenue, Las Vegas, NV 89119 (reservations 1-877 632 7800, front desk & casino 632 7777, www.mandalaybay.com). Bus Deuce, 104, 105/ self-parking & valet parking W Hacienda Avenue.
Rooms 2,791. **Rates** $109-$509 double.
Map p336 A9 ❺

Not only do the suits at MGM Mirage know not to mess with a good thing, they also know how to make it better. There's no finer example of this skill than the South Seas island-themed Mandalay Bay, one of the Strip's most luxurious resorts. At its heart has always been an 11-acre water park with a sandy beach, a wave pool, a lazy river, two additional pools and a jogging track set in lush green foliage, plus the Moorea Beach Club, a limited-access South Beach-esque retreat that transforms into a sultry hotspot on warm-weather weekend nights. But a $30-million expansion added a three-storey, climate-controlled, glass-fronted casino on the sand, where guests can enjoy beachside gambling, casual dining or sun-worshipping. Book one of the decked-out Villas Soleil, where you and 15 pals can take advantage of your own wet bar, MP3 player, flatscreen TV and private third-level pool.

The interior is just as impressive. An understated oasis of water features, lush foliage, huge aquariums and island architecture, it encompasses a sensuous spa, a classy collection of restaurants, a pair of wedding chapels, several theatres and the kid-friendly Shark Reef aquarium (*see p71*). Mandalay Place, a nice sky-bridge mall that connects the hotel with the Luxor, contains a number of upscale boutiques and restaurants, a chic barber and even Forty Deuce, a 'back-alley striptease lounge'. The convention facilities are among the city's best.

If all this doesn't work for you, there are two other hotels accessible from Mandalay Bay. A corridor off the lobby leads to the Four Seasons (*see p130*, which has its rooms on floors 35 to 39 but is run as a separate operation. Meanwhile, Thehotel at Mandalay Bay (*see p132*) is an all-suites, casino-free tower that eschews the island theme entirely.

Accommodation

All 2,791 guestrooms and suites at Mandalay Bay were remodelled a few years ago with a contemporary look and additional amenities: lofty pillow-top beds with triple sheeting, 42in plasma-screen TVs, iPod docks and high-speed net access. Bathrooms come with 15-in LCD TVs and giant tubs. Larger suites command excellent views of the Strip or the surrounding mountains and come with wet bars.

Eating & drinking

Mandalay Bay is unusual among the major resorts on the Strip in that it locates many of its eateries in a 'restaurant row' away from the casino, so you can dine without seeing – or, just as crucially, hearing – so much as a single slot machine. The top spot on the block is Michael Mina's Strip Steak, the first steakhouse by a chef previously known for his seafood. Other noteworthy spots include Hubert Keller's Fleur de Lys; Charlie Palmer's Aureole; Wolfgang Puck's Trattoria del Lupo; and Mary Sue Milliken and Susan Feniger's nouveau Mexican Border Grill. China Grill and Shanghai Lily serve Asian fare; Rumjungle is a Brazilian *rodizio* and rum bar/nightclub; and Red, White & Blue is a decent but too-pricey café.

You'll have to venture into the casino to sample the Cajun cooking at House of Blues, upstairs from the music venue. Try Sunday's soul-stirring Gospel Brunch or, if you can, the super-exclusive Foundation Room, which serves dinner to members and VIPs amid deluxe furnishings on the top floor. Ringing the casino are the nice 24-hour Raffles Café, the Noodle Shop and J-Pop, where music and sushi are the order of the evening. Over at Mandalay Place, carnivores can have theirs with lettuce and tomato at the Burger Bar; also here are RM Seafood (with two dining rooms, R-Bar-Café and the more intimate restaurant RM) and Chocolate Swan.

Entertainment

The 12,000-seat Mandalay Bay Events Center has a schedule of boxing events and concerts, but a better choice is the more acoustically reliable House of Blues, which features a concert roster rivalled only by the Pearl at the Palms. When the weather's warm, the hotel produces the Bay Rock Concert series.

Leaving aside Mix at Thehotel at Mandalay Bay, Hollywood import Forty Deuce, over in Mandalay Place, is the hottest nightclub, though Rumjungle draws a young, pretty crowd with pounding Latin beats, and the vodka selections at Red Square remain impressive. There's piano music in the casino's Orchid Lounge and, on weekends (6-8pm), at Charlie Palmer Steak inside the Four Seasons.

Gambling

The 135,000sq ft (12,500sq m) casino is airier than many, with 2,400 machines (including nickel video slots that take up to 45 or 90 coins), but you have to hunt for good video-poker machines. Table games – 122 of them – include blackjack, roulette, craps, Let it Ride, Caribbean stud, pai gow poker and mini baccarat. You'll also find a poker room where you can get your fix of seven-card stud and Texas or Omaha hold 'em. The race and sports book has 17 large screens, enough seating for some 300 sports fans, a bar and a good deli.
Amenities *Bars (10). Business centre. Concierge. Disabled-adapted rooms. Gym. Internet ($11.99). No-smoking floors. Pools (outdoor). Restaurants (21). Room service. Spa. TV: pay movies.*

Games *Baccarat ($100-$15,000); blackjack ($10-$15,000); Caribbean stud; craps (3x, 4x, 5x; from $10); keno; Let it Ride; mini baccarat ($25-$15,000); pai gow poker; pai gow tiles; poker (10 tables); roulette (single & double zero); three-card poker.*

★ Mirage

3400 Las Vegas Boulevard South, between Spring Mountain & W Flamingo roads, Las Vegas, NV 89109 (reservations 1-800 374 9000, front desk & casino 791 7111, www.mirage.com). Bus Deuce, 105, 202, 203/self-parking Spring Mountain Road/valet parking Las Vegas Boulevard South. **Rooms** 3,044. **Rates** $109-$699 double. **Map** p335, p336 A6 **⊙**

With its Polynesian village decor, lush landscaping, lagoon-like pool and waterfalls, the $650-million Mirage set the standard for modern resorts when it was opened by Steve Wynn in 1989. But in much the same way that the likes of the Tropicana and the Flamingo were left standing at the gate when the Mirage welcomed its first guests, so the Mirage was in turn overtaken by its sassier competitors, who shrewdly realised that there was money to be made from a younger, more fashionable generation.

The owners have pepped things up no end over the past few years. The hotel's dining options have vastly improved, nightclubs and lounges aimed squarely at the under-thirties rather than the over-forties have opened, and Christmas-camp Siegfried & Roy have been replaced with a vibrant Beatles-based show. The Mirage might not look like a different resort, but it certainly feels like one.

For all that, many of the old favourites remain. The mocked-up volcano at the front is no more realistic than it ever was, but its hourly shows (evenings only) remain a draw. Also still here are the 90ft rainforest atrium filled with fresh and faux palm trees and orchids, the much-imitated 20,000-gallon aquarium behind the registration desk, and the Secret Garden & Dolphin Habitat (*see p76*). And do make time to stop by the gorgeous pool area, which comprises a series of blue lagoons, inlets and waterfalls, plus two islands exotically landscaped with various palm trees and tropical flowers.

Accommodation

Decor in the rooms is on the conservative side of bold, with cranberries, greens and browns. Rooms are as comfortable as you'd expect, and very well appointed, with 42in TVs,

Eating & drinking

The Samba Brazilian Steakhouse, surf 'n' turf favourite Kokomo's and Cravings, hardly 'the ultimate buffet experience' but good nonetheless, have been joined by some eye-catching restaurants. Chief among them is Japonais, imported via Chicago and New York, and the swanky Stack, which places American cuisine into a tapas-style menu. Other

options include Onda, a smartish Italian restaurant; Chinese-oriented Fin ; the almost forcibly casual California Pizza Kitchen; and, from New York, the Carnegie Deli.

Entertainment

The big show at the Mirage is one of the biggest and best in the city: *Love,* Cirque du Soleil's surprisingly successful reinvention of the Beatles' back catalogue. Ventriloquist Terry Fator, an early winner of the *America's Got Talent* TV competition, has replaced the late, beloved impressionist Danny Gans.

The nightlife here has received a not-before-time overhaul of late, and the changes have made a huge difference to the atmosphere throughout the Mirage. The Cirque-designed Revolution Lounge grabs the headlines, with its novel interactive tables and moreish speciality cocktails; however, the putative Beatles theme doesn't extend as far as the soundtrack, which (with the exception of a BritPop themed Thursday) tends towards polite house. Things are a little livelier at chichi Jet, a little mellower at the wine lounge at Onda, and a little breezier at the poolside Dolphin Bar.

Gambling

The Mirage has nearly 100 blackjack tables, most dealt from six-deck shoes. Minimums are high: $10 for 21, craps and roulette, $15 for mini baccarat, $100 for baccarat. You can find a good game of poker at any hour; since many players are tourists, the action, both on the low- and high-limit tables, is plentiful. For a break, check out the high-limit slots. If you're polite, and it's not too busy, an attendant might offer you some freshly sliced fruit, normally reserved for players who insert $100 tokens five at a time (their generosity truly knows no bounds). The Red, White & Blue slot offers a $1 million jackpot.

Amenities *Bars (5). Business centre. Concierge. Disabled-adapted rooms. Gym. Internet (Wi-Fi $12.99). No-smoking floors. Pools (outdoor). Restaurants (14). Room service. Spa. TV: pay movies.*
Games *Baccarat ($100-$15,000); Big Six; blackjack ($10-$10,000); Caribbean stud; casino war; craps (3x, 4x, 5x; from $10); keno; Let it Ride; mini baccarat ($15-$15,000); pai gow poker; pai gow tiles; poker (30 tables); roulette (single zero & double zero); Spanish 21; three-card poker.*

Paris Las Vegas

3655 Las Vegas Boulevard South, at E Flamingo Road, Las Vegas, NV 89109 (reservations 1-877 603 4386, front desk & casino 946 7000, www.harrahs.com). Bus Deuce, 202/self-parking & valet parking Las Vegas Boulevard South or Audrie Street. **Rooms** 2,916. **Rates** $109-$499 double. **Map** p336 A7 **⊙**

What happens when the City of Lights collides with the City of Light? Versions of Paris's greatest monuments cut down to size, all-you-can-eat crêpes at

Mirage.

the buffet, reasonably polite waiters, ancient Rome across the street… and, of course, the lights never go out. If only the real Paris could be so accommodating. Even the French love Las Vegas.

To say that this huge resort in the heart of the Strip is one of the town's most eye-catching is to do its effervescent absurdity a rank injustice. Its reproductions of Parisian landmarks start with the 34-storey hotel tower modelled after the Hôtel de Ville, and also take in the Louvre, the Paris Opéra, the Arc de Triomphe and, of course, the half-scale replica of the Eiffel Tower, built using Gustav Eiffel's original plans, that plunges into the casino. The theming continues within, with French-themed restaurants, shops and even, though you'll need to look closely, the casino. It may seem rather sub-Disney at first glance, but it's by no means all haw-hee-haw cliché: you can also get a massage in a mock-Balinese spa, sun yourself by the rooftop pool or take in a show by that timeless international hitmaker Barry Manilow, who has moved across town from the Las Vegas Hilton and staged his own Paris occupation.

Accommodation
The smallish guestrooms are comfortable, prim and stately, decorated in rich Regency style; some are furnished with canopied beds and armoires. The spacious marble bathrooms are outfitted with vanities, a make-up mirror and soaking tubs.

Eating & drinking
Paris Las Vegas doesn't do too badly at living up to its theme city's culinary reputation, albeit without the breadth of styles you'll find at the Venetian or the Bellagio. Along with JJ's Boulangerie and La Creperie, serving sandwiches and delicious sweet and savoury crêpes, and the quaint Le Village Buffet, which features regional cuisine from five French provinces, the hotel has the Eiffel Tower Restaurant, located on the tower's 11th floor, and the bustling Mon Ami Gabi, a streetside brasserie serving classics such as *steak frites*. Les Artistes Steakhouse has a menu of rotisserie-style meats, fish and poultry, while Ah Sin is a chic place with patio dining that serves Thai and Chinese dishes along with Korean barbecue and sushi. Most ridiculous of all? Le Burger Brasserie, putatively a French take on American classics. Hmm.

Entertainment
If Paris Las Vegas's strolling mimes leave you unenthusiastic, there's a variety of ways to spend the

night wisely (or otherwise). The major show here is *Barry Manilow: Music & Passion* (see *p231*). If we all ignore hypnotist Anthony Cools, who performs six shows a week, perhaps he'll go away. A better bet is Risqué, a nightclub where old-world France meets contemporary Asian-tilted lounge, complete with house music and dessert bar. Downstairs, there's dance music under sparkly lights among the shady faux trees of Le Cabaret. And there are decidedly non-French duelling piano singalongs in Napoleon's (see *p181*), a champagne and cigar bar.

Gambling

Three of the Eiffel Tower's four legs plunge into the casino, which is smaller, noisier and more energetically crowded than most. The 100 table games and 2,000-plus slot machines are not as budget-friendly as they used to be, though there are still plenty of 25¢ slots. The race and sports book has big TVs and 'pari-mutuel' betting on horse racing. Theming is rampant, from Monet-influenced carpets and Paris Métro-style wrought-iron canopies above the games to security guards in gendarme uniforms. Check out the LeRoy Neiman paintings in the high-limit pit.
Amenities *Bars (6). Business centre. Concierge. Disabled-adapted rooms. Gym. Internet ($10.99). No-smoking floors. Pool (outdoor). Restaurants (11). Room service. Spa. TV: pay movies.*
Games *Baccarat ($100-$15,000); Big Six; blackjack ($5-$10,000); Caribbean stud; casino war; craps (3x, 4x, 5x; from $5); Let it Ride; mini baccarat ($15-$5,000); pai gow poker; poker (10 tables); roulette (single zero & double zero); Spanish 21; three-card poker.*

Venetian & Palazzo

3555 Las Vegas Boulevard South, between Sands Avenue & E Flamingo Road, Las Vegas, NV 89109 (reservations 1-877 883 6423, front desk & casino 414 1000, www.venetian.com). Bus Deuce, 105, 203/self-parking & valet parking Las Vegas Boulevard South or Koval Lane. **Rooms** *Venetian 4,049. Palazzo 3,025.* **Rates** *$179-$559 suite.* **Map** *p335, p336 B6* ❽
Sheldon Adelson's Venetian manages the neat trick of recreating the city of canals in the desert. To-scale replicas of the Rialto Bridge, the Doge's Palace and the Campanile are rendered with affection, and the singing gondoliers and itinerant 'street' performers in St Mark's Square perform with gusto and a wink. It's less tacky than you might expect.

Attractions here are, with the arguable exceptions of Andrew Lloyd Webber's *Phantom* and the adjacent Madame Tussaud's (see *p75*), pretty good. The Grand Canal Shoppes (see *p195*) is a meandering mall with flowing canals and faux façades that curve around to St Mark's Square. Another key draw is the Canyon Ranch SpaClub, which offers a full range of spa services along with movement and wellness classes, a climbing wall and a café. The resort connects to the Sands Expo (see *p311*); indeed, the

Venetian & Palazzo.

CONSUME

Venetian pulls in much of its business from conventioneers, especially midweek.

The adjacent Palazzo has an upper-crust Beverly Hills feel. The resort features a new mall, the Shoppes at Palazzo (see p196), connected to the Venetian via the Grand Canal Shoppes and anchored by Barneys department store.

Accommodation

The standard suites (there are no regular rooms) at the Venetian are far larger than the Vegas norm. The sumptuously appointed suites underwent renovations during 2007, no doubt to keep them on a par with the Palazzo. The 12-storey Venezia Tower atop the car park has rooms that are similar to those in the original tower, but that now come with some extra amenities (private elevators, complimentary newspaper delivery, access to the secluded Italian-style pool garden and arboretum). For more exclusivity, the tower's top five floors contain an old world drawing-room-style lounge and speciality baths.

Eating & drinking

Where to begin? The Venetian's restaurant roster reads like a Who's Who of top chefs. Thomas Keller (of French Laundry fame) oversees stellar brasserie Bouchon; Wolfgang Puck and Emeril Lagasse respectively run the San Francisco-style café Postrio and the Cajun Delmonico Steakhouse; Joachim Splichal's Pinot Brasserie brings a lighter taste of French cuisine; and Tom Moloney's AquaKnox serves Californian cuisine. This being ersatz Venice, there's plenty of Italian food: Piero Selvaggio's dual rooms Valentino and the Grill at Valentino; Zeffirino, a Genoan-style seafood restaurant with a fan club that includes Pavarotti; and Canaletto. Newer arrivals include Tao, an Asian bistro related to the fashionable New York restaurant-club; Mario Batali's B&B Ristorante and Enoteca San Marco; and David Burke's signature American restaurant. Less pricey options (it's all relative) include Noodle Asia for pan-Asian noodle dishes, Hong Kong dim sum and vegetarian specialities; the excellent 24-hour Grand Lux Café; and Taqueria Cañonita.

Entertainment

The Venetian has improved its night-time entertainment options, with the Blue Man Group and all-round entertainer Gordie Brown, as well as a snazzed-up Phantom. The Palazzo hosts Broadway hit Jersey Boys.

After numerous attempts at starting a nightclub scene stalled at the gates, the Venetian finally hit the bullseye with Tao, a pan-Asian boîte, nightclub and rooftop lounge that entertains thousands on weekends. For more lounge and less club, check out the sizzling minimalist V Bar (see p183).

Gambling

In the casino, the 140 table games include blackjack, craps, Caribbean stud, Let it Ride and pai gow. The casino's 2,600 slots are weighted toward reel games, with a large mix of $1 machines. For the player with pull, there are high-denomination machines – $5, $25 and $100 – in the casino's high-limit salon, which also includes a baccarat pit and 12 table games (blackjack starting at $10,000 a hand).

Amenities Bars (3). Business centre. Concierge. Disabled-adapted rooms. Gym. Internet ($10). No-smoking floors. Pools (outdoor). Restaurants (18). Room service. Spa. TV: DVD (selected rooms)/pay movies.

Games Baccarat ($100-$15,000); mini baccarat ($25-$10,000); Big Six; blackjack ($10-$5,000); Caribbean stud; casino war; craps (3x, 4x, 5x; from $10); keno; Let it Ride; pai gow poker; pai gow tiles; poker (39 tables); roulette (double zero). Gambling lessons (craps 11am Mon-Fri; roulette noon Mon-Fri; blackjack 12.15pm Mon-Fri).

★ Wynn Las Vegas & Encore

3131 Las Vegas Boulevard South, between E Desert Inn Road & Sands Avenue, NV 89109 (reservations 1-888 320 9966, front desk & casino 770 7000, www.wynnlasvegas.com). Bus Deuce, 203/self-parking & valet parking Las Vegas Boulevard South or (Tower Suites) Spring Mountain Road. **Rooms** *Wynn Las Vegas 2,716. Encore 2,034.* **Rates** *$199-$699 double.* **Map** *p335, p336 B6* **❾**

Before he'd even finished building his namesake hotel, Steve Wynn was, true to form, already planning an addition to it. However, Encore has since morphed into rather more than a mere addendum: it's another full-scale resort, complete with restaurants, bars and nightclubs. Wynn, after all, can't let himself be outdone by fellow mogul Sheldon Adelson and his neighbouring Palazzo (see p112). But in the meantime, Wynn Las Vegas has more than enough diversions to keep visitors busy.

Known as the man who brought Vegas entertainment curbside, Wynn went against his own convention and designed this resort from the inside out. Luxury is everywhere, as you'd expect from a casino that cost somewhere in the region of $2.7 billion. On the far side of the faux mountain (see p77 **The Wynn's Mysterious Mountain**), the Lake of Dreams fuses light, water, horticulture and architecture into a multimedia experience. The garden-themed Spa at Wynn houses 45 treatment rooms, a beauty salon and a fitness centre, while the 18-hole golf course (designed by Tom Fazio) is overlooked by 36 fairway villas.

The exclusivity extends to the Wynn Esplanade mall (see p196), where you'll find the crème de la crème of high-end fashion designers, including Louis Vuitton, Christian Dior, Oscar de la Renta and Brioni. If you can't fathom the thought of a hire car, there's also Penske Wynn Ferrari Maserati, Nevada's only factory-authorised Ferrari and Maserati dealership. There are several notable works of art hanging in the hotel's common areas. *Photo p114.*

CONSUME

Wynn Las Vegas & Encore. *See p113.*

CONSUME

Accommodation

The large and lavish (naturally) guestrooms offer floor-to-ceiling windows, signature Wynn beds with 320-thread-count European linens, a seating area with a sofa and ottomans, a dining table and chairs, flatscreen LCD TVs, spacious bath areas and bedside drapery controls. The suites set a new Vegas standard: some have their own massage rooms, VIP check-in areas, private pools and dining rooms. Don't even get us started on the villas.

Eating & drinking

Though Wynn has been partly responsible for the onslaught in Vegas of absentee celebrity chefs who slap their names on the marquees but mainly leave the cooking to others, the restaurants here are all run by the chefs whose names they bear. The signature spot is Alex, run by Alessandro Stratta; other options include Daniel Boulud, Eric Klein's SW Steakhouse, Mark LoRusso's Tableau, Stephen Kalt's Corsa Cucina and Paul Bartolotta's Bartolotta Ristorante di Mare. There's more casual food at Asian bistro Red 8, the poolside Terrace Pointe Café and the sumptuous Buffet. Parasol Up and Parasol Down, the hotel's lobby bars, offer everything from tea to cocktails.

Entertainment

Garth Brooks holds court in a close-up show at the intimate Encore theatre. And erstwhile Cirque du Soleil producer Franco Dragone was called on to design *Le Rêve*, named after the Picasso masterpiece that was initially the inspiration for the hotel itself. It has been continually revamped since opening night, but it still includes the same aerial acrobatics for which Dragone is known. The seductive Lure serves as Wynn's version of the ultralounge; Tryst is his answer to the nightclub scene.

Gambling

As you might expect, the action at Wynn is both sophisticated and decidedly pricey. Blackjack min-

imums start at $15, with a few single-deck games that pay the reduced 6:5 for naturals; hotel guests can also play 21 poolside at the Cabana Bar. Crap minimums are similar to blackjack. A single-zero roulette wheel is usually open in the high-limit room, though the minimums are dear. The slots run the gamut from pennies to a $5,000 machine. Amazingly, Wynn has tried to attract local video-poker players with full-pay machines at higher denominations (very rare), though the schedules change unexpectedly; check the *Las Vegas Advisor* for their comings and goings. The keno lounge is one of the most comfortable in town.

Amenities *Bars (6). Business centre. Concierge. Disabled-adapted rooms. Gym. Internet ($11.95; Wi-Fi in lobby). No-smoking floors. Pool (outdoor). Restaurants (18). Room service. Spa. TV: DVD (suites only)/pay movies.*

Games *Baccarat ($100-$15,000); Big Six; blackjack ($15-$10,000); Caribbean stud; casino war; craps (3x, 4x, 5x; from $10); Let it Ride; mini baccarat ($50-$10,000); pai gow poker; pai gow tiles; poker (26 tables); roulette (single & double zero); Spanish 21; three-card poker.*

Moderate

Bally's

3645 Las Vegas Boulevard South, at E Flamingo Road, Las Vegas, NV 89109 (reservations 1-877 603 4390, front desk & casino 967 4111, www.harrahs.com). Bus Deuce, 202/self-parking & valet parking Las Vegas Boulevard South or E Flamingo Road. **Rooms** 2,814. **Rates** $99-$459 double. **Map** p336 A7 ❿

A classic, Dan Tanna-esque *Vega$* experience can still be had at the grande dame of the Strip's Famous Four Corners. Though now owned by Harrah's, Bally's has stayed true to its Hollywood roots, albeit probably because management simply hasn't got around to renovating yet. The garish eight miles of ostentatious looping neon, part of a multi-million-dollar 'grand entry' that delivers tourists to the hotel's elegant porte cochère, is pretty ugly, but Bally's retains its classic appeal inside. Amenities include an oversized, heated pool with private cabanas; eight floodlit tennis courts next to a pro shop, where you can sign up for lessons (it's one of the last hotels on the Strip with tennis courts); a full-service health club; and access to the Caesars-owned Cascata golf course. The Bally Avenue Shoppes houses one-off boutiques.

Accommodation

The good-sized standard rooms are decorated with a West Coast casual elegance of bright velvet couches offset by muted earth tones. Of the 2,814 rooms, 265 are suites: the one- and two-bedroom Grand Suites, each with a huge jetted tub and wet bar, are slightly more contemporary. The 22nd Club offers access to private concierge services, free breakfast and evening cocktails with gorgeous Strip views.

Eating & drinking

The restaurant selection is like the rest of the resort: a throwback to old-school subtlety. It's no surprise that the best place to eat is an all-you-can-scoff affair: Sunday's Sterling Brunch, a spectacular linen-and-champers buffet for which booking is necessary. Al Dente offers contemporary Italian food, and the New England-style Steakhouse does grilled beef and seafood right. The only new addition: Yuk Sing Wong's Asia, serving regional specialities such as Hong Kong wun tun soup and Sichuan shrimp. Along with the Big Kitchen Buffet, there's a host of casual spots for sushi, ice-cream, sandwiches and Italian fast food, plus cocktails at the sport-and-slots bar Sully's and the Mexican-slanted Tequila Bar.

Entertainment

For an old-school Vegas show experience, *Jubilee!* is just the ticket: beautiful showgirls reprising world-famous production numbers with lavish sets and spectacular choreography (topless on the late run). A rotating line-up of local acts plays the Indigo Lounge.

Gambling

The casino is a large, rectangular space, an inviting atmosphere of soft lighting and art deco accents with 65 table games and 2,100 slot machines. Among them are 'champagne' $1,000 slots, with a top payout of a cool mil. Not surprisingly, you'll find all the latest creations from machine-maker Bally, including laser-disc versions of craps, roulette and blackjack; all are excellent practice tools before heading to the actual tables. The buy-ins at the tables start at $10 with an occasional $5 single-deck 6:5 21 game, though many players wager far more than the minimum. The video poker is pretty pitiful, but the sports book, on the lower level, is as classy and technically advanced as those at the Bellagio and the Hilton, and it's only crowded on big-game days.

Amenities *Bars (5). Business centre. Disabled-adapted rooms. Gym. Internet ($10.99). No-smoking floors. Pool (outdoor). Restaurants (12). Room service. Spa. TV: pay movies.* **Games** *Baccarat ($100-$15,000); blackjack ($5-$3,000); Caribbean stud; casino war; craps (3x, 4x, 5x; from $5); keno; Let it Ride; mini baccarat ($15-$5,000); pai gow poker; poker (9 tables); roulette (double zero); Spanish 21; three-card poker.*

Flamingo

3555 Las Vegas Boulevard South, at E Flamingo Road, Las Vegas, NV 89109 (reservations 1-888 902 9929, front desk & casino 733 3111, www.harrahs.com). Bus Deuce, 202/self-parking & valet parking Las Vegas Boulevard South or Audrie Street. **Rooms** 3,626. **Rates** $90-$450 double. **Map** p336 A7 ⓫

The Flamingo is the Strip's sleeping giant. Its location at the heart of the action couldn't be better; and

Bally's.

thanks to its beginnings under Bugsy Siegel, its name is virtually legendary. But while its competitors at Caesars and the Bellagio across the street are raising their game in an attempt to draw new crowds, the Harrah's-owned Flamingo seems content to coast along in third gear, happy to milk a gradually ageing clientele who apparently aren't interested in what the competition might be able to offer them.

Behind the signature pink neon sign, the resort is huge, with six guestroom towers. Hidden between them is the resort's centrepiece: a lush 15-acre tropical pool area with waterslides, waterfalls and jungle-like foliage enveloping four distinct pools (including Bugsy's oval-shaped original). Also outdoors are four tennis courts and an assortment of wildlife, including (yes) flamingos. So far so good, then, but the interior of the Flamingo is markedly less impressive, wedged some time in the 1980s and unable or unwilling to escape. The new Go guestrooms are a sign that change may be on the horizon, but it's going to be a long and difficult job.

Accommodation
The standard rooms at the Flamingo are smallish, fairly basic and profoundly old-fashioned, despite a relatively recent renovation. All of which makes the new Go guestrooms a bit of a surprise. Designed in a more modern style and done out with flatscreen TVs, iPod-friendly hi-fis and wireless access, they're more inviting than you'd expect from either the other rooms or, for that matter, the rest of the resort.

Note that while room rates at all Vegas properties vary from night to night, the differentials at the Flamingo are spectacular even by local standards. Guestrooms can be ridiculously cheap during the week and outrageously expensive at weekends.

Eating & drinking
The gastronomic revolution that's enlivened Vegas vacations over the last decade or so has yet to reach the Flamingo. Aside from a 24-hour coffeeshop and the inevitable buffet, visitors can choose from Italian (Ventuno), steaks and seafood (Steakhouse46) or sushi and teppanyaki (popular chain Hamada of Japan). None disgrace their surroundings, but when your signature restaurant is Jimmy Buffet's Margaritaville, a theme bar-restaurant decorated in colours loud enough to blind from 50 paces, perhaps a rethink is in order.

Entertainment
The 10pm slot is held down by George Wallace (the comedian, not the segregationist former governor of Alabama), a reliably funny man who seems to have found a gig for life. Further laughs are provided by Second City, a satellite branch of the Chicagoan improv troupe; late at night, its theatre is home to burlesque shows.

Gambling
The casino area, though a bit claustrophobic and loud, offers you a real chance to survive: crap and blackjack minimums are a reasonable $5 outside prime time. It's tougher to come out ahead in the slot area: none of the 2,100 machines are considered loose (after all, the last renovation cost $130 million). You'll also find a lively card room, a keno parlour, and a race and sports book.

Amenities *Bars (5). Business centre. Disabled-adapted rooms. Gym. Internet ($10.99, web TV $9.99). No-smoking floors. Pools (outdoor). Restaurants (9). Room service. Spa. TV: pay movies.*

Games *Baccarat ($10-$5,000); Big Six; blackjack ($5-$3,000); Caribbean stud; craps (3x, 4x, 5x;*

Flamingo. *See p115.*

CONSUME

Harrah's.

from $5); keno; Let it Ride; mini baccarat ($10-$5,000); pai gow poker; poker (14 tables); roulette (double zero); three-card poker. Gambling lessons (craps 11am Tue-Sat).

Harrah's

3475 Las Vegas Boulevard South, between Sands Avenue & E Flamingo Road, Las Vegas, NV 89109 (reservations 1-800 214 9110, front desk & casino 369 5000, www.harrahs.com). Bus Deuce, 105, 203/self-parking & valet parking Koval Lane. **Rooms** *2,667.* **Rates** *$60-$450 double.* **Map** *p336 A6*
This middle-of-the-road, middle-of-the-Strip resort might not have the same cachet as most of its neighbours, Caesars Palace and the Venetian among them, but its parent company is one of the most powerful in town. The acquisition in 2005 of the Imperial Palace, which sits between Harrah's and sibling property the Flamingo, might have been the catalyst for recent change. The 35-year-old resort still plays the tired Mardi Gras theme, but fresh entertainment options, new eateries and just-renovated guestrooms have injected the property with a little spirit.

Accommodation
The guestrooms and suites in Harrah's three towers are comfortable and festive. Many have minibars, some have jetted tubs. The deluxe rooms have updated decor and amenities.

Eating & drinking
There are no celeb chefs or brand-name chains here; all the restaurants are suitable for casual or smart-casual diners. If you're all dressed up, you'll feel most at home at the Range Steakhouse with its nice views of the Strip. Your next best bets are Penazzi Italian Ristorante and the Oyster Bar at Penazzi for Italian recipes, and Ming's Table, the gourmet restaurant formerly known as Asia, for crispy roast duck. Casual diners flock to remodelled buffet Flavors and the Café at Harrah's, which serves standard coffeeshop fare.

Entertainment
The family-friendly afternoon magic show delivered by the hugely likeable Mac King is popular. Budd Friedman's famous Improv comedy club brings in fresh comedians each week. And you can listen to live country music in Toby Keith's I Love This Bar & Grill or be dazzled by the flair bartenders in the Carnaval Court.

Gambling
Harrah's has a wide selection of table games, including Caribbean stud, Let it Ride and casino war. Most blackjack games are dealt from the shoe, but higher limits – at least $25 minimum – are dealt from hand-held decks. Beware the single decks, which have lower limits but pay a measly 6:5 for naturals. Occasionally, gracious pit bosses will bring out the European single-zero roulette wheel for high rollers. For lively action, take a seat in the cosily compact poker room; the race and sports book offers booths and table seating.
Amenities *Bars (7). Business centre. Disabled-adapted rooms. Gym. Internet ($11.95). No-smoking floors. Pool (outdoor). Restaurants (8). Room service. Spa. TV: pay movies.*
Games *Baccarat ($25-$10,000); blackjack ($10-$5,000); Caribbean stud; craps (3x, 4x, 5x; from $5); keno; Let it Ride; mini baccarat ($15-$5,000); pai gow poker; poker (15 tables); roulette (single & double zero); three-card poker.*

Imperial Palace

3535 Las Vegas Boulevard South, between Sands Avenue & E Flamingo Road, Las Vegas, NV 89109 (reservations 1-800 634 6441, front desk & casino 731 3311, www.imperialpalace.com). Bus Deuce, 105, 203/self-parking & valet parking Las Vegas Boulevard South. **Rooms** *2,640.* **Rates** *$66-$370 double.* **Map** *p336 A6*
You don't have to be royalty to stay at this oriental-themed hotel; in fact, with the Stardust's demise, there should be even more demand for an on-Strip property where rates often drop into double digits.

CONSUME

The monorail station on site helps you get around to the hipper places, but the resort does offer a few reasons to stay. The main attraction is the Auto Collections, which has more than 200 antique, classic and special-interest vehicles on display and for sale. You can even get your photo taken with an old car for free. Speaking of which, the IP's venerable *Legends in Concert* is still thriving. Indeed, it's spilling over into the remodelled casino, where, at the Dealertainers Pit, you might find Cher, primed to belt out a song from behind the blackjack table.

Accommodation

All guestrooms, from small standard rooms through to the King Suite, received much-needed facelifts a few years ago. Certain rooms come with a jacuzzi-driven 'luv tub'. The best penthouse suites have one or two bedrooms and an extra-large living room.

Eating & drinking

There are restaurants to satisfy most basic cravings, from the Burger Palace to the Pizza Palace, plus a couple of decent buffets in between. Head to the fifth floor for fancier places: Embers (steak), the Cockeyed Clam (seafood), Fireside (barbecue) and Ming Terrace (pan-Asian). The Rockhouse has a mean daiquiri bar, rock music, and free shots poured 24-7 by the Rockhouse Dancers. The IP recently added the Madhouse Bar, a frathouse saloon by Jeff Beacher (of Beacher's Madhouse infamy) where scantily clad servers produce 'bottle service' of mini beer kegs.

Entertainment

The Imperial Palace has what may be the busiest showroom in town, rotating Aussie boyband-turned-Motown tribute act Human Nature; Divas Las Vegas; and Japanese acrobatic troupe. From April to October, the pool transforms into a luau scene, with food and a Polynesian revue. Inside at Tequila Joe's, guests dance to DJs nightly.

Gambling

Thanks to its high-traffic location, the casino is always busy, though that doesn't necessarily mean it's particularly favourable. Typical central-Strip blackjack rules and video-poker paybacks gouge the first-time tourist; the rest of the games gouge the sucker, no matter how experienced. 'Dealertainers' in the IP's party pit impersonate Madonna, the Blues Brothers, Elvis and other pop stars while pitching cards and rockin' out to the loud music. If you have to fade the bad odds, this is a fun place to do it.
Amenities *Bars (8). Business centre. Concierge. Disabled-adapted rooms. Gym. Internet (Wi-Fi $9.99). No-smoking floors. Pool (outdoor). Restaurants (9). Room service. Spa. TV: pay movies.*
Games *Big Six; blackjack ($10-$500); Caribbean stud; casino war; craps (3x, 4x, 5x; from $3); keno; Let it Ride; pai gow poker; roulette (double*

zero); three-card poker. Gambling lessons (blackjack 9am daily; roulette 10am daily; craps 11am daily).

Luxor

3900 Las Vegas Boulevard South, at W Hacienda Avenue, Las Vegas, NV 89119 (reservations 1-888 777 0188, front desk & casino 262 4102, www.luxor.com). Bus Deuce, 104, 105/self-parking & valet parking Reno Avenue. **Rooms** 4,407. **Rates** $69-$599 double. **Map** p336 A9 ⓩ
Second only to New York New York in terms of the absurdity of its exterior, the Luxor impresses on scale long before you've set foot inside it. While some casinos limit theming to the interiors, leaving the buildings as smart but not altogether memorable towers, the 30-storey glass pyramid housing much of the Luxor makes one hell of a first impression. At night, a high-intensity light shoots skywards from the top; visible in space, it's also a beacon to a swarm of insects and bats during warmer months.

The homage to ancient Egypt continues inside, but to a far lesser extent than it did when the casino opened in 1993. The campiest elements of the theming evaporated years ago, but even more Egyptiana was mummified during a still-ongoing renovation that began in 2006, lending credence to rumours that the casino may rebrand itself as the Pyramid. The enjoyably silly King Tut Museum remains, but the theming around the pool has been toned down, and several of the hotel's Egyptian-slanted bars and restaurants have gone.

Accommodation

Only around half of the hotel's 4,407 guestrooms are actually located in the pyramid. These Strip-fronted rooms offer great views and are accessed by special elevators called 'inclinators', which rise, like enclosed ski lifts, at an angle of 39°. However, there are compensations if you don't get hooked up with a pyramid room: the guestrooms in the towers, just behind the pyramid, are larger.

Eating & drinking

The eating options here are best described as reliable. The Luxor Steakhouse and the Pharaoh's Pheast buffet both have good reputations and are probably the best bets in the casino. Elsewhere, the Backstage Deli apes New York Jewish food as only an Egyptian-themed casino in Nevada can, while Fusia offers upmarket Asian dishes. Burgers, pizzas and expensive coffees are available at the food court.

Entertainment

Supremely dislikeable prop comic Carrot Top features, along with magician Criss Angel's show, combined with the inevitable help of Cirque du Soleil. Late-night entertainment is provided by the underdressed dancers of the Fantasy revue (*see p228*). Überhip Los Angeles club LAX has an outpost inside the casino.

CONSUME

Gambling

The massive casino, decorated with hieroglyphics and ancient artefacts, is filled with the latest high-tech slot and video-poker machines. Expect $10 minimums at blackjack and craps, higher on weekends. For poker players, the card room offers weekend action so lively that Cleopatra herself would have been impressed. Take a few minutes to walk the perimeter of the circular casino and get your bearings; if you can't identify landmarks, you'll wind up going in circles.

Amenities *Bars (3). Business centre. Concierge. Disabled-adapted rooms. Gym. Internet (Wi-Fi $11.99). No-smoking floors. Pool (outdoor). Restaurants (6). Room service. Spa. TV: pay movies.*
Games *Big Six; blackjack ($10-$10,000); Caribbean stud; casino war; craps (3x, 4x, 5x; from $5); keno; Let it Ride; pai gow poker; poker (14 tables); roulette (single zero & double zero); three-card poker. Gambling lessons (poker 2pm daily).*

★ MGM Grand

3799 Las Vegas Boulevard South, at E Tropicana Avenue, Las Vegas, NV 89109 (reservations 1-877 880 0880, front desk & casino 891 7777, www.mgmgrand.com). Bus Deuce, 201/self-parking Las Vegas Boulevard South, Koval Avenue or E Tropicana Avenue/valet parking E Tropicana Avenue. **Rooms** 6,852. **Rates** $109-$499 double. **Map** p336 A8 ⑮

There is a spa here, of course. Not to mention a pool, a convention centre and a kid-friendly animal attraction (the popular Lion Habitat; *see p70*). However,

the MGM Grand really comes alive after dark, when this immense resort is at its vibrant, buzzing best.

For a time, the largest hotel on earth (with, it should be said, one of the ugliest exteriors) aimed itself squarely at families. When Vegas fashion started to move back towards the adult market, the MGM was by no means quickest to react. However, it's since thrown itself into the grown-up market with commitment and smarts, building an unlikely but deserved reputation as one of the liveliest resorts on the Strip. Billing itself as 'Maximum Vegas' takes the point a bit far, but there's little doubt that the MGM balances the needs of cash-happy big spenders, easygoing middle Americans and youthful club kids as well as any resort in the city does. *Photo p120.*

Accommodation

The 5,044 rooms (including 751 increasingly plush suites) in the main building are mostly done out with art deco-styled furnishings, designed to evoke back-lot bungalows from Hollywood's glamour age. They manage it pretty well, too, though you suspect Clark Gable and Louise Brooks would sooner be down the street at the Wynn. A fourth-floor guest services desk functions as an additional concierge, a massive plus in this huge hotel.

However, the real luxury is elsewhere on the lot. First to arrive was the Mansion, which contains 29 handsomely appointed and even more handsomely priced villas. In 2005, the hotel added 51 Skylofts, vast and chic two-storey accommodations designed by Tony Chi that remain among the town's more fashionable temporary addresses. And then there's the Signature, a luxurious condo-hotel development

CONSUME

Luxor.

CONSUME

MGM Grand. *See p119.*

with three 576-suite towers. Rooms have jacuzzi tubs and balconies; guests also get access to private pool areas, among other perks.

Eating & drinking
Quietly, steadily and with great savvy, the MGM Grand has spent the last ten years reinventing its once-moribund dining to the point where it now contains the best and most varied range of restaurants in the city. Many casinos make the 'something for everyone' claim about their eating options; the MGM comes closer than any to fulfilling the brief.

You can't move here for all the celebrity chefs, or at least the assistants who quietly do their bidding for them. The flagship operation is Joël Robuchon, devised by the notoriously inventive French chef; those diners unable to stretch to the $360 16-course tasting menu may prefer the fractionally more casual L'Atelier de Joël Robuchon. Among the high-end options are Tom Colicchio's Craftsteak, where the focus is on meat, fish and fowl from small farms; Fiamma, an Italian trattoria imported from New York; Japanese restaurant Shibuya and the all-Chinese Pearl; and two Michael Mina operations, Californian-style eaterie Nobhill and seafood haven Seablue.

Other star names with a toe in the MGM's restaurant pool include Cajun specialist Emeril Lagasse (Emeril's) and Wolfgang Puck (at the laid-back Wolfgang Puck Bar & Grill), both of which are very good options. Meanwhile, Diego deals in excellent Mexican food, while there's slightly more casual fare at the Rainforest Café, Colicchio's 'Wichcraft, the Stage Deli and the Grand Wok & Sushi Bar, which shares a kitchen with the 24-hour coffeeshop. The buffet is one of the best on the Strip.

Like its nightclubs Studio 54 and Tabú, the MGM's bars tend towards the hipper end of the scale. The splashiest is Centrifuge, with a large central bar upon which dancers sometimes do their thang. Zuri, a cigar bar of sorts, and the open-plan Rouge are more sophisticated options.

Entertainment
The entertainment options at the MGM are led, as is fast becoming customary in Las Vegas casinos, by Cirque du Soleil. The fourth Cirque production to launch in the city, *Kà* is a spectacular, high-concept piece of dramatic fluff that plays in a vast theatre accessible towards the rear of the main casino floor. The other full-time resident piece is *Crazy Horse Paris*, an adult show that nonetheless aims at a rather different audience than the Crazy Horse Too strip club on Industrial Road.

The 740-seat Hollywood Theatre hosts perhaps half a dozen acts on regular rotation for runs of anywhere from a week to a month. Ticket prices are high, but you're paying a premium for the privilege of seeing such big names as David Copperfield and Tom Jones in intimate confines. Intimacy isn't a word generally associated with the 16,800-seat MGM Grand Garden Arena, which stages a mix of concerts (the Police, Rush, Justin Timberlake and the like) and sporting events (boxing, ultimate fighting).

The nightlife here is strong and relentlessly fashionable. Studio 54 lacks the cocaine, celebrities and gay hookers that defined the New York original, but it's still a popular spot. Tabú continues to consolidate its reputation as the Strip's coolest lounge, though you'll pay for the privilege of sitting in it. Diego hosts Vida!, a Latin club, every Friday and Saturday.

Gambling

The MGM has four gaming areas (Entertainment, Hollywood, Monte Carlo and Sports) in which you'll find all the games, including Spanish 21. It's the largest casino in Las Vegas and boasts hundreds of tables. Table minimums can go down to $10 on weekdays, but most are higher; in the pit, you'll find $25 minimums and $15,000 maximums. There's also a large race and sports book with floor-to-ceiling screens, one of the best poker rooms in town, and 3,700 slots, from a nickel to $500.

Amenities Bars (7). Business centre. Concierge. Disabled-adapted rooms. Gym. Internet (Wi-Fi $11.99). No-smoking floors. Pool (outdoor). Restaurants (18). Room service. Spa. TV: pay movies.

Games Baccarat ($100-$15,000); Big Six; blackjack ($10-$10,000); Caribbean stud; casino war; craps (3x, 4x, 5x; from $5); keno; Let it Ride; mini baccarat ($25-$15,000); pai gow poker; pai gow tiles; poker (22 tables); roulette (single zero & double zero); Spanish 21; three-card poker.

Monte Carlo

3770 Las Vegas Boulevard South, between W Harmon & W Tropicana avenues, Las Vegas, NV 89109 (reservations 1-888 529 4828, front desk & casino 730 7777, www.montecarlo.com). Bus Deuce, 201/self-parking & valet parking Rue de Monte Carlo. Rooms 3,002. Rates $49-$599 double. Map p336 A8 ⑯

Modelled after the Place du Casino in (of course) Monte Carlo, this handsome but low-key resort is an appealing, mid-range option. The many attractive features, not least of which is the impressive exterior architecture (twin archway entrances, a big streetside fountain), suggest this $344-million resort might be on the same page as, say, the $1.4-billion Bellagio. The truth is that the Monte Carlo appeals to those after an approximation of high style at low prices.

Next to its neighbours, the Monte Carlo isn't an especially charismatic option, less energetic than New York New York and nothing like as fashionable as the MGM Grand. Still, its lack of flash and filigree is just what its admirers like about the hotel, which seems very popular with business travellers. The casino floor is about as mellow as they come, thanks to the bright lighting and high ceilings, and the rooms are simple and familiar. Attractions include not rollercoasters or animal shows but a waterfall-filled pool area. The front desk's picture windows look over the verdant water park, giving the best lobby view in town. *Photo p123.*

Accommodation

The Monte Carlo's tri-tower set-up contains 3,002 rooms, including 259 suites. The standard rooms exhibit a comfortable, vaguely old-world feel, with cherrywood furniture and plump furnishings. The decor gets progressively more opulent the further up the price scale you climb.

Eating & drinking

The Monte Carlo's signature eaterie is André's, the sole Strip location of André Rochat's venerable Downtown establishment. The name of the spacious, industrial-styled Monte Carlo Brewpub has been a little misleading since it stopped brewing its own beer, but never mind. There's also a steakhouse (Blackstone's), a casual Italian trattoria (Market City Caffè), the requisite 24-hour coffeeshop and buffet, and the Dragon Noodle Company.

Entertainment

A pianist plays from Thursday to Sunday in Houdini's Lounge.

Gambling

There are plenty of $5 blackjack tables and many 5¢ opportunities among the 2,200 slots, and a bright, casual atmosphere. Players appreciate the details: stools with backs at every machine, wide walkways throughout the casino and even single-zero roulette. The Monte Carlo attracts brisk traffic from neighbouring casinos, but the tables never seem crowded. Players stand a better chance of landing a one-on-one blackjack game with the dealer than at most Strip resorts.

Amenities Bars (3). Business centre. Concierge. Disabled-adapted rooms. Gym. Internet ($11.99). No-smoking floors. Pool (outdoor). Restaurants (8). Room service. Spa.

Games Baccarat ($25-$15,000); Big Six; blackjack ($5-$3,000); Caribbean stud; craps (3x, 4x, 5x; from $5); keno; Let it Ride; mini baccarat ($10-$5,000); pai gow poker; pai gow tiles; poker (9 tables); roulette (single & double zero); three-card poker. Gambling lessons (craps 11am daily).

New York New York

3790 Las Vegas Boulevard South, at W Tropicana Avenue, Las Vegas, NV 89109 (reservations 1-866 815 4365, front desk & casino 740 6969, www.nynyhotelcasino.com). Bus Deuce, 201/self-parking Las Vegas Boulevard South or W Tropicana Avenue/valet parking W Tropicana Avenue. Rooms 2,023. Rates $69-$549 double. Map p336 A8 ⑰

So good they named it twice? Well, yes, as it goes. The most audacious, preposterous example of hotel theming in Las Vegas – and, for that matter, perhaps even the world – remains a thrilling success more than a decade after it welcomed its first guests. Built at a cost of $460 million, it's been called the largest piece of pop art in the world.

A mini-New York Harbor, complete with tug-boats, a scaled-down Brooklyn Bridge and a giant Statue of Liberty, looms over the Tropicana/Strip intersection. Above it, the resort's skyline includes a dozen of the Big Apple's most famous landmarks, among them the Empire State Building, the Chrysler Building and the New Yorker Hotel but not the

World Trade Center; the hotel was themed after 1950s New York, long before the twin towers were built. Inside, along with representations of Times Square, Central Park, Greenwich Village and Wall Street, you'll find every New York cliché in the book: a Broadway subway station, graffitied mailboxes, steam rising from manhole covers… It sounds silly, but it's tremendous fun, and seems to inspire visitors to act as if they were out on the East Coast: it's got energy like no other casino floor in town.

The resort's greatest trick, one that New York City has yet to achieve, is to balance the needs of adult visitors with those of its younger guests. Grown-ups will enjoy the nightlife here, not to mention Cirque du Soleil's adult-oriented show *Zumanity* (see p227), but there's plenty for the young 'uns. The Coney Island Emporium (see p70) is nirvana for kids and wanna-be-kids-again, a mix of old-fashioned midway games, high-tech interactive videos and virtual-reality rollercoasters. The hotel's real rollercoaster, the Manhattan Express (see p71), twists, turns and rolls around the property. The pool and spa are, alas, real letdowns: a replica of the famous Vertical Club would have been fitting. Or, perhaps, the Central Park Reservoir. *Photo p124.*

Accommodation
NYNY's rooms are concealed behind (but not in) an assortment of towers and skyscrapers. The rooms are done fairly nicely, in art deco-styled woods with black accents, and are maintained to a high standard. Although they're pretty small, they're bargains in comparison to some of their Strip competitors, especially during the week. Check when you make your booking that the Manhattan Express doesn't rumble by your window, or you'll be continually disturbed by the squeals of riders.

Eating & drinking
The restaurants aren't a match for those in the city on which they're modelled, but if they lack subtlety (and they do), they're at least a vibrant bunch. The smartest by far is Gallagher's Steakhouse, a Big Apple import; there's also competent Italian at Il Fornaio, reasonable Mexican at Gonzalez y Gonzalez and serviceable Chinese at Chin-Chin. Nine Fine Irishmen is a rather hokey but locally popular Irish pub, while the sports-themed ESPN Zone is located by the sports book and gets rammed on game days. A food court fashioned after Greenwich Village (cobblestone streets, a subway station, apartment buildings) contains burgers, pizzas and fried fish, though – disappointingly – no knishes. However, the best eating option is the most straightforward: America, a 24-hour coffeeshop that delivers average-to-excellent renditions of dishes from all over the 50 states.

Entertainment
NYNY's leading show is Cirque du Soleil's *Zumanity*, an intriguing but only partly successful

attempt at mixing Cirque's ever-dazzling acrobatics with the sexiness of the Strip-standard adult revue. After Rita Rudner moved to Harrah's, the casino decided to replace her with a roster of temporary engagements, though it's rumoured that the space may be turned into a nightclub. The other entertainments are all participatory: duelling piano players lead boozy singalongathons all night, every night at the Bar at Times Square, while Coyote Ugly is a loud, lairy nightclub modelled on the film (which was, in turn, modelled on a New York City bar) of the same name. The Big Apple Bar, inspired by the supper clubs of the '30s, is a tad more sophisticated.

Gambling
The capacious casino is modelled on Central Park, without the muggers but with twice the crowds. Minimums for blackjack (practically all six-deck shoes) and craps are $10; it's $5 for roulette. The range of slots is one of the best on the Strip. Dim sum hors-d'oeuvres are served in the Asian-styled Dragon Pit, with saké, plum wine, Asian beer and teas.

Amenities *Bars (6). Business centre. Concierge. Disabled-adapted rooms. Gym. Internet ($11.99). No-smoking floors. Pool (outdoor). Restaurants (8). Room service. Spa.*
Games *Blackjack ($5-$5,000); Caribbean stud; casino war; craps (3x, 4x, 5x; from $10); Let it Ride; mini baccarat ($10-$5,000); pai gow poker; roulette (double zero); three-card poker. Gambling lessons (craps 11am daily).*

Planet Hollywood
3667 Las Vegas Boulevard South, between E Harmon Avenue & E Flamingo Road, Las Vegas, NV 89109 (reservations 1-877 333 9474, front desk & casino 785 5555, www.planethollywood resort.com). Bus Deuce, 202/self-parking & valet parking E Harmon Avenue. **Rooms** 2,600. **Rates** $69-$499 double. **Map** p336 A7 ⑬
The Aladdin rubbed its magic lamp for the last time in spring 2007 and out popped Planet Hollywood, a rather hipper casino version of the restaurant chain. Amenities include the Planet Hollywood Spa by Mandara, which promises to ready guests for their 15 minutes of fame; the adjacent Miracle Mile Shops (see p196), a galleria of familiar shops (Urban Outfitters, H&M) and eateries (Trader Vic's, Hawaiian Tropic Zone); and a modernised theatre. *Photos p126.*

Accommodation
Planet Hollywood's 2,600 movie-themed rooms and suites are done out in what is known as 'Hollywood hip' decor: contemporary shades of rich chocolate and royal purple, Googie-esque carpet and techie amenities such as high-definition plasma TVs.

PH Towers Westgate is a residential tower and boutique hotel located next to Planet Hollywood. The 56-storey building contains 1,201 suites ranging in size from 400- to 950-sq ft

CONSUME

Monte Carlo. *See p121.*

Eating & drinking

The new and improved dining scene features the obligatory slew of celebrity restaurateurs, including Alfredo of Rome, famous for creating the original fettuccine Alfredo; the Japanese-Californian fusion cuisine of Koi, already a haven for Hollywood's A-list; Yolos, a Mexican eatery complete with margarita fountain; and the Glazier family's Strip House, a sexy steakhouse that's anything but traditional. Smaller bites are served at the Earl of Sandwich, Pink's is famous for its hot dogs; and Planet Dailies is a high-energy coffeeshop. Polynesian-themed Trader Vic's and David Burke's Hawaiian Tropic Zone have joined beach-themed burger joint Cheeseburger at the Oasis in the Miracle Mile Shops (*see p196*). And the Spice Market Buffet is still one of the best in town, serving a variety of ethnic dishes (including many vegetarian options).

Entertainment

It's adults-only with *Peepshow*, that old Vegas staple, the topless review. And the ladies aren't left out either, with male revue *American Storm*. The Amazing Johnathan is magic strictly for grownups, while *Tony 'n' Tina's Wedding* re-creates the nuptials of a stereotypical Italian American family. Correspondents from TV's *Extra* interview celebrities from their new Vegas headquarters, the Extra Lounge. Privé and the Living Room, imports from South Beach, add a little sizzle.

Gambling

The years-long transition from the Aladdin into Planet Hollywood has reconfigured the casino endlessly. Well-heeled players frequent the high-limit pit on the second floor: the salon features 30 high-limit tables, including blackjack, roulette and baccarat, and 100 high-denomination slot machines.
Amenities *Bars (3). Business centre.*
Concierge. Disabled-adapted rooms. Gym. Internet (Wi-Fi $11.99). No-smoking floors. Pool (outdoor). Restaurants (7). Room service. Spa. TV: pay movies

Games *Baccarat ($100-$15,000); Big Six; blackjack ($5-$3,000); Caribbean stud; casino war; craps (3x, 4x, 5x; from $5); keno; Let it Ride; mini baccarat ($25-$5,000); pai gow poker; poker (10 tables); roulette (single zero & double zero). Gambling lessons (baccarat, blackjack, craps, poker & roulette 10am Mon-Fri).*

TI (Treasure Island)

3300 Las Vegas Boulevard South, at Spring Mountain Road, Las Vegas, NV 89109 (reservations 1-800 288 7206, front desk & casino 894 7111, www.treasureisland.com). Bus Deuce, 105, 203/self-parking or valet parking Las Vegas Boulevard South or Spring Mountain Road. **Rooms** *2,885.* **Rates** *$79-$999 double.*
Map p335, p336 A6 ⓲

An object lesson in what happens when you slavishly follow focus groups rather than your own commercial instincts. Treasure Island has struggled with an identity crisis in recent years – We're *Pirates of the Caribbean*! No, we're Robinson Crusoe! We're for families! No, adults! – and hasn't yet managed to make the transition from kid-friendly operation to more lucrative adult playground. Much of the campy pirate paraphernalia that lingered around the casino, leftovers from its original incarnation as a family resort, has been buried. But the general aesthetic doesn't quite match the fine assortment of adult-oriented shows, nightclubs and restaurants that the hotel has brought in to try and reposition itself in the market. It's not exactly helped by its signature event: the pyrotechnic pirate battle in the lagoon out front, which has dropped the kid-friendly content, employed some scantily clad women and rebranded itself *Sirens of TI*. It might be the most embarrassing and undignified spectacle in North America.

Still, though the hotel amounts to less than the sum of its parts, those parts are interesting and inviting enough to make Treasure Island an appealing option. The new line-up of restaurants is worlds better than what came before, as is the

CONSUME

New York New York. *See p121.*

nightlife. For those who think not of gimlets but of golf when they hear the word 'club', the hotel offers access to the exclusive Shadow Creek course, a perk reserved for guests of MGM Mirage resorts. The Wet Spa is disappointing, but the pool is a good one, surprisingly unheralded in the city. And though Treasure Island has little shopping to speak of on its own property, a pedestrian bridge provides easy access to the adjacent Fashion Show Mall (*see p197*).

Accommodation
The 2,885 rooms in TI's 36-storey Y-shaped tower are good enough for the price, decorated in appealing shades and without any undue ornamentation. Many have decent views of the Mirage volcano and the *Sirens* show below. The 220 suites are spacious, with living rooms, wet bars, two baths, jacuzzis and impressive TVs; they're a good deal if you feel like splashing out but not breaking the bank.

Eating & drinking
There's northern Italian fare at Francesco's and hunks of meat at the Steakhouse, two essentially by-rote Strip eateries that offer special packages combining dinner with tickets for Cirque du Soleil's *Mystère*, and snacks from Starbucks, Ben & Jerry's and Krispy Kreme. However, there are also plenty more charismatic options on site; indeed, the hotel's ongoing reinvention has been at its most successful when applied to its restaurants. The highlight is indisputably the Social House, a sleek, chic sushi bar located above Tangerine and operated by the all-conquering Pure group. Richard Sandoval's buzzing Mexican spot Isla, which offers a similar *Mystère* deal to the Steakhouse and Francesco's,

and the surprisingly interesting menu at the 24-hour Coffee Shop merit investigation. Other options include the obligatory buffet, a shiny offshoot of LA's Canter's Deli, and the slightly tacky Kahunaville.

Entertainment
Though the captivating pitch and tumble of Cirque du Soleil's *Mystère* is still good G-rated fun, the rest of TI's offerings run to more lascivious tastes. Along with *Sirens of TI*, the hotel has jumped on the burlesque bandwagon with Tangerine, where would-be exotic dancers do a tame bump and grind to live music and shimmy down to decorative undies at 9.30pm and 10.30pm (Thur-Sat only). The martini crowd shakes things up at Mist, the small, clubby lounge brought to you by the folks behind Bellagio's Light, Caramel and Fix.

Gambling
In the ever-crowded casino, you'll find all the usual games, as well as a race and sports book, but you're the one who's likely to be on the down side. As at the Mirage, table limits are high and six-deck shoes are the rule, but you can still find a few video-poker machines with good payback percentages.
Amenities *Bars (5). Business centre. Concierge. Disabled-adapted rooms. Gym. Internet (Wi-Fi $11.99). No-smoking floors. Pool (outdoor). Restaurants (11). Room service. Spa.*
Games *Baccarat ($100-$15,000); blackjack ($5-$15,000); Caribbean stud; casino war; craps (3x, 4x, 5x; from $5); keno; Let it Ride; mini baccarat ($25-$10,000); pai gow poker; pai gow tiles; poker (8 tables); roulette (double zero); Spanish 21; three-card poker.*

Budget

Bill's Gamblin' Hall & Saloon

3595 Las Vegas Boulevard South, at E Flamingo Road, Las Vegas, NV 89109 (reservations 1-866 245 5745, front desk & casino 737 2100, www.billslasvegas.com). Bus Deuce, 202/self-parking & valet parking Las Vegas Boulevard South. **Rooms** 200. **Rates** $59-$199 double. **Map** p336 A7 ⓴

Previously the Barbary Coast, a cosy slice of fin-de-siècle San Francisco with a prime mid-Strip location, the property was bought by Harrah's and renamed in 2007 for the firm's founder Bill Harrah. The casino remains atmospheric, done out with stained-glass and chandeliers.

Accommodation
You'll be pleasantly surprised by the Victorian wallpaper and paintings, etched mirrors and white lace curtains in the 200 guestrooms, some of which have four-poster brass beds, minibars and whirlpool tubs.

Eating & drinking
The Steakhouse at Bill's is the onsite eaterie.

Entertainment
Pete Vallee aka Big Elvis – you won't believe quite how big – plays in Bill's Lounge.

Gambling
This little Strip casino doesn't look like much, but it packs a decent punch: the casino often has lower minimums than its enormous neighbours. **Amenities** *Bars (2). Disabled-adapted rooms. Internet (Wi-Fi $10.99). No-smoking rooms. Restaurants (3). Room service. TV: pay movies.* **Games** *Blackjack ($5-$1,000); Caribbean stud; casino war; craps (3x, 4x, 5x; from $5); keno; pai gow poker; roulette (double zero); three-card poker. Gambling lessons (craps 10.30am daily).*

Casino Royale

3411 Las Vegas Boulevard South, between Sands Avenue & E Flamingo Road, Las Vegas, NV 89109 (reservations 1-800 854 7666, front desk & casino 737 3500, www.casino royalehotel.com). Bus Deuce, 105, 202, 203, self-parking Las Vegas Boulevard South/ no valet parking. **Rooms** 152. **Rates** $49-$179 double. **Map** p335, p336 A6 ㉑

Virtually the forgotten resort on the Strip, this independently operated, 152-room casino has nothing to do with the James Bond movie of the same name. Rather, it's a truly basic little casino-hotel that survives despite being surrounded by the city's major players. Favoured by budget travellers after cheap minimums and even cheaper drinks, it's a cheery place without much charisma but with plenty of value.

Accommodation
As you might expect from the cut-price room rates, the rooms here aren't anything special: they're basically motel-standard, though the handy mid-Strip location makes the ideal base from which to explore the city.

Eating & drinking
The Outback Steakhouse and Denny's are the closest things to signature restaurants here. The most notable feature of the bar is the dollar beers it offers around the clock.

Entertainment
You'll have to make your own here.

Gambling
There's not much to say about this place, though the minimums are low and it's the only casino on the Strip to offer 100x odds for craps, reducing the house edge to a mere 0.02%. **Amenities** *Bar. Disabled-adapted rooms. No-smoking floors. Pool (outdoor). Restaurants (2).* **Games** *Blackjack ($5-$1,000); Caribbean stud; craps (100x; from $3); keno; roulette (double zero); Spanish 21.*

Circus Circus

2880 Las Vegas Boulevard South, between Desert Inn Road & W Sahara Avenue, Las Vegas, NV 89109 (reservations 1-877 434 9175, front desk & casino 734 0410, www.circuscircus.com). Bus Deuce/self-parking S Industrial Road/valet parking Las Vegas Boulevard South or S Industrial Road. **Rooms** 3,773. **Rates** $39-$399 double. **Map** p335 B5 ㉒

When MGM Mirage purchased additional plots of land bordering Circus Circus, many in town muttered that it must be just a matter of time before Lucky the Laughing Clown is asked to fold up his Big Top and beat it. After all, he's been luring tourists into this garish casino for more than 40 years, a lifetime by Vegas standards, and not much has changed. Sure, MGM Mirage could ask performers from Cirque du Soleil to perform on the stage above the casino, and the carnie-style midway could be transformed into a futuristic arcade. But then there's a risk that the place would end up unrecognisable from its famous turn in *Fear and Loathing in Las Vegas*, and who wants that? *Photo p127.*

Accommodation
After several expansions, there are now 3,773 spartan rooms, mainly decorated with soft-blue carpeting, pastel bedspreads and upholstery, and dark wood furniture. The West Tower is the newest (built in 1997); the cheapest (and oldest) rooms are in the motel-like Manor section. Ask for a south-facing room in the Skyrise Tower for the best view of the Strip. Other amenities include pools and the 399-space Circusland RV Park.

Planet Hollywood. *See p122.*

CONSUME

Eating & drinking

The Steak House is a surprisingly high-quality dining room, while Mexitalia Xpress serves both Italian and Mexican. The Circus Buffet is mediocre, but its cheapness ensures its popularity.

Entertainment

Circus Circus never had a showroom; it no longer even has the G-string-clad pony girls, who used to ride plastic ponies on a ceiling-hung track, tossing balloons at the kiddies. But the midway and circus acts remain: acrobats, trapeze artists and magicians perform every half-hour (11am-midnight). The 23 rides and attractions at the Adventuredome (*see p78*) include Nickelodeon's Spongebob SquarePants 4-D thrill ride, a rollercoaster, a carousel and bumper cars. A must at Halloween, when the Adventuredome turns into the mega-haunted house (with rides in the dark) for the month of October.

Gambling

Connected by walkways and a monorail, each of the three casinos offers the same gaming options. The race book is located near the back of the resort, in the Skyways Tower area. A five-dollar bill is enough to get you started at most tables; it might take all day to find someone risking more than $10. You'll probably want to hide out in the casino; the rest of this place is a pre-pubescent madhouse.

Amenities *Bars (3). Business centre. Disabled-adapted rooms. Gym. No-smoking floors. Pool (outdoor). Restaurants (8). Spa.*

Games *Big Six; blackjack ($3-$3,000); Caribbean stud; casino war; craps (2x; from $3); keno; Let it Ride; pai gow poker; poker (8 tables); roulette (double zero); three-card poker. Gambling lessons (blackjack, craps, roulette 10.30am Mon-Fri).*

Excalibur

3850 Las Vegas Boulevard South, at W Tropicana Avenue, Las Vegas, NV 89109 (reservations 1-877 750 5464, front desk & casino 597 7777, www.excalibur.com). Bus Deuce, 201/self-parking & valet parking W Tropicana Avenue. **Rooms** 3,991. **Rates** $41-$501 double. **Map** p336 A8 ㉓

The jury's still out on whether or not this caricature of a castle will become the next generation's Circus Circus. MGM Mirage has been too busy transforming the pirate-themed Treasure Island and the Polynesian-tilted Mirage into hipper versions of their former selves, leaving Excalibur to fend for itself. However, there have been a few changes of note, in particular the addition of dining and entertainment options that eschew the family-friendly theme: a biker bar, the silly Dick's Last Resort, and the 'edgy' comedy of everyone's favourite fat guy, Louie Anderson. Identity crisis, anyone?

Accommodation

Housed in two towers behind the castle façade, the small rooms have none of the elegance of the hotel's adjacent sister resorts, the Luxor and Mandalay Bay. But a handful of spacious Parlor Suites have guest bathrooms, dining and living areas; with bold colours, dark wood furniture and wrought-iron fixtures, they're nowhere near as drab as those at Circus Circus.

Eating & drinking
Tops among the restaurants is Sir Galahad's Pub & Prime Rib House, where you'll find generous portions of prime rib and Yorkshire pudding. The Steakhouse at Camelot serves decent cuts, while Regale dishes out pastas. At biker-themed Octane, bartenders serve up such cocktails as Blood, Sweat & Gears and Tailpipe Wind, while Dick's Last Resort is a playfully tacky watering hole that serves massive cocktails and finger foods by the bucket. There's also a children's menu at the 24-hour Sherwood Forest Café and an extensive Round Table Buffet.

Entertainment
The medieval (and still child-friendly) orientation extends into the night with the entertaining Tournament of Kings, which features jousting, pyrotechnics and a surprisingly decent dinner. The Fantasy Faire Midway keeps children busy with two Magic Motion Machine film rides, medieval-themed midway games and an arcade. Comic Louie Anderson and hilarious male revue Thunder from Down Under provide adult-oriented fare.

Gambling
Neon knights slay neon dragons in the casino, one of the few in town where photography is allowed. Visitors are surrounded by images of playing-card kings and queens, but the table games are affordable for any commoner. Thousands of slots jam the joint; video poker is scarcer. When you're done throwing coins in machines, toss a few in the moat for good luck: they'll be donated to local charities.
Amenities Bars (4). Disabled-adapted rooms. Gym. Internet ($10.95). No-smoking floors. Pool (outdoor). Restaurants (7). Spa.
Games Blackjack ($5-$2,000); Caribbean stud; casino war; craps (3x, 4x, 5x; from $5); keno; Let it Ride; mini baccarat ($10-$2,000); pai gow poker; poker (14 tables); roulette (double zero); Spanish 21; three-card poker. Gambling lessons (blackjack, roulette 10.30am daily; poker 2pm daily).

INSIDE TRACK CHEF

When Comedy Central wanted Chef from the animated series *South Park* to have worked in a Vegas buffet, they chose the super-cheap, super-mediocre Circus Buffet at **Circus Circus** (*see p125*), famous for feeding up to 10,000 hungry souls a day.

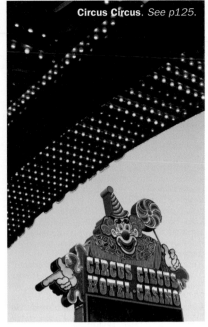
Circus Circus. *See p125.*

CONSUME

Hooters
115 E Tropicana Avenue, between Las Vegas Boulevard South & Koval Lane, Las Vegas, NV 89109 (reservations 1-866 584 6687, front desk & casino 739 9000, www.hchvegas.com). Bus Deuce, 201/self-parking & valet parking E Tropicana Avenue. **Rooms** 696. **Rates** $39-$399 double. **Map** p336 B6 ❷❹
How does the hotel version of Hooters differ from the restaurants familiar across middle America? Simple: instead of a handful of hot female service-industry workers in skimpy orange outfits, here there are dozens (200, if you're counting). At the bar, at the blackjack table, by the pool... even at the hotel's very own Hooters restaurant. If you (or your spouse) don't appreciate this amenity, stay somewhere else.

Accommodation
There are 696 rooms (including 17 suites); the standard ones are comfortable and take a beach-house theme. The pool is paradisical and the spa is a full-service operation with a workout room.

Eating & drinking
Cuisine here begins and ends with chicken wings, of course, but in between are a couple of fun surprises. Dan Marino (yes, the old Dolphins quarterback) has a slightly upscale restaurant that features dishes not included in his Nutrisystem diet plan. Pete &

Shorty's offers real Midwestern man cuisine (aka bar food), and the Dam Restaurant is a 24-7 café.

Entertainment
Hooters recently dumped its martini bar and turned it into a showroom for headliner Bobby Slayton, the 'Pit Bull of Comedy'. There's also live music at Nippers Pool Bar and the Porch Dogs club. Men of X provides equal opportunity leering time for the ladies.

Gambling
Hooters has struggled since it opened, which either explains or is a direct result of its tight casino (perhaps both). The blackjack has terrible rules: dealer hits soft 17, you can only double on 10 and 11, and all games pay 6:5 for naturals. Most tables have $10 or $25 minimums and some, mostly the ones in the Hooters Girls Fun Pit, are dealt by you know who. Beware of some of the video-poker schedules: they look typical, but some of the payouts are short. Craps isn't bad, with 3-5x odds and a field 12 paying triple. The players club returns a decent 1% for slot play and 0.5% for video poker, but only in comps: there's no cashback.

Amenities *Bars (4). Concierge. Disabled-adapted rooms. Gym. Internet ($12.95). No-smoking floors. Pool (outdoor). Restaurants (3). Room service. Spa. TV: pay movies.*
Games *Blackjack ($10-$2,000); craps (3x, 4x, 5x; from $10); keno; Let it Ride; pai gow poker; poker (3 tables); roulette (double zero); three-card poker.*

Riviera
2901 Las Vegas Boulevard South, between E Sahara Avenue & E Desert Inn Road, Las Vegas, NV 89109 (reservations 1-800 634 6753, front desk & casino 734 5110, www.rivierahotel.com). Bus Deuce, 108, 204/self-parking Riviera Boulevard or Paradise Road/valet parking Las Vegas Boulevard South. **Rooms** *2,100.* **Rates** $49-$199 double. **Map** p335 B5 ㉕
When the Riviera opened in 1955, Liberace headlined in its showroom. Though the original king of bling is long gone, the entertainment offerings at the Riv a half-century later are just as camp. The first high-rise hotel on the Strip continues to thumb its nose at family-style entertainment, staying true to its roots as an adult playground. Other throwbacks include two lighted tennis courts, an old-school pool (surrounded by hotel towers for too much shade) and guestrooms that haven't been dramatically upgraded for years. Still, there remains a market for this sort of hotel: unrepentantly old-fashioned, basic and – key to the entire operation's continued viability – cheap.

Accommodation
There are 2,100 rooms on five levels, two floors being all suites. The standard rooms are all in the original tower, while the deluxe rooms (better views) and suites are in the two newer towers. The newer tower rooms are smallish but not cramped, and decorated with dark wood furniture. Half the rooms have views over the pool; the rest face the surrounding mountains. Don't expect much – well, anything, to be honest – in the way of luxury.

Eating & drinking
As at most middlebrow resorts, there are a couple of smarter restaurants and a handful of low-end ones. At the top, there's Ristorante Italiano and Kristofer's Steakhouse, though the specials at Kady's coffeeshop are better bargains. Elsewhere, Hound Doggies tilts at a 1950s diner vibe, the World's Fare Buffet offers a range of international food, and the food court contains such staples as Pizza Hut and KFC.

Entertainment
Both of the two signature shows, and creaking topless fandango *Crazy Girls*, have been in residence five minutes short of forever. The Riviera Comedy Club presents two shows nightly, with a new line-up every week, while the once-swinging Le Bistro Lounge now runs a roster of shows that include Neil Diamond impersonator Jay White, comedy hypnotist Dr Scott Lewis and American Storm, a kind of cut-price Chippendales. The SynCity nightclub doesn't give the Palms any sleepless nights.

Gambling
The gaming area is an L-shaped expanse of red and mock gold with an elevated lounge and bar in the

Riviera.

centre (your best bet for a meeting place that everyone can find). Minimums at the tables are not as low as the surroundings would suggest: $5-$10 blackjack in a $2 setting. The lowest limits and nickel slots are found in a part of the casino dubbed Nickel Town, a plausible nickname for the whole resort.

Amenities *Bars (2). Business centre. Disabled-adapted rooms. Gym. Internet (Wi-Fi $9.99). No-smoking floors. Pool (outdoor). Restaurants (4). Room service. Spa. TV: pay movies.*
Games *Blackjack ($5-$2,000); Caribbean stud; craps (2x; from $5); keno; Let it Ride; mini baccarat ($25-$2,000); pai gow poker; poker (8 tables); roulette (double zero); Spanish 21; three-card poker. Gambling lessons (poker 2pm daily).*

Stratosphere

2000 Las Vegas Boulevard South, at W St Louis Avenue, Las Vegas, NV 89104 (reservations 1-800 998 6937, front desk & casino 380 7777, www.stratospherehotel.com). Bus Deuce, 108/self-parking & valet parking Las Vegas Boulevard South. **Rooms** 2,444. **Rates** $35-$319 double.
Map p335 C4 ㉖

The Stratosphere strives to be a destination resort out of necessity: it's between the Strip and Fremont Street, essentially no-man's land. Its lure starts at the summit, with a variety of rides atop the highest freestanding observation tower in the US (1,149ft/107m). There are indoor and outdoor observation decks, a revolving restaurant, and thrill rides with names such as Insanity (*see p78*). Down below are some 40 Tower Shops (not exactly the Fashion Show Mall), a remodelled casino and even a nightclub.

Accommodation

Guestrooms in the tower would be interesting, but all the Stratosphere's sleeping quarters are in separate buildings below. Some are in the original Vegas World mid-rise; a more recent tower brought the total to 2,444 rooms and suites. There are an overwhelming 13 different types of room, from the smallish standard rooms to the massive Premier Suites. On the eighth floor, there's a big pool and recreation deck.

Eating & drinking

Eating options run from the pricey Top of the World, which rotates once every 90 minutes, to McDonald's. Among those in the middle are Lucky's, a 24-hour café, and Roxy's, which has a '50s diner motif and rock 'n' roll singing waiters.

Entertainment

As impersonator shows go, the Strat's *American Superstars* is pretty good. If you like semi-nudity in your Vegas shows, *Bite* offers it… and vampires too. On the tower, there's an indoor/outdoor observation deck, plus a trio of terrifying rides (*see p78*).

Gambling

The casino area is spacious and comfortable, if not particularly noteworthy. The layout approximates a series of circles, which looks good but seriously complicates any attempt to get directly from one end of the complex to the other. The emphasis is on liberal machines and table-game gimmicks, which go some way to improve players' odds. The Stratosphere advertises a 98% return on more than 150 $1 dollar slots, a 100% return on some video-poker machines and 10x odds on craps, as well as double-exposure blackjack and crapless craps (with a bunch of cockamamie rules that aren't player-friendly).

Amenities *Bars (7). Business centre. Concierge. Disabled-adapted rooms. Gym. Internet (Wi-Fi in some rooms $9.95). No-smoking floors. Pools (outdoor). Restaurants (5). Room service. Spa. TV: pay movies.*
Games *Big Six; blackjack ($5-$3,000); Caribbean stud; craps (10x; from $5); Let it Ride; mini baccarat ($5-$1,000); pai gow poker; poker (6 tables); roulette (single & double zero); three-card poker. Gambling lessons (roulette 10.30am daily; craps 11am daily).*

Tropicana

3801 Las Vegas Boulevard South, at E Tropicana Avenue, Las Vegas, NV 89109 (reservations 1-888 826 8767, front desk & casino 739 2222, www.tropicanalv.com). Bus Deuce, 201/self-parking & valet parking Las Vegas Boulevard South, E Tropicana Avenue or Reno Avenue. **Rooms** 1,878. **Rates** $45-$329 double.
Map p336 A8 ㉗

Recently renovated, with a fresh, South Beach Miami-themed look and feel, the Tropicana was at the heart of the biggest bidding war in casino history when, in 2006, Columbia Sussex (owner of various Westin, Sheraton and Marriott hotels) paid $2.75 billion for the rights to redevelop the 50-year-old 'Tiffany of the Strip'. The Trop is worth a look if you want a really nice pool – between the hotel's two towers lie five acres of tropical landscaping with pools, lagoons, waterfalls, heated jacuzzis and swim-up blackjack tables – without paying too much for it.

Accommodation

The original two-storey motor inn buildings surround the pool and are thus conveniently close to it; although they're the oldest at the resort, they can be comfortable if you get one with a balcony and a pool view. The newer tower rooms are generally of a better standard.

Eating & drinking

Biscayne Steak, Sea & Wine, a reinterpretation of the classic Las Vegas steakhouse, serves up a colossal shrimp cocktail and tasty prime rib. Other choices include Bacio for classic Italian cuisine, and

CONSUME

Tropicana. *See p129.*

the South Beach Marketplace, home to a branch of Starbucks and the Pellegrino Pizza & Deli.

Entertainment

Once home to the carefully old-fashioned feathers-and-sequins spectacular *Folies Bergere*, which folded its pretty wings and flew back to Paris just shy of its 50th anniversary, the Tropicana now hosts a standing gig by pop-soul-R&B royalty Gladys Knight (sans Pips). She shares the Tiffany Theatre stage with *Xtreme Magic Starring Dirk Arthur*. There's also the Comedy Stop, which has a weekly rotation of stand-ups. But the biggest draw has to be Bodies: the Exhibition (*see p70*), 21 meticulously dissected human bodies that put under the microscope what happens to the lungs and liver after one too many trips to Vegas.

Gambling

The swim-up blackjack bar is the Tropicana's one unique gaming pull. Otherwise, there's the usual variety of games, with a bit less video poker than other places and some of the slots showing their age. The casino is on the smallish side, and cramped, with a tiny, dingy sports book at the bottom of a stairway at the back, hidden as if the hotel were embarrassed by it. Which it should be. *Photo p130.*

Amenities *Bars (3). Business centre. Disabled-adapted rooms. Gym. Internet (Wi-Fi in tower rooms $11.95). No-smoking floors. Pool (indoor/outdoor). Restaurants (5). Room service. Spa. TV: pay movies.*
Games *Blackjack ($5-$3,000); Caribbean stud; craps (3x, 4x, 5x; from $5); keno; Let it Ride; pai gow poker; poker (6 tables); roulette (double zero); three-card poker. Gambling lessons (blackjack, craps, poker 10am Wed-Sat).*

NON-CASINO HOTELS

Expensive

Four Seasons

3960 Las Vegas Boulevard South, at W Hacienda Drive, Las Vegas, NV 89119 (reservations 1-800 819 5053, front desk & casino 632 5000, www. fourseasons.com/lasvegas). Bus Deuce, 104, 105/no self-parking/valet parking Las Vegas Boulevard South. **Rooms** 424. **Rates** $270-$610 double. **Map** p336 A9 ㉘
The first boutique hotel to open on the Strip remains its most popular. It has its own private driveway, entrance, lobby, valet and crack concierge staff, as well as an award-winning spa, landscaped gardens

surrounding a secluded pool, restaurants and lounges. The twist is that the 424 rooms and suites are located in the Mandalay Bay resort, though they're accessed by private elevators. Guests may use Mandalay Bay's facilities, as well as those within Thehotel at Mandalay Bay (*see p132*).

The guestrooms are spacious and luxurious, especially the large marble bathrooms with sunken jacuzzis and L'Occitane products. Extra points are garnered for superior service: complimentary cocktails greet guests upon arrival, and repeat guests have room keys waiting for them at valet, while families will find rooms child-proofed and stocked with age-appropriate amenities (nappies for babies, Playstations for older children). Joggers get chilled water and towels after exercising. Dining options include Charlie Palmer Steak (*see p156*) and the popular Verandah Café (*see p166*), which features Italian-influenced American fare.

Amenities *Bars (1). Business centre. Concierge. Disabled-adapted rooms. Gym. Internet (Wi-Fi, $10). No-smoking floors. Pool (outdoor). Restaurants (2). Room service. Spa. TV: DVD/pay movies.*

Mandarin Oriental

CityCenter, 3752 Las Vegas Boulevard South, at E Harmon Avenue, Las Vegas, NV 89109 (reservations 1-888 881 9578, front desk & casino 590 8888, www.mandarinoriental.com/lasvegas). Bus Deuce, 202. **Rooms** *392.* **Rates** *$285-$2,650 double.* **Map** *p336 A7* **㉙**

Luxury is the keyword at Vegas's Mandarin Oriental. Along with the first US restaurant by star chef Pierre Gagnaire, 27,000sq ft is devoted exclusively to a spa and salon. One unusual attribute – an Eastern idiosyncracy – is that its breathtaking Sky Lobby is located on the 23rd of its 47 floors.

Accommodation

The Mandarin Oriental's 392 guestrooms and suites range from 850sq ft to a spacious 3,100sq ft, offering views of the Strip and the surrounding mountains. The hotel is LEED Gold certified, and the rooms are graced with electronic controls that conserve energy while controlling room temperature, drapes, lighting and the entertainment systems, which include a 42-inch flatscreen HD TV, and another TV in the bathroom. That the bedding and linens are luxe goes without saying.

Eating & drinking

The hotel immediately made its mark on the Vegas fine-dining scene with the arrival of Twist by chef Pierre Gagnaire. The first US restaurant by the Michelin-starred chef, Twist offers classic French cuisine, with a modern, well, twist. The Mandarin Oriental also offers MOzen Bistro, with its pan-Asian cuisine, and the Pool Café, on the eighth-floor deck. The Tea Lounge, off the lobby on the 23rd floor, has a serene view of a city in constant motion.

Mandarin Oriental.

CONSUME

Amenities *Bars (5). Business centre. Concierge. Disabled-adapted rooms. Gym. Internet (Wi-Fi). No-smoking floors. Pools (2 outdoor; 2 indoor lap pools). Restaurants (5). Room service. Spa. TV: pay movies.*

Thehotel at Mandalay Bay

3950 Las Vegas Boulevard South, at W Hacienda Avenue, Las Vegas, NV 89119 (reservations 1-877 632 7800, front desk & casino 632 7777, www.mandalaybay.com). Bus Deuce, 104, 105/self-parking & valet parking W Hacienda Avenue. **Rooms** 1,117. **Rates** $159-$1,799 suite. **Map** p336 A9 ㉚

The rather clumsy name of this property has reputedly caused cab drivers no end of confusion, to the point where a change has been rumoured. The hotel itself, though, needs no such alterations. Located around the back of Mandalay Bay (follow the signs carefully), Thehotel has filled a gap in the market that most major cities have plugged with a W Hotel. Which is to say that it's chic without being too fashionable, and a big hit with hipsters in their late twenties while being careful not to exclude everyone else.

The rooms here are all suites, decorated in rich colours and furnished with chairs and beds that manage to be both stylish and extremely comfortable. The restaurants, shows and gaming at Mandalay Bay are a corridor away, but the handsome hotel lobby is slot-free. Atop the hotel tower is Alain Ducasse's ultra-posh restaurant Mix, and its attached lounge. The Bathhouse spa is also excellent. The whole place doesn't feel like Vegas, which, for many guests, is part of the appeal. Recommended.

Amenities *Bar. Business centre. Concierge. Disabled-adapted rooms. Gym. Internet ($12). No-smoking floors. Pools (outdoor). Restaurants (2). Room service. Spa. TV: pay movies.*

Trump International

3128 Las Vegas Boulevard South, between Spring Mountain & Desert Inn roads, Las Vegas, NV 89109 (www.trumplv.com). Bus Deuce, 203. **Rooms** 1,200. **Rates** $200-$700 double. **Map** p335 A5 ㉛

Trump International.

A joint venture between 'The Donald' and Phil Ruffin, the owner of next door's New Frontier, Trump's first Vegas property – instantly recognisable with its gilding – is as posh as its sister properties in New York and Florida. When Donald Trump revealed his plans to build a condo-hotel tower here on *The Apprentice*, the condos were all reserved within three weeks. It was no surprise when, in a subsequent episode, he announced plans to build a second tower a little further down the line. The 1,200-plus spacious condo guestrooms feature floor-to-ceiling windows, whirlpool tubs, plasma TVs (in the bathrooms too) and, of course, lots and lots of marble.

Amenities *Business centre. Concierge. Disabled-adapted rooms. Gym. Internet (Wi-Fi). No-smoking rooms. Pool (outdoor). Restaurants (2). Spa. TV: pay movies.*

Vdara

CityCenter, 2600 W Harmon Avenue, at Las Vegas Boulevard South, Las Vegas, NV 89109 (reservations 1-866 745 7767, front desk & casino 590 2030, www.vdara.com). Bus Deuce, 202. **Rooms** 1,495. **Rates** $139-$600 suite.
Map p336 A7 **⓫**

Vdara calls itself 'a non-gaming, non-smoking, eco-friendly, all-suite boutique,' and as part of the CityCenter complex that has changed the Strip's very centre of gravity, it exemplifies an all-new Vegas, and an entirely new way of thinking about the city. With no gaming and no shows or distracting attractions, and no restaurants, save a lobby coffee bar, it's a distinctly serene and relaxing environment at the racing heart of the Strip. If the peace gets too quiet, walkways connect Vdara to siblings Aria and Bellagio.

Its embracingly curvilinear 57-storey tower houses 1,495 suites. Along with being eco-conscious – it has the world's first fleet of stretch limousines powered by clean-burning compressed natural gas – Vdara is very art-aware: pieces from CityCenter's fine art collection are showcased, including Frank Stella's 32-foot-long *Damascus Gate Variation I* at reception, and, viewed from the porte-cochère, Nancy Rubin's installation *Big Edge*, which looks like what would happen if dozens of canoes were attracted by a giant magnet. *Photo p137.*

Accommodation
Vdara's gentle arc-shaped structure complements the curves of its next-door-neighbour, the Aria. The open-plan suites, which range from 526 to 1,750sq ft, include fully equipped kitchens and high-tech media hubs, and are sold as private residences; owners have the option to lease their units as hotel rooms when they are not in residence.
Amenities *Business centre. Concierge. Disabled-adapted rooms. Gym. Internet (Wi-Fi). No-smoking floors. Pools (outdoor). Room service. Spa. TV: pay movies.*

Off-Strip

HOTEL-CASINOS
Expensive

Hard Rock

4455 Paradise Road, at E Harmon Avenue, Las Vegas, NV 89109 (reservations 1-800 473 7625, front desk & casino 693 5000, www.hardrockhotel.com). Bus 108/self-parking Paradise Road/valet parking E Harmon Avenue. **Rooms** 647. **Rates** $99-$549 double.
Map p336 C7 **㉝**

The exact point at which rock 'n' roll sold its soul is a mystery, but you can bet the Hard Rock took a healthy cut. The image of Sid Vicious adorns slot machines, Bob Dylan's lyrics line the elevators, and a notice reminds guests that smart dress is required, a rule that would bar more or less every one of the casino's icons. Still, despite its blazingly middle-American appropriation of rock imagery, the Hard Rock has been an unqualified success since its 1995 opening. The golf-shooting, Dockers-wearing baby-boomer brigade is here in force midweek, but on weekends the hotel draws a crowd of boisterous fun-seekers, A-list glitterati and local hipsters.

The Palms may have stolen some of its thunder over the past few years, particularly on the nightlife front, but the Hard Rock remains a premier party place. The casino design (circular, with a bar in the middle) is a beauty, and means the place always feels buzzing even when it's half-empty. Out back, the pool scene is even hotter: sandy beaches, waterfalls and swim-up blackjack. Amenities include the RockSpa (hey, don't shoot the messenger), electric purple limos and SUVs for guests, some terrific restaurants and the coolest sundries boutique in town: selling everything from liquor to lube, it embodies the concept of the convenience store. *Photos p134.*

Accommodation
The casino itself may be like a zoo, but the upstairs guestrooms are remarkably peaceful and minimalist, with mod space-agey furnishings that are sort of *Jetsons* meets the I-Ching. And thanks largely to the fact that the Hard Rock was built relatively recently, they're also very spacious. Most rooms have been decorated with museum-quality photos of rock stars. Try to get digs overlooking the pool.

Eating & drinking
The Hard Rock really excels with its eating options: there are only five of them, but each one is well worth a visit. Nobu offers the city's best sushi, while AJ's Steakhouse gave a retro, twentysomething twist to the meat-beat formula long before it was fashionable to do so. Simon Kitchen & Bar dishes out high-concept, high-calibre American comfort food; the Pink Taco specialises in gentrified Mexican cooking,

CONSUME

Hard Rock. *See p133.*

while also boasting a kinetic early-evening bar scene; and Mr Lucky's 24/7 is the city's coolest coffeeshop. For people-watching, try the Center Bar, in the middle of the circular casino, and the Viva Las Vegas Lounge. In summer, head out to the pool bar, or to Sunday's raucous Rehab pool party.

Entertainment
When it opened a decade and a half ago, the 3,000-capacity Joint helped bust any lingering music-industry stigma about playing Vegas, and it remains one of the strongest music venues in the city. There's more music, albeit of a rather lower grade, in the Viva Las Vegas Lounge. After-hours, the party continues in Body English, a fantastically fashionable nightclub full of fantastically fashionable women and the men who (would like to) love them. Avoid *Beacher's Madhouse*, a sporadically star-studded but ultimately dull variety show hosted each month by indefatigable self-publicist Jeff Beacher.

Gambling
A mid-1990s beast it may be, but this is still a hip and extremely popular gambling den. The casino remains small by Vegas standards: only 800 slots and video-poker machines, and 76 tables. The main floor is one big circle, with an outer hardwood walkway and an elevated bar in the centre. Dealers are encouraged to be friendly and enthusiastic; some will even give you a high-five if you hit a natural blackjack, a stunt that would give the pit boss a heart attack anywhere else.
Amenities *Bars (7). Concierge. Disabled-adapted rooms. Gym. Internet (Wi-Fi $11.95). No-smoking rooms. Pool (outdoor). Restaurants (5). Room service. Spa. TV: pay movies.*
Games *Baccarat ($100-$3,000); blackjack ($10-$5,000); Caribbean stud; craps (3x, 4x, 5x; from $5); Let it Ride; mini baccarat ($5-$2,000); pai gow poker; roulette (double zero); three-card poker.*

Moderate

Las Vegas Hilton
3000 Paradise Road, between E Sahara Avenue & E Desert Inn Road, Las Vegas, NV 89109 (reservations 1-888 732 7117, front desk & casino 732 5111, www.lvhilton.com). Bus 108, 204, 213/self-parking Paradise Road or Joe W Brown Drive/valet parking Paradise Road. **Rooms** 3,000. **Rates** $59-$319 double. **Map** p335 C5 **㉞**
Given that it has the biggest stake in Vegas's convention business, it's no surprise that the Hilton is as self-sufficient as resorts come. There are 3,000 rooms, a smörgåsbord of fine restaurants and an endless list of amenities – a full-service spa, a rec deck with tennis courts, wedding facilities (the only place where Elvis himself got married), a *Star Trek* theme park...

Accommodation
Just east of the Strip, the Hilton is perfect for those who want to be close to, but not in the middle of, the bustle. (The on-site monorail station can connect you to that in a hurry.) The seven room 'levels' each have their own decor, more than just increasingly plush renditions of the standard look. Park Avenue, for instance, is classic Manhattan style, while Classic goes for 1920s Hollywood. Some standard rooms are dark and claustrophobic. In addition to the standard ('deluxe') room, there are six 'levels' of suites.

Eating & drinking
Teppanyaki chain Benihana has an impressive 'Japanese village' setting, though the food is costly. Three other Asian spots (Garden of the Dragon, Teru Sushi, 888 Noodle Bar) join Andiamo (Italian), the Hilton Steakhouse and the *Star Trek*-themed Quark's Bar & Restaurant.

Entertainment
The Shimmer Cabaret is anchored by *Menopause: the Musical* and a music-and-dance show called

CONSUME

Sunset Strip. Star Trek: the Experience features two intergalactic adventures.

Gambling

Aside from the kitschy Space Quest Casino, which has $5 tables and sci-fi slots that offer the singular experience of starting the game by passing your hand though a laser beam, this is a high-roller haven, where class divisions are more conspicuous than at most casinos and minimums go through the roof when there's a big convention in town. The baccarat pit and high-limit tables are detached from the main gaming area, and the Platinum Plus slot machines, $5 and up per pull, have their own space. High limits dominate the main floor: the $100 tables are jumping year-round. Managers will only bring out a single-zero roulette wheel if you agree to bet $25-plus per spin. Sports bettors still flock to the 400-seat Super Book, where explanations on how to bet on various sports are posted to help novices.

Amenities *Bars (6). Business centre. Disabled-adapted rooms. Gym. Internet (Wi-Fi $10). No-smoking floors. Pool (outdoor). Restaurants (15). Room service. Spa. TV: pay movies.*
Games *Baccarat ($100-$15,000); Big Six; blackjack ($10-$10,000); Caribbean stud; casino war; craps (3x, 4x, 5x; from $5); keno; Let it Ride; mini baccarat ($25-$5,000); pai gow poker; poker (1 table); roulette (double zero; single zero on request); three-card poker. Gambling lessons (craps 10.30am & 4pm Mon-Fri; blackjack 2pm Mon-Fri).*

Palms

4321 W Flamingo Road, at S Valley View Boulevard, Las Vegas, NV 89103 (reservations 1-866 942 7770, front desk & casino 942 7777, www.palms.com). Bus 201/self-parking W Flamingo Road, S Arville Street or S Valley View Boulevard/valet parking W Flamingo Road. **Rooms** 798. **Rates** $89-$359 double.
Map p333 X3 ㉟

Ever since MTV's *Real World* took over a floor at the Palms, owner George Maloof has shown a Midas touch for keeping up with everybody from twentysomething hipsters to blue-rinse daytime gamblers. At night, the Palms attracts a Who's Who of Hollywood players and sports stars with nightclubs, a new concert hall, chic restaurants, a tattoo parlour, 'bachelor suites' replete with dancer poles and some rooms with giant beds (Maloof and his brother own the Sacramento Kings basketball team). But the magic also works on locals, with a movie theatre, a food court, a slots-driven casino and quality service. Connected to the hotel via a moving walkway called the SkyTube is Palms Place, a condo-hotel and spa.

Accommodation

The rooms at the Palms aren't giant, but many compensate by having great views – and you get to curl up on the same type of bed as you would find at the luxury Four Seasons. Two floors of Fantasy Suites include a Hugh Hefner Sky Villa with balcony pool; the Hardwood Suite, a vast playpen with a jacuzzi and a half-court basketball court; the Kingpin Suite, with a pool table and a bowling lane; and an Erotic Suite, with a circular, 8ft rotating bed with mirrored ceiling. The 'What happens in Vegas' line has surely been uttered more here than anywhere else.

Eating & drinking

Up in the penthouse of the original tower is Alizé , André Rochat's third French restaurant. Downstairs, there's Little Buddha, where you can dine on Asian dishes with a French twist or nosh with the beautiful people at the sushi bar. From Chicago comes N9ne, a steakhouse, champagne/caviar bar and celebrity hangout; the folks behind it also run Nove, an extravagant hotspot decked out in crystal chandeliers, purple leather and crocodile skins. Garduño's offers tasty Tex-Mex and the Sunrise Café is a serviceable 24-hour diner that's not as hip as it should be; there's also a buffet and food court.

CONSUME

Entertainment

The first Playboy Club to open in 25 years arrived in the Palms' Fantasy Tower in 2006. The first venue in town to combine gaming and lounging, Hef's haunt brought even more cachet to the Palms by injecting it with added sex appeal. Above it is Moon, a nightclub with a retractable roof.

Elsewhere, Pearl, an intimate concert hall, gives the House of Blues and the Joint serious competition. The three-storey Rain shines as a proper nightclub; high above it all (and with an equally lofty attitude) is the white-on-white Ghostbar, kind of LA East. When the weather heats up, so does Skin, a twice-weekly pool party complete with cavorting 'mermaids'.

Gambling

Underpinned by a classy hardwood floor, the casino includes 2,400 slots, 55 table games (many with $10 minimums), and a race and sports book. A survey conducted just after the casino opened found the slots to be the loosest in Las Vegas; judging from the video poker, this relative generosity lives on.

Amenities *Bars (6). Business centre. Concierge. Disabled-adapted rooms. Gym. Internet (Wi-Fi $11.99). No-smoking floors. Pool (outdoor). Restaurants (9). Room service. Spa. TV: DVD/pay movies.*

Games *Baccarat ($100-$10,000); blackjack ($10-$5,000); Caribbean stud; casino war; craps (3x, 4x, 5x; from $5); Let it Ride; mini baccarat ($10-$5,000); pai gow poker; poker (10 tables); roulette (double zero); three-card poker. Gambling lessons (poker noon Mon-Fri).*

Rio

3700 W Flamingo Road, at S Valley View Boulevard, Las Vegas, NV 89103 (reservations 1-866 746 7671, front desk & casino 777 7777, www.harrahs.com). Bus 201/self-parking & valet parking W Flamingo Road, S Valley View Boulevard or Viking Street. **Rooms** *2,563.*
Rates $90-$480 suite. **Map** p333 X3 ⏣

The Rio is another identity crisis in progress. In a bid to appeal to a younger audience, the all-suites Rio hired Prince to play here in 2006 and 2007, while Pure Management Group brought in hipster bowling lounge Lucky Strike. But some things remain unchanged: Masquerade Show in the Sky, a free parade with musicians and dancers, is still staged seven times daily. It's part of the hyperactive Masquerade Village, which features two storeys of dining, a variety of bars (from Irish pub to wine cellar), dancing, shopping and shows. Other amenities include four waterfall-filled pools complete with sandy beach and volleyball courts, three wedding chapels and a floor of honeymoon suites, the top-of-the-line Michael's Salon, a spa, and access to the Rio Secco golf course, a half-hour away. A shuttle bus runs between the Rio and the Strip (9am-1am daily).

Accommodation

The comfortable mini-suites feature floor-to-ceiling windows, big televisions and fridges. The full suites, measuring 1,600sq ft (150sq m), come with better sound systems and wet bars.

Eating & drinking

The range of options here is wide and appealing: the All-American Bar & Grille, the award-winning Indian Gaylord's, wildly popular chain Hamada of Japan, solid Italian at Antonio's, Buzio's for seafood and Bamboleo for Mexican. The Carnival World Buffet is a long-time favourite. Newest is the Italy-by-way-of-Philly Café Martorano, from East Coast restaurateur Steve Martorano, which goes nightclub after hours.

Entertainment

The postmodern comedic magic of Penn & Teller is the rock of the Rio, holding the fort in the Samba Theatre; the entrenched Chippendales do exactly what you'd expect.

The nightlife has improved, mostly thanks to Prince's Club 3121 and Cafe Martorano. Elsewhere, the tI-Bar combines natural earth elements (rock, water, light) with natural Vegas elements (dancing bartendresses in flesh-coloured costumes). The Flirt Lounge fits its billing as 'the haven for women to gather after seeing the Chippendales'. The formerly fashionable VooDoo Lounge offers ghastly decor, ordinary service and – the key – great views. Lucky Strike, a ten-lane hipster-heavy bowling alley contains a full-service restaurant and bar, retro decor and throbbing music.

Gambling

The casino is huge, sprawling for two blocks, and the predominant colours are green ($25) and black ($100): at weekends, it's hard to find $10-minimum blackjack. Smaller-stakes gamblers should aim for the lower-limit tables in the outlying areas of the casino; or better yet, walk across the street to the Gold Coast. Poker is offered – the Rio is home to the World Series of Poker – but it's a tough room filled with locals.

Amenities *Bars (10). Business centre. Concierge. Disabled-adapted rooms. Gym. Internet ($12.95, Wi-Fi in convention area). No-smoking floors. Pool (outdoor). Restaurants (13). Room service. Spa. TV: pay movies.*

Games *Baccarat ($100-$15,000); Big Six; blackjack ($15-$10,000); Caribbean stud; casino war; craps (3x, 4x, 5x; from $5); keno; Let it Ride; mini baccarat ($25-$10,000); pai gow poker; pai gow tiles; poker (8 tables); roulette (double zero).*

Westin Casuarina

160 E Flamingo Road, at Koval Lane, Las Vegas, NV 89109 (reservations 1-800 937 8461, front desk & casino 836 5900, www.starwood hotels.com). Bus Deuce, 202/self-parking & valet

parking E Flamingo Road. **Rooms** 826.
Rates $112-$299 double. **Map** p336 B7 ③
The first Westin-branded hotel in Las Vegas is a
low-key resort, which is just how the majority of its
guests like it. There is a small casino here, and even
(though you'll need to look to find it) a cosy little
showroom, but the Casuarina is aimed less at holi-
daymakers and more at the kind of business traveller who wants to get some work done but also
wants the bright lights of the Strip within easy
reach. There's a good deal of meeting space, and
rooms contain all the amenities a laptop-toting
workaholic could want. But it's also a comfortable
place to stop a while: the service is solid, the pool
area is relaxing, and the Hibiscus spa has 15 treatment rooms and a full-service salon.

Accommodation
The rooms here are everything you'd expect from a
Westin property, which is to say that they're comfortable, handsome (in a discreet way), immaculately
maintained and well equipped for the business traveller. The 'Heavenly Beds' live up to their names.

Eating & drinking
Suede, the hotel's sole restaurant, offers comfort food
24-7; there's also a Starbucks on site.

Entertainment
There is a showroom here, but no single show seems
to stick around for very long.

Gambling
The gambling here feels like an afterthought, with
300 machines and ten table games. However, it is

one of the few non-smoking casino areas in the city.
Amenities Bar. Business centre. Concierge.
Disabled-adapted rooms. Gym. Internet ($9.95).
No-smoking floors. Pool (outdoor). Restaurants (2).
Room service. Spa. TV: pay movies.
Gambling Blackjack ($5-$500); craps (2x; from
$5); roulette (double zero).

NON-CASINO HOTELS
Expensive

Platinum
211 E Flamingo Road, at Koval Lane, Las Vegas,
NV 89169 (reservations 1-877 211 9211, front
desk 893 0824, www.platinumlasvegas.com). Bus
201/no self-parking/valet parking E Flamingo
Road. **Rooms** 255. **Rates** $159-$399 suite.
Map p336 B7 ③
The second condo-hotel to open in Las Vegas (the
first was the Residences at the MGM Grand), this
highly impressive property sits within a five-minute
walk of the Strip. It's close enough for convenience,
but the location also allows it to retain a welcome
sense of distance. Free of both gambling and smoking, the Platinum is a refuge from the madness mere
metres away: perfect for the residents who snapped
up many of its 255 suites and now live here part-
time, but also great for visitors keen on retaining
their sanity while those all around them are losing
theirs. It's a very well-run operation, free of bustle
but retaining a certain urban style in its restaurant,
relaxed ground-floor bar and fabulously appointed
spa. And the suites themselves are both spacious
(the bathrooms in some suites are bigger than

CONSUME

Vdara. See p133.

guestrooms at a couple of hotels in town) and handsome, done out with high-spec amenities and very comfortable beds. The cannily designed indoor-outdoor pool on the fifth floor is another nice touch in a property that's quietly full of them.
Amenities *Bar. Disabled-adapted rooms. Gym. Internet ($12.99). No-smoking rooms. Pool (indoor/outdoor). Restaurant. Room service. Spa. TV: pay movies.*

Renaissance

3400 Paradise Road, between E Desert Inn Road & E Twain Avenue, Las Vegas, NV 89109 (reservations 1-800 750 0980, front desk 733 6533, www.renaissancelasvegas.com). Bus 108, 213/self-parking & valet parking Paradise Road. **Rooms** 548. **Rates** $119-$419 double. **Map** p335, p336 C6 ❸❾

This 15-storey, 548-room Marriott hotel south of the Las Vegas Convention Center seems all business, with a list of amenities that includes the highest-tech wireless internet service, ergonomic desk chairs and even 'Exhibitor Suites'. The hotel has a sophisticated executive level with a lounge, a pool area, spa service, comfy beds (with high-end linens and piles of pillows) and flatscreen televisions in every room. There's no mention of a nightclub or casino for good reason: the Renaissance is the city's largest non-gaming property. Still, there is one type of sin on site: Envy, a Richard Chamberlain steakhouse that serves a variety of rich comfort foods, from a Kobe filet mignon to truffle mac and cheese, with 1,500 bottles of wine. Escaping work is easy, with a monorail station nearby and the Strip a block away.
Amenities *Bars (1). Concierge. Disabled-adapted rooms. Gym. Internet (Wi-Fi $12.95). No-smoking hotel. Pool (outdoor). Restaurant. Room service. Spa. TV: pay movies.*

Moderate

Alexis Resort & Villas

375 E Harmon Avenue, between Koval Lane & Paradise Road, Las Vegas, NV 89109 (reservations 1-800 582 2228, front desk 796 3300, www.alexispark.com). Bus 108, 213/self-parking E Harmon Avenue. **Rooms** 495. **Rates** $79-$299 suite. **Map** p336 C8 ❹⓪

Built as an apartment complex and later transformed into an all-suites hotel (where local teenagers booked suites on prom night, until the resort wised up and began requiring guests to be 21), the gaming-free, Mediterranean-style Alexis is a surprisingly sedate little operation. The two-storey buildings, situated along winding pathways, house 500 well-appointed suites, ranging in size from 450sq ft to 1,275sq ft (42sq m to 120sq m) and offering a host of unexpected amenities (gas fireplaces, large bathrooms and, in some cases, upstairs lofts). But the main selling point? It's right by the Hard Rock (*see p133*).

Amenities *Bar. Business centre. Disabled-adapted rooms. Gym. Internet (Wi-Fi $5). No-smoking rooms. Pools (outdoor). Restaurant. Room service. Spa. TV: pay movies.*

Artisan

1501 W Sahara Avenue, at Highland Drive, Las Vegas, NV 89102 (reservations 1-800 554 4092, front desk 214 4000, www.theartisanhotel.com). Bus 204/self-parking W Sahara Avenue/no valet parking. **Rooms** 64. **Rates** $119-$179 double. **Map** p335 B4 ❹❶

This boutique hotel, housed rather unexpectedly in a former Travelodge in the shadow of I-15, shares a trait with most Strip resorts: it has a theme. The old-world European decor is inspired by art and artists; paintings, a mix of pieces by local artists and reproductions of iconic works by the likes of Rembrandt and Van Gogh, cover virtually every inch of wall space in the public areas, and even decorate the ceilings. The theme continues in the Artisan Lounge, a late-night hotspot frequented by local hipsters, and in the hotel's dining room. The 64 individually decorated guestrooms and suites are priced a little highly for their location, but they're likeable enough and a good option if you fancy steering clear of the Strip.
Amenities *Bar. Business centre. Concierge. Disabled-adapted rooms. Gym. Internet (Wi-Fi free). No-smoking floors. Pools (outdoor). Restaurant. Room service. Spa. TV: pay movies.*

Carriage House

105 E Harmon Avenue, between Las Vegas Boulevard South & Koval Lane, Las Vegas, NV 89109 (reservations 1-800 221 2301 ext 65, front desk 798 1020, www.carriagehouselasvegas.com). Bus Deuce, 201, 202/self-parking E Harmon Avenue or Audrie Street/no valet parking. **Rooms** 155. **Rates** $99-$145 double. **Map** p336 B8 ❹❷

Located next door to Grand Chateau, a new timeshare resort owned and operated by Marriott, the Carriage House is often overlooked by visitors. However, the moderately priced rooms are great value for the location, the best of any hotel not actually on Las Vegas Boulevard South. The rooms and suites are kept in decent shape; even the smallest ones have kitchenettes. Outside, there's a tennis court, a heated pool and a simple sun deck.
Amenities *Business centre. Concierge. Disabled-adapted rooms. Internet (Wi-Fi, free). No-smoking floors. Pool (outdoor). TV: DVD/pay movies.*

Comfort Inn

4350 Paradise Road, between E Flamingo Road & E Harmon Avenue, Las Vegas, NV 89109 (reservations 1-877 424 6423, front desk 938 2000, www.choicehotels.com). Bus 108/self-parking Paradise Road/no valet parking. **Rooms** 199. **Rates** $79-$109. **Map** p336 C7 ❹❸

In truth, this outpost of the ubiquitous national chain isn't anything special. However, it's a useful standby in the event that the rest of the town is booked solid or running at often ridiculously high weekend prices: the rates here never seem to change by more than ten bucks a night, regardless of the time of year or the time of week. The hotel offers a similar range of amenities to those delivered by Comfort Inns in the South-west: an outdoor pool, a very basic breakfast, and an assortment of kitchen utilities (microwave, coffeemaker) that no one ever seems to use. Still, it's kept in fair condition, and the location is terrific for hipsters: it's opposite the Hard Rock (see p133) and close to the Double Down Saloon.

Amenities *Disabled-adapted rooms. Gym. Internet (Wi-Fi, free). No-smoking floors. Pool (outdoor). TV: pay movies.*

Courtyard by Marriott

3275 Paradise Road, at E Desert Inn Road, Las Vegas, NV 89109 (reservations 1-800 661 1064, front desk 791 3600, www.marriott.com). Bus 108, 213/self-parking Paradise Road/no valet parking. **Rooms** 149. **Rates** $139-$269 double. **Map** p335 C5 **44**

While Las Vegas's status as the world's most ridiculous resort grabs the headlines, it's worth stressing that the city is also the convention capital of the US, welcoming millions of business travellers each year alongside all the leisure traffic. This outpost of Marriott's Courtyard chain is tilted squarely at those here for work purposes, and particularly at those who've flown in to attend an event at the Las Vegas Convention Center, right opposite the property. All rooms have work spaces and internet access, and decor that won't offer any distractions from the job at hand. It's one of several such chain-tied business hotels within walking distance of the LVCC; others include the immediately adjacent Residence Inn (3225 Paradise Road, 796 9300, www.marriott.com) and a tidy, well-equipped branch of the popular Embassy Suites hotel group (3600 Paradise Road, 893 8000, www.embassysuites.com).

Amenities *Bar. Business centre. Disabled-adapted rooms. Gym. Internet (Wi-Fi $9.95). No-smoking floors. Pools (outdoor). Restaurant. TV: pay movies.*

Budget

Aruba Hotel

1208 Las Vegas Boulevard South, at E Charleston Boulevard, Las Vegas, NV 89104 (reservations 1-866 383 3150, front desk 383 3100, www.arubalasvegas.com). Bus Deuce, 206/self-parking Las Vegas Boulevard South/no valet parking. **Rooms** 94. **Rates** $49-$99 double. **Map** p335 C3 **45**

The slightly shady stretch of Las Vegas Boulevard South between the Stratosphere and Charleston Boulevard is lined with old motels. Many of them are pretty sketchy places, as you'd expect given the signs out front advertising hourly rates and free adult movies, but a few stand out from the crowd. The Holiday Motel (2205 Las Vegas Boulevard South) is a pretty scruffy place, but its animated vintage neon sign is one of the most handsome in town. And up the road, the venerable Aruba at least makes an effort to elevate itself above its surroundings. This is still a pretty basic and thin-walled motel, sure, and the location isn't perfect. But a recent refurbishment has spruced it up a lot, with the management tilting at a vintage Vegas vibe, and the regular events in the Thunderbird Lounge (swing night on Fridays, occasional bands on Saturdays) are a nice touch.

Amenities *Bar. Disabled-adapted rooms. Gym. No-smoking rooms. Pool (outdoor). Restaurant. Room service. Spa. TV.*

Budget Suites

3655 W Tropicana Avenue, between S Valley View Boulevard & I-15, Las Vegas, NV 89103 (reservations 1-888 281 0480, front desk 739 1000, www.budgetsuites.com). Bus 201/self-parking Paradise Road/no valet parking. **Rooms** 480. **Rates** $199-$299/wk suite. **Map** p333 A8 **46**

Budget Suites is perfect for visitors planning on staying in Las Vegas for an extended period and who require some self-catering facilities. The daily rates are nothing special, but a one-bed apartment can be rented for around $250 a week, with further discounts for monthly rentals. Each secure 220- to 300-unit complex is made up of basic mini-suites, each with their own kitchen and bathroom. Maid service is available, but you can save on the expense by bringing your own linen and towels. There are four locations dotted around Las Vegas, but this is the closest to the Strip.

Amenities *Disabled-adapted rooms. Pool (outdoor).*

Sin City Hostel

1208 Las Vegas Boulevard South, at E Charleston Boulevard, Las Vegas, NV 89104 (reservations & front desk 868 0222, www.sincityhostel.com). Bus Deuce, 206/self-parking Las Vegas Boulevard South/no valet parking. **Rates** $19.50-$39. **Map** p335 C3 **47**

The lack of youth hostels in Vegas is easily explained by the fact that you can get a room in a Downtown casino for $30 or so. Still, despite its location in the Naked City, the Sin City Hostel has built up a nice reputation. The dorms are relatively cosy, and there are also semi-private doubles. Amenities include free laundry facilities, an internet terminal and a jacuzzi pool. Guests must produce a student ID or proof of international travel at check-in.

Amenities *Disabled-adapted rooms. No-smoking rooms.*

Lavish Loos

When you've got to go… you might as well go in luxury.

When you've gotta go, you gotta go. But in Vegas, where they've extended extravagance to even to the humblest of rooms – the rest room – you can choose to go in style.

Take a look at these posh potties: If you opt for the fantasy facilities at certain casinos and nightclubs, the business of doing your business may be the best part of your night.

The chandelier-lit ladies' room at Vanity nightclub at the **Hard Rock Hotel & Casino** (*see p133*) stuns with sheer scale – more lounge than loo at 2,000 square feet. Instead of sharing a mirror, patrons can prettify at individual vanity tables. Of course there are attendants to touch up hair and makeup and even fetch pricey cocktails – your may end up spending the whole evening in there.

Men not left out of the fun of the lavish lav: Decked out with (faux) snakeskin wallpaper, the men's room at Vanity sports flatscreen TV monitors mounted over the urinals; at the Mix Lounge at **TheHotel at Mandalay Bay** (*see p132*), a strip of windows runs atop the urinals, so gents can take in the view while they're relieving themselves. The men's at ESPN Zone at **New York New York** (*see p121*) has more than 100 screens, so sports fans won't miss a play. And in the men's room at **Main Street Station** (*see p141*), the urinals are embedded in a graffiti-covered segment of the actual Berlin Wall.

The newest trend in restrooms is the unisex bathroom, exemplified at its most enticing by the lounge at **Déjà vu Erotic Ultra Lounge** (*see p225*), which is hidden behind a waterfall and illuminated with coloured lights, featuring transparent toilet stalls that cloud over when occupied. And at RumJungle at **Mandalay Bay** (*see p109*), men and women alike can peer through gauzy peekaboo windows, perhaps to figure out, once and for all, what really goes on in the mysterious sanctuaries of the opposite sex.

Downtown

In 1906, people were gambling in what is now Downtown. Sawdust joints, casinos with wooden boardwalks and floors, attracted railroad workers, ranchers and the like. For classic Vegas, you should head here, where old neon turns night into day and casinos offer fewer sideshows to distract from gambling. The house rules at the casinos are often more liberal than on the Strip and minimum bets tend to be lower. Still, poor attitudes on the casino floors, a result of poorer management, leaves Downtown gambling a sad shadow of its former self.

HOTEL-CASINOS

Moderate

★ Golden Nugget

129 E Fremont Street, at S Casino Center Boulevard, Las Vegas, NV 89101 (reservations 1-800 846 5336, front desk & casino 385 7111, www.goldennugget.com). Bus Deuce & all BTC-bound buses/self-parking E 1st Street/valet parking S Casino Center Boulevard. **Rooms** 1,907. **Rates** $79-$189 double. **Map** p334 C1 ⓭

Following the improvements a few years ago, the Nugget has consolidated its position as the best casino on Fremont Street. The refurbishments have been dramatic, and almost entirely for the better. The casino floor now feels almost grand, complete with a new poker room and the city's most handsome sports book. A slew of new restaurants have revitalised what had become a fairly tired catering programme. And then there's the fabulous pool area, complete with private cabanas, its own lounge (the Dive Bar, tee hee) and water slides running through a central shark tank. Well, why not? *Photo p143.*

Accommodation

The rooms here are not as swanky as some would have you believe; the recent renovations under Landry's were almost entirely limited to the property's public areas. Still, the lodgings here are pretty decent, and better than those found at any other Downtown property. The three hotel towers contain a total of 1,907 rooms, a number of plush suites (some of which are spread over two levels). The suites atop the spa tower are in a more modern style, the ones atop the original tower positively old-Vegas opulence.

Eating & drinking

Key to dining at the Golden Nugget is the branch of Vic & Anthony's, with lighter fare offered at Lillie's Noodle House and the Italian-slanted Grotto. The Carson Street Café has been overhauled, but continues to serve a straightforward range of casual American classics, and the buffet rightly retains its reputation as the neighbourhood's finest. But perhaps the most dramatic addition is Rush Lounge, a nightclubby lounge that's worlds away from anything offered by its Fremont Street competitors.

Entertainment
The Nugget's 600-seater is currently home to impressionist Geordie Brown. Guest headliners add a little variety.

Gambling
The Nugget's elegant marble lobby may seem out of place on Fremont Street, and the high minimums (mostly $10 for craps and blackjack) in the nicely renovated casino are are unusual for Downtown. There's a segregated pit for players with larger bankrolls who want to play baccarat and blackjack without the hoi polloi; it's the only high-limit pit Downtown. However, there are also good selections of slot and video-poker machines from low to high denominations. The sports book was relocated to where the buffet used to be; it's now full-scale.
Amenities *Bars (4). Business centre. Concierge. Disabled-adapted rooms. Gym. Internet (Wi-Fi $11.99). No-smoking floors. Pools (outdoor). Restaurants (5). Room service. Spa. TV: pay movies.*
Games *Blackjack ($5-$2,500); Caribbean stud; casino war; craps (3x, 4x, 5x; from $5); keno; Let it Ride; mini baccarat ($5-$2,500); pai gow poker; poker (9 tables); roulette (double-zero); Spanish 21; three-card poker. Gambling lessons (blackjack, craps, poker, roulette 10am daily).*

Main Street Station
200 N Main Street, at E Stewart Avenue, Las Vegas, NV 89101 (reservations 1-800 713 8933, front desk & casino 387 1896, www.mainstreet casino.com). Bus Deuce & all BTC-bound buses/ self-parking & valet parking N Main Street. **Rooms** 430. **Rates** $40-$110 double. **Map** p334 C1 ㊼
Main Street Station is the nicest Downtown casino not called the Golden Nugget. Themed as a fin-de-siècle delight (check out the gaslamps that front the property), the casino is filled with antiques of all kinds, not all of them Victorian. Teddy Roosevelt's Pullman car is here, now a chic smoking lounge; a carved oak fireplace from Prestwick Castle in Scotland and a set of doors from an old London bank are also on display; and chunks of the Berlin Wall sit in the men's room. Accessible yet smart, upscale (for Downtown) yet fun, this isn't the most charismatic property, but it's likeable all the same.

Accommodation
The 430 guestrooms are comfortable, if rather basic.

Eating & drinking
The choice might be small, but it's all good stuff. Its name a nod to a railway theme that's delivered in fairly tasteful fashion, the Pullman Grille deals in

surf and turf favourites. It's fine, but the Triple 7 Brew Pub remains a better bet, the well-above-average burgers and sandwiches acting as perfect stomach-lining for the very decent beers brewed on site. Many locals swear by the Garden Court Buffet: the room is beautiful, the selections are excellent and the prices ($10.99 for dinner) are most definitely right.

Entertainment
Nothing, really.

Gambling
Main Street offers a good selection of slots and video poker, three-card poker and low limits at the tables; $5 single- and double-deck blackjack dominates, and the craps tables offer 20x odds. An illuminated sign over the roulette area depicts a single-zero wheel, but the wheel itself contains two zeros.
Amenities *Bar. Disabled-adapted rooms. No-smoking rooms. Restaurants (3). Room service.*
Games *Blackjack ($5-$1,000); craps (20x; from $5); keno; Let it Ride; pai gow poker; roulette (double zero); three-card poker.*

Budget

Binion's
128 E Fremont Street, at N Casino Center Boulevard, Las Vegas, NV 89101 (reservations 1-800 937 6537, front desk & casino 382 1600, www.binions.com). Bus Deuce & all BTC-bound buses/self-parking N Casino Center Boulevard, E Ogden Avenue or E Stewart Avenue/valet parking N Casino Center Boulevard or Ogden Avenue. **Rooms** 366. **Rates** $39-$79 double.
Map p334 D1 ㊿
Opened by Benny Binion as Binion's Horseshoe in 1951, this Fremont Street relic competes with the Flamingo and Caesars Palace for the title of the most iconic hotel-casino in Vegas history. Certainly, it's been one of the most influential. Binion, a fabulous character and a fairly unpleasant man, was arguably more responsible than any other individual for the tone of 21st-century gambling in the city; it was Binion who abolished table limits for the first time, and Binion who effectively established the World Series of Poker here in the early 1970s.

So much for the past. After the Horseshoe stumbled into financial disrepair under the auspices of Binion's daughter Becky Behnen, the property fell into corporate hands (first Harrah's, then MTR Gaming) and it's not been the same since. The Horseshoe name has been lost to history, while the World Series of Poker has decamped to the Harrah's-owned Rio. A recent refurbishment of the casino has sapped all atmosphere from the space, leaving this historic property as just another Downtown grind joint. Shame.

Accommodation
Eighty of the rooms are from the original casino; the other 286 were added when the hotel acquired the

CONSUME

Mint. The vast majority of them could use some fairly serious regeneration.

Entertainment
The main entertainment here comes courtesy of a mechanical bull, two words that could also be usefully employed when describing the recent remodelling of the casino.

Eating & drinking
Binion's Original Coffee Shop is still pretty decent, and there are excellent views from the 24th-floor Binion's Ranch Steakhouse, but there's otherwise not much here.

Gambling
When the Binions owned Binion's, you found savvy, renegade dealers – some of the best in town. But dramatic modifications have occurred since the change in ownership. Only four craps tables remain from what was once the centre of the dice universe. The blackjack pits have also shrunk, replaced by some newfangled poker derivatives that would've rendered Benny Binion apoplectic. Still, the video poker is only half bad; and the poker room is one of the largest in town. The race book occupies a former lounge in the West Horseshoe; the sports book is in a separate part of the casino.

Amenities *Bars (2). Disabled-adapted rooms. No-smoking rooms. Restaurants (3).*

Games *Blackjack ($5-$3,000); craps (3x, 4x, 5x; from $5); keno; Let it Ride; mini baccarat ($5-$3,000); poker (35 tables); roulette (double zero); three-card poker. Gambling lessons (poker 11am daily).*

El Cortez
600 E Fremont Street, at N 6th Street, Las Vegas, NV 89101 (reservations 1-800 634 6703, front desk & casino 385 5200, www.elcortezhotel casino.com). Bus Deuce & all BTC-bound buses/self-parking E Ogden Avenue/valet parking N 6th Street. **Rooms** 300. **Rates** $33-$110 double. **Map** p334 D2 ⑤

The owners pumped $20 million into the old El Cortez a few years ago, replacing smoke-saturated carpeting, widening the casino aisles, installing new table games, adding a wine cellar, revamping the valet entrance and remodelling the rooms. But the historic building's Spanish-style architecture is still intact, and so is another Vegas relic: Jackie Gaughan, who bought the property way back in 1963; she still walks the floors daily, single-handedly keeping the spirit of post-war Downtown alive. Gaughan's mission statement – 'Give the customer a good deal and he'll come back' – is nice to hear in the age of resorts run by corporations. And they do come back to Downtown's longest continuously running casino, for low-stakes slots, cheap guestrooms, prime rib at the Flame Steakhouse and nine-buck haircuts in the barbershop.

Accommodation
The rooms are spartan to say the least (what do you expect for 30 bucks?), but those in the main hotel have been freshened up a little. The Ogden House, across the street, has been remodelled and renamed the Cabana Suites.

Entertainment
You make your own fun here, though there are at least a number of new style bars just across the road.

Eating & drinking
If you fancy yourself as a character from *Fear and Loathing in Las Vegas*, you're in luck. The circular booths and kelly-green/hot-pink decor at Roberta's scream Tarantino; the porterhouse steak special here is a local favourite. Careful Kitty's, a 24-hour coffeeshop, provides local colour and late-night specials.

Gambling
The El Cortez is the place to go if you're short on cash and high on hope: there are plenty of penny and nickel video-poker machines, and some of the few remaining $3 blackjack tables in town. Craps minimums go as low as $3, but 10x odds are continuous. Roulette often has a 25¢ minimum; like the 40¢ keno, it's good for cheap entertainment. The casino hosts a twice-yearly social security number lottery: if your nine-digit number is drawn, you win $50,000.

Amenities *Bars (3). Disabled-adapted rooms. No-smoking rooms. Restaurants (2).*

Games *Blackjack ($3-$500); craps (10x; from $3); keno; Let it Ride; mini baccarat ($5-$1,000); poker (2 tables); roulette (double zero). Gambling lessons (craps 8.15am Tue, Fri).*

Fitzgeralds
301 E Fremont Street, at S 3rd Street, Las Vegas, NV 89101 (reservations 1-800 274 5825, front desk & casino 388 2400, www.fitzgeraldslas vegas.com). Bus Deuce & all BTC-bound buses/self-parking S 3rd Street/valet parking S 4th Street. **Rooms** 638. **Rates** $50-$179 double. **Map** p334 D1 ㊲

Luck might be a lady elsewhere in Vegas, but here she's a giant leprechaun, mounted on the roof and spilling a pot o' gold. The Irish theme aside, this is standard Downtown fare, though it does have some amusing lounge acts and an outdoor pool.

Accommodation
There are 638 guestrooms (including 14 suites) in the 34-storey hotel. There have been some modest attempts to modernise the property, including a new business centre.

Eating & drinking
Don B's Steakhouse has straightforward fare. If you're unsure, get food you can see first at Molly's Buffet. Plan C: Fitzgerald's proudly offers the only McDonald's on Fremont Street.

Golden Nugget. *See p140.*

CONSUME

Entertainment
The Fitz shows signs of life in its lounge, featuring acts such as the Spirit of the King Band (an Elvis tribute) and impersonator Larry G Jones, billed somewhat optimistically as 'the Man of 1,002 Voices'.

Gambling
A typical Downtown grind joint spread over two levels, the Fitzgeralds casino has low minimums for all the table games, especially roulette ($2, with quarter wheel chips). The blackjack is mostly six-deck. If you look hard enough, you can find full-pay video poker in quarter denominations. Upstairs is a smaller gaming area outside the restaurants, and there's also a small outdoor deck off the bar, the only one of its kind Downtown.
Amenities *Bars (3). Business centre. Disabled-adapted rooms. No-smoking rooms. Pool (outdoor). Restaurants (4).*
Games *Blackjack ($5-$500); Caribbean stud; craps (3x, 4x, 5x; from $3); Let it Ride, keno; pai gow poker; poker (6 tables); roulette (double zero); Spanish 21. Gambling lessons (craps, times vary Fri, Sat).*

Four Queens
202 E Fremont Street, at S Casino Center Boulevard, Las Vegas, NV 89101 (reservations 1-800 634 6045, front desk & casino 385 4011, www.fourqueens.com). Bus Deuce & all BTC-bound buses/self-parking E Carson Avenue/valet parking S 3rd Street. **Rooms** 690. **Rates** $50-$120 double. **Map** p334 D1 ⑲
Fresh off a 45th anniversary, the Four Queens are still ladies in waiting; specifically, waiting for a genuine Fremont resurgence. But for visitors who like

their gambling vacations cheap and to the point, this is a prime location for a taste of old-school Vegas.

Accommodation
The hotel's 690 guestrooms (including 45 suites) have been remodelled, but keep your hopes down. Still, the flatscreen TVs are a nice touch.

Eating & drinking
The best of Downtown's bunch might be Hugo's Cellar, a romantic, quintessentially old-school restaurant: long-stem roses handed out at the door, salad cart, steak and lobster, and, of course, the flaming table-side cherries jubilee. Magnolia's Veranda is a standard Downtown 24-hour café (complete with the standard prime-rib dinner), while the Chicago Brewery features microbrews, pizza and a cigar lounge. There's also a deli.

Entertainment
The Canyon Club, run by House of Blues expats, is a 600-capacity music venue.

Gambling
Cramped and crowded, for some reason the Four Queens packs 'em in nightly. It's not that the gambling here is any stronger than next door or across the street, though the beers are better thanks to the presence of a brewpub. The roulette chips are dollars, with a $5 minimum. A $5 toke to the cocktail waitresses earns a huge smile and frequent service.
Amenities *Bars (3). Disabled-adapted rooms. No-smoking rooms. Restaurants (5).*
Games *Blackjack ($5-$500); Caribbean stud; craps (5x; from $5); Let it Ride; keno; pai gow poker; roulette (double zero); Spanish 21.*

Fremont

200 E Fremont Street, at N Casino Center Boulevard, Las Vegas, NV 89101 (reservations 1-800 634 6182, front desk & casino 385 3232, www.fremontcasino.com). Bus Deuce & all BTC-bound buses/self-parking & valet parking N Casino Center Boulevard or E Ogden Avenue. **Rooms** 447. **Rates** $40-$150 double. **Map** p334 D1 ❻❹

Most of the original charm has disappeared from the Fremont after a half-century, and a tropical-island motif has moved in – along with a large Hawaiian clientele. The famous block-long neon sign still holds its own, except when outglared by the Fremont Street Experience that runs above it.

Accommodation

The hotel's 447 guestrooms (including 23 suites) are modern, and feature floral patterns in hues of emerald and burgundy.

Eating & drinking

The Fremont courts visitors from the Pacific Rim, hence the surprising Second Street Grill: an unexpectedly upscale and risk-taking fusion-focused dining room, it delights discerning visitors with mahi mahi and ono. The Paradise Café coffeeshop offers American and Chinese specialities in 'a rainforest setting', and Lanai Express is an Asian fast-food joint. There's also a Tony Roma's, reputedly the most successful in the nation. At night, the Paradise rolls out a buffet.

Entertainment

Nothing doing here.

Gambling

A nondescript grind joint in the middle of Grind Central, with nothing much to recommend it but also nothing much to criticise. There's usually a slot or slot-club promotion going on; if you're in the neighbourhood, enquire at the slot-club booth.
Amenities *Bars (4). No-smoking rooms. Restaurants (4).*
Games *Blackjack ($5-$1,000); Caribbean stud; craps (2x; from $5); Let it Ride; keno; pai gow poker; roulette (double zero); Spanish 21; three-card poker.*

Golden Gate

1 E Fremont Street, at S Main Street, Las Vegas, NV 89101 (reservations 1-800 426 1906, front desk & casino 385 1906, www.goldengate casino.net). Bus Deuce & all BTC-bound buses/ self-parking & valet parking S Main Street. **Rooms** 106. **Rates** $45-$70 double. **Map** p334 C1 ❻❺

Being the oldest and smallest of anything aren't normally qualities about which a Vegas property brags, but the Golden Gate manages to pull it off. Having celebrated its 100th birthday in 2006 (it's been known as the Golden Gate only since 1955; it was

opened as the Hotel Nevada), this 106-room property appears positively quaint alongside the flashy Golden Nugget, the enormous brash Plaza and the garish Fremont Street Experience. Owned by likeable local maverick Mark Brandenburg, who so far seems to have shown little inclination to drag his place into the modern world, the Golden Gate remains old Vegas at its most appealingly basic.

Accommodation

Many original 10ft-by-10ft bedrooms remain. Some have been updated with air-conditioning, but most are still characterfully old-fashioned, replete with mahogany doors, plaster walls and tiled bathroom floors. Aside from the addition of a relatively modern key-card system, there haven't been any major technological advances here since 1907, when the hotel announced that it had taken control of the first telephone in Nevada (boasting, of course, the number 1).

Eating & drinking

In 50 years, the 24-hour San Francisco Deli has served 25 million shrimp cocktails, tangy treats in tulip-shaped glasses, and among the best bargains in the city. The Bay City Diner offers a survey of American classics, dished out by waitresses seemingly borrowed from a Raymond Carver short story.

Entertainment

The piano player at the back of the casino is another fabulous nod to tradition. They're very good too.

Gambling

An old-time, no-frills, family-owned casino navigated by a multitude of wheelchair-required small ramps. The carpet's worn, the tables and machines are packed like sardines, and the bosses brook no nonsense. From the far dice-table closest to the deli, you can make a dash for the famous shrimp cocktail between rolls. The comps here are liberal: play $10 blackjack for an hour and ask for the coffeeshop for two.
Amenities *Bar. No-smoking rooms. Restaurants (2).*
Games *Blackjack ($3-$300); Caribbean stud; craps (5x; from $3); pai gow poker; roulette (double zero).*

Plaza

1 N Main Street, at E Fremont Street, Las Vegas, NV 89101 (reservations 1-800 634 6575, front desk & casino 386 2110, www.plazahotel casino.com). Bus Deuce & all BTC-bound buses/self-parking & valet parking S Main Street. **Rooms** 1,037. **Rates** $39-$149 double. **Map** p334 C1 ❻❻

This iconic Downtown property opened as Jackie Gaughan's Plaza, but Jackie is long Gaughan (he now owns El Cortez) and the Plaza is currently owned by the Tamares Group (which also owns the Vegas Club, the Western and the Gold Spike. Even so, the Plaza retains a resolutely old Vegas feel, from the majestically over-the-top lighting beneath the shelter outside its main entrance to the unpalatably smoky casino floor and the resolutely downmarket buffet. In truth, it's a fairly shambolic place that could really use a little TLC. Still, the prices are right, and the rooftop swimming pool is an appealing extra.

Accommodation
The Plaza can usually be relied upon to deliver some of Downtown's cheapest rooms. Once you've stayed in one, you'll understand why. All things considered, the basic lodgings here are in need of an upgrade.

Eating & drinking
While it retains a certain vintage Vegas charm and serves a creditable steak, the best things about the second-level Center Stage restaurant are the views straight down Fremont Street afforded from its window seats. The other eating options here are pretty much as you might expect: a round-the-clock diner, a super-cheap buffet (dinner is just $8.99) and a food court holding a handful of global chains.

Entertainment
The headline production here is *Shag with a Twist*, a surprisingly charming reanimation of 1960s culture aimed at those who enjoyed Broadway retro fave *Hairspray*. From 9pm to 1.30am, Thursdays to Sundays, the Omaha Lounge hosts the likes of shiny-shirted smooth jazz stylist David van Such and super-soft reggae quartet Island Tyme.

Gambling
The casino teems with 1,200 slot machines. In the pit, gamblers can play $1 craps or $5 blackjack. Seven-card stud, Texas hold 'em and Omaha hold 'em poker are played in the card room, where limits are low and the players are more gentlemanly than on the Strip. But if you really want to gamble on the cheap, the keno lounge is for you: the Plaza is the only place in the US that offers double keno (simultaneous action on two boards) with games starting at 40¢, a bargain, despite the rotten odds. The bingo room is on the third floor.
Amenities *Bars (5). Disabled-adapted rooms. Gym. No-smoking rooms. Pool (outdoor). Restaurants (4).*
Games *Big Six; bingo; blackjack ($5-$500); craps (5x; from $5); keno; Let it Ride; mini baccarat ($5-$500); pai gow poker; poker (7 tables); roulette (double zero); three-card poker.*

Vegas Club
18 E Fremont Street, at N Main Street, Las Vegas, NV 89101 (reservations 1-800 634 6532, front desk & casino 385 1664, www.vegasclub casino.net). Bus Deuce & all BTC-bound buses/self-parking & valet parking N Main Street. **Rooms** 410. **Rates** $64-$124 double. **Map** p334 C1 **57**

This 410-room old stager on Fremont Street is owned by the Tamares Group and is a good-value but feebly themed hotel-casino. As well as the Vegas Club and the Plaza (*see p144*), Tamares also owns a couple of other low-roller joints: these include the basic 110-room Gold Spike (400 E Ogden Avenue, 1-877 467 7453, 384 8444, www.goldspikehotel casino.com), and west of Las Vegas Boulevard, the spartan Western (899 E Fremont Street, 1-800 634 6703, 384 4620, www.westernhotelcasino.com).

Accommodation
While Downtown drags itself kicking and screaming into the 21st century, the Vegas Club's motel-standard guestrooms remain firmly stranded in 1987. Still, while the decor isn't the height of fashion, the rooms aren't in bad condition, especially compared to those at a few of their more downmarket neighbours. The guestrooms in the North Tower are in the best shape, something usually reflected in the prices.

Eating & drinking
The Great Moments restaurant aims for a vintage Vegas vibe, and sometimes gets away with it. Two sports-themed joints offer snacks: the Upper Deck and the 24-hour Seventh Inning Scoop.

Entertainment
Make your own.

Gambling
The casino here is bigger than it first appears, stretching around the ground floor to the newer wing along Ogden Avenue. In line with the rest of the hotel, it's in pretty good shape following a recent clean-up, though there's not much in the way of atmosphere. The blackjack has good rules, if you know how to take advantage of them using a slightly altered basic strategy. Find a long-time dealer and ask him or her for a little advice.
Amenities *Bars (2). Disabled-adapted rooms. No-smoking rooms. Restaurants (4).*
Games *Big Six; bingo; blackjack ($3-$500); craps (3x, 4x, 5x; from $5); keno; Let it Ride; pai gow poker; roulette (double zero); three-card poker.*

The Rest of the City
HOTEL-CASINOS
Expensive

Green Valley Ranch
2300 Paseo Verde Drive, at S Green Valley Parkway, Henderson, NV 89052 (reservations 1-866 782 9487, front desk & casino 617 7777, www.greenvalleyranchresort.com). Bus 111/self-parking & valet parking S Green Valley Parkway or Paseo Verde Parkway. **Rooms** 490. **Rates** $129-$349 double.

Silverton. *See p148.*

The Green Valley Ranch was a gem right out of the box in 2001, and it hasn't stopped polishing itself since. In its third expansion, the former boutique-style resort with the Argentinian cattle baron motif has doubled its guestroom capacity, improved the gambling options, and added a 500-seat entertainment lounge. Amenities already in place before the renovation included District, a main-street-style shopping mall (*see p197*), a great mix of restaurants and one of the hottest pool areas in town.

Accommodation
The guestrooms are done out with old-world decor, supplemented by goose-down pillows and fluffy robes. The huge penthouse suite comes complete with a baby grand, a dining table for ten, his and hers baths, a full kitchen and numerous plasma screens. There's a cutting-edge spa out back, part of the eight-acre Whiskey Beach area; rent a cabana and order bottle service at the private pool called the Pond.

Eating & drinking
The gaming area is lined with dining options, including a couple of Asian options (China Spice and Sushi & Sake), upscale Italian at Terra Verde, and a re-creation of vintage Vegas at Hank's, which boasts of 'fine steaks and martinis'. Still hungry? You need the Feast Around the World Buffet, a local favourite.

Entertainment
There are outdoor concerts at Whiskey Beach in summer, some at the 2,000-seat Grand Events Center, and in the Ovation Lounge, booking everything from

Grand Funk Railroad to Big Bad Voo doo Daddy. Every night, there's Vegas-club-style action at Whiskey, a high-flyin', star-attractin' club that insouciantly spills out to outdoor lounging in the beach area. Back inside, there's a 500-seat entertainment lounge and a ten-screen cinema. Adjacent to the hotel is the District shopping mall, with around 50 shops and restaurants.

Gambling
The pit, which surrounds the Drop Bar, is a bit cramped, though the slot areas are more expansive. A recent renovation brought a new 22-table poker room and a state-of-the-art sports book. Mini baccarat starts at $10 a hand. The video poker has been consistently strong over the past few years.
Amenities *Bars (12). Business centre. Disabled-adapted rooms. Gym. Internet ($12.99). No-smoking rooms. Pools (outdoor). Restaurants (14). Room service. Spa. TV: pay movies.*
Games *Blackjack ($5 $5,000); Caribbean stud; casino war; craps (3x, 4x, 5x; from $10); keno; mini baccarat ($10-$1,000); pai gow poker; roulette (double zero); Spanish 21; three-card poker.*

JW Marriott Summerlin
221 N Rampart Boulevard, at Summerlin Parkway, Summerlin (reservations 1-888 236 2427, front desk & casino 869 7777, www. jwlasvegasresort.com). Bus 207/self-parking & valet parking N Rampart Boulevard.
Rooms 555. **Rates** $194-$289 double.
This expansive Spanish-style spa and golf resort is not your typical Marriott. The resort sits on some 54

acres in the heart of Summerlin, and boasts spectacular views of the Red Rock Conservation Area and access to eight of the area's most sought-after golf courses. There's also a beautiful waterfall pool, a splendid spa, a full-service beauty salon, a fully equipped fitness centre, several restaurants and clubs, and a few shops. A complimentary shuttle provides access to the Strip.

Accommodation
Divvied up between two towers, the resort's spacious rooms are more luxurious than anything you'd usually encounter at a Marriott. All rooms feature oversized raindrop showers and separate whirlpool baths.

Eating & drinking
Local celebrity chef Gustav Mauler has carved a neat niche for himself with the Italian trattoria Spiedini. Shizen offers sushi and teppanyaki, while a lively standing-room crowd enjoys bangers 'n' mash and top-shelf Irish whiskey at JC Wooloughan's Irish Pub. Fine-dining options include Ceres, which serves breakfast, lunch and dinner amid gorgeous views of the resort's waterfalls; the intimate Carmel Room, which features fine continental cuisine served with Mediterranean flair; and, in season, light fare poolside at the Waterside Grille.

Entertainment
There's Celtic folk and rock in JC Wooloughan's.

Gambling
The Marriott casino is among Vegas's most expansive and luxurious, with a stunning, palm-painted backlit dome over the pit. The table and slot chairs are extremely swish, helping to make this a hugely comfortable place. There's a story behind it all: the casino was originally designed to attract affluent visitors, but few took the $50 cab ride from the Strip and the place went bankrupt. The new owners hired a veteran management group that instead targeted affluent Summerlin locals with unexpectedly low minimums and decent slot-club benefits.
Amenities *Bar. Business centre. Concierge. Disabled-adapted rooms. Gym. Internet ($9.95). No-smoking floors. Pools (outdoor). Restaurants (3). Room service. Spa. TV: pay movies.*
Games *Baccarat ($100-$5,000); blackjack ($5-$5,000); Caribbean stud; casino war; craps (3x, 4x, 5x; from $5); keno; mini baccarat ($5-$500); pai gow poker; roulette (double zero); Spanish 21; three-card poker.*

★ Red Rock Resort
11011 W Charleston Boulevard, at I-215, Las Vegas, NV 89135 (reservations 1-866 767 7773, front desk & casino 797 7777, www.redrocklas vegas.com). Bus 206/self-parking & valet parking W Charleston Boulevard. **Rooms** 815. **Rates** $149-$599 double.

Like Green Valley Ranch, it's located in an affluent suburb. And like Green Valley Ranch, there's a Rande Gerber-owned nightclub on site. But the comparisons between Red Rock and its sibling end there. This billion-dollar operation pays homage to the classic resort architecture of the early 1950s and '60s as well as the natural landscape that surrounds it. The rusty red and tan exterior mimics the colours of the nearby mountain range, while floor-to-ceiling glass walls afford spectacular views. There's even an Adventure Spa that takes full advantage of the desert surroundings by offering horseback riding, guided hikes and mountain biking. For pure relaxation, head to the Red Rock Spa.

Gold-leaf ceilings, Swarovski-crystal chandeliers and crocodile-leather wall panels are just a few of the more luxurious elements that set Red Rock apart from other neighbourhood casinos; indeed, the steakhouse, trendy nightclub and martini bar mirror the Strip's hipster aesthetic. The centrepiece is the palm tree-lined, circular Sandbar Pool, complete with a 'beach' with 19 private cabanas, six wading pools and, best of all, blackjack.

Accommodation
The guestrooms are fashionably outfitted with modern furniture and accessories that don't sacrifice comfort for style. Slip into the plush robe and slippers, plug in your iPod and pour yourself a drink from the self-service martini bar. Try the villa suite, which features a private patio complete with its own bar, a ten-person whirlpool spa and views of the beach area.

Eating & drinking
The choice here is wide and appealing. T-Bones Chophouse is an elegant steakhouse with a great wine list, while the authentic Italian dishes of Terra Rossa come courtesy of *Hell's Kitchen* winner Heather West. Salt Lick BBQ serves Texas-style 'cue; Cabo Cantina offers Baja-style Mexican; and Tides Oyster Bar dishes up creole-style po'boys and pan roasts. In the heart of the casino, you'll find the Lucky Bar, home to those red patent-leather crocodile panels as well as an awe-inspiring crystal chandelier. The Onyx Lounge specialises in signature martinis, while the Sand Bar serves cool poolside libations.

Entertainment
Cherry, nightclub impresario Rande Gerber's latest foray into Vegas, reigns supreme as the off-Strip hotspot, while house band Zowie Bowie keeps the Rocks Lounge jumping with dance covers. In warm months, the Sandbar hosts poolside shows from the likes of Damien Marley. There's a 16-screen multiplex with private viewing boxes and a 72-lane bowling alley.

Gambling
The name of the game here is machines: there are more than 3,200 of them, split evenly between slots

CONSUME

and video poker. Table minimums are reasonable. Look for the one-of-a-kind giant Wheel of Fortune Super Spin slot machine that seats several players around a big bubble (it's by the cinema entrance).

Amenities *Bars (15). Business centre. Concierge. Disabled-adapted rooms. Gym. Internet ($12.99). No-smoking rooms. Pool (outdoor). Restaurants (9). Spa.*

Games *Baccarat ($100-$10,000); bingo; blackjack ($5-$5,000); Caribbean stud; casino war; craps (3x, 4x, 5x; from $5); keno; mini baccarat ($5-$10,000); pai gow poker; poker; roulette (double zero); Spanish 21; three-card poker.*

Moderate

Orleans

4500 W Tropicana Avenue, between S Decatur & S Valley View boulevards, Las Vegas, NV 89103 (reservations 1-800 675 3267, front desk & casino 365 7111, www.orleanscasino.com). Bus 103, 104, 201/self-parking & valet parking W Tropicana Avenue, Cameron Street or S Arville Street. **Rooms** 1,886. **Rates** $60-$175 double. **Map** p333 X3 ⑤⑧

The theme at the Orleans is more Disneyland than French Quarter. Still, the locals don't seem to mind, mostly because the Vegas-style action is very real. Located very close to the Strip (and within a five-minute walk of the Palms), the Orleans is one of the few casinos at which locals and tourists happily mix in every part of the operation. The rooms aren't especially exciting, but they're kept in good condition and by no means offensively designed. In any case, it's hard to grumble at these prices.

The 11 restaurants run the casino-dining gamut, including steak and seafood (Canal Street), prime rib (Prime Rib Loft), buffet (French Market), Mexican (Don Miguel's) and the nearly ubiquitous Irish pub (Brendan's). The sure eating bet here is the grilled-to-order burger at Terrible Mike's.

Entertainment comes courtesy of the Orleans Arena, home of hockey's Wranglers and arena football's Gladiators; the Century Orleans 18 cinema (*see p244*); and the 70-lane bowling centre (*see p264*). You might occasionally find Bourbon Street-style jazz or modern rock in the 999-seat Orleans Showroom, though country and nostalgic rock are the norms.

But the gambling is the main draw for locals, with the casino offering lively, low-limit action. The poker room is one of the best in town, with 'bad-beat jackpots' (awarded to the player who loses with a very big hand) and regular tournaments. The blackjack is mostly double-deckers that pay 3:2 for naturals.

Amenities *Bars (7). Business centre. Disabled-adapted rooms. Gym. Internet (Wi-Fi $10.95). No-smoking floors. Pool (outdoor). Restaurants (11). Spa.*

Games *Bingo; blackjack ($5-$2,000); Caribbean stud; craps (2x; from $5); keno; Let it Ride;* mini baccarat ($5-$1,000); pai gow poker; poker; roulette (double zero); Spanish 21; three-card poker.

Silverton

3333 Blue Diamond Road, at I-15, Las Vegas, NV 89139 (reservations 1-866 946 4373, front desk & casino 263 7777, www.silvertoncasino.com). Bus 117/self-parking & valet parking Dean Martin Drive. **Rooms** 300. **Rates** $69-$199 double.

Its location, just off I-15 several miles south of the Strip, doesn't flatter the Silverton. However, this is a surprisingly attractive property that, while by no means offering the Palms or Caesars much competition in the coolness or extravagance departments, is nonetheless smarter and more stylish than you might expect. The rooms are decent if somewhat expensive for the location, and the casino offers the usual array of table games and slots.

Entertainment is by and large limited to shows from guitar bands that could politely be described as 'vintage'; hell, the hotel has even persuaded Hootie & the Blowfish to lend their name to the agreeably retro Shady Grove Lounge. Eating options are headlined by the Twin Creeks steakhouse, with the Sundance Grill offering round-the-clock American classics and Seasons providing all-you-can-eat buffet fare. Bonus: Just across I-15 is the Bootlegger (*see p174*).

The casino is surprisingly expansive and upscale, with 1,400 slots and nearly 50 table games; the video poker is good enough to attract the pros. *Photo p146.*

Amenities *Bars (5). Disabled-adapted rooms. Gym. Internet (Wi-Fi $10). No-smoking floors. Pool (outdoor). Restaurants (5). Room service. TV: pay movies.*

Games *Blackjack ($5-$2,000); craps (10x; from $5); keno; mini baccarat ($10-$3,000); pai gow poker; poker; roulette (double zero); three-card poker.*

South Point

9777 Las Vegas Boulevard South, at E Silverado Ranch Boulevard, Las Vegas, NV 89183 (reservations 1-866 791 7626, front desk & casino 796 7111, www.southpointcasino.com). Bus 117/self-parking E Silverado Ranch Boulevard/valet parking Las Vegas Boulevard South. **Rooms** 1,354. **Rates** $50-$180 double.

After effectively selling the Coast casino chain to Boyd Gaming in 2004, Michael Gaughan (son of legendary local casino operator Jackie) began working for his former competitors, watching as they spent more than $500 million building the South Coast casino on an isolated site several miles south of the Strip. When, after a year, it failed to achieve lift-off, Gaughan jumped in and bought the resort, first changing its name and then upgrading both its facilities and its image. It's an appealing place, its rooms decorated with attractive colours and without unnecessary ornamentation. Amenities include a 64-lane bowling alley, a 16-screen cinema and, right out of left field, a 4,400-seat equestrian arena. Dining is headlined by Michael's, recently relocated from Bill's Gamblin' Hall on the Strip; there's also an Italian eaterie (Don Vito's), a steakhouse (the Silverado), an oyster bar (Big Sur) and the obligatory buffet (the Garden). The big casino includes more than 2,400 machines (with decent video-poker schedules) and 60 table games, along with a 300-seat indie race and sports book. A shuttle bus runs to and from the southern end of the Strip.

Amenities *Bars (10). Business centre. Disabled-adapted rooms. Gym. Internet (Wi-Fi $10.99). No-smoking floors. Pools (outdoor). Restaurants (7). Room service. Spa. TV: pay movies.*
Games *Bingo; blackjack ($5-$2,000); Caribbean stud; craps (2x; from $5); keno; mini baccarat ($5-$5,000); pai gow poker; poker; roulette (double zero); three-card poker.*

Budget

Arizona Charlie's
4575 Boulder Highway, at E Twain Avenue, Las Vegas, NV 89121 (reservations 1-888 236 9066, front desk & casino 951 9000, www.arizona charliesboulder.com). Bus 107/self-parking & valet parking S Decatur Boulevard. **Rooms** 350. **Rates** $31-$125 double.

Arizona Charlie's is a no-frills, 258-room bunkhouse for serious players who need a place to drop. The theme is the Yukon gold rush, though you won't notice: the interior design is little more than a floor, a ceiling and rows of machines. One effort to keep up with the local competition was the replacement of the Yukon Grille with a link from the Outback Steakhouse chain. But the surest bet at Charlie's is still the Sourdough Café, where the steak-and-eggs special will set you back just $2.99. There's also a buffet. The Naughty Ladies Saloon plays host to a range of lounge acts. The blackjack games here are decent, with typical low minimums, as is some of the video poker. You can also find $2 craps at times, but often with only 2x odds. There's a strong selection of slots for nickel and quarter players.

Amenities *Bars (3). Disabled-adapted rooms. No-smoking floors. Pool (outdoor). Restaurants (3). TV: pay movies.*
Games *Bingo; blackjack ($5-$1,000); craps (2x, 5x; from $2); Caribbean stud; keno; Let it Ride; pai gow poker; roulette (double zero).*

Boulder Station
4111 Boulder Highway, at E Desert Inn Road, Las Vegas, NV 89121 (reservations 1-800 683 7777, front desk & casino 432 7777, www.boulder station.com). Bus 107, 213/self-parking & valet parking Boulder Highway. **Rooms** 300. **Rates** $49-$169 double.

This Victorian-styled Station casino on the Boulder Strip lures locals with solid entertainment. The

Railhead hosts a stable of B-list headliners (from Loverboy to Diane Schuur), and there are plenty of family-friendly amenities, such as an 11-screen movie theatre and a Kids Quest childcare centre, there are decent dining options too: the Feast Gourmet Buffet is popular, and the Broiler's Sunday champagne brunch is one of the best in Vegas (and only $19.99). The casino is typical for the Station chain, though the minimums in this part of town seem to run a little lower, with some $3 tables scattered about, 10x odds at craps, and 50¢ roulette chips. The newest machines seem to show up here first.

Amenities *Bars (5). Disabled-adapted rooms. Internet ($9.99). No-smoking floors. Pools (outdoor). Restaurants (6). Room service.*
Games *Bingo; blackjack ($3-$1,000); Caribbean stud; craps (10x; from $2); keno; Let it Ride; mini baccarat ($5-$1,000); pai gow poker; pai gow tiles; poker; roulette (double zero); three-card poker.*

Fiesta Rancho
2400 N Rancho Drive, at W Lake Mead Boulevard, Las Vegas, NV 89130 (reservations 1-888 899 7770, front desk & casino 631 7000, www.fiestarancholasvegas.com). Bus 103, 106, 210, 211/self-parking N Rancho Drive, W Lake Mead Boulevard or Carey Avenue/valet parking W Lake Mead Boulevard. **Rooms** 100. **Rates** $30-$250 double.

The slot-club at the Fiesta Rancho is known for regular triple-points days and no-hassle food comps. There's also a 300-seat bingo room and a drive-up sports-betting window, where you don't even have to get out of the car to bet on an upcoming game. There is also a poker room.

Besides the gaming, it's the party-style atmosphere that draws visitors to the north-west part of the city. A variety of acts play Club Tequila, where the emphasis is on Latin music; the obligatory Mexican food comes courtesy of Garduno's (with a ridiculous 300 flavours of margarita) and the Blue Agave Steakhouse. Escape the desert heat in the outdoor swimming pool or the NHL-size ice arena.

Amenities *Bars (4). Disabled-adapted rooms. Internet ($9.99). No-smoking rooms. Pools (outdoor). Restaurants (4). Room service. Spa. TV: pay movies.*
Games *Bingo; blackjack ($5-$1,000); casino war; Caribbean stud; craps (10x; from $2); keno; Let it Ride; pai gow poker; poker; roulette (double zero); three-card poker.*

Gold Coast
4000 W Flamingo Road, at S Valley View Boulevard, Las Vegas, NV 89103 (reservations 1-800 331 5334, front desk & casino 367 7111, www.goldcoastcasino.com). Bus 201/self-parking & valet parking S Valley View Boulevard, W Flamingo Road or Wynn Road. **Rooms** 711. **Rates** $44-$124 double. **Map** p333 X3 ⑮

CONSUME

Boyd Gaming took hold of Coast Casinos in 2006, renaming the Barbary Coast and leaving this spot as the oldest link in Michael Gaughan's chain. So far, it's relying on the same formula for success. Locals love the GC's machines and the players' club, both of which usually take top honours in the *Las Vegas Review-Journal*'s 'Best of Vegas' survey. There's plenty of $5 blackjack, $5 pai gow and $1 roulette for low rollers, one of the city's bigger bingo rooms (eight sessions daily) plus a 70-lane bowling alley. The 711 rooms have been upgraded with the seemingly mandatory 32in LCD TVs.

For food, choose from the Cortez Room, a mid-priced steakhouse; the all-Asian Ping Pang Pong; the Java Vegas coffeeshop; or the buffet, rated highly by locals. The one new addition is a noodle bar called Noodle Exchange.

Amenities *Bars (5). Business centre. Concierge. Disabled-adapted rooms. Gym. Internet ($10.99). No-smoking floors. Pool (outdoor). Restaurants (6). Room service. TV: pay movies.*
Games *Bingo; blackjack ($5-$2,000); Caribbean stud; craps (2x; from $2); keno; mini baccarat ($10-$1,000); pai gow poker; poker; roulette (double zero); Spanish 21; three-card poker.*

Palace Station

2411 W Sahara Avenue, at N Rancho Drive, Las Vegas, NV 89102 (reservations 1-800 634 3101, front desk & casino 367 2411, www.palace station.com). Bus 104, 204/self-parking & valet parking W Sahara Avenue, N Rancho Drive or Teddy Drive. **Rooms** *1,006.* **Rates** *$39-$299 double.* **Map** p336 A4 ⑥

The original Station casino has been a favourite of locals for more than 30 years, thanks largely to the popular gaming promotion. You'll find 1,800 slot and video-poker machines here, along with 57 gaming tables, a 600-seat bingo room, a nine-table poker room, a keno lounge, and a race and sports book. The hotel draws its share of tourists too, due to its close proximity to the Strip and cheap rooms.

Several of the restaurants offer fine neighbourhood fare: the Feast Gourmet Buffet; steaks and seafood in the Broiler; and a food court. There's lounge music in Sound Trax and Jack's, an Irish pub and the Cabo Bar. The 1,000-plus rooms and suites range from economy courtyard rooms to deluxe tower rooms.

INSIDE TRACK SUPER SPAS

Lots of the casinos have spas these days, offering self-indulgent treatments to make your Vegas visit even more sybaritic. Among the best in the city are the **Bathhouse** at Thehotel at Mandalay Bay, **Planet Hollywood Spa**, **Qua Baths & Spa** at Caesars Palace, **Red Rock Spa** and the **Spa at Wynn**. For all, *see p211.*

Amenities *Bars (4). Business centre. Disabled-adapted rooms. Gym. Internet (Wi-Fi, $9.99). No-smoking rooms. Pool (outdoor). Restaurants (7). Room service. TV: pay movies.*
Games *Baccarat ($10-$5,000); bingo; blackjack ($5-$3,000); Caribbean stud; craps (3x, 4x, 5x, 10x; from $5); keno; Let it Ride; pai gow poker; pai gow tiles; poker; roulette (double zero).*

Sam's Town

5111 Boulder Highway, at E Flamingo Road, Las Vegas, NV 89122 (reservations 1-800 897 8696, front desk & casino 456 7777, www.sams townlv.com). Bus 107, 115, 202/self-parking & valet parking Boulder Highway, E Flamingo Road or Nellis Boulevard. **Rooms** *646.*
Rates *$34-$250 double.*

If you like Old West-style casinos, this is your place. Though gunfire is kept to a minimum, the theme is nonetheless prevalent, from the saloon-style bars to Roxy's, the rowdy dance hall. There's even a quality western store (Sheplers). Elsewhere, modern amenities include a 24-hour bowling centre, an 18-screen movie theatre and Sam's Town Live!, a 1,100-seat multi-use venue that stages a variety of country and pop concerts. In the middle of all this is Mystic Falls Park, a ten-storey atrium whose indoor nature walk (with trees and chirping birds) gets interrupted four times daily by the Sunset Stampede, a laser light and water show. Check out the TV sets over the tables in some of the pits, and bet up to 20x odds at the crap tables. There are thousands of video-poker machines, though few, if any, are full-pay.

Amenities *Bars (6). Disabled-adapted rooms. Internet (Wi-Fi $10). No-smoking rooms. Pool (outdoor). Restaurants (5). TV: pay movies.*
Games *Bingo; blackjack ($5-$3,000); craps (20x; from $5); keno; Let it Ride; pai gow poker; poker; roulette (double zero).*

Santa Fe Station

4949 N Rancho Drive, at US 95 (junction 90A), Las Vegas, NV 89130 (reservations 1-866 767 7771, front desk & casino 658 4900, www. santafestationlasvegas.com). Bus 101, 102, 106, 219/self-parking & valet parking N Rancho Drive or Lone Mountain Road. **Rooms** *200.* **Rates** *$50-$190 double.*

Santa Fe staples include a 488-seat bingo room and a wide variety of slots, a state-of-the-art fitness centre, plus the Chrome Showroom and multiplex. Locals enjoy great Mexican fare at Cabo, where bartenders blend equally entertaining margaritas; other options include the endlessly popular Feast Buffet and unexpectedly impressive Charcoal Room for steak and seafood. Santa Fe also operates a Kids Quest childcare and entertainment centre.

The smallish casino has low-limit table games, though with no competition nearby, the rules are not altogether favourable. The video poker is typical for

Gold Coast. *See p149.*

Station: there are a few 99% machines, but the rest lower. There is also a 24-hour poker room and a new sports book.
Amenities *Bars (8). Business centre. Disabled-adapted rooms. Gym. Internet ($9.99). No-smoking rooms. Pool (outdoor). Restaurants (7). Room service. TV: pay movies.*
Games *Blackjack ($5-$1,000); craps (10x; from $5); Let it Ride; pai gow poker; roulette (double zero); three-card poker.*

Suncoast
9090 Alta Drive, at N Rampart Boulevard, Las Vegas, NV 89145 (reservations 1-877 677 7111, front desk & casino 636 7111, www.suncoast casino.com). Bus 207/self-parking & valet parking Alta Drive & Rampart Avenue. **Rooms** 427. **Rates** $50-$180 double.
This Coast casino shares the qualities of its siblings but with one major difference: it's in Summerlin, and thus surrounded by 81 holes of world-class golf, and an assortment of upper-scale shopping and dining options. Stay on site, though, and you'll find a large and player-friendly casino floor, with 50 table games, plenty of slots and some full-pay video poker, bingo, a race and sports book, and a progressive players' club that plies regulars with comps.

Entertainment is focused on the 500-seat showroom, which stages the unlikely likes of Air Supply and the Smothers Brothers. There's also a 64-lane bowling alley plus, as is the case at many locals' joints, a 16-screen movie theatre. Foodwise, there's a standard buffet and a coffeeshop, but you'd be better off with the steaks, seafood and lamb at Primo's, or Señor Miguel's tasty Mexican specialities. The Kid's Tyme childcare centre is open seven days a week; there's also a beauty salon and fitness centre.
Amenities *Bars (6). Disabled-adapted rooms. Gym. Internet (Wi-Fi $11). No-smoking rooms.*

Pool (outdoor). Restaurants (7). Room service. TV: pay movies.
Games *Baccarat ($15-$2,500); bingo; blackjack ($5-$2,000); Caribbean stud; craps (2x; from $5); keno; Let it Ride; pai gow poker; poker; roulette (double zero); Spanish 21; three-card poker.*

Sunset Station
1301 W Sunset Road, between N Stephanie Street & I-515, Henderson, NV 89014 (reservations 1-888 786 7389, front desk & casino 547 7777, www.sunsetstation.com). Bus 114/self-parking & valet parking Stephanie Street, W Sunset Road, Marks Street or Warm Springs Road. **Rooms** 457. **Rates** $59-$189 double.
Slot-clubbing locals keep every inch of the capacious Sunset Station casino buzzing. The usual table games, with $5-$10 minimums (and 10x odds at craps), are situated under a stained-glass ceiling. There are wide ranges of slots and video-poker machines, though the full-pay variety are few and far between.

Naturally, there are plenty of other ways in which to spend your money. A 13-screen Regal Cinema (*see p244*), a Kids Quest childcare centre and a very with-it bowling centre all appease both adults and kids; grown-ups may prefer the Club Madrid, where you'll find big-name acts in an intimate lounge. During swimming season, big-name entertainers (from Styx to Clint Black) perform at the 5,000-seat amphitheatre by the Mediterranean-style pool. But the restaurants are the steady draws, with cuisine that ranges from wings at Hooters to the smarter Sonoma Cellar Steakhouse. In between, there's the worth-the-wait Feast Buffet, plus the Guadalajara Bar & Grille and its sweet little tequila collection. And don't miss the gaudy Gaudi Bar in the centre of the action.

Amenities *Bars (11). Disabled-adapted rooms. Internet ($9.99). No-smoking rooms. Pool (outdoor). Restaurants (8). Room service.*
Games *Bingo; blackjack ($5-$5,000); craps (10x; from $2); keno; Let it Ride; mini baccarat ($5-$1,000); pai gow poker; poker; roulette (double zero); three-card poker.*

Texas Station

2101 Texas Star Lane, at N Rancho Drive, between W Lake Mead Boulevard & Vegas Drive, Las Vegas, NV 89032 (reservations 1-800 654 8888, front desk & casino 631 1000, www. texasstation.com). Bus 103, 106, 210, 211/self-parking N Rancho Drive/valet parking W Lake Mead Boulevard or N Rancho Drive. **Rooms** 200. **Rates** $40-$25 double. **Map** p333 X1 ⑥①

Bigger is better in this Lone Star-themed hotel, which features a 60-lane bowling centre, an 18-screen movie theatre, a 5,000sq ft (470sq m) arcade, and 2,300 very popular slot and video-poker machines. In the poker room, the game of choice is, inevitably, Texas hold 'em. And where would Texas be without a steakhouse? The award-winning Austins is a fine example of what a steakhouse should be: prime steaks dry-aged for 21 days, hand-cut on the premises and then marinated in Austins' secret sauce. Texas-style entertainment can be found in Club Armadillo and the 2,000-seat Dallas Events Center with the likes of Merle Haggard. Surprisingly, there are only 200 rooms, making the hotel side of this casino almost boutique. Texas also has a Kids Quest childcare and entertainment centre.
Amenities *Bars (8). Disabled-adapted rooms. Internet ($10.99). No-smoking rooms. Pool (outdoor). Restaurants (5). Room service. TV: pay movies.*
Games *Bingo; blackjack ($5-$1,000); craps (10x; from $5); keno; Let it Ride; pai gow poker; poker; roulette (double zero); three-card poker.*

NON-CASINO HOTELS

Expensive

Loews Lake Las Vegas

101 Montelago Boulevard, off Lake Las Vegas Parkway, Henderson, NV 89011 (reservations 1-800 235 6397, front desk 567 6000, www.loews hotels.com). No bus/self-parking & valet parking Lake Las Vegas Parkway. **Rooms** 493. **Rates** $144-$399.

Despite changing hands (it used to be a Hyatt), this Lake Las Vegas property still has a Moroccan theme and most of the same amenities. But Loews has upgraded the rooms, resurfaced the pools and given the hotel a facelift. Most dramatically, the small casino has gone, converted into a venue for weddings, meetings and, yes, ballroom dancing (every Saturday).

As for food, Marssa has taken over from Japengo but still serves Pacific Rim cuisine and sushi

prepared by master chef Osamu Fujita. Café Tajine serves breakfast, lunch and dinner in a bright, laid-back atmosphere. The Arabesque Lounge has beautiful views of the lake and mountains; for outdoor dining, try the SandsaBar Grill.

Along with hiking, biking and birdwatching, the major sports are on a 320-acre private man-made lake (sailing, canoeing, kayaking, windsurfing and fishing), and three golf courses. There's a well-groomed white-sand beach as well as a sports area with a small putting green, basketball, volleyball and tennis.
Amenities *Bars (2). Business centre. Concierge. Disabled-adapted rooms. Gym. Internet (Wi-Fi $9.95). No-smoking floors. Pools (outdoor). Restaurants (5). Room service. Spa. TV: pay movies.*

Ravella Lake Las Vegas

1610 Lake Las Vegas Parkway, off E Lake Mead Parkway, Henderson, NV 89011 (reservations 1-800 241 3333, front desk 567 4700, www. ravellavegas.com). No bus/self-parking & valet parking Lake Las Vegas Parkway. **Rooms** 349. **Rates** $179-$1,500.

Carefully isolated within the Lake Las Vegas community, roughly 20 miles south-east of the Strip, this former Ritz-Carlton is one of the most luxurious resorts in the Vegas metropolitan area, in no small part because it doesn't really feel much like Las Vegas. Key to this, of course, is the lack of an in-house casino: gamblers can wander next door to the Casino Montelago (939 8888, www.casinomonte-lago.com), but the Ritz-Carlton remains unsullied by the incessant blinking lights and tinkling melodies that characterise most major resorts in the region.

The hotel itself offers all the luxury you'd expect to find in a Ritz-Carlton property. The rooms themselves are handsome without being needlessly flashy, kitted out with plush beds and chairs, fabulously generous bathrooms and most conceivable amenities (minibars, internet access and so on). The lobby bar, Firenze, delivers worthwhile cocktails, decent sandwiches and, on weekend afternoons at 1pm, a Florentine-style high tea. The real culinary action is downstairs in the renowned Medici, which serves a winning range of Mediterranean-influenced American dishes for breakfast, brunch (Sundays only), lunch and dinner.

The luxury extends to the hotel's capacious spa, rightly regarded as one of the city's best. Nearby amenities include the Falls and Reflection Bay golf courses, which essentially adjoin the hotel, and Montelago Village, a sort of upscale Italianate theme park dotted with expensive boutiques, restaurants and bars.
Amenities *Bar. Business centre. Concierge. Disabled-adapted rooms. Gym. Internet (Wi-Fi; included in $25 resort fee). No-smoking floors. Pools (outdoor). Restaurants (2). Room service. Spa. TV: pay movies.*

Restaurants & Buffets

Bye bye buffet. Hello haute cuisine.

Nowhere in Las Vegas is the power of cash more evident than in its array of restaurants. For years, food here was designed purely to provide stomach-lining for drinkers and fuel for gamblers. The sole aim of catering crews was to get diners in and out of their restaurants as quickly as possible, sending them back to the gambling tables where the real profits were to be made. The choice of cuisine didn't extend far beyond all-you-can-eat buffets, 24-hour coffeeshops and, for the rich visitor, swanky steakhouses. These days all that has changed as big-name chefs vie for customers.

THE VEGAS RESTAURANT SCENE

Since the arrival in 1992 of Wolfgang Puck, the first star chef to open a restaurant in the city, Las Vegas's dining scene has been turned on its head. The range of restaurants in the casinos is broader than ever, catering to more or less every taste and budget. The casino moguls have spent millions luring the world's best chefs to the city, forking over even more cash on spectacular interior design and fresh ingredients, flown in from around the country every day of the year. The buffets and all-night eateries remain, but many of them have been upgraded and are virtually unrecognisable from days of yore.

Despite all the welcome improvements, things aren't perfect. Many of the star chefs who've lent the weight of their names and/or reputations to restaurants in the city don't cook here, though that doesn't stop them from setting extremely high prices. There's still plenty of mediocrity: overpriced steakhouses, inauthentic Chinese eateries, dreary breakfast bars and the like. And a few of the town's high-end, big-name restaurants coast along on autopilot after an initial marketing blitz, when reputations are made and trends are set. But many others sustain a high standard. Indeed, the smart restaurateurs are aware that even in a resort town such as this, word-of-mouth is a powerful tool, especially now that foodie blogs and restaurant review apps mean that everyone can be a critic.

Away from the Strip, things are less consistent but often impressive. Carnivores are well served by a fine array of steakhouses and barbecue joints; a handful of excellent low-key, high-value Asian restaurants sit tucked away in unlikely strip-mall locations; and there's even a plethora of Middle Eastern eateries. Follow the recommendations in this chapter, and you can't go far wrong.

PRACTICALITIES

The ebb and flow of visitors through Las Vegas is so unpredictable that making reservations, while not always necessary, is nonetheless recommended for all major Strip restaurants, especially those at the higher end of the scale. Weekends are busy, but many eateries do a brisk trade during the week thanks to the influx of conventioneers. Aside from some special Sunday feeds (such as the **Sterling Brunch** at Bally's; *see p178*), casino buffets don't accept reservations; prepare to queue at busy times. Away from the Strip, you'd do well to book for Friday and Saturday nights.

Vegas is a pretty casual town – that shlump in cargo shorts and flip-flops

> ❶ Blue numbers given here correspond to the location of restaurants marked on the street maps. *See pp333-336.*

INSIDE TRACK TIPPING TIPS

Tipping is a way of life in the US and workers in service industries rely on gratuities. Restaurant waiting staff should get 15-20 per cent.

might be a billionaire — and only a few restaurants enforce a dress code that moves much beyond an insistence on shoes and a shirt. You should be all right if you employ common sense: you can get away with almost anything at the **Burger Bar** (*see p156*), but men would do well to wear a jacket when dining at **Picasso** (*see p163*). If in doubt, it's always advisable to ask staff when you make your reservation.

Restaurants

THE STRIP

America

New York New York *3790 Las Vegas Boulevard South, at W Tropicana Avenue (740 6451, www. nynyhotelcasino.com). Bus Deuce, 201.* **Open** 24hrs daily. **Main courses** $12-$24. **Map** p336 A8 ❶ **American & steakhouses**
Like the casino in which it's housed, America is terrific fun. In both, a simple concept is executed with wonderfully playful enthusiasm. The all-purpose menu offers innumerable dishes from across the country, many of them inspired by a particular corner of the US: chicken quesadillas by way of

Albuquerque, for example, or Philadelphia cheese steaks. It's not really about the authenticity, mind; this is just good, solid cooking served with an exclamation mark, a wide smile and a heartfelt 'have a nice day!'

★ American Fish
Aria, CityCenter *3746 Las Vegas Boulevard South, at W Harmon Avenue (877 230 2742, www.arialasvegas.com.com). Bus Deuce, 202.* **Open** 11am-2.30pm, 5-10.30pm Mon-Thur; 11am-10.30pm Fri-Sun. **Main courses** *Lunch* $15-$22. *Dinner* $20-$38. **Map** p336 A7 ❷ Seafood
Chef Michael Mina's take on the classic seafood restaurant takes sustainability – in the ingredients and in the decor, made from reclaimed materials – as its mission. Mina creates fresh and saltwater fish dishes with another unique touch: the cooking water itself is drawn from various oceans and lakes.

Aquaknox
Venetian *3555 Las Vegas Boulevard South, between Sands Avenue & E Flamingo Road (414 3772, www.aquaknox.net). Bus Deuce, 105, 203.* **Open** 5-11pm Mon-Thur, Sun; 5-11.30pm Fri, Sat. **Main courses** $28-$65. **Map** p335, p336 B6 ❸ Seafood
The prevalence of so many excellent seafood restaurants in this desert resort town remains baffling to outsiders, and understandably so, but Aquaknox stands as solid proof that with a little expense and a good deal of effort, it's possible to conjure up excellent fish out of next to nothing. Served in a sleek room that nods constantly to the cuisine's watery theme, Tom Moloney's food lets its fresh ingredients do the work. Good idea.

American Fish.

★ L'Atelier de Joël Robuchon

MGM Grand *3799 Las Vegas Boulevard South, at E Tropicana Avenue (693 7223, www.mgm grand.com). Bus Deuce, 201.* **Open** 5-10.30pm Mon-Thur, Sun; 5-11pm Fri, Sat. **Main courses** $14-$54. **Map** p336 A8 **❹ French**
This workshop-style dining room, right next door to Robuchon's signature restaurant (*see p159*), features a few tables and a counter at which you can sit and watch some of the world's best dishes (simpler and cheaper than at the other place) being prepared. Push the boat out and go for the discovery tasting menu; it's worth the $150 price tag.

Aureole

Mandalay Bay *3950 Las Vegas Boulevard South, at W Hacienda Avenue (632 7401, www.charlie palmersteak.com). Bus Deuce, 104, 105.* **Open** 6-10.30pm daily. **Set menu** $69-$85. **Map** p336 A9 **❺ American & steakhouses**
Where else can you dine within sight of a four-storey, 4,500-bottle wine tower, up and down which float harnessed wine angels, fetching your choice on demand? The food, orchestrated by Charlie Palmer and overseen by Vincent Pouessel, is also a delight, with seasonal American dishes including caramelised Sonoma duck and fennel steamed Alaskan salmon. Megan Romano's ethereal sweets make breaking your diet well worthwhile.
▶ *For the Charlie Palmer Steakhouse, see p156.*

Barmasa/Shaboo

Aria, CityCenter *3600 Las Vegas Boulevard South, at W Flamingo Road (693 8181, www. toddenglish.com). Bus Deuce, 202.* **Open** 11am-2.30pm, 5-10.30pm Mon-Thur; 11am-10.30pm Fri-Sun. **Main courses** *Lunch* $15-$22. *Dinner* $20-$38. **Map** p336 A7 **❻ American & steakhouses**
Entering this austerely room with its vast-seeming darkened vaulted ceiling, one feels instantly at ease – it's like joining a sophisticated nighttime picnic in an urban backyard. The first Las Vegas restaurant by star chef Masayoshi Takayama (his Masa restaurant in New York City's Time Warner Center, is one of the world's most expensive), is divided into two: Bar Masa is elegantly casual a la carte Japanese cuisine; the smaller, more exclusive (and expensive) Shaboo offers an omakase-style chef-designed experience that is different every night.

Bartolotta Ristorante di Mare

Wynn Las Vegas *3131 Las Vegas Boulevard South, between E Desert Inn Road & Sands Avenue (770 7000, www.wynnlasvegas.com). Bus Deuce, 203.* **Open** 5.30-10.30pm daily. **Main courses** $35-$100. **Map** p335, p336 B6 **❼ Seafood**
If you're lucky, you'll land a table with a view of the water outside at this posh, but by no means flashy, eaterie within the Wynn resort – all the better to get you in the right frame of mind for Paul Bartolotta's

cultured take on the Mediterranean seafood tradition. (That said, the menu also features pasta and a few meat options.) The expensive prices mean it's probably one best saved for those really special occasions.

Beso

Crystals, CityCenter *3720 Las Vegas Boulevard South, at W Harmon Avenue (254 2376, www. besolasvegas.com). Bus Deuce, 202.* **Open** 11am-3.30pm, 5.30pm-11pm daily. **Main courses** *Lunch* $15-$22. *Dinner* $20-$38. **Map** p336 A7 **❽ American & steakhouses**
One of many celebrity owned restaurants in Las Vegas, Beso – its patron is *Desperate Housewives* star Eva Longoria – is one of the few that earns its keep. Tucked into the entrance of the Crystals shopping centre, a Housewives hangout if there ever was one, the candlelit restaurant fuses steakhouse classics with Latin fire and flair.

Boa Steakhouse

Caesars Palace (Forum Shops) *3570 Las Vegas Boulevard South, at W Flamingo Road (733 7373, www.boasteak.com). Bus Deuce, 202.* **Open** noon-10pm Mon-Thur; noon-11.30pm Fri, Sat; noon-10pm Sun. **Main courses** $27-$45. **Map** p336 A7 **❾ American & steakhouses**
The austere, clinical design is contemporary and a long way from the gentlemen's-club standard fittings that decorate more traditional steakhouses, but then the menu at Boa (an LA import) goes beyond surf 'n' turf cliché. The classics are rendered well here, though there's plenty of fun to be had on a list of appetisers that might include such novelties as truffle nachos and goat's cheese baklava. Prices are high.

THE BEST RESTAURANTS

For a brilliant breakfast
Bouchon (*see p156*), **Hash House a-Go Go** (*see p175*) or Sunday brunch at the **Verandah Café** (*see p166*).

For a lovely lunch
Corsa Cucina (*see p157*), **NM Café** (*see p161*) or **'Wichcraft** (*see p168*).

For a sneaky snack
Luv-It Frozen Custard (*see p169*) or **Pink's** (*see p163*).

For a divine dinner
Craftsteak (*see p158*), **Joël Robuchon** (*see p159*) or **Le Cirque** (*see p157*).

For a midnight meal
America (*see left*), **Bootlegger Bistro** (*see p174*) or **Mr Lucky's 24/7** (*see p170*).

CONSUME

Border Grill

Mandalay Bay *3950 Las Vegas Boulevard South, at W Hacienda Avenue (632 7403, www. bordergrill.com). Bus Deuce, 104, 105.* **Open** 11.30am-10.30pm daily. **Main courses** $10-$30. **Map** p336 A9 ⑩ **Mexican**
Imported from Santa Monica, this Angeleno take on Mexican food is not especially authentic, but works a treat regardless. Mary Sue Milliken and Susan Feniger, frontwomen of popular show *Too Hot Tamales*, have given some classic dishes a twist (the quesadillas are a great call), but also look to their home state for inspiration: witness the deep-fried snapper, served over refried beans. Lively stuff.

★ Botero

Encore *3131 Las Vegas Boulevard South, at Sands Avenue (770 3463, www.wynnlas vegas.com). Bus Deuce, 202.* **Open** 6-10.30pm Mon-Thur, Sun; 6-11pm Fri, Sat. **Main courses** *Dinner* $31-$100. **Map** p336 A7 ⑪ **American & steakhouses**
The voluptuous flavours and atmosphere of Chef Mark LoRusso's contemporary cosmopolitan dinner-only steakhouse are inspired by the artwork of namesake Fernando Botero – several of his sculptures are featured on the poolside premises. It's a steakhouse, yes, but LoRusso has an unforgettable way with seafood, too, as evidenced by his Dungeness crab agnolotti and loup de mer with niçoise vegetables.

Bouchon

Venetian *3555 Las Vegas Boulevard South, between Sands Avenue & E Flamingo Road (414 6200, www.frenchlaundry.com). Bus Deuce, 105, 203.* **Open** 7-10.30am, 5-11pm Mon-Fri; 8am-2pm, 5-11pm Sat, Sun. *Oyster bar* 3-11pm daily. **Main courses** *Breakfast* $8-$22. *Lunch & dinner* $17-$33. **Map** p335, p336 B6 ⑫ **French**
Inside this bistro and oyster bar, much-garlanded Thomas Keller serves authentic French country fare modelled after the cuisine served in the original *bouchons* of Lyon. Indoors or on poolside seating in the gardens, indulge in Bouchon french toast for breakfast, served bread-pudding style with warm layers of brioche, custard and fresh fruit with maple syrup; or, for dinner, try the *truite aux amandes*, pan-roasted trout with almonds, brown butter and green beans.

Bradley Ogden

Caesars Palace *3570 Las Vegas Boulevard South, at W Flamingo Road (731 7410, www. harrahs.com). Bus Deuce, 202.* **Open** 5-11pm daily. **Main courses** $37-$175. **Map** p336 A7 ⑬ **American & steakhouses**
Ogden has cultivated relationships with regional suppliers and boutique growers across the US, with everything from Utah salt to Oregon seafood purchased direct from specialist providers. The result is an American cuisine that doesn't come cheap, but

if melt-in-the-mouth rack of Colorado lamb or slow-roasted muscovy duck with purple artichokes and rhubarb ring your bell, consider this an essential stop. The best bit? Ogden sticks around to cook it.

Burger Bar

Mandalay Bay *3950 Las Vegas Boulevard South, at W Hacienda Avenue (632 9364, www. mandalaybay.com). Bus Deuce, 104, 105.* **Open** 10.30am-11pm Mon-Thur, Sun; 10am-3am Fri, Sat. **Main courses** $8-$60. **Map** p336 A9 ⑭ **American & steakhouses**
Cast images of McBurgers out of your mind: the burgers at this chic yet amenable spot are fresh, meaty and deeply delicious, especially once you've garnished them with your choice of toppings. (Veggie options are available.) Ironically, it took a Frenchman to reinvent this most American of meals: it's the brainchild of Hubert Keller, the chef behind Fleur de Lys (*see p159*).

Canter's Deli

Treasure Island *3300 Las Vegas Boulevard South, at Spring Mountain Road (894 7111, www.treasureisland.com). Bus Deuce, 105, 203.* **Open** 10.30am-11pm daily. **Main courses** $6-$17. **Map** p335, p336 A6 ⑮ **Jewish**
New York-style cheesecake served in a famous LA restaurant? Welcome, of course, to Las Vegas. The original Canter's Deli is a glorious old shambles, its 75-year-old Naugahyde fittings lit by too-bright fluorescence and overseen by Jewish dears who've seen it all before. By comparison, the Vegas outpost lacks charm, but the sandwiches and soups hold their own.

Carnegie Deli

Mirage *3400 Las Vegas Boulevard South, between Spring Mountain & W Flamingo roads (866 339 4566, www.carnegiedeli.com). Bus Deuce, 105, 202, 203.* **Open** 7am-2am daily. **Main courses** $14-$21. **Map** p335, p336 A6 ⑯ **Jewish**
Las Vegas has long delighted in bringing the world to its doorstep and reconstituting it for a theme-park crowd, a trend that reached its absolute apogee with the arrival of this Manhattan institution. Gone are the wisecracking staff and gigantic sandwiches; in their place are polite servers and surprisingly expensive (yet still sizeable) meals. It's not bad, but anyone who's been to the original may feel let down.

Charlie Palmer Steak

Four Seasons *3960 Las Vegas Boulevard South, at W Hacienda Drive (632 5120, www.charlie palmersteak.com). Bus Deuce, 104, 105.* **Open** 5.30-10.30pm daily. *Lounge* 5pm-midnight daily. **Main courses** $24-$42. **Map** p336 A9 ⑰ **American & steakhouses**
Every upscale steakhouse chain in America has an outpost in Vegas. However, Charlie Palmer (who, alongside Megan Romano, is also at the helm of

Mandalay Bay's Aureole; *see p155*) stays a cut above the rest by offering ever-changing variations on the staple steak-spuds-seafood fare, thanks to resident chef de cuisine Stephen Blandino. There are classic cuts to please even the most jaded of palates, plus Romano's fantastic desserts.

Le Cirque

Bellagio *3600 Las Vegas Boulevard South, at W Flamingo Road (693 7223, www.bellagio.com). Bus Deuce, 202.* **Open** 5.30-10pm daily. **Set menus** $105-$145. **Map** p336 A7 ⓭ **French**
This Vegas version of the New York institution is overseen by Mario Maccioni, who grew up playing and working in his father Sirio's original. Chefs come and go at Le Cirque; some of the best in the world have passed through the kitchens of its various locations. But the unparalleled French cuisine

and world-class service never change, and this incarnation has one attribute that none of the three New York locations could ever boast: views of the Bellagio's elegant Lake Como.

Corsa Cucina

Wynn Las Vegas *3131 Las Vegas Boulevard South, between E Desert Inn Road & Sands Avenue (770 3463, www.wynnlasvegas.com). Bus Deuce, 203.* **Open** 5-10.30pm Mon, Tue; 11.45am-2.30pm, 5-10.30pm Wed-Sun. **Main courses** *Lunch* $17-$24. *Dinner* $24-$46. **Map** p335, p336 B6 ⓳ **Italian**
Chef Steven Kalt takes everyday Italian cuisine and infuses it with novel gourmet touches in this recently remodelled spot. The results will please diners in the market for something traditional or experimental. Try the cannelloni, made with sheep's milk ricotta,

---

Meet Your Sommelier

Las Vegas's relationship with wine is a new one, but it's getting stronger.

Not that long ago, Las Vegas's reputation for wine could be summed up in one imaginary but by no means implausible conversation.

> Waiter: 'Red or white?'
> Diner: 'Yes.'

While there are still some restaurants in which that conversation continues to take place, the wine in many restaurants is much better, much more expensive and much more likely to complement that Kobe beef steak. And it will be expertly selected and uncorked at the table by somebody whose sole responsibility is to select and uncork wines.

Every restaurant worth its salt in Vegas these days has a sommelier, if not a full-on director of wine. It's hardly surprising, given the number of vintages on offer. **Alizé** (*see p172*) at the Palms has a 65-page wine menu; and wine director William Sherer at **Aureole** (*see p155*) has filled a wine tower that's so high (four storeys) and mighty (55,000 bottles) that it has a computer tablet for a menu and 'wine angels' who rope up in search of your choice.

For all the changes, which began with the improvement of the town's dining in the early 1990s, Las Vegas's wealth actually stems more from the beer-drinking legions of visitors from middle America. So why the demand for sommeliers? Jaime Smith, a former wine director at MGM Grand who now works at Las Vegas mega-distributor

Southern Wine & Spirits, has a theory. 'As opposed to large metro areas where, generally speaking, the public is in tune with wine and seeking it out, here people come to turn their brains off. They need someone to help them decide.

Aureole.

CONSUME

spinach and a sauce of butter, walnuts and aged pecorino romano. And the tomato and mozzarella appetiser – a modern spin on the classic caprese salad with chopped tomato, basil and balsamic vinegar, beautifully arranged in the shape of a rose – is not to be missed.

Craftsteak

MGM Grand *3799 Las Vegas Boulevard South, at E Tropicana Avenue (891 7800, www.craft restaurant.com). Bus Deuce, 201.* **Open** 5.30-10pm Mon, Sun; 5-10pm Tue-Thur; 5-10.30pm Fri, Sat. **Main courses** $26-$110. **Map** p336 A8 ⑳
American & steakhouses
The selection of meats (grass-fed veal, lamb shank, filet mignon, braised short ribs) is impressive, but the sides and the quiet invention shown in the kitchen both elevate Tom Colicchio's Craftsteak from more run-of-the-mill casino steakhouses. Ingredients come from small family farms and other below-the-radar sources, and you can tell. It's all served in a cultured atmosphere, if a slightly noisy one.

Daniel Boulud

Wynn Las Vegas *3131 Las Vegas Boulevard South, between E Desert Inn Road & Sands Avenue (770 3463, www.wynnlasvegas.com). Bus Deuce, 203.* **Open** 5.30-10.30pm daily. **Main courses** $26-$44. **Map** p335, p336 B6 ㉑
Modern European
New York superstar Boulud received a special exemption from Steve Wynn's edict that every head chef in his hotel must work there full-time. But his absence isn't evident in this perfectly executed brasserie, which gives diners a chance to sample his less formal fare (burgers, raw bar selections, sweetbread schnitzel). The casually cultured dining room has an incredible view of the hotel's man-made waterfall and surrealist light show.

Diego

MGM Grand *3799 Las Vegas Boulevard South, at E Tropicana Avenue (891 7800, www.mgm grand.com). Bus Deuce, 201.* **Open** 5.30-10pm Mon-Thur, Sun; 2-10pm Fri, Sat. **Main courses** $17-$40. **Map** p336 A8 ㉒ **Mexican**
The experience at MGM's lively *cocina* starts as soon as you see the bold colours and backlit tequila-bottle tower. Traditional Mexican recipes are exemplified and often modernised; Oaxacan *carne asada* (mesquite-grilled chilli-marinated beef), Yucatan-style braised pork, cactus and tequila salsa, and so on. A tasting menu offers even more unique bites, such as braised pit-style goat and table-made shrimp cocktail.

Eiffel Tower Restaurant

Paris Las Vegas *3655 Las Vegas Boulevard South, at E Flamingo Road (948 6937, www. eiffeltowerrestaurant.com). Bus Deuce, 202.*

Fleur.

Open 11am-3pm, 5-10pm Mon-Thur, Sun; 11am-3pm, 5-10.30pm Fri, Sat. **Main courses** $30-$50. **Map** p336 A7 ㉓ **French**
The food – lamb, foie gras, steaks – which is to say high-class French dishes with subtle twists, doesn't live up to the location, but then how could it? Eleven floors above the Strip in the Eiffel Tower (with great views of the Bellagio's fountains) and designed with a beautifully modern sophistication, it's a stunner. The prices reflect this state of affairs, but then this is more about occasion than cuisine.

Fiamma

MGM Grand *3799 Las Vegas Boulevard South, at E Tropicana Avenue (891 7800, www.mgm grand.com). Bus Deuce, 201.* **Open** 5.30-10.30pm Mon-Thur, Sun; 5.30-11pm Fri, Sat. **Main courses** $21-$39. **Map** p336 A8 ㉔ **Italian**
Stephen Hanson remodelled the once-proud Olio into this beautiful if oversized trattoria, a sister to his Fiamma Osteria in New York's SoHo. A favourite for its cosy, trendy bar scene, Fiamma also dishes up Italian faves, such as lobster gnocchi and short rib raviolini, as well as a few chophouse-style steak, seafood and poultry dishes. Save room for the crochette dessert, three ridiculously delicious fried doughnuts.

Fin

Mirage *3400 Las Vegas Boulevard South, between Spring Mountain & W Flamingo Roads (791 7337, www.mirage.com). Bus Deuce, 105, 202, 203.* **Open** 11am-2pm, 5-11pm daily. **Main courses** *Lunch* $13-$22. *Dinner* $14-$295. **Map** p335 & p336 A6 ㉕ **Chinese**
The menu isn't anything out of the ordinary; certainly, there's nothing on here to frighten the horses. But Chi Choi's renditions of Chinese classics, some slightly adapted for the modern world, are nonetheless very good, and the space in which they're served is sublime and cultured. There are options suitable for most wallets.

Fix

Bellagio *3600 Las Vegas Boulevard South, at W Flamingo Road (693 8400, www.bellagio.com). Bus Deuce, 202.* **Open** 5pm-midnight Mon-Thur, Sun; 5pm-2am Fri, Sat. **Main courses** $30-$60. **Map** p336 A7 ㉖ **American & steakhouses**
The idea at Fix, the first of the three sexy Light Group eateries in town, is to bring you the 'scene and the cuisine': rather than sequestering its cast of primped diners, it opens its classy, undulating interior design to the casino so everyone can smell the wood-fired surf 'n' turf. We suggest a lounge seat, a pomegranate martini, and salmon and caviar forks.

★ Fleur

Mandalay Bay *3950 Las Vegas Boulevard South, at W Hacienda Avenue (632 9400, www.mandalaybay.com). Bus Deuce, 104, 105.* **Open** 5.30-10pm Mon-Thur, Sun; 5.30-10.30pm Fri, Sat. **Set menus** $79-$99. **Map** p336 A9 ㉗ **French**
Fleur de Lys features 30ft walls of cultured stone, a floral sculpture containing more than 3,000 fresh-cut roses, semi-private cabana tables and in, in the wine loft, a private dining area. There are DJs in the lounge, but the USP remains Hubert Keller's contemporary French cuisine. For the last word in indulgence, the Fleurburger, a Kobe burger served with truffles and foie gras, and accompanied by a bottle of 1990 Château Petrus, costs a cool $5,000.

Isla

Treasure Island *3300 Las Vegas Boulevard South, at Spring Mountain Road (894 7349, www.treasureisland.com). Bus Deuce, 105, 203.* **Open** 4-10.45pm Mon, Thur, Sun; 4-9.15pm Tue; 4-11.45pm Wed, Fri, Sat. **Main courses** $9-$18. **Map** p335 & p336 A6 ㉘ **Mexican**
Treasure Island's rebranding from family resort to adult pleasure palace hasn't been wholly successful, but the dining is certainly a vast improvement. The reinvention has been led by Richard Sandoval's Isla, which really adds a spark to some of the old Mexican favourites (burritos, chicken mole) while also bringing a slightly Californian angle to some less familiar dishes. There's an enormous variety of tequila and

staff will be happy to recommend the perfect cocktail to accompany your dinner or dessert choices.

★ Jaleo

Cosmopolitan *3708 Las Vegas Boulevard South, at W Harmon Avenue (877 551 7776, www.jaleo.com). Bus Deuce, 202.* **Open** 11am-2.30pm, 5-10.30pm Mon-Thur; 11am-10.30pm Fri-Sun. **Main courses** *Lunch* $15-$22. *Dinner* $20-$38. **Map** p336 A7 ㉙ **Tapas**
Loud and fun, a visit to Jorge Andres' tapas restaurant feels like sitting al fresco at a streetside café in Madrid. Located on the third floor of the Cosmopolitan – that's the prime people-watching area of the city's hippest new casino – diners share small plates like bacon-wrapped dates, fried eggplant with honey and *jamon* Serrano with sangria and flan, and watch the unsurpassable parade of hyped-up humanity.

Japonais

Mirage *3400 Las Vegas Boulevard South, between Spring Mountain & W Flamingo roads (792 7979, www.mirage.com). Bus Deuce, 105, 202, 203.* **Open** 5-10.30pm Mon-Wed, Sun; 5-11pm Thur-Sat. **Main courses** $14-$65. **Map** p335, p336 A6 ㉚ **Japanese**
Jun Ichikawa offers only the most traditional styles of sushi, shunnin g fusion cuisine and American-style rolls. Meanwhile, French-trained Gene Kato offers a large selection of entrées and hot appetisers. *Robata* (Japanese charcoal grill) is a speciality. The lounge is located under the Mirage's domed atrium, with a 110ft (34m) glowing red firewall alongside a multi-level main dining room. *Photo p161.*

Jean Georges Steakhouse

Aria, CityCenter *3600 Las Vegas Boulevard South, at W Flamingo Road (693 8181, www.todd english.com). Bus Deuce, 202.* **Open** 11am-2.30pm, 5-10.30pm Mon-Thur; 11am-10.30pm Fri-Sun. **Main courses** *Lunch* $15-$22. *Dinner* $20-$38. **Map** p336 A7 ㉛ **American & steakhouses**
Named for chef Jean-Georges Vongerichten and, well, steak, this entry brings some contemporary, international angles and curves to the traditional steak and seafood house. Starters include watermelon gazpacho, exquisitely presented platters of oysters, shrimp cocktail and a Crispy Sushi Sampler. The meal culminates with perhaps a Maine Lobster with smoked chilli and almond, or a 10-oz. Filet Mignon or a 26oz. Australian Tomahawk Chop, which you can dress with house-made hot sauce or soy-miso butter.

★ Joël Robuchon

MGM Grand *3799 Las Vegas Boulevard South, at E Tropicana Avenue (693 7223, www.mgm grand.com). Bus Deuce, 201.* **Open** 5.30-10pm Mon-Thur, Sun; 5.30-10.30pm Fri, Sat. **Main courses** $25-$155. **Set menus** $225 6 courses; $360 16 courses. **Map** p336 A8 ㉜ **French**
The only US fine dining restaurant by the so-called 'Chef of the Century' has a lot to live up to. But what

CONSUME

goes on in the kitchen, from Robuchon's famous *pommes purées* to dishes such as confit of lamb with couscous, is even more spectacular than the five-room space, which feels like a 1930s Parisian mansion. It comes at a price, of course. But once you're here, you might as well splash out on the exquisite tasting menus.

Joe's Seafood, Prime Steak & Stone Crab

Caesars Palace (Forum Shops) *3500 Las Vegas Boulevard South, at W Flamingo Road (792 9222, www.icon.com/joes). Bus Deuce, 202.* **Open** 11.30am-10pm Mon-Thur, Sun; 11.30am-11pm Fri, Sat. **Main courses** $18-$50. **Map** p336 A7 ㉝ Seafood

When it opened a few years back, Joe's (affiliated with the legendary Miami restaurant) impressed many with its fresh-daily seafood, bone-in steaks and gracious service. Since then, more pricey seafood and steak joints of higher pedigree have elevated local expectations. Still, Joe's represents rare value in the field of upscale Vegas dining, and is one of the gems of the Forum Shops expansion.

Julian Serrano

Aria, CityCenter *3733 Las Vegas Boulevard South, at W Harmon Avenue (877 230 2742, www.arialasvegas.com). Bus Deuce, 202.* **Open** 11.30am-11pm Mon-Thur, Sun; 11.30am-11.30pm Fri, Sat. **Main courses** *Lunch* $15-$22. *Dinner* $20-$38. **Map** p336 A7 ㉞ American & steakhouses

Serrano serves up Spanish cuisine at its sexiest at his colourful new tapas restaurant at CityCenter's Aria. Lobster gazpacho, stuffed bacon-wrapped dates, Iberian pork shoulder and divine risotto and paella. The $10 Spanish sandwiches are one of the best deals in the city, for the quality and flavour.

Mariposa

Neiman Marcus, Fashion Show Mall, 3200 Las Vegas Boulevard South, at Spring Mountain Road (697 7330, www.neimanmarcus.com). Bus Deuce, 105, 203. **Open** 11.30am-3pm Mon-Sat. **Main courses** $9-$23. **Map** p335, p336 A6 ㉟ Modern European

Only a few tottering stiletto steps from the temples to haute couture on the second floor of Neiman Marcus, David Glass's equally fashionable temple to haute cuisine mixes American classics with Asian, nouveau continental and Mediterranean flavours. Think truffle asiago mac and cheese; black angus burger with melted gorgonzola, caramelised onions and Belgian fries; or miso-glazed ahi tuna burger. Request a seat by the floor-to-ceiling windows, and you'll enjoy unobstructed views of the Strip.

Mastro's Ocean Club

Crystals, CityCenter *3729 Las Vegas Boulevard South, at W Harmon Avenue (798 7115, www.*

mastrosrestaurants.com). Bus Deuce, 202. **Open** 4pm-1am daily. **Main courses** *Lunch* $15-$22. *Dinner* $20-$38. **Map** p336 A7 ㊱ **American & steakhouses**

Cantilevered out over the austere white environs of the high-end Crystals shopping centre, Mastro's is a restaurant within a sculpture – from the outside it looks like a Jules Verne rendering of a sailing/starship; inside feels warm, inviting and classically comfortable. The menu is substantial surf and turf, with fantastic steaks and grilled lobster tails – don't miss the lobster mashed potatoes.

▶ *For shopping at Crystals, see p194.*

Mesa Grill

Caesars Palace *3570 Las Vegas Boulevard South, at W Flamingo Road (731 7410, www.mesagrill.com). Bus Deuce, 202.* **Open** 11am-3pm, 5-11pm Mon-Fri; 10.30am-3pm, 5-11pm Sat, Sun. **Main courses** *Brunch* $13-$24. *Lunch* $15-$24. *Dinner* $23-$45. **Map** p336 A7 ㊲ **American & steakhouses**

Rather like Bobby Flay, the celebrity chef behind this popular restaurant, the Mesa Grill is a little on the brash side. The room itself is dazzling in all the best ways, a flourish-packed riot of colour and energy. But the nuevo-American food, like Flay, could do with a little more subtlety. The likes of pork tenderloin with sweet potato tamale and crushed pecan butter are fine, but they read better than they sound and don't justify their high price tags.

★ Michael Mina

Bellagio *3600 Las Vegas Boulevard South, at W Flamingo Road (693 7223, www.michaelmina.net). Bus Deuce, 202.* **Open** 5.30-10pm daily. **Main courses** $38-$85. **Set menus** $85-$105. **Map** p336 A7 ㊳ Seafood

Michael Mina's flagship restaurant in Vegas may have changed its name (it was formerly Aqua), but it still delivers what is, next to Mina's SeaBlue restaurant, the best seafood anywhere on the Strip. His caviar parfait is legendary, but the ever-changing menu also features such deep-sea delights as savoury black mussel soufflé and a miso-glazed Chilean sea bass.

▶ *For SeaBlue, see p165.*

Mix

Thehotel at Mandalay Bay *3950 Las Vegas Boulevard South, at W Hacienda Avenue (632 9500, www.mandalaybay.com). Bus Deuce, 104, 105.* **Open** 6-10.30pm daily. **Main courses** $35-$55. **Map** p336 A9 ㊳ French

The food isn't cheap, but it appears that culinary legend Alain Ducasse might not be taking his Vegas eaterie as seriously as his more expensive restaurants in other cities. Both service and preparation seem rushed as the staff turn out more meals than perhaps they can manage. It's hard to fault the view from the 43rd floor, but you'll get the same view, and more bang for your buck, in the lounge next door (*see p189*).

★ Mon Ami Gabi

Paris Las Vegas *3655 Las Vegas Boulevard South, at E Flamingo Road (944 4224, www. monamigabi.com). Bus Deuce, 202.* **Open** 1.30am-11pm Mon-Thur, Sun; 11.30am-midnight Fri, Sat. **Main courses** $12-$32. **Map** p336 A7 ❹
French

Chicago-based Lettuce Entertain You Enterprises (ouch!) is responsible for, among others, the Eiffel Tower Restaurant (*see p158*) and this spot on the ground floor. While the Eiffel is decidedly upscale, Mon Ami Gabi wears its French theming more casually. As such, it's enjoyable; and if the food sometimes fails to live up to expectations, it's a people-watching paradise, especially from the alfresco bit.

NM Café

Neiman Marcus, Fashion Show Mall, 3200 Las Vegas Boulevard South, at Spring Mountain Road (697 7340, www.neimanmarcus.com). Bus Deuce, 105, 203. **Open** 11am-6pm Mon-Sat; noon-6pm Sun. **Main courses** $9-$18. **Map** p335, p336 A6 ❹ **American & steakhouses**

Next door to Neiman Marcus's ultra-chic Mariposa (*see p160*) sits its trendier sibling, more Juicy Couture than Chanel. Perch at the sleek bar nibbling on classic Middle Eastern fare from the meze sampler or sip cosmos on the shaded patio. Fashionistas flock here to see and be seen, but also to try exec chef Jason Horwitz's shrimp *chermoula* and greek salad, and NM's famous chocolate chip cookies.

Nobhill Tavern

MGM Grand *3799 Las Vegas Boulevard South, at E Tropicana Avenue (693 7223, www. michaelmina.net). Bus Deuce, 201.* **Open** 5.30-10pm Mon-Thur, Sun; 5.30-10.30pm Fri, Sat. **Main courses** $29-$62. **Map** p336 A8 ❹ **American & steakhouses**

A classy San Franciscan treat on the Strip, Michael Mina's Nobhill serves such Bay Area classics as chicken *tetrazzini*, lobster pot pie and North Beach *cioppino*. Just as popular are his contemporary creations, particularly Niman Ranch rack of lamb. Cosy up in a bar booth made for two, throw back a few Cable Cars, slather sourdough bread in cheese fondue and polish off a tarte tatin for dessert.

Noodles

Bellagio *3600 Las Vegas Boulevard South, at W Flamingo Road (693 7111, www.bellagio.com). Bus Deuce, 202.* **Open** 11am-2am Mon-Thur; 11am-3am Fri-Sun. **Main courses** $12-$30. **Map** p336 A7 ❹ **Pan-Asian**

Once a gem showcasing the subtle, modern elegance of Tony Chi's pan-Asian dishes, Noodles has somewhat declined in recent years. Nevertheless, you'll still enjoy the urban diner feel, the late hours, and the selection of dim sum (lunch), Hong Kong barbecue and, of course, the hot and chilled noodle dishes from across Asia. Reliable, at the very least.

CONSUME

Japonais. *See p159.*

Olives

Bellagio *3600 Las Vegas Boulevard South, at W Flamingo Road (693 8181, www.toddenglish.com). Bus Deuce, 202.* **Open** *11am-2.30pm, 5-10.30pm Mon-Thur; 11am-10.30pm Fri-Sun.* **Main courses** *Lunch $15-$22. Dinner $20-$38.* **Map** p336 A7 ㊹ **American & steakhouses**

A revamp by Jeffrey Beers has breathed new life into Todd English's 'casual' Las Vegas establishment overlooking the Bellagio's lake. Boston-based English (the original Olives is in Charlestown, MA)

keeps his 'interpretive Mediterranean' cuisine alive and well with such innovations as white clam pizza and butternut-squash tortellini.

Pampas

Planet Hollywood *3667 Las Vegas Boulevard South, between E Harmon Avenue & E Flamingo Road (737 4748, www.planethollywoodresort.com). Bus Deuce, 202.* **Open** *11.30am-10pm daily.* **Set menus** *Lunch $19. Dinner $37.* **Map** p336 A7 ㊺ **Brazilian**

Extreme Eating

What buys what at each end of the price scale.

The most venerable and beloved snack in Las Vegas is the shrimp cocktail at the **Golden Gate** (*see p144*). For $1.99 (gone is the day of the classic 99-cent shrimp cocktail), you get six ounces of firm, white, cold-water shrimp in a tulip glass with cocktail sauce, lemon and crackers. But for the meal deal of the millennium, try the steak-dinner special at **Ellis Island** (4178 Koval Lane, at E Flamingo Street, 733 8901, www.ellisislandcasino.com), where $7.95 buys you a ten-ounce filet-cut (thick, cooked to order) top sirloin, salad, a potato, green beans and rolls.

Moving up a few pay grades, a dozen steak specials can buy you a single burger at Mandalay Bay's **Burger Bar** (*see p156*). Not just any burger, mind: this one is made

with Kobe beef, truffles and foie gras. For the same $85, sit down to the **Sterling Brunch** at Bally's (*see p178*), with caviar, lox, leg of lamb, duck, ostrich, rabbit and good champagne. Alternatively, try a 42-ounce porterhouse – USDA Prime, dry-aged and cooked only rare – at **Charlie Palmer Steak** (*see p156*), a snip at $110.

Moving up the scale, the 16-course tasting menu at **Joël Robuchon** (*see p159*) costs $360; wine's not included. Plan on spending $1,250 on dinner for two. And if that's not flashy enough, try the FleurBurger 5000 at Mandalay Bay's **Fleur** (*see p159*). The burger itself (Kobe, with truffles and goose pâté) is 'only' $75, but the bottle of Château Petrus 1990 to accompany it will set you back an extraordinary five grand.

Golden Gate.

CONSUME

This Brazilian *churrascaria rodizio* restaurant is an all-you-can-eat establishment where various barbecued meats are paraded from table to table on large skewers, and sliced right there and then for hungry diners. Not an ideal venue for vegetarians, perhaps, but carnivores will be licking their lips with delight at the very idea.

Panevino
246 Via Antonia Avenue, at S Gillespie Street (222 2400, www.panevinolasvegas.com). Bus Deuce. **Open** 11am-3pm, 5-10pm Mon-Fri; 5-10pm Sat, Sun. **Main courses** Lunch $11-$30. Dinner $15-$45. **Map** p333 X4 **46 Italian**
The number-one reason to eat at Panevino is the panoramic view, offered through architecturally enhanced windows that run the length of the restaurant and frame the action at McCarran International Airport. The food, though, comes a close second: the menu has plenty of interesting offerings, including risottos, pastas, pizzas and seafood.

Pâtisserie Jean-Philippe
Bellagio *3600 Las Vegas Boulevard South, at W Flamingo Road (693 8788, www.bellagio.com). Bus Deuce, 202.* **Open** 7am-11pm Mon-Thur, Sun; 7am-midnight Fri, Sat. **Pastries** $3.50-$6. **Map** p336 A7 **47 French**
The cascading chocolate fountain stops passers-by in their tracks, but it's pastry chef Jean-Philippe Maury's biscotti, truffles, macaroons, jellies and jams that lure them inside. This European-style pâtisserie sells an impressive range of sweet and savoury luxuries for people on the go (limited seating is available), plus exotic teas and coffees. Don't miss the Nutella brioche filled with caramelised hazelnuts.

Pearl
MGM Grand *3799 Las Vegas Boulevard South, at E Tropicana Avenue (693 7223, www.mgm grand.com). Bus Deuce, 201.* **Open** 5.30-10pm daily. **Main courses** $16-$48. **Map** p336 A8 **48 Chinese**
A quiet, time-honoured winner on the Strip's upscale restaurant scene, Pearl offers a fresh take on classic Chinese cuisine from Canton and Shanghai provinces with dishes that rotate to reflect the changing of the seasons. There are also plenty of memorable touches off the menu, including an exotic-tea cart and an elegant contemporary room designed by Tony Chi.

Picasso
Bellagio *3600 Las Vegas Boulevard South, at W Flamingo Road (693 8105, www.bellagio.com). Bus Deuce, 202.* **Open** 6-9.30pm Mon, Wed-Sun. **Set menu** $95-$105. **Map** p336 A7 **49 French**
When your room is lined with $20 million of Picasso paintings, you have to work pretty hard to make an impression. No matter: Julian Serrano usually manages it. Unlike a lot of celebrity chefs with

high-profile restaurants in Vegas, Serrano actually cooks at Picasso, building two crisp, daisy-fresh and wonderfully uncomplicated French-slanted menus nightly. Service is a treat and the wine list is stellar.

Pink's
Planet Hollywood *3667 Las Vegas Boulevard South, between E Harmon Avenue & E Flamingo Road (785 5555, www.pinkshollywood.com). Bus Deuce, 202.* **Open** 8am-5pm daily. **Main courses** $6-$7. **Map** p336 A7 **50 American & steakhouses**
You're unlikely to catch the great and the good of Hollywood here, as you might if you spend enough time hanging around by the 70-year-old LA original. However, if you're in the mood for a diet-busting dog topped with all manner of greasy gloop, there's really nowhere else in town for such superior junk food.

Pinot Brasserie
Venetian *3555 Las Vegas Boulevard South, between Sands Avenue & E Flamingo Road (414 8888, www.venetian.com). Bus Deuce, 105, 203.* **Open** 7-10am Mon-Fri; 11.30am-3pm, 5.30-10pm daily. **Main courses** Lunch $14-$17. Dinner $21-$37. **Map** p335, p336 B6 **51 French**
Joachim Splichal gives his French cuisine a lighter touch, with pastas, seafood, steak and wild game. The homey decor is *très rustique*, with copper pots, leather club chairs and paintings depicting wildlife frolicking in the French countryside. The bistro also has a large rotisserie and oyster bar.

★ Postrio
Venetian *3555 Las Vegas Boulevard South, between Sands Avenue & E Flamingo Road (796 1110, www.wolfgangpuck.com). Bus Deuce, 105, 203.* **Open** 11.30am-10pm daily. **Main courses** Lunch $9-$28. Dinner $9-$50. **Map** p335, p336 B6 **52 American & steakhouses**
The most intimate – and, some say, best – restaurant in Wolfgang Puck's Vegas collection, Postrio blends San Francisco and Venice to achieve a romantic atmosphere. Food fuses Mediterranean and Asian influences; seasonal specials include pan-roasted Vermont farm quail with sweet potato gnocchi, and Peking-style roasted duck with warm sesame crêpes. The desserts are a must: try the warm chocolate tart with crumbled toffee ice-cream and fresh raspberries.

Prime
Bellagio *3600 Las Vegas Boulevard South, at W Flamingo Road (693 7223, www.bellagio.com). Bus Deuce, 202.* **Open** 5-10pm daily. **Main courses** $25-$48. **Map** p336 A7 **53 American & steakhouses**
Prime indeed. In fact, one could go further: first class, superior and pre-eminent pretty much sum

CONSUME

CONSUME

Strip Steak. See p166.

up Jean-Georges Vongerichten's steakhouse, where the striking setting comes with a perfect view of the Bellagio's fountains. There's magic on the plate, too: steaks are the highlights, but don't overlook the free-range chicken, seared ahi tuna, wood-grilled veal chop and a selection of 11 sauces and seven mustards.

Rao's

Caesars Palace *3570 Las Vegas Boulevard South, at W Flamingo Road (731 7410, www. harrahs.com). Bus Deuce, 202.* **Open** *11am-3pm, 5-11pm daily.* **Main courses** *Lunch $14-$25. Dinner $18-$31.* **Map** p336 A7 ❸ **Italian**
The original Rao's has been operating in New York City for over 110 years, and is known as one of the toughest reservations in the Big Apple. The Caesars Palace spinoff is a lot easier to access, although you'll still need to book in advance. And the food is well worth the wait, classic Italian recipes that have been fine-tuned by the same family for more than a century. The house speciality is lemon chicken, but everything on the menu is sure to please.

Red 8

Wynn Las Vegas *3131 Las Vegas Boulevard South, between E Desert Inn Road & Sands Avenue (770 3463, www.wynnlasvegas.com). Bus Deuce, 203.* **Open** *11am-11pm Mon-Thur, Sun; 11am-1am Fri, Sat.* **Main courses** *$10-$88.* **Map** p335, p336 B6 ❺ **Pan-Asian**

Many of the restaurants at Wynn set the sky as their limit when pricing their dishes, but this pleasingly simple Asian bistro keeps things so affordable that even the riff-raff can eat here. Stick with the noodle dishes and you won't be disappointed.

Restaurant Guy Savoy

Caesars Palace *3570 Las Vegas Boulevard South, at W Flamingo Road (731 7410, www. harrahs.com). Bus Deuce, 202.* **Open** *5-11pm Wed-Sun.* **Set menus** *$190 4 courses; $290 10 courses.* **Map** p336 A7 ❺ **French**
Managed by Guy's son Franck Savoy, with Adam Sobel presiding over the kitchen, this is among the most expensive dining rooms in Vegas. However, it's worth every penny, providing a level of culinary sophistication rarely glimpsed here. Highlights include artichoke and black truffle soup served with toasted mushroom brioche, and a guinea hen cooked inside a pig's bladder to preserve the moisture. If you have the cash, try the ten-course *menu prestige*.

★ RM

Mandalay Bay *3950 Las Vegas Boulevard South, at W Hacienda Avenue (632 9300, www.mandalaybay.com). Bus Deuce, 104, 105.* **Open** *5.30-10.30pm daily.* **Main courses** *$22-$70.* **Map** p336 A9 ❺ **Seafood**
Rick Moonen moved to Vegas from New York to ensure that everything at his restaurant lives up to his initials. As a result, the room is cosily contemporary, the service is classic and the seafood is out of

this world. For about half the price, you can sample Moonen's cooking bistro-style downstairs at the R Bar Café, which features a raw menu.

SeaBlue

MGM Grand *3799 Las Vegas Boulevard South, at E Tropicana Avenue (891 7800, www.michael mina.net). Bus Deuce, 201.* **Open** 5.30-10pm Mon-Thur, Sun; 5.30-10.30pm Fri, Sat. **Main courses** $27-$75. **Map** p336 A8 🟤 Seafood
Following on from Nobhill at the MGM Grand (*see p161*) and his eponymous seafood restaurant at Bellagio (*see p160*), Michael Mina's third Las Vegas venture is intimate and well designed, but aren't they all? Fish entrées grilled over wood and/or baked in clay are tasty, but what makes this place stand out is its big raw bar. Even the gimmicky lobster corn-dog appetiser is worth a bite.

Sensi

Bellagio *3600 Las Vegas Boulevard South, at W Flamingo Road (693 7223, www.bellagio.com). Bus Deuce, 202.* **Open** 11am-2.30pm, 5-10pm daily. **Main courses** *Lunch* $14-$22. *Dinner* $22-$42. **Map** p336 A7 🟤 Italian
Japanese firm Super Potato designed this culinary theatre to complement Martin Heierling's world cuisine, a combination of Italian and Asian influences, grilled dishes and seafood classics. Four glass-enclosed kitchens in the middle of the room provide an interactive stage: watch curries plunge into a red-hot tandoori oven on the Asian stage; spot focaccias with vacherin cheese and black truffles slipped into a wood-fire oven in the Italian corner; and see Blue Point oysters shucked in the raw section.

Shibuya

MGM Grand *3799 Las Vegas Boulevard South, at E Tropicana Avenue (891 7800, www.mgm grand.com). Bus Deuce, 201.* **Open** 5.30-9.30pm Mon-Thur, Sun; 5.30-10pm Fri, Sat. **Main courses** $22-$54. *Teppanyaki* $42-$105. **Map** p336 A8 🟤 Japanese
Shibuya is really three beautiful restaurants in one: a 50ft (15m) marble sushi bar; a collection of traditional *teppanyaki* (table cooking) grills under hot pink stainless steel canopies; and a pair of modern rooms where guests can indulge in chef Stephane Chevet's French spin on modern Japanese cuisine. Guests in any section are free to order from the various menus, and everything is easily shared.

★ Sinatra

Encore *3121 Las Vegas Boulevard South, at E Desert Inn Road (770 3463, www.wynnlas vegas.com). Bus Deuce, 202.* **Open** 5.30pm-10pm daily. **Main courses** $31-$59. **Map** p336 A7 🟤 American & steakhouses
Inspired, of course, by Frank himself, this dinner-only Italian restaurant is subtly decorated with Ol' Blue Eyes memorabilia – including the Oscar

Sinatra won for his role in *From Here to Eternity* – and transports visitors back to a finer, more elegant moment of Vegas history. Start with signature Sinatra Smash cocktails and move on to the lobster risotto, osso bucco 'My Way' and veal Milanese.

★ Social House

Crystals, CityCenter *3720 Las Vegas Boulevard South, at W Harmon Avenue (693 8181, www.purelv.com/social). Bus Deuce, 202.* **Open** 5-10pm Mon-Thur; noon-11pm Fri, Sat; noon-10pm Sun. **Main courses** *Lunch* $15-$22. *Dinner* $20-$38. **Map** p336 A7 🟤 American & steakhouses
Chef Joseph Elevado staked his claim as a major food force on the Strip when Social House opened at Treasure Island. Now relocated to Crystals, the austere high-end shopping centre at CityCenter, the food is still great, with sushi a speciality, and the atmosphere is also a treat. Living up to its name, Social House ingeniously converts itself into a stylish nightclub after dinner; the tables even lower themselves to coffee table level – perfect for cocktails.

Spago

Caesars Palace (Forum Shops) *3500 Las Vegas Boulevard South, at W Flamingo Road (369 6300, www.wolfgangpuck.com). Bus Deuce, 202.* **Open** *Café* 11am-11pm Mon-Thur, Sun; 11am-midnight Fri, Sat. *Restaurant* 5.30-10pm daily. **Main courses** *Lunch* $8-$33. *Dinner* $14-$68. **Map** p336 A7 🟤 American & steakhouses
The eatery that reinvented Vegas dining in 1992, Spago has managed to stay smart with the tourists and power-lunchers by regularly reinventing itself, most recently with the addition of art by Vegas success stories David Ryan and Tim Bavington. Options in the formal dining room include seasonal specialities (lobster, truffles) and organic vegetarian offerings; in the indoor patio café, there are signature salads, pizzas and sandwiches.

Stack

Mirage *3400 Las Vegas Boulevard South, between Spring Mountain & W Flamingo roads (792 7801, www.mirage.com). Bus Deuce, 105, 202, 203.* **Open** 5-11pm Mon-Thur, Sun; 5pm-midnight Fri, Sat. **Main courses** $17-$44. **Map** p335, p336 A6 🟤 American & steakhouses
The name refers to the design by the Graft Lab of Berlin, in which the mahogany walls have a canyon-like appearance. It will lure you in; the American-style cuisine (giant steaks, Kobe burgers, whipped potatoes and comfort desserts such as modern-day cookies and milk) will make you glad you stayed.

Steak House

Circus Circus *2880 Las Vegas Boulevard South, between W Sahara Avenue & Desert Inn Road (794 3767, www.circuscircus.com). Bus Deuce.*

CONSUME

Open 5-10pm Mon-Fri, Sun; 5-11pm Sat. **Main courses** $28-$38. **Map** p335 B5 **65 American & steakhouses**
The casino in which it's housed neuters some of the sophistication, but this is still an excellent choice if you've a yen for a large lump of cow. The steaks here are aged for 21 days and then mesquite-grilled; even more so than usual, order rare or miss out on some of the flavour. What's more, the prices are well below those of other beef emporia along the Strip. A Vegas legend of sorts.

Strip Steak
Mandalay Bay *3950 Las Vegas Boulevard South, at W Hacienda Avenue (632 7414, www.michaelmina.net). Bus Deuce, 104, 105.* **Open** 5.30-10.30pm daily. **Main courses** $28-$85. **Map** p336 A9 **66 American & steakhouses**
Star chef Michael Mina's first steakhouse is also his first slight misstep. It's not that the food is bad, because it isn't. But at prices this high ($50 for a 10oz filet mignon, eight bucks for a side of baked potato), it needs to be dazzling, and it's rarely quite that good. The slow-poached prime rib is the best bet, but that said, do try one of the supreme desserts. The open-plan restaurant area can get pretty loud when it's busy, which is reasonably often. *Photos p164.*

Sushi Roku
Caesars Palace (Forum Shops) *3700 Las Vegas Boulevard South, at W Flamingo Road (733 7373, www.sushiroku.com). Bus Deuce, 202.* **Open** noon-10pm Mon-Thur, Sun; noon-11.30pm Fri, Sat. **Main courses** $22-$49. **Map** p336 A7 **67 Japanese**
As if Las Vegas wasn't enough like LA, in slinks this Santa Monica/Hollywood hotspot, all dressed up and ready for some celebrity action. With similar prices to Nobu (*see p171*) but less of the cachet, Sushi Roku proves that getting super-fresh fish in the desert isn't cheap. Fanatics are split on whether it's worth the price tag, but anyone worth their $300 jeans knows that the Strip views and loungey bar scene are draws equal to the sensational sashimi.

Tableau
Wynn Las Vegas *3131 Las Vegas Boulevard South, between E Desert Inn Road & Sands Avenue (770 3463, www.wynnlasvegas.com). Bus Deuce, 203.* **Open** 8am-10.15am, 11.30am-2.15pm, 5.30-10pm Mon-Fri; 8am-2.30pm, 5.30-10pm Sat, Sun. **Main courses** *Breakfast & brunch* $11-$25. *Lunch* $19-$25. *Dinner* $38-$49. **Map** p335, p336 B6 **68 American & steakhouses**
Mark LoRusso cut his teeth working for increasingly visible chef Michael Mina; you can tell, and in a very, very good way. While Mina reigns more or less supreme towards the south of the Strip, LoRusso's cultured take on American cuisine is among the best restaurants at this end of the boulevard, his kitchen displaying a real lightness of touch when dealing

with variations on classic themes such as rack of lamb. A real gem of a restaurant.

Tao
Venetian *3555 Las Vegas Boulevard South, between Sands Avenue & E Flamingo Road (388 8338, www.taolasvegas.com). Bus Deuce, 105, 203.* **Open** 5pm-midnight Mon-Thur, Sun; 5pm-1am Fri, Sat. **Main courses** $20-$88. **Map** p335, p336 B6 **69 Pan-Asian**
This ever-fashionable NYC import is best known these days as a nightclub and lounge (*see p261*) that attracts the beautiful people and microcelebs with money to burn. However, the pan-Asian food is also pretty good, especially when twinned with one of the club's speciality drinks.

Trevi
Caesars Palace (Forum Shops) *3500 Las Vegas Boulevard South, at W Flamingo Road (735 4663, www.trevi-italian.com). Bus Deuce, 202.* **Open** 11am-11pm Mon-Thur, Sun; 11am-midnight Fri, Sat. **Main courses** $13-$30. **Map** p336 A7 **70 Italian**
For the most part, Caesars and the adjacent Forum Shops wear their theming fairly lightly. One notable exception is this Italian eatery, named for the fountain and located right by its Vegas reworking. It's a replacement for long-serving Bertolini's, and previous visitors may not notice a great deal of difference in its menu of Italian comfort food. But this is still a reliable option; and next to its competitors in the Forum Shops, it's pretty fairly priced.

Valentino
Venetian *3555 Las Vegas Boulevard South, between Sands Avenue & E Flamingo Road (414 3000, www.valentinorestaurantgroup.com). Bus Deuce, 105, 203.* **Open** 5.30-10.30pm daily. **Main courses** $34-$42. **Map** p335, p336 B6 **71 Italian**
Piero Selvaggio's take on Italian cuisine, delivered by executive chef Luciano Pellegrini, is authentic in almost every regard but the prices, which are a good deal higher than they need to be. Still, this is the Venetian; and in any case, the food here is pretty impressive, delivered in a room that stays the right side of a line separating handsome from gauche.

Verandah Café
Four Seasons *3960 Las Vegas Boulevard South, at W Hacienda Drive (632 5121, www.fourseasons.com). Bus Deuce, 104, 105.* **Open** 6.30am-10pm Mon-Fri; 7am-10pm Sat, Sun. **Main courses** *Breakfast* $16-$23. *Lunch* $18-$25. *Dinner* $16-$34. **Map** p336 A9 **72 American & steakhouses**
Outfitted in everything from suits to tennis shorts, rock stars, real-estate magnates and other riff-raff find this comfortable California country club-styled spot irresistible. The under-promoted yet popular Sunday brunch is an all-you-can-savour taste treat, putting

Sin City's Sweet Tooth

Get your fix of sugar on the Strip.

Las Vegas is justifiably famous and infamous as a place to indulge cravings and vices: it's identified internationally as *the* place to drink, smoke, gamble and make sextime, anytime. From all over the world, people come here to indulge their dream of excess, to forget the bitter and taste the sweet. There's a particulary Vegas attitude to indulging and overindulging: no one wants to hear 'Oh I really shouldn't,' no matter how bad you're being.

But Sin City has an unspoken vice and it's an open secret: Vegas has a raging sweet tooth. Often called an adult Disneyland, the Strip is more like Candyland, a 21-and-over Willy Wonka factory where everyone has a golden ticket.

Always candy-coloured, in the past decade the Strip has been sugarcoated and dipped in chocolate, with sprinkles on top. We're not talking humble Raisinettes or Red Vines – or even 100 Grand chocolate bars. Like all the other human desires that have been tarted up here, candy has been Vegasized, from the bedazzled $25 'couture' lollipops at outposts of the **Sugar Factory** (*see p206*) at Paris and other casinos – a favourite of the Kardashian klan and the *Jersey Shore* gang – to the all-chocolate dinner at **Payard** at Caesars

Palace (*see p104*) and the carefully tended Zen gardens of gelato and frozen yogurt emporiums at just about every casino. At **Serendipity 3**, a very pricey ice-cream parlour fronting Caesars Palace, specialities of the house are a $10 frozen hot chocolate, $12 cotton-candy martinis and a $1,000 sundae – topped with edible gold leaf – that you have to order 48 hours in advance.

One of the most crowded spots at the always crowded Bellagio is the **Jean-Philippe Patisserie** (*see p103*), where tourists and locals alike gather to gawk at the world's largest chocolate fountain – it's no accident that there's also an outpost of this high-end sweets shop at the very heart of the new **Aria** casino (*see p104*) at CityCenter, where the sweet stuff is laid out erotically, like lingerie or jewels.

Perhaps this explains the enduring appeal of sugar on the Strip: winning is its own reward; for those who lose, candy offers instant comfort and solace – orally administered – when the big prize didn't pay out as planned. You may leave Las Vegas with any and all manner of mementos — but you're almost certain to go home with a jacked-up glycemic index and sticky fingers for souvenirs.

CONSUME

Jean-Phillippe Patisserie.

other buffets to shame at a price that says it should. A poolside dining area (request when booking) spirits you away to Santa Barbara for bellinis and blintzes.
► *For more buffets, see p177.*

'Wichcraft

MGM Grand *3799 Las Vegas Boulevard South, at E Tropicana Avenue (891 3166, www.craft restaurant.com). Bus Deuce, 201.* **Open** 10am-6pm Mon-Thur, Sun; 10am-8pm Fri, Sat. **Main courses** $6-$9. **Map** p336 A8 ⑦ **American & steakhouses**
Tom Colicchio's overexcited little sibling to Craftsteak (*see p158*) peps up the previously dreary world of American sandwich culture; visitors used to Subway-standard sandwiches will be dazzled. Generally speaking, the more appetising the description, the nicer the sandwich, so skip the so-so roast turkey in favour of the more exotic varieties. There's plenty for vegetarians, a novelty in such a meat-oriented town. Breakfast is served all day.

Wing Lei

Wynn Las Vegas *3131 Las Vegas Boulevard South, between E Desert Inn Road & Sands Avenue (770 3388, www.wynnlasvegas.com). Bus Deuce, 203.* **Open** 5.30-10.30pm daily. **Main courses** $26-$88. **Set menus** $78-$128. **Map** p335, p336 B6 ⑦ **Chinese**
As if naming your casino after yourself wasn't outlandish enough, Steve Wynn has also lent his identity to this super-smart restaurant: Wing translates as 'Wynn' in Chinese. Happily, the mogul's vanity doesn't extend to taking charge of the kitchen: chef Richard Chen looks after that side of the operation, dispensing cultured Chinese food in a predictably luxurious environment.

Wolfgang Puck Bar & Grill

MGM Grand *3799 Las Vegas Boulevard South, at E Tropicana Avenue (891 3000, www.wolfgang puck.com). Bus Deuce, 201.* **Open** 11.30am-11pm Mon-Thur; 11.30am-11.30pm Fri; 10am-11.30pm Sat; 10am-11pm Sun. **Main courses** $17-$28. **Map** p336 A8 ⑦ **American & steakhouses**
Styled on a California beach bungalow, and a very modish one at that, this Puck outpost offers a contemporary take on Californian cuisine. Signature dishes include truffled potato chips with blue cheese, duck bratwurst and Puck pizzas; all of it is very edible indeed, and perfectly suited to a lazy lunch.

STRATOSPHERE AREA

Florida Café

Howard Johnson *1401 S Las Vegas Boulevard South, at W Charleston Boulevard (385 3013, www.floridacubancafe.com). Bus Deuce, 206.* **Open** 8am-10pm Mon-Thur; 7am-11pm Fri-Sun. **Main courses** $8-$17. **Map** p335 C3 ⑦ **Latin American**

CONSUME

Origin India. *See p171.*

A rather scruffy-looking motel at the wrong end of Las Vegas Boulevard provides the unlikely setting for the most popular Cuban restaurant in Las Vegas. This isn't subtle food, by any means, and nor is it especially healthy. But don't let that stop you – as comfort cooking goes, it's just exotic enough to stand out from the pack. Try a Cuban sandwich if you're not absolutely ravenous.

Luv-It Frozen Custard

505 E Oakey Boulevard, at Las Vegas Boulevard South (384 6452, www.luvitfrozencustard.com). Bus Deuce. **Open** 1-10pm Tue-Thur; 1-11pm Fri, Sat. **Main courses** $3-$6. **No credit cards. Map** p335 C3 **⑦ American & steakhouses**
This little shack doesn't look like much, but it dispenses the most moreishly delicious desserts in the city. Frozen custard looks like ice-cream and even tastes a bit like ice-cream, but it's richer and smoother than anything either Ben or Jerry could conjure. Now run by Greg Tiedemann, whose grandparents opened the business in 1973, Luv-It offers four flavours a day, served in cups, sundaes and shakes. A Western sundae's a good start, but you can't go wrong with any of it.

Thai BBQ

1424 S 3rd Street, at Las Vegas Boulevard South (383 1128). Bus Deuce. **Open** 11am-10pm daily. **Main courses** $7-$18. **Map** p335 C3 **⑦ Thai**
Despite its gritty locale, Thai BBQ remains one of the best Thai eateries in town. The friendly and helpful service makes choosing from the large menu of Thai specialities simple; the hearty portions of such classics as pad Thai are worth the trip. Highlights include papaya salad, excellent satay, and rich and spicy beef noodle soup.

Top of the World

Stratosphere *2000 Las Vegas Boulevard South, at W St Louis Avenue (380 7711, www.topof theworldlv.com). Bus Deuce, 108.* **Open** 11am-3pm, 5.30-10.30pm Mon-Thur, Sun; 11am-3pm, 5.30-11pm Fri, Sat. **Main courses** *Lunch* $10-$15. *Dinner* $33-$60. **Map** p335 C4 **⑦ American & steakhouses**
The views are the main selling point of this restaurant at the top of the Stratosphere, and with good reason: they're spectacular, especially on a clear night. However, the food is better than it needs to be, a brisk, cultured mix of American and French-influenced classics. Prices are almost as high as the restaurant itself; you can just stop by for a drink if the food is out of budgetary range.

EAST OF THE STRIP

AJ's Steakhouse

Hard Rock *4455 Paradise Road, at E Harmon Avenue (693 5500, www.hardrockhotel.com).*

Bus 108. **Open** 6-11pm Tue-Sat. **Main courses** $19-$37. **Map** p336 C7 **⑧⑩ American & steakhouses**
The vibe outside AJ's upholstered door may be Hard Rock, but it's a Rat Pack state of mind within. Named after the father of Hard Rock founder Peter Morton, AJ's is a flashback to old Vegas. Powerful martinis at the bar, a pianist crooning standards and some of the finest cuts of meat in town are just a few reasons that so many stars make it a regular haunt.

Envy

Renaissance *3400 Paradise Road, between E Desert Inn Road & E Twain Avenue (784 5716, www.envysteakhouse.com). Bus 108, 213.* **Open** 6.30am-2pm; 5-10.30pm daily. **Main courses** *Breakfast* $11-$19. *Lunch* $12-$18. *Dinner* $28-$56. **Map** p335 C6 **⑥⑤ American & steakhouses**
Plenty of big deals are hammered out at this modern steakhouse during convention season. House specialities include American Kobe (or more properly, Wagyu) beef, and a bone-in filet served with foie gras and preserved cherry sauce; lobster arrives with a decadent vanilla-infused butter. Wash everything down with one of the 1,500 bottles of wine housed in a candlelit, walk-in cellar and wine wall.

Esmerelda's

1000 E Charleston Boulevard, between E Charleston Boulevard & S 10th Street (388 1404). Bus 109, 206. **Open** 11am-9pm daily. **Main courses** $6-$15. **Map** p334 D3 **⑥② Latin American**
There are a few Mexican dishes on the menu, a nod to the origins of its clientele. But the real reason to visit this unprepossessing storefront eatery is for its range of calmer but still hearty Salvadorean specialities. Chow down on a *pupusa* or two, a flat corn tortilla stuffed variously with cheese or any number of different meats. Subtlety isn't a strong point of the kitchen here, but you'll leave replete.

Firefly

3900 Paradise Road, between E Flamingo Road & Sands Avenue (369 3971, www.fireflylv.com). Bus 108. **Open** 11.30am-2am Mon-Thur; 11.30am-3am Fri; 5pm-3am Sat; 5pm-2am Sun. **Main courses** $11-$20. *Tapas* $3-$10. **Map** p336 C6 **⑥③ Tapas**
This popular tapas bar is populated by a parade of pretty locals almost every night of the week. Music (downtempo to Latin house) competes with sangria-fuelled chatter, as small plates – scrumptious bacon-wrapped dates, mushroom tarts, shrimp ceviche – emerge from the busy kitchen. The loungey scene and reasonable prices conspire to let you spend as little or as much as you'd like.

Gandhi

4080 Paradise Road, at E Flamingo Road (734 0094, www.gandhicuisine.com). Bus 108, 202.

Open 11am-2.30pm, 5-10.30pm daily. **Main courses** *Lunch buffet* $11. *Dinner* $10-$23. **Map** 336 C7 ❷ **Indian**
Good Northern Indian and Southern Indian cuisine, including a fine selection of vegetarian dishes, are combined at this longtime local favourite. The all-you-can-eat lunch buffet is nice and spicy, and stars such dishes as chicken pakora, keema naan (stuffed bread with minced lamb) and chicken tikka masala for next to nothing.

Hofbrauhaus
4510 Paradise Road, at E Harmon Avenue (853 2337, www.hofbrauhauslasvegas.com). Bus 108. **Open** 11am-11pm Mon-Thur, Sun; 11am-midnight Fri, Sat. **Main courses** *Lunch* $9-$15. *Dinner* $15-$25. **Map** p336 C8 ❻ **German**
Planting this near-identical replica of the famous Munich beerhall across from the Hard Rock was a great idea, but the results are hot and cold. To wit: pretzel girls, hot; the rest of the menu, not. Still, while the authentic German grub is mostly bland, the beer makes up for it. Unlike the Munich original, the *biergarten* (beer garden) has a roof, making it feel like little more than a glorified cafeteria.

Komol
Commercial Center, 953 E Sahara Avenue, between S 6th Street & S Maryland Parkway (731 6542, www.komolrestaurant.com). Bus 109, 204. **Open** 11am-10pm Mon-Sat; noon-10pm Sun. **Main courses** $8-$18. **Map** p333 Y2 ❻❻ **Thai**
Despite its location in the run-down Commercial Center, where it competes with the nationally renowned Lotus of Siam and a pair of nationally infamous sex clubs, Komol remains hugely popular for its authentic rendering of Thai cuisine, a vast vegetarian menu, plus 1950s Americana such as egg foo yung, all at bargain prices. Specify the degree of heat you'd like, and the kitchen will try to comply.

★ Lotus of Siam
Commercial Center, 953 E Sahara Avenue, between S 6th Street & S Maryland Parkway (735 3033, www.lotusofsiamlv.com). Bus 109, 204. **Open** 11.30am-2pm Mon-Fri; 5.30-9pm daily. **Main courses** *Lunch buffet* $8. *Dinner* $8-$29. **Map** p333 Y2 ❻ **Thai**
The knowledgeable folks at *Gourmet* magazine have rated this the best Thai restaurant in the US. We might not go quite that far, but Lotus of Siam is certainly a rare and unexpected treat in an unprepossessing strip mall otherwise dominated by gay bars and swingers' clubs. Saipin Chutima puts her specialities on the easy-to-read menu, and isn't afraid to make her food spicy. However, many diners opt for the excellent and super-cheap lunch buffet.

Mr Lucky's 24/7
Hard Rock *4455 Paradise Road, at E Harmon Avenue (693 5592, www.hardrockhotel.com). Bus 108.* **Open** 24hrs daily. **Main courses** $9-$19. **Map** p336 C7 ❻ **American & steakhouses**
The prices have gone up a little, the servings seem to be smaller, and the previously hush-hush $7.77 steak-and-shrimp special is now advertised on a cue card placed on every table. However, the Hard Rock's mid '90s reinvention of the classic diner otherwise rolls on unchanged, dishing out burgers, sandwiches and breakfast classics (try the *huevos*

N9ne. *See p172.*

CONSUME

rancheros) to a disparate pre- and post-party crowd. Great people-watching too.

Nobu

Hard Rock *4455 Paradise Road, at E Harmon Avenue (693 5090, www.hardrockhotel.com). Bus 108.* **Open** 6-11pm daily. **Main courses** $11-$80. **Map** p336 C7 ❽ **Japanese**
Plenty of imitators have emerged in recent years, trying to replicate chef Nobu Matsuhisa's Japanese fusion cuisine and ultra-hip room. But Nobu remains the original, one reason why it will probably never lose its credibility or its appeal. Big prices and little slices follow the leads of its New York and London brethren. If you can, indulge in the chef's Omakase tasting menu.

Origin India

4480 Paradise Road, at E Harmon Avenue (734 6342, www.originindiarestaurant.com). Bus 108. **Open** 11.30am-11.30pm daily. **Main courses** $10-$23. **Map** p336 C7 ❿ **Indian**
Having reigned unchallenged for years, Gandhi (*see p169*) has some genuine competition for the title of Vegas's best Indian eatery. The lowlit swank of Origin India differentiates it from its competition, but the pleasingly spicy food is also a class apart, with classics such as *saag gosht* (lamb with spinach) and a creamy chicken *makhani* rendered in technicolour brilliance. *Photos p168.*

Pamplemousse

400 E Sahara Avenue, at Paradise Road (733 2066, www.pamplemousserestaurant.com). Bus 108, 204. **Open** 5.30-10.30pm Tue-Sun. **Main courses** $18-$29. **Map** p335 C4 ❾ **French**
Along with André's (*see p173*) and the Bootlegger (*see p174*), Georges La Forge's eaterie is one of a very few non-casino old Vegas classics, having served country-style French fare to such regulars as Wayne Newton and Robin Leach for years. The menu-less tradition continues today: the staff recite the choices, so be sure to pay attention. Dishes include fettuccini a la Georges, reportedly invented when Frank Sinatra asked La Forge to create him a dish he'd never forget.

Pink Taco

Hard Rock *4455 Paradise Road, at E Harmon Avenue (693 5000, www.hardrockhotel.com). Bus 108.* **Open** 11am-10pm Mon-Thur, Sun; 11am-midnight Fri, Sat. **Main courses** $8-$14. **Map** p336 C7 ❿ **Latin American**
Only the Hard Rock could get away with giving a restaurant such a jaw-droppingly euphemistic name. Happily, though, this Mexican eaterie transcends its rather smutty moniker. The menu doesn't hold any surprises, at least not if you stick to the favourites (burritos, enchiladas). Join the buzzing bar scene between 4pm and 7pm during the week for two for one beers and margaritas, plus half-price appetisers.

Nove. *See p172.*

Simon Kitchen & Bar

Hard Rock *4455 Paradise Road, at E Harmon Avenue (693 4440, www.hardrockhotel.com). Bus 108.* **Open** 6-10.30pm Mon-Fri; 6-11pm Sat, Sun. **Main courses** $22-$44. **Map** p336 C7 ❿ **American & steakhouses**
Rumours persist that Simon, arguably the city's first scene eaterie, might be short on life. But for now, the scene is very much alive and kicking. When he's in town, Kerry Simon acts the consummate host, while groovy music provides the backdrop to top-shelf retro comfort food (massive shrimp cocktail, meatloaf, giant bowls of cotton candy). No matter if your album hasn't hit platinum: the hosts do a great job of making everyone a star.

CONSUME

Togoshi Ramen

855 E Twain Avenue, at Swenson Street (737 7003). Bus 203. **Open** 11.30am-9.30pm daily. **Main courses** $6-$12. **Map** p333 Y3 ❾❹
Japanese
If the only ramen you've tried is the bulk, packaged, grocery-store ramen with powdered flavouring, hike here and try the real stuff. Known for its Japanese comfort-food fare, such as tonkatsu, gyoza and curry rice, this place specialises in much more than noodle soup. The menus are in English, but the specials are listed on the walls in Japanese and appeal to the true Japanese palate. Food is inexpensive.

WEST OF THE STRIP

Alizé

Palms *4321 W Flamingo Road, at S Valley View Boulevard (951 7000, www.alizelv.com). Bus 201.* **Open** 5.30-10pm daily. **Main courses** $30-$50. **Map** p333 X3 ❾❺ **French**
Up on the 56th floor, venerated local André Rochat (of longstanding Downtown restaurant André's; *see p173*) has hired chef Mark Purdy to maintain his classics and deliver some fresh takes on French cuisine. Many of the seasonal dishes – pan-seared muscovy duck with peach and foie gras tarte tatin – taste as great as they sound. It comes at a price, but Rochat, who's been cooking foie gras in Vegas since Dan Tana was around, is the business.

Gaylord

Rio *3700 W Flamingo Road, at S Valley View Boulevard (777 2277, www.gaylordlv.com). Bus 202.* **Open** 11.30am-2.30pm, 5-11pm daily. **Main courses** $14-$28. **Map** p333 X3 ❾❻ **Indian**
The best in-casino Indian restaurant in Las Vegas is also, the last time we checked, the only in-casino Indian restaurant in Las Vegas. Still, that's not to underplay the quality of the cooking at Gaylord, which remains higher than you might expect. Although the food does seem to have been toned down for an American audience, and prices are high, it retains a reassuring hint of authenticity. The decor is pleasing, and service is both friendly and efficient.

Golden Steer Steak House

308 W Sahara Avenue, between Las Vegas Boulevard South & S Industrial Road (384 4470, www.goldensteerlv.com). Bus 204. **Open** 5-11pm daily. **Main courses** $25-$85. **Map** p335 B4 ❾❼ **American & steakhouses**
The enormous (and, yes, golden) steer that signposts this old-school steak place on Sahara Avenue also advertises its decor. Discreet it certainly is not: think updated bordello crossed with an Old West saloon and you're almost there. But the steaks are classic: large, juicy and perfectly grilled, albeit served at prices that could stun a cow at 20 paces. Sinatra and Dino both ate here; four-plus decades later, it remains vintage Vegas at its most unreconstructed.

Little Buddha

Palms *4321 W Flamingo Road, at S Valley View Boulevard (942 7778, www.littlebuddha lasvegas.com). Bus 201.* **Open** 5.30-11pm Mon-Thur, Sun; 5.30pm-midnight Fri, Sat. **Main courses** $16-$50. **Map** p333 X3 ❾❽ **French**
Buddha Bar's sexy baby sister serves decent fusion food in a dramatic setting. For want of space, the now-larger sushi bar is in the back room, but you can still belly up to the main room bar to bark your sashimi order over the soundtrack. Come here for the lively scene, the sounds and the sushi, and be sure to look as fabulous as possible, but leave the Asian cooking to the restaurants a mile north at Chinatown Plaza, where similar fare can be had for a lot less money.

N9ne

Palms *4321 W Flamingo Road, at S Valley View Boulevard (933 9900, www.n9nesteaks.com). Bus 201.* **Open** 5.30-10pm Mon-Thur, Sun; 5.30-11pm Fri, Sat. **Main courses** $25-$150. **Map** p333 X3 ❾❾ **American & steakhouses**
Superb steak and seafood? Absolutely. A quiet spot for a date? Absolutely not. A busy bar scene, a DJ, busy lighting and acoustics seemingly designed to force diners to yell make N9ne, feel like a nightclub – and it's all intentional. The appetisers and sides are well-executed complements to the mains, and the flaming s'mores dessert is a show unto itself. A Saturday booking requires an A-list name or months of planning. *Photo p170.*

Nove

Palms *4321 W Flamingo Road, at S Valley View Boulevard (942 6800, www.n9negroup.com). Bus 201.* **Open** 5-11pm daily. **Main courses** $20-$60. **Map** p333 X3 ❶⓿⓿ **Italian**
This expensive sister to N9ne (*see above*) sits atop the Palms' super-luxury Fantasy Tower and boasts one of the best views in town, along with beautiful modern decor. The steaks are mediocre and the service is steeped with attitude. But for all that, the only complaint you'll hear about the Nove spaghetti, prepared with lobster, shrimp, crab, scallops, calamari and basil, will relate to its $42 price tag. *Photos p171.*

Omelet House

2160 W Charleston Boulevard, at S Rancho Drive (384 6868, www.omelethouse.net). Bus 206. **Open** 7am-3pm daily. **Main courses** $5-$9. **Map** p335 A3 ❶⓿❶ **American & steakhouses**
Omelettes aren't just the speciality at this basic, unassuming little diner: they're more or less the only thing on the menu. Sure, they make 'em in around 60 varieties, but eggs is eggs is eggs, and the kitchen here does 'em as well as anyone. Making plans for a subsequent dinner is unnecessary: each omelette is made with a preposterous six eggs, and will have you napping at the table until the heartburn wakes you up.

DOWNTOWN

André's
401 S 6th Street, at E Lewis Avenue (385 5016, www.andresfrenchrest.com). Bus Deuce, 206. Open 6-11pm Mon-Sat. Main courses $28-$65. Map p334 D2 ● French
Check out the expense-account crowd at this Downtown institution, with patio dining that's oh-so-New York. Chef and owner André Rochat (also of Alizé; *see left*), a local legend of sorts, serves French haute cuisine accompanied by a world-class wine cellar (though with few bargains).

Chicago Joe's
820 S 4th Street, between E Gass & Hoover avenues (382 5637, www.chicagojoes restaurant.com). Bus Deuce, 206. Open 11am-10pm Tue-Fri; 5-10pm Sat. Main courses $10-$39. Map p334 C2 ● Italian
The kind of no-frills, fair-prices locals' favourite that everyone loves, CJ's – located in a tiny 1932 brick house – has lasted 30 years, thanks to its solid southern Italian cooking and regional specialities (Chicago spicy lobster), and its homey, authentic but quirky setting. Joe's is far removed from the $50 pasta joints on the Strip, and that's the whole point.

Doña Maria's
910 Las Vegas Boulevard South, at E Charleston Boulevard (382 6538). Bus Deuce, 206. Open 8am-10pm daily. Main courses *Lunch* $8-$12. *Dinner* $12-$15. Map p334 C3 ● Mexican
The prices are good and the location is central, but Doña Maria's is very popular with the city's large Mexican community for one reason above all others: the loud and occasionally boisterous place offers some of Vegas's best Mexican food. The tamales (spicy chopped meat and ground corn, served in a corn husk) are the real draw, but the *tortas* (sandwiches) and fiery salsas help keep the place busy.

El Sombrero
807 S Main Street, at E Gass Avenue (382 9234). Bus Deuce. Open 11am-4pm Mon-Thur; 11am-8.30pm Fri, Sat. Main courses $7-$13. Map p334 C2 ● Mexican
The oldest continuously operating non-casino eaterie in the city approaches its 60th birthday much as it neared its 50th: with a shrug. Curiously, gloriously oblivious to the last two decades of Strip development, this small hut continues to dispense unflashy but hearty Mexican peasant food to its patrons, many of whom have been coming here for years. Definitely a better bet than its rival Casa Don Juan just down the street.

Grill on Charleston
241 W Charleston Boulevard, between Las Vegas Boulevard South & I-15 (380 1110, www.lv grill.com). Bus 206. Open 11am-2pm, 5pm-10pm

daily. Main courses *Lunch* $8-$16. *Dinner* $12-$35. Map p335 A3 ● American & steakhouses
This little spot in the Holsum Lofts started out American, but new management brought an Italian slant to the menu in 2007. Expect fuss-free Italian classics (*caprese*, fresh-baked pizza), plus imported wines and beers.

Hugo's Cellar
Four Queens *202 E Fremont Street, at S Casino Center Boulevard (385 4011, www.four queens.com). Bus Deuce & all BTC-bound buses.* Open 5-10pm daily. Main courses $38-$60. Map p334 D1 ● American & steakhouses
One of Vegas's original fine-dining establishments. Hugo's old traditions are still ones to be good ones: pampering wait staff, a tableside visit from the famous salad cart, a solid wine list and a rose for the lady. The menu is vintage Vegas gourmet rather than fusion; heavy on the meat and seafood (steak and lobster are the stars), and just what you'd expect for dessert (cherries jubilee, bananas Foster).

Kabob Korner
507 E Fremont Street, at Las Vegas Boulevard South (384 7722, www.kabobkornerlv.com). Bus Deuce & all BTC-bound buses. Open 10am-11pm daily. Main courses $7-$9. Map 334 D2 ● Middle Eastern
A tidy, tiny and unassuming urban storefront bang in the middle of fast-rising Fremont Street, Kabob Korner is a family-run and relatively inexpensive boîte. It serves a broad menu with something for everyone: burgers, subs and pitta sandwiches, as well as Halal-certified selections (try the tikka and kebab dishes). This stretch of Fremont Street is fast filling with increasingly fashionable bars, but this agreeably basic enterprise remains its best eating option at present.

Mickie Finnz Fish House
425 E Fremont Street, at Las Vegas Boulevard South (382 4204). Bus Deuce & all BTC-bound buses. Open 11am-2am daily. Main courses $6-$17. Map p334 D1 ● American & steakhouses
Part of a Fremont Street triple threat (alongside Irish pub Hennesseys and upscale Brass), this vaguely tiki spot is perfect for the laid-back Downtown crowd. Don't let the name trick you into thinking seafood is the main menu staple: although the grilled fish tacos really are delicious, the menu also offers a large selection of bar food and snacks (nachos, burgers, pizzas) intended to lay a good foundation for the drinking later on. Music at weekends (from local bands) veers from the unfortunate to the unexpectedly good.

Triple George
201 N 3rd Street, at E Ogden Avenue (384 2761, www.triplegeorgegrill.com). Bus Deuce & all BTC-

bound buses. **Open** 11am-4pm Mon; 11am-10pm Tue-Thur; 11am-11pm Fri; 4-11pm Sat. **Main courses** *Lunch* $9-$27. *Dinner* $17-$34. **Map** p334 D1 **111 American & steakhouses**
A lunch haven for business suits but an evening haunt for more casually clad Downtowners, this subtly chic art deco room was conceived as a San Francisco-style chophouse, with a central wooden bar surrounded by several private dining enclosures. The steaks, seafood and chops are good, but it's the Louis salads and own-made soups that are the real highlight here. A valiant, upmarket addition to the area.

Vic & Anthony's

Golden Nugget *129 E Fremont Street, at S Casino Center Boulevard (386 8399, www.golden nugget.com). Bus Deuce & all BTC-bound buses.* **Open** 5-11pm daily. **Main courses** $22-$85. **Map** p334 C1 **112 American & steakhouses**
Modelling itself as a classic Vegas steakhouse, with a live Maine lobster tank, masculine decor and attentive service, Vic & Anthony's manages to make a meal in a new restaurant feel like a step back in time. Start off the experience with a strong cocktail and a tray of fresh Blue Point oysters, then move on to mains of various seafood dishes, grain-fed beef or lamb and veal chops. A smart start to a vintage Vegas weekender.

THE REST OF THE CITY

Agave

10820 W Charleston Boulevard, between I-215 & S Town Center Drive, Summerlin (214 3500, www.agavelasvegas.com). Bus 206. **Open** 24hrs daily. **Main courses** $11-$26. **Latin American**
This 24-hour cantina has emerged from its honeymoon period as a gathering place more than a restaurant. The menu reflects the adventurous decor, which offers a central Mexican vibe via imported Guadalajaran fixtures. Dishes such as goat tacos and a *chile relleno* stuffed with rock shrimp complement the numerous tequilas. The secluded patio is a wonderful spot to while away a happy hour.

Ambiance Bistro

3980 E Sunset Road, at Annie Oakley Drive, Henderson (454 3020, www.ambiancelasvegas. com). Bus 212. **Open** 11am-9pm Mon-Thur; 10am-9pm Fri, Sat. **Main courses** $14-$20. **French**
Though more and more people are discovering this lovely French bistro/bakery, it remains the province of those in the know (or in Cirque du Soleil, members of which frequent the place). Speaking French helps you get by, but staff will serve anyone with an appetite for proper pastries and French fare. For dinner, there's an upscale bistro menu.

Big Mama's Rib Shack

2230 W Bonanza Road, at N Rancho Drive, North Las Vegas (597 1616, www.bigmamasribs.com).

Bus 106. **Open** 11am-9pm Mon-Thur; 11am-10pm Fri, Sat; noon-8pm Sun. **Main courses** $3-$18. **Map** p333 X1 **113 American & steakhouses**
Other restaurants in town have their fans, but, at least for our money, this spartan place on a slightly sketchy stretch of Bonanza Road is the best barbecue joint in Las Vegas. Eat here two or three times a week, and you'll figure out why Mama got to be Big: this stuff is rich, hefty and irresistible.

Bleu Gourmet

8751 W Charleston Boulevard, between S Rampart Boulevard & S Durango Drive (363 2538, www.bleugourmet.com). Bus 206. **Open** 10am-10pm daily. **Main courses** $13-$32. **Italian**
Occupying the intersection of a Venn diagram consisting of a deli, a café, a wine bar and a bistro, this noble operation is all things to all people. Well, to some people, anyway: Bleu Gourmet never seems as busy as it deserves to be. However, it's worth the detour: the short, Italianate menu, available for eat-in or takeout, is cultured, and the wine and beer lists are both excellent. There's free Wi-Fi too.

Bonjour Bistro

9055 S Eastern Avenue, at E Pebble Road, Henderson (270 2102, wwwbonjourvegas.com). Bus 110. **Open** 5-10pm daily. **Main courses** $19-$25. **French**
Expat natives of Cannes operate this cheerful Green Valley bistro, where the service and the food more than justify the prices. A recent move has allowed for somewhat fancier decor, although the casual neighbourhood vibe remains. A well-chosen selection of wines complements a lengthy list of French Riviera traditions in appetisers (frogs' legs, onion soup), salads and mains (seafood, *steak au poivre*).

Bootlegger Bistro

7700 Las Vegas Boulevard South, at Blue Diamond Road, South of Strip (736 4939, www.bootleggerlasvegas.com). No bus. **Open** 24hrs daily. **Main courses** *Breakfast* $5-$13. *Lunch* $7-$13. *Dinner* $10-$31. **Italian**
This operation comes with a flamboyance that's two parts Italian, one part Las Vegan and three parts pure showbiz. There's a full menu here, Italian staples sold at prices several dollars too high. But the entertainment is the key: lounge acts with patter as

---

INSIDE TRACK AS SEEN ON TV

The Strip's high-end restaurants now provide a glitzy and instantly recognisable backdrop for many popular competitive reality shows, including *Top Chef* and *Next Food Network Star*. Many of the chefs who've been made stars on those popular shows end up opening restaurants here.

CONSUME

Lindo Michoacan.

old as the city itself. The fact that the owner is the Lieutenant Governor of Nevada, a lounge artist in her own right who'll happily do a turn when prompted, makes perfect sense. A 24-hour classic.

Casa di Amore
2850 E Tropicana Avenue, at S Eastern Avenue, East Las Vegas (433 4967, www.casadiamore.com). Bus 110, 201. **Open** 24hrs daily. **Main courses** *Lunch $8-$10. Dinner $13-$24.* **Map** p333 Z3 ⑭ Italian
The vibe in this cosy, clubby Amer-Italian spot is overwhelmingly '60s Vegas. The Rat Packmosphere and extended hours draw old-school Las Vegans around the clock for classic pizzas, authentic recipes (baked clams, chicken pasta soup) and seafood; however, it's at its busiest after-hours on weekends, when musicians entertain the crowds.

Gaetano's
10271 S Eastern Avenue, at Sienna Heights Drive, Henderson (361 1661). Bus 110. **Open** 5-10pm Mon-Thur; 5-10.30pm Fri, Sat; 5-9pm Sun. **Main courses** $12-$27. Italian
Henderson isn't known for its fine dining, but this *ristorante* holds its own among the Italian big boys thanks to mom-and-dad attention to detail. The charming Gaetano Palmeri and family are always there to ensure a good experience in this handsome dining room, where the tasty northern Italian menu features the likes of gnocchi and osso buco.

Hash House a-Go Go
6800 W Sahara Avenue, at S Rainbow Boulevard (804 4646, www.hashhouseagogo.com). Bus 101, 204. **Open** 7.30am-2.30pm, 5-9.30pm Mon-Thur; 7.30am-2.30pm, 5-10pm Fri, Sat; 7.30am-2.30pm Sun. **Main courses** $10-$27. **American & steakhouses**
'Twisted farm food', advertises the menu, an altogether less appetising prospect than the excellent comfort cooking that's actually served at this capacious roadhouse. The dinners (chicken and biscuits, meat loaf) are great if pricey, and the lunches (sandwiches, burgers as big as your head) also impress. But to see the Hash House at its best, come for the phenomenal breakfasts and weekend brunches, which'll fill even the emptiest of stomachs.

Hedary's
7365 W Sahara Avenue, at S Buffalo Drive, West Las Vegas (873 9041, www.hedarys.com). Bus 204. **Open** 11am-3pm Mon-Sat; 5-10pm Mon-Thur; 5-11pm Fri, Sat. **Main courses** *Lunch $9-$17. Dinner $13-$22.* **Middle Eastern**
This comfortable outpost of the Lebanese Hedary family's Texas original offers fabulous, fresh renditions of falafel, houmous, tabouleh and *kibbeh*, plus plenty of speciality items (*ftayir, mqaniq*, lamb kebabs). For vegetarians, the tasting meze offers a never-ending supply of incredibly good small plates.

Lindo Michoacan
2655 E Desert Inn Road, between S Eastern Avenue & S Pecos Road, East Las Vegas (735 6828, www.lindomichoacan.com). Bus 110, 213. **Open** 11am-10pm Mon-Thur; 10am-midnight Fri; 8am-midnight Sat; 8am-11pm Sun. **Main courses** *Lunch $5-$7. Dinner $6-$17.* **Map** p333 Z3 ⑮ Mexican
Las Vegas's favourite neighbourhood Mexican, Lindo is housed in a colourful, bigger-than-it-looks

building out on Desert Inn, and is busy at virtually all times of day. The lunch specials are good value, but dinner is more enjoyable, with the menu of standards brought to life by an atmosphere that's never less than lively. The same family runs Bonito Michoacan on the west side (3715 S Decatur Boulevard, 257 6810) and Viva Michoacan in Henderson (2061 Sunset Road, 492 9888).

M&M's Soul Food

3923 W Charleston Boulevard, at S Valley View Boulevard, West Las Vegas (453 7685, www.mmsoulfoodcafe.com). Bus 104, 206. **Open** 7am-8pm daily. **Main courses** $12-$20. **American & steakhouses**
Comfort food doesn't get much heartier than the soul food dished up here. It's a pretty basic room; indeed, it feels a tad dreary after dark. But the food is fabulous: chicken, short ribs and other goodies dished up a variety of ways with an array of moreish sides (try the yams and the macaroni cheese). Get there in good time, mind: it closes early.

Montesano's Deli & Restaurant

3441 W Sahara Avenue, between S Valley View Boulevard & S Rancho Drive, South-west Las Vegas (876 0348, www.montesanos.com). Bus 104, 204. **Open** 10am-9pm Mon-Sat. **Main courses** $7-$18. **Map** p333 X2 ⑯ **Italian**
It might feel like a kitschy pop-culture joint, but this long-time family-run establishment is an authentic slice of Brooklyn in Vegas that pre-dates *The Sopranos* by decades. In the deli/bakery, folks line up daily for fresh-baked bread, decadent desserts and tasty take-away. In the dining room, eggplant *parmigiana* and gnocchi with pink cream sauce compete with an extensive and original selection of pizzas. The tiramisu, cannoli and Italian cheesecakes are also superb.

Paymon's Mediterranean Café & Market

4147 S Maryland Parkway, at E Flamingo Road, University District (731 6030, www. paymons.com). Bus 108, 202. **Open** *Café* 11am-1am Mon-Thur; 11am-3am Fri, Sat; 11am-5pm Sun. *Market* 9am-8pm Mon-Fri; 10am-5pm Sat. **Main courses** $7-$15. **Map** p333 Y3 ⑰ **Middle Eastern**
Long before the idea caught on, Paymon Raouf was serving the kind of ethnic food that the college crowd adores. Even now, when so many Middle Eastern restaurants have opened up in Vegas, the Med – decent for dinner but best for lunch – still wins out, simply because its kebabs and salads are better than anyone else's. Next door's Hookah Lounge (*see p188*) makes an unlikely but effective companion.

Sapporo

9719 W Flamingo Avenue, at I-215, West Las Vegas (216 3080, www.sappororestaurants.com).

Bus 202. **Open** 4-11pm daily. **Main courses** $9-$16. **Japanese**
This suburban Las Vegas outpost of a Scottsdale favourite was reworked a few years ago to capitalise on the popularity of its indoor/outdoor lounge. The food is secondary to the socialising, but it's still very good. Most of the diners are supping sushi, but a decent Pacific Rim menu and *teppanyaki* tables are available if you tire of the trendy bar scene.

Satay Malaysian Grille

3755 Spring Mountain Road, at S Valley View Boulevard (362 2828, www.sataygrille.com). Bus 104, 203. **Open** 11am-11pm Mon-Thur, Sun; 11am-3am Fri, Sat. **Main courses** $8-$20. **Map** p333 X3 ⑬ **Malaysian**
The chic, low-lit interior of this eaterie looks expensive, and the presence of an upscale cocktail menu raises fears that perhaps the owners have concentrated on style over substance. Happily, this is not the case. The food has few such ambitions, and remains firmly and pleasingly grounded in Malaysian tradition. The kitchen's rendition of *nasi goreng* is unflashy and thoroughly appetising, but the menu yields plenty of variety if you're in the mood for being adventurous.

Shanghai Noon

3943 Spring Mountain Road, at S Valley View Boulevard, West Las Vegas (257 1628). Bus 104, 203. **Open** 11am-11pm daily. **Main courses** $7-$14. **Map** p333 X3 ⑲ **Chinese**
The best Chinese food in Vegas? Perhaps. But unless you have the stomach for adventure, you'll be relegated to raving about the incredible noodles. This immensely popular hole-in-the-wall cockily struts out one gorgeous, low-priced plate after another of exotic, otherworldly sounding delights (seafood, hotpots; all translated on the specials menu) to giddy patrons who know their way around.

Table 34

600 E Warm Springs Road, between Bermuda & Paradise roads, South-east Las Vegas (263 0034). Bus 217. **Open** 11am-3pm Mon; 11am-3pm, 5-9.30pm Tue-Fri; 5-9.30pm Sat. **Main courses** $14-$28. **American & steakhouses**
The comfortably modern decor serves as a palate cleanser for Puckish pizza (chef Wes Kendrick is a Wolfgang protégé), home-made soups and New American mains such as braised pot roast, and mac and cheese with smoked ham and English peas, all of which is surprisingly affordable.

Terra Rosa

Red Rock *11011 W Charleston Boulevard, at I-215, West Las Vegas (797 7576, www. redrocklasvegas.com). Bus 206.* **Open** noon-10pm Mon-Thur, Sun; noon-11pm Fri, Sat. **Main courses** $16-$46. **Italian**

Red Rock's signature Italian restaurant is too nice a room to suffer the indignity of shorts and T-shirts, and yet it does. A Tuscan menu (with some Italian-American choices) treats guests to own-made pasta, fresh fish specialities and the ubiquitous wood-fired pizza. Want something lighter? Dress well, snag a seat at the tiny bar and take a wine flight (from the 1,500-bottle wine room) with antipasto.

Vintner Grill

10100 W Charleston Boulevard, at Hualapai Way, Summerlin (214 5590, www.vglasvegas.com). Bus 206. **Open** 11am-10pm Mon-Thur, Sun; 11am-11pm Fri, Sat. **Main courses** $17-$34. **American & steakhouses**

The Corrigan family elevates the neighbourhood dining experience with this well-hidden New American bistro. With a dramatic interior design reminiscent of old Hollywood, and a large patio area segmented into cosy dining nooks, Vintner almost overnight became the hottest table for well-heeled Summerlin folks. Could it be the Mediterranean-influenced menu (lamb osso bucco, wood-fired pizza)? The comfortable lounge? The sexy crowd?

Zaba's Mexican Grill

3318 E Flamingo Road, at S Pecos Road, East Las Vegas (435 9222, www.zabas.com). Bus 111, 202. **Open** 10.30am-10pm Mon-Sat; 11am-8pm Sun. **Main courses** $5-$8. **Map** p333 Z3 ⓬⓪ **Mexican**

¡Aye-aye-aye! Part of the ever-growing trend of burrito and taco chains, Zaba's is as fresh as salsa fresca, with tender grilled meats and delectable guacamole. The decor is stark but the selections are miles away from fast food, despite the speed with which they're prepared. *¡Muy delicioso!*

Buffets

The idea of the buffet started in the 1940s at the original El Rancho. Looking to keep customers in his casino after the show, Beldon Katleman dreamed up the Midnight Chuckwagon Buffet, promising 'all you can eat for a dollar'. His idea of treating guests to a feast for a small price was soon copied and expanded upon by other hotels: why not offer it all day long?

Casino buffets typically serve breakfast, lunch and dinner, with many also offering an extended brunch at weekends. At most resorts, buffets cost $8-$15 for breakfast, $10-$17 for lunch and $15-$25 for dinner. Prices are lower in the locals' casinos away from the Strip; kids often eat for less (generally half-price). But whatever the price and time, all buffets work in the same way: you pay your money at the start and then stuff yourself silly from a range of at least 50 food selections, featuring everything from salads to cakes.

However, a few rules do apply to all buffets. Eat as much as you want while you're there, but don't take anything away with you.

Country Club at Wynn. See p178.

CONSUME

Health codes oblige you to take a new plate every time you return; leave your plates and a small tip on the table, to be picked up by the staff. And to avoid queuing, arrive early for breakfast, late for lunch and early for dinner.

In addition to the buffets detailed below, other hotel buffets are notable, whether by dint of luxuriance (**Country Club** at **Wynn**; *photo p177*), bounty and display (Aria, Bellagio), size (the buffet at **Circus Circus** (*see p126*) serves up to 10,000 diners a day), price (**Palace Station** (*see p150*) is among the best of the cheaper options) or quality of food (the **Mirage** (*see p110*), **Main Street Station** (*see p141*) and **Caesars Palace** (*see p104*) all offer decent spreads). Locals' casinos such as the **Suncoast** (*see p151*) and **Sunset Station** (*see p151*) offer ordinary food at ridiculously cheap prices. And for the best-kept buffet secret in town, visit the **Verandah Café** at the Four Seasons (*see p166*) for weekend brunch.

Bay Side Buffet

Mandalay Bay *3950 Las Vegas Boulevard South, at W Hacienda Avenue (632 7777, www.mandalaybay.com). Bus Deuce, 104, 105.* **Buffets** *Breakfast* 7-11am daily. *Lunch* 11am-2.45pm daily. *Dinner* 2.45-10pm daily. **Prices** $9.25-$12.75 breakfast; $11.50-$15.50 lunch; $19.75-$22.75 brunch or dinner. **Map** p336 A9 ⓬①
Flexing its marketing muscle in the direction of the sophisticated, moneyed traveller, Mandalay Bay has chosen not to make a big deal about its good quality buffet. A pity: while the selection isn't anything remarkable, it's very well executed and is decent value to boot.

Big Kitchen Buffet/Sterling Brunch

Bally's *3645 Las Vegas Boulevard South, at E Flamingo Road (967 4111, www.harrahs.com). Bus Deuce, 202.* **Buffets** Big Kitchen Buffet: *Brunch* 7am-4pm daily. *Dinner* 4-10pm daily. Sterling Brunch: 9.30am-2.30pm Sun. **Prices** *Big Kitchen Buffet* $12.95 brunch; $18.95 dinner. *Sterling Brunch* $58. **Map** p336 A7 ⓬②
The daily Big Kitchen Buffet at Bally's is one of the town's best. However, Sunday's swanky Sterling Brunch, which is held in a separate space, really takes the biscuit …and the caviar, the lobster, the beef tenderloin and the champagne cocktail. Skip church and indulge yourself.

★ Buffet at Bellagio

Bellagio *3600 Las Vegas Boulevard South, at W Flamingo Road (693 7111, www.bellagio.com). Bus Deuce, 202.* **Buffets** *Breakfast* 8-10.30am Mon-Fri. *Brunch* 8am-3.30pm Sat, Sun. *Lunch* 11am-3.30pm daily. *Dinner* 4-10pm Mon-Thur, Sun; 4-11pm Fri, Sat. **Prices** $13.95 breakfast; $21.95 brunch; $17.95 lunch; $25.95-$33.95 dinner. **Map** p336 A7 ⓬③

The Buffet at Bellagio is very much like the rest of the hotel: smart yet approachable, stylish yet undemonstrative, expensive yet probably just about worth it. Usual buffet fare gets upgraded with extras such as venison, steamed clams and crab legs.

Carnival World Buffet

Rio *3700 W Flamingo Road, at S Valley View Boulevard, West of Strip (777 7777, www.harrahs.com). Bus 202.* **Buffets** Carnival World Buffet: *Breakfast* 7-11am Mon-Fri; 7.30-10.30am Sat, Sun. *Brunch* 10.30am-3.30pm Sat, Sun. *Lunch* 11am-3.30pm Mon-Fri. *Dinner* 3.30-10pm daily. Village Seafood Buffet: *Dinner* 4-10pm Mon-Thur, Sun; 4-11pm Fri, Sat. **Prices** *Carnival World Buffet* $13.99 breakfast; $23.99 brunch; $16.99 lunch; $23.99 dinner. *Village Seafood Buffet* $34.99. **Map** p333 X3 ⓬④
A favourite among locals, the pioneering Carnival World Buffet journeys the planet for its food. It's an idea that several other casinos have since copied, but no one has yet topped the Rio's intercontinental spreads, which take in everything from lasagne to Peking duck. The separate Seafood Buffet offers sushi, oysters and lobster, as well as a surprising range of meat dishes.

Golden Nugget Buffet

Golden Nugget *129 E Fremont Street, at S Casino Center Boulevard, Downtown (385 7111, www.goldennugget.com). Bus Deuce & all BTC-bound buses.* **Buffets** *Breakfast* 7-10.30am Mon-Fri. *Brunch* 8am-3.30pm Sat, Sun. *Lunch* 10.30am-3.30pm Mon-Fri. *Dinner* 3.30-10pm daily. **Prices** $8.99 breakfast; $15.99-$16.99 brunch; $9.99 lunch; $16.99-$19.99 dinner. **Map** p334 C1 ⓬⑤
Downtown's smartest buffet more than delivers the goods that its reputation demands of it. The room isn't particularly cosy, but the quality of the food more than compensates. The offerings are near the top of the Vegas food chain, especially the carvery and the excellent desserts.

Le Village Buffet

Paris Las Vegas *3655 Las Vegas Boulevard South, at E Flamingo Road (946 7000, www.harrahs.com). Bus Deuce, 202.* **Buffets** *Breakfast* 7-11am daily. *Brunch* 11am-3.30pm Sun. *Lunch* 11.30am-3.30pm Mon-Fri. *Dinner* 3.30-10pm daily. **Prices** $12.95 breakfast; $24.95 brunch; $17.95 lunch; $24.95 dinner. **Map** p336 A7 ⓬⑥
The one French-themed casino in town really should offer a good buffet, and so it does. The 400-seat Le Village Buffet has stations representing five French provinces, and dishes up a variety of fine foods (it's especially good for meat-lovers). But go easy on starters and mains, so as to save room for the fresh pastries and desserts.

Bars & Lounges

Drink with mermaids? Only in Vegas.

You're sporting a furry ushanka to ward off the sub-zero temperatures. You're sipping banana-flavoured vodka. You're staring at a giant bronze head of Lenin. You're in the 'vodka locker' (read: freezer) of **Red Square**, a bar that, by taking its theme to the zenith of ridiculousness, is perfectly, archetypally Vegas.

The hallucinatory creativity that built a neon oasis in the desert has also been employed in the construction of the city's bars. The resorts are dotted with the kind of piano bars, meat markets and casual lounges you might expect to find. However, you can also sink beers with swimming mermaids, down martinis on a revolving carousel, and piss on the Berlin Wall. Should these gimmicks fail to inculcate a sense of wonder, a bacon martini may do the trick.

Wherever you prefer to take your libations, one thing you won't hear very often is the phrase 'last call'. Liquor flows as freely at five in the morning as it does at five in the evening: most of the bars in town, including at least one in every casino, are open 24 hours a day, though it should be noted that you're just as likely to be refused service here as in other cities.

Although there are a few exceptions, among them the **Artisan** and the **Downtown Cocktail Room**, the bartops at most off-Strip, non-casino hangouts are lined with video poker machines. Indeed, many such bars are kept afloat as much by gambling revenue as by alcohol sales. If you're gambling, drinks are usually free with a minimal deposit (usually $10 to $20) into your nearest machine; always ensure that the bartender knows you're playing.

In addition to the bars listed below, small music venues such as the **Bunkhouse Saloon** also function as bars; *see p252-256*. A number of restaurants also have busy bars, among them **Aureole** (*see p155*), with its spectacular central wine tower. And keep an eye out for the likeable, western-themed **Roadrunner** mini-chain (www.roadrunnerlasvegas.com).

THE LAW

You have to be 21 to consume or buy alcohol in Nevada. If you look less than 40, you'll regularly be required to produce photo ID, such as a driver's licence or passport. Las Vegas's drink-driving laws are as harsh and

uncompromising as in any major US city, and the cops don't let too many woozy fish swim by. So leave the car behind: you can easily walk back and forth between bars on the Strip and Fremont Street, and a taxi ride to and from most of the more distant joints will be cheap. Cabs are plentiful around the Strip; elsewhere, the bartender will be happy to call one for you. For the law on smoking, *see p315*.

THE STRIP

Bar at Times Square

New York New York *3790 Las Vegas Boulevard South, at W Tropicana Avenue (236 0374, www.newyorknewyork.com). Bus Deuce, 201.* **Open** 11am-2.30am daily. **Map** p336 A8 ❶
Bellowing voices pour from this packed bar, where duelling pianos provide the upbeat entertainment. Sure, there's beer behind the emotion, but there's also a lot of genuine fun being had. The musicians can and will play anything if you've got the money to tip 'em. The best of the city's piano bars.

Caramel

Bellagio *3600 Las Vegas Boulevard South, at W Flamingo Road (693 8300,*

---

❶ Green numbers given in this chapter correspond to the location of each bar as marked on the street maps, *pp334-336*.

Centrifuge.

www.lightgroup.com). Bus Deuce, 202.
Open 5pm-4am daily. **Map** p336 A7 ❷
With opaque marble tables, one-way windows on to the casino floor and a sophisticated, ultra-modern atmosphere, Caramel seems less like a lounge than a private club. And that, naturally, comes at a price: $15 speciality martinis are the norm. As the night wears on and the crowds thicken, the swanky couches are reserved for parties willing to pony up about $300 or more for bottle service.

★ Chandelier
Cosmopolitan *3708 Las Vegas Boulevard South, at W Harmon Avenue (698 7979, www.cosmopolitanlasvegas.com). Bus 109, 201.* **Open** 4pm-4am daily. **Map** p336 A7 ❸
The Chandelier is at the centre of the new Vegas bar scene – and a three-storey chandelier is at the centre of this gorgeous, multi-level bar. You'll be surrounded by sparkle, and dazzled by your fellow cocktailers as you sip a Fire-Breathing Dragon – or ask your bartender to come up with something to commemorate the moment.

Centrifuge
MGM Grand *3799 Las Vegas Boulevard South, at E Tropicana Avenue (891 7777, www.mgm grand.com). Bus Deuce, 201.* **Open** 2pm-2am Mon-Thur; noon-2am Fri-Sun. **Map** p336 A8 ❹
Having dramatically remade its range of restaurants, the MGM turned its attention to its bars. Along with Rouge, the Centrifuge is the most eye-catching, a circular bar near the front of the casino with TV screens, dancing girls and excellent cocktails. It's more expensive than it should be, but worth a look nonetheless.

Coyote Ugly
New York New York *3790 Las Vegas Boulevard South, at W Tropicana Avenue (740 6969, www.coyoteuglysaloon.com/vegas). Bus Deuce, 201.* **Open** 6pm-4am daily. **Map** p336 A8 ❺

Belly-baring servers stomp to choreographed dances in this saloon, based on the New York bar that was the subject of a ghastly movie. The schtick goes that the girls invite boozed-up revellers to join them up on the bar, while simultaneously hurling insults at the crowd below. To add injury to insults, there's nowhere to sit, and it takes a lot of expensive liquor to make you forget the $10 cover charge (after 9pm).

Fix
Bellagio *3600 Las Vegas Boulevard South, at W Flamingo Road (693 8300, www.lightgroup.com). Bus Deuce, 202.* **Open** 5pm-midnight Mon-Thur, Sun; 5pm-2am Fri, Sat. **Map** p336 A7 ❻
This upscale bar and restaurant is known for its tasty appetisers and tantalising beverages, striking a careful balance between sleekness and comfort in both decor and menu. The waiting staff seems to have been selected from a genetic pool that counts hotness as the main determinant of survival.

Gold
Aria CityCenter *3730 Las Vegas Boulevard South, at W Harmon Avenue (693 8300, www.arialasvegas.com). Bus Deuce, 201.* **Open** 5pm-4am Tue-Sat. **Map** p333 Y3 ❼
Located adjacent to the Viva Elvis theatre, which showcases Cirque du Soleil's tribute to the King, this gleaming boutique lounge is said to be inspired by Graceland, including furnishings and design patterns found in Presley's home. But with all the gold-dipped tones – even the bartenders and servers seem golden – it feels more like it was inspired by *Goldfinger*.

I Love this Bar & Grill
Harrah's *3475 Las Vegas Boulevard South, between Sands Avenue & E Flamingo Road (369 5000, www.harrahslasvegas.com). Bus Deuce, 203.* **Open** 11.30am-2am Mon-Thur, Sun; 11.30am-3am Fri, Sat. **Map** p336 A6 ❽
Boot-scoot your way on down here for a cold domestic and some Southern-fried fun. Named after his hit

single 'I Love this Bar', Toby Keith's place is tinged with country. But even those repelled by cowboy hats might find it's their kind of place, since it doesn't smash you over the ten-gallon hat with its theme.

Jimmy Buffet's Margaritaville

Flamingo *3555 Las Vegas Boulevard South, at E Flamingo Road (733 3302, www.margaritavillelas vegas.com). Bus Deuce, 202.* **Open** 8am-2am Mon-Thur, Sun; 8am-3am Fri, Sat. **Map** p336 A7 ⑨
You've heard of Deadheads, right? Well, here you'll find their ornithological equivalent: parrotheads, men dressed in khaki shorts and floral shirts with parrots perched on their heads, united in their devotion to the self-described 'gulf and western' music of Jimmy Buffet. The ambience is not for the faint of heart or the sophisticated of taste.

Napoleon's

Paris Las Vegas *3655 Las Vegas Boulevard South, at E Flamingo Road (1-877 603 4586, www.parislasvegas.com). Bus Deuce, 202.* **Open** 4pm-2am Mon-Thur, Sun; 2pm-3am Fri, Sat. **Map** p336 A7 ⑩
There are 100 varieties of champagne on offer at this longstanding hangout within the Paris resort. They're a better choice than the rather over-inventive cocktails, and certainly more authentic than the obligatory duelling pianists, who work their way through Parisian classics such as, er, 'Goodbye Yellow Brick Road' and 'Living on a Prayer' at 9pm nightly.

★ Parasol Up/Parasol Down

Wynn Las Vegas *3131 Las Vegas Boulevard South, between E Desert Inn Road & Sands Avenue (770 7000, www.wynnlasvegas.com). Bus Deuce, 203.* **Open** *Parasol Up* 11am-4am Mon-Thur, Sun; 11am-5am Fri, Sat. *Parasol Down* 11am-2am daily. **Map** p335, p336 B6 ⑪
Whether you're up or down, there's a Parasol cocktail for you. These two pricey, Euro-chichi hangouts

THE BEST BARS

For new Vegas sophistication
Downtown Cocktail Room. *See p184.*

For making your day, punk
Double Down Saloon. *See p183.*

For joining in on the chorus
Bar at Times Square. *See p179.*

For the benefit of Mr Kite
Revolution. *See p182.*

overlooking the waterfall, itself projected with images and colours, have more charm than standard casino bars, and are full of the sort of beautiful, wealthy people who like to hang out at this most chichi of resorts.

★ Peppermill's Fireside Lounge

2985 Las Vegas Boulevard South, at Convention Center Drive (735 4177, www.peppermilllas vegas.com). Bus Deuce, 203. **Open** 24hrs daily. **Map** p335 B5 ⑫
Known for the seats around the combination firepit-fountain and for the luxuriant dresses worn by the bosomy waitresses, this place is old Vegas at its best. Or, at least, it was, until they put flatscreen TVs on every available surface and ruined the vintage feel. Still, the drinks are impressive; try a Scorpion, which will arrive in a glass that's bigger than your head.

★ Red Square

Mandalay Bay *3950 Las Vegas Boulevard South, at W Hacienda Avenue (632 7407, www.mandalaybay.com). Bus Deuce, 104, 105.* **Open** 4pm-1am Mon-Thur; 4pm-2am Fri, Sat. **Map** p336 A9 ⑬

CONSUME

Peppermill's Fireside Lounge.

The vodkas here are so good they made Lenin lose his head. Well, that's the only rational explanation for the enormous decapitated statue of the father of the Soviet Union over the entrance, though you can always ask the barman what happened to Vlad's missing body part (it's in the walk-in 'vodka locker', on ice). The food is fine and the drinks are strong.

Revolution

Mirage *3400 Las Vegas Boulevard South, between Spring Mountain & W Flamingo roads (693 8300, www.lightgroup.com). Bus Deuce, 202, 203.* **Open** 10am-4am Mon, Wed-Sun. *Abbey Road* noon-4am daily. **Map** p335, p336 A6 ⑭
If you want to drink to a Beatles soundtrack, arrive early, before the group is ditched in favour of a more contemporary soundtrack. That aside, the Fab Four theme of this spot is generally carried out pretty well, with subtle and not-so-subtle nods to classic songs (crystals hanging from the ceiling, portholes behind the bar). Interactive tabletops, like giant Etch-a-Sketches, are a highlight. For a more low-key spot, try the Abbey Road Bar just in front of Revolution.

Rockhouse

Imperial Palace *3535 Las Vegas Boulevard South, between Sands Avenue & E Flamingo Road (735 0977, www.therockhousebar.com). Bus Deuce, 203.* **Open** 10am-4am daily. **Map** p336 A6 ⑮
The Rockhouse is like an adolescent searching for his identity before realising that it's easier to find large-breasted women. Other attractions include a mechanical bull, go-go dancers, bottle service, multiple American flags, a stage, and a whole lot of people standing around, not quite sure what to do with themselves. If in doubt, ogle.

Shadow Bar

Caesars Palace *3570 Las Vegas Boulevard South, at W Flamingo Road (1-877 427 7243, www.harrahs.com). Bus Deuce, 202.* **Open** 4pm-2am Mon-Thur; 2pm-3am Fri, Sat; 2pm-2am Sun. **Map** p336 A7 ⑯
Question: how do you get naked women to shake, writhe and strut their stuff without showing any flesh? Answer: shadow play. This saucy spot continues Las Vegas's hesitating shimmy towards bringing strip clubs to the Strip without having any stripping. The ladies concerned, silhouetted on screens, play up what comes naturally (or, possibly, surgically), while expensive drinks add a haughty note. The dress code is smart-casual.

Switch

Encore *3121 Las Vegas Boulevard South, at E Desert Inn Road (248 3463, www.wynnlasvegas.com). Bus Deuce, 108, 203.* **Open** 11am-midnight Mon, Sun; 4pm-midnight Tue; 4pm-3am Wed, Thur; 11am-3am Fri, Sat. **Map** p333 Y3 ⑰
Encore and Wynn offer many choices, as far as bars go, but if you pick Switch, you'll feel like you've barhopped several times during your session, without every leaving. The decor cleverly changes every 30 minutes – the wallpaper and ceiling actually 'switch'. Otherwise, Switch is primarily a steakhouse, and the cocktail prices are, well, pricey.

★ Todd English PUB

CityCenter *3720 Las Vegas Boulevard S, at W Harmon Avenue (489 8080, www.toddenglishpub.com). Bus Deuce, 201.* **Open** 11am-2am daily. **Map** p333 Y3 ⑱
Celebrity chef English's new gastropub – in the CityCenter complex cosied right up to the enormous Aria casino-hotel – established itself on arrival as

CONSUME

Revolution.

One More for the Road

The drink never stops flowing on and around the Strip.

Drinking on the cheap is easy in Vegas. Gamblers always drink for free, though tipping your waitress will result in more frequent service. And even if you're not gambling, you can usually find one-dollar draft or bottled beers at Strip venues such as **Casino Royale** (*see p125*) and **Slots-a-Fun** (2890 Las Vegas Boulevard South, 734 0410), and similarly cheap drinks along Fremont Street.

Further from the Strip, the happy hour at **Firefly** (3-6pm Mon-Thur, 3-5pm Fri; *see p169*) includes half-price cocktails, meaning martinis are four bucks and mojitos $3.25. Nearby, the bar at **Pink Taco** (*see p171*) offers two-for-one deals on margaritas and beers during happy hour (4-7pm Mon-Fri). And from here, nip across to the **Divebar** (4-8pm Mon-Fri; *see p255*) for two-buck domestics and three-dollar import beers.

Such bargains are old Vegas through and through. New Vegas, though, demands luxury, and luxury demands expense. Start

at **N9ne** Steakhouse (*see p172*) with an 'ultimate margarita', made from Herradura Seleccion Suprema tequila and priced at $69. Then, head to **Aureole** (*see p155*) for a shot of Hardy Perfection cognac from a Lalique crystal bottle – yours for $350. But for the price of three Hardys, you could sample Chivas Regal 50-Year Salute, from one of 255 bottles produced from Queen Elizabeth II's coronation cask and released to celebrate her Golden Jubilee in 2002. Offered at the Bellagio's **Prime** restaurant (*see p163*), a single measure is $1,050.

Picasso (*see p163*), the gourmet room at Bellagio, was declared the eighth most expensive restaurant in the United States in a 2005 survey, mostly because of its wine list. A bottle of 1945 Chateau Mouton Rothschild retails for $16,888, with a 1947 Cheval Blanc going for $15,610. And at $13,500, the 1961 Chateau Petrus Classic makes the five-grand bottles at **Fleur de Lys** (*see p159*) look like bargains.

one of the most comfortable, personable and delicious bars in a town full of bars. The impressive array of beers on tap – more than 30, including a smart selection of craft beers and seasonals – is matched by English's witty touch on saloon fare, including hand-carved roast beef, a raw bar, sweet potato fries, (organic) corn dogs and a sublime variation on the New England lobster roll. *Photo p184.*

V Bar
Venetian *3555 Las Vegas Boulevard South, between Sands Avenue & E Flamingo Road (414 3200, www.venetian.com). Bus Deuce, 119, 203.* **Open** 5pm-3am Mon-Wed, Sun; 5pm-4am Thur-Sat. **Map** p335, p336 B6 ⑲
Brought to you by the creators of the Big Apple's Lotus and LA's Sunset Room, V Bar is as basic, simple and understated as its name. The young, attractive and affluent clientele put on a show for lesser mortals peeking in through small slits in the wall-length frosted-glass windows. Dress smart-casual unless you want to join them on the outside.

View Bar
Aria *CityCenter, 3730 Las Vegas Boulevard South, at W Harmon Avenue (414 3200, www.aria lasvegas.com). Bus 109, 201.* **Open** 5pm-2am Mon-Wed, Sun; 5pm-3am Thur-Sat. **Map** p333 Y3 ⑳
Aria at CityCenter is one of the best new sights in the city – and its lobby bar, called View Bar – is one of the best new spots for people-watching, centrally

located as it is in the airy lobby, across from the check-in stations. But you're paying – and quite dearly – for the views: cocktails run from $15 to $20.

OFF-STRIP
East of the Strip

Double Down Saloon
Paradise Plaza, *4640 Paradise Road, between E Harmon & E Tropicana avenues (791 5775, www.doubledownsaloon.com). Bus 108.* **Open** 24hrs daily. **No credit cards. Map** p336 C8 ㉑
No head for drink? Then hand over $20 for puke insurance: if you barf, staff'll clean up. Otherwise, you're on your own at this darkly chaotic bar. 'The Happiest Place on Earth', they bill it, and with good reason: the music is loud, whether from the impeccably punkish jukebox or the regular bands, and the vibe is welcoming. Specialities include Ass Juice and bacon martinis (no one's ever had two). Beers are a better bet.

West of the Strip

Artisan Lounge
Artisan *1501 W Sahara Avenue, at Highland Drive (214 4000, www.theartisanhotel.com). Bus 204.* **Open** 24hrs daily. **Map** p335 B4 ㉒
Gold-framed prints and paintings cover the walls and ceiling here, almost to the point of absurdity;

Todd English PUB.
See p182.

there are even empty frames suspended in the air, and statues interspersed with shelves full of books. Somehow, it all works. A unique amalgam of lodge, bar and gallery, the Artisan is arty Vegas's living room away from home. Thanks to the lack of gambling, it's also one of the quietest lounges in town.

Ghostbar
Palms *4321 W Flamingo Road, at S Valley View Boulevard (942 6832, www.palms.com). Bus 201.* **Open** 8pm-4am daily. **Admission** $10 Mon-Thur; $25 Fri-Sun. **Map** p333 X3 ㉓
Suspended 51 floors above the city (check out the see-through patio with a view all the way to the ground), decked out in blues and space-age silvers, Ghostbar is a dramatic spot. Enter via the private elevator (and prepare to pay the private cover charge of $10-$25), and try to get here before the glamorous masses: it starts to get busy from 11pm.

Little Buddha
Palms *4321 W Flamingo Road, at S Valley View Boulevard (942 7778, www.littlebuddhalasvegas. com). Bus 201.* **Open** 5.30-11pm Mon-Thur, Sun; 5.30pm-midnight Fri, Sat. **Map** p333 X3 ㉔
This restaurant and bar, a smaller version of Paris's famed Buddha Bar (it's operated by the same people), has a low-key and sophisticated air, as smooth and relaxing as the popular ambient DJ compilations created in its name. The bar area is small and crowded, but it's still worth a look for the Asian decor, the drinks and the sushi.

DOWNTOWN

★ Beauty Bar
517 E Fremont Street, at Las Vegas Boulevard South (598 1965, www.thebeautybar.com). Bus
Deuce & all BTC-bound buses. **Open** 9pm-2am daily. **Map** p334 D2 ㉕
The 'martinis and manicures' concept featured on *Sex and the City* was made famous by the New York version of this chain; a shame, then, that cosmetology laws forbid full manicures here. The '50s decor was salvaged from the Capri Salon of Beauty in Trenton, NJ, with lighting from the old Algiers hotel in Vegas; it's matched by delightful themed cocktails, such as the Platinum Blonde, the Prell and the Red Head. Bands and DJs entertain more or less nightly.

Dino's
1516 Las Vegas Boulevard South, at W Utah Avenue (382 3894). Bus Deuce, 206. **Open** 24hrs daily. **No credit cards. Map** p335 C3 ㉖
The sign on the side, advertising this as 'The last neighbourhood bar in Las Vegas', is hyperbole. Still, this local dive offers an upbeat mix of hipsters, freaks, drunks and, on the karaoke nights hosted by Elton John doppelgänger Danny G (Thur-Sat), off-key crooners and wannabes. Bar regulars compete to join the Drunk of the Month Club.

★ Downtown Cocktail Room
111 Las Vegas Boulevard South, at E Fremont Street (880 3696, www.downtownlv.net). Bus Deuce & all BTC-bound buses. **Open** 4pm-2am Mon-Fri; 7pm-2am Sat. **Map** p334 D2 ㉗
Despite its name, this chic, upscale bar will make you forget you're in Downtown; or, at least, downtown Las Vegas. Perhaps the most casually dramatic addition to the area, done out in deep, sexy reds and sheer curtains you can close for added nook privacy, this understated lounge will put you in the mood to leave with a date even if you didn't come in with one. DJs entertain nightly, though the music is generally pitched at conversation-friendly levels.

★ Frankie's Tiki Room

*1712 W Charleston Boulevard, at Shadow
Lane (385 3110, www.frankiestikiroom.com).
Bus 109, 206.* **Open** 24hrs daily. **Map** p333 Y3 ②
Once your eyes get acclimatised to the dimness, the
decor and details of this newish variation on the
classic tiki lounge begin to emerge: a jukebox
stuffed with surf-rock, Hawaii-themed movies on
the screens, and, of course, neon-hued tropical
drinks, served in fanciful, Vegas-themed ceramic
tumblers designed by tiki artists (you can buy them
as souvenirs). Even if you leave this place after
dark, you might want to put on your sunglasses –
the outside world will seem unbearably bright.
Photos p187.

★ Griffin

*511 E Fremont Street, at Las Vegas Boulevard
South (382 0577). Bus Deuce & all BTC-bound
buses.* **Open** 5pm-4am Mon-Sat; 9pm-4am Sun.
Map p334 D2 ②
Though it's at street level, this putatively Brit-styled
joint on Fremont Street is the place to go medieval.
Windowless with an eerie but romantic glow fed by
candlelight and fireplaces, Griffin doubles as an
after-work beer pub and a late-night indie-rockin'
haunt. Tattooed hotties pull Stellas while a dollar
stirs T-Rex and the Smiths from the juke.

Hogs & Heifers

*201 N 3rd Street, at E Ogden Avenue (676 1457,
www.hogsandheifers.com). Bus Deuce & all BTC-
bound buses.* **Open** 1pm-4am daily. **No credit
cards. Map** p334 D1 ③
'Is that the sound you make when he takes you from
behind?' yells a classy maven in boots from her roost
on top of the bar. To some onlookers, Hogs & Heifers
isn't pretty or fun; still, those onlookers seem to fall
in the minority. The schtick here is similar to Coyote
Ugly, but less choreographed and more raunchy.
Arrive on your Harley if you're fixin' to fit right in.

Huntridge Tavern

*1116 E Charleston Boulevard, at S Maryland
Parkway (384 7377). Bus 109, 206.* **Open** 24hrs
daily. **No credit cards. Map** p334 D3 ③
For decades, this hangout has been everything a
dive bar should be: low-estate without being seedy,
intriguing without being dangerous, careworn
without being ugly. Presumably, the fiftysome-
things who warm the stools here do go home to
their families once in a while. Still, with
brews this cheap, you couldn't blame them if they
just stayed put.

Rush Lounge

Golden Nugget *129 E Fremont Street, at S
Casino Center Boulevard (385 7111, www.golden
nugget.com). Bus Deuce & all BTC-bound buses.*
Open 6pm-2am Mon-Thur, Sun; 6pm-4am Fri,
Sat. **Map** p334 C1 ③
Before 2007, 'contemporary' wasn't an adjective that
applied to the Golden Nugget casino. However, it's
just about the most accurate description for its
upscale Rush Lounge, swathed in sexy reds, browns
and horizontal stripes. A rare find among
Downtown casinos, not least because it prefers table
games to video poker.

Sidebar

*201 N 3rd Street, at E Ogden Avenue (259 9700,
www.sidebarlv.com). Bus Deuce & all BTC-bound
buses.* **Open** 3pm-midnight Mon-Thur; 3pm-2am
Fri, Sat. **Map** p334 D1 ③
Shake up vintage Vegas appeal with 21st-century
style and you have Sidebar, a louche spot attached
to the Triple George steakhouse (*see p173*).
Martinis are the speciality, drunk to a soundtrack
provided by a piano player and with picture windows looking out to 3rd Street. An ideal place to
while away a few hours, perhaps discussing the difference between gentrification and revitalisation in
America's downtowns.

CONSUME

Beauty Bar.

Thunderbird Lounge

Aruba *1215 Las Vegas Boulevard South, at Park Paseo (383 3100, www.arubalasvegas.com). Bus Deuce, 206.* **Open** 4pm-8am Mon-Thur, Sun; 24hrs Fri, Sat. **Map** p335 C3 ❸❹

With a dark wood bar and an occasionally dingy ambience, this is an old Vegas haunt through and through. There's a darker feel here than at, say, the Peppermill (*see p181*), mostly down to the hotel's location surrounded by quickie chapels, bail bondsmen and hourly-rate motels. Bands play from time to time.

Triple 7 Brew Pub

Main Street Station *200 N Main Street, at E Stewart Avenue (387 1896, www.mainstreet casino.com). Bus Deuce & all BTC-bound buses.* **Open** 11am-7am daily. **Map** p334 C1 ❸❺

The Triple 7 serves fair beer and above-par bar food, and has an unbeatable $1-a-drink happy hour. But the real reason to visit this microbrewery is to gawk at the multi-million-dollar collection of antiques and collectibles, which even extends to the restroom: gents are able to express their opinion on communism by relieving themselves on a portion of the Berlin Wall.

Mix it Up, Baby

Cocktails that have 'Vegas' written all over them.

Sensi.

Throughout its history, Las Vegas has taken other people's ideas and twisted them into something altogether different. Alcoholically speaking, this tendency has borne fruit in many of the city's bars, which are constantly regenerating their cocktail menus to include an array of only-in-Vegas beverages. There's only one heavenly Cucumber Lavender Mojito in town, and it's at **Parasol Up** (*see p181*). And while the combination of Sauza tequila, cilantro, cucumber and tabasco known as an Amante Picante is the perfect accompaniment to a Cuban cigar, it's served only at **Casa Fuente** (*see p209*).

The cocktail revival in Vegas began when Steve Wynn hired Tony Abou-Ganim, the best cocktail guy in the business, to help him open the Bellagio in 1998. Abou-Ganim worked with chefs to create

cocktail lists while also teaching bartenders about spirits: how to mix them, how to serve them and how to tell their stories. A year later, Nevada's top liquor distributor, Southern Wine & Spirits, brought to town champion mixer Francesco Lafranconi, who raised the bar with his cocktails – visit **Wynn Las Vegas** (*see p114*) and Casa Fuente for evidence – while also launching the one-of-a-kind Academy of Spirits & Fine Service.

These days, you're behind the times if you don't rotate your cocktail menu seasonally, draw ingredients fresh from organic farms or employ at least one master mixologist who's trying to outdo the guy at the next resort. Fancy, house-invented drinks are the rage up and down the Strip. However, the Bellagio is still *the* place to soak up the cocktail zeitgeist. Drew Levinson, who oversees the resort's 140 bartenders and their 30,000 daily pours, has even derived what he loosely calls the 'Bellagio Crawl', an informal tour of some of the city's best signature beverages.

The quick version of the tour starts with a sampling of the Levinson-designed cocktail menu at **Sensi** (*see p165*), where you can try a seasonal 'salad in a glass' martini called the Caprese (tomato water and vodka muddled with basil) and a treat called a Regalo. Translating from the original Italian as 'gift', it contains Bacardi orange rum, orangecello, Alize red passion liqueur, orange juice, lime and passion fruit. Over at the **Petrossian** bar, try a fresh Bella Peach, the resort's new bestseller, or a Bellagio Breeze, invented and served by much-decorated bartender Darren West. Other stops should include **Michael Mina**'s restaurant (*see p160*) for one of Abou-Ganim's Cable Cars.

CONSUME

Frankie's Tiki Room. *See p185.*

THE REST OF THE CITY

Brendan's Irish Pub

Orleans *4500 W Tropicana Avenue, between S Decatur & S Valley View boulevards, West Las Vegas (365 7111, www.orleanscasino.com). Bus 103, 104, 201.* **Open** 5pm-1am Mon-Thur; 10am-2am Fri-Sun.
The scene is fairly generic for an Irish pub with sports-bar leanings. But while the setting is a little bland, the entertainment on weekends spices things up, with everything from Irish bands to zydeco troupes on the agenda. The bands' daffy groupies are sometimes even more of a lark than the music.

Champagnes Café

3557 S Maryland Parkway, between E Desert Inn Road & E Twain Avenue, East Las Vegas (737 1699, www.champagnescafe.blogspot.com). Bus 109. **Open** 24hrs daily. **No credit cards.** **Map** p333 Y3 ㊱
With velvety flock wallpaper, Frank and Dino on the jukebox, and a shrine (a martini, a coffee cup and a cigarette) dedicated to former manager Marty, this vintage bar is a Dom Perignon '53 among Vegas saloons. Hipsters, barflies and discerning locals head here at all hours for cheap drinks; many find it understandably hard to leave.

Crown & Anchor Pub

1350 E Tropicana Avenue, at S Maryland Parkway, University District (739 8676, www.crownandanchorlv.com). **Open** 24hrs daily. **Map** p333 Y3 ㊲
The British-themed Crown & Anchor manages the feat, difficult in this town, of being a free-standing, independent pub, separate from a casino or a strip mall. Collegiate types and football-shirted expats head here to down pints of Boddingtons, tuck into fish 'n' chips and bash away hopefully at Thursday's quiz night. It gets packed during football matches.

Davy's Locker

1149 E Desert Inn Road, at S Maryland Parkway Avenue, East Las Vegas (735 0001, www.davys lockerlv.com). Bus 109, 213. **Open** 24hrs daily. **No credit cards. Map** p333 Y3 ㊳
Sadly, the interior of this long-standing fixture can't match the sign out front, a truly evocative old glory that's surely destined for the Neon Museum if the bar ever closes. After more than four decades, though, it seems pretty firmly ensconced, a calm, slightly divey little wellspring of cheap drinks and melancholy on a forlorn stretch of Desert Inn Road.

Dispensary Lounge

2451 E Tropicana Avenue, at S Eastern Avenue, East Las Vegas (458 6343). Bus 110, 201. **Open** 24hrs daily. **Map** p333 Z3 ㊴
You can look at the waterwheel, you can listen to the waterwheel, but you certainly can't touch it.

Sort of like the waitresses. The Dispensary is a throwback to old Vegas, complete with shag carpets, fake plants and leotard-clad serving staff who become more boisterous and less balanced as the night wears on (well, you try wearing high heels on a shag carpet). A dark, quiet answer to a bright and frenetic city.

Drop Bar

Green Valley Ranch *2300 Paseo Verde Drive, at S Green Valley Parkway, Henderson (617 7777, www.greenvalleyranchresort.com). Bus 111.* **Open** 24hrs daily.
It's easy to be tricked into feeling that you're not old enough to be lounging with a glass of pinot noir on the frightfully white bar stools and leather couches at Drop. By contrasting the whites with deep, dark floors and walls, the designers have achieved a seriously sexy look, with sheer curtains providing separation from the lively casino. A luxurious place to celebrate a win or to lick your wounds.

Freakin' Frog

4700 S Maryland Parkway, at E Tropicana Avenue, University District (597 9702, www. freakinfrog.com). Bus 109, 201. **Open** 2pm-4am daily. **Map** p333 Y3 ㊵
Despite its irritatin' name, the Frog is a locals' favourite, and not just because of the 400-strong beer selection. Located across the road from UNLV, this

is about as close as Vegas gets to a college bar. Order some fried mac 'n' cheese triangles or a corn dog to accompany your discussion of Peruvian beer versus, say, Colt 45 (both of which are stocked). There's a whiskey bar upstairs.

Herbs & Rye
3713 Sahara Avenue, at S Valley View Boulevard, Westside (982 8036, www.herbsandrye.com). Bus 104, 204 109. **Open** *5pm-3am Mon-Sat.* **Map** *p333 Y3* ⓐ
Mixologists reign at the bar of this Italian/tapas restaurant, which aspires to a 1920s speakeasy feel. The bartenders focus on quality, tradition and innovation – the cocktail menu is arranged according to the history of spirits, with a chapter on Prohibition. Ask for a Bee's Knees – a '20s-era nectar of gin, honey and lemon.

Hookah Lounge
Paymon's Mediterranean Café & Market, 8380 W Sahara Avenue (804 0293, www.hookah lounge.com). Bus 204. **Open** *5pm-1am daily.*
In this dark and ornate haven, a stark contrast to the adjoining Mediterranean Café (*see p176*), you'll be served at low tables by a hookah jockey, who dispenses cocktails and water pipes. Flavours range from the flowery to the fruity, but we recommend something nutty and traditional, like Turkish pistachio. Take a couple of puffs and then pass it on. There's food and herbal smoke before 9pm; afterwards, the kitchen closes and the real tobacco is brought out.

Shady Grove Lounge
Silverton *3333 Blue Diamond Road, at I-15, South Las Vegas (263 7777, www.silverton casino.com). Bus 117.* **Open** *4pm-midnight Thur-Sat;10am-midnight Sun.*

Freakin' Frog.
See p187.

With decor that includes an Airstream trailer equipped with two mini bowling lanes, the Shady Grove is a curious place, but in a good, raising-the-brows kind of way. The Hootie references and memorabilia are noticeable enough to grab fans but subtle enough not to distract the rest of us.

Lucky Bar
Red Rock Resort *11011 W Charleston Boulevard, at I-215, West Las Vegas (797 7518, www.redrocklasvegas.com). Bus 206.* **Open** *10am-3am daily.*
Summerlin's sister to the Drop Bar is an impressive, round and deep-red room well-hung with expensive crystal and furnished with flatscreens, comfortable banquettes and rotating Austin Powers love seats. The drinks are mixed well, and it only gets crazy on weekend nights, making this a nice escape.

★ Mermaid Bar & Lounge
Silverton *3333 Blue Diamond Road, at I-15, South Las Vegas (263 7777, www.silverton casino.com). Bus 117.* **Open** *11am-1am daily.*
While you're sitting and sipping your Shark Attack and gazing into the 117,000-gallon aquarium, it might occur to you to wonder: where are the mermaids? Don't fret: they, and their companion mermen, will be along in a while, diving in on the hour in the evenings (except Tue) and performing underwater versions of *Swan Lake*. Cheap drinks and jellyfish tanks add to the eccentric appeal.

Lounges

Many visitors to Vegas leave town arguing that a number of the big shows staged in Strip casinos really aren't strong enough to merit an admission charge. But as long as people are willing to pay $50 to see a Neil Diamond impersonator or drop $25 to hear an impressionist, the casinos will be more than happy to take the money and run.

Conversely, few visitors make the case that the resorts should start charging for the free entertainment offered in their lounges. Traditionally, Vegas lounges have been reserved for acts on their way up or down the showbiz ladder: Louis Prima revived his career in the Sahara's Casbah Lounge, and others have made their name by playing Vegas lounges for little more than a tip and a wink. These days, though, the musicians who provide a soundtrack to the increasingly drunken gambling are of a rather lower grade.

There's a limit on the number of classic rock covers any sane person can stomach, and many visitors will have a similarly low tolerance for the too-smooth jazzers and *American Idol* wannabes who try just that little bit too hard o catch the eyes and ears of passing punters.

Carnaval Court.

Even so, pleasant musical surprises aren't as rare as you might expect, and even the worst rendition of 'Don't Stop Believing' can get the head nodding and the nostalgia flowing after a liberal infusion of vodka.

THE STRIP

Le Cabaret
Paris Las Vegas *3655 Las Vegas Boulevard South, at E Flamingo Road (1-877 603 4586, www.parislasvegas.com). Bus Deuce, 202.* **Open** 2pm-3am daily. **Map** p336 A7 43
Le Cabaret has more character than most antiseptic casino lounges. With its faux shady trees and sparkling lights, you'll almost feel like you're doin' the 'Neutron Dance' in gay Paree. Or, at least, you will after the eighth drink of the evening.

Carnaval Court
Harrah's *3475 Las Vegas Boulevard South, between Sands Avenue & E Flamingo Road (369 5000, www.harrahs.com). Bus Deuce, 203.* **Open** noon-1am Mon-Thur, Sun; noon-2am Fri, Sat. **Map** p336 A6 44
At this outlandish outdoor bar, the show-off entertainment is just as prevalent among the bartenders as the musicians: it's not uncommon to see a barkeep pouring shots into the upturned mouths of waiting patrons, like baby birds begging to be fed. For a Vegas kitsch sensation, check out entertainer Cook E Jarr, who performs here on Fridays and Saturdays from 6pm to 8pm.

Indigo Lounge
Bally's *3645 Las Vegas Boulevard South, at E Flamingo Road (731 7778, www.ballyslasvegas.com). Bus Deuce, 202.* **Open** 9pm-2am Mon-Fri, Sun; 9pm-3am Sat. **Map** p336 A7 45
Right next to the Bally's/Paris Las Vegas walkway, this casual, enjoyable lounge features a scattering of pop, dance, Motown and R&B acts.

Mizuya Lounge
Mandalay Bay *3950 Las Vegas Boulevard South, at W Hacienda Avenue (632 6112, www.mandalaybay.com). Bus Deuce, 104.* **Open** 11.30am-11pm daily. **Map** p336 A9 46
Dance bands play at Mandalay Bay's largest music lounge and sushi bar, beyond restaurant row, and draw energetic crowds nightly. A mellower vibe can be found in the Orchid Lounge.

THE REST OF THE CITY

Bourbon Street Cabaret
Orleans *4500 W Tropicana Avenue, between S Decatur & S Valley View boulevards, West of Strip (365 7111, www.orleanscasino.com). Bus 103, 104, 201.* **Open** 6pm-3am Tue-Sun. **Map** p333 X4 47
Local bands play a mix of rock, pop, Latin and disco in this small lounge six nights a week. It's styled like a French Quarter courtyard and adorned with wrought-iron decorations, with grand pianos suspended overhead. There's usually a two-drink minimum in effect.

Chrome
Santa Fe Station *4949 N Rancho Drive, at US 95 (junction 90A), North Las Vegas (658 4900, www.santafestationlasvegas.com). Bus 101, 102, 106, 219.* **Open** varies.
If 1980s music is your guilty pleasure, get over to this sleek club/showroom. Wednesdays, Fridays and Saturdays draw national touring blues performers, who always go great with bourbon.

Rock's Lounge
Red Rock Resort *11011 W Charleston Boulevard, at I-215, West Las Vegas (797 7777, www.redrocklasvegas.com). Bus 206.* **Open** varies.
Fake smoke pours out of the lounge of this swanky neighbourhood casino, a thick haze that either beckons or repels you from the cheese-o-rama.

CONSUME

Discover the city from your back pocket

Essential for your weekend break, 30 top cities available.

POCKET SIZED *from* £6.99 / $11.95

Shops & Services

Our advice? Bring a spare suitcase…

Taking in a show? Check. Dining at a star-studded restaurant? Check. Rolling the dice or doubling down? Check. But… buying a pair of Manolos? Really? Yes, it's true. Though few predicted it 20 years ago, the way in which tourists now enjoy Vegas has changed dramatically since the Forum Shops opened at Caesars Palace in 1992. According to the Las Vegas Convention & Visitors Authority, more than half of the city's 40 million visitors spend time shopping. The key is in the old something-for-everyone cliché: there's Nike Golf for the weekend duffer, Prada and Tom Ford for the label hound, and the Gap for just about everybody else.

THE SHOPS

Change in the Vegas shopping scene has been rapid and dramatic. The 2004 opening of the cool, urban **Mandalay Place** was followed by dramatic renovations and expansfion at the **Fashion Show Mall**, the christening of a new wing at the Forum Shops, the unveiling of the **Wynn Esplanade**'s selection of super-smart stores, and the 2007 remodelling (and renaming) of the **Miracle Mile Shops**. And that's just on the Strip: the **Las Vegas Premium Outlets** in Downtown has been a huge success, while the conversion of a landmark bakery into the **Holsum Design Center** has brought small local businesses into focus.

Further south on Las Vegas Boulevard, the **Town Square** mall has 150 stores, 12 restaurants, a buzzy, locals-heavy club scene and a multiplex with an IMAX theatre. While the aforementioned Las Vegas Premium Outlets has a store count of 150.

So go ahead, shop till you drop – if you do, your hotel room is more often than not just an elevator ride away: many of the newest, highest-end malls are built right into the casino resorts.

The **Shoppes at the Palazzo** (*see p196*), the Venetian's new sibling, is now home to Barneys, Las Vegas's first branch of the department store favoured by New York's funky fashion elite.

And now, outsparkling them all, is **Crystals** (*see p194*), the ultraluxe shopping complex that fronts the new **CityCenter** complex on the Strip, with its elegant angles designed by

architect Daniel Libeskind. With its vast ceilings and pristine all-white settings, Crystals looks like a museum of shopping designed by a sci-fi art director, and it features boutiques by Balenciaga, Dior, Pucci, Gucci and Fendi, Stella McCartney, Paul Smith and Tom Ford.

Right next door there's the even newer **Cosmopolitan** (*see p194*), the choice of the international hipoisie (and locals, who took to the place immediately). Its collection of boutiques will send them off kitted out to be noticed.

If all this sounds too serious, rest assured that good taste hasn't completely taken over Vegas. You'll still be able to find all the kitschy knick-knacks you could possibly want in the town's many souvenir stores. Certainly, **Bonanza Gifts** (*see p208*), which declares itself the 'World's Largest Gift Shop', isn't getting any smaller…

SERVICE WITH A SMILE?

It may come as a surprise, but service is not always a strong point here. Attendants can veer from wonderfully helpful to downright rude in seconds; it might seem rather odd in a city so completely based on pleasing its visitors, until you work out that this is just

INSIDE TRACK SALES TAX

An 8.1 per cent sales tax will be added to your purchases at the till.

about the only major service industry in town where the professionals stand no chance of being tipped handsomely for their work.

General

DEPARTMENT STORES

The following stores stock a broad range of products, from fashion to homewares. In addition, the numerous branches of **Target** (www.target.com) in Vegas offer trendy designer labels (Isaac Mizrahi, Liz Lange, Mossimo) at discount prices. And be sure to look out for **Barneys**: New York's most fashionable export has opened a branch in the Venetian's new Shoppes at the Palazzo.

Dillard's

Fashion Show Mall, 3200 Las Vegas Boulevard South, at Spring Mountain Road (733 2008, www.dillards.com). Bus Deuce, 105, 203.
Open 10am-9pm Mon-Sat; 11am-6pm Sun.
Map p335 B6.
The American west's equivalent of Marks & Spencer has excellent beauty aisles, a good selection of women's shoes, and a great range of men's suits at decent prices. By the same token, there's not much to quicken the pulse.
Other locations throughout the city.

Macy's

Fashion Show Mall, 3200 Las Vegas Boulevard South, at Spring Mountain Road (737 8708, www.macys.com). Bus Deuce, 105, 203.
Open 10am-9pm Mon-Sat; 10am-8pm Sun.
Map p335, p336 B6.
The king of department stores, Macy's offers a variety of quality merchandise at competitive prices. Clothing, strong on both men's and women's lines, ranges from classic (Ralph Lauren) to hip (Ben Sherman) to utilitarian.
▶ *The homewares-only branch on Spring Mountain Road has frequent sales.*
Other locations throughout the city.

Neiman Marcus

Fashion Show Mall, 3200 Las Vegas Boulevard South, at Spring Mountain Road (731 3636, www.neimanmarcus.com). Bus Deuce, 105, 203. **Open** 10am-8pm Mon-Fri; 10am-7pm Sat; noon-7pm Sun. **Map** p335, p336 B6.
The world's best designers are on display at this upmarket department store, among them the catwalk-friendly likes of Prada, Manolo Blahnik, Escada, Missoni and Chanel. It also has a good range of accessories, make-up, lingerie and perfumes, and a fantastic homewares selection. It's nicknamed 'Needless Mark-Up' for a reason, but there are discounted goods down at the Fashion Outlets of Las Vegas in Primm (874 2100; *see p198*).

Nordstrom

Fashion Show Mall, 3200 Las Vegas Boulevard South, at Spring Mountain Road (862 2525, www.nordstrom.com). Bus Deuce, 105, 203.
Open 10am-9pm Mon-Sat; 11am-6pm Sun.
Map p335, p336 B6.
Those who swear by Nordstrom agree that it's a good place for style-conscious people of any age to find great stuff at reasonable prices and with

Crystals at CityCenter.
See p194.

CONSUME

excellent service. Both the men's and women's shoe departments are worth a look. Harking back to the days when shopping used to be an 'experience', Nordy's even treats its customers to piano music and a fine café. Those of lesser means should try its Henderson outlet.

Other locations Nordstrom Rack, 9851 S Eastern Avenue, at E Silverado Ranch Boulevard, Henderson (948 2121).

Saks Fifth Avenue
Fashion Show Mall, 3200 Las Vegas Boulevard South, at Spring Mountain Road (733 8300, www.saksfifthavenue.com). Bus Deuce, 105, 203. **Open** 10am-8pm Mon-Wed; 10am-9pm Thur, Fri; 10am-7pm Sat; noon-6pm Sun. **Map** p335, p336 B6.
For those with discriminating taste and a heavy-weight bank account, a trip to Saks is like a visit to church: you go once a week to pay homage and hear the word. The men's and women's apparel sections are especially strong (Marc Jacobs, Dolce & Gabbana, Hugo Boss).
▶ *If you've got the taste but not the money, check out Off 5th, Saks's outlet store at the Las Vegas Outlet Center (263 7692; see p198).*

MALLS
Casino malls

Casino malls tend to attract the high-end brands and big-name chains, rather than any discount outlets. For designer labels, head to the brand-new **Crystals** (Balenciaga, Dior, Pucci, Gucci and Fendi, Stella McCartney, Paul Smith and Tom Ford), the **Wynn**

THE BEST SHOPS

For a bit of everything
Forum Shops *See p194.*

For the folks back home
Gamblers General Store. *See p208.*

For local literature
Dead Poets Books. *See p198.*

For an indelible souvenir
Pussykat Tattoo Parlor. *See p212.*

Esplanade (Chanel, Gaultier, Manolo Blahnik), **Via Bellagio** (Prada, Gucci, Fendi) and the **Forum Shops** (Marc Jacobs, Pucci, Carolina Herrera). The latter also houses a number of high-street staples (Gap, Banana Republic), as does Planet Hollywood's **Miracle Mile Shops**.

Le Boulevard
Paris Las Vegas *3655 Las Vegas Boulevard South, at E Flamingo Road (946 7000, www.parislasvegas.com). Bus Deuce, 202.* **Open** 9am-11pm daily. **Map** p336 A7.
Just about every shop in this small but divine mall (it's basically an extended hallway) comes with a strong but delightful French influence. La Boutique offers a well-edited collection of high-end accessories from such French labels as Celine, Hermès and Cartier; Les Enfants has Madeline, Babar the Elephant and Eloise toys and dolls; and Les

CONSUME

Mémoires sells sweet-smelling boudoir and bath gifts. La Cave has cheeses, pâtés and wine, while Lenôtre is known for its bread and pastries. There's even a 24-hour gift shop (Le Journal) where you can purchase everything from a Paris Las Vegas T-shirt to Diet Coke and cigarettes.

★ Cosmopolitan

CityCenter *3708 Las Vegas Boulevard South, between E Harmon Avenue & E Flamingo Road (1-877 551 7778, 698 7000, www.cosmopolitan lasvegas.com). Bus Deuce, 202.* **Open** 10am-11pm daily. **Map** p336 A7.

Cosmopolitan set out to be different from anywhere else in Las Vegas, and it has achieved this goal with style, sophistication and wit. The choice of the international and hip, as well as chic locals, Cosmo attracts a younger, more urbane crowd, who like to look at each other as much as they like to gamble – maybe more. The unusual vertical layout (three storeys, centred around a chandelier that even Liberace himself couldn't have envisioned), is studded with unusual shopping options, including Amsterdam's outré, avant-garde Droog assemblage of conceptual furniture. You'll also find an option of the UK's All Saints Spitalfields, the Beckley luxury boutique, the discerning Stitched menswear collections, and Skins 6/2 Cosmetics, which sells potions with 'retail theater'. Once you have your look together, grab a cocktail and head for the third floor, an endless people-watching parade, with an amusing collection of vintage mid-modern furniture for striking a pose upon.

★ Crystals at CityCenter

CityCenter *3720 Las Vegas Boulevard South, at E Harmon Avenue (1-866 754 2489, 590 9299, www.crystalsatcitycenter.com). Bus Deuce, 202.* **Open** 10am-11pm daily. **Map** p336 A7.

Hollywood should stage the Academy Awards at the new Crystals shopping centre at the CityCenter complex. God knows it's big enough, with its soaring ceilings and vast expanses of white stone. And all the designer labels favoured by celebrities and socialites are in place: Balenciaga, Dior, Pucci, Gucci and Fendi; Stella McCartney, Paul Smith and Tom Ford, as well as jewellers-to-the-stars Bulgari, Cartier, Tiffany, Van Cleef and Arpels, Mikimoto and Harry Winston. Between bouts of browsing and buying, there are restaurants by Wolfgang Puck and Todd English (his PUB. is a fantastically fun casual saloon), the pan-Asian Social Club and the lavish, retro-futuristic Mastro's Ocean Club, which perches over the fabulous fray. Since precious few can afford the baubles on display, there's often plenty of room inside the boutiques, where it's often 'look but don't touch'. But the biggest draw at Crystals, its water-themed public art, is definitely look and touch: one work features giant obelisks of ice that emerge then slowly thaw, creating fantastic shapes and textures via heat, wind, and the touch of thousands of tourists; another offers rainbow-hued whirlwinds within plexiglass cylinders. *Photo p192.*

▶ *For more art in Las Vegas, see pp245-247.*

★ Forum Shops

Caesars Palace *3500 Las Vegas Boulevard South, at W Flamingo Road (1-877 427 7243, 893 4800, www.caesars.com). Bus Deuce, 202.* **Open** 10am-11pm Mon-Thur, Sun; 10am-midnight Fri, Sat. **Map** p336 A7.

Sure, it might be trying too hard with the faux-Roman vibe – classical pillars, statues, huge replica of the Trevi Fountain – but with more than 160 boutiques

Where to Shop

Where to find what you want.

THE STRIP

Most shoppers remain confined to the Strip, and not without good reason: the majority of the town's more interesting and popular malls are found on it. The new high-end shopping complex Crystals (*see p194*) at CityCenter is the crown jewel of Strip shopping.

DOWNTOWN

Fremont Street is pathetically devoid of decent shops. However, the Arts District is crammed with vintage stores and galleries; the Holsum Design Center offers an array of gift shops; and the Las Vegas Premium Outlets (*see p198*) is great for bargains. The new mixed-use

buildings (Juhl, Soho Lofts, Newport Lofts) also have street-level retail.

THE REST OF THE CITY

The new Town Square outdoor shopping/ dining/entertainment complex (*see p197*), south of the Strip, has quickly become a favourite among locals, and many tourists find it worth their while to make the quick trip too. Along Maryland Parkway, you'll find a few vintage clothing stores that appeal to UNLV students. Otherwise, take your pick from any of the plentiful malls. The best of Las Vegas's independent retailers are in strip malls or stand-alone buildings all around the city. It really does pay to travel.

Forum Shops.

(414 4500, www.grandcanalshoppes.com). Bus Deuce, 203, 213. **Open** 10am-11pm Mon-Thur, Sun; 10am-midnight Fri, Sat. **Map** p336 A6.

The Grand Canal Shoppes felt like a second-rate Forum Shops when it opened in 1999. In places, that's what it still resembles. The walkways are narrow and cramped, but the smaller space does at least give a reasonable impression of an intimate city streetscape – and it's studded with cafés, such as the Grand Lux and San Genaro Grill. With its faux-alfresco feel, the outpost of Wolfgang Puck's Postrio here is one of the most pleasant places in the city to dine; and the scene at Tao Asian Bistro becomes one of the city's hottest clubs at night. Let's not overlook the novelty of browsing shops along one of Vegas's wonders: a Venetian canal, paddled by singing gondoliers. Oh, then there are the shops, of course: Lladró, Movado, Jimmy Choo, St John Sport, BCBG/MaxAzria and Burberry are among the best of the generally high-end retailers. If it all becomes a bit too much, there's an on-site oxygen bar called Breath. And the Grand Canal may be the only mall with its own branch of the famous Madame Tussaud's Interactive Wax Museum.

▶ For a review of Postrio, see p163. For Tao Asian Bistro, see p261.

Mandalay Place
Mandalay Bay 3950 Las Vegas Boulevard South, at W Hacienda Avenue (632 9333, www. mandalaybay.com). Bus Deuce, 104, 105. **Open** 10am-11pm daily. **Map** p336 A9.

What separates this smallish retail experience from other Strip malls is its vow to 'break the chains': it leases its stores only to companies otherwise absent from Vegas. It's a savvy move, and one that brought the city its first Urban Outfitters (which has since also opened in the Miracle Mile Shops); an outpost of Frederick's of Hollywood lingerie; unusual art offerings, including the Art of Music and Peter Lik Gallery, featuring beautiful palmwood furniture by Aussie designer Bruce Dowse. The handful of great boutiques includes Fornaria, Nora Blue, Elton's Men Store and Max&Co; other highlights include the modern furniture, lighting and accessories at Blankspace, and Lush Puppy, which carries fashion-conscious accessories for cats and dogs.

For nibbles, try Rick Moonen's RM Seafood (Moonen is TV-famous from his appearances on the Top Chef reality show; and food-famous for his commitment to sustainable seafood cuisine). The Burger Bar (see p156) continues to be popular, with its baroque twists (foie gras!) on the humble hamburger. And when you need to chill out, pop into the Minus5 Ice Lounge, an all-ice cocktail bar – where you'll be outfitted with a parka and gloves before you sip your vodka from an ice goblet. The mall is located on a bridge that connects Mandalay Bay to the Luxor, and is accessible from either resort. Photo p196.

and shops under its trompe l'oeil, always-twilit Italian sky, the Forum Shops rakes in a whopping $1,300 in sales per square foot each year, the nation's highest per-square-foot revenue. And that's a lot of square feet – the Forum Shops recently added 175,000 square feet and additional levels that extend the mall to the Strip. Far and away the best of the casino malls, you could spend your entire visit here. (And keep your eyes peeled for Celine Dion – she works in the building).

In the main mall, mid-range chains (Banana Republic, Gap, Abercrombie & Fitch, Diesel, Kenneth Cole) punctuate the serious designer line-up: Elie Tahari, Dolce & Gabbana, Christian Lacroix, Robert Cavalli, Valentino, Ermenegildo Zegna, John Varvatos, et al. Accessorise your outfit at Chopard, David Yurman, Bulgari, De Beers, Harry Winston or Tiffany & Co. But the real jewels are the refined shops that front directly on to the Strip. Spiral escalators and marble floors help create a swanky setting for tenants such as fashion powerhouses Kate Spade, Marc Jacobs, Pucci, Thomas Pink and Carolina Herrera. Recent arrivals include H&M, Judith Ripka, Miss Sixty and Ron Herman. There are attractions at either end of the mall: statues come to life at one extremity, with Atlantis rising from the waves at the other. When your feet or credit cards are exhausted, head for the Qua Baths & Spa or pop by Numb Bar for one of their frozen cocktails.

Grand Canal Shoppes
Venetian 3377 Las Vegas Boulevard South, between Sands Avenue & E Flamingo Road

CONSUME

Mandalay Place. *See p195.*

★ Miracle Mile Shops

Planet Hollywood *2667 Las Vegas Boulevard South, between E Harmon & E Flamingo roads (1-888 800 8284, www.miraclemileshopslv.com).* Bus Deuce, 202. **Open** 10am-11pm Mon-Thur, Sun; 10am-midnight Fri, Sat. **Map** p336 A7.
Formerly the Desert Passage, this 1.2-mile loop-mall recently underwent a multi-million-dollar makeover, transforming it from a Moroccan-style market into a contemporary urban centre. The Hollywood-style facelift added trendier, younger labels to attract the kind of hipsters usually found hanging at the Palms or the Hard Rock, among them Ben Sherman, H&M, Bettie Page Las Vegas, Metropark, Quiksilver, Marciano and Urban Outiftters. What makes it stand out are the scores of eating options – grab a cheeseburger at the Oasis or head to Trader Vic's for mai tais and chicken curry – and the entertainment venues studded throughout the mall, plus a free hourly 'thunderstorm' show that brings everyone to a halt. *Photos p199.*

Shoppes at Palazzo

Palazzo *3327 Las Vegas Boulevard South, between Sands Avenue & W Flamingo Road (414 4525, www.theshoppesatthepalazzo.com).* Bus Deuce, 202. **Open** 10am-11pm Mon-Thur, Sun; 10am-midnight Fri, Sat. **Map** p333 X3.
Anchored by the fashionista magnet Barney's New York, the sophisticated sibling of the Venetian offers an upscale array of shops, including Bottega Veneta, Catherine Malandrino, Chloé, Fendi and von Fürstenberg, Thomas Pink and Tory Burch.

Shoe-hounds will want to slip into Christian Louboutin and Jimmy Choo. Las Vegas is not a town that generally celebrates or venerates reading, so it's encouraging to discover Bauman's Rare Books, a bibliophile's dream, nestled amid the boutiques. Food experiences include the eclectic menu of First Food & Bar and the lavish LAVO, offering Italiante cuisine in an atmosphere inspired by Roman bathhouses.

Via Bellagio

Bellagio *3600 Las Vegas Boulevard South, at W Flamingo Road (693 7111, www.bellagio.com).* Bus Deuce, 202. **Open** 10am-midnight daily. **Map** p336 A7.
In line with its upmarket image, the Bellagio's small mall contains ten of the smartest designer names this side of Wynn Las Vegas. Long-standing tenants such as Tiffany & Co, Prada, Gucci, Chanel, Dior, Giorgio Armani and Hermès have been joined of late by the likes of Fendi and Bottega Veneta. If your wallet can't cope, at least pop in to enjoy the location: the venue is a shrine to materialism, with daylight streaming through the vaulted glass ceilings on to opulent walkways and tidy storefronts. The food is a cut above regular mall fodder too: try Todd English's Olives (*see p162*), a Mediterranean bistro overlooking the lake, with a marvellous view of the hourly Bellagio fountain show.

★ Wynn Esplanade

Wynn Las Vegas *3131 Las Vegas Boulevard South, between E Desert Inn Road & Sands*

Avenue (770 7000, www.wynnlasvegas.com). Bus Deuce, 203. **Open** 10am-11pm Mon-Thur, Sun; 10am-midnight Fri, Sat. **Map** p335, p336 B6.

Steve Wynn took Oscar de la Renta on a personal tour of the then under-construction Wynn Las Vegas, in an attempt to convince the couturier that it would be the finest resort in town. It worked. De la Renta located his signature shop inside the Wynn Esplanade, as have Alexander McQueen, Jean-Paul Gaultier, Hermès, Brioni, Manolo Blahnik (the second signature store in the US) and Jo Malone perfumers, to name but a few. Peppered throughout the rest of the resort are other interesting spots, such as Shoe In (an assortment of designer shoes from Stuart Weitzman, Christian Louboutin and Giuseppe Zanotti), Outfit (ready-to-wear clothes from Zac Posen, Narciso Rodriguez and Martin Margiela) and Wynn LVNV (home accessories that include the Wynn's dreamy beds, Murano chandeliers and chocolates by Frédéric Robert). There's also the requisite collection of designer labels, among them Chanel, Dior and Louis Vuitton, and the mustn't-miss Ferrari-Maserati showroom and logo gift shop ($10 admission required – unless you're buying a car).

Non-casino malls

Even without its casino malls, Vegas caters efficiently and effectively for shoppers. The revamped **Fashion Show Mall** leads the way, with a host of chain and department stores, supplemented by the more prosaic **Boulevard Mall** and other less notable developments.

In addition, Las Vegas now has its very own 'lifestyle centres', open-air complexes that 'serve as multi-purpose leisure-time destinations' (according to the International Council of Shopping Centers). The best is the **District** out in Green Valley. Others include **Rampart Commons** (1055 S Rampart Boulevard, at W Charleston Boulevard, Summerlin), home to Nevada's first Pottery Barn, and the nearby **Boca Park Fashion Village** (8950 W Charleston Boulevard, at S Rampart Boulevard, Summerlin), with boutiques such as **Talulah G** (*see p202*).

Boulevard Mall

3528 S Maryland Parkway, at W Desert Inn Road, East Las Vegas (732 8949, www.boulevard mall.com). Bus 109, 213. **Open** 10am-9pm Mon-Sat; 11am-6pm Sun. **Map** p333 Y3.

A bastion of the Las Vegas shopping scene and the first mall of its type to open in the city; it's centrally located, reasonably priced and loaded with familiar favourites such as Sears, Dillard's, Macy's and JC Penney. When you're weighed down with bags and nearing collapse, head to the Panorama Café's food court for cheap international cuisine.

The District

Green Valley Ranch *120 S Green Valley Parkway, between Paseo Verde Parkway & I-215, Henderson (564 8595, www.thedistrictatgvr.com). Bus 114.* **Open** 10am-9pm Mon-Sat; 11am-7pm Sun.

Highlights at the open-air District, across the street from the lush Green Valley Ranch casino-resort in Henderson, include REI, Anthropologie, Coldwater Creek and Francesca's Collection, a sweet little accessories and gift shop. Eateries, among them Lucille's Smokehouse Bar-B-Que, Kennedy's, the splendid King's Fish House, the high-energy burger joint Al's Garage and the deliciously authentic Settebello Pizzeria Napoletana, are an important part of the mix. The District crossed over Green Valley Parkway to include the city's second Whole Foods Market (*see p207*), its first West Elm furniture showcase and chic women's boutique Chelsea.

Fashion Show Mall

3200 Las Vegas Boulevard South, at Spring Mountain Road (369 0704, www.thefashion show.com). Bus Deuce, 105, 203. **Open** 10am-9pm Mon-Sat; 11am-7pm Sun. **Map** p335, p336 B6.

True to its name, the Fashion Show Mall offers live runway shows every Friday through Sunday, from noon to 6pm on the hour, with models showcasing styles from the scores of retailers within the malls's vast compound. A $1-billion expansion of the Fashion Show Mall included the addition of the Cloud, an amazing image projection screen/sunshade that hovers over the front of the shopping centre and broadcasts to the Strip. However, it's the line-up of shops that's the real eye-catcher. The mall has nearly doubled in size; original tenants such as Macy's, Neiman Marcus and Saks Fifth Avenue have been joined by anchor tenants including Bloomingdale's Home, Nordstrom and speciality shops such as Paul Frank, Apple, Puma, Teavana and Zara. Other recent arrivals include a cheaper, more casual version of J.Crew called Madewell, and the metropolitan Ruehl, Abercrombie & Fitch's take on clothing for young professionals. The range of restaurants is also very fine: try Ra Sushi and Capital Grille. *Photos p200.*

★ Town Square

6605 Las Vegas Boulevard South, at the intersection of I-15 & I-215 (269 5000, www. mytownsquarelasvegas.com). Bus 114. **Open** 10am-9.30pm Mon-Thur; 10am-10pm Fri, Sat; 11am-8pm Sun.

Though it's somewhat off the Strip – just south of Mandalay Bay – this new addition to the city's shopping and entertainment scene is worth the cab ride. Vegas locals often opt for the stylised street scene and less-overwhelming outdoor plaza of Town Square over the Strip: shopping options include just about everything you'd want, from Abercrombie & Fitch and Armani Exchange to White House/Black Market to a design district. There are a host of dining choices, the best of which may be the outdoor patio

CONSUME

at Brio; you'll also find a Whole Foods Market (*see p207*), a Barnes & Noble books-and-everything-else store, a state-of-the-digital-art multiplex with an IMAX screen, and a cluster of busy, buzzy clubs, including Blue Martini, Cadillac Ranch, Yard House and Pete's Dueling Piano Bar.

Discount malls

For brand-name bargains, you can't beat a discount mall, where stores sell last season's stock at a fraction of its original price. Vegas has two of its own (*see below*), but there are more bargains south of the city: the **Fashion Outlets of Las Vegas** mall in Primm (32100 Las Vegas Boulevard South, 874 1400, www. fashionoutletlasvegas.com) houses over 100 stores, among them big-names such as **Old Navy** and **Gap**.

Swap meets, at which new and used goods are hawked at bargain rates, are also worth a look. Both the **Broadacres Open Air Swap Meet** (2934 Las Vegas Boulevard North, at N Pecos Road, North Las Vegas, 642 3777) and the **Fantastic Indoor Swap Meet** (1717 S Decatur Boulevard, at W Oakey Boulevard, South-west Las Vegas, 877 0087) are both open Friday to Sunday.

Las Vegas Outlet Center
7400 Las Vegas Boulevard South, at E Warm Springs Road, South of Strip (896 5599, www. premiumoutlets.com). Bus Deuce, 117.
Open 10am-9pm Mon-Sat; 10am-8pm Sun.
Now owned by the same company as the newer Las Vegas Premium Outlets, this long-established outlet centre has decent bargains from Calvin Klein, Off 5th (the Saks Fifth Avenue discount outlet), Nike, Adidas, Harry & David Coach and Bose. The giant carousel should keep the kids content.

Las Vegas Premium Outlets
875 S Grand Central Parkway, at W Charleston Boulevard, Downtown (474 7500, www.lasvegas premiumoutlets.com). Bus 105, 106, 108, 207.
Open 10am-9pm Mon-Sat; 10am-8pm Sun.
Map p335 C2.
As the name suggests, this excellent outdoor outlet mall is geared to the higher end of the fashion market. Labels include Armani, Dolce & Gabbana, Brooks Brothers, Lacoste, Theory and Ralph Lauren, to name but a few. *Photo p203.*

Specialist
BOOKS & MAGAZINES

Reading is not a priority in Las Vegas (whatever reading goes on takes place by the pool), and independent bookstores have had even more of a hard time of it than in other cities. There are branches of book chain **Barnes & Noble** in Las Vegas; the nearest to the Strip is at 3860 S Maryland Parkway (at E Flamingo Road, 734 2900, www.barnes andnoble.com).

Specialist

Gamblers Book Club
5473 Eastern Avenue South, near McCarran International Airport, between Tropicana Avenue E and Russell Road E (382 7555, www.gamblers book.com). Bus 202, 203. **Open** 9am-7pm Mon-Fri; 9am-6pm Sat. Map p334 D3.
Recently moved from old Downtown to a new location near the airport, the Gamblers Book Club is supposedly the world's largest distributor of gambling books, be they coffee-table tomes, industry histories or tips on beating the system. If you don't just want to read about gambling, there are also cards, chips and gambling-related software for sale.

Used & antiquarian

Bauman Rare Books
3327 Las Vegas Boulevard South, between Sands Avenue & W Flamingo Road (1-888 982 2862, 948 1617, www.baumanrarebooks). Bus Deuce, 202. **Open** 10am-11pm daily.
Need a breath of civilisation and civility? Step into the hushed, luxe halls of this antiquarian purveyor of vintage volumes, modelled after Bauman's famous Madison Avenue shop – but open 13 hours a day, seven days a week, for the high-roller with a taste for rare books. The 2,300sq ft gallery has offered desirable documents and books, including first editions of Chaucer, Joyce and Twain.

Dead Poet Books
937 S Rainbow Boulevard, between W Charleston Boulevard & Alta Drive, West Las Vegas (227 4070). Bus 101, 206. **Open** 10am-6pm daily.
You'll find a charming hotchpotch of antiquarian books here on almost every topic; specialities include metaphysical cookbooks (yes, really), military histories and first editions.

CHILDREN
Fashion

Gap Kids and **BabyGap** can both be found in the Miracle Mile Shops (862 4042; *see p196*); check www.gap.com for other locations. **Las Vegas Premium Outlets** (*see above*) also has a whole slew of children's stores, among them **OshKosh B'Gosh** (221 1400), **Strasburg Children** (676 1459), **Carter's** (386 3082) and **Stride Rite Keds Sperry** (388 2055).

Along Came a Spider

Fashion Show Mall, 3200 Las Vegas Boulevard South, at W Spring Mountain Road (735 2728). Bus Deuce, 105, 203. **Open** 10am-9pm Mon-Sat; 11am-6pm Sun. **Map** p336 B6.

Along Came a Spider is an upscale boutique favoured by stage mums who tussle over designer apparel by Juicy Couture, Diesel, Phat Farm and Flowers by Zoe for their budding 'Idol'. There's also a great selection of dress-up clothes.

Dagerman's Just For Kids

2370 S Rainbow Boulevard, at W Sahara Avenue, West Las Vegas (798 5437, www.dagermans. com). Bus 101, 204. **Open** 10am-6pm Mon-Sat; noon-5pm Sun.

This family-owned boutique is one of the most popular children's stores in town. Alongside upscale clothes, it also sells strollers, toys, bedding and other accessories for infants.

Janie & Jack

Fashion Show Mall, 3200 Las Vegas Boulevard South, at Spring Mountain Road (892 9571, www.janieandjack.com). Bus Deuce, 105, 203. **Open** 10am-9pm Mon-Fri; 10am-8pm Sat; 11am-7pm Sun. **Map** p336 B6.

This precious addition to the Gymboree family relies on a sugar-coated colour palette to dress up its sweet ensembles for babies and toddlers. Personalised baby gifts include embroidered fleece blankets.

Toys

Build-a-Bear Workshop
Planet Hollywood (Miracle Mile Shops)
3667 Las Vegas Boulevard South, between E Harmon Avenue & E Flamingo Road (836 0899, www.buildabear.com). Bus Deuce. **Open** 10am-11pm Mon-Thur, Sun; 10am-midnight Fri, Sat. **Map** p336 A7.

Miracle Mile Shops. *See p196.*

MIRACLE MILE SHOPS at planet hollywood resort & casino

SHOP THE PLANET

An individual teddy bear makes a cute gift for the one you love, or indulge the kids by letting them pick out their own gift. Choose your bear's fur colour, eye colour, costume (the range is huge) and stuffing type, and watch as it is assembled by teddy experts. A real treat for children and the young at heart.
Other locations Fashion Show Mall (*see p197*; 388 2574).

Five Little Monkeys
Mandalay Bay (Mandalay Place) *3950 Las Vegas Boulevard South, at W Hacienda Avenue (632 9382, www.5littlemonkeys.com). Bus Deuce, 104, 105.* **Open** 10am-11pm daily.
The toys here are organised by theme (fairies, pirates, dinosaurs) and feature such brands as Calico Critters, Whoozit and Corolle dolls. There are also arts and crafts to distract the little ones during dinner.

ELECTRONICS & PHOTOGRAPHY
General

Best Buy (3820 S Maryland Parkway, at E Flamingo Road, 732 8283, www.bestbuy.com) and **Circuit City** (3778 S Maryland Parkway, at E Flamingo Road, 731 0374, www.circuit city.com), national chains dealing in audio, visual and computing kit of every stripe,

have stores throughout the city. For troubleshooting, Best Buy also offers a **Geek Squad** (1-800 433 5778), who are available 24 hours a day for any computer-related emergencies (in store or call-out).

For affordable, non-digital film processing, head to one of the myriad branches of chain drugstores **Walgreens** (*see p210*) or **Smith's** (*see p206*). **Ritz Camera** (Sahara Pavilion, 2580 S Decatur Boulevard, at W Sahara Avenue, South-west Las Vegas, 889 1998), part of the Wolf Camera group, will also develop film.

Fry's Electronics
6845 Las Vegas Boulevard South, at I-215, South of Strip (932 1400, http://frys.com). Bus Deuce, 105. **Open** 8am-9pm Mon-Fri; 9am-9pm Sat; 9am-7pm Sun.
This San Jose-based retailer is best known for out-fitting Silicon Valley's dotcommers during the boom. This branch stays true to Fry's not-so-humble roots, but also caters for those who merely want high quality computing, audio and video equipment – most of it at very competitive prices.

Sahara Camera Centre
2305 E Sahara Avenue, at S Eastern Avenue, East Las Vegas (457 3333). Bus 110, 204. **Open** 9am-6pm Mon-Fri; 10am-5pm Sat. **Map** p333 Z2.

Fashion Show Mall. *See p197*.

CONSUME

Claiming to be 'Nevada's largest full-service camera store', the Sahara Camera Centre pretty much has – and does – it all, with rentals and repairs, quality new and used equipment, knowledgeable staff and one-hour photo processing. Prices are fair.

Specialist

For hi-fi buffs, the Fashion Show Mall (*see p197*) houses branches of audio-visual high-flyer **Bang & Olufsen** (731 9200) and the **Apple Store** (650 9550; also at Town Square, south of the Strip). You'll find the latest Sony technology at **Sony Style** (697 5420) in the Forum Shops at Caesars.

FASHION

Las Vegas's wild and unexpected growth as a shopping destination has benefited one industry above all others: fashion. Every major chain is represented here, and a good many designer labels have also shown up to claim their stake. Some savvy European shoppers now come to Las Vegas instead of New York for a chance to restock their wardrobes at US prices. However, the city does still lack its own fashion scene: there aren't many local designers working here, just plenty of very well-dressed Las Vegans.

There's a lot more to shopping in Vegas than the stores mentioned below, and the vast malls

can make for an overwhelming experience. To get the most out of your limited shopping time, check out the malls' websites for a little pre-trip browsing and planning.

Designer

Most international design houses have stores in Vegas, which are to be found in the casino malls. **Via Bellagio** (*see p196*) offers **Prada** (866 6886) and **Giorgio Armani** (893 8327), while the **Wynn Esplanade** (*see p196*) features **Jean Paul Gaultier** (770 3490), **Oscar de La Renta** (770 3487), **Brioni** (770 3440) and **Dior Homme** (770 3496). Across at the **Grand Canal Shoppes** (*see p195*), you'll find British brand **Burberry** (735 2600).

Dolce & Gabbana (892 0880) and rarely seen imports such as **Christian Lacroix** (731 0990) and classic London shirtmaker **Thomas Pink** (731 0263) reside at the **Forum Shops** (*see p194*), which also offers menswear from the likes of **Brooks Brothers** (369 0705), **Ralph Lauren** (650 5656) and **Roberto Cavalli** (893 0369). And **Mandalay Place** (*see p195*) also has a few stores that you won't find elsewhere, most notably Italian boutiques **Fornarina** (215 9300) and **Max&Co** (795 1015).

C Level

Boca Park Fashion Village, 750 S Rampart Boulevard, at W Charleston Boulevard, Summerlin (933 6867, www.clevel-lv.com). Bus 206. **Open** 11am-7pm Mon-Sat; 11am-6pm Sun.
Budding socialites visit this two-storey loft space to keep up with owner Edith Castillo's well-edited, ever-changing collection of established and emerging designer labels (for men and women), including Heather Hawkins, Eugenia Kim and Rachel Pally.

Indra Grae

6085 S Fort Apache Road, between W Russell & W Sunset roads, West Las Vegas (636 9700). No bus. **Open** 10am-7pm Mon-Sat; noon-6pm Sun.
Taking its cue from fashion capitals around the country (New York, LA, San Francisco), this shop stocks trendy labels with an eye for detail, including Charlotte Ronson, Rebecca Beeson and Free People. There's also a fabulous selection of affordable jewellery and handbags.

Intermix

Caesars Palace (Forum Shops) *3500 Las Vegas Boulevard South, at W Flamingo Road (731 1922/www.intermixonline.com). Bus Deuce, 202.* **Open** 10am-11pm Mon-Wed, Sun; 10am-midnight Thur-Sat. **Map** p336 A7.
The Keledjian brothers stock a mix of European and American designer womenswear in this growing chain of eclectic boutiques. They prefer to help

customers mix and match pieces (hence the name) from different collections by designers such as Chloé, Stella McCartney, Matthew Williamson and Missoni, rather than buy a whole look from one collection.

Ice Accessories

Caesars Palace (Forum Shops) *3500 Las Vegas Boulevard South, at W Flamingo Road (696 9700). Bus Deuce, 202.* **Open** 10am-11pm Mon-Thur, Sun; 10am-midnight Fri, Sat. **Map** p336 A7.

Beaded evening bags, dazzling costume jewellery and funky hair accessories from such designers as Konstantin, Isabelle Fiore and LuLu Guinness. There's also a selection of chic home accessories.

John Varvatos

Caesars Palace (Forum Shops) *3500 Las Vegas Boulevard South, at W Flamingo Road (939 0922, www.johnvarvatos.com). Bus Deuce, 202.* **Open** 10am-11pm Mon-Thur, Sun; 10am-midnight Fri, Sat. **Map** p336 A7.

This men's lifestyle collection has been going since 2000, finding bad-boy credibility by using the likes of Chris Cornell, Iggy Pop and Velvet Revolver to front its ad campaigns. Shop here for eclectic tailored suits, funky sportswear, accessories and great boots.

Mojitos Resort Wear

Wynn Las Vegas (Esplanade) *3131 Las Vegas Boulevard South, between E Desert Inn Road & Sands Avenue (770 3545, www.wynnlasvegas.com). Bus Deuce, 203.* **Open** 9am-10pm Mon-Thur, Sun; 9am-11pm Fri, Sat. **Map** p335, p336 B6.

This high-end boutique caters to vacationing jet-setters with designer labels for men, women and kids.

Scoop

Caesars Palace (Forum Shops) *3500 Las Vegas Boulevard South, at W Flamingo Road (734 0026, www.scoopnyc.com). Bus Deuce, 202.* **Open** 10am-11pm Mon-Thur, Sun; 10am-midnight Fri, Sat. **Map** p336 A7.

This NY-based boutique chain has been hugely successful with its 'ultimate closet' concept, allowing hip shoppers (men, women and children) to find everything they need under one roof. Prices vary, with clothes, accessories and shoes from the likes of James Perse, Marc Jacobs and Lolita Jaca.

Talulah G

Fashion Show Mall, 3200 Las Vegas Boulevard South, at Spring Mountain Road (737 6000, www.talulahg.com). Bus Deuce, 105, 203. **Open** 10am-9pm Mon-Sat; 11am-7pm Sun. **Map** p336 B6.

Owner Meital Grantz is a New York expat with a fantastic eye. Her strong selection includes pieces by Sonia Rykiel, Matthew Williamson, Havaianas and Citizens of Humanity, and her obvious success

in Las Vegas has led to a branch in Newport Beach's Fashion Island.

Other locations Boca Park Fashion Village, 750 S Rampart Boulevard, at W Charleston Boulevard, Summerlin (932 7000); Red Rock Resort, 11011 W Charleston Boulevard, at I-15, Summerlin (797 7848).

General

Miracle Mile (*see p196* has a good range of trendy stores for those on a budget, among them **Urban Outfitters** (733 0058), **H&M** (369-1195) and **Ben Sherman** (688 4227), while the **Grand Canal Shoppes** (*see p195*) include branches of **Kenneth Cole** (836 1916) and **Ann Taylor** (731 0655).

However, as is often the case, the **Forum Shops** (*see p194*) comes out on top by a long way. Stores here include the pick of the US chains, among them **Abercrombie & Fitch** (731 0712) and perennial favourite **Banana Republic** (650 5623), alongside chic accessible designer labels such as **DKNY** (650 9670).

The **Fashion Show Mall** (*see p197*) mixes upscale with casual in a similar way to the Forum Shops, and with almost as much success. Among those present are **Quiksilver** (734 1313) and femme favourite **Betsey Johnson** (735 3338), plus the trendier likes of **Lucky Brand** (369 4116), **Diesel** (696 1055) and the youthful brand **Paul Frank** (369 2010). Don't forget the town's discount malls (*see p198*): you'll find over 150 different labels at the **Las Vegas Premium Outlets** (*see p198*), among them **Tommy Hilfiger** (383 8660), **Calvin Klein** (366 9898) and **Timberland** (386 3045).

Francesca's Collections

Green Valley Ranch (District) *120 S Green Valley Parkway, between Paseo Verde Parkway & I-215, Henderson (435 3288, www.francescas.net). Bus 114.* **Open** 10am-9pm Mon-Sat; 11am-7pm Sun.

Stocked with a treasure trove of trendy street fashions, girly baubles, glittering hair accessories and playful gifts, Francesca's is the perfect place to pick up that last-minute gift for the girls back home, at very affordable prices.

Lacoste

Caesars Palace (Forum Shops) *3500 Las Vegas Boulevard, at W Flamingo Road (791 7616, www.lacoste-usa.com). Bus Deuce, 202.* **Open** 10am-11pm Mon-Thur, Sun; 10am-midnight Fri, Sat. **Map** p336 A7.

The polo shirt, created by French tennis champion René Lacoste in the 1930s, bears the crocodile logo that comes from his nickname. There are cheaper goodies in its store at Las Vegas Premium Outlets.

Other locations Fashion Show Mall (*see p197*; 796 6676).

Las Vegas Premium Outlets. *See p198.*

CONSUME

Suite 160
9350 W Sahara Avenue, at S Fort Apache Road, West Las Vegas (562 6136). Bus 204, 213. **Open** 10am-7pm Mon-Sat; 1-6pm Sun.
The street-chic brainchild of former skateboarder Jeffrey Brown. Look for old-school favourites plus new urban lines by (among others) Elwood.

Ted Baker
Caesars Palace (Forum Shops) *3500 Las Vegas Boulevard South, at W Flamingo Road (369 4755, www.tedbaker.co.uk). Bus Deuce, 202.* **Open** 10am-11pm Mon-Thur, Sun; 10am-midnight Fri, Sat. **Map** p336 A7.
This London-based label – there is no 'Ted Baker' per se – stocks well-cut, tidy but fun apparel for men and women. Their collection of shirts, suits and traditional (but quirky) gentlemen's accessories particulary stand out.

Used & vintage

Attic
1018 S Main Street, at E Charleston Boulevard, Downtown (388 4088, www.atticvintage.com). Bus 105, 106, 108, 207. **Open** 10am-5pm Mon-Sat. **Map** p335 C3.
Its claim to be the largest vintage store in the world is as silly as the $1 admission charge (refundable on purchase, but that's not the point). Despite this, and its high prices, the Attic is still the best vintage store

in Vegas. The ground floor has homewares and custom-made clothing; shoes and accessories are upstairs. If clothing could speak: imagine the high-rollers and lowlife characters that stepped lively in these retro duds!

Buffalo Exchange
4110 S Maryland Parkway, at E Flamingo Road, University District (791 3960, www.buffalo exchange.com). Bus 109, 202. **Open** 10am-8pm Mon-Sat; 11am-7pm Sun. **Map** p333 Y3.
For first-rate secondhand, this countrywide vintage chain is more popular than ever, especially with students at nearby UNLV. Its prices range from budget to middling; the clothing from shop clearances rounds out the stock.

D'Loe House of Style
220 E Charleston Boulevard, at S 3rd Street, Downtown (382 5688, www.houseofstyle thenandnow.com). Bus Deuce, 105, 106, 108, 204. **Open** noon-6.30pm Tue-Sat. **Map** p334 C3.
D'Loe's, like the Attic retro store, is a Downtown institution that qualifies as a vintage Vegas destination. Mario D'Loe cut his teeth as a costume designer for Vegas shows before filling this store with finds from the 1960s and '70s.
► *A few blocks away is Valentino's Zoot Suit Connection (906 S 6th Street, at E Charleston Boulevard, 383 9555), which offers similar vintage fare with the emphasis on eveningwear.*

CONSUME

FASHION ACCESSORIES & SERVICES

Clothing hire

Al Phillips (*see below*) also hires out men's formalwear. For details on weddings in Vegas, *see p271-275.*

David's Bridal

2600 W Sahara Avenue, at S Rancho Drive, West of Strip (367 4779/www.davidsbridal.com). Bus 106, 204. **Open** 11am-9pm Mon-Fri; 10am-6pm Sat; noon-6pm Sun.
Off-the-rack gowns at reasonable prices in a variety of styles are this store's speciality. There are also tons of accessories, including frocks for the bridal party and dyeable shoes.

I&A Formalwear

3345 S Decatur Boulevard, between W Desert Inn & Spring Mountain roads, West Las Vegas (364 5777, www.iaformalwear.com). Bus 103, 213. **Open** 9am-6pm Mon-Fri; 9am-5pm Sat.
The biggest range of designer-name tuxedos (Cardin, de la Renta, Dior) in Las Vegas.

Williams Costume Company

1226 S 3rd Street, at W Colorado Avenue, Downtown (384 1384). Bus Deuce, 105, 108, 206. **Open** 10am-5pm Mon-Sat. **Map** p335 C3.
The only place in town that carries sufficient ancient Egyptian, Renaissance gentry and Elvis costumes to dress the bride, groom and all the guests in your chosen theme.

Cleaning & repairs

Al Phillips (www.alphillips-thecleaner.com) has locations all over Vegas; the most central is at 4130 Koval Lane (at E Flamingo Road, 733 1043). All branches provide dry-cleaning, laundry and repairs, and hire men's formalwear.

Cora's Coin Laundry

1097 E Tropicana Avenue, at S Maryland Parkway, University District (736 6181). Bus 109, 201. **Open** 8am-8pm daily. **No credit cards. Map** p333 Y3.
Just two miles off the Strip, Cora's is popular with UNLV folk, offering self-service or drop-off laundry, dry-cleaning and – of course – video poker.

Shoe Lab

3900 Paradise Road, between Sands Avenue & E Flamingo Road, East of Strip (791 2004, www.shoelabworld.com). Bus 108. **Open** 8am-6pm Mon-Fri; 9am-4pm Sat. **Map** p335 C5.
The Shoe Lab can work miracles on any broken shoe or damaged handbag. It also sells leather care accessories such as polish, brushes and shoe trees.

Jewellery

Hit the jackpot? Vegas is the place to flash your cash on blinging baubles. Blow your winnings, or simply max out the credit cards at **Via Bellagio** (*see p196*) by picking up a tiara from **Tiffany & Co** (697 5400), or indulge your loved one with a string of diamonds by **Fred Leighton** (693 7050). Trip the light fantastic with understated luxury at **Harry Winston** (933 7370) or invest in a future family heirloom from **Cartier** (733 6652), both to be found at the **Forum Shops** (*see p194*). Smaller spenders might prefer the pirate's treasures of **Jewelers of Las Vegas** (2400 Western Avenue, at W Sahara Avenue, West of Strip, 382 7411, www.thejewelers.com). Some of the shops listed under **Luggage** (*see right*) also carry jewellery and fashion accessories.

Chrome Hearts

Caesars Palace (Forum Shops) *3500 Las Vegas Boulevard South, at W Flamingo Road (893 9949, www.chromehearts.com). Bus Deuce, 202.* **Open** 10am-11pm Mon-Thur, Sun; 10am-midnight Fri, Sat. **Map** p336 A7.
Free your inner rock wild side at this fine silver and leather shop. Its signature handcrafted silver jewellery is adorned with skulls, crossbones, crucifixes and flames, but the store also sells some of the softest and most stylish leather jackets, trousers and coats money can buy.

Lingerie & underwear

Agent Provocateur

Caesars Palace (Forum Shops) *3500 Las Vegas Boulevard South, at W Flamingo Road (696 7174, www.agentprovocateur.com). Bus Deuce, 202.* **Open** 10am-11pm Mon-Thur, Sun; 10am-midnight Fri, Sat. **Map** p336 A7.
The smarties behind Agent Provocateur know that there's something rather empowering about wearing fine lingerie, whether or not you share it. Look for some of the most titillating and trashy yet tasteful creations currently on the market.

Bare Essentials Fantasy Fashions

4029 W Sahara Avenue, at S Valley View Boulevard, West of Strip (247 4711, www.bare essentialsvegas.com). Bus 104, 204. **Open** 10am-7pm Mon-Sat; noon-5pm Sun. **Map** p333 X2.
Whatever your fantasy (or gender), Bare Essentials will do you right. The camp-as-cowboys owners are correct in their claim that they make women feel at ease, but there are also men's essentials, costumes and 'accessories'.

Love Jones

Hard Rock *4455 Paradise Road, at Harmon Avenue, East of Strip (693 5007, www.love*

jones.com). Bus 108. **Open** 10am-11pm Mon-Thur, Sun; 10am-1am Fri, Sat. **Map** p336 C7.

Fur-lined handcuffs, paddles, silk stockings, garter belts and lingerie from the likes of Honey Dew and Christie's make this a mentionable unmentionables boutique. It also sells a few flavoured lotions, potions and toys (but nothing electric). Hotel guests have access to 24-hour room service.

Luggage

Bloomingdale's Home (*see p212*) and **Macy's** (*see p192*) also stock a variety of travel bags and luggage in the lower price ranges.

Bags, Belts & Baubles

Wynn Esplanade *3131 Las Vegas Boulevard South, between E Desert Inn Road & Sands Avenue (770 3555, www.wynnlasvegas.com). Bus Deuce, 203.* **Open** 9am-11pm Mon-Thur; 9am-midnight Fri, Sat. **Map** p335, p336 B6.

Leather goods, handbags, jewellery, sunglasses and other accessories by the likes of Bottega Veneta, Nancy Gonzalez and Adrienne Landau are displayed like miniature works of art in this well-designed shop. It's the perfect accompaniment to Outfit, the chic women's clothing store at Wynn.

Corsa Collections

Caesars Palace (Forum Shops) *3500 Las Vegas Boulevard South, at W Flamingo Road (733 9442). Bus Deuce, 202.* **Open** 10am-11pm Mon-Thur, Sun; 10am-midnight Fri, Sat. **Map** p336 A7.

Handbags are this store's speciality. The designer collection includes bags by Marc Jacobs, Michael Kors, Longchamp, Furla, as well as luggage from Tumi, Kipling and Swiss Army.

Shoes

There are plenty of brand-name shoe stores scattered around the Strip, whether your taste is for slingbacks or sneakers. The selection at the **Grand Canal Shoppes** (*see p195*) is led by super-chic **Jimmy Choo** (733 1802) and the more casual **Rockport** (735 5082), while the **Fashion Show Mall** (*see p197*) has smart-casual Brit-import **Clarks** (732 1801), sports label **Puma** (892 9988) and the all-conquering **Skechers** (969 9905). Over at the **Forum Shops** (*see p194*), you'll find Italian designer **Salvatore Ferragamo** (933 9333), the very Californian footwear of **Donald J Pliner** (796 0900) and **Niketown** (650 8888).

Designer Shoe Warehouse

2100 N Rainbow Boulevard, at W Lake Mead Boulevard, West Las Vegas (636 2060, www.dsw shoe.com). Bus 101, 210. **Open** 9am-9pm Mon-Sat; 10am-7pm Sun.

The finest selection of discounted designer cobbling in town, with footwear stacked from floor to ceiling. While the shoes may be not be this season's latest design, they're still fabulous. Accessories are available in the form of handbags and scarves.

Other locations Sun Mark Plaza, 671 Marks Street, at W Sunset Road, Henderson (547 0620).

New Rock Boots

804 Las Vegas Boulevard South, at E Gass Avenue, Downtown (614 9464). Bus Deuce. **Open** 11am-8pm Mon-Sat. **Map** p334 C3.

Cross John Fluevog's edgy style with the Doc Martens aesthetic, stir in the 1970s rock 'n' roll style of Kiss, and lo: New Rock Boots. Decorative touches such as buckles, straps, flames and skulls make the boots popular with punks, goths and bikers, but there's also a wide selection of stilettos.

★ Shoe In

Wynn Las Vegas *3131 Las Vegas Boulevard South, between E Desert Inn Road & Sands Avenue (770 3460, www.wynnlasvegas.com). Bus Deuce, 203, 213.* **Open** 10am-11pm Mon-Thur, Sun; 10am-midnight Fri, Sat. **Map** p335, p336 B6.

Shoe In specialises in fine footwear (boots, stilettos, Mary Janes, flip-flops) by well-know designers such as Christian Louboutin, Emma Hope and Stuart Weitzman. It's the best selection of unique shoes outside a department store in the city.

FOOD & DRINK

Bakeries

Cupcakery

9680 S Eastern Avenue, at E Silverado Ranch Boulevard, Henderson (207 2253, www.the cupcakery.com). Bus 110. **Open** 8am-6pm Mon-Fri; 10am-6pm Sat; noon-6pm Sun.

Tickle Me Pink, Boston Dream, Kir Royale... the fanciful little cakes taste as good as they sound, and with their specially designed sugar crystals, they sparkle as much as the city. Staff can even print a digital photo on the top, and they take custom orders – see if you can coax one of the salespeople into spilling the sweet-tooth secrets of the Cupcakery's celebrity clientele.

Nothing Bundt Cake

9711 S Eastern Avenue, at E Silverado Ranch Boulevard, Henderson (314 0520, www.nothing bundtcakes.com). Bus 110. **Open** 9am-6pm Mon-Fri; 9am-4pm Sat.

The chocolate-chocolate-chip is a crowd-pleaser, but the carrot Bundt cake (it's a corruption of German Bund cake) is the real show-stopper. Other flavours include lemon, pineapple-upside-down, spice and plain chocolate.

Other locations 8512 W Sahara Avenue, at S Durango Drive, West Las Vegas (871 6301).

CONSUME

CONSUME

Candy & sweets

Las Vegas has lots of secrets, but this one hides in plain site – the 'grownups' playground' has a seriously sweet tooth. Candy emporia have popped up in nearly every casino in town, and it's not unusual to see high-rollers, showgirls and clubgoers licking a lolly.

Lick

Mandalay Bay *3930 Las Vegas Boulevard South, between W Russell Road & W Tropicana Avenue, (207 4881, www.marshallretailgroup.com). Bus Deuce, 202.* **Open** 9am-11pm Mon-Thur; 9am-midnight Fri, Sat. **Map** p333 X4.
Lick's tagline is 'what colour is your tongue' – visitors can sample the treats and then step into a photobooth for a snapshot of their own, now brightly hued licker. Setting it apart from the candy pack: an 'adult' candy section at the back of the store.

M&Ms World

3785 Las Vegas Boulevard South, at E Tropicana Avenue (736 7611). Bus Deuce, 202. **Open** 6am-midnight daily. **Map** p336 A7.
Walking in to M&M's World reminds you immediately of Willy Wonka. And then it makes you wonder why no one has built a Willy Wonka World on Las Vegas's Strip. It's a world of pure M&Mmmmmmmagination, where you can buy not only the sweet stuff – and design your own colour combos – but also logo-branded wearables, toys and, yes, home decor.

Rocket Fizz

5130 Fort Apache Road S, between W Tropicana Avenue & W Hacienda Avenue 889 4292, www.rocketfizz.com). Bus Deuce, 202. **Open** 10am-9pm. **Map** p336 B9.
This suite of sweets offers 'the world's biggest selection of bottled soda pops', plus nostalgia-inducing vintage candy from the '50s to the '90s.

Sugar Factory

Paris Las Vegas *3655 Las Vegas Boulevard South between E Harmon Avenue & E Flamingo Road, (866 0777, www.sugarfactory.com). Bus Deuce, 202.* **Open** 8am-1am Mon-Thur; 7am-2am Fri- Sun. **Map** p336 A7.
The sugar-shock shack of choice for candy-coloured celebrities such as the Kardashians, Britney Spears, Lindsay Lohan and the *Jersey Shore* gang, the Sugar Factory has every kind of sweet thing in stock. But its signature item is a 'couture' lollypop with a dazzling holder, in flavours like champagne, of course. They retail for upward of $25. Which is the genius and evil of Las Vegas – on a stick.
Other locations: Mirage (*see p110*); Planet Hollywood (*see p123*); Bally's (*see p115*).

Drinks

Las Vegas has the usual liquor stores, plus several options for wine buffs. **Bleu Gourmet** (*see p174*) also has a superb selection of wines.

Lee's Discount Liquor

3480 E Flamingo Road, at S Pecos Road, East Las Vegas (458 5700). Bus 111, 202. **Open** 9am-10pm Mon-Thur; 9am-11pm Fri, Sat; 9am-9pm Sun. **Map** p333 Z3.
The enormous 'wall of vodka' is a sight worth a pilgrimage; old favourites, hard-to-find European wines and dirt-cheap prices make Lee's the best liquor store in town. There's a surprisingly good range of beers from around the planet, and a few ciders as well. **Other locations** throughout the city.

Marché Bacchus

2620 Regatta Drive, at Mariner Way, West Las Vegas (804 8008, www.marchebacchus.com). Bus 210. **Open** 10am-10pm Mon-Sat; 10am-3pm Sun.
This fabulous little French store sells fine wines, champagnes, pâtés, cheeses, some sandwiches and salads, and tasting kits. There are also monthly wine-tasting sessions, and outdoor seating on a terrace by the lake where you can enjoy an à la carte Sunday brunch (10am-4pm).

Valley Cheese & Wine

1770 W Horizon Ridge Parkway, at Arroyo Grande, Henderson (341 8191, www.valleycheese andwine.com). Bus 114. **Open** 10am-8pm Mon-Sat; 11am-5pm Sun.
This gourmet wine and cheese shop supplies Las Vegas with artisanal and handcrafted wine, beer, speciality food and cheeses. Owner Bob Howald will be happy to help select wines to match your food.

General

There isn't a major supermarket on the Strip, but all the main chains have branches within easy reach. Just east of the Strip, the branches of Safeway-owned **Vons** (1131 E Tropicana Avenue, at S Maryland Parkway, 798 8697, www.vons.com) and **Smith's** (2540 S Maryland Parkway, at E Sahara Avenue, 735 8928, www. smithsfoodanddrug.com) are both open 24 hours daily. In Downtown, try **Albertsons** (1760 E Charleston Boulevard, at S Bruce Street, 366 1550, www.albertsons.com), open 6am to midnight daily.

British Foods

3375 S Decatur Boulevard, at W Desert Inn Road, South-west Las Vegas (579 7777, www.british grocers.com). Bus 103, 213. **Open** 10am-6pm daily.
British Food offers Las Vegas's 40,000 resident expats a taste of home: HP sauce, Heinz baked beans, proper marmalade, teas and so on.

Vosges Haut-Chocolat.

Trader Joe's
2101 S Decatur Boulevard, at W Sahara Avenue,
West Las Vegas (367 0227, www.traderjoes.com).
Bus 103, 204. **Open** 9am-9pm daily.
A hip, eco- and health-conscious twist on the old-style grocery store: all products in the chain's constantly changing stock are tested to ensure that they are 'the best' (it claims). You can find gluten-, sodium- and GM-free produce as well as chocolate cookies and party foods. Other locations throughout the city.

Whole Foods
6605 Las Vegas Boulevard South, at intersection
of I-15 & I-215 (254 8655, www.wholefoods
market.com). Bus 206. **Open** 7am-10pm daily.
The produce and meat sections at this leading natural and organic grocer are great, but don't miss the seafood case, the deli (for wonderful cheeses and breads) and the impressive prepared foods.
Other locations 100 S Green Valley Parkway, at Paseo Verde Parkway, Henderson (361 8183), 8855 W Charleston Boulevard, at S Fort Apache Road, Summerlin.

Specialist

Chocaholics in Vegas shouldn't miss the **Ethel M Chocolates** factory in Henderson (*see p96*), but in central Vegas there are only really three options. The most distinctive is Chicago-based chocolatier **Vosges Haut-Chocolat** (at the Forum Shops; 836 9866), which offers some glorious truffle concoctions. Otherwise, Belgian confectioner **Godiva** is at the Forum Shops, Miracle Mile, the Grand Canal Shoppes and the Fashion Show Mall, while Swiss chocolatier **Teuscher** is at Miracle Mile (866 6624).

Gee's Oriental Market
4109 W Sahara Avenue, at S Arville Street,
West Las Vegas (362 5287). Bus 104, 204.
Open 8am-8pm Mon-Sat; 9am-5pm Sun.
The best place for Chinese, Thai, Vietnamese and Filipino groceries, with first-rate fresh produce and seafood. Should you have developed a craving, this is the only place in Las Vegas that sells the delicacy *meang da na* (a cockroach-like insect).

International Marketplace
5000 S Decatur Boulevard, at W Tropicana
Avenue, West Las Vegas (889 2888). Bus 103,
201. **Open** 9am-6pm Mon-Sat.
This huge building is basically a warehouse containing every kind of imported edible goodie and gadget, with prices on the better side of cheap.

Rainbow's End Natural Foods
1100 E Sahara Avenue, at S Maryland Parkway,
East Las Vegas (737 1338, www.rainbowsend

CONSUME

lv.info). Bus 109, 204. **Open** 9am-8pm Mon-Fri; 10am-8pm Sat; 11am-5pm Sun. **Map** p333 Y2.
The closest place to the Strip to buy good quality fresh fruit also offers a broad range of herbs, vitamins and bodycare items.

Siena Deli
2250 E Tropicana Avenue, at S Eastern Avenue, East Las Vegas (736 8424, sienadeli.com). Bus 110, 201. **Open** 8am-6pm Mon-Sat. **Map** p333 Z3.
Siena's Italian owner continues to bring the best of Italian cuisine to Vegas. Prices can be quite steep (119-year-old balsamic vinegar at $149.95!) but the high quality is beyond doubt. Siena also stocks Italian cookware.

GIFTS & SOUVENIRS
Las Vegas souvenirs

As the cash-spending hordes schlep through the malls buying stuff you can pick up in any US city, savvy shoppers go off the beaten track for local souvenirs with more charisma. If you're after something specific to Las Vegas, the Strip is dotted with tatty shops selling everything from snow domes (it's the desert, folks!) to dice clocks, and more gambling mementos than you could shake a croupier's rake at. For unique works of art, try Dale Chihuly's gallery at Via Bellagio.

Bonanza Gifts
2460 Las Vegas Boulevard South, at W Sahara Avenue (385 7359, www.worldslargestgift shop.com). Bus Deuce, 204. **Open** 8am-midnight daily. **Map** p335 C4.
Bonanza's huge sign declares it to be the 'world's largest gift store'; certainly, it's hard to imagine one much bigger. The store sells everything from postcards to place mats, Elvis shot glasses to dice clocks, playing cards to earrings. Harkening back to the days of Route 66 gift shops, there's also plenty of American Indian turquoise and silver jewellery.

Chihuly Store
Bellagio (Via Bellagio) *3600 Las Vegas Boulevard South, at W Flamingo Road (693 7995, www.portlandpress). Bus Deuce, 202.* **Open** 10am-midnight daily. **Map** p336 A7.
It's fitting that glass sculptor Dale Chihuly should open his first signature gallery inside the Bellagio: his largest sculpture, with more than 2,000 pieces of glass, hangs from the ceiling of the hotel lobby. While mainly focusing on affordable Chihuly glass editions, which sell like hot cakes, the store also has some more elaborate (and expensive) pieces.

Gamblers General Store
800 S Main Street, at E Gass Avenue, Downtown (382 9903, www.gamblersgeneralstore.com). Bus

Deuce, 105, 106, 108. **Open** 9am-6pm daily. **Map** p334 C2.
This well-stocked shop is packed with gift ideas for that special gambler in your life. There's something to suit all budgets, from a single casino chip costing a couple of coins to vintage video poker machines. Along with the collectibles are pretty much everything you need to play any of the casino games, including a library of 'how to' gaming books.

Jack Gallery
Venetian (Grand Canal Shoppes) *3355 Las Vegas Boulevard South, at Sands Avenue (866 6813, www.s2art.com). Bus Deuce, 105, 203, 213.* **Open** 10am-11pm Mon-Thur, Sun; 10am-midnight Fri, Sat. **Map** p336 A6.
This amazing lithograph shop specialises in limited editions of Hollywood movie posters and classic French posters, which it produces on 130-year-old printing presses in the Downtown Arts District (at the S^2 Art Group Atelier).
Other locations Mandalay Place (*see p195*; 632 4770); Fashion Show Mall (*see p197*; 731 0074).

Rainbow Feather Dyeing Company
1036 S Main Street, at E Charleston Boulevard, Downtown (598 0988, www.rainbowfeatherco.com). Bus Deuce, 105, 106, 108. **Open** 9am-4pm Mon-Fri; 9am-1pm Sat. **Map** p335 C2.
Master feather-crafter Bill Girard sells big, beautiful, colourful and handmade boas to everyone from showgirls to Cirque du Soleil at his unassuming store in the emerging Arts District.

Sex & erotica

The best of the adult bookstores, the **Rancho Adult Entertainment Center** (4820 N Rancho Drive, at W Lone Mountain Drive, North-west Las Vegas, 645 6104), is open 24-7. Its staff are friendly and they welcome female shoppers.

Adult Superstore
3850 W Tropicana Avenue, at S Valley View Boulevard, West of Strip (798 0144). Bus 104, 201. **Open** 24hrs daily. **Map** p333 X3.
There are four branches of this locals' favourite, but this is the biggest of them. The magazine and video sections are devoted to every fetish and fantasy that's legal in Nevada, and there's an unequalled selection of toys, fetish gear and sexy food items.
Other locations throughout the city.

Love Boutique
3275 Industrial Road, at Spring Mountain Road, West of Strip (731 5655, www.dejavu.com). Bus 105, 203. **Open** 10am-4am daily. **Map** p336 A6.
Located next to the Déjà Vu (*see p225*), Love sells an extensive collection of lingerie and novelty gift items. Kick off a bachelor/bachelorette party here.
Other locations throughout the city.

Paradise Electro Stimulations
1509 W Oakey Boulevard, at S Western Avenue (474 2991, www.peselectro.com). Bus Deuce, 105, 108. **Open** 10am-6pm Mon-Thur; 10am-7pm Fri; noon-6pm Sat. **Map** p335 B3.

'The Studio' is known for its electric muscle stimulation devices: dildos, plugs and sheaths, all composed of clear plastic and attachable to an electrical impulse control unit that stimulates the user from the inside out, 'harmonising with the body's own electrical impulses'. If you say so.

Tobacconists

Casa Fuente
Caesars Palace (Forum Shops) *3500 Las Vegas Boulevard South, at W Flamingo Road (731 5051). Bus Deuce, 202.* **Open** 10am-11pm Mon-Thur, Sun; 10am-midnight Fri, Sat. **Map** p336 A7.

The first store from the Arturo Fuente brand is halfway between a shop and a cigar bar. The enormous walk-in humidor holds cigars from around the world. They also stock a huge array of cigar-smoking accessories.

Havana Cigar Bar
3900 Paradise Road, between E Flamingo Road & Sands Avenue, East of Strip (892 9555, www. havanasmoke.com). Bus 108. **Open** 9am-2am Mon-Thur; 9am-1am Fri; 2pm-1am Sat; 2-10pm Sun. **Map** p336 C7.

Aficionados swear this cigar and wine bar is the best place in town to some take time out, sit down and enjoy the pleasure of a fine cigar and a good glass of wine. Its range of accessories is as strong as that of its cigars.

Las Vegas Cigar Co
2510 E Sunset Road, at S Eastern Avenue (262 6100, www.lvcigar.com). Bus 110. **Open** 8am-10pm daily. **Map** p336 A8.

The Las Vegas Cigar Co's 12 established varieties of cigar are hand-rolled daily, in-house, using Cuban-seed tobacco imported from Ecuador and the Dominican Republic.

HEALTH & BEAUTY
Complementary medicine

Body Works Massage Therapy
5025 S Eastern Avenue, between E Tropicana & E Hacienda Avenues, East Las Vegas (736 8887). Bus 110, 201. **Open** by appt. **Map** p333 Z4.

For more than ten years, Body Works' masseurs and masseuses have been kneading, prodding and pounding, with treatments including Swedish deep tissue and Chinese mix, as well as hot-stone therapies, muds and salts.

T&T Ginseng
Chinatown Mall, 4115 Spring Mountain Road, between S Arville Street & Wynn Road, West Las Vegas (368 3898). Bus 104, 203, 213. **Open** 10am-8.30pm daily.

At this fascinating store and Chinese herbal pharmacy in Las Vegas's Chinatown, diagnosis and treatment are handled with ancient wisdom and extreme care. An oriental medical doctor and herbalist are on duty every day.

Worton's Palmistry Studios
4644 W Charleston Boulevard, at S Decatur Boulevard, West Las Vegas (386 0121). Bus 206. **Open** by appointment. **No credit cards.**

The first licensed psychic in Las Vegas, Worton's has been offering professional palmistry and astrology readings since 1958.

Hairdressers & barbers

ARCS: A Robert Cromeans Salon
Mandalay Bay (Mandalay Place) *3950 Las Vegas Boulevard South, at W Hacienda Avenue (632 6130, www.robertcromeans.com). Bus Deuce, 104, 105.* **Open** 9am-7pm Mon-Fri; 8am-8pm Sat; 10am-6pm Sun. **Map** p336 A9.

The prices at crazy coiffeur Cromean's trendy Paul Mitchell salon are about the same as his California salons: in other words, eye-watering.

Globe Salon
900 Las Vegas Boulevard South, between W Charleston Boulevard and E Bonneville Ave, Downtown (938 4247, www.globesalon.com). Bus 103, 206. **Open** 11am-4pm Tue; 11am-7pm Wed, Thur; 9am-4pm Fri; 9am-5pm Sat.

This award-winning Bumble+Bumble network hair and skin care salon is run by Vegas native and 'hairstylist to the hip' Staci Linklater, who oversees a team of professionals in a mod-style Downtown space.

Opticians

Frame Fixer (3961 W Charleston Boulevard, at S Valley View Boulevard, West Las Vegas, 735 7879) does fast, friendly and gentle repairs.

Lunettes
Fashion Show Mall, 3200 Las Vegas Boulevard South, at Spring Mountain Road (733 7624). Bus Deuce, 105, 203. **Open** 10am-9pm Mon-Sat; 11am-7pm Sun. **Map** p335, p336 B6.

Shades are a must in a city that sees an average of 320 days of sun per year. Lunettes sells products by designers including Gucci, Oliver Peoples, Cartier and Kia Yomoto.
► *Also in the Fashion Show Mall, Sunshades (731 3598) has a similarly strong selection, including sportier shades from Oakley and fancier specs from Kate Spade.*

CONSUME

Nu Vision Cyclery/Sport Optics

8447 W Lake Mead Boulevard, at N Rampart Boulevard, Summerlin (228 1333, www.nuvision cyclery.com). Bus 210. **Open** 10am-6pm Mon-Fri.
Mike Hileman, a licensed optician and avid cyclist, runs this one-stop shop where sportspeople can find cool prescription eyewear that stays on the head, no matter how rough the play. Hileman sells and services Oakley Rx, Adidas, Rudy Project and Dragon Optical, and also stocks sports goggles for swimming and skiing.

Oculus

Caesars Palace (Appian Way Shops) *3570 Las Vegas Boulevard South, at W Flamingo Road (731 4850/www.oculusltd.com). Bus Deuce, 202.* **Open** 10am-8pm Mon-Thur, Sun; 10am-9pm Fri, Sat.* **Map** p336 A7.
This outpost of Dr Ed Malik's stylish Eyes & Optics boutique offers an excellent selection of frames from designers such as Oliver Peoples and Alain Mikli, plus eye examinations, spectacle repairs and sunglasses. The optician is also available for prescription emergencies.

Pharmacies

You'll find drugstores all over the city. There's a 24-hour branch of **Walgreens** (www.walgreens.com) near the MGM Grand on the Strip (3765 Las Vegas Boulevard South, 739 9645). There's another 24-7 branch Downtown (495 E Fremont Street, at S 5th Street, 385 1284), though the pharmacy is open limited hours (9am-7pm Mon-Fri; 9am-6pm Sat; 10am-6pm Sun).

Shops

The major department stores (*see p192-193*) stock all the big-name brands. Canadian giant **MAC** has a store (369 8770) in the Forum Shops.

Aveda

Planet Hollywood (Miracle Mile Shops) *3667 Las Vegas Boulevard South, between E Harmon Avenue & E Flamingo Road (732 3290, www.aveda.com). Bus Deuce.* **Open** 10am-11pm Mon-Thur, Sun; 10am-midnight Fri, Sat.
Divine-smelling, all-natural hair care, skin care and beauty products. The signature lip balm is a must. **Other locations** Fashion Show Mall (*see p197*; 733 6660); Aveda Institute, 4856 S Eastern Avenue, at E Tropicana Avenue, East Las Vegas (459 2900).

Fresh

Caesars Palace (Forum Shops) *3500 Las Vegas Boulevard South, at W Flamingo Road (631 5000, www.fresh.com). Bus Deuce, 202.*

Open 10am-11pm Mon-Thur, Sun; 10am-midnight Fri, Sat. **Map** p336 A7.
Clean gets tasty with Fresh bath products, made with sugar, milk, soya and even saké. The line also includes some great perfumes and basic cosmetics in natural-looking hues for all skin tones.

Kiehl's

Caesars Palace (Forum Shops) *3500 Las Vegas Boulevard South, at W Flamingo Road (784 0025, www.kiehls.com). Bus Deuce, 202.*
Open 10am-11pm Mon-Thur, Sun; 10am-midnight Fri, Sat. **Map** p336 A7.
The simplicity of the skin- and hair-care products sold at Kiehl's is part of their appeal, as is its commitment never to test on animals. It sells lotions

Tattoo You

Ink is in in Sin City.

One way or another, Las Vegas is going to leave its mark on you. Whether it's the sudden absence of heft in your wallet or your savings account, or the extra 10lbs you carry after eating at buffets and sipping suds at casinos, Vegas is known for leaving a lasting impression.

Within the past decade, Sin City has opted to make it easy for visitors to leave with souvenirs that last a lifetime – just about every casino and shopping plaza has its own tattoo parlour. There are more than 50 listed in Las Vegas, most of them open from around noon until 4am. (Getting tattooed is a famously impulsive life decision, and there's not much of a demand at breakfast time).

And several of them boast celebrity affiliations – albeit skuzzy celebrities – Vince Neil of Motley opened **Vince Neil Ink** at O'Shea's Casino (3555 Las Vegas Bvd, www.vinceneilink.com), a fratty place specialising in beer pong and dwarf-tossing. Motocross star Corey Hart is behind **Hart & Huntington Tattoo Co** at the Hard Rock (*see p132*), which features resident tattooists and visiting guest artists. Tattoo star (there is such a thing) Mario Barth reigns at King Ink at the **Mirage** (*see p110*), and Linkin Park's Chester Bennington is a partner in Club Tattoo at **Planet Hollywood** (*see p123*).

After catching *The Lion King* at Mandalay Bay (*see p109*), why not pop in to **Barth's Starlight Tattoo** and get 'Hakuna Matata' emblazoned on your … whatever? You won't remember where you got this idea from, anyway.

rizona transplant, now comfortably the best store in town, buys and sells music and s, trading with recording companies as well man off the street. It even deals in vinyl.

RT & FITNESS

wo best general sports stores are s. Both **Big 5** (2797 S Maryland /ay, at E Sahara Avenue, 734 6664, big5sportinggoods.com) and **Sports ority** (2620 S Decatur Boulevard, at ara Avenue, 368 3335, www.sports ity.com) sell a wide range of clothing quipment from multiple locations d the city. Fashion sportswear is ell represented: the Forum Shops ne to a **Niketown** (650 8888), while owcase Mall has America's first as Sports Performance Store 373).

Pro Shops Outdoor World S Industrial Road, at Blue Diamond Silverton (730 5200, www.basspro.com). 17. **Open** 9am-10pm Mon-Sat; pm Sun. firing range, a gunsmith, an archery range custom tie shop (for anglers), this massive s a lesson in retail as entertainment. The dis-include a host of animal trophies from around rld: a stuffed giraffe, a pride of lions and a's own state animal, the bighorn sheep.

rt Rock Sports W Charleston Boulevard, between S Buffalo urango drives, West Las Vegas (254 1143, lesertrocksportslv.com). Bus 206. **Open** pm daily. t Rock carries super-cool climbing, hiking, ng and backpacking gear for the outdoor iast, as well as stuff for children and dogs. n rent equipment at next door's Powerhouse Climbing Center (254 5604).

hie's S Fort Apache Road, at W Flamingo South-west Las Vegas (252 8077, cghies.com). Bus 204. **Open** 10am-7pm ri; 10am-6pm Sat; 10am-5pm Sun. siness for 40 years, McGhie's embraced the oarding craze in the early 1990s, and later mountain biking to its ski (both water and goods. Rentals, plus advice on the area's better tion areas, are also available.

Cyclery W Charleston Boulevard, at Antelope West Las Vegas (228 9460, www.pro .com). Bus 206. **Open** 10am-7pm ri; 10am-5pm Sat.

This long-term fixture on the Vegas cycling scene is a great source of gear for both hire and purchase. Experienced cyclists and novices are all made to feel welcome.

REI

Green Valley Ranch (District) 2220 Village Walk Drive, at S Green Valley Parkway, Henderson (896 7111, www.rei.com). Bus 111. **Open** 10am-9pm Mon-Sat; 11am-6pm Sun. In 1938, 20 mountain climbing enthusiasts formed a co-operative so they could purchase some of the better gear available in Europe. Recreation Equipment Inc now has over two million members worldwide, and 70 store locations. This shop is great for backpacking, biking, mountain-climbing and kayaking gear.

Subskates

9151 W Sahara Avenue, at Fort Apache Road, Summerlin (258 3635). Bus 101, 208. **Open** 11am-6.30pm Mon-Sat; noon-5pm Sun. Anyone in Las Vegas with a fondness for balancing on a board heads here to buy their gear. The stock includes everything from boards to bearings, plus all the accessories you're likely to need. Other essen-tial gear includes clothes and shoes from the likes of Fallen and Etnies. **Other locations** 9151 W Sahara Avenue, at S Fort Apache Road, Summerlin (233 3842).

TICKETS

Ticketmaster (474 4000, www.ticketmaster. com) sells tickets for many events, although the booking fees can be high. They may be slightly lower at Ticketmaster desks in **Macy's** (see p192) and branches of **Smith's** (see p206).

TRAVELLERS' NEEDS

For **airlines**, see p308; for **car hire firms**, see p310. If you're in need of extra suitcases to hold all that excess shopping, your best bets on the Strip are **Bloomingdale's Home** (see p212) and **Macy's** (see p192), though prices are more reasonable at **Target** (see p192).

You can rent mobile phones on a weekly or daily basis from **Roberts Rent-a-Phone** (1-800 964 2468, www.roberts-rent-a-phone. com), which delivers to any US address within 24 hours. However, it may be cheaper simply to buy a phone from a store such as **Best Buy** (see p200). For more on phones, see p315.

If your laptop fails, try the Best Buy Geek Squad (see p200), available 24 hours a day. Mac users should try the **Apple Store** (see p201).

and potions for all skin and hair types, created with the entire family in mind.

Sephora

Venetian (Grand Canal Shoppes) 3377 Las Vegas Boulevard South, between Sands Avenue & E Flamingo Road (735 3896, www.sephora. com). Bus Deuce, 105, 203. **Open** 10am-11pm Mon-Thur, Sun; 10am-midnight Fri, Sat. **Map** p335 & p336 B6. The most comprehensive cosmetics emporium in town contains stock from Dior and Yves Saint Laurent, hip offerings from Smashbox, Nars, Paul & Joe, and an impressive and good-value own-brand range. Test out the goods in the application areas or let a pro get to work on you. **Other locations** Miracle Mile (see p196; 737 0550).

Spas & salons

The odds are that you didn't travel to Las Vegas to consult a nutritionist, improve your sleeping habits or (shudder) detox. There's only one thing that most visitors want from a spa in Sin City: pleasure. Many casinos have spas these days, those listed below are among the best in the city.

Bathhouse

Thehotel at Mandalay Bay 3950 Las Vegas Boulevard South, at W Hacienda Avenue (1-877 632 9636, 632 9636, www.mandalaybay.com). Bus Deuce, 104, 105. **Open** 6am-8.30pm daily. **Daily pass** Hotel guests $30. Visitors $35. All free with spa services over $50. **Map** p336 A9. The first clue that the Bathhouse differs from other Vegas spas is revealed the moment you step into the long, suede-lined hallway and are greeted gra-ciously by staff clad in slick, space-age uniforms before a backdrop of textured slate, frosted glass, cool running water and hints of shocking char-treuse. Indulge in an Asian tea bath (chai or green) capped off by the bamboo sugar scrub. Not a rub-ber ducky in sight.

Planet Hollywood Spa by Mandara

Planet Hollywood 3667 Las Vegas Boulevard South, between E Harmon & E Flamingo Roads (785 5772, www.mandaraspa.com). Bus Deuce, 202. **Open** 6am-7pm daily. **Daily pass** $25. **Map** p336 A7. With its variety of resurfacing facials, miracle lip and eye therapies and scalp massages, the Planet Hollywood spa will have you ready for your 15 minutes of fame. If you really want to be pampered like an A-lister, book the signature Mandara mas-sage, a blend of Japanese shiatsu, Hawaiian lomi lomi, and Swedish and Balinese massage tech-niques, performed by two experienced therapists. Lights, camera, relax.

Qua Baths & Spa

Caesars Palace 3570 Las Vegas Boulevard South, at W Flamingo Road (731 7776, www.quabathsandspa.com). Bus Deuce, 202. **Open** 6am-8pm daily. **Daily pass** $35; free with spa services over $75. **Map** p336 A7. Housed in the Augustus Tower, Caesars' luxurious spa is themed after Roman baths. Within tubs of mineral-rich waters, a Laconium sauna (inspired by ancient Roman steam baths) and an arctic ice room (heated floors and benches under falling snow), therapists practise ritualistic therapies. Take Qua's Mystic Journey and enjoy a bamboo body exfoliation, a lotus-flower and water-lily wrap, and an essential-oil facial and scalp massage. When in Rome…

Red Rock Spa

Red Rock 221 N Rampart Boulevard, at Summerlin Parkway, West Las Vegas (798 7878, www.redrocklasvegas.com). Bus 206. **Open** 6am-8pm daily. **Daily pass** Hotel guests free. Visitors $35; free with spa services. This modern retreat is frequented by local socialites as much for its proximity to their homes as for its sleek aesthetic. Situated next to the lush pool, the treatment suites appear to float on water. After a hike, order a Champagne Pedicure and Caviar Creams: this champagne cocktail for you and your feet includes 80 minutes of deep exfoliation, soothing masques, moisturising caviar lotion and menthol foot balm massage, plus, of course, a glass of cham-pagne. Cheers!

Spa at Wynn

Wynn Las Vegas 3131 Las Vegas Boulevard South, between E Desert Inn Road & Sands Avenue (770 3900, www.wynnlasvegas.com). Bus Deuce, 203, 213. **Open** 9am-7pm daily. **Daily pass** $25; free with salon services over $75. **Map** p335 B6. Reserve one of the 45 treatment rooms inside this Asian-inspired retreat and indulge in a bamboo-lemongrass body scrub, a saké body treatment or a shiatsu massage. The Good Luck Ritual is based on feng shui, with a 50-minute heated Thai herb massage, a moisturising hand and foot massage, and a wild-lime botanical scalp treatment. Hotel guests are able to use the lavish spa facilities with-out booking a salon session; non-guests can only use the spa by booking a salon treatment (Mon-Thur only).

Tattoos & piercings

Hart & Huntington Tattoo Company

Palms 4321 W Flamingo Road, at S Valley View Boulevard, West of Strip (942 7777, www.hartandhuntingtontattoo.com). Bus 201. **Open** 11am-2am Mon-Fri; 10am-2am Sat, Sun. **Map** p333 X3.

CONSUME

Motocross legend Carey Hart and club promoter John Huntington (the man behind the original Pimp 'n' Ho Costume Ball) have set up this hip tattoo parlour inside the Palms, and promptly landed their own TV show, *Inked*. Huntington has since sold the shop to Hart, but the patrons hardly seem to care. Guests can book a slot at the same time as they make their hotel reservations.

Pussykat Tattoo Parlor

4972 S Maryland Parkway, at E Tropicana Avenue, University District (597 1549). Bus 109, 201. **Open** hours vary. **Map** p333 Y3.
Owner/artist Dirk Vermin is a Vegas native and local legend who has dedicated his life to bettering the local subculture. His tattoo work is well known among aficionados; you will need to book ahead to see Vermin himself.

HOUSE & HOME
Antiques

Charleston Antique Mall

307 W Charleston Boulevard, at S Western Avenue, Downtown (228 4783). Bus Deuce, 104, 105, 108, 206. **Open** 10am-6pm Mon-Sat; 11am-5pm Sun. **Map** p335 B3.
Formerly part of the Red Rooster Antique Mall, the old 7-Up bottling company has been restocked and renovated with 35 vendors. If you like the look of that tiki bar, snap it up: the good stuff goes fast.

Funk House

1228 S Casino Center Boulevard, at E Colorado Avenue, Downtown (678 6278, www.thefunkhouse lasvegas.com). Bus Deuce, 104, 105, 108, 206. **Open** 10am-5pm Mon-Sat.
Cindy Funkhouser's ever-growing collection is especially strong in late-1950s and early-'60s pieces, and there's a wide variety of glass, jewellery and toys. One of the best antiques stores in town, the Funk House is also ground zero for First Friday (*see p219*).

Gypsy Caravan Antique Village

1302 S 3rd Street, at W Colorado Avenue, Downtown (868 3302). Bus Deuce, 104, 105, 108, 206. **Open** 10am-5pm Tue-Sat. **Map** p335 C3.
This colourful antiques avenue comprises several historic bungalows. There are particularly strong selections of Victorian light fixtures, furnishings and typewriters. Be sure to investigate the courtyard and its medley of patio furnishings.

Main Street Antiques

500 S Main Street, at Bonneville Avenue, Downtown (382 1882). Bus Deuce, 104, 105, 108. **Open** 9am-6pm daily. **Map** p335 B3.
Two stories of vendors sell vintage merchandise, including unique Vegas-style antiques such as glass-encased showgirl costumes.

Red Rooster Antique Mall

1109 S Western Avenue, at W Charleston Boulevard, Downtown (382 5253). Bus Deuce, 104, 105, 108, 206. **Open** 10am-6pm Mon-Sat; 11am-5pm Sun. **Map** p335 B3.
A labyrinth of cluttered rooms and individually run stalls, with racks of dusty magazines holding shelf space next to $100 antique bottles. There's fabulous casino memorabilia: ashtrays, chips and postcards.

General

Among the best homewares stores in town is **Unicahome** (3901 West Russell Road, www.unicahome.com), which stocks everything from books to flatpack furniture by the likes of Tom Dixon.

Blank Space

Mandalay Bay (Mandalay Place) *3950 Las Vegas Boulevard South, at W Hacienda Avenue (632 9399). Bus Deuce, 104, 105.* **Open** 10am-11pm daily. **Map** p336 A9.
The only modern home-accessories store on the Strip, this well-curated shop stocks furniture and homewares from Vitra Design, Cassina, Kartell, Mooi and Jonathan Adler.

Bloomingdale's Home

Fashion Show Mall, 3200 Las Vegas Boulevard South, at Spring Mountain Road (784 5400, www.bloomingdales.com). Bus Deuce, 105, 203. **Open** 10am-8pm Mon-Wed; 10am-10pm Thur-Sat; 11am-7pm Sun. **Map** p335, p335 B6.
The only Bloomingdale's in Vegas (and the Nation's first Bloomingdale's Home) is a furnishings store carrying bath and bedding (DKNY, Michael Kors, Natori), cookware and bakeware (All-Clad, Cuisinart, Calphalon), home decor (Nambe, Waterford, Kosta Boda) and luggage (Tumi, Victorinox).

Durette Studios

1007 S Main Street, at W Charleston Boulevard, Downtown (368 2601, www.durettecandito design.com). Bus Deuce, 206. **Open** 9am-5pm Mon-Fri; by appt Sat.
Durette Candito's Arts District studio is Nevada's most prestigious supplier of decorative hardware, lighting and home accessories, many of which are exclusive, handcrafted imports from some of the best clans of craftsmen around the world. Candito's architectural and interior-design skills are also superb.

Lik Design

Mandalay Bay (Mandalay Place) *3950 Las Vegas Boulevard South, at W Hacienda Avenue (736 5227). Bus Deuce, 104, 105.* **Open** 10am-11pm daily. **Map** p336 A9.
In addition to his photography gallery, Peter Lik presents Pacific Green furniture by Aussie designer

Bruce Dowse. The one-of-a-kind furniture collection is built of palm wood from unwanted coconut palms, and is therefore eco-friendly.

MUSIC & ENTERTAINMENT

In the age of downloads, **Blockbuster** stores can still be found; to find a branch, use the store locator at www.blockbuster.com. Alternatively,

try the lower-key **Hollywood** hollywoodvideo.com). Some release CDs are sold at mass **Best Buy** (*see p200*).

Zia Record Exchange

4225 S Eastern Avenue, at Fl East of Strip (735 4942, www Bus 110, 202. **Open** 10am-m

---

Go Western!

The National Finals Rodeo is a shopping bonanza.

One unexpected benefit of the ten-day **National Finals Rodeo** (NFR; *see p221*), held in the city each December, is that it gives the city's mainstream retailers a well-deserved cowboy-booted kick in the ass. If you're looking to refurnish your ranch, saddle your horse or outfit your nearest and dearest cowboy or cowgirl, bring your biggest pick-up truck and prepare to fill 'er up at one of three separate fairs, selling everything from homewares to jeans, linens to leather goods. There are even experts on hand who can steam your stetson and bend it to your liking.

The North Hall at the Las Vegas Convention Center (*see p311*) houses the **Original Cowboy Christmas**, the NFR's only officially sanctioned western shopping experience. Fans can find licensed goods from the NFR among the 400 vendors, as well as fashion shows and autograph signings. And in recent

years, a few savvy souls hav gift shows as competition fo Cowboy Christmas: the Sand the **Country Western Gift E** the NFR, while Mandalay Bay **Cowboy Marketplace**.

Good news: the renegade bring more stuff to town. Bac lot of times, it's the same st the booths at each site char shoppers looking for big bra Strauss, Tony Lama, et al) w them at all three sites. Sma meanwhile, tend to shop at wholesale outlets, and so th the same or similar items. H look closely, you'll find a few top-notch antique and vintag as some talented craftsmen hawking their own one-of-a-k

National Finals Rodeo.

Arts & Entertainment

Calendar

Las Vegas is all about celebration.

Las Vegas has a habit of attracting the kind of parties that don't happen anywhere else. As the spiritual home of gambling, it's obvious that the city should host the **World Series of Poker**, while a town that revels in the nickname Sin City is a natural location for the **Fetish & Fantasy Halloween Ball**. Still, that doesn't explain the presence of **Pet-a-Palooza**, several rodeo competitions, and innumerable events dominated by vintage cars, bikes and scooters.

For information on temporary attractions in town, check the free *Las Vegas Weekly*, *Seven* or *CityLife* magazines.

ARTS & ENTERTAINMENT

SPRING

NASCAR Nextel Cup
Las Vegas Motor Speedway *7000 N Las Vegas Boulevard, at Speedway Boulevard, North Las Vegas (644 4444 information, 1-800 644 4444 tickets, www.lvms.com). No bus.* **Tickets** $40-$150. **Date** early Mar.
One of the biggest auto-racing weekends of the year, the Vegas leg of NASCAR's Nextel Cup sees thousands of enthusiasts descend upon the city. Visitors should book accommodation well in advance. For details of other events at the Las Vegas Motor Speedway, *see p262*.

Monster Jam World Finals
Sam Boyd Stadium *7000 E Russell Road, at Boulder Highway, South-east Las Vegas (739 3267, www.monsterjamonline.com). Bus 201A.* **Tickets** $30-$40. **Date** mid Mar.
Bring out your inner 13-year-old with this feast of automotive carnage, featuring an array of giant trucks with enormous wheels; the 2007 champion, Batman the Monster Truck, was basically a hulked-out Batmobile. The pit party is also worth a look.

St Patrick's Day
Around Las Vegas. **Date** 17 Mar.
Vegas more than makes up for its lack of Irish heritage on St Patrick's Day. There's a parade in downtown Henderson and a three-day party at New York New York's Nine Fine Irishmen bar, which sprawls on to the casino's mini-Brooklyn Bridge. Elsewhere, Hennesseys on the Fremont Street Experience celebrates with music, drink and 'Irish nachos'.

Extreme Thing Festival
Desert Breeze Skate Park *8275 W Spring Mountain Road, at S Durango Drive, South-west Las Vegas (474 4000, www.extremething.com). Bus 203.* **Tickets** $17-$20. **Date** late Mar.
Extreme sports, such as skateboarding, BMX and wrestling championships. Extreme body modification, chiefly piercing and tattoos. And extreme music: punk, lots of it. Expect teenage aggression.

Pet-a-Palooza
Location varies (www.mix941.fm). **Date** late Mar.
Rock bands share the stage with animal performers at this pet-friendly festival. The fairgrounds are lined with booths hosted by animal rescue and non-profit organisations, and there are pet-oriented vendors hawking their wares.

Viva Las Vegas
Orleans Hotel & Casino *4500 W Tropicana Avenue (1-562 496 4287, www.vivalasvegas.net).*

THE BEST FESTIVALS

For roaring engines
NASCAR Nextel Cup. *See above.*

For fab fancy dress
Halloween. *See p220.*

For boring drunks
New Year's Eve. *See p221.*

Bus 103, 201. **Tickets** $115-$150.
Date Easter wknd.
In order to dance to old-school rockabilly bands from all over the world, check out the burlesque competition and shop for the perfect '50s cocktail dress at the swap meet, you'll have to buy a pricey ticket. However, the breathtaking hot-rod car show is open to all. Dress in Sailor Jerry tattoos and Brylcreem to blend in.

Mardi Gras Celebration
Fremont Street, at Las Vegas Boulevard South, Downtown (www.vegasexperience.com). Bus Deuce & all BTC-bound buses. **Map** p334 D2.
Date early Apr.
The only reason Mardi Gras is New Orleans' festival is because Las Vegas didn't think of it first. That doesn't stop the Fremont Street Experience from hosting its own version slightly later in the year, with more celebrations at the Rio and Orleans hotels.

UNLVino
Paris Las Vegas *3655 Las Vegas Boulevard South, at E Flamingo Road (946 7000). Bus Deuce, 202.* **Tickets** $75-$100. **Map** p336 A7.
Date early Apr.
More than 100 international wine-growers participate in this fundraiser for UNLV. There are auctions of wine-themed art and vintage crates, but the real treat is chatting with the growers and sampling the wines. Designated drivers are thoughtfully provided.

Clark County Fair & Rodeo
Clark County Fairgrounds, on I-15, Logandale (1-888 876 3247, www.ccfair.com). No bus.

Admission *Fair* $7-$9. *Rodeo* $19-$21.
Season pass $21. Free under-5s.
Date mid Apr.
For a taste of hometown Southwestern life sans glitter, drive a little way north for all kinds of ropin', ridin', country music and carnival fun.

Epicurean Affair
Location varies (878 2313, www.nv restaurants.com). **Tickets** $125-$150.
Date late Apr-late May.
Local restaurants unveil their latest attempts to outdo each other in this industry festival of culinary hedonism. Expect a full-blown onslaught of the senses from exotic food, drink and spectacle.

Cinco de Mayo
Lorenzi Park, 3333 W Washington Avenue, at N Rancho Drive, North-west Las Vegas (229 1087). Bus 106, 208. **Map** p333 X1. **Date** wknd closest to 5 May.
The city's Mexican community comes together in a show of pride with all-day dancing, mariachi bands, fireworks and traditional cuisine. Festivities also take place at the Fremont Street Experience.

Helldorado Days
Various locations (870 1221, www.elkshell dorado.com). **Date** mid May.
Instituted in 1935 to attract tourists to the area after the completion of the Hoover Dam, this revived celebration of Las Vegas's beginnings plays up the city's Western roots while also including golf and poker tournaments, trap-shooting contests, rodeos, art auctions, trail rides and a Downtown parade.

ARTS & ENTERTAINMENT

Monster Jam World Finals.

House of Vegas Heritage

Enjoy a huge collection of all kinds of Vegas artefacts on Nevada Day.

Dr Lonnie **Hammargren's** home is a grand old place, three connected houses that form a 12,500-square-foot (1,150-square-metre) mansion with ten bedrooms and nine bathrooms. However, it's what sits inside and outside the house that's really notable. A retired neurosurgeon, Hammargren was Nevada's lieutenant governor from 1994 to 1998. These days, though, he's best known for his enormous collection of... well, stuff. By accident and design, Hammargren has accumulated a huge, dazzling collection of Nevada-related memorabilia.

Peering into the Hammargren's backyard, you can see everything from a montage of ungulate antlers to the actual railcar in which Howard Hughes came to Las Vegas. Indeed, transportation is a recurring theme in the collection: the yard contains a submarine, an experimental plane, a train engine (straight out of an old mining operation) and an authentic space capsule used for training Apollo astronauts. When the Stratosphere's High Roller 'coaster was removed in 2006, guess where a large portion of it ended up?

Other unusual items include a missile silo, the doors to the first Clark County jail, the hand and torch from a scale model of the Statue of Liberty, and Liberace's last dressing room. The front façade of the buildings is a replica of a Mayan Mexican governor's palace. Hammargren has also haunted all the casinos that have closed in the past 30 years and rounded up signs, bars, decorations and other junk to add to his collection. Also indoors are an observatory and a planetarium, a 19th-century western saloon, a dinosaur from a 1930s movie and miles of train tracks (with working trains).

The collection can be viewed on **Nevada Day** (31 Oct, www.nevadadays.org) when Hammargren and long-suffering wife Sandy hold an open house, which draws crowds of up to 20,000. But if you just want to drive past for a quick peek, they're at 4318 Ridgecrest Drive. Head east on Flamingo Road from the Strip for about four miles, then turn right on South Sandhill Road. The collection in the backyard is visible from Sandhill; go round the front, turn right on Rosecrest Circle, then left on to Ridgecrest.

Hammargren's.

Rockabilly Rod Reunion
Las Vegas Motor Speedway *7000 Las Vegas Boulevard North, at Speedway Boulevard, North Las Vegas (644 4444, www.rockabillyrod reunion.com). No bus.* **Admission** $15-$50; $6 reductions; free under 5s. **Date** Late May.
More than a hot rod car show and automotive swap meet, the Rockabilly Rod Reunion mixes vintage dragsters, rockabilly bands, DJs and burlesque acts. Don't miss the burnout contest from hell.

Vegas Cruise
Fremont Street, at Las Vegas Boulevard South, Downtown (www.lasvegascarshows.com). Bus Deuce & all BTC-bound buses. **Map** p334 D2. **Date** late May/early June.
This three-day classic-car event sees enthusiasts showing off gleaming vintage vehicles on Fremont Street. Onlookers may be blinded by all that shiny chrome.

SUMMER

World Series of Poker
Rio *3700 W Flamingo Road, at S Valley View Boulevard, West of Strip (777 7777, www.wsop. com). Bus 202.* **Date** June-July. **Map** p333 X3.
It's a matter of conjecture whether the popularity of poker fuelled the popularity of this two-week tournament or vice versa. Either way, the WSOP is loved worldwide. In 2010, more than 7,000 competitors took part and $8.9 million was awarded to winner Jonathan Duhamel. *Photo p220.*

Black & White Party
Cosmopolitan *3708 Las Vegas Boulevard South (382 2326, www.afanlv.org). Bus Deuce.* **Tickets** $40. **Map** p333 X3. **Date** late Aug/early Sept.
Affordable but still satisfyingly posh, the city's main AIDS fundraiser brings the community together with black-and-white costumes, food from the best chefs in town, and risqué amusements such as a spanking booth.

Las Vegas Harvest Festival
Cashman Center *850 Las Vegas Boulevard North, at E Washington Avenue, Downtown (1-415 447 3205, www.harvestfestival.com). Bus 113.* **Admission** $9; free under-12s. **Map** p333 Y1. **Date** early Sept.
Hundreds of artisans from across the country bring their hand-blown glass, silver jewellery and jars of chutney to this fair.

Star Trek Las Vegas Convention
Rio *3700 W Flamingo Boulevard (1-818 409 0960, www.creationent.com). Bus 202.* **Tickets** $314. **Map** p333 X3. **Date** mid Aug.
Sci-fi celebrities and obscure memorabilia make it a holy pilgrimage for Trekkies, though non-fans will be unfazed.

AUTUMN

San Gennaro Feast
Location varies (227 0295, www.sangennaro feast.net). **Admission** $7-$8. Additional $25 for carnival ride pass. **Date** Sept.
So popular it is staged three or four times a year, this Italian-American outdoor festival is mostly about the food, but it also includes carnival rides and a traditional procession.

SuperRun
Henderson (643 0000, www.superrun.com). **Date** mid/late Sept.
The area's largest classic-car show takes over downtown Henderson for three days with hundreds of classic vehicles, from fully-built custom hot rods to a well-preserved hearse used when the Mob ran Vegas.

Greek Food Festival
St John the Baptist Greek Orthodox Church *5300 S El Camino Road, at E Hacienda Road, South-west Las Vegas (221 8245, www.lasvegas greekfestival.com). No bus.* **Admission** $6. **Date** late Sept.
One of Las Vegas's few true ethnic festivals. Enjoy four days of folk dancing, retsina and *souvlaki* with a boisterous crowd.

Las Vegas BikeFest
Cashman Center *850 Las Vegas Boulevard North, at E Washington Avenue, Downtown (1-866 245 3378, 450 7662, www.lasvegas bikefest.com). Bus 113.* **Tickets** $25-$40. **Map** p334 D2. **Date** late Sept/early Oct.
Even non-bikers can enjoy the classic Harleys, demo rides and 'Artistry in Iron' master-builder championships at this get-together for the black-leather set.

Pure Aloha Festival
Silverton Casino Lodge *3333 Blue Diamond Road (604 9438, www.vizzun.com). Bus 115.* **Admission** $5; $2 reductions. **Date** early Oct.
Immerse yourself in two days of Polynesian food, music, art and dance. The city's community of

---

INSIDE TRACK FIRST FRIDAY

One of the city's most popular festivals is its most regular. Held from 6pm to midnight on the first Friday of every month in the Downtown Arts District and Fremont East, First Friday (www.firstfriday-lasvegas.org) is essentially a massive block party with an artistic bent. Local galleries and shops stay open late into the night; bands and DJs play on the specially erected stages; and there's tons of great street food and drinks on offer.

World Series of Poker. *See p219.*

transplanted Hawaiians help to make the festival rich in traditional and contemporary interpretations of aloha.

Fright Dome
Adventuredome at Circus Circus *2880 Las Vegas Boulevard (www.frightdome.com). Bus Deuce.* **Tickets** *$34.95-$50.* **Map** p335 B5. **Date** wknds Oct, 7pm-midnight, Fri-Sun.
Colourful lasers, roaming characters, performances and several haunted houses. It's too scary for small kids – only 12-year-olds and older are allowed in.

Age of Chivalry Renaissance Fair
Silver Bowl Park *6800 E Russell Road, Henderson (474 4000 tickets, www.lvrenfair.com).* **Admission** *1 day $10; $5 reductions. 3 days $25; $10 reductions-5s.* **Date** Oct.
Chivalrous battles, costumed maidens and other displays of questionable historical accuracy. We can recommend the roast turkey leg.

Professional Bull Riders Tour
MGM Grand *3799 Las Vegas Bouleard South, at E Tropicana Avenue (1-719 242 2800 information, 474 4000 tickets, www.pbrnow.com). Bus 109, 201.* **Tickets** *$18-$83.* **Map** p336 A8. **Date** Oct.
It isn't as prestigious as the National Finals Rodeo, but this competition provides a more affordable chance to rub shoulders with the world's finest bull riders and their fans and see some of the action up close.

Grand Slam for Children
Wynn *3131 Las Vegas Boulevard South (227 5700 information, www.agassifoundation.org).*

Bus Deuce. **Tickets** *Concert $50-$90.* **Map** p335 B6. **Date** late Oct.
Andre Agassi hosts an exclusive gala auction and dinner to benefit his children's foundation each year, bursting with the country's great and good, who have paid a lot of money to attend. The concert that follows is always given by an A-list performer.

Halloween
Around Las Vegas. **Date** 31 Oct.
Nearly every nightclub and bar hosts a fancy-dress party for Halloween, many overflowing with grownups playing naughty dress-up. The Fetish & Fantasy Ball, held in 2011 at the South Point hotel (*see p149*), reigns supreme for debauchery, dazzling costumes and Vegas-calibre spectacle. For something a bit less risqué, hit the Beaux Arts Ball at Studio 54 (*see p261*): it features some of the best entertainers on the Strip and an over-the-top costume contest, with all proceeds going to AIDS charity Golden Rainbow.

Vegas Valley Book Festival
Various locations (www.vegasvalley bookfestival.org). **Tickets** *free-$10.* **Date** early Nov.
Local authors, historians and poets get a chance to shine in this three-day celebration of bibliophilia that brings local literary heroes and such names as Chuck Palahniuk to town for readings, signings debates and panel discussions.

Motor Trend International Auto Show
Las Vegas Convention Center *3150 Paradise Road, at Convention Center Drive, East of Strip (892 0711, www.motortrendautoshows.com/*

lasvegas). Bus 108, 213. **Admission** $9; $6 reductions. **Map** p335 C5. **Date** late Nov.
A chance to see all the shiniest new models and prototypes from the world's automobile manufacturers before anyone else, though sadly you can't drive them away. Free parking is available at the Convention Center's Silver Lot 3.

WINTER

National Finals Rodeo

Thomas & Mack Center *4505 S Maryland Parkway, at E Tropicana Avenue, University District (1-888 637 7633 information, www.nfr-rodeo.com). Bus 109, 201.* **Tickets** $75-$1,000. **Map** p333 Y3. **Date** early Dec.
Cowboys and girls set Vegas ablaze for nine days as part of this massive event. Tickets are distributed by lottery a year beforehand, but you can watch proceedings on TV at the Gold Coast (*see p150*). Buy western duds from the Original Cowboy Christmas (*see p213*), then party at Sam's Town (*see p150*).

New Las Vegas Marathon & Half-Marathon

Around the city (731 1052, www.lvmarathon.com). **Date** early Dec.
Beginning in the early evening, the marathon starts and ends at Mandalay Bay (*see p109*), has a rock 'n' roll theme, with bands playing along the route. If you want to run, register online; the earlier you do so, the cheaper the fee.

Christmas

Around Las Vegas. **Date** Dec.
The most spectacular festive event in the region is the annual Light the Night display in the cactus garden at Ethel M Chocolates in Henderson (*see p96*). The space is dotted with millions of lights, while carol-singers reel off all the festive favourites. Be sure to get yourself into the factory before 7pm for free chocolate samples.

Other events around the city bring good cheer in similar ways during December. A drive-through trail entitled A Gift of Lights winds through the whole of Sunset Park (E Sunset Road, at S Eastern Avenue, East Las Vegas), with some proceeds going to charities. The Magical Forest at Opportunity Village (6300 W Oakey Boulevard, between S Jones Boulevard & S Torrey Pines Drive) contains a castle, giant candy canes, a forest of decorated trees and two million lights. And numerous watercraft sail around Lake Mead as part of the Parade of Lights.

New Year's Eve

Around Las Vegas. **Date** 31 Dec.
Las Vegas Boulevard and Fremont Street become absolutely rammed on New Year's Eve, a night filled with parties, one-hit celebrities, air displays, fireworks and general chaos. Room rates soar; to be honest, the whole thing is probably best avoided.

African American History Month

West Las Vegas Library *951 W Lake Mead Boulevard, at Concord Street, West Las Vegas (507 3980, www.lvccld.org). Bus 210, 214.* **Date** Feb.
The West Las Vegas Library houses a permanent collection of artefacts, photographs and documents relating to African-American history in the West. During February, its theatre hosts a celebration of African-American community and culture in the region, with spoken word, dance, theatre and music.

High Rollers Scooter Weekend

Around the city (www.lvscooterrally.com). **Date** mid Feb/early Mar.
Rockers on motorbikes steer clear: this weekend of mod rock and showing off is for sharp-looking multi-mirrored scooters and the aficionados who love them.

Chinese New Year Celebration & Asian Food Festival

Las Vegas Chinatown Plaza, 4255 Spring Mountain Road, between S Valley View & S Decatur boulevards, South-west Las Vegas (221 8448, www.lvchinatown.com). Bus 104, 203. **Admission** $3; $1 reductions; free under 5s. **No credit cards. Date** 25 Feb.
The Chinese New Year celebrations in Vegas are actually pan-Asian; they also celebrate Japanese, Tahitian and Thai culture. Expect traditional lion and dragon dances and a feast of Eastern delicacies.

Chinese New Year Celebration.

ARTS & ENTERTAINMENT

Adult Entertainment

Silicone Valley.

The past 20 years have been a rollercoaster ride for Sin City. As Las Vegas has changed from a far-flung hedonistic escape to a world-class tourism destination, the growing pains have sometimes been traumatic. First came the ill-fated attempt to ditch the sin and catch the family market. Topless showgirls started to conceal the surgeon's skill, and pushchairs became de rigueur on the Strip. Then, when the absurdity of Vegas aping Disneyland sank in, the *Swingers*-inspired New Rat Pack tried to recapture the bacchanalian spirit of the city in its heyday. Upscale strip clubs offered elaborate interiors, and risqué showroom revues were again the norm. In other words, sin was in.

Now, as the city eases into its second decade as a 21st-century city, modern Las Vegas has emerged as a mostly respectable destination. Sex hasn't been stripped from Vegas; indeed, there are more adult clubs and shows than ever. But the mainstreaming of US adult entertainment has forced it to share centre stage, as Las Vegas now caters efficiently for all of the seven deadly sins. Even the 'what happens here, stays here' ad campaign played off this fact: were the girls really just shopping and eating last weekend, or was something more naughty going down? After all, every vice, from drinking to dirty dancing, is available 24-7, with no breaks for penance.

One result of the local population growth has been an increase in the breadth of adult entertainment. While the industry still caters mostly to the straight male libido, there are now several places at which women can grasp at men's G-strings. The Playgirl Lounge at **Sapphire** (*see p224*) stages *Men: the Show* on weekend nights, while the **Olympic Garden** (*see p224*) hosts the *Men of OG*. It's a trend that has moved into the casinos, with the likes of *American Storm* at the **Riviera**, the Chippendales at the **Rio**, the *Men of X* at **Hooters** and *Thunder From Down Under* at **Excalibur** (for all, *see p224*). While women have no problem getting attention (and lap dances) from female dancers at mainstream clubs, gay men still find themselves admiring the go-go boys at the city's gay clubs.

Adult entertainment falls into three categories: casino clubs and revues; topless

or nude clubs; and swingers' clubs. For adult shops, *see p208*. Whatever your pleasure, remember that prostitution is illegal in Clark County, in which Las Vegas sits. (It is legal at the brothels in nearby Pahrump, 30 minutes away in Nye County). No matter what the ads, pamphlets or signs say, pay to play and you run the real risk of being busted, or worse.

CASINO CLUBS & REVUES

A few years ago, rumours were rife that strip clubs would soon open in casinos. At the time, owning a topless strip club (with a limited gaming licence) appeared to be a cash generator second only to operating a full-blown casino.

The feverish speculation has cooled, but it's no secret that upscale adult clubs, many of them situated right off the Strip, are leeching cash from casinos. That's why many high-end gambling halls are skating the legal line by adding as much nudity as permissable in the form of topless pool areas, risqué performances and even old-school burlesque clubs.

Still, while joints such as Ivan Kane's **Forty Deuce** (*see p259*) entice patrons with the promise of theatrical burlesque, the stage shows, however impressive, are far too brief. Once the girls have gone, it's just another nightclub where the emphasis is on the bar tab.

In all, there are 11 adult-themed shows to be found in casino showrooms, ranging from the **Riviera**'s long-running, campy *Crazy Girls* to the revamped *Crazy Horse Paris* at the **MGM** (for both, *see p228*). The classic feathers and sequins show *Jubilee!* (at **Bally's**, *see p233*) is the only one of its kind on the Strip; more modern adult shows can take the tack of the lesbian-chic rock 'n' roll vampires of *Bite* at the **Stratosphere** (*see p228*), the Cirque du Soleil cabaret *Zumanity* at **New York New York** (*see p227*), or the Broadway-meets-burlesque *Peepshow* at **Planet Hollywood** (*see p227*). For all adult-oriented shows, *see p227-229*.

TOPLESS BARS

Southern Nevada was once home to scores of tiny, smoky topless clubs, most little more than a dive bar with a small stage. For better or for worse, few of these seedy hangouts remain, but if you do still fancy walking into a Bukowski short story, try the gloriously unpretentious **Larry's Villa** (2401 W Bonanza Road, at N Rancho Drive, 647 2713).

These days, most of these former dives have either upscaled with a plush refit or are aspiring to do so. Many are crowded at weekends, for sporting events and during conventions (also, not coincidentally, when the best and best-looking dancers make the roster). But a quiet midweek visit can be more fun, as you won't have to scramble for a seat. A continuous parade of strippers shimmies to DJ music, stripping down to a G-string, a pair of stilettos and, if you're lucky, a smile.

Topless dancers must be at least 21 years old and are more chatty than those in nude clubs. The clubs all have full bar service (some with bottle service and food) and are open to patrons aged 21 and over. Most are located in dark warehouse areas, so you're best catching a cab. Be sure to specify which club you want to visit: it's not unheard of for cabbies to be paid kickbacks by door staff for dropping tourists at particular venues. All admission prices are for visitors; locals who can show a Nevada ID usually pay less.

Badda Bing
3500 W Naples Drive (between W Flamingo Road & W Tropicana Avenue), between I-15 & S Valley View Boulevard, West of Strip (581 5316, www.baddabinglv.com). Bus 104. **Open** 4pm-late Mon, Tue, Thur-Sun; 11.30am-late Wed. **Admission** $30. **Map** p333 X3.
Formerly known as the Men's Club, open since 2007, this is the most unusual strip club in town. At first, it feels like the house party of a wealthy libertine: the Euro-gothic style, combined with plush finishes, beautiful people, diverse music and a 10,000-bottle wine cellar gives the place real class. The main room has a performance stage on two levels, and a raised glass walkway for observing the dancers from below. A welcome alternative to the mega-clubs.

Cheetahs Topless Club
2112 Western Avenue, between W Wyoming & W Sahara avenues, West of Strip (384 0074, www.ch3lv.com). Bus 105, 204. **Open** 24hrs daily. **Admission** $30 after 8pm. **Map** p335 B4.
This remains Vegas's most relaxed topless bar, neither seedy nor pretentious. Large enough to have five stages yet as homey as a neighbourhood sports bar, Cheetahs has a reputation as a locals' hangout. It's packed during football season, when Monday Night Football parties offer $10 'touchdown dances'. Girls have less silicone than at other clubs; bouncers and bartenders are friendly enough.

Crazy Horse III
3525 W Russell Road, between S Valley View Boulevard & Polaris Avenue, West of Strip (673 1700, www.ch3lv.com). Bus 105, 204. **Open** 24hrs daily. **Admission** $30 after 8pm. **Map** p335 B4.
The history of the Crazy Horse strip clubs (this is iteration no.3) is a fascinating one and reveals much about the political environment of this company town. But that's not what brings in the customers at this upscale 40,000sq ft playground west of the Mandalay Bay casino, complete with raised 'gladiator seating'.

Girls of Glitter Gulch
20 E Fremont Street, at N Main Street, Downtown (385 4774). Bus Deuce & all BTC-bound buses. **Open** 1pm-4am daily. **Admission** 2-drink min. **Map** p333 C1.

Crazy Horse III.

ARTS & ENTERTAINMENT

This diminutive club is the only one in town located on a piece of prime real estate. The interior has been spiffed up nicely, and the proximity to Downtown's casinos is a boon. The small size makes it hard to blend in and enjoy a drink as the entertainers work the room for dances, but you could do worse.

Jaguars

3355 S Procyon Avenue, at W Desert Inn Road, West of Strip (732 1116, www.scoreslas vegas.com). Bus 104, 213. **Open** 24hrs daily. **Admission** $20.

The topless club formerly known as Scores (it's main claim to fame being that it was radio star Howard Stern's favourite strip joint) has reverted to its Jaguars title, taking advantage of extensive remodelling courtesy of Scores. Now known as a 'gentlemen's cabaret', the plush environmment remains, and the stages and seating have been vastly improved. The hourly erotic aerialist performances and the free happy-hour buffet (5-6pm daily) are added attractions.

Olympic Garden

1531 Las Vegas Boulevard South, at E Wyoming Avenue, Stratosphere Area (385 9361, www.og vegas.com). Bus Deuce. **Open** 24hrs daily. **Admission** $5 plus $10 for 2 drink tickets. **Map** p335 C3.

Locals call the city's original upscale club 'the OG'; thanks to its location on Las Vegas Boulevard between Downtown and the Strip, it remains popular. Two storeys, multiple stages and dozens of often surgically enhanced hotties keep everyone happy. Upstairs, the Men of Olympus entertain female visitors (Wed-Sun). Men and women are welcome to go back and forth between floors. Handily, it's within walking distance of Luv-It (*see p169*) and the Arts District.

Sapphire

3025 S Industrial Road, at Stardust Road, West of Strip (869 0003, www.sapphirelasvegas.com). Bus 105. **Open** 24hrs daily. **Admission** $30. **Map** p335 B5.

The largest adult club in the world features a pulsing main room that's almost too big, bottle service, 13 private (and pricey) skyboxes, and the Playgirl Lounge, offering male dancers at weekends. Swing shift (11pm onwards) generally sees the best of the topless dancers, though on a busy weekend it can be a madhouse. Be aware that a cocktail will set you back upward of $15 – there are no less than five ATM machines located throughout the club.

Spearmint Rhino

3344 Highland Drive, at W Desert Inn Road (access via Spring Mountain Road), West of Strip (796 3600, www.spearmintrhinolv.com). Bus 105. **Open** 24hrs daily. **Admission** $30. **Map** p335 A5.

Something about this comfortable spot captivates the young and stylish, making it the choice for the nightclub-hopping crowd. It might be the diverse parade of entertainers – from bleached blondes to tattooed rockers – and their eclectic music choices that make it so fun. Popular with locals and couples, it's busy on nights when other clubs are sleepy.

Treasures

2801 Westwood Drive, at Highland Drive, West of Strip (257 3030, www.treasureslasvegas.com). Bus

Sapphire.

105. **Open** 4pm-6am Mon-Thur, Sun; 4pm-9am Fri, Sat. **Admission** $20-$30. **Map** p335 A4.

With its two storeys, mansion-styled room and two primary stages, Treasures reads like an OTT version of Jaguars, and lives up to its slogan: 'the most luxurious gentlemen's club in the world'. In the main room, dancers perform on poles under special lighting and fog machines. With its pleasant service and upscale ambience, Treasures is Vegas's Playboy mansion.

NUDE CLUBS

Nude clubs are similar to topless bars save for one important difference: the full-nudity licence prohibits alcohol, and so the clubs (except for the **Palomino**) are open to anyone over 18. Without the cash cow of alcohol sales, the environments are much less plush and attract less affluent patrons. It's easy to be a star guest by tipping well and smiling. As the focus is elsewhere, there's less silicone and more emphasis on pole tricks and personality.

Déjà Vu Showgirls
3247 Industrial Road, between Stardust Road & W Sahara Avenue, West of Strip (894 4167, www.dejavushowgirlslasvegas.com). Bus 105, 204. **Open** 11am-6am Mon-Sat; 6pm-4am Sun. **Admission** $25 (inc unlimited non-alcoholic drinks). **Map** p336 A5.

Dancers at Déjà Vu have an honest-to-goodness personality that's hard to find in the land of silicone sameness. Look out for theme nights, from oil wrestling to shower parties on the two stages, and the neighbouring Déjà Vu Adult Emporium. Dress: no tank tops.

Little Darlings
1514 Western Avenue, at W Wyoming Avenue, Stratosphere Area (366 1141, www.littledarlings vegas.com). Bus 105. **Open** 11am-6am Mon-Sat; 6am-4am Sun. **Admission** $20 plus $10 for unlimited non-alcoholic drinks. **Map** p335 B3.

Stark lighting, annoying DJs and plastic soda cups are indicative of the tarted-up recreation hall feel at this Déjà Vu-run club. Many of the dancers look like they just stepped out of the indie rock bar down the block. Amateur nights can get pretty sexy and private dances can be wild, but the performers aren't chatty. Dress: no tank tops.

Palomino Club
1848 Las Vegas Boulevard North, at E Owens Avenue, North Las Vegas (642 2984). Bus 113. **Open** 4pm-5am daily. **Admission** $30. **No credit cards.** **Map** p333 Y1.

The granddaddy of Vegas clubs is ragged, but merits its reputation as the city's most atmospheric nude club: it's the only one with a liquor licence. Upstairs, an egalitarian roster of dancers works a small stage, while downstairs (open weekends and busy seasons)

Spearmint Rhino.

'feature dancers' (porn actresses, centrefolds) take to the catwalk. Changes in North Las Vegas may soon spell the end of adult entertainment here, so get your drink and your nudity while you can.

SWINGERS' CLUBS

The euphemistically named 'couples scene' in Las Vegas is finally getting comfortable with itself. Swingers' clubs don't offer gambling or alcohol (you can bring your own), but they often have pool tables, dancefloors and stripper poles. You pay an entrance fee (or 'donation'), which is usually $40-$50 for each single male, about $10 less for couples, and next to nothing for single women.

Notable for its ethnic eateries and gay bars, the down-at-heel Commercial Center strip mall (953 E Sahara Avenue) also contains three swingers' clubs: **Red Rooster** (732 2587), the **Fantasy Social Club** (893 3977, www.fantasy socialclub.com) and the wildly popular **Green Door** (732 4656, www.greendoorlasvegas.com). The former two are open from early evening until 5am, while the Green Door opens at 1pm and stays open until 7am on weekends; prime time is 10pm-1am. The **Red Rooster** in old Henderson (451 6661, www.vegasred rooster.com), unaffiliated to the other Red Rooster, attracts a more mature, old-school 'lifestyle' crowd to a 'party house' well on the eastern outskirts of town.

ARTS & ENTERTAINMENT

Casino Entertainment

Gambling and putting on a show: what this city's all about.

Las Vegas pridefully calls itself 'the entertainment capital of the world', and arguably it is – depending on how you define 'entertainment'. If you think of it under the wide rubric of 'diversion', then perhaps the city has earned its crown. But the live entertainment on offer here represents a very narrow band of the performance spectrum. Here, even the new is almost inevitably the old, recycled, remixed – repackaged for a crowd that craves the comfort of unchallenging familiarity. If it was a hit on radio or TV from the '60s to the '90s, you can still find it somewhere on the Strip, or touring cyclically (if not cynically) through one of its concert venues.

THE ENTERTAINMENT SCENE

During the late 1990s and early 21st century, Las Vegas entertainment was turned on its head. The tired old revues that had defined the city for years were ushered out of the door, replaced by big-budget, high-concept pieces of populist performance art delivered by **Cirque du Soleil** (of whom more in a moment). A generation of tired comics and hoarse singers was replaced by still-popular stand-ups and musicians who remained on speaking terms with the charts. And the grinning showgirls were gradually pensioned off, in favour of dancers prepared to show a little more than their feathers. (The female and male strip-shows of the Strip are hardly as naughty as they are purported to be – for that 'anything goes, everything shows' ethos, you have to go a few blocks off the Strip; *see pp222-225* **Adult Entertainment**.)

After such a dramatic shift in priorities, Las Vegas has lately been content simply to consolidate. Indeed, when it comes to entertainment, the city remains an impersonator rather than an innovator. The musical headliners are big names who won't frighten your parents (Celine Dion, Donny & Marie, Barry Manilow, Elton John). And after Cirque du Soleil's first show, *Mystère*, broke box-office records, every casino on the Strip

wanted one just like it. As a result, there are no fewer than seven Cirque productions in town, with at least one more – a Michael Jackson tribute – on the way. Heaven only knows what Sinatra and Elvis would make of it all... especially since the latter now 'stars' in a Cirque production of his own.

INFORMATION AND TICKETS

Although most of the shows listed in this section are expected to run for the shelf-life of this guide, others open and close all the time. For the most up-to-date information, check 'Neon' in Friday's *Las Vegas Review-Journal*, free magazines such as *What's On*, the town's three alternative weeklies and www.vegas.com. In any given week, there are also a few big-name acts working short engagements in the city, either filling in for vacationing headliners or working in auditoria that only deal with temporary bookings (such as the **Hollywood Theatre** at the MGM Grand).

You're always best off buying tickets at the hotel-casino's own box office, either in person, by phone or online. If you get stuck, try **Ticketmaster** (*see p214*), but prepare to pay over the odds. If you book by phone or online, pick up the tickets at the 'will call' window. Try and book as far ahead as possible for the big shows. However, even if the show has sold out, it's worth calling the box office, especially midweek, to check for cancellations. You can also find half-price tickets to some shows at **Tix4Tonight** (1-877 849 4868, www.tix4tonight.com) in the Fashion Show Mall, Showcase Mall and Hawaiian Marketplace ; the booth opens at noon daily.

Shows are expensive in Las Vegas. The cheapest tickets for most big shows go for upwards of $50, and the best seats are routinely priced at three-figure sums. Some quoted prices include tax, others don't; many shows include a drink in their prices. However, there are bargains. Many shows offer discounts with coupons found on flyers or in magazines. If you're a heavy gambler, you might even get comped into a show in the casino in which you've been playing.

Tickets for many shows allocate the theatregoer specific seats. If you have tickets for a show that offers only 'general admission' (unnumbered) seating, which is relatively rare these days, arrive early if you want a good spot. If you're not satisfied with your seat's location, try discreetly tipping the maître d' $10 or $20. Some shows, especially those with a degree of nudity, come with age restrictions; always check if you have kids in tow.

For music venues, *see p252-256*; for nightclubs, *see p257-261*.

Resident Shows

Las Vegas's first stage productions were known as 'floor shows'. When Sophie Tucker performed at the El Rancho and Jimmy Durante played the Flamingo in the 1940s and '50s, they were preceded by a line of girls, a comic or a magician, and a speciality act (a juggler, say).

Entertainment in the city changed radically when the Stardust premièred *Lido de Paris* in

1958. The fabulous spectacle played to packed houses and set the template for productions such as **Folies Bergere** and **Jubilee!**; both remain, dated yet enjoyable examples of what visitors to Las Vegas in the 1960s would have enjoyed in the city's showrooms.

There are still plenty of production shows on display, though they've moved on a little bit since the town's tits-and-feathers heyday. **Cirque du Soleil** now has no fewer than seven shows here, all built especially for Vegas, but many other big-budget shows have been tried and tested elsewhere before being picked up by the casino moguls. **Phantom**, for example, made millions on Broadway and in London's West End before shipping out to the desert.

Elsewhere, magicians still draw the crowds: even with Siegfried & Roy gone, there's still plenty of choice. Other options include celebrity impersonator shows, in which lookalikes sing or lip-synch in imitation of pop-culture heroes and heroines, and adult revues, featuring a parade of hardbodies taking it off for crowds of women and (more often) men. And many casinos carry on the time-honoured tradition of booking star headliners, with full-timers such as **Rita Rudner** joined by semi-resident performers such as **Elton John** and regular guests such as **Jay Leno**.

ADULT REVUES

Peepshow
Planet Hollywood *3667 Las Vegas Boulevard South, West of Strip (1-800 745 3000, 785 5555, www.lasvegaspeepshow.com). Bus Deuce, 108, 119, 202.* **Shows** 9.30pm Mon, Tue, Fri, Sun; 8pm, 10.30pm Thur, Sat. **Tickets** $84.55-$154. No under-18s. **Map** p333 X3.

A fresh, flashy – and fleshy – take on that old Vegas staple, the topless burlesque revue, Peepshow is that rarity of rarities: a Strip stripper act you can take your wife or girlfriend to. Directed with Broadway-style jazz and pizazz by Jerry Mitchell, who staged the musical versions of *Hairspray* and *The Full Monty*, Peepshow stars Holly Madison, the former paramour of Hugh Hefner who has appointed herself Las Vegas's ambassador to the world. She's adorable, as is the rest of the cast of near-naked lovelies, in a bijou setting. There are all manner of variations on the classic stripper-pole moves, and the aerobically stimulating dance numbers send performers frolicking in an aquarium full of milk and literally swinging over the audience's heads.

Zumanity
New York New York *3790 Las Vegas Boulevard South, at W Tropicana Avenue (1-866 606 7111, 740 6815, www.zumanity.com). Bus Deuce, 201.* **Shows** 7.30pm, 10.30pm Wed-Sun. **Tickets** $69-$146.45. No under-18s. **Map** p336 A8.

Peepshow.

ARTS & ENTERTAINMENT

The idea of asking Cirque du Soleil to compile its own adult revue was an unexpected one. In parts, it pulls it off, most notably the more comic stretches and the two-women-in-a-fishtank section towards the start of the show. A little too often it seems unsure whether it's better off trying to dazzle or arouse the audience, but those on the love seats (or, as the box office coyly calls them, 'duo sofas') seem to go upstairs happy enough. The Vienna-inspired jewelbox cabaret theatre, all sensual curves and touchable textures, may inspire your own performance later.

Male revues

Ladies, why let the guys have all the fun in Vegas when there are chiselled male specimens available to gyrate for your pleasure? Equal parts sensuality and humour, these four male revues makes for the perfect bachelorette, birthday or divorce party setting. Be warned: the performers won't let you just sit back and passively take it all in; arriving drunk and uninhibited ensures a much better time.

American Storm
Planet Hollywood *3667 Las Vegas Boulevard South, West of Strip (1-866 932 1818, 260 7200, www.american-storm.com). Bus Deuce, 108, 119, 202.* **Shows** 10pm Fri; 11.30pm Sat. **Tickets** $55-$58.65. No under-18s. **Map** p333 X3.

Chippendales
Rio *3700 W Flamingo Road, at S Valley View Boulevard, West of Strip (1-888 746 7784, 777 7776, www.riolasvegas.com). Bus 104, 202.* **Shows** 8pm Mon-Thur, Sun; 8pm, 10.30pm Fri, Sat. **Tickets** $39.95-$59.95. No under-18s. **Map** p333 X3.

Men of X
Hooters *115 E Tropicana Avenue, West of Strip (1-866 584 6687, 739 9000, www.hooters casinohotel.com). Bus Deuce, 201.* **Shows** 8pm Fri-Sun. **Tickets** $34.95-$59.95. No under-18s. **Map** p333 X3.

Thunder From Down Under
Excalibur *3850 Las Vegas Boulevard South, at E Tropicana Avenue, East of Strip (1-800 933 1334, 597 7600, www.excalibur.com). Bus 202.* **Shows** 9pm Mon-Thur, Sun; 9pm, 11pm Fri, Sat. **Tickets** $40.95-$50.95. No under-18s. **Map** p333 X3.

Female revues

Each of these revues has some distinguishing characteristic, but at the (soft) core, each one is all about waiting for the big reveal.

Bite
Stratosphere *2000 Las Vegas Boulevard South, at E St Louis Avenue, East of Strip (1-800 998 6937, 380 7777, www.stratospherehotel.com). Bus Deuce, 109, 204.* **Shows** 9pm Mon, Wed-Sun. **Tickets** $49.95. No under-18s. **Map** p336 A9.

Fangs for the memories. The camp-vampire *Bite* revue was on to the beautiful-undead theme before *Twilight* and *Vampire Diaries* and the rest of the bloodsucking crew. Performers tease the crowd against a soundtrack of classic rock snippets (avoiding the licensing fees, are we?).

Crazy Girls
Riviera *2901 Las Vegas Boulevard South, between E Sahara Avenue & E Desert Inn Road, West of Strip (1-877 892/7469, www.riviera hotel.com). Bus Deuce, 108, 204.* **Shows** 9.30pm Mon, Wed-Sun. **Tickets** $50-$67. No under-18s. **Map** p335 B5.

'Girls! Girls! Crazy girls!' goes the infernally catchy theme song. Well, crazy they ain't, and, if local legend is to be believed, the butts displayed in bronze outside the Riviera by way of advertisement – touching them has become a rite of passage, and the patinaed statue has the shiny patches to prove it – aren't all female. Regardless, this low-budget titfest, which has been around for 25 years, is a giggle: about as arousing as a kick in the teeth, granted, but lovers of Vegas camp will be in heaven.

Crazy Horse Paris
MGM Grand *3799 Las Vegas Boulevard South, at E Tropicana Avenue, West of Strip (1-877 880 0880, 891 7800, www.mgmgrand.com/ entertainment). Bus Deuce, 201.* **Shows** 8pm, 10.30pm Mon, Wed-Sun. **Tickets** $50.50-$60.50. No under-18s. **Map** p336 A8.

Formerly known as *La Femme*, *Crazy Horse Paris* claims to 'reinvent the female form as art', a boast that somehow doesn't go unfounded. Lighting effects and film, ballet and cabaret, canvasses and zodiac signs: all add up to a show with worldly flair. Its 'international collection' of a dozen stars have performed with the original Crazy Horse dance troupe in Paris, a company dating back to 1951. Who says Vegas has no sense of history?

Fantasy
Luxor *3900 Las Vegas Boulevard South, at W Hacienda Avenue, East of Strip (1-800 557 7428, 262 4400, www.luxor.com). Bus Deuce, 104, 105.* **Shows** 10.30pm daily. **Tickets** $39-$52. No under-18s. **Map** p336 A9.

Fantasy stages and interprets an array of top-shelf seduction scenarios. Charismatic host Sean Cooper keeps energy and anticipation running high with his comedic impersonations, singing and dancing, but you may find that you've seen this all before, and less rigidly, in your dreams.

THE BEST SHOWS

For the Beatles on trapezes
Love. See p234.

For Broadway in Vegas
Jersey Boys. See p233.

For big names in a small space
Hollywood Theatre. See p226.

For afternoon magic
Mac King. See p230.

For late-evening laughs
George Wallace. See p230.

But if you only have time
for one show...
O. See p235.

X Burlesque

Flamingo *3555 Las Vegas Boulevard South, at E Flamingo Road, West of Strip (1-800 221 7299, 733 3333, www.flamingolasvegas.com). Bus Deuce, 104, 105.* **Shows** 10.30pm daily. **Tickets** $44.95-$55.95. No under-18s. **Map** p336 A9.

The pretty birds of *X Burlesque* share a hotel, if not a stage, with squeaky-clean Donny & Marie. The half-dozen dancers play with fanciful props, and the old-school mid-show comics try to keep your attention while the dancers exchange one skimpy costume for the next.

CELEBRITY IMPERSONATORS

★ Divas Las Vegas

Imperial Palace *3535 Las Vegas Boulevard South, between E Flamingo & Sands avenues (1-888 777 7664, 794 3261, www.imperial palace.com). Bus Deuce, 108, 204.* **Shows** 10pm Mon-Thur, Sat, Sun. **Tickets** $39-$79. **Map** p335 B5.

Glamour boy Frank Marino, the long-reigning Queen of the Strip – with more than 25 years of performing in high heels and higher hair – thoroughly enjoys being a girl. And so does his cast of top-notch female impersonators, who present an eye-popping parade of top-shelf pop-culture doppelgängers: the Madonna, Beyoncé and Britney bits are snatched from their latest tours (the real Britney Spears wishes she looked as good as her double); the Celine Dion act is so artfully exact it will make you appreciate anew just how much Celine puts into being Celine.

Gordie Brown

Golden Nugget *129 E Fremont Street, between N Main Street & N Las Vegas Boulevard (1-866 946/5336, www.goldennugget.com).*
Bus Deuce, 105, 203. **Shows** 7.30pm Tue-Sat. **Tickets** $33-$71.50. No under-16s.
Map p334 D1.

De Niro, Eastwood and Nicholson; Dylan, Pavarotti and Armstrong... Only a very few high-profile entertainers escape the attentions of this energetic singer/comic/actor/impressionist, a former political cartoonist from Canada who made his Vegas name at the Golden Nugget. Some have accused Brown of trying too hard, of sacrificing himself to his characters, but it's a likeable enough show.

Legends in Concert

Harrah's *3475 Las Vegas Boulevard South, between E Flamingo Road & Sands Avenue (1-800 214 9110, 369 5111, www.harrahs lasvegas.com). Bus Deuce, 119, 203, 213 105.* **Shows** 7pm, 9.30pm daily. **Tickets** $55.45-$65.45; $34.95-$44.95 reductions.
Map p336 A6.

Sorry you missed Elvis? Can't afford Cher's show down the street? Wish Britney Spears, Lady Gaga and Barbra Streisand didn't charge $500 a ticket? Worry not: they're all here in this long-running tribute show. Unlike other shows of this type, these performers – backed by a fine band and surrounded by showgirls – actually sing, usually doing several numbers or a medley of top hits.

The Rat Pack is Back

Rio *3700 W Flamingo Road, between Las Vegas Boulevard South & S Valley View Boulevard, West of Strip (1-888 727 6966, 737 5540, www. greekislesvegas.com, www.riolasvegas.com). Bus Deuce, 202.* **Shows** 8.15pm daily. **Tickets** $62.10-$95.10. **Map** p335 B5.

For those who miss the Vegas of yore, when it was a town for grown-ups – before the pool parties, candy and bijou shops and digital slot machines – here's a tribute to the era when Frank, Dino, Sammy and Joey reigned supreme. A re-creation of their classic act from the Copa Room at the Sands – complete with a 12-piece band, and all the off-colour jokes and locker-room razzing you remember.

Terry Fator

Mirage *3400 Las Vegas Boulevard South, between Spring Mountain & W Flamingo roads (1-800 963 9634, 792 7777, www. mirage.com). Bus Deuce, 105, 202, 203.* **Shows** 7.30pm Tue-Sat. **Tickets** $54.99-$149.99. No under-5s.
Map p335, p336 A6.

Replacing the late and much-loved impressionist Danny Gans was no small order. Fortunately for ventriloquist Terry Fator and the Mirage, Fator has a similar family-friendly appeal, plus a national fan base from his wins on the *America's Got Talent* TV show. And Fator (and his cast of puppet personas) can do comic and musical impressions too – he's particularly good at razzing such fellow Strip draws as Garth Brooks and Cher – all without moving his lips.

COMEDIANS

Carrot Top
Luxor *3900 Las Vegas Boulevard South, at W Hacienda Avenue (1-800 557 7428, 262 4400, www.luxor.com). Bus Deuce, 104, 119.* **Shows** 8.30pm Mon, Wed-Sun. **Tickets** $49.95-$65.95. No under-18s. **Map** p336 A9.

Carrot Top is inescapable in Las Vegas – his blazing ginger hair and freckled face leers out from billboards and bus sides. And even if you think he's too juvenile, it's guaranteed that if he coaxes you into the theatre, one way or another, you're going to laugh. Once you get past the 'zany prop comic' stigma, it's easy to see why his popularity has endured. Lightning-quick, with an ADD attention span, inventing visual puns by the truckload, Carrot Top combines subtle political, social and cultural commentary with music, video and – yes – those infamous props for a comedic concoction like no other in town.

George Wallace
Flamingo *3555 Las Vegas Boulevard South, at E Flamingo Road (1-800 221 7299, 733 3333, www.flamingolasvegas.com). Bus Deuce, 202.* **Shows** 10pm Tue-Sat. **Tickets** $49.95-$75. No under-5s. **Map** p336 A7.

George Wallace's evenly paced, conversational style, with up-to-the-second topical comedy and social criticism, makes audiences think as well as laugh. Named one of Comedy Central's 100 greatest stand-ups of all time, Wallace veers between 'Yo' mama' jokes, comic bewilderment at the English language and audience interaction; and you never know who (Jerry Seinfeld, Chris Tucker) might show up. Don't be surprised to find him mingling on the casino floor after the show.

Rita Rudner
Venetian *3355 Las Vegas Boulevard South, between Sands Avenue & E Flamingo Road*

Criss Angel: Believe.

(1-866 641 7469, 414 9000, www.venetian. com). Bus Deuce, 203. **Shows** 8.30pm Mon-Wed, Sat. **Tickets** $59-$109. No under-7s. **Map** p336 A6.

In the mood for comedy that's not too blue-blooded, blue-collar or just plain blue? The former chorus girl's adult but pointedly clean brand of observational material is witty without being wanton, classy instead of crass. You'll be hard-pressed to find anyone with better bits on relationships, family and shopping, nor will you find a more earnest, likeable performer on the Strip. After years as a mainstay at Harrah's, she's now, appropriately, in the more elegant environs of the Venetian.

Magicians

Amazing Johnathan
Harmon Theater (Planet Hollywood) *3663 Las Vegas Boulevard South #600, at E Harmon Avenue (1-800 634 6787, 836 0836, www. harmontheater.com). Bus Deuce, 108, 119, 202.* **Shows** 9pm Tue-Sat. **Tickets** $59.95-$65.95. No under-18s. **Map** p335 C4.

Tagged as 'the Freddy Krueger of comedy', John Szeles delivers an adult-oriented show that relies heavily on audience participation, sight gags, explosive language and outrageous effects; not to mention the 'aid' of his goofily loveable sidekick, Psychic Tanya. The Amazing Johnathan doesn't toe the line when it comes to good taste: he makes it disappear in a puff of smoke.

Criss Angel: Believe
Luxor *3900 Las Vegas Boulevard South, at W Hacienda Avenue, East of Strip (1-800 557 7428, 262 4400, www.luxor.com). Bus Deuce, 104, 119.* **Shows** 7pm Wed, Thur; 7pm, 9.30pm Tue, Fri, Sat. **Tickets** $64.90-$176; $29.50 reductions. **Map** p336 A9.

After a blizzard of hype – Cirque invested $100 million – TV illusionist Criss Angel's show still stands on its own at the Luxor, and remains the most controversial act in town. Framed by the most beautiful proscenium on the Strip – a gilded steampunk fantasia – Angel runs through an erratically paced routine of vanishing tricks and anticlimactic set pieces, all with a faux-Goth flair straight out of a New Jersey strip mall. If you don't get comps or dramatically discounted tickets, you will have to suspend your disbelief at how Angel made your money disappear.

Mac King
Harrah's *3475 Las Vegas Boulevard South, between Sands Avenue & E Flamingo Road (1-800 392 9002, 369 5222, www.harrahslas vegas.com). Bus Deuce, 119, 203, 213.* **Shows** 1pm, 3pm Tue-Sat. **Tickets** $32.95. No under-5s. **Map** p336 A6.

One of the real gems of Vegas's family entertainment roster is also one of its cheapest shows. Sure,

Celine Dion.

there are no big bangs or grand illusions here: the budget extends to a pack of cards, some rope, a box of Fig Newtons and a silly suit. But King's warm manner, gentle humour and casually dazzling tricks keep the audience hooked, even now that King has moved to a bigger showroom. Look out for discount coupons in the local magazines, but even if you don't find them, this is well worth full price. A highly likeable afternoon.

Nathan Burton

Flamingo *3555 Las Vegas Boulevard South, at E Flamingo Road (1-800 221 7299, 733 3333, www.nathanburton.com). Bus Deuce, 202.* **Shows** 4pm Tue-Sun. **Tickets** $34-$44; $17-$22 reductions. **Map** p336 A7.
Like Carrot Top, Nathan Burton is as much comic as he is magician, and many of his tricks involve very silly props and Rube Goldberg-esque contraptions. Clean-cut and casual, Burton gives and his showgirl assistants add goofy new twists to time-honoured tricks. Burton's halftime act, droll jongleur Michael Holly, is worth the price of admission all by himself. A well-spent afternoon, indeed.

Penn & Teller

Rio *3700 W Flamingo Road, at S Valley View Boulevard, West of Strip (1-888 746 7784, 777 7776, www.pennandteller.com). Bus Deuce, 202.* **Shows** 9pm Mon-Wed, Sat, Sun. **Tickets** $75-$95. No under-5s. **Map** p333 X3.
Burly man-mountain Penn Jillette and the mute, mono-monikered Teller are the Reservoir Dogs to most other magicians' Ocean's Eleven: edgy, angry, and always seemingly on the verge of going off. They've become scourges of the Magic Circle by showing the audience how tricks are done, but they deserve equal credit for the pzazz with which they pull off the illusions that they don't explain. The closing bullet routine is the only one that falls flat, but the rest of the evening is very entertaining. Bonus: stick around afterwards for the inevitable autograph signings, and you may hear Teller speak.

Steve Wyrick: Ultra Magician

Las Vegas Hilton *3000 Paradise Road, between E Sahara Avenue & E Desert Inn Road, East of Strip (1-800 222 5361, 732 5111, www.lvhilton.com). Bus 108, 204, 213.* **Shows** 7.30pm daily. **Tickets** $39.95-$125. **Map** p336 A7.
Magician Wyrick, who specialises in manly magic – like making jets and motorcycles appear – has been doing something of a disappearing act himself of late, having been forced to move from his self-titled entertainment complex at Planet Hollywood due to bankruptcy. He's since remonetised and rematerialised, moving to the Las Vegas Hilton. For fast-paced, no-frills magic performed in an intimate setting, his act can't be beat.

Musical headliners

Barry Manilow: Music & Passion

Paris Las Vegas *3655 Las Vegas Boulevard South, between E Flamingo Road & E Harmon Avenue (1-800 745-3000, 946 7000, www.parislasvegas.com). Bus Deuce, 108, 204, 213.* **Shows** 8pm Fri-Sun. **Tickets** $95-$299. **Map** p335 C5.
Barry Manilow has long been a titan on the Strip; now he has staged a one-man occupation of Paris. Adorably elfin, winking and twinkling in a black brocade jacket, he holds his 'fanilows' rapt, and wins over even the sceptical by evening's end. This go-round was directed and choreographed by Jeff Hornaday (*High School Musical*), and though there seems to be a lot of energy up there, like the similarly sixtysomething Cher, Manilow makes the most of minimal movements. The Paris show is somewhat less relentless than his long-running shows at the Las Vegas Hilton, with dips into his greatest-hits albums celebrating this or that decade. But he always goes back to the hits, culminating with the mandatory 'Copacabana', set against a backdrop of animated rococo psychedelia on the giant high-res screen behind him.

★ Celine Dion

Colosseum at Caesars Palace
3570 Las Vegas Boulevard South, at W Flamingo Road (1-877 432 5463, 866 1400, www.caesarspalace.com). Bus Deuce, 202. **Shows** 7.30pm Mon-Wed, Fri-Sun **Tickets** $55-$250. **Map** p336 A7.
After 'taking a break' after her five-year Vegas run with a world tour, Celine Dion returns triumphant. (Bette Midler and Cher kept the stage – which was built for Dion – warm for her.) The new show, which features a 31-piece orchestra, tributes to movie music and Michael Jackson – and a duet with a hologram of herself – scales back the excess (and the French-Canadian dancer/acrobats) of her Cirque-directed spectacle, in favour of keeping the focus on Las Vegas's biggest star. Elvis who?

ARTS & ENTERTAINMENT

Donny & Marie.

ARTS & ENTERTAINMENT

★ Donny & Marie

Flamingo *3555 Las Vegas Boulevard South, at E Flamingo Road (1-800 221 7299, 733 3333, www.flamingolasvegas.com). Bus Deuce, 202.* **Shows** 7.30pm Tue-Sat. **Tickets** $95-$260. **Map** p336 A7.

Go ahead and smirk, but the toothy Mormon brother-and-sister act fit right in on the Strip; in fact, you might even say they dominate it. Entertainers since conception, they work the Flamingo's human-scaled showroom like lifelong politicians – running on an antidepressant platform – and no one can grin, wave, point, wink, dance on tables or kiss hands like they can. There's a few duets, some Broadway, country, even cod-opera, and they work out their comic sibling rivalry with a comic dance-off. By evening's end, you'll find yourself with a lump in your throat as they roll a montage of their entire televised lives, including a galaxy of stars, featuring just about everyone who has ever played Vegas.

Elton John

Colosseum at Caesars Palace *3570 Las Vegas Boulevard South, at W Flamingo Road (1-888 435 8665, 866 1400, www.caesarspalace.com). Bus Deuce, 202.* **Shows** (50 performances a year) 8pm Wed-Sun; dates vary. **Tickets** $55-$250. **Map** p336 A7.

Having signed a new three-year contract that began in September 2011, the Queen of England renews his lease on Las Vegas with a show called the *Million-Dollar Piano*. The show – scheduled for 50 performances a year – is named for a custom-built Yamaha piano. Elton's second residency as a Strip headliner will be another rummage through his endless back catalogue of hits, supported by his longtime band, collection of custom spectacles and couture costumes.

★ Garth Brooks

Encore Theater at Wynn Las Vegas *3131 Las Vegas Boulevard South, between E Desert Inn Road & Sands Avenue (1-877 654 2784, 770 1000, www.wynnlasvegas.com). Bus Deuce, 202.* **Shows** (2nd & 4th wk of the mth) 8pm, 10.30pm Fri, Sat. **Tickets** $253. **Map** p336 A7.

You might call him the world's highest-paid busker. Country idol Garth Brooks is in the midst of his five-year contract as a solo act at the intimate (by Vegas standards) Wynn showroom, and when we say solo, we mean just the man and his guitar, often doing two shows a night. It's a thrillingly up-close, gimmick-free encounter with a showbiz legend (thrilling if you like country music, that is, and even if you don't). He's funny, self-effacing – and he takes requests! To woo Brooks, casino mogul Steve Wynn famously bought Brooks his own jet, so he can 'commute' back home for his kids' soccer games. Mrs Brooks – country star Tricia Yearwood – takes the stage now and then for a duet.

Gladys Knight

Tropicana *3801 Las Vegas Boulevard South, at Tropicana Avenue (1-800 829 9034, 739 2411, www.troplv.com). Bus Deuce, 201.* **Shows** 8pm Tue-Sat. **Tickets** $40-$105. **Map** p336 A7.

The venerable Trop has been spruced up with a South Beach, Florida feel, and its owners have ensconced headliner Gladys Knight (sans Pips) in what was previously known as the Tiffany Theater, the oldest showroom on the Strip. Knight's show is called *A Mic and a Light*, and that's really all this veteran entertainer needs to outshine everyone else in town.

Human Nature

Imperial Palace *3535 Las Vegas Boulevard South, between E Flamingo Avenue & Sands Avenue (1-888 777 7664, 794 3261, www.imperialpalace.com). Bus Deuce, 108, 204.* **Shows** 7.30pm Mon-Thur, Sun. **Tickets** $49.95-$59.95. **Map** p336 A7.

Having passed puberty, the Australian boyband wisely grew up musically, studied the Motown song-book (and style guide), and flew east to Vegas. Sponsored by Vegas resident Smokey Robinson himself, the sharp-dressed quartet currently reigns at the Imperial Palace showroom with their tight, snappy revue of classic Motor City hits.

PRODUCTION SHOWS

★ Absinthe
Caesars Palace *3570 Las Vegas Boulevard South, at W Flamingo Road (1-800 745 3000, www.absinthevegas.com). Bus Deuce, 202.* **Shows** 8pm Wed; 8pm, 10pm Tue, Thur-Sat. **Tickets** $69-$99. No under-18s. **Map** p335, p336 B6.
This pop-up show instantly became the toast of Las Vegas when it pitched its Spiegeltent in front of Caesars Palace at the corner of Flamingo Road. It's as if a bunch of crazy carnies colonised the Strip with their acro-cabaret with a touch of Cirque and more than a touch of *Rocky Horror*'s sexy camp.

Blue Man Group
Venetian *3555 Las Vegas Boulevard South, between Sands Avenue & E Flamingo Road (1-866 641 7469, www.blueman.com). Bus Deuce, 203.* **Shows** 7pm, 10pm daily (subject to change). **Tickets** $74.90-$147.50. No under-5s. **Map** p335, p336 B6.
It's no surprise that Blue Man Group is such an international phenomenon: their witty, rhythmic and colourful appeal is universal – meaning no language barrier for foreign visitors – and very carefully pitched at all age groups. In this industrial-themed theatre at the Venetian, the three blue baldies cull comedy from multimedia high jinks, a festival environment from audience reactions, and

music from just about everything they can get their hands on. Few performers express so much while saying so little.

Jubilee!
Bally's *3645 Las Vegas Boulevard South, at E Flamingo Road (1-800 237-7469, 967 4567, www.ballyslasvegas.com). Bus Deuce, 202.* **Shows** 7.30pm, 10.30pm Mon-Thur, Sat, Sun. **Tickets** $57.50-$117.50. No under-18s. **Map** p336 A7.
If you enjoyed the movie *Showgirls*, then *Jubilee!* is a must-see, as this is the over-the-topless spectacular that inspired the set-pieces in that awful classic. *Jubilee!*'s staging of the sinking of the *Titanic* and Samson's destruction of the Philistines in the temple are beyond lame – rather, they're lamé. But the production numbers in this long-running camp folly, which feature endless parades of beauties wearing nothing more than outlandishly coloured (hot pink and tangerine predominate) feathers, headdresses and rhinestones (and chorus boys in riotously hilarious studded leather codpieces), make it one of a kind – and, somewhat sadly, the last of its kind.

★ Jersey Boys
Palazzo *3325 Las Vegas Boulevard South, between Sands Avenue & E Flamingo Road, East of Strip (1-866 641 7469, 414 9000, www.palazzo.com). Bus Deuce, 108, 203.* **Shows** 7pm Wed-Fri, Sun; 6.30pm, 9.30pm Tue, Sat. **Tickets** $73.10-$260.10. No under-14s. **Map** p335 C5.
About all that remains of the short-lived dream of a 'Broadway West' in Las Vegas, *Jersey Boys* is the one to make it work. It's a perfect show for the Strip. It might as well be nicknamed *Dreamboys*, as it

Jubilee!.

ARTS & ENTERTAINMENT

Le Rêve.

ARTS & ENTERTAINMENT

traces the four-decade rise and fall of Frankie Valli and the Four Seasons through a jukebox full of hand-clapping, hip-swiveling hits – 30, in fact. The dancing and singing are as razor-sharp as the suits and haircuts: *Jersey Boys* makes you pine for a time when men had style.

★ Kà

MGM Grand *3799 Las Vegas Boulevard South, at E Tropicana Avenue (1-877 880 0880, 531 3826, www.mgmgrand.com). Bus Deuce, 201.* **Shows** 7pm, 9.30pm Tue-Sat. **Tickets** $69-$150; half-price 5-11s. No under-5s. **Map** p336 A8.

The stage is the star of this Cirque spectacular, which is like a cross between videogames, Japanese manga comics and an IMAX movie screen. Having pushed the boat out for *O* (literally, in a couple of scenes), Cirque du Soleil had to work hard to top it in this multi-million-dollar extravaganza, in which the colossal stage platform rotates, revolves and stands on end, conjuring ocean depths, arctic cliffs and desert islands. Set in an ornate theatre that calls to mind a Jules Verne steampunk fantasia, Kà differs from other Vegas-based Cirque shows in that it has a plot (about twins struggling to reunite). The story gets a bit lost in an array of ever more breathtaking routines; yet for all the excess, the most touching moment in the piece is a section involving hand-shadows, the simplest of theatrical effects.

Love

Mirage *3400 Las Vegas Boulevard South, between Spring Mountain & W Flamingo roads (1-800 963 9634, 792 7777, www.mirage.com). Bus Deuce, 202, 203.* **Shows** 7pm, 9.30pm Mon,

Thur-Sun. **Tickets** $79-$155. No under-5s. **Map** p335, p336 A6.

This could have been horrific, a parade of paperback writers coming together in Sgt Pepper's yellow submarine to help Jude get back, or something. Sure, Cirque du Soleil's Beatles show is a little too literal with the lyrics in places, but from its spectacular opening until its cheesy climax, *Love* is mostly great fun, packed with Cirque's trademark acrobatics and punctuated with playful humour. Oh, and the music's never sounded better.

Menopause: The Musical

Luxor *3900 Las Vegas Boulevard South, at W Hacienda Avenue, East of Strip (1-800 557 7428, 262 4400, www.luxor.com). Bus Deuce, 104, 119.* **Shows** 5.30pm Mon, Wed-Sun; 8pm Tue. **Tickets** $49.95-$65. No under-14s. **Map** p335 C5.

The *Menopause* musical juggernaut finds a home in a city known for its own frequent hot flushes. Set in the lingerie department of Bloomingdale's, *Menopause* unites not only its four stars but women everywhere who are tackling 'the change', head-on through dialogue and two dozen pop parodies. Women under 45 and men of all ages should stay as far away as possible.

Mystère

Treasure Island *3300 Las Vegas Boulevard South, at Spring Mountain Road (1-800 392 1999, 894 7722, www.treasureisland.com). Bus Deuce, 203.* **Shows** 7pm, 9.30pm Mon-Wed, Sat, Sun. **Tickets** $69-$109. **Map** p335, p336 A6.

The first Cirque du Soleil show to reach Vegas, *Mystère* holds up very well next to the more spectacular and expensive siblings that have joined it. The reason? It doesn't take itself too seriously, and plays for slapsticky laughs as much as it does for astonishment (*taiko* drumming, *bunraku* puppetry, dazzling gymnastic exhibitions). The design is showing its age a little, but otherwise, this long-runner is in rude health. As with all Cirque shows, you'd do well to arrive early, as the pre-show clowning with the audience is charming.

O

Bellagio *3600 Las Vegas Boulevard South, at W Flamingo Road (1-888 488 7111, 693 7722, www.bellagio.com). Bus Deuce, 202.* **Shows** 7.30pm, 10pm Wed-Sun. **Tickets** $93.50-$155. No under-5s. **Map** p336 A7.

It's been surpassed in the extravagance stakes by *Kà* (see *p234*), but some say this is still the best Cirque du Soleil production in town, and maybe the best show on the Strip. *O* – a pun on *eau* – is a spectacle of Fellini-esque tableaux coupled with acrobatic feats performed by 70-plus swimmers, divers, aerialists, contortionists and clowns in, on, above and around a pool/stage containing 1.5 million gallons of water. None of which goes any way towards describing just how beautiful it all is.

Phantom

Venetian *3355 Las Vegas Boulevard South, between Sands Avenue & E Flamingo Road (1-866 641 7469, 414 9000, www.venetian.com). Bus Deuce, 203.* **Shows** 7pm, 9.30pm Mon, Sat; 7pm Tue-Fri. **Tickets** $79-$184.90. No under-6s. **Map** p335, p336 B6.

One of the most beloved musicals of all time is now one of Vegas's most seductive shows. Housed in a theatre designed to evoke the show's own Paris Opera House, the abbreviated, snazzed-up *Phantom* claims to challenge the dramatic superiority of the original Lloyd Webber production. In truth, there's really nothing new to see here, but the production remains thrilling all the same.

★ Le Rêve

Wynn Las Vegas *3131 Las Vegas Boulevard South, between E Desert Inn Road & Sands Avenue (1-888 320 7110, 770 9966, www.wynn lasvegas.com). Bus Deuce, 203.* **Shows** 7pm, 9.30pm Mon, Tue, Fri-Sun. **Tickets** $99-$195. **Map** p335, p336 B6.

Named after mogul Steve Wynn's favourite Picasso painting, this big-budget spectacular features diving, acrobatics and amazing choreography, all performed in an aqua-theatre with intimate, in-the-round seating and an ever-changing circular pool that creates towering fountains and fathomless depths. With sexy, swimsuit-clad aquatic acrobat/dancers, out-of-the-box aesthetics and an independent vision (courtesy of several very public overhauls), it's pretty to watch, but it fades from memory as fast as a dream itself. But in the baking desert of the Strip, this show is like entering a pleasant humidifier for 90 minutes, and the emotionally evocative scent of chlorine is what really lingers long after the show ends.

Tony 'n' Tina's Wedding

Planet Hollywood (Miracle Mile) *3667 Las Vegas Boulevard South, West of Strip (949 6450, www.tonyandtinavegas.com). Bus Deuce, 108, 119, 202.* **Shows** 7.30pm Mon, Fri-Sun. **Tickets** $89.99-$139.99. **Map** p336 A7.

In this inventive, interactive dinner-show – sort of a live-action *Jersey Shore* – ticket-holders become wedding guests taking in the nuptials and reception of an Italian-American couple coping with comically stereotypical families, a pregnant maid of honour, a drunk priest and more. The set-up is just hokey enough to make you want to brush up on your singing and dance moves (think 'YMCA'). But once dinner is served (an Italian buffet, naturally), you'll want to hightail it like a groom on the business end of a shotgun.

Tournament of Kings

Excalibur *3850 Las Vegas Boulevard South, at W Tropicana Avenue (1-800 933 1334, 597 7600, www.excalibur.com). Bus Deuce, 119, 201.* **Shows** 6pm Mon, Wed; 6pm, 8.30pm Thur-Sun. **Tickets** $56.95 ($44.35 without dinner). **Map** p336 A8.

The phrase 'dinner and a show' takes on new meaning at this year-round indoor olde worlde fayre. Kids and those with time-period fetishes will dig the jousting knights, dancing maidens and galloping horses, as King Arthur and company recreate a bygone era with fine-tuned costumes, dialogue and mannerisms. One meal sans utensils is cool and all, but you may find you prefer to dive knife-and-fork-first into any number of casino buffets.

V: The Ultimate Variety Show

Planet Hollywood (Miracle Mile) *3667 Las Vegas Boulevard South, between E Harmon & E Flamingo Roads (1-866 932 1818, www.vthe show.com). Bus Deuce, 108, 119, 202.* **Shows** 7pm, 8.30pm daily. **Tickets** $59-$89; half-price 2-12s. **Map** p336 A7.

The V Theater features an ever-rotating array of shows during the day and evening hours, from '60s tributes and hypnotists to pole-dancing classes and pet acrobatics. And then there's *V: The Ultimate Variety Show*, which mashes them all up in a blender of comedy, magic, music, juggling and daredevil stunts. You never know who or what's going to be on the bill, but you can be assured that it will be fast-paced and family-friendly, though the action can get a little schizoid at times.

Viva Elvis

Aria at CityCenter *3730 Las Vegas Boulevard at E Harmon Avenue (1-877 253 5847, www.*

ARTS & ENTERTAINMENT

arialasvegas.com). Bus Deuce, 119, 202. **Shows** 7pm, 9.30pm Tue-Sat. **Tickets** $69-$175. **Map** p336 A8.

Elvis Presley is the subject of this Cirque du Soleil attempt at a bio-musical. The Canadian spectacle factory cherry-picked scenes from the life of the King, dipped them in cheese, deep-fried them, sprayed on a hard-candy coating and dished the whole thing up on a stick. Gimmicky, bright and loud, with a big scoop of kitsch Americana – the requisite jukeboxes, poodle skirts, finned Cadillacs – it plays like a *Grease* reunion, with an amped-up, remixed Elvis soundtrack and the usual array of uncanny acrobatics involving trampolines, wall-walkers and roller skates. Strangely, even though images and impressions of him abound, Elvis himself feels absent, save for a cinematic montage of the man and his earthy magic that renders much of the gimmickry mundane. Next up for the Cirque-itous treatment: Michael Jackson.

COMEDY CLUBS

Comics are as much a Vegas staple as magicians, showgirls and second-mortgage-inducing blackjack losses. In addition to marquee funnymen such as **Jerry Seinfeld** and **Jay Leno**, who make regular pilgrimages to Vegas's biggest showrooms, and acts such as **Rita Rudner** (*see p230*) and **George Wallace** (*see p230*), who have nightly residencies here, the city boasts a number of pretty good comedy clubs. Shows typically run for about 80 minutes and feature two or three stand-ups plus an MC.

Brad Garrett's Comedy Club

Tropicana *3801 Las Vegas Boulevard South, at E Tropicana Avenue (1-800 829 9034, www.brad garrettcomedy.com). Bus Deuce, 201.* **Shows** 8pm Mon-Thur, Sun; 8pm, 10pm Fri, Sat. **Tickets** $39-$59. **Map** p336 A8.

Formerly the Comedy Stop, this is now named for a co-star of the sitcom *Everybody Loves Raymond*, who adds a bit of star power to the 'three comics and a mic' routine at this 300-capacity room. Performers tend to be in residence for a week at a time, and there's surprisingly little repetition of acts.

Improv at Harrah's

Harrah's *3475 Las Vegas Boulevard South, between Sands Avenue & E Flamingo Road (369 5223, www.harrahslasvegas.com). Bus Deuce, 203.* **Shows** 8.30pm, 10.30pm Tue-Sun. **Tickets** $29.05-$44.95. No under-21s. **Map** p336 A6.

After more than 40 years in the funny business, the jokes here at the Improv are still pretty fresh. The comedy isn't improv at all – it's actually straightforward stand-up, delivered by a weekly-changing roster of three comics.

Louie Anderson Theater

Palace Station *2411 W Sahara Avenue, at South Rancho Drive (367 2411, www. palacestation.com). Bus Deuce, 119, 204.* **Shows** 8.30pm Tue-Sat. **Tickets** $49.95-$99.95. **Map** p336 A8.

The large and in-charge comic guarantees himself a place to perform his show, called *Louie LOL*, with his self-branded room at the downtown Palace Station. When Anderson isn't around, the club is filled with a rotating array of comics, including Marty Allen and the Bonkerz Comedy All-Stars.

Playboy Comedy

Palms *4321 W Flamingo Road, at S Valley View Boulevard, West of Strip (474 4000, www.palms.com). Bus 104, 202.* **Shows** (one weekend a mth) 8pm Thur, Fri; 8pm, 10pm Sat. **Tickets** $47-$68. No under-21s. **Map** p333 X3.

This normally dark lounge lights up one weekend a month with Playboy Comedy, studded with hip comics such as Marc Maron and other relatively well-known names you may recognise from Comedy Central, HBO or TV shows on other channels.

Riviera Comedy Club

Riviera *2901 Las Vegas Boulevard South, between E Sahara Avenue & E Desert Inn Road (1-800 634 3420, 794 9433, www.riviera hotel.com). Bus Deuce, 108, 204.* **Shows** 9pm daily. **Tickets** $24.99-$34.99. No under-18s. **Map** p335 B5.

The Riviera's comedy club does pretty much what you might expect, booking three (or sometimes four) solid acts for two shows nightly in a fairly dreary room. The line-ups change weekly.

SHOWROOMS

Many hotel-casinos have smallish showrooms that host touring productions, concerts and other special events. Prices vary by performer and location: tickets for big-name acts at Strip venues (David Copperfield at the MGM, say) will set you back around $100, while past-their-prime hitmakers can often be seen for a mere $20 or so.

The best showroom on the Strip is the **Hollywood Theatre** at the **MGM Grand** (*see p119*), a cosy, 740-seat room that regularly hosts Tom Jones, Howie Mandel and the aforementioned David Copperfield among its roster of regular guests. There are also strong selections of name-brand entertainment at theatres within several locals' casinos, chiefly the 800-seater **Orleans** (*see p148*), the larger **Sam's Town** (*see p150*) and the more intimate **Suncoast** (*see p151*). For larger venues that host big-name bands and other one-night stands, *see pp252-255* **Music**.

ARTS & ENTERTAINMENT

Elvis Hasn't Left the Building

Long live the King!

After Elvis Presley's death, Las Vegas was swamped by impersonators, who would perform on any stage, jump from aeroplanes and throw out the first pitch at ballgames. According to people who keep these sorts of statistics, there were more Elvises (Elvi?) in Nevada than in Tennessee.

Three decades after Presley went way down for the last time, he's conspicuous by his absence in Vegas. The Elvis-a-Rama museum on Industrial Road closed its doors in 2006, and most Elvis impersonators have left town. Maybe it's because the new, slicker Vegas has little use for old-fashioned rock 'n' roll. But still, although the King is no longer omnipresent, he's by no means gone.

Pete Vallee is the biggest Elvis impersonator in Las Vegas. Literally. Revelling in the self-explanatory stage name of **Big Elvis**, the once-obese singer, who recently lost weight, performs sweat-soaked shows more or less daily in the lounge at Bill's Gambling Hall & Saloon (*see p125*). Pretending to be neither the young nor the old Presley, Vallee had – until his recent weight loss – been more like the Ghost of Elvis Future, assuming the King had continued to wolf down fried banana sandwiches at the same rate for the next 35 years.

The city's flashiest Elvis is **Trent Carlini**, who fashions himself after the younger, thinner Elvis, but with a generous amount of Vegas-style rhinestones. The show, at the Las Vegas Hilton (*see p134*), covers the music from Presley's rockabilly beginnings in the 1950s to the comeback songs of the late '60s.

But the biggest tribute in town has to be **Viva Elvis** (*see p235*), Cirque du Soleil's gimmicky and gaudy take on the life of the King, set amid the expected acrobatics, wall walkers and skaters – as well as a big spoonful of '50s kitsch Americana. But fans may find little of the real Elvis in the show. At the time of writing the show was taking a break for some tweaking.

True Elvis fans, meanwhile, can live out the ultimate fantasy and have the King consecrate their marriage. The **Viva Las Vegas** (*see p275*) and **Graceland** wedding chapels (*see p273*) both offer Elvis packages that include low-key performances, *Blue Hawaii* themes and, sometimes, commemorative T-shirts. Remember: the more you pay, the younger and thinner your Elvis will be. You'll also have to pay extra for one who actually performs the ceremony, and doesn't just show up with a boombox to belt out a couple of songs.

ARTS & ENTERTAINMENT

Viva Elvis.

Children

Vegas is no Disneyland, but there's still a world of magic out there.

The rebranding of Treasure Island says a lot about the target audience for 21st-century Las Vegas. The resort spent a lot of money sexing up its wholesome past as the family-friendly Treasure Island; in the process, it got rid of the free pirate show, a must-see back in the family-oriented days of the '90s. Oh, there's still a show, and it's still free, but the stars are now the scantily clad, silicone-enhanced Sirens of TI. Like most Las Vegas attractions today, kids might enjoy the show, but it's not designed with their enjoyment in mind.

ARTS & ENTERTAINMENT

CHILD-FRIENDLY ENTERTAINMENT

Although Vegas has focused on entertaining adults of late, where there's a gap in the market, someone in Las Vegas will be only too happy to fill it, which is why there are still plenty of child-friendly amusements in the city. Video arcades and rollercoasters line the Strip; and even without Siegfried & Roy, animals remain perhaps the ultimate all-ages crowd-pleaser. Most of the major shopping malls offer an array of amusements alongside the stores. And in the showrooms, the old staples – magicians, impersonators and variety acts – still thrive. With Cirque du Soleil alone now offering seven different shows (though one of them, *Zumanity,* is unsuitable for kids; another, Criss Angel's magic act, is too loud and potentially frightening), there's no shortage of entertainment options.

A free outdoor Strip show that's more suitable for youngsters than the Sirens of TI is the reimagined volcano at the nearby **Mirage** (*see p110*), designed by the fire-and-water techno-magicians that created the

Bellagio fountains. Set to a heart-pounding worldbeat score by former Grateful Dead drummer Mickey Hart, the Mirage's magic mountain blows its fiery top every night at 8pm and does it all over again every hour on the hour until midnight.

There's also plenty of choice if you want to take in a movie or go bowling, especially if you're prepared to leave the Strip. Las Vegas has more bowling lanes per capita than any place on earth, and they all seem to have the latest high-tech stuff and gimmicks (cosmic bowling, anyone?). Even the upscale Red Rock Casino has a 72-lane centre. And for something completely different, try the **Las Vegas Springs Preserve** (*see p240* **Going Green**), a 180-acre eco-park.

THE LAW

State law forbids under-21s from lingering on casino floors. Children are allowed to pass through casino areas when accompanied by an adult, but they cannot stay by any of the gaming tables or machines. If they do, a security guard is likely to ask them – politely, but firmly – to leave the casino. Parents are not permitted to bet when they have youngsters in tow.

A Clark County curfew dictates that unaccompanied under-18s are not allowed on the Strip after 9pm on weekends and holidays. Off the Strip, the curfew is 10pm, or midnight on Fridays and Saturdays and during school holidays. Teenagers have the roughest time because, until they're 21, they can't go into bars, nor most clubs or showrooms.

THE BEST KIDS' STUFF

For earth
Las Vegas Springs Preserve. *See p240.*

For wind
Rides at the **Stratosphere**. *see p239.*

For fire
The volcano at the **Mirage**. *See above.*

WHERE TO STAY

Many hotel-casinos on the Strip have an arcade and/or a cinema to help keep kids entertained. That said, some resorts are more family-friendly than others: the best are **Circus Circus** (*see p126*), **Excalibur** (*see p127*), the **Luxor** (*see p118*) and **Mandalay Bay** (*see p109*), all of which are owned by MGM Mirage. The **Monte Carlo** (*see p121*) is a good, lower-priced option, while **New York New York** (*see p122*) gets a gold star for its efforts to keep the kids happy. The gambling-free **Four Seasons Las Vegas** (*see p131*) doesn't offer flashy entertainments, but the service is child-friendly, and the hotel is attached to the attraction-filled Mandalay Bay.

Off the Strip, the **Stratosphere** (*see p129*) and **Palms** (*see p135*) have good childcare facilities, as do a number of the locals' casinos, particularly **Boulder Station** (*see p149*), **Santa Fe Station** (*see p151*), **Sunset Station** (*see p151*) and **Texas Station** (*see p152*). Out at the **Loews Lake Las Vegas** (*see p152*), great family amenities include water activities and a special kids' programme. For more on the city's accommodation, *see pp98-152*.

EATING & DRINKING

As in most towns, the best family restaurants are heavily themed and often quite loud. The **Rainforest Café** in the MGM Grand (*see p119*; 891 8580, www.rainforestcafe.com, open 8am-11pm Mon-Thur & Sun, 8am-midnight Fri & Sat) is filled with fake foliage, life-size robotic animals and large aquariums with (real) fish. There's even the odd 'thunderstorm'. Sports fans will enjoy the **ESPN Zone** at New York New York (*see p122*), with fun food and a cool arcade.

SIGHTSEEING

Animal & water attractions

The off-Strip **Southern Nevada Zoological Park** (*see p93*) is too far out for many visitors. However, if you combined the numerous animal habitats along the Strip, you'd have a pretty good menagerie, albeit one that's rather old-fashioned and not very politically correct.

Siegfried & Roy may not perform any more, but the duo's **Secret Garden** is still open for business at the Mirage (*see p110*). Check out the lions, the tigers and the playful Asian elephant, before adjourning to the **Dolphin Habitat**. There are more big cats over at the MGM Grand's slight but satisfying **Lion Habitat** (*see p70*). Even if the lions are asleep, they'll probably be lying on top of a glass tunnel through which you can walk

Adventuredome. *See p240.*

for a closer look. Wait at both spots to see the animals being fed and handled by the staff. But the best animal attraction is Mandalay Bay's **Shark Reef** (*see p71*): it features more than 75 species of fish and reptiles. At the touch pool, kids can get their hands wet touching sharks, rays and horseshoe crabs.

Over at the Mystic Falls Park at **Sam's Town** (*see p150*), a four-times-daily laser and water show, **Sunset Stampede**, tells the story of the Western pioneer experience.

ARTS & ENTERTAINMENT

Going Green

Vegas? The environment? Las Vegas Springs Preserve brings them together.

Down on the Strip, there are resorts devoted to New York City, Venice and Paris, to Italian luxury and Egyptian history, to the circus, to Hollywood and even to medieval England. However, a few miles north-west, Las Vegas's newest attraction boasts a rather different theme to any of its high-profile neighbours. How do geology, green issues and desert history grab you?

The $250-million, 180-acre **Las Vegas Springs Preserve** (for listings, *see p92*) attempts to educate visitors about how best to live on this troubled planet. As you park under a canopy topped by photovoltaic cells (capturing solar energy) and walk down a path that's shaded by an undulating roof of corrugated steel (representing flowing water), you'll start to realise that this is no typical Vegas attraction. However, it's far from the earnest, desert-dry enterprise you might expect. The creators promise that all its educational medicine will go down with a nice big spoonful of sugar.

The many cool presentations include a flash-flood experience: in a cave-like room, you'll stand on a rock above a gully as a rainstorm causes a raging torrent around you. Your kids can also pretend to be 1930s dam workers, riding perilously high on a

pulley cart (thanks to a large-scale diorama). Outside, there's a life-size Anasazi pit house (the ancients knew a thing or two about sustainable homebuilding), a Pullman train car, a lizard pit and a bat cave.

Down a path is the Desert Living Center, an incarnation of the concept of 'green' living. One of its core exhibits, Inside Out, shows visitors the sustainable secrets of several buildings, from a cut-out showing straw-bale wall insulation to roofing rigged for catching rainwater. Across the way, the Sustainability Gallery offers an array of interactive exhibits and demonstrations of recycling, conservation and alternative energy. While Dad finds out how a Toyota Prius runs so efficiently, the kids can crawl on a rubber compost pile.

Other attractions include the Botanical Gardens; a children's playground with a mini-amphitheatre surrounded by concrete terrain featuring peepholes, crawl spaces and a giant snake; and trails that take you through Las Vegas at its most natural desert state. Perhaps the kids will appreciate the constructive irony that, in the land of glitz and excess, sustainability is the central theme of the attraction. Or perhaps they'll just enjoy a fun day out.

Arcades & rides

Most major casinos have games arcades. Some consist of little more than a room with a dozen old video games, but others boast superlative arcades and even fairground attractions. Those at both the **Excalibur** (on the Fantasy Faire level; *see p127*) and **Circus Circus** (where the games surround a central ring with circus acts; *see p126*) are decent, but the best are the **Coney Island Emporium** (*see p70*) at New York New York, the **Games of the Gods** arcade at the Luxor (*see p118*) and, especially, the non-casino **GameWorks** (*see p72*) in the Showcase Mall.

Of the clutch of theme parks in the city, the indoor **Adventuredome** (*see p78*) at Circus Circus rules the roost, yet it's never so busy that you'll spend the bulk of your time in queues. The Canyon Blaster is a short but furious double-loop, double-corkscrew rollercoaster; other exciting rides include the head-rushing Inverter and the Rim Runner water flume (yes, you will get wet). There are half a dozen low-intensity rides for the

little ones, plus carnival games, miniature golf and the Xtreme Zone, where you can test your mettle with rock climbing and bungee jumping.

Other rides in town range from the ridiculous to the heart-stoppingly thrilling. Arguably the most harrowing is the **Manhattan Express** rollercoaster (*see p71*), which twists and loops through New York New York. Further north is the Stratosphere, which hosts three monstrous thrill rides some 1,000 feet (300 metres) above the Strip: **X Scream**, the **Big Shot** and **Insanity: the Ride** (for all, *see p78*).

The **Forum Shops** (*see p194*) at Caesars Palace has free animatronic shows in the mall – the 'ancient" statues come to life – and an IMAX 3-D ride called Race For Atlantis. Off the Strip, the **Las Vegas Mini Gran Prix** (1401 N Rainbow Boulevard, at US 95, 259 7000, www.lvmgp.com) features an indoor arcade, a miniature rollercoaster and four go-karting tracks, where the size and speed of the vehicles match the increasing age and skill of the young drivers. Height and weather restrictions apply for many thrill rides in Las Vegas.

Educational attractions

Aside from the **Las Vegas Springs Preserve** (*see left* **Vegas Goes Green**), there's the **Lied Discovery Children's Museum** (*see p88*), tilted, as the name implies, at kids.

Parks

Sunset Park (E Sunset Road & S Eastern Avenue), **Lorenzi Park** (W Washington Avenue & N Rancho Drive) and **Floyd Lamb State Park** (Tule Springs Road, off US 95 north of Las Vegas) are a trio of large, grassy parks with lakes and volleyball courts; Sunset and Lorenzi Parks also have tennis facilities. For details on all parks, call 455 8200.

ARTS & ENTERTAINMENT

Aside from the stand-alone **UA Showcase 8** (*see p244*) movie theatre on the Strip, many off-Strip casinos have in-house cinemas, with those at the **Orleans** (*see p148*) and the **Palms** (*see p147*) closest to the Strip. Many of the Station casinos have movie theatres; **Sam's Town**, another locals' casino, counts an 18-screen multiplex among its selling points.

Most shows on the Strip are adult-oriented, whether in terms of explicit content or complex themes; tickets for those that are suitable for children, such as Cirque du Soleil's original, fabulous *Mystère* (*see p234*), exotic, aquatic *O* (*see p235*) and Beatles-themed *Love* (*see p234*), can cost more than $100. However, there are some bargains: comedy magician Mac King (*see p230*) produces the expected rabbits and doves – and unexpected laughs – in his shows, which have cross-generational appeal and are conveniently staged in the afternoons.

DIRECTORY
Babysitting & children's supplies

Several agencies in Las Vegas offer licensed babysitters who have been cleared through the sheriff's department and by the FBI. Every hotel worth its salt can arrange babysitting services; many even offer on-site babysitters. Many hotels can also arrange the delivery of children's supplies (strollers, cots, car seats, even video games); if yours can't, try **Baby's Away** (1-800 560 9141, 458 1019, www.babysaway.com).

Nurseries & activity centres

Although few of the large Strip resorts have nurseries, many of the town's neighbourhood hotel-casinos do run some kind of childcare centre. Most such operations require written consent from the parents and may ask you to leave valid ID; they may also insist that the child is potty trained and no longer in nappies. Most centres have a three-hour time limit; only the person who drops off the children can collect them. You don't have to be an overnight guest at the hotel, but you do have to remain on the premises while your child is in the nursery.

In addition to **Kids Quest** (*see below*), the **Kids Tyme** facilities at the Orleans (*see p148*) and the Suncoast (*see p151*) have licensed supervisors to entertain kids with movies, toys and crafts. Each has a five-hour limit.

Kids Quest

Various locations. **Open** *Summer* 9am-midnight Mon-Thur; 9am-1am Fri-Sun. *Winter* 9am-11pm Mon-Thur, Sun; 9am-1am Fri, Sat. **Rates** $6-$8/hr. Kids Quest has all manner of attractions, including a Barbie area, a big cliff and jungle area and, of course, computer games. Kids aged from six weeks to 12 years can be dropped off for up to three and a half hours, but parents must remain on site. Kids Quests are located at Santa Fe and Sunset (for both, *see p151*), Boulder (*see p149)* and Texas Stations (*see p152*), as well as at the Palms (*see p135*) and the Red Rock (*see p147*).

TRIPS OUT OF TOWN

Don't miss the assortment of natural and man-made attractions just outside town. **Hoover Dam**, **Valley of Fire State Park**, **Red Rock Canyon** and **Bonnie Springs/Old Nevada** are all great for exploring with children (for all, *see p278-284*). Further afield, children love the Desperado rollercoaster and other rides at Buffalo Bill's resort in **Primm**.

Sam's Town. See p239.

Film

The big picture.

With Las Vegas slowly but surely attaining the status of an honorary suburb of LA, it was only a matter of time before the city immersed itself completely in the glitzy twin worlds of film and fame. In the past, Vegas occasionally served as a location for movies, many of them iconic. But in the last decade, with its popularity speedily soaring among the Hollywood jet set, the city has found itself creeping into more and more feature films and TV shows – reality shows in particular – its instantly recognisable profile rising even faster than the condo towers on Las Vegas Boulevard.

For moviemakers, Vegas is now more attractive than it has ever been. But for moviegoers, it's a different story. Although the city is based on alluring distractions, and cinema is hardly its top priority, it's not hard to find the big-ticket Hollywood blockbusters in one of the city's enormous multiplexes, most of which are housed in off-Strip casinos. But of these, only Cinemark's **Century Suncoast 16** has shown any commitment to non-mainstream fare, leaving the non-casino-tied **Regal Village Square 18** as Vegas's independent/foreign cinema destination.

That said, inroads are being made. The city's cinematic calendar is pepped up by a variety of movie-related events, from one-night marathons to the **CineVegas Film Festival**. The festival typically runs for about nine days in mid June, but it took an economy-related break in 2010; check its website (www.cine vegas.com) for information on future festivals. Past festivals have seen such Vegas-y events as a 'dive-in' night-time screening of The Beatles' *Yellow Submarine* at the Mandalay Bay resort swimming pool. The fad of 'red carpet' publicity events has taken firm root in Las Vegas, which brings the stars of screen to town for, if not premières, at least photo opportunities, which the public can watch for free.

INFORMATION AND TICKETS

The *Las Vegas Review-Journal's* Friday 'Neon' supplement, and the free alt-weeklies *CityLife* and *Las Vegas Weekly* all provide cinema schedule information. On your mobile phone, the Fandango app is a godsend; you can also call **MovieFone** (222 3456); knowing your zip code beforehand will help you select the closest multiplex. Online, head to http://lasvegas.mr movietimes.com for details of what's on.

Tickets can be bought from box offices, or by phone and online through **Fandango** (1-800 326 3264, www.fandango.com).

MOVIE THEATRES

A score of movie houses populate the Vegas Valley. Those listed here are among the most notable and/or accessible.

Visitors after a break from the Hollywood norm have a handful of options in addition to those detailed below. The **Winchester Cultural Center** (3130 S McLeod Drive, East Las Vegas, 455 7340, www.clarkcountynv.gov) and the **Charleston Heights Arts Center Theater** (800 S Brush Street, North-west Las Vegas, 229 6383, www.artslasvegas.org) both showcase left-of-centre cinema, with themed monthly series throughout the year. Meanwhile, the **Clark County Library** serves as Las Vegas's de facto revival movie house.

★ Brenden Las Vegas 14

Palms *4321 W Flamingo Road, at S Valley View Boulevard, West of Strip (507 4849, www.brenden theatres.com). Bus 202.* **Tickets** *Regular screens* $10.50; $7 reductions; $8 before 6pm. *Screenings* 3D $3.50 extra. *IMAX* $16.50; $13.50 reductions, and before 6pm. **Map** p333 X3.

Countless consumer awards and regular high-profile premières pay tribute to the Brenden Palms' central role in the Vegas movie-going experience. With the exception of June's CineVegas Film Festival, block-busters dominate, with one major feature usually configured for the sole IMAX screen.

Set in Vegas

The Strip on celluloid.

Using Las Vegas as a backdrop for film productions is a risky manoeuvre, owing to the city's proclivity for upstaging nearly every actor who tries to stand in front of it. Practically everyone knows what the town looks like, not to mention what kind of story to expect when a movie opens, as so many have, with an aerial shot of the Strip. Perhaps because of Las Vegas's star quality, the city's grand mythos is slowly being whittled down to a handful of visual clichés: lines of showgirls mid-kick, slot machines disgorging fountains of coins, disembodied hands sweeping cards off blackjack tables. Reality TV shows, for this exact reason, love the city as a backdrop, and the anything-you-need convenience of the massive resort hotels makes for easy and cheap mass production of celebrity chef competitions and serial-dating contests.

The newest wave of Las Vegas-set movies hit screens in the late 2000s, and *What Happens in Vegas*, *21* and *The Hangover* indicated the demographic shift away from Rat Pack nostalgia to a younger, more casual, club-hopping crowd.

Made in 1960, **Ocean's 11** defined Vegas as metonymic of a particular cultural epoch. Its five Rat Packers are practically golden as they hustle their way through a five-casino heist without breaking a sweat. The effect that the film had on every heist movie that followed is indisputable, but it also started a long and fruitful cinematic streak for Vegas.

Some Sin City films, such as Elvis Presley's **Viva Las Vegas** (1963), were vehicles for performers. Others placed unlikely characters in the Vegas mix, such as Sean Connery's ageing Bond in **Diamonds Are Forever** (1971). The latter, a lesser chapter in Hunter's Bond tenure but one of the best Vegas films, played fast and loose with Howard Hughes (named 'Willard Whyte' for the film), while also presenting the town in a glamorous light that hasn't dimmed in the three decades since.

Martin Scorsese's **Casino** (1995) manages to perfectly evoke the same period in Vegas's history. It's a fictionalised account of the life of Frank 'Lefty' Rosenthal (Sam 'Ace' Rothstein in the film), one of the most colourful Vegas figures alleged to have been involved in organised crime. Rosenthal's attorney, a man who also represented Tony 'The Ant' Spilotro and Meyer Lansky, was asked by Scorsese to reprise his role for the film. The attorney, one Oscar Goodman, readily agreed; five years on, he became Mayor Goodman; he was recently succeeded in the post by his wife, Carolyn Goodman.

Las Vegas's most famous cinematic wipeout is Paul Verhoeven's **Showgirls** (1995). Filmed in part at Cheetahs, though the interiors were shot at the San Diego branch of the club, the movie is the anti-*Ocean's 11*; if the Sinatra film is Vegas in a sharp suit, *Showgirls* is the city in a filthy raincoat. Yet even the Vegas of *Showgirls* has a strange cinematic appeal; the film has developed a cult following in recent times. To experience the endangered species of camp extravaganzas that *Showgirls* celebrates, visit the topless revue *Jubilee!* at Bally's casino on the Strip – they actually sink the *Titanic* on stage.

Other movies have approached Vegas in more general terms. Tim Burton managed to get some spectacular footage in **Mars Attacks!** (1996), including the real-life destruction of the saucer-topped Landmark Hotel. **Honeymoon in Vegas** (1992), while only mildly funny, did offer viewers the Flying Elvis troupe, performing a heroic parachute drop in front of Bally's. Three years later, star Nicolas Cage returned to the city in **Leaving Las Vegas**, playing failed screenwriter Ben Sanderson, who proceeded to drink himself to death. Doug Liman's **Swingers** (1996) almost single-handedly revived swing music and Vegas culture; even people who haven't seen the movie have been known to utter its rallying cry: 'Vegas, baby. Vegas!' And in 1998, Terry Gilliam's funny, fever-dream interpretation of Hunter S Thompson's **Fear and Loathing in Las Vegas** had its own kind of swing, the kind one gets after chasing Elvis-sized fistfuls of painkillers with a swig of rum.

But perhaps most significant was Steven Soderbergh's 2001 re-creation of **Ocean's Eleven**. Opening with thrilling aerial shots of the city and closing with a dialogue-free sequence set against the Bellagio fountains, the film expresses the romance that Las Vegas effuses on its best days. You truly believe that somehow you could win your way into the kind of life you've seen in the movies.

ARTS & ENTERTAINMENT

Century Orleans 18

Orleans *4500 W Tropicana Avenue, between S Decatur & S Valley View boulevards, West of Strip (227 3456, 889 1220, www.cinemark.com). Bus 103, 104, 201.* **Tickets** *$10; $7 reductions; $8 before 6pm. 3D screenings $13.25; $11.25 before 6pm.* **Map** *p333 X3.*

This 18-screener at the Orleans ushered Las Vegas into the multiplex era with such amenities as stadium seating and THX-equipped auditoria. Although it isn't as chic as its chief competitor, the nearby Brenden Las Vegas 14 at the Palms (*see p242*), it has remained one of the valley's most loved movie theatres. Every so often, the roster includes a major studio-sanctioned art flick.

Century Suncoast 16

Suncoast *9090 Alta Drive, at N Rampart Boulevard, North-west Las Vegas (869 1880, www.cinemark.com). Bus 207.* **Tickets** *$10; $8.50 before 6pm.*

The 16-screen theatre at the Suncoast is a popular choice among Summerlin residents, while Vegas cineastes willing to make the trek also enjoy the CineArts series, which includes anywhere from one to three independent and foreign films. Cinemark also runs a number of other movie theatres in the city, all based in casinos and all specialising in mainstream fare. Among them are the Century 18 Sam's Town (547 1732), the Century Stadium 16 Rancho Santa Fe (645 5518) and the Century 16 South Point (260 4061). For all, *see venue index.*

UA Showcase 8.

Regal Cinemas

Boulder Station 11 *4111 Boulder Highway, at E Desert Inn Road, East Las Vegas. Bus 107, 213.*
Colonnade 14 *8880 S Eastern Avenue, at E Pebble Road, Green Valley. Bus 110.*
Green Valley Ranch 10 *2300 Paseo Verde Drive, at S Green Valley Parkway, Henderson. Bus 111.*
Red Rock Resort 16 *11011 W Charleston Boulevard, at I-215, West Las Vegas. Bus 206.*
Sunset Station 13 *1301-A W Sunset Road, between N Stephanie Street & I-515, Henderson. Bus 212, 402.*
Texas Station 18 *2101 N Texas Star Lane, at N Rancho Drive, between Lake Mead Boulevard & Vegas Drive, North Las Vegas. Bus 103, 106, 210, 211.*
Village Square 18 *9400 W Sahara Avenue, at S Fort Apache Road, North-west Las Vegas. Bus 204.*
All venues *221 2283, www.regmovies.com.* **Admission** *$10.75; $7-$10.50 reductions; $8 matinée. Additional fees for 3D screenings.*

The Regal cineplexes are among the busiest in town: partly due to their locations in the popular Station Casinos, but also thanks to the variety of programming. The best by far is the cinephile-favoured Village Square 18-screener, which shows as many as five non-mainstream films (plus concert simulcasts) at any given time. The Red Rock location is the city's newest.

UA Showcase 8

Showcase Mall, 3769 Las Vegas Boulevard South, at W Tropicana Avenue (221 2283, www.reg movies.com). Bus Deuce, 201 113, 215, 501. **Admission** *$10.75; $7 reductions; $8 matinée. Additional fees for 3D screenings.* **Map** *p336 A8.*

You can catch the latest blockbuster at the only movie theatre on the Strip, but don't expect lots of locals, nor any great luxury or cutting-edge cinema technology at this ageing multiplex just north of the MGM Grand. Parking in the Showcase garage is free with validation; if, that is, you can get past the parking lot that is Las Vegas Boulevard.

West Wind Las Vegas 5 Drive-In

4150 W Carey Avenue, at N Rancho Drive, North-west Las Vegas (646 3565). **Tickets** *$6.50 per person; $1 children; $4.50 Tue.* **No credit cards.**

This 50-year-old institution has survived several changes in ownership and the increasing popularity of indoor multiplexes, leaving it as Vegas's only remaining drive-in. It's ideal for traditionalists and cheapskates who favour bringing their own drinks and snacks, though lights emanating from the surrounding sprawl have affected visibility. Five screens offer double features of current releases; sound is available through your FM radio.

ARTS & ENTERTAINMENT

Galleries

Yes, there is art in Sin City.

Let's face it: the majority of Las Vegas-bound travellers did not choose the city for its plethora of cultural attractions. Yet the self-proclaimed entertainment capital of the world does have a lively visual-arts scene, concentrated for the most part in the Arts District towards the southern edge of Downtown. The economic crisis of recent years made art – and the art market – a low priority in this money-dominated desert city, and the arts scene took several critical blows with the loss of the esteemed Las Vegas Art Museum, the Venetian's franchise of the Guggenheim Hermitage Museum, and several prominent taste-making galleries, including Dust and Michele Quinn's G-C Arts. The arrival of the **Emergency Arts Center**, a collective gallery space carved from an unused medical building, revived the pulse of arts enterprise, but it, too, is in critical condition.

ARTS & ENTERTAINMENT

THE ART SCENE

The most prominent hub of activity in the Arts District is the **Arts Factory**, a collection of studios and gallery spaces at the intersection of Charleston and Casino Center boulevards. The **Holsum Lofts** (at Charleston Boulevard and Grand Central Parkway) is home to shops and galleries; due south, the **Commerce Street Studios** (at Commerce Street and Wyoming Avenue) holds 11 studio spaces. One focus of the Arts District's cultural activity is **First Friday** (*see p219*), a monthly event that draws thousands of revellers – locals, mainly – to the area.

Beyond First Fridays, Las Vegas offers a handful of artistic experiences that you won't find in any other metropolis. Take, for example, the reservation-only **Neon Boneyard**, a three-acre dirt lot in which massive, defunct neon signs spend their limbo, awaiting resurrection as refurbished artefacts of the city's bygone years. Or visit the **Bellagio Gallery of Fine Art** and experience a true culture clash: clanging slot machines one minute and an urbane exhibition of master works of art the next.

Indeed, fine art is a serious part of hotel design in contemporary Las Vegas, a trend that has supplanted the 1990s era of fancifully themed hotels. Public art was one of the fundamental concepts uniting the architects of the massive new **CityCenter** resort-condo-casino complex), which features sculptures by Henry Moore, Maya Lin and Claes Oldenburg, and surprising artistic and artisanal touches throughout all the buildings: the Jenny Holzer light installation in the parking area of the **Aria** casino (3730 Las Vegas Boulevard, 1-866 359 7757, www.arialasvegas.com) has been known to shock some patrons with its moral admonitions. Elsewhere, the blue-chip decor of **Thehotel at Mandalay Bay** (*see p131*) includes a massive Arturo Herrera painting behind the front desk, while the serious modern collection that spruces up the **Red Rock** (*see p147*) includes works by the likes of Takashi Murakami and Robert Indiana.

GALLERIES & ART MUSEUMS

In addition to the galleries listed, space inside the **Funk House** antiques shop (*see p212*) is also dedicated to art by local artists. And don't

---

THE BEST GALLERIES

For emerging artists
Donna Beam Fine Art Gallery. See p246.

Vegas's artistic heartbeat
Emergency Arts Center. See p247.

For affordable art
Trifecta Gallery. See p247.

Trifecta Gallery.

forget the **Neon Boneyard**, open for tours by appointment (*see p86* **A Paean to Neon**).

Bellagio Gallery of Fine Art
Bellagio *3600 Las Vegas Boulevard South, at W Flamingo Road (693 7871, www.bellagio.com). Bus Deuce, 202.* **Open** 10am-6pm Mon, Tue, Thur, Sun; 10am-7pm Wed, Fri, Sat. **Admission** $15; $12 reductions. **Credit** AmEx, DC, Disc, MC, V. **Map** p336 A7.
The longest-standing gallery on the Strip stages a strong selection of shows; they're here on a temporary basis, but the last three have been in residence for a year apiece. Following a wildly popular and meaty Monet exhibition leased from the Museum of Fine Arts, Boston, another Impressionism show and an exhibition of Ansel Adams photographs, the gallery launched a show devoted to Picasso's ceramics.

City of Las Vegas Galleries
Bridge Gallery *2nd Floor, City Hall, 400 E Stewart Avenue, at Las Vegas Boulevard South (229 6383). Bus Deuce & all DTC-bound buses.* **Map** p334 D1.
Charleston Heights Art Center *800 S Brush Street, between W Charleston Boulevard & Evergreen Avenue, North-west Las Vegas (229 6383). Bus 103, 206, 207.*
Reed Whipple Cultural Center *821 Las Vegas Boulevard North, at E Washington Avenue, North Las Vegas (229 6211). Bus 113.* **Map** p334 D1.
West Las Vegas Art Center *947 W Lake Mead Boulevard, between I-15 & N Martin Luther King Boulevard, West Las Vegas (229 4800).* **All** *www.artslasvegas.org.* **Open** *Bridge Gallery* 8am-5pm Mon-Fri; *Others* 11am-9pm Tue-Fri; 10am-6pm Sat, Sun.
The City of Las Vegas puts a great deal of thought into the shows it exhibits in its municipal galleries. All four spaces offer satisfying exhibits by serious artists from across the US, many of whom demonstrate a decidedly academic bent. The West Las Vegas Art Center stages shows by and for the largely African-American community in the neighbourhood. Artists without local representation who show at Reed Whipple will sometimes sell work at a big discount owing to the space's non-profit status.

Donna Beam Fine Art Gallery
Alta Ham Fine Arts Building, UNLV, 4505 S Maryland Parkway, between E Flamingo Road & E Tropicana Avenue, University District (895 3893, http://finearts.unlv.edu/galleries). Bus 109, 201. **Open** 9am-5pm Mon-Fri; 10am-2pm Sat. **Map** p333 Y3.
A bit tricky to find, this gallery is best visited on a weekday, when you're sure to run into an art student who can point you towards it. During the academic year (Sept-May), it hosts work by students and faculty of UNLV's fine-art programme, along with the occasional travelling exhibit.

Paint to the Rhythm

Local artist Tim Bavington translates songs into paintings.

Tim Bavington.

As Las Vegas continues to develop the kind of sophisticated art scene one would expect to find in a metropolitan area of nearly two million people, several locally based artists are making names for themselves, and the city, elsewhere around the world. One of them is Tim Bavington.

Bavington was born in London but transplanted to the US in his teens. His career began to bloom when he fell under the tutelage of prominent art critic and curator Dave Hickey at UNLV in the late 1990s. Since then, his work has struck a chord – literally and figuratively – with art enthusiasts who share his affinity for rock 'n' roll. Bavington has landed on a visual riff that allows him to translate popular rock tunes into paintings, with notes assigned a hue and a width. The resultant brilliantly coloured stripe paintings have been compared to those of Gene Davis and others, but are arguably much more fun.

Although Bavington lives in a mid-century modern house in Downtown and works out of a spacious studio in the industrial district just west of the Strip, he rarely shows in Las Vegas. The late, lamented G-C Arts had a show in 2006, one painting hangs along a restaurant-and-retail corridor at Wynn Las Vegas, and there's another at Spago (*see p165*) in the Forum Shops. But after sold-out gallery shows in Los Angeles, New York, London and Paris, and the acquisition of one of his works by the Museum of Modern Art in New York, Bavington has as good a chance as any top contemporary artist today of becoming a household name.

ARTS & ENTERTAINMENT

★ Emergency Arts Center
520 Fremont Street, at 6th Street, Downtown (www.emergencyartslv.com). Bus Deuce, 105, 108, 206. **Open** noon-5pm, 7pm-midnight Mon; noon-5pm Tue, Thur; noon-8pm Wed; noon-5pm, 6-9pm Fri; 10am-1pm Sat. **Map** p334 D2.
After the Las Vegas Art Museum closed its doors due to the brutal economy, the Vegas arts scene seemed to go on life support. Here to save the day is the Emergency Arts Center, which has carved a collective of 35 gallery spaces from an old two-storey medical building across from the El Cortez hotel and casino. It not only resuscitated the scene, but now provides the area's art heartbeat.

S2 Art Group Atelier
1 E Charleston Boulevard, at S Main Street, Downtown (868 7880, www.s2art.com). Bus Deuce, 108, 206. **Open** 9am-5pm Mon-Fri. **Map** p335 C3.
S2 reproduces fine-art lithographs and sells them at various venues, among them the three Jack Gallery locations at Mandalay Bay, the Venetian and the Fashion Show Mall. The 19th-century French and German presses turn out reproductions of posters by Mucha and Toulouse-Lautrec, vintage film ads and other old favourites, as well as contemporary works. Visitors can watch the presses while touring the large selection of prints.

Trifecta Gallery
Arts Factory, 107 E Charleston Boulevard, #135, between S Main Street & Casino Center Boulevard, Downtown (366 7001, www.trifecta gallery.com). Bus Deuce, 108, 206. **Open** 11am-5pm Mon-Fri (until 10pm 1st Fri of mth); 11am-3pm Sat, Sun. **Map** p335 C3.
Tiny Trifecta is the labour of love of Las Vegas artist Marty Walsh, whose masterful, nostalgic paintings memorialise mid-century modern appliances and other artefacts. She also has an ingenious curatorial eye, and alternates showings of her own work with pieces by talented emerging painters. With many of the shows held here regularly selling out, Trifecta is the perfect place for serious art collectors on a budget.

Gay & Lesbian

Vegas is coming out with a vengeance.

You'd be forgiven for thinking that the original Sin City would be a natural playground for gays. After all, what other city in America can claim such a judgement-free, libertarian attitude, especially when it comes to late-night revelry? However, for years, the opposite has been the case. It's hard to say who has squandered the potential of Las Vegas's LGBT community more: the city itself or its own homosexual populace. The city missed a lucrative opportunity when Nevada declined to legalise gay marriage; it's now going to have to play catch-up with New York as a gay wedding destination. Nevertheless, the scene has been coming out with a vengeance recently, and visitors have been the main beneficiaries. Showrooms now lean heavily on Broadway spectacles, and hotels such as **Wynn** (*see p114*) and **Paris Las Vegas** (*see p111*) have recently made concerted efforts to market themselves to the international gay community.

THE GAY SCENE

The Strip is home to **Krave** (*see p250*), the town's first gay megaclub; the **Blue Moon Resort** (2651 Westwood Drive, 784 4500, www.bluemoonlv.com), a gay-oriented lodge with swimming pool, spa services and other amenities, is a fun and friendly place to meet other men visiting Vegas.

The local scene is also starting to look up, if gradually. The majority of gay venues reside in two dominant LGBT hubs where tourists and locals mingle freely: the so-called **Fruit Loop**, the streets around the intersection of Paradise Road and E Harmon Avenue, and **Commercial Center**, up on Sahara Avenue. Gay bars dot the valley, from old stagers such as **Snick's Place** to newer venues such as **Piranha**. The city's springtime **Pride** event has grown enough to take over Downtown for a weekend. Unlike most US cities, which hold their Pride in midsummer, Vegas tries to avoid the blasting heat with an earlier parade and indoor festival.

LESBIAN LAS VEGAS

There aren't any lesbian bars in Vegas, and women make up a very small constituent of the city's gay nightlife. However, gay bars – and even some casinos – are devoting an increasing number of nights to female-tilted events. **FreeZone** (*see p250*), the town's

unofficial lesbian hangout, throws the popular Lick Her Bust party every Tuesday; **8½** (*see p251*) welcomes the ladies to Orchid on Wednesdays; and **Krave** holds the LA-originated GirlBar event every Saturday in its lounge. Alternatively, **Betty's Outrageous Adventures** (991 9929, www.bettysout.com) is a social group that brings lesbians together for everything from movie nights to camping trips. Most events are all-inclusive, though some are women-only.

BARS

As well as the gay bars below, a few places self-identify as 'alternative', essentially proclaiming themselves as gay-friendly operations.

Backdoor Lounge

1415 E Charleston Boulevard, at S 15th Street, Downtown (385 2018). Bus 206. **Open** 24hrs daily. **Admission** $5 Fri, Sat. **Map** p334 E3.
The Backdoor caters to Latino guys and their admirers. It's like any other Vegas bar during the week, but plays things up for the weekend with dance parties, drag shows and beauty contests.

Badlands Saloon

Commercial Center, 953 E Sahara Avenue, between S 6th Street & S Maryland Parkway,

Strip Search

You need to know where to look for gay life on the Strip.

You'll find no shortage of people-watching opportunities in Las Vegas, but for gay men looking for like-minded types in town, it's not as easy as just prowling the casinos (though apps such as Grindr and Scruff have taken most of the guesswork – and a lot of the thrill – out of the manhunt). True, separating the average tourists from the Dolce & Gabbana set isn't difficult. But although there are numerous gay bars, clubs and spas elsewhere in town, looking for a gay scene on the Strip itself can be a challenge.

Those with cash to splash may want to try the casino spas. Gay men tend to favour **Nurture** at the Luxor (*see p118*),

Mandalay Bay's **Spa Mandalay** (*see p109*) and the **Bathhouse** (Thehotel at Mandalay Bay; *see p131*), but physical interaction is absolutely not encouraged; for that sort of scene, you'll need to go off-Strip to a non-casino spa.

It's hard to find many gay men in one place when the clubs are closed; the resort-hosted pool parties are oppressively heterosexual. However, gay men frequent the high-end malls such as the **Forum Shops** (*see p194*) and the **Fashion Show Mall** (*see p197*). Both centres feature a wide variety of gay-friendly fashion from the likes of Diesel; window-shopping isn't necessarily limited to the clothes.

East of Strip (792 9262). Bus 109, 204. **Open** 24hrs daily. **No credit cards**. **Map** p333 Y2.
The smaller of the city's two Western gay bars, Badlands is an intimate space patronised in the main by men over 30 and Commercial Center loyalists. A game of pool will set you back a mere quarter, making it the cheapest in Vegas (if not the state).

Buffalo
Paradise Plaza, 4640 S Paradise Road, between E Harmon & E Tropicana avenues, East of Strip (733 8355). Bus 108, 201. **Open** 24hrs daily. **No credit cards**. **Map** p336 C8.
The true Fruit Loop alternative, Buffalo is the destination for leather and bear enthusiasts, though they don't always represent the majority of the bar's patrons. There's no diva posturing or twinky snobbery here, just cheap drinks and chatty customers.

Charlie's Las Vegas
5012 Arville Street, at W Tropicana Avenue, South-west Las Vegas (876 1844, www.charlies lasvegas.com). Bus 103, 201, 202. **Open** 24hrs daily. **No credit cards**.
Gay country fans and followers of the Nevada Gay Rodeo Association head to this Western-themed bar with a large space for both line-dancing and socialising. The place attracts both men and women, especially on Sundays for the $5 beer bust (4-7pm) and Miss Kitty's ever popular drag show (9pm).

Escape Lounge
4213 W Sahara Avenue, between S Decatur & S Valley View boulevards, West of Strip (364 1167, www.escapeloungelasvegas.com). Bus 103, 104, 204. **Open** 24hrs daily.
Escape is the closest thing to a gay sports bar in Vegas. Expect disco and top-40 tunes to be playing

over the game; even if you're not a sports buff, Escape has one of the warmest vibes in the local scene.

★ Fun Hog Ranch
495 E Twain Avenue, between Paradise Road & Swenson Street, East of Strip (791 7001, www.funhogranchlv.com). Bus 103, 104, 204. **Open** 24hrs daily. **Map** p335, p336 C6.
The delightfully and evocatively named Fun Hog is rowdy and rustically decorated. It's a 'come as you are' place, with fetish and leather wear encouraged.

Las Vegas Eagle
3430 E Tropicana Avenue, at S Pecos Road, East Las Vegas (458 8662). Bus 111, 201. **Open** 24hrs daily. **Map** p334 Z3.
The Eagle is a favourite among older men and the Levi's/leather crowd, but the demographic expands for the Wednesday and Friday underwear parties, where those looking to drink for free must hand over their trousers at the door.

★ Las Vegas Lounge
900 E Karen Avenue, between Paradise Road & S Maryland Parkway, East of Strip (737 9350, www.lasvegaslounge.com). Bus 108, 109, 204. **Open** 24hrs daily. **No credit cards**. **Map** p333 Y3.
Everyone on the Vegas scene has a story about how they went into the seemingly nondescript Las Vegas Lounge and suddenly realised that they were at a tranny bar – the only such establishment in the state of Nevada. You'll find all the colours of the homo rainbow here; transsexual and cross-dressing go-go dancers perform more or less nightly.

Snick's Place
1402 S 3rd Street, between E Charleston & E Oakey boulevards, Stratosphere Area

ARTS & ENTERTAINMENT

(385 9298, www.snicksplace.com). Bus Deuce, 206. **Open** 24hrs daily. **No credit cards.** **Map** p335 C3.

Ask longtime gay Vegans where they first began meeting other similarly inclined men, and they'll probably mention Snick's, the oldest LGBT watering hole in town. Sure, it's seen better days, but it still retains a loyal following.

★ Spotlight Lounge

Commercial Center, 957 E Sahara Avenue, between S 6th Street & S Maryland Parkway, East of Strip (696 0202, www.spotlightlv.com). Bus 109, 204. **Open** 24hrs daily. **No credit cards.** **Map** p333 Y2.

Commercial Center's most beloved neighbourhood bar, Spotlight is favoured for its down-to-earth guys, regular liquor busts and free-pizza nights. A firm favourite among the leather crowd.

NIGHTCLUBS

Casino-housed clubs often host LGBT promotions – check the free gay publications and alternative weeklies for ads. Of course you'll find gay revellers in most of the popular joints. For more, *see p257-261.*

Flex Lounge

4347 W Charleston Boulevard, at S Arville Street, West Las Vegas (385 3539, www.flexlas vegas.com). Bus 103, 104, 206. **Open** 24hrs daily. **Admission** $5 Sat after midnight.

This enduring venue attracts a very diverse crowd within the gay community. The drag/stripper revue on Fridays and the hip hop party on Saturdays are the most popular events, but there's something going on here most nights.

Krave.

FreeZone

610 E Naples Drive, at Paradise Road, East of Strip (794 2300, www.freezonelasvegas.com). Bus 108, 213. **Open** 24hrs daily. *Food served* 6pm-2am Mon-Wed; 6pm-3am Thur-Sat. **No credit cards.** **Map** p336 C8.

If the line at Piranha is too long, FreeZone is the next best Fruit Loop option. Thursday's boys' night party remains a draw; weekends are reserved for the Queens of Las Vegas, the city's longest-running drag show. Lick Her Bust on Tuesdays is a ladies' affair, but you'll find the lesbian community well represented on any night.

GoodTimes

1775 E Tropicana Avenue, at Spencer Street, University District (736 9494, www.goodtimes lv.com). Bus 201. **Open** 24hrs daily. **No credit cards.** **Map** p333 Y3.

GoodTimes has always been renowned for its youth-oriented Monday-night liquor bust. But competition from Piranha has motivated management to abolish the cover and adopt a $1 well and draft beer promotion. Attendance is smaller during the rest of the week.

Krave

3663 Las Vegas Boulevard South, at E Harmon Avenue (836 0830, www.kravelasvegas.com). Bus Deuce, 201, 202. **Open** 10.30pm-6am Mon-Sun. **Admission** free locals (except Tue); $5-$20 non-locals. **Map** p336 A7.

INSIDE TRACK VEGAS PRIDE

As the Las Vegas gay community expands, so too do May's **Pride** festivities. What began in 1983 with around 100 revellers has become a fully fledged ten-day extravaganza attended by some 10,000 people. A series of small pageants, picnics and parties leads up to a Downtown parade, held just after twilight on the second Friday of May. it's held after dark and in the springtime not because of closet-shame, but because it gets too hot in Vegas for the traditional June-to-midsummer celebration of Pride. The following day, a family-friendly, all-day festival at the Clark County Amphitheatre welcomes local and national entertainers. For more, call 615 9429 or see www.lasvegaspride.org.

Various enterprises have come and gone in this Strip space, but Krave has thrived as a true alternative club. Gay men constitute the venue's main clientele, though every demographic is made to feel welcome. There are Latin, hip hop, goth and lesbian promotions; Saturday's Everything You Desire is the most popular night in the club, if not the entire gay scene.

★ Piranha & 8½

4633 Paradise Road, between E Harmon & E Tropicana avenues, East of Strip (791 0100, www.piranhalasvegas.com). Bus 108, 213. **Open** from 9pm-late daily. **Admission** free locals; $10-$20 non-locals. **No credit cards. Map** p336 C8.
Done out with velvet curtains, a marble-topped bar and gigantic piranha aquariums, the $5-million Piranha dance hall and connecting 8½ Lounge is gay Vegas's most beautiful nightlife palace. Go-go boys and girls are on display in Piranha, while guests take over the stage in 8½; the Skybox VIP rooms give welcome respite from the usual crowds. Cocktails can be expensive and low on booze, but it's easy to see why this complex has been a hit right out of the gate.

SHOPS

Get Booked

Paradise Plaza, 4640 Paradise Road, between E Harmon & E Tropicana avenues, East of Strip (737 7780, www.getbooked.com). Bus 108. **Open** 10am-midnight Mon-Thur, Sun; 10am-2am Fri, Sat. **Map** p336 C8.
This is the last remaining general gay retail shop in Las Vegas. It is located in the Fruit Loop and divides its offerings between all the usual merchandise (T-shirts, books, greeting cards, CDs, gifts) and the naughty stuff (videos, DVDs, underwear, lubricants, adult magazines).

CRUISING

With the rise of electronic 'dating' devices – apps such as Grindr and Scruff will seek and find available men in the vicinity and provide their stats and make overtures – the most popular non-nightclub cruising spots are now virtual. Try gay.com, which usually has two and sometimes three chatrooms filled with randy surfers 'looking around', as the blushed parlance goes. Also popular are manhunt.net and adam4adam.com, which run (often explicit) user profiles for those in the city or visiting soon, while cruisingforsex.com surveys high-traffic peek-a-boo and public-sex spots. Even lasvegas.craigslist.com has become a cruising HQ; you can post or search ads on pages devoted to men seeking men, casual encounter and erotic services.

In addition to the venues below, it's worth checking out the adult stores and the area around Commercial Center.

Entourage Vegas

Commercial Center, 953 E Sahara Avenue, between S 6th Street & S Maryland Parkway, East Las Vegas (650 9191, www.apollospa.com). Bus 109, 204. **Open** 24hrs daily. **Admission** $15 day pass; $25 with a locker, $30 room. **Map** p333 Y2.
If hotel spas seem a little chaste, you can rely on this Greek-themed facility (formerly Apollo Spa) for a more bacchanalian experience. The closest thing to a bathhouse in the city, Entourage offers all the standard spa accoutrements (heated pool, sauna, steam room, two jacuzzis, workout equipment), plus an internet café, community video room, private booths with video feeds and an on-staff masseur.

Hawk's Gym

Commercial Center, 953 E Sahara Avenue, between S 6th Street & S Maryland Parkway, East of Strip (731 4295, www.hawksgymlv.com). Bus 109, 204. **Open** 24hrs daily. **Admission** $7; locker $14; private dressing room $24. **No credit cards. Map** p333 Y2.
There is workout equipment here, of course. But with rooms such as the Cockpit and a blackout promo night (where, as the advertisement states, 'you almost have to feel your way around'), it's clear that Hawk's is no 24-Hour Fitness. Fetish wear is 'greatly encouraged.'

Get Booked.

ARTS & ENTERTAINMENT

Music

There's musical life in bars and basements as well as big casinos.

Las Vegas's long-time reputation as the last stop for any musical performer worth his or her salt is as far in the past as the Rat Pack's residency at the Sands. Sure, there's not much jazz, blues or classical music here. But when you combine the rock, pop, hip hop and country megastars appearing at major casino venues with the less refined gigs in bars and basements around town, it becomes clear that Sin City is gradually improving its musical image.

Big-name stars passing through town tend to perform at the often-sizeable concert halls and clubs inside the Strip's resorts. Smaller bands and local groups tend to perform in venues that are slightly more makeshift, either bars acting as part-time music clubs or fledgling theatres with few luxuries and hit-or-miss sound systems. Such a state of affairs is due in no small part to gambling regulations: venues with gambling machines are forbidden by law from charging admission, which means shows at the likes of the **Double Down Saloon** and the **Cooler Lounge** are free.

INFORMATION AND TICKETS

For information on what's on, pick up one of the free weeklies – *Seven, Las Vegas Weekly* or *CityLife* – or check online at www.vegas.com or www.yourlocalscene.com. Note that most small rock and jazz venues are restricted to patrons aged 21 and over; the main exceptions being the larger-scale casino venues, where age restrictions vary.

Tickets can generally be bought direct from venues and/or through **Ticketmaster** (474 4000), and prices vary wildly. Shows in bars rarely come with a cover of more than $10, and many are free. However, tickets for shows at the bigger casino venues can run into three figures, with no price too high for some shows by big names at the **MGM Grand Garden Arena**.

ROCK, POP & HIP HOP

Casino venues

Don't let the rather safe programme of music offered at the Colosseum in Caesars Palace put you off Vegas's grand casino venues. The MGM Grand, Mandalay Bay, the Hard Rock and now the Palms and

Cosmopolitan all house credible concert venues that showcase touring acts in most genres on an almost nightly basis.

Downtown, the best options are the 400-seat **Ballroom Theatre** (385 7111) at the Golden Nugget (*see p140*), home to occasional headliners playing everything from smooth jazz to alt-rock; and the 600-seat **Canyon Club** at the Four Queens (*see p243*). Newish venues are **Ovation** at the Green Valley Ranch (*see p146*), with 500 seats, and **Fever**, a hybrid showroom-nightclub at South Point (*see p149*). The latter offers Strip-style luxuries at a more reasonable cost, such as bottle service at a fraction of the on-Strip price.

★ House of Blues

Mandalay Bay *3950 Las Vegas Boulevard South, at W Hacienda Avenue (632 7600, www.mandalaybay.com). Bus Deuce, 104, 105.* **Tickets** $16-$75. **Map** p336 A9.
Though this is just one of several folk-art-filled locations across the US, the House of Blues' exciting mix of up-and-coming and established artists makes it feel like a homegrown champion. The multi-level main floor is surrounded by three bars and tiered balcony seating. Kitschy cover bands play on weekend nights; it's 'Gospel Brunch' on Sundays.

★ Joint

Hard Rock *4455 Paradise Road, at E Harmon Avenue, East of Strip (693 5000 information, 474 4000 tickets, www.hardrockhotel.com).* *Bus 108.* **Tickets** $20-$250. **Map** p336 C7.

Recently expanded and renovated – its 2009 grand reopening double-header featured as Vegas's own the Killers one night, Sir Paul McCartney the next – the Joint remains one of the strongest mid-sized rock venues in Las Vegas, playing host to acts as diverse as Stevie Nicks, Judas Priest and Roger Daltry performing the Who's *Tommy*. Carlos Santana has a long-running residency, cementing the Joint's classic rock supremacy. The main floor is a standing-room-only space; there's reserved table seating available on the balcony.

Mandalay Bay Beach

Mandalay Bay *3950 Las Vegas Boulevard South, at W Hacienda Avenue (632 7777 information, 474 4000 tickets, www.mandalaybay.com). Bus Deuce, 104, 105.* **Tickets** $10-$100. **Map** p336 A9.

Las Vegas's clement weather makes Mandalay Bay's man-made beach ideal for outdoor gigs, and its summer concert series draws in a variety of crowd-pleasing favourites, including Billy Idol, the B-52s and the Go-Gos. If standing in the sand (or water), watching the action up-close isn't your thing, shell out a few bucks more and enjoy the concert from Moorea Beach Club, an open-air lounge outfitted with its own pool, cabanas, bar, loungers and video screens displaying the performance from a safe (and dry) distance.

Mandalay Bay Events Center

Mandalay Bay *3950 Las Vegas Boulevard South, at W Hacienda Avenue (632 7777 information, 474 4000 tickets, www.mandalaybay.com). Bus Deuce, 104, 105.* **Tickets** $25-$250. **Map** p336 A9.

Though this massive arena isn't specifically a music venue per se (it also hosts expositions, boxing matches and awards ceremonies), it draws the biggest and the best international musical acts, from Aerosmith to Keith Urban. Getting in and out of the Events Center (and, for that matter, the casino) becomes a logistical nightmare during big crowd-pullers, so plan accordingly.

We Love the Daylife

'Daylife' has taken over from nightlife, with poolside concerts and parties.

The money-mad masterminds of Las Vegas have learned to make summer actually almost endless – and endlessly lucrative – making the hottest season even hotter by stretching it from April to October. Early in the 2000s, the concept of nightlife was ingeniously extended to hotel pools, which were once reserved as a mandatory but unimaginative amenity for registered guests only. The concept of 'daylife' was born with the arrival of the Hard Rock's Sunday **Rehab** pool parties (*see p260*), all that under-monetised outdoor space suddenly emerged as a fountain of cash. The casinos keep trying to outdo each other with more and more deluxe pool areas – they're called 'ultrapools' now – and parties, concerts and other fun.

The daylong pool-party scenes at Rehab, **Liquid** (Aria), **Lavo** (Palazzo) **Wet Republic** (MGM Grand), **Surrender** (Encore Beach Club), **Bare** (Mirage) and their ilk may be intimidating for those of us with mortal bodies, packed as these fleshfests are with glistening, uninhibited, impossibly hard-bodied girls and guys gone wild. The phenomenon has changed seasonal travel patterns in this resort city – along with what people can get away with wearing (or not wearing) – inside casinos.

But Vegas pools have learned to offer outdoor entertainment for all of us. Swimming has been relegated to a mere afterthought at these tricked-out, tarted-up watering holes, which take the simple concept of 'swimming pool' to ridiculously sublime extremes. The water itself is eclipsed by the rentable cabanas, outfitted with Wi-Fi, cable TV, mini-fridges and attendants who will bring a bounty of frosty, fruity drinks that amount to very expensive spiked Kool-Aid. Along with the mandatory DJ-driven pulsing, pounding soundtrack, you can also expect to find amusements such as floating island dancefloors, floating beer pong and bikini bull riding.

Daytime and evening poolside concerts featuring top pop names have made a splash too, but here's perhaps the coolest twist on Vegas' trendy aquaculture: Mandalay Bay and some other casino-resorts have been offering 'dive-in movies' – screenings of beachy-keen summer-fun films like *Fast Times at Ridgemont High* (almost certainly chosen in honour of Phoebe Cates' unforgettable exiting-the-pool-in-a-bikini scene).

We built this city on dreams; we built this city on rock and roll.

Beauty Bar.

ARTS & ENTERTAINMENT

★ Marquee
Cosmopolitan *3708 Las Vegas Boulevard South, at W Hacienda Avenue (333 9000, www. marquelasvegas.com). Bus Deuce, 104, 105.* **Tickets** $25-$200. **Map** p336 A9.
The first Vegas club to integrate nightlife and 'daylife' from the outset, Marquee has established itself as an instant favourite with visitors and locals, with three distinctly atmospheric rooms – including the Library, a chilled space stocked with hundreds of Vegas-centric books – an outdoor space and a host of resident DJs, including DJ Vice and DJ Redfoo from LMFAO. Upon opening, Marquee eclipsed other clubs as the place to see the coolest 'un-Vegas' bands and other live acts that rarely, if ever, set foot on the Strip – none other than Morrissey was an early booking, if that gives you any indication.

★ MGM Grand Garden Arena
MGM Grand *3799 Las Vegas Boulevard South, at E Tropicana Avenue (891 7777 information, 1-877 880 0880 tickets, www.mgmgrand.com). Bus Deuce, 201.* **Tickets** $70-$400. **Map** p336 A8.
From Britney Spears and U2 to Alan Jackson and the Police, this massive arena showcases the world's rock and pop royalty, as well as occasional special events such as the Billboard Music Awards. There are different vehicle drop-off points at the venue, so be prepared for a possible ten-minute hike through the casino if you enter via the Strip.

Ovation
Green Valley Ranch *23000 Paseo Verde Parkway (617 7777, www.greenvalleyranch resort.com). Bus Deuce, 201.* **Admission** usually free; bigger acts $30-$250. **Map** p336 A8.
Locals love this mid-sized music venue, located about 20 minutes off the Strip in Henderson. The Ovation, inside the Green Valley Ranch casino complex, hosts a range of acts from reggae greats to soft rockers such as Kenny Loggins to the heavy-metal spoofery of Steel Panther.

Pearl
Palms *4321 W Flamingo Road, at S Valley View Boulevard, West of Strip (942 7777 information, 944 3200 tickets, www.palmspearl.com). Bus 201.* **Tickets** $25-$200. **Map** p333 X3.
Since opening, the Palms has appeared very keen to steal the Hard Rock's thunder: first with its boutique accommodation, then with its numerous rooftop clubs and finally with this music venue, which stages many big-name acts. With a capacity ranging from 1,100 (seated) to 2,500 (standing), all within 120 unobstructed feet (35m) of the stage, the Pearl comes with an intimacy rarely found in a venue of this size.

★ Planet Hollywood Theatre for the Performing Arts
Planet Hollywood *3667 Las Vegas Boulevard South, at E Harmon Avenue (785 5000, www. planethollywoodresort.com). Bus Deuce.* **Tickets** $45-$110. **Map** p336 A7.
It was already one of the best-sounding concert halls in Vegas before a $25-million makeover in 2000, which explains why this gem was left standing even as the original Aladdin was razed. The programming is eclectic – from Nine Inch Nails to Jamie Fox.

Railhead
Boulder Station *4111 Boulder Highway, at E Desert Inn Road, East Las Vegas (432 7777 information, 547 5300 tickets, www.boulder station.com). Bus 107, 213.* **Tickets** free-$65.
Don't let the suburban, local-casino location fool you: the intimate Railhead still rocks, albeit a little bit more slowly and quietly than some of its distant Strip cousins. Bands who play here tend to be at the down-but-not-yet-out stage of their careers.

Non-casino venues

What with the emergence of the Killers, the uninitiated might be forgiven for assuming that the local music scene in Vegas is thriving.

In truth, while it's not dead, it's never been particularly vibrant, relegated as it is to the back-rooms of bars and a continual revolving door of opening and closing all-ages venues.

However, the scene has had a resurgence of late, thanks mostly to a combination of Downtown revitalisation initiatives and hipster musical interests. The opening of the **Beauty Bar** (*see p184*), which stages frequent indie rock shows alongside its DJ nights and other special events, coincided with plans for the Fremont East Entertainment District, and the hangout has since been joined by other bars in the same neck of the woods. Indie rock bands have found a home in Downtown venues.

In addition to the venues listed below, a number of other spots offer regular music. Punk and alternative rock still rule at the **Double Down Saloon** (*see p183*), and **Dino's** (*see p184*) has live music every Friday night. While the **Freakin' Frog** (*see p187*) hosts jazz, experimental and rock bands almost nightly.

Bunkhouse Saloon
124 S 11th Street, at S Fremont Street, Downtown (384 4536, www.bunkhouselv.com). Bus 109, 207. **Open** 24hrs daily. *Shows* times vary. **Admission** free-$15. **Map** p334 E2.
This place is all about contrasts: though no longer a country bar, it has kept the animal heads and cowboy paraphernalia, but the place packs in hipsters in skinny pants throwing back Pabst Blue Ribbon every weekend. The Bunkhouse's stage showcases a variety of live music, ranging from blues and punk to indie rock and electronica, every night.

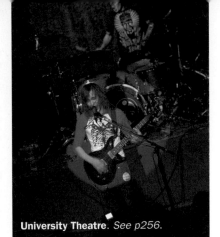

University Theatre. *See p256.*

Cheyenne Saloon
3103 N Rancho Drive, at W Cheyenne Avenue, North-west Las Vegas (645 4139). Bus 106, 218. **Open** 24hrs daily. **Admission** free-$13.
If you're looking for hard rock, you could do worse than to make the trip out here for some cheap beer and loud music. The stage is sizeable, the sound system is impressively robust, and the sunken dance floor is an unexpected touch that makes this rough-edged strip-mall dive a local favourite.

Cooler Lounge
1905 N Decatur Boulevard, at W Havelina Street, North-west Las Vegas (646 3009, www.cooler lounge.com). Bus 103, 210. **Open** 24hrs daily. **Admission** free. **No credit cards**.
For years, this cramped strip-mall dive bar has been drawing crowds for some of the best punk, metal and hard-rock bands in the region, and perhaps even the country. Notable names to have graced the tiny proto-stage include Michale Graves, TSOL, the Bad Samaritans, the Supersuckers and Dr Know.

Divebar
3035 E Tropicana Avenue, between S Eastern & S Pecos avenues, East Las Vegas (435 7526, www.vegasdivebar.com). Bus 201. **Open** 24hrs daily. **Admission** free. **Map** p333 Z3.
It's questionable whether Divebar lives up (or down) to its name, but the popularity of this drinking hole-cum-music venue isn't in doubt. The space is divided into two rooms, one with pub tables and the other, divided by a cutaway wall, is home nightly to everything from open-mic nights to garage-rock bands. Above-average bar food is available 24-7.

Double Down Saloon
4640 Paradise Road, at E Naples Drive (791 5775, www.doubledownsaloon.com). **Admission** free. **Open** 24hrs daily.
Dive-y atmosphere, free admission and live punk bands. Bands the place has featured include TSOL,

Bunkhouse Saloon.

Dickies and Richard Cheese. It's also known for its jukebox filled with ska, surf, psychobilly, punk and cowpunk music.

Thomas & Mack Center, UNLV

4737 S Maryland Parkway, at W Tropicana Avenue, University District (895 3761 information, 474 4000 Ticketmaster, www.thomasandmack.com). Bus 109, 201. **Open** events only, times vary. **Map** p333 Y3.
When a big touring event comes to town, from the circus to a monster-truck rally to *American Idol* or *Glee* live tours, this UNLV arena, almost walking distance from the Strip, is first choice.
► *This venue also hosts Rebels basketball games (see p263) and international robotics competitions.*

University Theatre

4737 S Maryland Parkway, at W Tropicana Avenue, University District (895 3801 information, 474 4000 Ticketmaster). Bus 109, 201. **Open** varies. **Admission** free. **Map** p333 Y3.
The first fully fitted concert hall to open in Vegas for some time, the 450-capacity University Theatre provides a smoke- and alcohol-free environment that packs in the kids for shows from touring alternative, punk and metal bands. It's an all-ages venue, though there's a bar next door for over-21s. *Photo p255.*

JAZZ, BLUES & ACOUSTIC MUSIC

Given the fact that it's widely perceived to hold an overabundance of lounge acts, the jazz scene in Las Vegas is surprisingly slight. Most casino lounges have been overrun by pop cover bands; those that haven't offer the kind of light jazz of which only Kenny G would be proud. Still, there are a few standard-bearers: in addition to the venues listed below, the **Bootlegger Bistro** (*see p174*) welcomes renowned jazz pianist Guy Mancuso on

Wednesdays, while the **Italian American Club** (2333 E Sahara Avenue, at S Eastern Avenue, 457 3866) hosts the 18-piece Carl Lodico Ghost Band every Thursday.
It's a similar story for acoustic music, with many of the bigger nights in town slowly dying off. However, the **House of Blues** (*see p252*) fills some of the gaps with its weekly Unplugged Thursdays, featuring acoustic acts in its courtyard.

CLASSICAL MUSIC

UNLV is key to classical music in Vegas. As well as providing a home for the **Las Vegas Philharmonic** and the **Charles Vanda Master Series** (895 2787, http://pac.unlv.edu), it hosts concerts by big names on a more or less monthly basis from autumn until spring.
Occasional performances by the **UNLV Symphony Orchestra** complete the classical-music picture. And the university's music department is also home to a number of ensembles and bands that perform regularly on campus. For details, see http://music.unlv.edu.

Las Vegas Philharmonic

Artemus Ham Concert Hall, 4505 S Maryland Parkway, between E Flamingo Road & E Tropicana Avenue, University District (895 2787, www.lvphil.com). Bus 109, 201. **Tickets** $38-$78. **Map** p333 Y3.
Since emerging in 1998, Las Vegas's resident orchestra gradually gained recognition under music director Harold Weller; today, director David Itkin and associate conductor Richard McGee continue the effort. Its repertoire has remained largely highbrow, with new works occasionally commissioned from contemporary composers. Aside from the concerts at Ham Hall, the Phil also perform pop classics to family audiences in annual recitals timed to coincide with holidays such as Christmas and Independence Day.

Las Vegas Philharmonic.

Nightclubs

Clubbing with the Kardashians.

In terms of quality, quantity and diversity, there are few cities in the US with a nightlife scene to rival that of Las Vegas. That said, an element of homogeneity has crept into the local scene of late, bringing the same music (MTV-cloned hip hop and poorly mixed mash-ups), the same overpriced bottle service and the same long queues to venues all over town.

There are some new twists and tweaks to the classic formula, of course, most notably a new generation crazy for cocktails, made-to-order with esoteric ingredients by highly trained mixologists. Celebrity guest hosts – the most popular being from such reality shows as MTV's *Jersey Shore* and *Keeping Up With the Kardashians* – are the new Vegas royalty, crowd magnets that reign over the hordes from behind velvet-roped VIP areas. And the traditional nightlife has ceded ground to 'daylife', with the prevalence of poolside bars and their attendant pool parties (*see p253* **We Love the Daylife**).

ARTS & ENTERTAINMENT

THE SCENE

The success of the Light Group, which runs a half-dozen venues, and the Pure Management Group, which operates nearly a dozen spots, has resulted in many clubs run in very similar fashion. There are advantages: the firms command enough bargaining power to retain big-name residents (such as Kaskade at the Cosmopolitan's **Marquee** club, or on another level, *Jersey Shore*'s Pauly D, who spins at **Rain** and other clubs at the Palms as part of his residency), and clubbers know they can expect certain standards of service. But at the same time, door policies, DJ programming and even venue design have become standardised.

If you're looking for less-mainstream sounds, whether drum 'n' bass, trance or garage rock, a number of weekly promotions at local bars draw their own scenes. Most notable among them is the **Beauty Bar** (*see p184*), where you might find DJs spinning anything from indie rock to vintage soul.

INFORMATION AND TICKETS

For information on what's on, check the free weekly magazines *Seven*, *Las Vegas Weekly* or *CityLife*. While some venues don't offer advance ticket sales, most of them allow patrons to reserve a table in advance if they're willing to fork out for bottle service (*see p260*

High Spirits). It's also a good idea to speak to your hotel concierge before settling on a venue: they may be able to offer guest-list privileges to clubs affiliated to the hotel.

Men: your power is in your wallets, not in your numbers. Large groups of guys are rarely admitted to clubs; conversely, women still get preferential treatment, often not even having to pay the cover charge. Admission prices listed below are for visitors, and can vary depending on the night; locals with Nevada ID usually pay less. And if you're under 21, forget it: the bouncers here are expert at checking IDs.

NIGHTCLUBS

The Bank
Bellagio *3600 Las Vegas Boulevard South, at E Flamingo Road, East of Strip (693 8300, www.lightgroup.com). Bus 108.* **Open** 10.30pm-4am Thur-Sun. **Admission** $30 men; $20 women. **Map** p336 A7.
Maybe they should have just called the Bank something more direct, like ATM Machine, or Your Entire Wallet. The upscale club, which features a mix of expensive-sounding hip hop and rock from its resident DJs, has a capacity of 1,000, and that number or more is packed in when one of the frequent celebrity guest hosts – the Kardashian klan is inescapable – is in the house.

Rain. *See p260.*

Chateau

Paris *3655 Las Vegas Boulevard S, at W Flamingo Road, West of Strip (776 7770, www.chateaunightclublv.com). Bus 108.* **Open** 10pm-4.30am Tue, Fri-Sun. **Admission** $30 men; $20 women. **Map** p336 A7.

The new Chateau club at Paris has all the expected nightlife amenities, with attractive outdoor options: a balcony with a view of the Strip and the Bellagio fountain show, and a beer garden, which is all the rage in Las Vegas. The sister club of Planet Hollywood's Gallery, Chateau shares its roster of celebrity DJs, reality show hosts, and UFC celebu-thugs.

Cherry

Red Rock Resort *11011 W Charleston Boulevard, at I-215, West Las Vegas (797 7180, www.midnightoilbars.com). Bus 206.* **Open** 10pm-late Thur-Sat. **Admission** $20 men; free-$10 women.

Rande Gerber's first full-on Vegas club (he also created ultralounge Whiskey; *see p261*) is a polished spot, smaller than those on the Strip. The red-toned, wood-and-steel interior creates a warm, intimate environment, and opens out to a gorgeous pool. Even the restrooms are a delight, with holographic projections, voyeuristic mirrors and mouth-shaped urinals. Expect a slightly older, well-heeled locals' crowd.

Empire Ballroom

3765 Las Vegas Boulevard South, between E Harmon & E Tropicana avenues (737 7376/ www.empireballroom.com). Bus Deuce, 201. **Open** hrs vary. **Admission** free-$20. **Map** p320 A8.

Formerly the home of pioneering dance den Club Utopia, this big space (with a great patio) remains the only independent nightclub on the Strip. The club's independent-spirited tradition continues with after-hours promotion Late Night Empire (from 3am, Thur-Sat nights), which delivers the kind of house music that's rarely heard in Vegas.
► *The Empire is also a part-time music venue, hosting acts as varied as the Killers and Lady Sovereign.*

Godspeed

Mandalay Bay *3950 Las Vegas Boulevard South, at W Hacienda Avenue (632 7777, www.hob.com). Bus Deuce, 104, 105.* **Open** 11pm-5am Mon. **Admission** $30. **Map** p336 A9.

The House of Blues' exclusive Foundation Room atop Mandalay Bay opens its doors to non-members on Mondays. Resident and guest DJs provide a sexy house soundtrack, which, when combined with the lush Asian-inspired decor and breathtaking city views, creates an indulgent jet-set atmosphere.

Haze

Aria, CityCenter *3730 Las Vegas Boulevard S, at E Harmon Avenue, East of Strip (693 8300, www.hazenightclub.com). Bus 108.* **Open** 10.30pm-4am Thur-Sat. **Admission** $30 men; $20 women. **Map** p336 A8.

Expect your recollection of the night before to be a little, well, hazy after a good night at one of the Strip's newest clubs, at CityCenter's Aria casino-hotel. A queue of black-clad beauties indicates you are near the entrance to the bi-level, subterranean space, which has a Manhattan feel to it, with booths overlooking the dancefloor. The club is designed to feel close, intimate and voyeuristic.

Ivan Kane's Forty Deuce
Mandalay Bay *3950 Las Vegas Boulevard South, at W Hacienda Avenue (632 9442, www. fortydeuce.com). Bus Deuce, 104, 105.* **Open** 10.30pm-4am (sometimes until 5am) Mon, Thur-Sun. **Admission** $25. **Map** p336 A9.
Burlesque-oriented clubs started re-emerging in Sin City a few years ago, but only Forty Deuce is founded entirely on the combination of stage-trained dancers and DJ-spun club sounds. Though smallish and lacking a sufficient dancefloor, this offshoot of an LA original is worth a visit.
▶ *You can buy the dancers' costumes in the adjacent Champagne Suzy's boutique (632 7800).*

Jet
Mirage *3400 Las Vegas Boulevard South, between Spring Mountain & W Flamingo Roads (792 7900, www.lightgroup.com). Bus Deuce, 105, 202, 203.* **Open** 10.30pm-4am Mon, Fri, Sat. **Admission** $30. **Map** p335, p336 A6.
As at sister club Light (*see right*), the main dancefloor at Jet is a sunken rectangle surrounded by VIP seating and two bars. Hip hop and mash-ups keep the dancefloor packed, and clubbers drink cocktails served by gorgeous staff. But the real reasons to visit are the two side rooms, one with the latest in house and the other pumping out rock and '80s dance music.

LAX
Luxor *3900 Las Vegas Boulevard S, at W Tropicana Avenue, West of Strip (262 4529, www.laxthenightclub.com). Bus 108.* **Open** 10.30pm-4am Fri, Sat. **Admission** $30 men; $20 women. **Map** C7.
It would hardly be surprising if someone discovered a secret portal directly from Las Vegas's McCarran International Airport to LAX. Not the Los Angeles airport – the nightclub at the Luxor casino-resort.

INSIDE TRACK
GIRLS! GIRLS! GIRLS!

Men, here's a bit of a reality check: if you notice a preternatural preponderance of pretty young things queuing up in front of a club in little black dresses and towering heels, there's a good chance that they're for hire. No, not that way! The clubs import bevvies of local beauties as decor, and as a lure for the free-spending young men that are the target market. Which is not to say these girls won't be friendly to you inside the club. You just have to buy them a drink.

It's that crowded. Such demi-celebs as Snooki from reality show *Jersey Shore* keep packing them in to the club, which has a gothic feel, deep within the Strip's famous pyramid.

Light
Bellagio *3600 Las Vegas Boulevard South, at W Flamingo Road (693 8303, www.lightlv.com). Bus Deuce, 202.* **Open** 10.30pm-4am Thur-Sun. **Admission** $30. **Map** p336 A7.
Light set the pace for the modern Las Vegas nightclub, introducing bottle service, exclusive door policies and a return to upscale dress codes. Though it has dumbed down a little in both its music (ubiquitous hip hop, bad rock remixes) and dress code, some things never change: groups of men larger than six are not allowed, VIP booths are scarce and the dancefloor is packed. But hey, it's all part of the experience.

Lure
Wynn Las Vegas *3131 Las Vegas Boulevard South, between E Desert Inn Road & Sands Avenue (770 3350, www.wynnlasvegas.com). Bus Deuce, 203.* **Open** 9pm-late Tue-Sat. **Admission** free-$30. **Map** p335 & p336 B6.
Lure has never quite carved out a proper niche for itself, teetering between intimate, sexy cocktail lounge and low-key nightclub. Dimly lit in soothing blues and draped with delicate fabrics, it's a gorgeous space, often overlooked in the dizzying array of nightspot options in Sin City. A laid-back alternative to busier, more boisterous clubs elsewhere.

★ Marquee
Cosmopolitan *3708 Las Vegas Boulevard S, between E Flamingo Avenue and E Tropicana Avenue (333 9000, www.marqueelasvegas.com). Bus 108.* **Open** 10pm-5am Mon, Thur, 9.30pm-5am Fri, Sat. **Admission** $30 men; $20 women. **Map** p336 A7.
For review, *see p254.*

Mix
Thehotel at Mandalay Bay *3950 Las Vegas Boulevard South, at W Hacienda Avenue (632 7777, www.mandalaybay.com). Bus Deuce, 104, 105.* **Open** 5pm-2am Mon-Thur, Sun; 5pm-3am Fri, Sat. **Admission** $20-$25. **Map** p336 A9.
Surrounded by 30ft-high windows, the lounge at Alain Ducasse's dynamic restaurant (*see p160*) atop Thehotel at Mandalay Bay attracts locals with its impressive panoramic views. Mix also comes with the overly clubby feel that's attached to so many of the city's other towering venues. Its intimate atmosphere is enhanced by house and lounge sounds, though there's no proper dancefloor.

Moon
Palms *4321 W Flamingo Road, at S Valley View Boulevard, West of Strip (942 6832, http://moon-las-vegas.n9negroup.com).*

ARTS & ENTERTAINMENT

Bus 201. **Open** 8pm-4am daily. **Admission** $10 Mon-Thur; $25 Fri-Sun. **Map** p333 X3.
In space, no one can hear you scream. However, they sure can see you dance, at least if they happen to be looking through Moon's retractable roof. The club's space-age design has a retro feel, but its location 53 floors up the Palms' Fantasy Tower offers incredible views from its two balconies and its bead-curtained, floor-to-ceiling windows. The music can be a bit schizophrenic, ranging from top-40 remixes to hip hop/rock mash-ups and occasional house nights. Most evenings, admission includes access to the Playboy Club via a direct escalator.

OPM
Caesars Palace (Forum Shops) *3570 Las Vegas Boulevard South, at W Flamingo Road (369 4998, www.o-pmlv.com). Bus Deuce, 202.* **Open** 10pm-late Wed-Sun. **Admission** $20-$30. **Map** p336 A7.
It took a while for OPM, located on the top floor of Wolfgang Puck's Chinois in the Forum Shops, to find its identity. However, it's now become the prime destination for the upscale, hip hop crowd in Las Vegas. DJs also spin reggae and R&B; the urban sounds and intimacy of the venue keep the blinging patrons grinding week after week.

★ Pure
Caesars Palace *3570 Las Vegas Boulevard South, at W Flamingo Road (731 7873/www. purethenightclub.com). Bus Deuce, 202.* **Open** 10pm-4am Tue, Fri-Sun. **Admission** $20-$30. **Map** p336 A7.
Soon after opening in 2005, Pure became the hottest megaclub in Las Vegas, and remains so several years down the line. Its multiple levels, including a massive terrace overlooking the Strip, are always packed with patrons vying for a glimpse of the latest Hollywood celebs hosting parties in the labyrinthine venue. Attached is the Pussycat Dolls Lounge, in which its namesake burlesque troupe perform at regular intervals nightly.

Rain
Palms *4321 W Flamingo Road, at S Valley View Boulevard, West of Strip (942 6832, www.rainat thepalms.com). Bus 201.* **Open** 11pm-4am Fri, Sat. **Admission** $25. **Map** p333 X3.
One of the last Vegas clubs built in an oversized, industrial style, Rain now looks a bit dated. However, it's still the best at what it does, with the non-stop dance music and eyebrow-searing pyrotechnics perhaps best heard and viewed from one of the private cabanas that overlook all the action from upstairs. *Photo p258.*

★ Rehab
Hard Rock *4455 Paradise Road, at E Harmon Avenue, East of Strip (693 5555, www.rehab lv.com). Bus 108.* **Open** 10.30pm-4am Fri-Sun. **Admission** $30 men; $20 women. **Map** p336 C7.
The pool party to end all pool parties, the Hard Rock's Sunday Rehab is still the one to beat after more than five nearly-naked years and a reality show observing the goings-on in and out of the water. Rehab season (each party is followed by an evening bash called, appropriately, Relapse) runs for about 20 Sundays, from April to October. It's hard to get over the sight of a limousine pulling up to the casino and disgorging a dozen bikini-clad women in towering heels, or the queue of tatted men and women that stretches into the dim cool depths of the casino.

Risqué
Paris Las Vegas *3655 Las Vegas Boulevard South, at E Flamingo Road (967 4589, www. harrahs.com). Bus Deuce, 202.* **Open** 10pm-4am Thur-Sun. **Admission** free-$10. **Map** p336 A7.
Though it bills itself as an ultralounge, Risqué defies categorisation. It's less spacious than most nightclubs but more involving than a mere bar, with modern Asian decor complementing a space with private

ARTS & ENTERTAINMENT

High Spirits

The pros and cons of bottle service.

Las Vegas's ascension as an upscale nightlife destination has brought with it the curse of VIP bottle service, first popular in Miami but now creeping into clubs all over the US. In order to reserve a table at many casino clubs, you'll need to buy an entire bottle of booze at a mark-up nearing 1,000 per cent: it's not uncommon to pay $300 (including mixers, excluding service) for a bottle of vodka. Many venues even run a two-bottle minimum.

There are 300 green-backed reasons why bottle service is a pretty unappealing trend. But if you're desperate to go to a particular venue and there are a number of people in your party (four to six is ideal), it's a surprisingly attractive way to approach the night ahead. (At least if you arrive promptly: latecomers have been known to have their 'reserved' table sold out from under them for more money.)

Paying the premium means no waiting in line, no snobby stares from the host and no cover for at least some of the party (all of them, if they're female). Men love VIP seating as a way to attract women; women love it as a way to escape men. And with cover charges running to $30 and poorly mixed martinis going for close to $20, it even makes financial sense. Sort of.

balconies overlooking the Strip, an intimate salon (with its own events), a proper dancefloor and occasional performances from burlesque-style dancers.

Rumjungle

Mandalay Bay *3950 Las Vegas Boulevard South, at W Hacienda Avenue (632 7408, www.mandalaybay.com). Bus Deuce, 104, 105.* **Open** 11pm-4am Mon, Wed, Fri, Sat; 11pm-2am Tue, Thur, Sun. **Admission** $10-$30. **Map** p336 A9.
The fire-and-water theme at Rumjungle perfectly complements the music, which varies from hip hop to reggaeton to Latin dance (especially during promotions such as Wednesday's Rumba). It's particularly popular with the college-age set, but its semi-strict dress code keeps out the rubes, and it's now far less crowded since the once-legendary swank contingent dispersed to newer venues.

Studio 54

MGM Grand *3799 Las Vegas Boulevard South, at E Tropicana Avenue (891 1111, www.mgmgrand.com). Bus Deuce, 201.* **Open** 10pm-5am Tue-Sat. **Admission** $10-$20. **Map** p336 A8.
This 21st-century revamp of the legendary New York disco has a high-ceilinged entranceway with lounge seating, VIP areas on the upper levels and a private lounge for the DJ and his or her hangers-on. It remains a favourite with locals and visitors, thanks to top-notch sound and lighting, a cool, industrial feel and some of the most innovative promotions in Vegas.

Tabú

MGM Grand *3799 Las Vegas Boulevard South, at E Tropicana Avenue (891 7183, www.mgmgrand.com). Bus Deuce, 201.* **Open** 10pm-3am Mon, Wed-Sun. **Admission** free-$20. **Map** p336 A8.
Lots of spaces in Las Vegas call themselves ultralounges, but Tabú was the first and probably remains the best. Despite its lack of dancefloor and overabundance of seating, DJs manage to keep people on their feet all night in the upscale, modern space – especially during Super Slide Sundays, when B-boys and -girls tear up the floor as if *Breakin' 3* were being filmed right there in the room.

★ Tao

Venetian *3555 Las Vegas Boulevard South, between Sands Avenue & E Flamingo Road (388 8588, www.taolasvegas.com). Bus Deuce, 105, 203.* **Open** 10pm-4am Thur, Fri; 9.30pm-4am Sat. **Admission** $20-$30. **Map** p335, p336 B6.
This NYC import rivals Pure as the favourite party-spot of celebs visiting Vegas. And who can blame them? The Zen- and Buddhist-themed decor is intoxicating, and the multiple lounges and VIP areas lend an air of exclusivity to the venue. Other attractions include an adjacent gourmet Asian fusion restaurant, a cosy Strip-facing patio, a rooftop pool party (summer only), gorgeous bathing ladies (really)

and some of the town's hottest house DJs, though the music is more mainstream at weekends.

Tryst

Wynn Las Vegas *3131 Las Vegas Boulevard South, between E Desert Inn Road & Sands Avenue (770 3375, www.wynnlasvegas.com). Bus Deuce, 203.* **Open** 10pm-4.30am Thur-Sun. **Admission** $20-$30. **Map** p335 & p336 B6.
Descend the stairs and follow a passage through a womb-like hallway into a dark, sensual space. The dancefloor extends outside to overlook a private lagoon and 94ft (29m) waterfall, with waterside bottle service and corset-wearing servers. The atmosphere is completed by the Library, a VIP area with bookshelf-lined walls and a stripper pole. A decadent nightlife experience for those who can afford it.

Vanity

Hard Rock *4455 Paradise Road, at E Harmon Avenue, East of Strip (693 5555, www.vanitylv.com). Bus 108.* **Open** 10pm-4am Fri-Sun. **Admission** $30 men; $20 women. **Map** p336 C7.
Vanity is one of the Seven Deadly Sins, and this club at the Hard Rock makes room for the other six, especially Lust, Gluttony and Greed. As the name suggest, mirrors are everywhere – the better to check yourself out, and check yourself out being checked out in the 'look at me' atmosphere. This is one of the more dance-oriented spaces in town, and the music ranges from house and hip hop to pop and hard rock, with the dancing reaching out into the poolside areas.

Whiskey

Green Valley Ranch *2300 Paseo Verde Drive, at S Green Valley Parkway, Henderson (617 7777, www.greenvalleyranchresort.com). Bus 111.* **Open** 6pm-2am Mon-Thur, Sun; 6pm-4am Fri, Sat. **Admission** free.
Rande Gerber's first foray into Vegas nightlife has evolved over the years from a lounge into something approaching a suburban nightclub. The amenities are headed by the adjacent Whiskey Beach: one of the most breathtaking pool areas in the desert and host to all manner of outdoor concerts, it also affords unexpectedly fantastic views of the Strip.

★ XS

Encore *3131 Las Vegas Boulevard S, at Sands Avenue (770 0097, www.xslasvegas.com). Bus 108.* **Open** 10pm-4am Fri-Sun. **Admission** $30 men; $20 women. **Map** p336 C7.
Steve Wynn doesn't do things halfway, and the opulent gold-plated nightclub at his casino-hotel sets a new standard of luxe. The 13,000sq ft indoor-outdoor space is gilded with rotating gold chandeliers, golden moulds of cocktail waitresses and balconies surrounding the 1,000sq ft dance floor. The club's signature drink, the Ono, combines Dom Perignon, Rémy Martin Black Pearl cognac – and men's and women's jewellery – for a mere $10,000.

ARTS & ENTERTAINMENT

Sport & Fitness

A sporting chance.

Far be it from us to detract from the enjoyment of betting on your team, a predictably popular pastime in this town, but getting your heart rate pumping from sideline enthusiasm doesn't count as exercise. Happily, the word 'sports' isn't always followed by the word 'book' in Las Vegas: there are plenty of opportunities in and around the city for watching and taking part in an array of games. That said, Vegas remains the largest US city without either a major-league team or a major-league-quality sporting arena.

(see p267 Jump to it)

THE POLITICS OF SPORT

During his tenure, Mayor Oscar Goodman appeared determined to bring a major-league team to the city, and he didn't seem fussy about which sport got here first. In 2005, he wooed the Florida Marlins baseball team; the following year, in the wake of Hurricane Katrina, the suddenly homeless New Orleans Saints of the NFL seemed another possibility. And in 2007, Vegas even managed to host the NBA All-Star Game. But neither the Marlins nor the Saints made the leap, and NBA commissioner David Stern then announced that basketball wouldn't be returning to Sin City unless or until a major-league calibre arena is built.

For now, the only options for spectators not keen on auto racing are minor-league or college sports. And there's always – always – **mixed martial arts** (MMA), which also goes by the name ultimate fighting: the no-holds-barred cage-match bashes that have caught on big-time worldwide. The violent sport/spectacle has made Vegas its unofficial home, and many of its major bouts are broadcasted from here.

The choices are broader if you're keen to get active. Bowling, tennis, swimming, cycling, horse riding and a bizarre homegrown activity known as **Sky Zone** (*see p267* **Jump to it**) are all popular options, and Vegas is packed with excellent health clubs and spas. And despite being in the middle of the desert, the city is dotted with world-class golf courses. Further out, **Red Rock Canyon** (*see p282*) is good for hiking, cycling and rock climbing, and **Lake Mead** (*see p280-281*) is great for fishing and even scuba diving. Indeed, one of the many peculiarities about Las Vegas is that you can go water skiing (on Lake Mead) and skiing (at Mount Charleston) on the same day and still be back in the hotel for dinner, at least if you're prepared to get up miserably early and don't mind returning home exhausted.

Outside the inferno-like summer months, the climate here is pleasant and sunny. Be sure to drink plenty of water and load up on sunscreen. In summer, plan outdoor activities for early in the day to avoid the midday sun.

SPECTATOR SPORTS

Auto racing

With two paved ovals, a dirt course and a drag strip, the 1,500-acre **Las Vegas Motor Speedway** (7000 Las Vegas Boulevard North, 644 4444, www.lvms.com) reverberates with events throughout the year, among them the VW frenzy that is October's **Bugorama**. The biggest is the **NASCAR 400 Nextel Cup** race in March, which draws more than

150,000 fans to Las Vegas (and, irony of ironies, creates huge traffic jams to and from the event).

Baseball

The AAA affiliate of the **Toronto Blue Jays**, the **Las Vegas 51s** (www.lv51.com) plays 72 games between April and September at **Cashman Field** (850 Las Vegas Boulevard North, at Washington Avenue, Downtown, 386 7200) from April to September. Although the 51s is among the most consistently successful teams in the Pacific Coast League, the 10,000-seat stadium is generally about half-full, and tickets ($8-$13) are usually available on the gate. The ballpark opens in March with an exhibition game featuring major-league stars.

Basketball

If this wasn't Vegas, you might get away with saying the **UNLV Runnin' Rebels** (www.unlv rebels.com) are the only game in town. Most recently the stars of the HBO Sports documentary film *Runnin' Rebels of UNLV*, the Las Vegas university team, coached by Lon Kruger, made it all the way to the Sweet 16 of the NCAA tournament in 2007. There hadn't been this much excitement around the team since the days when Jerry Tarkanian, aka Tark the Shark, led them to the NCAA title in 1990. Between November and March, games are played at the Thomas & Mack Center (E Tropicana Avenue & Swenson Street); call 739 3267 for tickets, which cost $15-$30.

The Lady Rebels, UNLV's women's basketball team ($9 a game), play at the Cox Pavilion (739 3267, www.unlvrebels.com), next door to the Thomas & Mack. The team has been posting as many wins as the men of late.

Boxing

With blood, sweat and spit, boxing draws the richest of the rich and the poorest of the poor, just like Vegas itself. The hotels used regularly for big bouts are **Mandalay Bay** (which also hosts numerous 'ultimate fighting' events; *see p109*, the **MGM Grand** (*see p119*) and **Caesars Palace** (*see p104*). Call each hotel or Ticketmaster (745 3000) ahead of the fight for tickets, which can cost several thousand dollars but nonetheless often sell out quickly.

Football

The **UNLV Rebels** college team plays under coach Bobby Hauck at **Sam Boyd Stadium** (Boulder Highway & Russell Road, 739 3267, www.unlvrebels.com) between September and December. Tickets, on sale from July, cost $15-

Las Vegas Motor Speedway.

$30. Sam Boyd Stadium also hosts the **Maaco Bowl Las Vegas**, which features the best of the Mountain West Conference.

Golf

Because of its year-round golf-friendly climate and resort ambience, the Las Vegas area is home to more than 40 golf courses – including Las Vegas National, site of Tiger Woods' first PGA victory, and backdrop to scenes from *Casino*. The area annually hosts many PGA tournaments and other high-calibre events. In a particularly, peculiarly Vegas twist on the normally sedate game, the inaugural **World Series of Golf** tournament (www.worldseriesofgolf.com) was held in 2007, in Primm, 45 minutes south of Las Vegas. The game manages to combine golf with, you guessed it, poker: players get to pass, bet or fold on each shot.

Ice hockey

The city's resident team, the **Las Vegas Wranglers** (284 7777, www.lasvegaswranglers. com), takes to the ice between October and April at the 9,000-seat **Orleans Arena** (*see p148*). Competing in the West division of the National Conference, the team is a feeder club for the NHL's Calgary Flames. At $17.50-$38, tickets are worth their weight in body slams, ice brawls and speeding-puck action; the crowd's enthusiasm is even hotter than the temperatures outside.

Mixed martial arts/ultimate fighting

Vegas is a frequent host and headquarters for the MMA/UFC craze, which is on the verge of surpassing boxing as a big-ticket draw, and is

UNLV Rebels. *See p263.*

pulling a younger and considerably rowdier crowd. Big bouts, which are often broadcast live via pay-per-view cable, take place at the **Palms**, **Mandalay Bay** and **MGM Grand Garden Aren**a. Visit www.ufc.com and www.mmafighting.com for scheduled events; call each hotel or Ticketmaster (474 4000) ahead of the fight for tickets.

Rodeo

Every December, the **National Finals Rodeo** (*see p221*) sweeps into town, packing the Thomas & Mack Center with riders who make riding a bucking bronco look as easy as sitting on a carousel horse. See www.nfr experience.com for details of events. The relatively new **South Point Equestrian Center** (796 7111, www.southpointevents center.com) hosts events year-round, including the Western States Championship Ranch Rodeo.

In October, the best professional bull riders in the world come to the Thomas & Mack to compete in the **Built Ford Tough World Finals**. For tickets, call 1-877 632 7400 (first weekend) or 1-866 727 7469 (second weekend), or see www.pbrnow.com.

Tennis

Home to world-famous tennis pros Andre Agassi and Steffi Graf, Las Vegas is the site of many professional tennis tourneys. Half a dozen casino resorts have tennis facilities, and there are four good public courts, including the **Darling Tennis Center** (7901 W Washington Avenue, 229 2100, www.darling tenniscenter.net), which each year hosts the **Tennis Channel Open** (Feb-Mar, www. tennischannelopen.com), a high-profile, round-robin tournament.

ACTIVE SPORTS

Auto racing

If you'd like to get out of the stands and into the car, contact the **Richard Petty Driving Experience** (1-800 237 3889, www.drive petty.com) or the **Mario Andretti Racing School** (1-877 722 3527, www.andretti racing.com). Both offer the chance to sit in the passenger seat (around $150) or behind the wheel (roughly $400) of a speeding motor.

Bowling

A number of casinos have huge, 24-hour alleys, among them the **Suncoast** (64 lanes; *see p151*), **Sam's Town** (56 lanes; *see p150*) and the **Red Rock** (72 lanes ,with a VIP section; *see p147*). There are also alleys with slightly more limited hours at the **Gold Coast** (70 lanes; *see p150*), the **Orleans** (70 lanes; *see p148*) and **Santa Fe Station** (60 lanes; *see p151*). The newish **Strike Zone** at **Sunset Station** (72 lanes; *see p151*) is a little more modern, while the bowling and nightclub worlds collide at **Lucky Strike** at the **Rio** (10 lanes; *see p135*) with surprisingly delightful results. For all, call ahead before making a special trip: local bowling leagues take over entire alleys on selected nights, and some alleys are open only to over-21s at night.

Cycling

Looking around Vegas, you'd think that the only cyclists are Mormon missionaries. Don't be put off: although urban areas are incredibly auto-centric, there are thrilling cycle trails surrounding the city, even if you have to drive to get there.

McGhie's Ski Bike & Board (4035 S Fort Apache Road, between W Flamingo Road & W Saddle Avenue, 252 8077, www. mcghiesbikes.com) rents out road and mountain bikes (from $35 a day), and can arrange group tours. McGhie's is the official bicycle tour operator for Red Rock Casino Resort, the closest resort to beautiful Red Rock Canyon and the most breathtaking biking spots in the area.

Possible routes include the eight-mile off-road **Cottonwood Valley Loop** near Red Rock (head west on Highway 160 and look for a dirt road six miles past the junction with Highway 159) and the **River Mountain Peak**, a ten-mile trek between Las Vegas and Henderson (drive along I-93/95 to Equestrian Drive and turn east). There's also an unofficial mountain bike trail on the north-west corner of Tropicana Avenue and Decatur Boulevard. It's steep and challenging but well worn, running through one of the few undeveloped parcels of land in town.

Fishing

Lake Mead (see p280-281) is stocked with half a million rainbow trout annually, and also contains black and striped bass; the upper Overton Arm of the lake is good for crappie, bluegill and catfish. **Lake Mohave** is also good for rainbow trout. In the city, check out **Lorenzi Park** (Rancho Drive & Washington Avenue), **Sunset Park** (Sunset Road & Eastern Avenue) or **Floyd Lamb State Park** (see p283).

To fish from any Nevada shore, you'll need a Nevada fishing licence ($18 for the first day, $7 for subsequent days); a special stamp is required for trout fishing. To fish from a boat on Lake Mead, you'll also need a stamp from Arizona, as the two lakes share jurisdiction of the lake. For details on all aspects of fishing in Nevada, contact the **Nevada Division of Wildlife** (486 5127, www.ndow.org), ask at a ranger station for the current hotspots or consult **Fish Incorporated** (565 8396, www.fishincorporated.com).

Golf

Las Vegas has about half the courses it needs to meet demand; call several weeks ahead and show up with a three-figure sum if you want to play on any of the best. **Las Vegas Preferred Tee-Times** (1-877 255 7277, www.lvptt.com) can arrange reservations at a number of courses. Rates are cheaper in the heat of summer and later in the afternoon. Most courses are open from 7am to dusk; one exception is the par-three **Cloud Nine** course

at Angel Park (254 4653, www.angelpark.com), where nine of the 12 holes are floodlit. Sharpen up your game at **Butch Harmon's School of Golf** at the Rio Secco Golf Club (777 2444, www.butchharmon.com).

Bali Hai Golf Club
5160 Las Vegas Boulevard South, at W Russell Road, South of Strip (597 2400, www.balihai golfclub.com). Bus Deuce, 104. **Green fees** *June-Aug* $175-$195; $125-$150 twilight. *Sept-May* $265-$325; $189-$229 twilight. **Map** p336 A9.
This challenging par-71 track includes seven acres of water features, 2,500 palm trees, Augusta white sand and more than 100,000 tropical plants.

Craig Ranch Golf Course
628 W Craig Road, between N Martin Luther King Boulevard & Losee Road, North Las Vegas (642 9700). No bus. **Green fees** $19-$35; $5-$16 juniors.
Established in 1962, Las Vegas's first public course is a favourite with locals, thanks in part to the fabulously inexpensive prices.

Desert Pines Golf Club
3415 E Bonanza Road, at N Pecos Road, East Las Vegas (366 1616, www.golfdesertpines.com). Bus 111, 215. **Green fees** *June-Aug* $69-$79; $39-$49 twilight. *Sept-May* $99-$129; $69-$79 twilight. **Map** p333 Z1.
The public course at Desert Pines has been recognised as one of the premier upscale courses in the country by *Golf Digest*, with a tight, 6,810-yard, par-71 layout, tree-lined fairways and nine holes on water. The climate-controlled practice facility is the best in Las Vegas.

Las Vegas Golf Club
4300 W Washington Avenue, between N Decatur & N Valley View boulevards, North Las Vegas (646 3003, www.americangolf.com). Bus 103, 208. **Green fees** $69-$89, $49-$69 twilight.
This is the oldest course in the Valley, dating back to 1938. But with $5 million in improvements, you'd never know it. The 6,319-yard, par-72 public course is popular, and it's easy to see why. Book ahead.

Legacy Golf Club
130 Par Excellence Drive, at Green Valley Parkway, Henderson (897 2187, www.thelegacy

> ## INSIDE TRACK
> ## CALLING ALL ALIENS
>
> The **Las Vegas 51s** are named after Nevada's mysterious and legendary alien home base, **Area 51** (*see p302*).

gc.com). Bus 114. **Green fees** June-Sept $75-$90; $55 twilight. Oct-May $100-$155; $75-$85 twilight. This handsome, 7,233-yard, par-72 course is host each year to US Open qualifying, but is also a popular choice with the public.

Royal Links
5995 E Vegas Valley Drive, east of S Nellis Boulevard, East Las Vegas (450 8123, www. royallinksgolfclub.com). No bus. **Green fees** June-Aug $95-$155; $75-$85 twilight. Sept-May $175-$275; $135-$175 twilight.
The Royal Links course is modelled on 11 different courses used for the Open championship; there's a replica of the Postage Stamp at Troon, and the Road Hole at St Andrew's.

TPC at the Canyons
9851 Canyon Run Drive, at Town Center Drive, Summerlin (256 2000, www.tpc.com). No bus. **Green fees** June-Aug $125-$150; $75 twilight. Sept-May $225-$275; $170-$190 twilight.
One of two courses to host the annual Frys.com Open, this 6,772-yard layout was co-designed by Bobby Weed and Ray Floyd.

Gyms & sports centres

Most major hotel-casinos have some sort of fitness facility on the premises.

Gold's Gym
Gold's Plaza, 3750 E Flamingo Road, at Sandhill Road, East Las Vegas (451 4222, www.golds gym.com). Bus 111, 202. **Open** 24hrs daily. **Rates** $15/day; $35/wk. **Map** p333 Z3.
Touted as a no-frills gym, Gold's offers all the aerobics classes, free weights, weight machines and CV equipment an exercise buff could handle.
Other locations throughout the city.

Las Vegas Athletic Club
2655 S Maryland Parkway, at Karen Avenue, East Las Vegas (734 5822, www.lvac.com). Bus 109, 204. **Open** 24hrs daily. **Rates** $15/day; $35/wk. **Map** p333 Y2.
All five Vegas branches have pools, saunas, jacuzzis, Nautilus, free weights and dozens of classes, plus childcare services. Most locations are open 24 hours.
Other locations throughout the city.

24 Hour Fitness
2605 S Eastern Avenue, at E Sahara Avenue, East Las Vegas (641 2222, www.24hour fitness.com). Bus 110, 204. **Open** 24hrs daily. **Rates** $15/day. **Map** p333 Z2.
In addition to gym facilities, 24 Hour has a kids' club and rock climbing. Larger branches also have pools and basketball courts. The latest branch is at the Molasky Building in Downtown (100 City Parkway).
Other locations throughout the city.

Hiking

The **Sierra Club** (732 7750, www.sierraclub. com), the granddaddy of environmental outfits, organises hikes around Red Rock Canyon, Mount Charleston and the Lake Mead area.

Horse riding

See p282 and p283.

Hunting & shooting

Call the **Nevada Division of Wildlife** (486 5127, www.ndow.org) for information on hunting dove, quail and waterfowl in the Lake Mead area, and details of seasonal hunting of deer, elk, antelope and bighorn sheep. A hunting licence for non-residents costs $142.
The **American Shooters Supply & Gun Club** (3440 Arville Street, between W Desert Inn & Spring Mountain roads, 362 1223, www. americanshooters.com) has the only 50-yard indoor range in Las Vegas. Meanwhile, the **Gun Store** (2900 E Tropicana Avenue, between McLeod & Harrison drives, 454 1110, www.thegunstorelasvegas.com) offers more shooting options, from M16s to machine guns. Ladies shoot for free on Tuesday nights.

Pool & billiards

Cue Club
953 E Sahara Avenue, at S Maryland Parkway, East of Strip (735 2884, www.lvcueclub.com). Bus 109, 204. **Open** 24hrs daily. **Map** p333 Y2.
There's 15,000 square feet of ball-banging action at Vegas's largest pool hall.

Rafting & kayaking

See p279 **Rolling on the River.**

Rock climbing

If you don't fancy trekking to Red Rock Canyon (see p282), you can practise at the **Nevada Climbing Center** (3065 E Patrick Lane, between S Eastern Avenue & S Pecos Road, 898 8192, www.nevadaclimbing.info), **GameWorks** (see p72) and Circus Circus's **Adventuredome** (see p240).

Scuba & skin diving

See p281.

Snow sports

The mountains are closer (and snowier) than you think. Just 47 miles away, the **Las Vegas**

Jump to the Beat

Bouncy castles for grown-ups.

The walls are padded. The floor too. The people just keep bouncing and bouncing and bouncing. But there are no straitjackets in sight, nor nurses with pill cups. So what gives?

Descriptions make it sound like an insane asylum, but the **Sky Zone Indoor Trampoline Park** (4915 Steptoe Street, at E Tropicana Avenue, 436 6887, www.skyzone sports.com) is all in good fun. It's a room filled with a large grid of conjoined trampolines on which kids and adults bounce like popcorn to blaring music as they spring up and down, knees buckling and faces beaming with sweaty smiles.

This bouncy 'court' was created a few years ago for Sky Zone, a team sport in which players soar through the air and attempt to put a ball into the hoop (sometimes following it through the goal in the process). But the game's creators decided that the court shouldn't be limited to Sky Zone players, and opened it for all kinds of bouncing activities. Some of them are organised, such as 3-D Dodgeball and SkyRobics (aerobics on trampolines). However, there are also hours set aside for open jumping and pizza parties; for the latter, get the digesting done before you start jumping. It's doubtful that trampoline jumping while passing a ball will ever achieve full Olympic status. Still, that's not really the point. The best part of Sky Zone is that it allows adults to rekindle the joy of childhood bouncy castle parties. Trust Las Vegas to patent something so offbeat and over-the-top, yet also so alluring.

Ski & Snowboard Resort (385 2754, 593 9500 snow conditions, www.skilasvegas. com) at Lee Canyon on Mount Charleston (*see p283*) offers action for all abilities, and has a half-pipe and terrain park. In good years, the season runs from November to April, with the park open 10am-4pm.

A three-hour drive from Vegas on I-15 and SR 145 is the two-mountain, all-abilities **Brian Head Ski Resort** in Utah (1-435 930 1010, www.brianhead.com). Full-day lift passes are $40, or $47 during holidays.

Swimming

Almost every hotel and motel in Las Vegas has a pool, although most are leisure-oriented and not ideal for high-speed lap swimming. Open seasonally from early morning until twilight, the poshest hotel pools on the Strip include **Caesars Palace** (*see p104*), the vast **MGM Grand** (*see p119*), the **Rio** (with a beach for volleyball; *see p135*) and **Mandalay Bay** (*see p109*); many have sections given over to topless sunbathing. Downtown, the pool at the **Golden Nugget** (*see p140*) has an integrated shark tank. Most hotel pools are available only to guests at the resort (or, in some cases, at an affiliated property), but some of them reopen to all comers for evening pool parties in summer; the **Rehab** pool party (*see p260*) at the Hard Rock on Sundays is always popular.

Tennis

It's becoming more difficult to find a tennis court on the Strip; unsurprising, given the price of land. However, some hotels still maintain courts. At **Bally's**, **Flamingo**, **Las Vegas Hilton**, **Paris**, **Plaza** and **Riviera** guests have priority, but they're also open to the public. **Bally's** (*see p115*) has eight courts, twice as many as the **Flamingo** (*see p116*). You can also play at some sports centres and parks, such as **Sunset Park** (Sunset Road & Eastern Avenue, 455 8241, $3-$5/hr), and at the **Darling Tennis Center** (*see p264*; free-$5.50/hr).

Water-skiing

Behind the Hoover Dam, huge **Lake Mead** (*see p280-281*) offers great water-skiing. **Invert Sports** at Lake Mead Marina (1-888/205 7119, www.invertports.com) hires out the necessary equipment, and organises trips and lessons in water-skiing, tubing and wakeboarding.

Theatre & Dance

Move away from the Strip for a different kind of performance.

Theatre in Las Vegas is dominated by the extended-engagement productions on the Strip: much larger than life, and always condensed for tourist audiences who are presumed not to speak English, and certainly not to be in the market for three hours of Brecht. You'll find little in the way of intricate storylines or even two-act structures in these bank-busting shows, but the levels of talent and professionalism can make for an engrossing spectacle.

There were hopes that Vegas would become a standard second stage for major Broadway hits, but less-than-stellar sales saw the arrival and departure of *Avenue Q, Hairspray, The Producers,* Monty Python's *Spamalot* and *Mamma Mia!* (which lasted five years at Mandalay Bay). In their place are the established Cirque and Cirque-esque spectacles, and the return of such dependable solo and duo headline acts as Barry Manilow and Donny and Marie Osmond. (For these and other casino-based shows, *see p226-237.*)

(For these and other casino-based shows, *see p226-237.*)

OFF-STRIP THEATRE

Off-Strip community theatre in Las Vegas lives very much in the shadow of these big-ticket blockbusters, but it's there if you know where to look. Companies such as the newish **Stagedoor Entertainment** and the well-established **Las Vegas Little Theatre** stage high-quality productions; the LVLT has both a 155-capacity main stage and the smaller Fischer Black Box at its disposal, and occasionally rents the latter to outside companies. For more alternative fare, look into the fringey, ambitious productions of **Insurgo Theater Movement**, a spunky, funky troupe that has been rattling sensibilities within the city's nascent arts subculture, particularly in and around Downtown.

Tucked away within the sizeable **UNLV** campus is a thriving and forward-thinking theatre department. Major productions play in the 550-seat **Judy Bayley Theatre**; smaller shows are staged at the more intimate **Paul Harris Theatre** and the **Black Box**, which is also used for student projects and many of the more low-key productions put together by the **Nevada Conservatory Theatre**. Alongside the university's theatre programme, UNLV's Department of Dance is responsible for many of the more worthwhile dance performances, both from UNLV students and visiting troupes.

The city's library system contains three modern, comfortable spaces. The theatres at **Summerlin Library** and **West Las Vegas Library** both have proscenium stages and seat roughly 300; the auditorium at **Clark County Library** features a thrust stage and seats 400. Details of performances are at www.lvccld.org; for details of libraries around the city, *see p313.*

INFORMATION & TICKETS

CityLife, the *Las Vegas Weekly* and the 'Neon' supplement in Friday's *Las Vegas Review-Journal* all carry theatre listings. For advance tickets, which aren't always necessary, contact the theatres direct rather than an outside agent such as Ticketmaster.

THEATRE COMPANIES

★ Insurgo Theater Movement

900 E Karen Avenue #D114, Commercial Center, South-east Las Vegas (771 7331, www.insurgotheater.org). Bus 104, 203. **Tickets** $10-$20.

The city's brashest, brattiest and brightest alternative theatre is a hive of energy and audaciousness, located in an eccentric strip mall that houses a

No Pain, No Gain

Swing Shift Side Show makes art out of pain.

White tigers, disappearing aeroplanes, campy pop singers... Las Vegas certainly isn't short of entertainment options. But for visitors looking for something above and beyond the Strip-standard parlour tricks and showtunes, there's a more visceral option. Much more visceral.

While most people spend their lives generally avoiding discomfort, Andrew S and Kelvikta have turned direct interaction with sharp blades, skin-piercing skewers and broken glass into an art form with the truly fearsome **Swing Shift Side Show**. In a city known for its mysteries and illusions, their double act is the real deal, pushing their bodies to mental and physical extremes in the name of entertainment.

Andrew admits that he has been 'weird' since he was a young lad. However, about ten years ago, the Hawaii native started honing that weirdness to creative effect, developing the kind of freak-show skills that he continues to put to good use in his performances. 'I took everything that was controlling me and learned how to benefit from it,' he says.

Since the group's inception several years ago, Swing Shift Side Show has performed for all manner of curious audiences, from jaded indie rockers to corporate executives, tattoo conventions to college psychology classes. Sometimes accompanied by part-time collaborators Aaron Zilch, Lady Diablo and the deliciously named Jenn O Cide, the duo swallow swords, walk on glass, breath fire and accomplish a number of other feats that you're unlikely to find elsewhere on the Strip. Gents: once you've seen what thay can do with a guy's reproductive organs, no kick in the groin will ever hurt as much again.

Irony of ironies? By day, Andrew is a massage therapist, specialising in deep-tissue treatments. 'Half the week I hurt other people for a living,' he chuckles. 'The other half, I hurt myself.'

● For details of forthcoming performances, see www.swingshiftsideshow.com.

plethora of wig shops, swingers' clubs and a renowned Thai restaurant. Insurgo focuses mostly on presenting bold new work, with some classics. When the young troupe tackles Shakespeare – or Gilbert & Sullivan – it may have the late playwrights spinning in their graves, although it often sends their works spinning into a new light of insight.

Las Vegas Academy
Lowden Theater for the Performing Arts
entrance at S 9th Street & Clark Avenue, Downtown (information 799 7800 ext 5103, 6.30am-3pm Mon-Fri, tickets 1-800 585 3737, www.lvacademytheatre.org). Bus Deuce, 206. **Tickets** $7-$25. **Map** p334 D2.
Las Vegas's oldest secondary school was nearly razed in the early 1990s, but instead found new life as a magnet school for performing arts and international studies. The LVA's new Lowden Theater for the Performing Arts is a state-of-the-art facility that hosts technically impressive shows in a variety of genres: recent seasons included productions of *Sweeney Todd, Cats, Miss Saigon* and *The Grapes of Wrath*. These kids are far better than they should be.

Las Vegas Little Theatre
Schiff City, 3920 Schiff Drive, at Spring Mountain Road & S Valley View Boulevard, South-west Las Vegas (362 7996, www.lvlt.org). Bus 104, 203, 213. **Tickets** $15-$24; $14-$21 reductions.

Las Vegas's oldest community theatre company has settled well into its new space, with both the main stage and the Fischer Black Box regularly hosting sell-out productions. The companion Insomniac Project occasionally features less-mainstream works; fledgling companies also sometimes rent the building for their productions and to hold workshops.

Rainbow Company
Charleston Heights Arts Center, 800 S. Brush Street (229 6553, www.rainbowcompany.org). **Tickets** $7; $3-$5 reductions.
This youth-theatre group stages about a half-dozen different family-friendly productions each year. Shows are staged at the Charleston Heights Arts Center (*see p246*).

Stagedoor Entertainment
581 5008, www.stagedoorlv.com. **Tickets** $6-$18.
A newer company known chiefly for its often small-scale productions staged at the Fischer Black Box in the Las Vegas Little Theatre, Stagedoor does produce at least one full-size affair at the outdoor Super Summer Theatre venue at Spring Mountain Ranch. In 2011, it was *Annie*, the well-known musical about a depression-era orphan abandoned by her parents on the steps of a New York orphanage.
► *For more about Super Summer Theatre, see p270.*

ARTS & ENTERTAINMENT

★ Super Summer Theatre
Spring Mountain Ranch State Park,
Red Rock Canyon (594 7529, www.super
summertheatre.org). No bus. **Tickets** $15.
No credit cards.
Super Summer Theatre is staged in the coolest place
in town – quite literally. On a summer evening, the
temperature at the outdoor stage in Red Rock
Canyon is a good 20 degrees below that of the swel-
tering city. Complete with looming rock walls and
flittering bats, this outdoor amphitheatre is an
appealingly novel place to catch a musical production – the 20-minute sunset drive from the city is as
moving and dramatic as anything onstage. The season runs from June to August (bring your bug spray
and, yes, a sweater) and usually features three or
four populist shows performed in rotation; most of
the leading performers are veterans of Strip revues.
Patrons rent chairs or spread out on blankets with
picnic baskets; get there early for a good spot.
Tickets are available from the UNLV ticket centre
(*see below*).

UNLV Theatre Department
4505 S Maryland Parkway, between E Flamingo
Road & E Tropicana Avenue, University District
(895 2787, http://theatre.unlv.edu). Bus 109, 213.
Tickets $20-$25. **Map** p333 Y3.
Together with the Nevada Conservatory Theatre,
a highly ambitious crew that includes seasoned
pros from all over the world as collaborators in the
classroom and on stage, UNLV presents a large
spread of productions during spring and autumn
in the Judy Bayley Theatre. Great productions can
also be found in the Paul Harris Theatre and in the
Black Box, where the MFA playwriting programme workshops pieces by students and faculty.
An annual series of student-penned one-act plays
in spring and autumn typically yields some memorable stuff.

Dance companies

Nevada Ballet Theatre
243 2623, www.nevadaballet.org. **Tickets** $25-$85.
Associated with UNLV, the Nevada Ballet Theatre
remains Las Vegas's only fully professional ballet
company and training academy, favouring classical works and other time-tested pieces likely to
entertain even complete neophytes. However, artistic director James Canfield, formerly of the Joffrey
Ballet, is spearheading a push to present new work
and forms in the hope of attracting new audiences.
Most shows are held at UNLV's Judy Bayley
Theatre, though larger productions are staged at
the nearby Artemus Ham Concert Hall, also on the
university campus.

UNLV Dance Theatre
4505 S Maryland Parkway, between E Flamingo
Road & E Tropicana Avenue, University District
(895 3827, http://dance.unlv.edu). Bus 109, 213.
Tickets free-$25. **Map** p333 Y3.
UNLV's dance programme features a mix of per-
formances by faculty, students and guest artists.
Classical ballet and modern works are both repre-
sented, with productions held at the Artemus Ham
Concert Hall and the Judy Bayley Theatre.

Nevada Ballet Theatre.

Weddings

Chapels of love.

Nevada authorities never saw fit to enforce a waiting period on couples wanting to apply for a marriage licence. So when couples realised that they'd have to wait a whole three days for a marriage licence in California (thanks to the Gin Law, enacted in 1912 to dissuade drunken lovers from taking the plunge), whirlwind elopements to Vegas quickly became the fashion. The trend was begun by Hollywood celebrities such as Betty Grable and Rita Hayworth, but legions of ordinary couples soon followed. The lenient state laws continue to draw impatient sweethearts, keen to get spliced without a moment's delay: the world's top destination for star-crossed lovers, Las Vegas hosts around 120,000 weddings each year.

WEDDINGS VEGAS-STYLE

In the early days, weddings were performed in hotel rooms or, more often, by a justice of the peace at the county clerk's office. The first wedding chapel to provide a one-stop service centre was founded by the Reverend JD Foster in 1933. But the wedding business didn't really take off until the '40s, when diminutive white steeples started popping up like pointy mushrooms along Las Vegas Boulevard. The industry suffered from the general slump that befell the city in the 1970s, but it bounced back with the glittering '90s renaissance, as hotel-casinos began to provide increasingly luxurious alternatives to the independent chapels that still stand south of Downtown.

In the past, couples were attracted by two main attributes to a Vegas marriage: the casual modernity of an instant wedding; and the price. Today, though, the once-trendy thing-to-do has become a tradition of sorts, with a unique all-American romance of its own. And it's still pretty cheap. On the Strip, you can get married on a spacecraft, atop the Eiffel Tower or on a gondola. Or you could head north towards Downtown to one of the town's old-school independent chapels, where Elvis himself (sort of) could preside over the ceremony.

A basic package wedding at an independent Downtown chapel can cost as little as $50. However, this price excludes a number of crucial services ('donation' to the minister, tip for the limo driver, flowers, and so on),

all of which can result in a heftier bill than anticipated. Set charges tend to be rather higher at resort chapels, but the packages include more options and extras. Before making your decision, call around; there'll be something to suit your budget. And whether your cultural touchstone for the experience is Joan Didion's comic essay 'Marrying Absurd' or the episode of *Friends* in which Ross and Rachel get spliced after getting drunk in their hotel room, the lavish and loopy or lavishly loopy Vegas wedding of your dreams can be yours.

HOW TO DO IT

Before taking the plunge, both bride and groom will need a marriage licence. The happy couple should present themselves at the **Marriage Bureau** (201 E Clark Avenue, at S Casino Center Boulevard, Downtown, 671 0600, www.co.clark.nv.us/clerk) with $60 in cash and valid photo ID; the office is open a hard-working 8am to midnight every day. To save time, download the marriage licence application form from the website and fill it out before you arrive. You'll need to be able to prove that you are who you say you are and that you're at least 18 years of age; US citizens will need their social security numbers, while foreigners should bring ID in English. If either of you have been married before, you'll need to give the date and time the marriage ended (whether through divorce, death or annulment), although you won't need to produce any certificates.

ARTS & ENTERTAINMENT

Once you've got a marriage licence, you'll need to hold the wedding ceremony within a year. It must be conducted in the state of Nevada by a licensed person, who will present you with a marriage certificate once the deed has been done. The quickest and cheapest option is to walk the two blocks from the bureau to the **Commissioner of Civil Marriage** (1st floor, 309 S 3rd Street, at Bridger Avenue, Downtown, 455 3474, open 2-6pm Mon-Thur, Sun, 8am-10pm Fri, Sat). Bring a witness and you can finish the job for the bargain price of $50 (cash only; they don't give change). But with so many more charismatic chapels within walking or drive-through distance, it's best to look around.

You may not need a reservation at many of the city's freestanding chapels. However, it's always best to make one in advance in order to avoid queues or disappointment, especially at weekends or other busy times (Valentine's Day, for example). The whole procedure could all be over in no time at all, but some ceremonies are more time-consuming; it all depends on how much fuss you want to make (and how much you're willing to spend).

Non-US citizens will need certified copies of both the marriage licence and the marriage certificate for their union to be recognised at home. Both are available at nominal cost from the Marriage Bureau and the office of the Commissioner of Civil Marriage respectively, at the time or thereafter by post. Non-US citizens may also require an apostille in order that their marriage is recognised as legally binding in their home country. This is easily obtainable (for a small fee) from the Notary Division of the Secretary of State; further details are available on the Marriage Bureau's website.

WEDDING CHAPELS
Hotel-chapel weddings

Resort chapels are more formal than their Downtown counterparts; couples should plan on booking ahead. The two newest Strip venues, CityCenter and the Cosmopolitan, do not offer wedding services.

THE BEST WEDDINGS

For classic Vegas romance
Little Church of the West. *See p274.*

For modern Vegas opulence
Venetian. *See p273.*

For only-in-Vegas speed
A drive-through wedding. *See p274.*

Artisan
1501 W Sahara Avenue, at Highland Drive, West of Strip (1-800 554 4092 ext112/214 4000 ext 201, www.theartisanhotel.com). Bus 204. **Map** p335 A4.
Antiques and gilt-framed prints make the Artisan an elegant, funky and very un-Vegas spot for a wedding. The Gothic chapel is delightfully spooky, and the bar and the dining hall are perfect for a chic reception.

Bellagio
3600 Las Vegas Boulevard South, at W Flamingo Road (1-888 987 3344, 693 7700, www.bellagio.com). Bus Deuce, 202. **Map** p336 A7.
Whether you choose the grand South chapel or the intimate East chapel, Bellagio offers a Vegas take on old-fashioned European opulence. The Deluxe package starts at $2,000; the Cosa Bella is a cool $25,000.

Excalibur
3850 Las Vegas Boulevard South, at W Tropicana Avenue (1-800 811 4320, 597 7278, www.excalibur.com). Bus Deuce, 202. **Map** p336 A8.
Get dressed up in ermine-trimmed Renaissance garb to marry the king or queen of your heart in the Excalibur's fairytale Canterbury Chapel.

Flamingo
3555 Las Vegas Boulevard South, at E Flamingo Road (1-800 933 7993, 733 3111, www.flamingolasvegas.com). Bus Deuce, 202. **Map** p336 A7.
Apparently, Bugsy Siegel's private suite was torn down to make room for the Flamingo Garden chapel, which remains one of the most elegant and old-school Strip-resort settings in which to marry.

Las Vegas Hilton
3000 Paradise Road, between E Sahara Avenue & E Desert Inn Road, East of Strip (1-866 945 5933/697 8750/www.lvhilton.com). Bus 108, 204, 213. **Map** p335 C5.
The Hilton offers classic old-Vegas opulence, but you can also get married on the bridge of the *Enterprise* in the Star Trek Experience attraction, with a Klingon as your witness and a reception in Quark's *(see p134)*.

Paris Las Vegas
3655 Las Vegas Boulevard South, at E Flamingo Road (1-877 650 5021, 946 7000, www.parislasvegas.com). Bus Deuce, 202. **Map** p336 A7.
Whether you marry in the cavernous, 90-capacity chapel or choose a ceremony for 12 guests atop the Eiffel Tower, this is one way to say you got married in Paris and Las Vegas. For $69.99, bag yourself one of the resort's risqué wedding-cake toppers.

Little Chapel of the Flowers.

Rio
3700 W Flamingo Road, at S Valley View Boulevard, West of Strip (1-888 746 5625, 777 7986, www.riolasvegas.com). **Bus** 202. **Map** p333 X3.
Short of taking a helicopter or a hot-air balloon, the 50th-floor terrace at the Rio is the highest place to get wed in Vegas. Packages start at $150, but it's better to build your own from the extensive list of options.
▶ *Afterwards, head down to watch (of course!) Tony 'n' Tina's Wedding (see p235).*

★ Venetian
3555 Las Vegas Boulevard South, between Sands Avenue & E Flamingo Road (1-866 548 1807, 414 4280, www.venetianweddings.com). **Bus** Deuce, 203. **Map** p335, p336 B6.
There's a traditional chapel here, but you can also say 'I do' on a gondola afloat a faux-canal in faux-Venice or on a footbridge under the blue faux-sky painted with faux-clouds. It's more charming than it sounds, though you'll pay for it: weddings range from $2,000 to $16,500.

Independent weddings

A Christian Pastor 2U
378 7000, www.spiritofprophecy.org.
Pastor Rick and his family offer an evangelical Christian wedding service, which is something of a novelty in Vegas. The pastor is willing to travel to Cathedral Rock, Mount Charleston or elsewhere to conduct the ceremony; prices start at $349.

Cupid's Wedding Chapel
827 Las Vegas Boulevard South, at Gass Avenue, Downtown (1-800 543 2933, 598 4444, www.cupidswedding.com). **Bus** Deuce, 206. **Open** 10am-6pm Mon-Thur, Sun; 10am-1am Fri, Sat. **Credit** AmEx, Disc, MC, V. **Map** p334 C3.
This chapel's classic heart-shaped sign is one of the most striking beacons in the vicinity. Staff can be a little rude, but with packages starting at $179 (for the 'You Send Me wedding'), who's complaining?

Graceland Wedding Chapel
619 Las Vegas Boulevard South, at Bonneville Avenue, Downtown (1-800 824 5732, 382 0091, www.gracelandchapel.com). **Bus** Deuce, 206. **Open** 9am-11pm daily. **Map** p334 C2.
Rose bushes on the patio and a dove motif on the stained-glass windows complete the tidy air of this 'Elvistablishment,' where options run from $199 to $499 (for the 'Famous Dueling Elvis' package). The King will perform at any ceremony but he can only officiate at renewals.
▶ *For more on Vegas's continuing love affair with the King, see p237 Elvis Hasn't Left the Building.*

A Hollywood Wedding
2207 Las Vegas Boulevard South, between E St Louis & E Sahara avenues (1-800 704 0478, 731 0678, www.ahollywoodweddingchapel.com). **Bus** Deuce, 204. **Open** 10am-8pm Mon-Fri, Sun; 10am-10pm Sat. **Map** p335 C4.
Deals at this spot just north of the Sahara range from $99 to an all-inclusive top-end deal for $499. Add $100 and Elvis will sing and walk the bride down the aisle.

Las Vegas Wedding Specialists
Suite 4-210, 10120 W Flamingo Road, West Las Vegas (1-888 638 4673, 496 2613, www.lasvegasweddingspecialists.com). **Bus** 202. **Open** by app.
Multiple rooms (including a traditional chapel) and costumes make this a good choice for a themed wedding, though they'll even come to your hotel room if you're feeling really lazy. Saying 'I do' in a hot-air balloon above the desert costs $675. Daphne will provide religious ceremonies for same-sex couples.

Little Chapel of the Flowers
1717 Las Vegas Boulevard South, at E Oakey Boulevard (1-800 843 2410, 735 4331, www.littlechapel.com). **Bus** Deuce. **Open** 9am-9pm Mon-Thur; 9am-10pm Fri, Sat. **Map** p335 C4.
There are actually three chapels at this well-kept, popular and very professional facility, along with a florist and a photography studio. The chapel even offers couples the opportunity to broadcast weddings live on the internet, so the folks at home can share the joyful occasion. Prices start at $195; $3,755 will buy you a wedding on the floor of the Grand Canyon, with helicopter flights included in the deal.

ARTS & ENTERTAINMENT

★ Little Church of the West

4617 Las Vegas Boulevard South, at W Russell Road (1-800 821 2452, 739 7971, www. littlechurchlv.com). Bus Deuce. **Open** 10am-midnight daily. **Map** p333 Y4.

Voted the city's best chapel for the last ten years by the *Las Vegas Review-Journal*, the quaint Little Church is in the National Registry of Historical Places. Celebs such as Zsa Zsa Gabor and Angelina

Jolie have wed here; hopefully, your marriage will last a little longer.

Little White Wedding Chapel

1301 Las Vegas Boulevard South, at Park Paseo, Downtown (1-800 545 8111, 382 5943, www.alittlewhitechapel.com). Bus Deuce, 206. **Open** 8am-2am Mon-Thur, Sun; 24hrs Fri, Sat. **Map** p335 C3.

Drive-Through Love

Regrets? I've had a few.

Two recently acquainted people stumble down Las Vegas Boulevard with a yard of margarita in one hand and ads for in-room strippers in the other. Making out under the Eiffel Tower, inspiration strikes. The pair decide, after craps and blackjack and maybe another drink, to go full-on Vegas (baby!) and get hitched. A short ride to the Marriage Bureau ensues, followed by the filling out of applications, each party glancing over the other's shoulder to learn their partner's surname.

Turning in their forms, they glance around the tiny office and privately make bets as to which of the other swaying couples will 'make it'. The all-night clerk doesn't bother to check a most-wanted list for bi-coastal bigamist killers stopping off from the desert leg of a cross-country rampage and, instead, turns the form into a licence.

So, where to go? How about the famous Little Church of the West? Perhaps one of the chapels whose signage inadvertently advertises random celebrity couplings, such as Joan Collins and Michael Jordan? Or maybe they could be married by Elvis! Yes! But, dammit, you have to book an Elvis in advance, and time seems short. Then one of them remembers you can

get married in Vegas without even leaving your car. They drive up, roll down the window and greet an internet-ordained minister leaning out to exchange electroplated wedding bands for cash.

The ceremony, long on brevity and short on belief structures, is pleasant but unlikely to be remembered in its entirety. A few items survive the haze: the wedding photo (the happy couple show off their rings from the front seats), a CD from an Arizona goth band that they used in place of a wedding march and a congratulatory gift pack from the chapel containing, among other things, a heart-shaped key ring and coupons for deodorant.

Las Vegas is beautiful in the morning, but with daylight comes sobriety, and a reminder that night is only night but daytime is Real Life. The legally bound strangers emerge from a Downtown motel, dry-mouthed and slightly confused, and take a long look at each other. Or a short one. Back in their respective home towns, they initiate divorce proceedings, surprised and disappointed to learn that there isn't a drive-through for that too, and, upon imparting their now-famous-among-friends Vegas story, are often asked: 'So, did you get fries with that?'

It's not so little, actually: there are five chapels at this Vegas classic, where Frank Sinatra married Mia Farrow in 1966. The drive-through Tunnel of Love was designed for those with physical handicaps who perhaps found it difficult to leave their vehicles, but it's now popular with anyone after a quickie wedding in true only-in-Vegas style.

Mon Bel Ami

607 Las Vegas Boulevard South, at E Bonneville Avenue, Downtown (1-866 503 4400, 388 4445, www.monbelami.com). Bus Deuce, 206. **Open** 10am-10pm daily. **Map** p334 C2.

This well-landscaped and inviting chapel schedules its ceremonies a full hour apart. Hair and make-up artists, a manicurist and a massage therapist are among the services that can be arranged for couples. The 'Just for Two' package starts at $99; the 'Crème de la Crème 'costs $1,799 and includes the release of a white dove. Add Elvis to your wedding for an additional $150.

A Special Memory Wedding Chapel

800 S 4th Street, between E Bonneville Avenue & E Charleston Boulevard, Downtown (1-800 962 7798, 384 2211, www.aspecialmemory.com). Bus Deuce, 206. **Open** 8am-10pm Mon-Thur, Sun; 8am-midnight Fri, Sat. **Map** p334 C2.

The original drive-through wedding costs just $199 plus gratuity. However, the inside of this three-chapel facility is bright and inviting; it even looks like a real church, albeit one with a lot of lights. Ceremonies in the chapels cost anywhere from $199 to $1,095. Grand Canyon, Valley of Fire and Red Rock packages are also available.

Sweethearts Wedding Chapel

1155 Las Vegas Boulevard South, between E Charleston & E Oakey boulevards, Downtown (1-800 444 2932, 385 7785, www.sweethearts chapel.com). Bus Deuce, 206. **Open** 10am-10pm daily. **Map** p335 C3.

This modest chapel seats 35 and has a bridal boutique on site. The $759 special includes a wedding gown, a headpiece, an underskirt, shoes and a tux. Items can also be selected on an à la carte basis.

Vegas Adventure Wedding Chapel

1600 Las Vegas Boulevard South, at E Wyoming Avenue (1-888 463 1399, 270 2522, www.vegas adventureweddings.com). Bus Deuce. **Open** 10am-8pm daily. **Map** p335 C3.

This outfit essentially has two settings: traditional and extreme. You can get married in the chapel, where all weddings are scheduled at least an hour apart, or go for one of the helicopter-based options. The chapel is able to rent formalwear to guests.

Vegas Wedding Chapel

320 S 3rd Street, between E Bridger & E Lewis avenues, Downtown (1-800 823 4095, 933

3464, www.702wedding.com). Bus Deuce & all BTC-bound buses. **Open** 9am-midnight daily. **Map** p334 C2.

This two-chapel venue is perfect for walk-ins: it's one of the closest to the Marriage Bureau. Packages start at $199, with the 'Indulge' package at $2,499; outdoor options include trips to Lake Mead and the Grand Canyon. Staff are able to broadcast weddings live on the internet.

Viva Las Vegas Chapel

1205 Las Vegas Boulevard South, at Park Paseo, Downtown (1-800 574 4450, 384 0771, www. vivalasvegasweddings.com). Bus Deuce, 206. **Open** 9am-8pm Mon-Thur, Sun; 9am-10pm Fri, Sat. **Map** p335 C3.

Known for its themed weddings, which range from sci-fi to western via the obligatory Elvis-slanted ceremony, Viva Las Vegas has more sets than some movie studios. Same-sex commitment ceremonies are treated with care.

★ Wee Kirk o' the Heather

231 Las Vegas Boulevard South, at Bridger Avenue, Downtown (1-800 843 5266, 382 9830, www.weekirk.com). Bus Deuce & all BTC-bound buses. **Open** 10am-8pm Mon-Thur, Sun; 9am-9pm Fri, Sat. **Map** p334 D2.

This tiny chapel has been going since 1940 and is one of the oldest still in operation. Done out to resemble a toy version of a Scottish church, it's also one of the cutest. Prices range from $87 to $777.

Outdoor weddings

Many chapels can organise outdoor weddings, but how about exchanging vows on the rooftop of the 25 storey-tall Binion's Hotel overlooking the Strip? (580 9617, www.thelas vegasweddingcompany.com). For a more sedate experience, charter the 200-capacity **Desert Princess** paddle steamer (www. lakemeadcruises.com) and get married on Lake Mead.

ARTS & ENTERTAINMENT

A world
of inspiration

Escapes & Excursions

Valley of Fire State Park, Nevada. *See p297.*

Day Trips

Get out of Vegas, baby.

Man cannot live on free cocktails and enormous buffets alone. After a while, iridescent sun will become more attractive than fluorescent striplights, and fresh air will appeal more than cranked-to-the-max air-conditioning; even if, as is the case in summer, the temperatures outside are well into three figures. Happily, the roads leading out of Las Vegas offer some terrific escape routes, with opportunities for some great trips. Within 50 miles of the city, you'll find desert parks (**Red Rock Canyon**, **Valley of Fire**), boating and fishing (on **Lake Mead**), man-made marvels (**Hoover Dam**) and even somewhere to ski (**Mount Charleston**).

Heading East

THE HOOVER DAM

The bare facts are staggering enough. It's 726 feet (221 metres) high. At its base, it's 660 feet (200 metres) thick; at its crest, it's 1,244 feet (379 metres) wide. It weighs 6.6 million tons. The building of it used enough concrete to pave a highway between San Francisco and New York. Its reservoir is 110 miles long and around 500 feet (150 metres) deep, and can hold enough water to cover the entire state of Nevada six inches deep. So far, so impressive. But then you actually catch sight of the **Hoover Dam**, and you can scarcely believe your eyes.

Without the Hoover Dam (née Boulder Dam, but renamed in 1947 for President Herbert Hoover, under whose administration the project was begun), much of the Southwest would not exist. The dam controls the Colorado River, providing electricity and water to nearly 20 million people in Nevada, California and Arizona, and makes it possible for cities and farmland to flourish in one of the driest, hottest and most inhospitable regions of the world.

In the early 20th century, the sheer power of the Colorado River made the building of the Hoover Dam both necessary and terrifying. Black Canyon was chosen as the location for the project, which was overseen by the Bureau of Reclamation and came with four main aims: flood prevention, silt control, water storage and electrical-energy generation.

Building it was a mammoth task. The Colorado had to be temporarily diverted so the dam wall could be constructed. The concrete would have taken 100 years to set if left under normal conditions, so the cooling process was sped up by pumping ice-cold water through a network of pipes laid into each block of concrete. Vast pipes some 30 feet in diameter, known as penstocks, were lowered from an overhead cableway 800 feet (250 metres) above the canyon floor and squeezed into tunnels blasted out of the side walls. A vast army of 16,400 workers – remember, the project was built at the height of the Depression – laboured day and night for four years, finishing in February 1935… two years ahead of schedule.

The dam straddles the border between Arizona and Nevada. The skinny, perennially congested **Highway 93** passes over the top, although traffic was significantly eased with the October 2010 opening of the four-lane **Hoover Dam Bypass** a quarter of a mile south of the dam. Officially named the Mike O'Callaghan-Pat Tillman Memorial Bridge (after former Nevada governor Mike O'Callaghan, who died in 2004, and professional footballer Pat Tillman who left his career to enlist in the army after 9/11, and was killed by friendly fire in Afghanistan), it is nearly 2,000 feet (610 metres) long, with a 1,060-foot twin-rib concrete arch. The $240 million bridge spans the Black Canyon and connects the Arizona and Nevada approach highways nearly 900 feet (275 metres) above the Colorado River.

Even if you've seen the Hoover Dam before, this spectacular new bridge calls for another visit. You can walk across it: there's a sidewalk entrance on the north side of the bridge.

The 459-car parking garage (parking $7; there are free lots on the Arizona side of the bridge) and the visitors' centre are on the Nevada side of the border. The latter is something of a necessary evil, through which the bulk of the 'Discovery' tour is conducted. Booking isn't required, but early arrival is recommended to beat both crowds and traffic. (The 'Hard Hat' tours, which took visitors closer to the action, were suspended post 9/11 and seem unlikely to resume.)

The **tour** ($11, $9 reductions, free under-7s) is a mixed bag. The films are informative, but the constant waiting in line is frustrating and the way in which visitors are herded in and out of cinemas and galleries, while no fault of the knowledgeable, enthusiastic staff – it's to do with the hamfisted design of the centre itself – is an irritation. However, in between the movie and the exhibition, you'll get to see inside the dam, specifically a long hall that contains eight huge generators.

Back outside, note a few interesting features on or near the dam. Chief among them are a pair of 30-foot sculptures, the *Winged Figures of the Republic*, flanking a flagpole above a terrazzo floor inlaid with a celestial map; it marks Franklin D Roosevelt's dedication of the dam in September 1935. The white mark on the shoreline indicates the flood level in 1983 when Lake Mead rose to within seven feet of the top. But while these are nice diversions, they won't be what you remember. That'll be the sheer size of the place, one of the greatest man-made constructions on the planet.

Getting there

To reach the Hoover Dam from Las Vegas, take US 93 south for 32 miles. You'll pass through Boulder City en route.

Tourist information

For information on tours, call 1-866 730 9097 or 494 2517, or see www.usbr.gov/lc/hooverdam. The **visitors' centre** is open 9am to 6pm daily; tours end at 5.15pm.

Rolling on the River

Go kayaking on the Colorado for stunning views of the Hoover Dam.

Lake Mead, the reservoir that sprawls off the Colorado, is man-made; as, of course, is the Hoover Dam, which diverts water into it. Amid such man-made monsters so close to a city defined by artifice, it's easy to forget that the Colorado River itself is a living, breathing watercourse. But so it goes and so it flows, winding its way down through the Southwest towards the Gulf of California. You can join in for a while.

One of several firms that operates kayaking trips on the Colorado, **Desert Adventures** (293 5026, www.kayaklas vegas.com) offers visitors unique views of the Hoover Dam from the water below. Sign up to DA's half-day kayaking tour ($120 per person) and you'll set off from close to the dam's base; from here, you'll cruise eight miles downriver in the company of a guide, stopping for a packed lunch en route.

It can get windy down on the surface, but the dam and the width of the river both help mitigate against whitewater. It's perfect for novices, not least because it's surprisingly easy to learn. The views are amazing and the exercise bracing. And after the awful traffic approaching the dam, all that open space will come as a glorious relief.

Hoover Dam.

Lake Mead.

BOULDER CITY

Driving down Highway 93 from Vegas, you'll pass some small motels, the odd restaurant and a few stalls selling Mexican pottery and other handicrafts. Only slowly do you realise that something's missing. Built in 1931 to house the workers at the dam, **Boulder City** is the only town in Nevada where gambling is illegal.

Triangular in shape, Boulder City was the first 'model city' in the US, built according to progressive planning theories. The Bureau of Reclamation, government buildings and a park sit at the apex of the triangle, with the workers' houses radiating down from there. It was never intended to be a permanent settlement, it got a second wind during World War II and is now flourishing. There's more on the area at the **Boulder City/Hoover Dam Museum** (294 1988, www.bcmha.org, $1-$2) within the Boulder Dam Hotel.

Where to stay, eat & drink

Boulder City is small-town Americana, and a good eating option in that vein is **Milo's Best Cellars** (538 Nevada Highway, 293 9540, www.miloswinebar.com), which has a nice, lightish menu. Those who prefer the grain to the grape are directed to the newly opened **Boulder Dam Brewing Company** (453 Nevada Highway, 243 2739, www.boulderdambrewing.com).

If the atmosphere appeals, stay at the historic **Boulder Dam Hotel** (1305 Arizona Street; 293 3510, www.boulderdamhotel.com); it counts Howard Hughes among its former guests. In the basement, **Matteo's Underground Lounge** (293 0098, www.matteodining.com) stages regular shows by local bands.

Getting there

Boulder City is 25 miles south of Vegas (seven miles west of Hoover Dam) on US 93. To see the historic district, turn off at the business loop, which rejoins US 93 on the far side of the town.

Tourist information

In the Boulder Dam Hotel, the **Chamber of Commerce** (293 2034, www.bouldercity chamberofcommerce.com) has maps and local information.

LAKE MEAD

Around ten million visitors come to Lake Mead's 550 miles of shoreline each year to sail, fish, swim, water-ski, camp and generally enjoy watery pleasures in the desert. Wholly artificial, the lake was created when the Colorado was blocked by the Hoover Dam. It's an incongruous sight, a large blue splodge surrounded by barren mountains and canyon-tops.

The lake is the centrepiece of the huge **Lake Mead National Recreation Area**, which also includes Lake Mohave to the south (formed when the Colorado River was stemmed again in 1953 by the Davis Dam) and the desert east to the edge of Grand Canyon National Park (*see p285*) and north to Overton. There's a $10 permit fee per car (or $5 per person), which grants seven days' access to the whole area.

Lakeside Scenic Drive (Highway 146) and Northshore Scenic Drive (Highway 167) skirt the western and northern sides of Lake Mead for nearly 60 miles. The route isn't very scenic, but it's the access road for the concession-operated marinas along the Nevada shoreline, several of which have been closed or forced to relocate due to continually dropping water levels at Lake Mead. All have small ranger stations, grocery stores and some form of restaurant; some also have swimming beaches (without lifeguards), picnic sites, motels, showers and gas stations. **Lake Mead Marina** on Boulder Beach (293 3484, www.riverlakes.com), which had to be relocated three miles south (and closer to Boulder City) in 2008 due to lowering water levels, and the **Las Vegas Boat Harbor** (293 1191, www.lasvegasboatharbor.com) are the largest, closest and busiest marinas; further north are the **Callville Bay Marina** (565 8958,

www.callvillebay.com), the **Echo Bay
Resort** (394 4000, www.echobay7c.com)
and the **Overton Beach Resort** (394 4040,
www.overtonbeachmarina.net).

The best way to explore the lake is by boat.
There are numerous secluded coves, sandy
beaches and narrow canyons accessible only
by water, and the warm, clear lake is ideal for
swimming: the water temperature averages
78°F (26°C) in spring, summer and autumn. You
can hire a boat from the marinas; expect small
fishing boats to cost around $20-$40 for two
hours or $60-$120 per day, with large ski boats
roughly three times the price. Alternatively, take
a cruise on the *Desert Princess* paddlesteamer
($39, $18 reductions), run by **Lake Mead
Cruises** (293 6180, www.lakemeadcruises.com).

Lake Mead offers some of the best year-round
sport **fishing** in the country, but it's also one
of the country's top freshwater **scuba diving**
destinations. Visibility averages 30 feet (nine
metres) and can reach double that in winter,
better enabling divers to see the dramatic drop-
offs and boat wrecks. The most popular location
is **Scuba Park**, adjacent to Lake Mead Marina.
You can rent equipment for around $35 a day
from **American Cactus Divers** (3985 E
Sunset Road, Henderson, 433 3483, www.
americancactusdivers.com).

Where to stay, eat & drink

For an eaterie on the water try the **Las
Vegas Boat Harbor House Café** (293 1191).
Seven Crown Resorts (1-800 752 9669,
www.7crown.com) runs motels at **Echo Bay**
(394 4000, rates $60-$115) and **Lake Mead
Lodge** (293 2074, rates $85-$180). There are
campgrounds (293 8491, rates $10) at all
marinas bar Overton and Willow Beach. Close
by is upscale **Lake Las Vegas** (*see p96*).

Getting there

The visitors' centre is 27 miles south of Vegas
on Highway 93, at the junction with Lakeshore
Scenic Drive (Highway 146). To reach Las
Vegas Bay, Boulder Beach and Lake Mead
marinas, bypassing the visitors' centre, take
Boulder Highway south from Vegas and turn
left at Lake Mead Drive (Highway 146), or take
I-15/US 93 north to exit 45 in North Las Vegas
and turn on to Lake Mead Boulevard east
(Highway 147). Both routes join the shore road.

Tourist information

Consult the NPS website (www.nps.gov/lame).
The **Alan Bible Visitor Center** (293 8990,
8am-4.30pm daily) on US 93 has maps and
details on activities. There are also information
stations at Overton Beach, Echo Bay, Callville
Bay, Las Vegas Bay and Temple Bar.

VALLEY OF FIRE STATE PARK

An hour north-east of Las Vegas lies a natural
marvel that's every bit as spectacular as the
resorts on the Strip. Bounded by the grey
limestone Muddy Mountains to the south and
west, **Valley of Fire** was the first state park in
Nevada, and is still one of its most breathtaking.

The main attractions are the red sandstone
formations, created from sand dunes deposited
135 to 150 million years ago and sculpted by
wind and water into bizarre, anthropomorphic
shapes: look for **Elephant Rock** and **Seven
Sisters** along Highway 169, the east–west road
through the park. A two-mile loop road runs past
some of the most dramatic rock formations.

The park is easily explored in a day. Hiking
is permitted, but there are few marked trails,
and all are very short. Get advice on hiking
and a trails map from the visitors' centre (*see
below*). The road north from the centre offers a
panoramic view of multicoloured sandstone at
Rainbow Vista and ends at the White Domes
picnic area. An easy trail from Rainbow Vista
leads to spectacular rocks at **Fire Canyon**,
from where you can see the spot where Captain
Kirk met his doom in *Star Trek: Generations*.

Atlatl Rock, on the scenic loop road, has a
number of petroglyphs, while others are visible
on the short trail to **Mouse's Tank**, a natural
water basin used in the 1890s as a hideout by
a renegade Indian known as Mouse. Visit the
Lost City Museum in Overton (397 2193,
www.comnett.net/~kolson), eight miles north of
the park, to learn about the Indian inhabitants,
from the ancient Basketmaker people and the
Puebloans (Anasazi) to the Paiute, whose
descendants still live in southern Nevada.

Summer highs top 110°F (43°C); as such,
the best times to visit are spring and autumn.
If you're lucky, you may spy a desert tortoise
(Nevada's state reptile) and you're sure to see
antelope ground squirrels (aka chipmunks).
Don't feed or pet them: they're suspected of
carrying the fleas that transmit bubonic plague.

Getting there

Head north on I-15 for 33 miles to Highway
169: it's 17 miles to the park's western entrance.
You can also enter the park from Lake Mead,
off Northshore Scenic Drive (*see left*).

Tourist information

Advice on hiking and a trails map are available
from the **visitors' centre** (397 2088, http://
parks.nv.gov/vf.htm), which also has displays

ESCAPES & EXCURSIONS

on the area's geology, ecology and human history. Signposted along Highway 169, it's open 8.30am-4.30pm daily. Park entrance is $10.

Heading West

RED ROCK CANYON & AROUND

A mere 20 miles from the gaming tables of Vegas is one of Nevada's most beautiful outdoor areas. The cool, deep-cut canyons of the **Red Rock Canyon National Conservation Area** make it a popular hiking spot year-round, while climbers come here from all over to enjoy some of the best rock climbing in the US.

Part of the Spring Mountains, Red Rock Canyon has as its centrepiece a nearly sheer escarpment of Aztec sandstone, the remnant of ancient sand dunes that covered the area 180 million years ago. Roughly 65 million years ago, the Keystone Thrust Fault pushed older grey limestone over younger sandstone, reversing the normal layering and resulting in today's dramatic landscape. The red and cream Calico Hills are more rounded, as they're not protected from erosion by a higher limestone layer.

Attracted by the water, Native Americans have used Red Rock Canyon since about 3500 BC: evidence remains in the form of rock art (etched petroglyphs and painted pictographs), as well as artefacts such as arrowheads and ceramics. More than 45 mammal species also inhabit the park, among them mountain lions, coyotes, kangaroo rats, mule deer and the near-mythical desert bighorn sheep, but you'll be lucky to spot any. The most visible animals are the non-native burros (donkeys), around 50 of which live around Red Rock Canyon. Observe from a distance and never feed them (it's illegal and dangerous).

Stop first at the visitors' centre (clearly signed) for information and a map, before exploring the one-way, 13-mile scenic drive (also popular with cyclists) through the canyon. The road gives access to numerous hiking trails and three picnic sites. Some trails are not marked clearly and require some scrambling; so take a topographic map (available at the visitors' centre) and a compass.

A good introduction to the Calico Hills at the start of the drive is the two-and-a-half-mile **Calico Tank** trail from Sandstone Quarry. Just above the tank is a fine view (smog permitting) of the valley and the Strip's casino monoliths. Other good, short summer hikes include **Ice Box Canyon** and **Pine Creek Canyon**. For further details of the scores of other trails, pick up a copy of the BLM's trail leaflet. Guided hikes are led by park staff at the weekends

and some weekdays, and by the Sierra Club (732 7750, www.nevada.sierraclub.org).

Red Rock is popular with rock climbers. Stop at **Desert Rock Sports** (*see p214*) for gear and some practice on the indoor wall, before calling in at the visitors' centre. There's further detail in three guides: Joanne Urioste's *The Red Rocks of Southern Nevada* and *The Red Book Supplement* (both Verex Press, $21.95 & $19.95), and Todd Swain's *Rock Climbing: Red Rocks* (Falcon Press, $30). Alternatively, get to know the Old West like an old Westerner with **Cowboy Trail Rides** (387 2457, www.cowboy trailrides.com), which can saddle you up and take you on a tour of Red Rock. Rides ($69-$250) are accompanied by a guide; first-timers are welcome, and booking is required.

If you'd prefer something less physical, head further west on Highway 159 to the green oasis of **Spring Mountain State Park**, at the base of the dramatic Wilson Cliffs. Admission to the park includes entrance to the New England-style ranch house, where the $9 day-use fee is payable (875 4141, http://parks.nv.gov/smr.htm, 10am-4pm daily). Stroll around the buildings in the fenced grounds and picnic on a grassy meadow. There are walking tours year-round, and open-air theatre and concerts in summer.

Bonnie Springs Old Nevada

1 Gun Fighter Lane, off Highway 159 (875 4191, www.bonniesprings.com). No bus. **Open** *May-Oct* 10.30am-6pm daily. *Nov-Apr* 10.30am-5pm daily. **Admission** $20/car. **Credit** MC, V.
South on Highway 159 sits this mock Wild West town, with a melodrama and hanging staged daily (times vary by season). It's rather dilapidated but good fun; visitors can take a horse ride ($30), and there's also a free petting zoo, a restaurant and a motel (875 4400, rates $65-$145).

Getting there

To reach the visitors' centre, head west on Charleston Boulevard (Highway 159) for 20 miles. If you're staying near the southern end of the Strip, drive south on I-15, take Highway 160 (towards Pahrump), then turn right on to Highway 159, passing Bonnie Springs and Spring Mountain en route to Red Rock Canyon.

Tourist information

The Red Rock Canyon visitors' centre (515 5361, www.nv.blm.gov/redrockcanyon), offers information, maps and a chance to pay the $7-per-car fee. The centre is open daily from 8am to 4.30pm; however, the scenic drive itself is open longer hours (6am-8pm Apr-Sept; 6am-7pm Oct, Mar; 6am-5pm Nov-Feb).

ESCAPES & EXCURSIONS

Arizona

The astounding and amazing Grand Canyon.

Of Arizona's two major towns, sprawling Phoenix has little to offer the visitor except sun and golf, while the more characterful Tucson is too far away to visit comfortably in a couple of days. It's no surprise, then, that most visitors to Arizona from Las Vegas head as directly west as the roads allow, towards one of the world's great natural wonders: the Grand Canyon. You'll have seen pictures, TV footage, maybe even an IMAX film on a larger-than-life-size screen. Yet nothing will prepare you for your first glimpse of the epic, breathtaking, unknowable Grand Canyon.

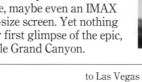

Grand Canyon National Park

Grand Canyon National Park sprawls across a length of 277 miles, most of which is difficult to reach and rarely visited; just a tiny portion is accessible from the **South Rim**, where most visitors congregate. The canyon is misnamed: it's not just one rip in the earth, but a series of canyons surrounding the central gorge cut by the Colorado River, a staggering 5,000 feet (1,500 metres) from top to bottom. At an average elevation of 7,000 feet (2,150 metres), the South Rim isn't unbearably hot in summer, but temperatures a mile further down at the bottom can edge beyond 110°F (43°C). The best months to visit are April, May, September and October, avoiding the relatively rainy (and tourist-packed) summer months and the snowbound winters.

Entrance to the park costs $25 per car ($12 per person for pedestrians, cyclists and motorcycles), valid for seven days. Although it's possible to make a see-it-and-scram round trip in one long day, we recommend that you stay at least two nights, allowing ime to explore the village, spin around the rim drives, take in the lookout points and venture into the canyon itself.

EN ROUTE TO THE SOUTH RIM

Some 150 miles west of the South Rim, the Grand Canyon forms the northern boundary of the Hualapai Indian Reservation. Although it's not as spectacular as the South Rim, the western canyon is closer

to Las Vegas and will give you a taste of the grandeur to be found further east.

Roughly an hour south-east of Las Vegas, there's the option of a detour to a high-concept, high-budget attraction within the reservation. Opened in 2007, the **Grand Canyon Skywalk** (1-877 716 9378, 1-702 220 8372, www.grand canyonskywalk.com) is a free-standing glass bridge that extends directly over the canyon, giving visitors the opportunity to stand 4,000 feet (1,200 metres) above the earth and look down into it. So far so good, until you take into account the breathtaking $73 admission fee – all individuals are required to purchase a Legacy pass to enter the reservation ($43.05 adults; $35.03 children $39.85 seniors) plus pay the additional cost for the Skywalk ($29.95 adults; $26.96 children; $26.96 seniors) – and the fact that cameras aren't allowed on the damn thing.

If money is no object and you have a photographic memory, then head to Skywalk by taking a left off US 93 on to Pierce Ferry Road, 40 miles south of the Hoover Dam, and then turning right on to Diamond Bar Road 28 miles

---

INSIDE TRACK ARIZONA TIME

Note that Arizona observes Mountain Standard Time year-round, without daylight saving time in summer. This means that from the first Sunday in November until the second Sunday in March, Arizona is one hour ahead of Las Vegas, but is effectively in the same time zone for the remainder of the year.

later. From here, it's a simple drive to the reservation's other attractions, such as rafting tours (**Hualapai River Runners** 1-928 769 2636), camping and helicopter rides. The tribal headquarters are further south in **Peach Springs**, where the **Hualapai Lodge** (900 Route 66, 1-928 769 2230) provides lodging and dining facilities along with permits for sightseeing, fishing and camping. For details, see www.bestgrandcanyondestinations.com.

If you choose to pass on the walk and continue along US 93, you'll hit **Kingman**. From here, you have a choice. If you're in a hurry, take speedy I-40 east. But if you've a little more time and a little more romance about your person, head along what is now the longest surviving portion of the iconic Route 66. Much of the 2,448-mile Mother Road, which originally linked Chicago with Santa Monica, has been bypassed or replaced by major highways, a victim of the motor travel whose population its construction predicted. But this portion survives, just about. In Kingman, swing by the **Route 66 Museum** (120 Andy Devine Drive, 1-928 753 9889, www.kingmantourism.org), before driving west through dusty **Hackberry**, the aforementioned Peach Springs and on to **Seligman**, where you can reconnect with I-40.

Continuing west along I-40 will bring you to the town of **Williams**, 60 miles south of the National Park. Some use the town as a staging post en route to the canyon, the entrance to which is 60 miles due north along Route 64 or along a picturesque, narrow-gauge

steam railway (*see p289*). Others, though, prefer the larger **Flagstaff**, 35 miles east. Situated at the base of the **San Francisco Peaks**, the highest mountains in Arizona, this pleasant railroad and university town has motels, restaurants, cafés and a brewpub, as well as the **Lowell Observatory** (www.lowell.edu), from which the planet Pluto was first spotted in 1930. For more information, contact the Chamber of Commerce (101 E Route 66, 1-928 774 4505, www.flagstaffchamber.com).

THE SOUTH RIM

The majority of the annual five million visitors to Grand Canyon National Park head for the **South Rim** and the restaurants, shops and sights of **Grand Canyon Village**, on the edge of the canyon. Inevitably, it's crowded, but it remains remarkably untouristy; or, in some cases, pleasantly retro-touristy. It's also closer to the Colorado River than the North Rim and affords much better views into the canyon.

If you have sufficient patience to avoid driving straight to the rim, park your car and take a free shuttle bus to the **Canyon View Information Plaza**, where you'll find a visitors' centre and bookstore (open 8am-5pm daily). Pick up a variety of literature from here, offering comprehensive information on sights, transportation, facilities and activities, and ask the rangers for tips on hikes. Stroll to **Mather Point** for your first gob-smacking view of the canyon, before riding the shuttle bus from Information Plaza into Grand Canyon Village.

Grand Canyon Skywalk. *See p285.*

ESCAPES & EXCURSIONS

Grand Canyon Village

Travellers have been coming to gawp at the Grand Canyon since the 19th century, and Grand Canyon Village remains proud of its history. The village is dotted with historic buildings, many of them built by pioneering female architect Mary Colter for the Fred Harvey Travel Company. Pick up a leaflet and take the self-guided walking tour around the village's historic district, starting at the **Santa Fe Railway Station** (1909), the terminus for the **Grand Canyon Railway** (*see p289*). Across the road on the canyon's edge is the luxurious **El Tovar Hotel**, a wooden structure in hunting-lodge style that cost a cool $250,000 to build in 1905. Next to it is the **Hopi House**, designed by Colter in 1904 as a showroom for Indian handicrafts. Colter modelled the building on a terraced Hopi dwelling, using local stone and wood, and employing Hopi builders. Nearby is **Verkamps**, completed in 1906 and one of the canyon's oldest continuously operating stores.

Walking west from the hotel along the Rim Trail, you'll pass the modern **Kachina** and **Thunderbird** lodges, and the pioneer-style, stone-and-log **Bright Angel Lodge**, designed by Colter in 1935. If you're here in winter, warm your hands at the fabulous 'geological' fireplace, the design of which mimics the layers of rock in the Grand Canyon. The hearth is made from stone from the bed of the Colorado River; at the top of the chimney breast sits a layer of Kaibab limestone.

Just beyond Bright Angel Lodge is the **Bucky O'Neill Cabin**, which dates from the 1890s and is the oldest surviving building on the rim, and the **Lookout Studio** (Colter, 1914), which now houses a gift shop. Perched on the edge of the precipice, the studio was designed as an observation building from which visitors could view the canyon. Colter didn't want the building to detract from its surroundings, and created a stone structure that merges with the surrounding rock. From a distance, the structure is almost invisible.

The nearby **Kolb Studio** was built by pioneering photographers Ellsworth and Emery Kolb, who started snapping mule riders here in 1902. The lack of water on the rim meant the brothers were required to hike halfway down the canyon to their developing tent at Indian Gardens to process the photos, then clamber back to the top before the mules returned. (To this day, all water at the South Rim is pumped up from inside the canyon; look for the trans-canyon pipeline on the Bright Angel Trail.) The Kolbs were also the first to film a boat trip down the Colorado, in 1912. The studio houses a bookstore and gallery, and has displays on the brothers' work. Beyond here is the head of the Bright Angel Trail (*see p291*).

Along the South Rim

Two roads lead west and east from the village along the canyon rim, each providing very different views into the canyon. You can also walk along the edge of the rim on the 12-mile, pedestrian-only **Rim Trail**. The village section of the trail is paved; elsewhere it can get rocky.

The eight-mile **Hermit Road** is closed to private vehicles. Instead, visitors are encouraged to take the shuttle bus that departs from the western edge of the village to **Hermit's Rest**, built by Mary Colter as a refreshment stop in 1914. The building, now in use as a gift shop, is deliberately primitive in style, and was designed to blend with its natural surroundings (fortunately, a Swiss chalet design was rejected). From here, you can set off on the Hermit Trail into the canyon (*see p291*).

The shuttle bus stops at various observation points on its way west. Among them is the spectacular **Abyss**, where the Great Mohave Wall drops 3,000 feet (900 metres) to the Tonto Platform above the Colorado River. On its return, the bus stops only at Mohave Point and **Hopi Point**. If you're planning to watch the sunset, check the time of the last bus before you leave to avoid a long, dark walk back to the village.

Along the East Rim, **Desert View Drive** runs 25 miles in the opposite direction as far as the park's eastern entrance. On the way, the road passes several excellent lookout points, with access to the **South Kaibab** and **Grandview Trails** (for both, *see p291*). Near the end of the drive, there's an 800-year-old ruin of an Anasazi pueblo and the **Tusayan Museum**, which provides somewhat scanty information on the history and culture of the canyon's Native American inhabitants.

The drive finishes at **Desert View**, which offers the clearest views of the Colorado River. This is also the location of the **Watchtower**, a circular, 70-foot (21-metre) tower regarded as Colter's masterpiece. A remarkable re-creation of the ancient Indian towers Colter had seen at Mesa Verde and Canyon de Chelly, its ground-floor room is modelled after a kiva (or sacred ceremonial chamber), while the roof provides a panoramic view of the Grand Canyon, the Painted Desert and the San Francisco Peaks, 40 miles to the south. The centrepiece is the **Hopi Room**, decorated with vivid Hopi designs depicting various gods and legends.

To learn more about the geology, history and archaeology of the South Rim, join one of the National Park Service's ranger-guided walks or activities. Check the park's website or ask at the visitors' centre for a programme schedule.

Where to eat & drink

There are three restaurants, two self-service cafés and a takeaway snack bar in the Grand Canyon Village, all open daily. The splendid, dark wooden dining room (with its large Indian murals) at the **El Tovar Hotel** is very popular:

you can take your chances at breakfast (6.30-11am) and lunch (11.30am-2pm), but must book for dinner (5-10pm; 1-928 638 2631 ext 6432); hotel guests take priority over non-guests.

Nearby are the less formal **Bright Angel Restaurant** (6.30am-10pm) and the **Arizona Room** steakhouse (4.30-10pm, also 11.30am-3pm during peak season; closed Jan and Feb). **Maswik Lodge** has a sports bar (open 11am-11pm) and an inexpensive but rather institutional cafeteria (6am-10pm); there's a larger cafeteria at **Yavapai Lodge** (6.30am-9pm). Wherever you dine, have a drink in the lounge at the El Tovar (11am-11pm), decorated by the ubiquitous Colter. There are also snack bars at Hermit's Rest (9am-5pm) and Desert View **Marketplace** (9am-5pm) at Market Plaza, and a deli at Market Plaza (8am-7pm).

Where to stay

There's plenty of accommodation in Grand Canyon Village, but demand is high: book as far ahead as you can (we're talking months, not weeks). That said, there are sometimes rooms available for walk-in visitors at Yavapai and Maswik Lodges, occasionally even in high season. Book through **Xanterra Parks & Resorts** (1-888 297 2757, 1-303 297 2757, www. grandcanyonlodges.com). Generally speaking, the more expensive rooms at the hotels and lodges listed below come with a canyon view.

Complete with a grand lobby adorned with stuffed animal heads, the **El Tovar Hotel** (double $178-$426), offers the most splendid lodging in the village. Try to get a room with a spacious private balcony overlooking the rim. Other options are the 1930s **Bright Angel Lodge** (double $81-$340) and the more modern, motel-style **Kachina** and **Thunderbird Lodges** (double $173-$184), also on the edge of the canyon. **Maswik Lodge** (double $92-$173) and **Yavapai Lodge** (double $114-$163) are located in a pine forest a short walk away.

There are also two campsites at the South Rim, run by the National Park Service. There are more than 300 pitches at the **Mather Campground**, but booking is recommended from March to mid November (1-877 444 6777, www.recreation.gov). Outside these times, campsites are available on a walk-up basis, and the standard $18 fee drops by $3. Roughly 25 miles east of Grand Canyon Village, **Desert View Campground** is open from mid May to mid October on a walk-up basis ($12).

A few miles south of Grand Canyon Village, just outside the park, is **Tusayan**. At the National Geographic Visitor Center, there's a supremely superfluous IMAX cinema and a rather more useful park fee pay-station, which will mean you don't have to queue on entry.

Among the basic motels are the **Red Feather Lodge** (1-866 561-2425, 1-928 638 2414, www. redfeatherlodge.com), the **Best Western Squire Inn** (1-800 622 6966, 1-928 638 2681, www.grandcanyonsquire.com) and a **Holiday Inn Express** (1-888 465 4329, 1-928 638 3000, www.grandcanyon.hiexpress.com). A free shuttle-bus service runs between Tusayan and the village. There are also plenty of motels in Flagstaff and Williams.

For lodging options in the canyon, *see p292.*

Getting there

By air

Several companies offer scheduled flights from the Las Vegas area to Grand Canyon Airport at Tusayan. Among them are **Air Vegas** (1-800 940 2550, 1-702 433 1677, www.airvegas.com), which operates several flights a day from the airport at Boulder City; a return flight costs $179. For details of sightseeing flights over the Grand Canyon, *see p317.*.

By bus

Bus service between Flagstaff, Williams and Grand Canyon Village is offered by **Open Road** (1-855 563-8830, 1-602 997-6474, www.openroad tours.com), which charges $95 roundtrip adult; $55 child between Flagstaff and the Grand Canyon. **Greyhound** (*see p208*) runs bus services from Las Vegas to Flagstaff (6hrs; $117-$145 return).

By car

To reach the South Rim, head south-east on US 93 to I-40 east, then turn left (north) on to Highway 64 at Williams. It's 290 miles from Vegas and the journey takes about five hours. As an alternative, drive to Williams and board the Grand Canyon Railway (*see below*).

By rail

The **Grand Canyon Railway** (1-800 843 8724, 1-928 773 1976, www.thetrain.com) runs train services from the depot in Williams to the old **Santa Fe Station** in the heart of Grand Canyon Village. Trains leave Williams at 9.30am and depart from the Grand Canyon at 3.30pm. There are various 'classes' of service in an assortment of historic 'carriages', and characters in costume entertain passengers en route. The trip takes 2hrs 15mins; tickets, which exclude the park fee, cost $70-$190 ($40-$110 children, who are not allowed in the Observation Dome or luxury coaches).

Getting around

To encourage a more serene appreciation of nature, the park service has limited private-vehicle access in some areas and is expanding

pedestrian and bicycle routes around the South Rim. The bus shuttles are a pleasant and workable alternative to private transport.

By bus

A free shuttle-bus service operates on three interconnecting routes around the South Rim: the **Village Route**, serving Canyon View Information Plaza and the main village destinations; the **Hermit's Rest Route**, along the rim from the west side of the village to Hermit's Rest; and the **Kaibab Trail Route**, from Canyon View to Yaki Point. A route for visitors needing mobility assistance operates from Canyon View to Mather Point.

By car

Canyon View Information Plaza, Mather Point, Yaki Point Road and Hermit Road are not accessible to private vehicles.

By coach

Choose from various Xanterra-run sightseeing trips around the canyon rim, including the **Hermit's Rest Tour** ($26 per person, children under 16 free when accompanied by paying adult), the **Desert View Tour** ($45), and popular 90-minute **Sunrise** and **Sunset** tours ($20.50). For reservations, call 1-888 297 2757 or 1-303 297 2757; alternatively, visit the desks at Bright Angel, Maswik and Yavapai Lodges, or at Canyon View Information Plaza.

By taxi

A 24hr taxi service is available on 1-928 638 2822.

THE NORTH RIM

From the South Rim, you can see lightning forks hit the **North Rim** ten miles across the canyon. However, to reach it, you'll have to hike down to the bottom and back up again, drive 220 miles all the way around the canyon, or catch the daily shuttle bus.

The North Rim is 1,000 feet (300 metres) higher than the South Rim and is only open from mid May to mid October. It has fewer facilities and, thus, fewer visitors than the South Rim, which is why many longtime visitors prefer it up here; the tranquil atmosphere can still evoke what it may have been like to visit the canyon in the early days. That said, you should book ahead for lodging, which is at a premium during busy seasons. Facilities include a visitors' centre, a grocery, a camping shop and a post office.

Where to stay, eat & drink

Run by Forever Resorts, the **Grand Canyon Lodge** (1-877 386-4383, www.grandcanyon lodgenorth.com) is the only lodging inside the

ESCAPES & EXCURSIONS

Grand Canyon Railway

park at the North Rim. Cabins cost $121-$187; there's also a dining room and a campsite (Jan-mid Apr 1-928 645 6865; mid May-mid Oct 1-928 638 2611), as well as the Grand Canyon chuck-wagon cookout experience (June-Sept, $22-$35), for which booking is advisable. There are also lodging and eating facilities at **Kaibab Lodge** (1-928 638 2389, www.kaibablodge.com, cabin $85-$155) and **Jacob Lake Inn** (1-928 643 7232, www.jacoblake.com, double/cabin $89-$138), respectively 18 and 45 miles north of the park.

Getting there

By bus
The only public transport to the North Rim is the **Trans Canyon Shuttle** bus service, (www.trans-canyonshuttle.com), which leaves the South Rim at 1.30pm daily and makes the return ride at 7am (mid May-mid Oct only). The journey takes about 4hrs 30mins and costs $80-$65 ($120-$150 round trip). Call 1-928 638 2820 for details.

By car
From Las Vegas, head north on I-15, then east on Hwy 9, Hwy 59 and US 89A to **Jacob Lake**. The park entrance is 30 miles south of Jacob Lake on Hwy 67; the rim is a further 14 miles. At a distance of 263 miles, the North Rim is nearer to Las Vegas than the South Rim, but the journey takes longer.

EXPLORING THE CANYON
Hiking in the canyon

However limited your time may be, try to hike at least part of the way into the canyon.

As jaw-dropping as the views undoubtedly are from the rim, the gulf is almost too huge to allow a full appreciation of this unique environment. Really, you need to get closer: to soak up the stunning colours of the cliffs, to identify the different geological layers of rock, and to see the turbulent brown waters and hear the roar of the Colorado River. The basic rule of hiking into the canyon is that it takes twice as long to hike up as down; if you have three hours, turn around after an hour.

Although the upper trails teem with crowds, remember that you're not at a theme park. The extremes of terrain and climate are dangerous: always seek and heed advice from rangers, and ensure you're in decent physical shape and properly equipped. Note, too, that overnight hikes (and camping stays) require a backcountry permit, which is issued on a strictly limited basis. Always try and apply for one in advance via the website; you can take your chances on the day and turn up at the **Backcountry Information Center** at 8am, but you may find yourself with a lengthy wait.

Hikers should note that mule riders have priority on the Bright Angel, South Kaibab and North Kaibab trails. Stop walking when the mules approach, and follow any instructions given by the rider leading the tour.

Backcountry Information Center
Grand Canyon National Park, PO Box 129, Grand Canyon, AZ 86023 (1-928 638 7875, 1-5pm Mon-Fri). **Open** mid May-mid Oct (walk-in visitors) 8am-noon, 1-5pm daily. **Rates** *Permit* $10, plus $5 per person, per night. **No credit cards**.

Apply here for a backcountry permit, required for all overnight camping trips except those that involve designated campgrounds (where fees range from $10-$23 per night). Applications open four months prior to the month in which you plan to hike; for example, applications for hiking trips in May are processed from 1 January. Apply as early as possible.

Bright Angel Trail

Grand Canyon Village to Plateau Point.
Round trip 19.2 miles. **Duration** 2 days.
This popular trail follows the line of a wide geological fault, which shifted the layering of the rock strata; as you descend, you'll notice that the layers on the left are much higher than those on the right. Water is usually available (May-Sept) at the rest houses 1.5 miles and three miles from the trailhead. They're good day-hike destinations but can get crowded. Experienced hikers could head for the campground at Indian Gardens (4.5 miles); the tall cottonwoods here, planted in the early 1900s, can be seen from the rim. From Indian Gardens, continue to Plateau Point (6.1 miles) for a view into the river gorge.

Grandview Trail

Grandview Point to Horseshoe Mesa.
Round trip 6.4 miles. **Duration** 1 day.
This unmaintained trail is steep and should only be attempted by experienced hikers. There's no water en route, but there are toilet facilities at Horseshoe Mesa, the site of an abandoned mining works.

Hermit Trail

Hermit's Rest to Colorado River.
Round trip 18.4 miles. **Duration** 2-3 days.

This difficult trail passes Hermit Gorge, Santa Maria Spring and the Redwall Formation en route to the Colorado River and is recommended for experienced desert hikers only. A precipitous side trail leads for 1.5 miles to Dripping Springs. There is no drinking water on the trail; spring water must be treated.

North Kaibab Trail

North Rim to Colorado River Bridge.
Round trip 29.2 miles. **Duration** 3-4 days.
The North Kaibab trail starts about 1.5 miles from Grand Canyon Lodge on the North Rim and begins with a beautiful but steep hike through the trees. The Supai Tunnel (1.8 miles) is an ideal day hike with a great view of the canyon, plus water and toilet facilities. There is little shade beyond this point. More experienced hikers might make it to Roaring Springs, but should not attempt to go further than this and back in one day. Beyond Roaring Springs, the trail continues to Phantom Ranch (13.8 miles) and the Colorado River Bridge (14.6 miles).

South Kaibab Trail

Yaki Point to Phantom Ranch.
Round trip 12.6 miles. **Duration** 2 days.
This trail, which starts five miles east of Grand Canyon Village, is shorter but steeper than Bright Angel trail, dropping 5,000ft (1,500m) in six miles. The route follows a series of ridge lines, crossing the Colorado at the Kaibab Suspension Bridge on its way to Phantom Ranch. There is no campground or drinking water en route; hike to the tree-dotted plateau of Cedar Ridge (1.5 miles) if you're short of time.

Grand Canyon.

ESCAPES & EXCURSIONS

Mule rides

Mule rides into the canyon are operated by **Xanterra** (*see p288*), and booking is essential. The three-hour day trip ($120.65 per person) takes you 3,200 feet (1,000 metres) down the **Bright Angel Trail** to **Plateau Point**. On the one-night ride ($497.89 one person, $879.43 two people, $394.46 each additional person), you'll go down the **Bright Angel Trail**, eat lunch at **Indian Garden**, then proceed over the Colorado River on a suspension bridge, and stay overnight in a cabin at **Phantom Ranch** (*see below*). You can even defy saddle-soreness with a three-day trip, which includes two nights at Phantom Ranch ($701.38 one person, $1,170.05 two people, $495.53 each additional person). All rates include accommodation and food.

Plane & helicopter rides

Plane and helicopter rides over the rim are a major cause of air and noise pollution in the canyon, reducing visibility and disturbing the area's natural tranquillity. Rides are not available from within the park. However, if you must get a bird's-eye view, various outfits operate services out of Grand Canyon Airport in Tusayan. Plane rides start from around $100-$145; helicopter rides are more expensive. For flights departing from Las Vegas, *see p310*.
Grand Canyon Airlines *1-866 235 9422, 1-928 638 2359, www.grandcanyonairlines.com*.
Papillon Grand Canyon Helicopters *1-886 357 272, 1-702 736 7243, www.papillon.com*.

River rafting

Follow in the wake of one-armed explorer Major John Wesley Powell, who in 1869 became the first man to navigate the length of the Colorado River by boat, by taking a river trip through the rapids of the Grand Canyon. It's a major undertaking: you'll need at least eight days to travel the 277 miles downriver from Lees Ferry at the far eastern end of the Grand Canyon to Pearce Ferry on Lake Mead, and you'll have to book months in advance. A list of approved operators is on the NPS's Grand Canyon website.

You can take a shorter trip by hiking in or out of the canyon. Firms such as **Canyoneers** (1-800 525 0924 outside Arizona, 1-928 526 0924 within Arizona, www.canyoneers.com) also offer shorter trips that start or finish at **Bright Angel Beach** near Phantom Ranch. Trips such as these entail less time on the river, and you'll also have to hike in or out of the canyon at the beginning or end of your trip.

For whitewater trips from **Diamond Creek** in Grand Canyon West, roughly a four-hour drive from the South Rim, *see p286*.

Staying in the canyon

Phantom Ranch, down at the bottom of the canyon, was designed by Mary Colter in 1922 and is a welcome oasis after the rigours of a strenuous hike. Hikers who stay here do not need backcountry permits, but will need to book months in advance: the dorms ($43.09 bed) are usually filled to capacity. Duffel service (where your pack is carried by mule) is an additional $64.64 each way. Non-guests can eat here, but must book meals in advance ($21.13 breakfast, $12.39 packed lunch, $26.69-$42.20 dinner).

There are campsites at **Indian Gardens**, **Bright Angel** (next to Phantom Ranch) and **Cottonwood Springs** (May-Oct, accessible from the North Rim on the North Kaibab Trail). You'll need a backcountry permit to stay at any of them; *see p290*.

TOURIST INFORMATION

For general information, call the **National Park Service** on 1-928 638 7888. Alternatively, check the detail-packed if slightly convoluted website at www.nps.gov/grca, which has information on accommodation, hiking and backcountry permits, plus maps of the area.
Arizona Office of Tourism *1-866 275 5816, 1-602 364 3700, www.arizonaguide.com*.

California

A different side of the Golden State.

The relationship between Nevada and southern California has always been an uneasy one. Nevadans view their near-neighbours with wariness, while California natives look back with downright suspicion. And yet the traffic between the two states has never been greater. The route between the two states takes the driver through pioneer country, traversed in the 19th century by migrants heading westwards, celebrated in the 20th century in Hollywood Westerns, and now offering 21st-century trippers a dramatic landscape. Don't forget that parts of southern California are uninhabited and often scorching. Take suitable precautions when driving and hiking (*see p294* **Inside Track**).

ESCAPES & EXCURSIONS

ALONG I-15

You can throw the dice one last time at a pair of mini-gambling resorts along I-15, south of Las Vegas but before the border with California. **Jean**, the closest of the pair to Vegas, is soon to get a shot in the arm from MGM Mirage, which plans to build a planned mixed-use community on the site of the closed Nevada Landing casino. Until it does, the sole reasons to stop here are to throw a few dollars in the direction of the **Gold Strike** (1-800 634 1359, www.stopatjean.com), a pretty basic casino-hotel, or to visit the ghost town of **Goodsprings**, which hit the headlines in 1942 when Clark Gable waited for news of the plane crash that killed his wife, Carole Lombard.

Right on the Nevada–California border, **Primm** is a three-resort cluster of more modern aspect. The success of **Whiskey Pete's**, the Primm family's first casino-hotel, was so great that they followed it with two more, **Primm Valley** and **Buffalo Bill's** (1-800 386 7867, www.primmvalleyresorts.com for all three). However, the main reason to pull in here is the presence of **Fashion Outlets Las Vegas** (874 1400, www.fashionoutletlasvegas.com), a better-than-you'd-expect outlet mall that features a number of familiar brands that aren't present at either Vegas outlet enterprise.

Continuing south, the I-15 passes through stunning scenery along the northern boundary of **Mojave National Preserve** (*see below*). The small town of **Baker**, 90 miles south of Vegas, makes a convenient gateway to this

wilderness, and is home to the world's tallest thermometer, which measures 134 feet (40 metres) top to toe. West, the I-15 continues through stark desert for 60 miles until it reaches **Barstow**, a bleak town notable primarily for its location on historic Route 66. Beyond the high-desert hick-town of **Hesperia**, I-15 takes you through the pine-capped wilderness of the San Bernardino Mountains until it hits the Los Angeles sprawl.

MOJAVE NATIONAL PRESERVE

Covering a gigantic rectangle bordered by I-15 to the north and I-40 to the south, the 2,500-square-mile **Mojave National Preserve** is a Cinderella park: it has no honeypot attractions, low visitorship and few facilities, and is really best approached as a giant desert sampler. The meeting point of three of the four types of North American desert (Mojave, Great Basin and Sonoran), it contains a variety of terrains, features and ecosystems, including the human.

Because its protected status is relatively recent, historical relics of inhabitants and would-be conquerors, from early man right through to 20th-century ranchers, dot the landscape. Spanish explorers, western pioneers and routefinders, soldiers, navvies and settlers passed this way, leaving behind roads and railroads still in use today. The best times to visit are spring or autumn; it's brutally hot from mid May to mid September, often over 110°F (43°C). Whenever you visit, admission is free.

INSIDE TRACK DESERT SAFETY

Don't underestimate the dangers of travelling in the desert just because you'll be in an air-conditioned car: even the most modern of cars can overheat and even break down under extreme conditions. If you're planning to drive on any unpaved roads, check local conditions before you set out. Turn off air-conditioning on uphill stretches to lessen the chance of overheating the engine. Leave a window open if you park for any length of time in the heat, and use a fold-up windscreen shade. Outside your vehicle, use lots of sunscreen and don't exert yourself in the midday sun. In or out of your car, carry plenty of water: you need to drink at least one gallon (four litres) a day.

Mojave National Preserve has been developed only minimally: there are just four paved roads and three marked trails, and gas and lodging are available only on its borders. You can see plenty by car and on short walks, but those with four-wheel-drive vehicles will find it an off-road paradise. The numerous unpaved roads include the 140-mile east–west Mojave Road, a Native American track developed by successive users.

If you're coming from Vegas along I-15, be sure to fill up with both gas and drinking water at the town of Baker. If you've only a few hours, a 67-mile triangular drive from Baker, via the Kelbaker Road, Kelso–Cima Road and Cima Road, to rejoin I-15 at the end of the trek, is a good introduction to the sights.

You'll pass the reddish humps of over 30 young volcanic cones before reaching **Kelso**; once a major passenger stop on the Union Pacific Railroad, it was named after a local railroad worker when his name was the first one pulled from a hat by colleagues looking to christen the site. The grand, Spanish Mission-style depot, built in 1924 and closed in 1985, has been converted into a visitors' centre. From here, you can detour to the 500-foot (150-metre) Kelso sand dunes by heading south on the Kelbaker Road and turning right after about seven miles on to a signed dirt road.

Back in Kelso, turn left towards **Cima**, passing the 7,000-foot (2,150-metre) Providence Mountains (currently closed to visitors) en route. At Cima, you can take Cima Road towards I-15 past the gently swelling Cima Dome, which has the largest stand of Joshua trees in the world. Alternatively, head along Morning Star Mine Road to Nipton Road in the Ivanpah Valley, then either take a left to I-15 or a right to tiny **Nipton**, at the preserve's northern

edge. Here you'll find a railroad crossing, a town hall and the charming **Hotel Nipton** (*see below*).

An interesting diversion from I-40 is a stretch of the old Route 66, featuring the kind of bleak desert landscapes beloved of cinematographers and the similarly iconic Americana of photogenic **Amboy**. To the east, 66 crosses I-40 and dips back into the preserve to **Goffs**, a lonely spot despite its status as 'the Desert Tortoise Capital of the World'. Further south is **Joshua Tree National Park** (www.nps.gov/jotr/index.htm), worth a look in its own right.

Where to stay & eat

Lodgings within the park are limited to a pair of campgrounds. **Mid-Hills** is usually cooler than Hole-in-the-Wall (www.nps.gov/moja/plan yourvisit/campgrounds.htm), and always much prettier. You'll need to drive some reliable but not always comfortable dirt roads to get here; Hole-in-the-Wall is accessible on blacktop from I-40. The fee at each is $12, and pitches are distributed on a first-come, first-served basis.

On the edge of the park, Baker has a clutch of basic non-chain motels as well as the rammed and rated **Mad Greek Diner** (1-760 733 4354), where both Greek and American fast food is served to motorists. However, the pick of the park-side lodging options is the **Hotel Nipton** (1-760 856 2335, www.nipton.com, rates vary by season), a century-old hotel in splendid desert isolation (except, that is, for its Wi-Fi access). If the main building is full, stay in one of the eco-cabins scattered behind the main building. Also here is the **Whistle Stop Oasis** (1-760 856 1045, 107355 Nipton Road), a basic-looking shack where Bill Sarbello's food (especially the burgers) is better than it has any right to be.

Getting there

By car

Baker is 90 miles south of Las Vegas on I-15. Nipton is located on Hwy 164, accessible via I-15 or Hwy 95, 63 miles south of Las Vegas. To reach Joshua Tree, take Kelbaker Road through the Mojave National Preserve and head south via Amboy until you reach Twentynine Palms; it's 130 miles from Baker.

Tourist information

Mojave National Preserve: Kelso Depot Visitor Center *Kelbaker Road, Kelso (1-760 252 6108, www.nps.gov/moja)*. **Open** 9am-5pm daily.
Mojave National Preserve: Hole-in-the-Wall Information Center *Essex & Black Canyon roads, north of I-40 (1-760 928 2572, www.nps. gov/moja)*. **Open** *May-Sept* 10am-4pm Fri-Sun. *Oct-Apr* 9am-4pm Wed-Sun.

DEATH VALLEY NATIONAL PARK

Enlarged and redesignated a national park under the 1994 Desert Protection Act, Death Valley is now the largest national park outside Alaska, covering more than 5,156 square miles. It's also, famously, one of the hottest places on the planet. The park's website calmly offers that 'Death Valley is generally sunny, dry and clear throughout the year'. True, but the word 'generally' masks a multitude of curiosities. Air temperatures regularly top 120°F (49°C) in July and August; fearsome by anyone's standards.

However, while the park is usually parched, receiving fewer than two inches of rain in an average year, it's not immune from water. In August 2004, terrifying flash floods hit Death Valley, killing two tourists and destroying parts of Highway 190. Reconstruction of the road was completed a couple of years later, but the same thing could happen again at any time.

Get your bearings at the **Death Valley Visitor Center** (*see p296*) at **Furnace Creek**, where you'll find an excellent bookshop, decent exhibits, a useful orientation film and helpful staff. Stop in for advice on current weather and road conditions (some tracks are only accessible to 4-wheel-drive vehicles), pay your fee of $20 per car and take the opportunity to fill up at one of the park's three expensive gas stations.

However, if you've entered the park on Highway 190 from Las Vegas, you'll pass two of the most amazing sights en route to Furnace Creek, and it may save time to stop at them before hitting the visitors' centre. Roughly 13 miles off the main road and standing 5,475 feet (1,669 metres) above sea level, **Dante's View** is a great place from which to survey the park's otherworldly landscape. And three miles south of Furnace Creek lies **Zabriskie Point**, famed for the eponymous 1970 Antonioni film but recognisable by its ragged, rumpled appearance.

There's more to see further south of Furnace Creek. At **Golden Canyon**, there's a simple two-mile round-trip hike that's best walked in the late afternoon sunlight, when you'll see how the canyon got its name. Continuing south, the landscape gets plainer. Nine miles down the road is the **Devil's Golf Course**, a striking, scrappy landscape formed by salt crystallising and expanding; a few miles further is bleak, eerie **Badwater**, just two miles as the crow flies from Dante's View but more than 5,000 feet (1,524 metres) lower. Indeed, this is the lowest point in the Western Hemisphere, 282 feet (86 metres) below sea level. Unexpectedly, it's only 85 miles

Opera in a Ghost Town

Tiny Death Valley Junction is home to a unique kind of opera house.

It's not your archetypal ghost town, Death Valley Junction. It was settled not by travelling pioneers or gold-hungry prospectors but by the Pacific Coast Borax Company, which built it in the mid 1920s to house its workers. When they left, the town crumbled, until a fortysomething ballet dancer arrived from New York in 1967, took over a derelict community hall and began to fashion from it her own American dream.

Renovating the building as the **Amargosa Opera House**, Marta Becket turned coffee-cans into spotlights and filled the room with garden chairs. She even painted an audience on the walls, which made performing in an empty hall, as she often did, easier to bear. Eventually word spread, and people travelled to see both Becket's theatre and her self-devised, folk art-ish performance pieces. In the early 1980s, Becket finally bought the property; audiences, fascinated by this tale of devotion and self-imposed isolation, continued to come.

Tom Willett (aka Wilget), Becket's longtime partner, died of a stroke in

2005, but the octogenarian Becket has continued without him, staging shows every Saturday night. There's nowhere quite like it.

Amargosa Opera House
Death Valley Junction, intersection of SR 190 & SR 127, just E of Death Valley National Park (1-760 852 4441, www. amargosaoperahouse.com). **Tickets** $15 adults; $12 children. Booking essential.

Death Valley National Park.

from the highest point in the lower 48 states, the 14,494-foot (4,420-metre) Mount Whitney in the Sierra Nevada. An annual 'ultramarathon' race is held between the two, though it no longer extends all the way to Whitney's summit.

Heading north from Furnace Creek offers a greater variety of sights. The remains of the **Harmony Borax Works** have been casually converted into a short trail; there's a similarly simple walk, less historic but more aesthetically pleasing, at nearby **Salt Creek**. Following the road around to the left will lead you past the eerie **Devil's Cornfield**, the frolic-friendly **Sand Dunes**, which rise and dip in 100-foot (30-metre) increments, and on to the small settlement at **Stovepipe Wells**. Taking a right and driving 36 miles will lead you to the luxurious **Scotty's Castle**; built in the 1920s for Chicago millionaire Albert Johnson, it was named after Walter Scott, his eccentric chancer of a friend. Rangers tell the story on 50-minute tours (usually hourly, 9am-5pm, $11 adults; $6-$9 reductions).

It's often too hot to hike, but there are plenty of trails in Death Valley, short and long. The options include the 14-mile round trip to the 11,000-foot (3,300-metre) summit of **Telescope Peak**, a good summer hike (the higher you climb, the cooler it gets). Starting at Mahogany Flat campground, you climb 3,000 feet (900 metres) for some spectacular views of Mount Whitney. In winter, only experienced climbers with ice axes and crampons should attempt it.

Where to stay & eat

Set into the hillside above Furnace Creek Wash, the **Furnace Creek Inn** (1-760 786 2345, www. furnacecreekresort.com, closed mid May-mid Oct, double $265-$455) was built in the 1930s, and retains a cultured dignity reminiscent of the era from which it emerged. The rooms are charming and well equipped, the landscaped gardens are picture-perfect and the pool is a delight. The inn's restaurant, where the upscale Californian food is far better than you might expect, is the best eating option in the area.

Elsewhere, the **Furnace Creek Ranch** (1-760 786 2345, www.furnacecreekresort.com, $138-$219) has 200 motel-style rooms and cabins, as well as a pool, tennis courts and the world's lowest golf course, plus a pretty basic restaurant and bar. The 83-room **Stovepipe Wells Village** (1-760 786 2387 www.escapetodeath valley.com, double $80-$145) also has food on offer, but few other amenities. Four of the park's nine campgrounds are free, with the others costing between $12 and $18 a night. The most central, and the only one for which reservations are taken, is at **Furnace Creek** (1-877 444 6777, 1-760 786 2441, www.recreation.gov).

Getting there

By car
From Vegas, head south on I-15 towards LA, exit on to Blue Diamond Road (at Silverton), then head west on Hwy 160 over the Spring Mountains. A few miles after Pahrump, take Bell Vista Road to Death Valley Junction and Hwy 190 into the park (120 miles). (Returning to Vegas via Death Valley Junction, note that Bell Vista Road is labelled State Line Road.) Alternatively, take US 95 to Beatty and then head south on Hwy 374.

Tourist information

Death Valley Visitor Center *Furnace Creek, Death Valley National Park (1-760 786 3200, www.nps.gov/deva).* **Open** 8am-5pm daily.
Scotty's Castle Visitor Center *Scotty's Castle, Death Valley National Park (1-760 786 2392, www.nps.gov/deva).* **Open** *Summer* 9am-4.30pm daily. *Winter* 8.30am-5pm daily.

ESCAPES & EXCURSIONS

Nevada

The wild, wild west – and some extraterrestrials.

Those who claim that there's plenty more to Nevada outside Las Vegas are overstating their case a little. Those who aver that there's plenty more *of* Nevada outside Las Vegas, on the other hand, are right on the money. Although the state is the seventh largest in the Union, almost three-quarters of its residents live within 40 miles of Las Vegas, with half the remainder in the Reno-Sparks urban area. That leaves an awful lot of not very much.

Yet after Vegas, an awful lot of not very much can be just what one needs. The under-visited **Valley of Fire State Park** is stunning. The drive north-west from Vegas to **Reno** on I-95 offers a desert landscape alternately bleak and beautiful under skies as big as you'll ever see. The smattering of towns along it are scruffy but fascinating, all in thrall to the prospectors and chancers who established them a century ago. And then there's the **Extraterrestrial Highway,** named after the many extraordinary tales of UFO sightings and other sinister goings-on at the Nevada Test Site's infamous Area 51.

THE ROAD TO RENO

US 95 leaves the lights of Las Vegas behind in a hurry. As the road roars out through the city's north-western corner, the landscape visible from the driver's seat empties from urban sprawl into endless desert. Get used to the view. You'll have seen a lot like it by the time your 450-mile ride from Vegas to Reno is complete. Soon, you'll be rolling past **Mount Charleston** (*see p283*). On the right sits **Nellis Air Force Range,** a vast tract of desert that, with an area of 5,200 square miles, is slightly larger than the state of Connecticut.

From 1951 until 1995, the US government, which owns more than 80 per cent of the land in Nevada, used the **Nevada Test Site,** which is flanked on three sides by the Nellis Range, to test atomic weapons, both above ground and beneath it. Day-long tours of the site, which leave from the **Atomic Testing Museum** in Las Vegas (itself worth a visit; *see p80*), are available to those prescient enough to book two months ahead and prepared to supply all manner of information to pass security screenings. For details, see www.nv.doe.gov or call 295 0944.

Shortly after Indian Springs, you'll leave Clark County and enter Nye County. At 18,147 square miles, it's the third largest county in the US, but it's also one of the emptiest: the 2008 census tagged the population at 44,375. At **Amargosa Valley,** close to the junction of US 95 and SR 373 (leading towards Death Valley), an unprepossessing cluster of buildings houses a bar, a gas station and a brothel, making it perhaps America's ultimate travellers' rest area. Across the road sits a bar; nearby, on SR 373, sits Jackass Airport, named for the animal rather than the idiocy of the local pilots. And that's more or less it.

For years, the government has planned to use **Yucca Mountain,** just north of Amargosa Valley, as the repository for the country's spent nuclear waste. The Department of Energy even set a date for the site's opening: 31 March 2017. However, Nevada senator (and, as of 2007, Senate majority leader) Harry Reid has insisted that the plan will never come to pass; this one looks set to run and run. Tours of the mountain, which sits inside the Nevada Test Site, are available to those who book well in advance; call 821 8687 or see www.ocrwm.doe.gov.

Head 30 miles north-west of Amargosa Valley and you'll find **Beatty,** established – as were so many towns at the turn of the 20th century – by prospectors ambitious to make

ESCAPES & EXCURSIONS

ESCAPES & EXCURSIONS

their fortunes. When word got around that Ed Cross and Frank 'Shorty' Harris had discovered a goldmine in the hills, hundreds of hopefuls descended on the area, leading Walter Beatty to set up a town on his homestead. The volunteer-run **Beatty Museum** (417 Main Street, 1-775 553 2303, www.beattymuseum.com) offers exhibits and anecdotes about these early days.

Beatty is now a ramshackle collection of casinos and bars, but at least it's still alive, which is more than can be said for nearby **Rhyolite**. An archetypal gold rush town, it sprung up after gold was found in August 1904. The first lots were sold in February 1905; by 1908, 10,000 locals were served by schools, hospitals, 50 bars, an opera house and a red-light district. But by 1910, all but a few hundred had moved on to the next boomtown, leaving the town to crumble. Today, a handful of buildings sit in various states of disrepair, weather-beaten and neglected but refusing to vanish; hand-drawn street signs remind visitors that these tracks were once busy thoroughfares. It's a fascinating, melancholy place. To reach it, take SR 374 south from Beatty (towards Death Valley) for about four miles, then take a right. Also here is the **Goldwell Open Air Museum** (870 9946, www.goldwellmuseum.org), a haunting spot that comprises half a dozen works by Belgian artists who settled in the area 20 years ago. Look out for Albert Szukalski's sculpture *The Last Supper*; although, to be honest, it's pretty hard to miss.

Some 50 miles north of Beatty sits **Goldfield**, another former mining town whose population surged from nothing to 10,000 between 1902 (when gold was discovered here) and 1907, and then doubled in the following three years. It didn't last, but Goldfield refused to die: a population of 500 makes it a sizeable settlement for this part of the world. If several grand stone buildings, including the Goldfield Hotel, the courthouse and the imposing former fire station, are poignant reminders of the town's heyday, the Mozart Club bar offers evidence that not everybody got lucky.

It's 26 miles from here to **Tonopah**, on US 95 at about the halfway point between Vegas and Reno. Jim Butler found silver here in 1900; over the next 15 years, almost $150 million of ore was dug from the small mines that dot the area. The **Central Nevada Museum** (1900 Logan Field Road, 1-775 482 9676, www.tonopahnevada.com, closed Mon & Tue) details this history, though you might be better off heading for the century-old buildings at the **Tonopah Historic Mining Park** (520 McCulloch Street, 1-775 482 9274, www.tonopahnevada.com, closed Mon & Tue Nov to Feb, $5).

From here, the landscape gets plainer. Settlements seem further apart – the next town of any note, **Hawthorne**, is 100 miles down

the road – and there's little to engage the senses save the freedom of an open road. Until, that is, a few miles after Hawthorne, when you find US 95 narrowing and curving – quite a shock after 300 miles of mainly straight highway – as it forces its way around a sizeable body of water.

In prehistoric times, **Walker Lake** covered much of western Nevada. These days, though still 20 miles long, it's in decline: with the Walker River diverted for irrigation purposes, the lake has dropped 100 feet (30 metres) since 1930. While not spectacularly beautiful, the lake and the state park that frames it are popular spots for swimming, boating and camping; call the state park on 1-775 867 3001 for more details on park activities, or see http://parks.nv.gov/walk.htm.

Past **Schurz**, a town every bit as unbecoming as its name, there are several routes to Reno. The quickest is to take US 95 north to Fallon, then pick up US 50 and Alternate US 50 to the surprisingly picturesque I-80, and head west on the Interstate into Reno. A slightly slower, slightly more scenic option is to head west on Alternate US 95 at Schurz, via the pleasant town of **Yerington** and the enjoyably green **Fort Churchill Historic State Park** in Silver Springs (1-775 577 2345, www.parks.nv.gov/fc.htm, admission $7), and then pick up I-80 to Reno near Fernley. The slowest option is to take this latter route as far as Silver Springs, then take US 50, SR 341 and US 395 into Reno via **Virginia City** (*see p302*). Our advice? Take the speedy run into Reno, but return to Vegas via Virginia City.

Where to stay, eat & drink

In Tonopah, the large **Tonopah Station** casino (1137 S Main Street, 1-775 482 9777, www.tonopahstation.com) has a dark gaming area, rooms, a restaurant and a wonderful collection of old chrome slot machines in the basement. **El Marques** (1-775 482 3885) serves decent, good-value Mexican food.

Hawthorne has a number of motels and one casino, the **El Capitan** (540 F Street, 1-775 945 3321, www.elcapitanresortcasino.com). **Maggie's** (US 95 at 785 E Street, 1-775 945 3908) serves burgers, salads and sandwiches.

Tourist information

For information about **Tonopah**, contact the Chamber of Commerce at 301 Brougher Avenue (1-775 482 6336, www.tonopahnevada.com).

RENO

Popular culture flags the differences between Nevada's largest cities. In song, Las Vegas is the town that set Elvis's soul on fire; Reno is where

Johnny Cash shot a man just to watch him die. On film, Vegas looks glamorous, stealing scenes from every actor dumb enough to compete with it. The finest Reno movie is Paul Thomas Anderson's *Hard Eight* (aka *Sydney*), a bleak tale set in the shadows of the town's gaming industry.

To visitors, Reno can't compete with Las Vegas. The casinos are smaller and shabbier, the neon less dazzling, the dining not as varied and the entertainment decidedly wearier. But to suggest that Reno is Vegas in miniature is to do it a disservice: after all, it's never attempted to compete with its glossier, more glamorous rival. Reno hardly sees itself as a gambling town at all; rather, it's a pretty little city with numerous and varied attractions, one of which is casinos.

Reno long ago made a deliberate decision not to become Las Vegas. In the 1950s, the city fathers passed a law that limited gambling to downtown Reno, then sat back and let Vegas explode in popularity, population and wealth. The 25-year law expired in 1978; since then, just enough (but not too many) casinos have opened, attracting just enough (but not too many) gamblers. At the same time, Reno has diversified its economy and tourism marketing focus, growing at a controlled pace.

Locals are proud of their town and disparaging about their putative rival; there's little love lost between Renoites and Las Vegans. In truth, gambling aside, the two cities have as little in common as San Francisco and Los Angeles. Where Vegas is an anything-goes, 24-7 kind of town, Reno is slower, prettier and more conservative. The flow of the Truckee River through downtown is attractive; if the Riverwalk that's been built around it doesn't differ wildly from the formula that's been applied in countless other American cities (a few shops, a handful of restaurants), it's no less pleasant for its lack of originality.

Reno also benefits from the variety of its seasons. Winter can be cold, but you won't hear a word of complaint from the skiers who jam the slopes of the 20-plus resorts within an hour of town. Summer, meanwhile, is usually balmy, with outdoor events galore. The biggest is **Hot August Nights** (www.hotaugustnights.net), a 1950s-themed mix of classic cars and rock 'n' roll, but **Street Vibrations** in September

Burn, Baby, Burn

Burning Man has become a mega-event.

To say the **Burning Man Festival** isn't really like most other events in Nevada is to say that Las Vegas isn't really like most other cities. Each year, in the week leading up to Labor Day, more than 50,000 people gather in the isolated Black Rock Desert to build a temporary, self-contained city, the physical, spiritual and symbolic centre of which is a 50-foot effigy that's set aflame at the end of the event. What goes on beforehand defies both belief and easy description:

the event will be unlike anything you've ever experienced before. Self-expression is prized above all else, with self-reliance second; temperatures can range from 0°C to 40°C (32°F to 104°F). Either way, for one week you'll be part of the world's most eccentric, creative and fascinating community. In the lead up to its 25th anniversary in 2011, tickets for the previously unlimited event sold out. For more, see www.burningman.com.

(www.road-shows.com), the Harley-Davidson equivalent, keeps pace with it.

Sightseeing

The **Nevada Museum of Art** (160 W Liberty Street, 1-775 329 3333, www.nevadaart.org, closed Mon, $1-$10), housed in a striking black building, has a strong permanent collection, the majority of pieces from the last century, plus temporary shows: check online for details.

The **National Automobile Museum** (10 S Lake Street, 1-775 333 9300, www.automuseum. org, $4-$10) is the best museum in Reno, and one of the finest in the state. The building holds more than 200 cars spanning a timeframe of more than a century, from an 1892 Philion Road Carriage – imagine a throne stuck on top of an outsized perambulator – to altogether less dignified Ed

Roth Kustom creations. The cars, including 1940s Lincolns, a 1930s Mercedes and a divine 1957 Cadillac, are all beautifully maintained.

Reno's other attractions sit on the University of Nevada campus. At the **Fleischmann Planetarium** (1650 N Virginia Street, 1-775 784 4811, http://planetarium.unr.edu), star shows run alongside 70mm nature films. A stone's throw away at the **Nevada Historical Society** (1650 N Virginia Street, 1-775 688 1190, www.museums. nevadaculture.org), there's a fine primer on the history of the state and a good bookstore.

Casinos

Though there are a handful of casinos out of the centre, notably the monstrous **Grand Sierra Resort** (formerly the Reno Hilton; 2500 E 2nd Street, at US 395, 1-775 789 2000, www.grand

Losers' Lounge

The winner takes it all, but not in this Laughlin bar.

Most of us are losers. That's all there is to it. Tinhorns. Pikers. Punters. We keep going to casinos and keep getting ground up into chopped meat. And then we keep playing.

Sure, sure: it's about the fun, about the recreation value, about spending the same money on gambling that you might use to buy tickets to a concert or a ballgame or an amusement park. And yeah, it's about risking your bankroll for the excitement of the casino, the adrenaline of the action, and, to some extent, the dream of a once-in-a-lifetime monster run. But mostly, it's about seeing how your luck is holding up, and finding out that it's not holding up very well. Gambling is all about trying for the acute fun of winning, but facing the chronic pain of losing to do so.

There is a shrine to all of us losers in Nevada, but it's not in Las Vegas, which takes itself way too seriously to even consider having a little fun at the expense of those who line its pockets. To find it, you'll have to head south on US 95 for 70 miles and then east on Highway 163 to **Laughlin**, a scruffy little low-rollers' haven founded in 1969 by Don Laughlin on the border with Arizona. Inside the **Riverside** (1-800 227 3849, www.riversideresort.com), the town's original hotel-casino, sits one of the most imaginative bars in Nevada. A lot of thought, planning and collecting went into the decorations at the **Losers' Lounge**, which dares to point out that the emperor isn't really wearing anything.

The setting is typical for a bar: a stage, a dancefloor, a balcony, bars, barstools and tables. But the decor is anything but ordinary, especially for a casino. The decorations pay homage to many of recent history's most famous fall guys and gals, who wound up on the wrong side of some track or another and went down in high-visibility flames.

A big presidential campaign mirror decorates the main bar, touting 'Nixon and Agnew – a Team of Honesty and Integrity'. A photograph of John Belushi hangs on the wall; on his face is etched one of the most desperate expressions ever captured on camera. Also commemorated here are the Hindenburg, Ma Barker and her boys, General Custer, Buffalo Bill and Mike Tyson, shooting stars to a man (and woman). Movie posters commemorate the spectacular failure of the Attack movies, among them *Attack of the 50-Foot Woman* and *Attack of the Puppet People*.

On the stairs up to the balcony are displays spotlighting such notables as Timothy McVeigh, Tonya Harding, OJ Simpson and Marcia Clark (side by side), and Ted Kaczynski. The balcony walls are (dis)graced by Imelda Marcos, Ethel and Julius Rosenberg, Eddie Fisher and Debbie Reynolds (in an old poster for a movie they co-starred in), Bonnie and Clyde, and Gary Hart. You can easily spend an hour here perusing the losers. But don't be surprised if your own photo is up there on the wall.

Reno.

sierraresort.com) and the colourful **Peppermill** (2707 S Virginia Street, at W Grove Street, 1-866 821 9996, www.peppermillreno.com), Reno's gambling is mostly downtown. Some of the names in lights will be familiar, among them the characterless **Harrah's** (219 N Center Street, at E 2nd Street, 1-775 786 3232, www. harrahs.com) and the family-friendly **Circus Circus** (500 N Sierra Street, at W 5th Street, 1-800 648 5010, www.circusreno.com).

Other casinos, though, are unique to Reno. The **Eldorado** (345 N Virginia Street, at W 4th Street, 1-800 648 5966, www.eldoradoreno.com) is the most pleasant operation, while the upscale **Silver Legacy** (407 N Virginia Street, at W 4th Street, 1-800 687 8733, www.silverlegacyreno. com) boasts a lobby filled with treasures from Tiffany's. It's in contrast to the basic **Club Cal-Neva** (38 E 2nd Street, at N Virginia Street, 1-877 777 7303, www.clubcalneva.com).

Where to eat & drink

Stay in or near a casino, as almost all visitors to Reno do, and you'll probably eat a number of your meals there. Of the downtown spots, the Eldorado and Harrah's offer the best dining; try Roxy's at the former and the Steak House at the latter. The Cal-Neva Virginian attracts the bargain-hunters. Out of the centre, the Grand Sierra and the Peppermill are among the strongest for food: the Peppermill's buffet is Reno's best and its White Orchid offers the finest dining in town. For all, *see above*.

Outside the casinos, you can find fine and messy Mexican food at **Bertha Miranda's**

(336 Mill Street, at Lake Street, 1-775 786 9697), heavy traditional Basque scran at **Louie's Basque Corner** (301 E 4th Street, at Evans Avenue, 1-775 323 7203) and splendid coffee at **Java Jungle** (246 W 1st Street, at S Arlington Avenue, 1-775 329 4484). You can sink microbrews at the attractive, slightly tucked-away **Silver Peak** (124 Wonder Street, at Holcomb Avenue, 1-775 324 1864, www.silverpeakbrewery.com), which serves upscale bar food.

Where to stay

Roughly 25,000 rooms are available in Reno, running the pricing gamut from dirt-cheap to sky-high. Prices peak in August (it's worth booking) but are cheap in winter: you can often get a room in one of the downtown casinos or motels for under $30. Note that rooms in casinos that have a sister Vegas hotel won't necessarily be in an identical mould.

Tourist information

Reno's visitor centre is in the lobby of the **National Bowling Stadium**. Alternatively, phone the information line at the Reno-Sparks CVA (1-800 367 7366, www.visitrenotahoe.com).

AROUND RENO
Carson City

As state capitals go, **Carson City**, 30 miles south of Reno on US 395, is not one of the more

Virginia City.

demonstrative. Still, what it lacks in pomposity it makes up for in quaintness, albeit a quaintness balanced by a string of casinos on Carson Street, the town's main drag, and also US 395.

Cynics suggest that the real balance of power in Nevada is held by the casino owners in Las Vegas, but the politicos of Carson City can still pack a punch when they need to. The centres of their activity are the **Nevada State Capitol** (N Carson Street, at Musser Street), a handsome domed structure dated 1871, and the **State Legislature**, a dreary building erected nearby a century later. The Kit Carson Trail, a two-mile walk detailed on a map available from the Chamber of Commerce (1900 S Carson Street, 1-775 882 1565, www.carsoncitychamber.com), offers a decent overview of the town's history.

Most of these buildings are closed to the public, but one that isn't is the suitably grand old US Mint Building at 600 N Carson Street, which for the last 60 years has served as the eclectic **Nevada State Museum** (1-775 687 4810, www.nevadaculture.org). The state's historic railroad comes under the microscope at the **Nevada State Railroad Museum** (2180 S Carson Street, 1-775 687 6953, www. nsrm-friends.org). Rides on old trains are offered most weekends outside winter. Still, the few casinos aside, there's not much nightlife here, and Carson City is best taken in during a day trip from Reno or Lake Tahoe.

Virginia City

A pleasant half-hour drive from Reno (south on US 395 for eight miles, then east on SR 341 for another eight miles) will take you to one of the most authentic historic mining towns in the West, where the discovery of gold and silver in nearby mines on the land of Henry Comstock sparked a furious bonanza in the 1860s. Of course, **Virginia City** is now also one of the most touristy towns in the West, its thin main drag soaked with themed bars, tatty museums – try the **The Way It Was Museum** (118 N C Street, 1-775 847 0766, www.visitvirginiacity.org), which looks like the Smithsonian next to some of its neighbours – photo studios and other less easily categorisable attractions ('See the Suicide Table!').

That said, provided you avoid summer weekends, when C Street can get claustrophobic with tourists, it's great fun. If you take the time to wander off the main drag, it's even a little bit more than that. The Walking Tour, available from the town's visitor centre, takes in the town's most fascinating buildings, among them the regenerated **Piper's Opera House** (1 N B Street, 1-775 847 0433, www.pipers operahouse.com). Visitors should note that many of the town's sights close during the viciously chilly winters.

Eating and drinking options in Virginia City are hardly varied, but you can wash down your sandwich or burger with a beer or a Coke in any number of establishments. There aren't too many places to stay, reflecting Virginia City's status as a day-tripper's paradise; in fact, you're best off driving back to Reno to find a bed for the night. And if you've got time, take the long way round – south on SR 341, then west on US 50 and back north on US 395 – in order to stop in at the magnificent **Chocolate Nugget** candy factory (56 SR 341, 1-775 849 0841) and pick up a couple of bags of sugar-rush.

Lake Tahoe

After you've driven through miles of desert, Reno's verdant trim comes as a pleasant surprise. But it's as nothing compared to **Lake Tahoe**, which sits on the California border, a 45-minute drive from Reno (south on US 395 for eight miles, then west on SR 431 for 25 miles). Some 22 miles long and 12 miles wide, it's one of the world's most beautiful alpine lakes.

Tahoe's two main settlements are at either end of the lake, both within a few miles of the state line. **Incline Village**'s population of 9,952 is swelled in winter by skiers (the slopes of **Mount Rose-Ski Tahoe** and **Diamond Peak** are nearby, with **Northstar-at-Tahoe** and the well-regarded **Squaw Valley USA** just across the state line), and in summer by hikers and people here for outdoor sports. Three miles west, in **Crystal Bay**, on the state line, are a handful of casinos; the best of them is the **Cal-Neva** (1-800 225 6382, www.calnevaresort.com).

South Lake Tahoe, meanwhile, also has its casinos, temptingly positioned on the Nevada edge of the state line. Among those offering accommodation are the **Montbleu** (formerly Caesars Tahoe; 1-888 829 7630, www.montbleuresort.com), **Harrah's** (1-800 427 7247, www.harrahslaketahoe.com), and its relation **Harveys** (1-775 588 6611, www. harveystahoe.com). On the California side sit restaurants, bars and motels. Skiers flock here in winter – **Heavenly**, **Sierra-at-Tahoe** and **Kirkwood** are the nearest slopes – while summer brings a more demure holidaymaker.

THE EXTRATERRESTRIAL HIGHWAY & AREA 51

Of course, you won't see anything. No one ever does. And if you're thinking about walking into the desert for a closer look, think again: you may find yourself greeted by employees of the US government wielding the kind of weaponry that'll encourage you to turn around in a hurry.

Still, SR 375 continues to draw tourists year-round. A few are here to plane-spot the military aircraft that roar overhead. A handful are on their way north to Ely. But the reason most people are ploughing up and down SR 375 is its now-official nickname, and what reputedly rests just a few miles west of the road.

If you've taken US 95 north to Reno, you'll already have skirted the western edge of the Nellis Air Force Range (see p297). Well, if you take SR 375, a plain-as-day desert road that links US 93 with US 6 in central Nevada, you'll be edging along its eastern perimeter. No one gave this much thought until the 1980s, when physicist Bob Lazar, in a series of interviews with local news gadfly George Knapp, claimed he had worked at Papoose Lake inside the range on alien spaceships. He also gave details – scant, but enough to light the touchpaper of conspiracy theorists – of the previously unknown dry-bedded Groom Lake, allegedly a

test site for top-secret new military aircraft and, more contentiously, the centre of government investigations into alien life. After the numbered grid square in which the base sits on maps of the test site, it's become known as **Area 51**; as a result of its notoriety, SR 375 has been nicknamed the **Extraterrestrial Highway**.

The US government refuses to acknowledge the existence of Area 51. Rumours persist that the notoriety of the base forced the government to move its operations from here to Utah during the 1990s. Either way, sightings of UFOs near the road are predictably common, and just as predictably difficult to substantiate.

Take care: someone is watching your movements. Don't cross into the military zone: you'll be arrested, questioned and fined. Armed guards are authorised to use 'deadly force' on trespassers. The border is not marked on maps and is often hard to detect: it's defined by orange posts, some topped with silver globes, and occasional 'restricted area' signs, but no fence.

The only town on SR 375 is **Rachel**, a scruffy collection of houses and huts that's home to a little under 100 people. This number is swelled by tourists staying at the **Little A'Le'Inn**, a slightly scruffy motel-bar-restaurant combo stocked with cheaply made, dearly priced alien ephemera and staffed by chatty people unafraid of engaging customers in a conversation about politics (tip: if you're a Democrat, keep your mouth shut).

Since 1995, when the military annexed more land, the only view of Area 51 is from **Tikaboo Peak**, 26 miles from the base. You get superb views of the desert, but even with binoculars, all you'll see of the base is a few distant buildings. It's a strenuous hike, best done in summer and early in the morning, before heat haze distorts the view. The best route is via a dirt road off US 93 at milepost 32.2, south of Alamo. It's just over 22 miles to Badger Spring and then a two-hour hike to the summit, but it's easy to get lost.

Where to stay, eat & drink

The aforementioned **Little A'Le'Inn** (1-775 729 2515, www.aleinn.com) has seven rooms in run-down trailers: you get a shared bathroom, a communal kitchen-cum-living room and UFO photos. The bar serves beer and burgers.

Getting there

By car
Take US 93 north for 107 miles to the junction with SR 375, aka the Extraterrestrial Highway. Rachel is 36 miles north-west of the junction. When driving, watch not so much for aliens but wandering cows: much of the road is an open range, and collisions occur regularly.

Utah

The rock formations of southern Utah are wonders of nature.

Utah will come as a culture shock after Las Vegas. It can be hard just to find a bar that serves alcohol here, or a restaurant that stays open past 9pm. If Las Vegas is a 24-hour city, then Mormon-dominated Utah, suspicious of outsiders and deeply mistrustful of its Nevadan neighbours, is a 12-hour state. But southern Utah is a unique place, not to say a spectacular one. National Park follows National Recreation Area follows National Monument, and hulking rock formations give way to vistas by turns peculiar and pretty. Zion National Park is a bit of both.

ZION NATIONAL PARK

A few hours north from Las Vegas, Zion National Park is a glorious introduction to the canyon country of south-east Utah. Zion's 2,000-foot (600-metre) cliffs and towering rock formations were discovered by early Mormon travellers in the 1880s. Originally called Mukuntuweap (roughly 'like a quiver', a description of the canyon's shape), its name was changed to Zion, an ancient Hebrew word meaning 'place of refuge', when it became a national park in 1919. With more than 2.5 million visitors annually, Zion is busy all year. However, it's best avoided in winter, when snow and ice make the trails tough to negotiate, and summer, when temperatures top 110°F (43°C).

The main entrance to the park is in the south, near the pretty town of **Springdale** (admission $25 per car, valid for seven days). Just beyond the entrance are the park's two campgrounds (*see p305*) and visitors' centre (staff are wonderfully helpful), with the tidy new **Zion Human History Museum** a further half-mile inside the gates. From April to October, when parts of the park are off-limits to cars, visitors should leave their cars at the south entrance or in Springdale, then take a free bus into the park. The rest of the park is open to private cars, but vehicles wider than 7ft 10in (2.39m) or higher than 10ft 4in (3.15m) must be escorted through the Zion–Mount Carmel tunnel ($25 per vehicle), which can lead to delays.

The majority of the park's sights and trails are accessible or visible from the six-mile

dead-end **scenic drive**, which starts at the main entrance and winds through the Virgin River gorge. (It's one of the aforementioned sections of the park that's closed to private cars from April to October.) The names of the vividly coloured Navajo sandstone rock formations along the drive echo the first visitors' religious sensibilities: the **Great White Throne**, **Angel's Landing**, the **Three Patriarchs**, the **Pulpit** and the **Temple of Sinawava**. Scan the sheer rock faces and you may see the ant-like figures of climbers; routes are detailed in Eric Bjornstad's *Desert Rock: Rock Climbs in the National Parks* (Falcon), an excellent resource for any traveller wanting to go climbing in this part of the world.

There are plenty of hiking trails off the scenic drive. The busiest are the short easy routes along the valley floor, such as **Weeping Rock** (0.5 miles, 30 minutes) and the **Riverside Walk** (two miles, one and a half hours), but the best views are at the end of the **Watchman Trail** (two and a half miles, two hours; shade on the route is minimal) and the five-mile, four-hour trail to and from **Angel's Landing**. Don't even attempt the latter if you're afraid of heights: the last half mile follows a steep, narrow ridge fitted with chains.

Perhaps the most spectacular hike is through the 16-mile **Narrows**, with canyon walls up to 2,000 feet (600 metres) high and at times only 20-30 feet apart. Be prepared to wade (or swim) through cold water and check conditions at the visitors' centre: there can be flash floods in summer. For hikers travelling from the top

Zion National Park.

down, a permit is required (fee based on group size: 1-2 people $10; 3-7 $15; 8-12 $20). For all hikes leaving from the bottom and heading up, as far as Big Springs, there is no permit fee through the Narrows.

East from Springdale and the scenic drive, you'll travel along the twisting **Zion–Mount Carmel Highway**, an engineering miracle when it was built in 1930. The impressive route leads through two long, narrow tunnels, passing scenery that is completely different from the landscapes of Zion Canyon. This is slickrock country: vast white, orange and pink rock formations, eroded into domes and buttes and marked with criss-cross patterns, loom next to the road. You can't miss the huge white monolith of **Checkerboard Mesa**.

Kolob Canyons, which is located in the park's north-western corner, has its own entrance (at exit 40 off I-15) and visitors' centre, from where a stunning five-mile drive leads into the red-rock **Finger Canyons**. There are also two hiking trails to embark on from here; the longer trail culminates at **Kolob Arch**, which, at 310 feet (95 metres), is possibly the world's largest natural arch.

Where to eat & drink

Inside the park, the **Red Rock Grill** restaurant at **Zion Lodge** (*see below*) is open for breakfast, lunch and dinner. Reservations are recommended for the last, especially in summer; call 1-435 772 7760.

Springdale has plenty of cafés and restaurants, but – this is Utah, folks – a

shortage of bars. The closest you'll find is the **Bit & Spur** (1212 Zion Park Boulevard, 1-435 772 3498, www.bitandspur.com, main courses $12-$25), a Mexican-slanted restaurant with outdoor seating. **Oscar's Café** (948 Zion Park Boulevard, 1-435 772 3232, main courses $10-$18) serves sturdy burgers, a vegetarian and vegan menu, Mexican dishes and other straightforward treats, while the family-friendly **Wildcat Willie's Ranch Grill & Saloon** at the Bumbleberry Inn (897 Zion Park Boulevard, 1-435 772 3224, www.wildcat willies.com) has a nice line in breakfasts.

Where to stay

Within the park sits the rustic-style **Zion Lodge** (1-888 297 2757, www.zionlodge.com), built in 1925 by the Union Pacific Railroad. Accommodation at the lodge includes six suites, 40 cabins and 75 motel-style rooms; prices range from $160 to $200 depending on the time of year and availability; you'll need to book well in advance between April and October.

There are also three campgrounds inside the park. The **Watchman Campground** is open all year (rates $16-$20); reservations are taken from March to early November (1-877 444 6777, www.reservations.nps.gov), with pitches allocated on a first-come, first-served basis at other times. The **South Campground** is open only from March to October and operates on a walk-up basis only (rates $16). Group campgrounds are also available to organised groups of nine to 40 people by booking in

advance (1-877 444 6777, http://reservations.
nps.gov, rates $3 per person).

There are many places to stay in Springdale,
including the 40-room **Cliffrose Lodge &
Gardens** (281 Zion Park Boulevard, 1 800
243 8824, 1-435 772 3234, www.cliffroselodge.
com, double $159-$399) and, perhaps most
appealingly, the **Desert Pearl Inn** (707 Zion
Park Boulevard, 1-888 828 0898, 1-435 772 8888,
www.desertpearl.com, double $143-$300).
For details of other options, contact the **Zion
Canyon Visitors' Center**; note that not all of
the town's hotels and motels are open in winter.

Getting there

To reach the park (164 miles from Vegas),
take I-15 north, watching your speed once you
leave Nevada (and being particularly careful
in Arizona, where the police aren't slow to stop
speeding cars). Head through the pleasant
Mormon town of St George and turn right at
exit 16 on to Highway 9 to Springdale. To visit
the Kolob Canyons area, continue for 25 miles
on I-15 until you reach exit 40.

Tourist information

Kolob Canyons Visitors' Center *3752 E Kolob
Canyon Road, New Harmony (1-435 586 9548,
www.nps.gov/zion).* **Open** *Spring-early summer,
autumn* 8am-5pm daily. *Summer* 8am-6pm daily.
Winter 8am-4pm daily.
Zion Canyon Visitors' Center Springdale
1-435 772 0170/3256, www.nps.gov/zion). **Open**
Spring-early summer, autumn 7am-6pm daily.

Summer 7am-8pm daily. *Winter* 8am-4.30pm daily.
Zion Canyon Visitors Bureau *1-888 518 7070,
www.zionpark.com.*

BEYOND ZION

At **Mount Carmel Junction**, east of the
park, Highway 9 joins up with US 89 for access
to the rest of Utah and Arizona, and scenery
that is arguably even more spectacular and
other-worldly than in Zion.

Heading north on US 89 and then east on
SR 12 takes you to **Bryce Canyon National
Park** (1-435 834 5322, www.nps.gov/brca),
where the landscape of vast rock hoodoos is
breathtakingly odd. It's dramatically snow-
cloaked in winter but mild during the summer
months, making it ideal for the casual hiker.
Try the Tower Bridge Trail, a three-mile round-
trip through some extraordinary scenery, or
venture out on to the Rim Trail, which affords
astonishing views of this peculiar landscape.
Admission to the park is $25 for private vehicles,
a pass that's valid for seven days. The website
above has details on accommodation.

Travelling north up Highway 12 from Zion,
through **Dixie National Forest**, brings you
to the **Capitol Reef National Park** (1-435
425 3791, www.nps.gov/care). While it's by
no means as spectacular as its neighbours, and
doesn't offer anything like the variety of hikes
that you'll find at Bryce Canyon or Zion, it's
geologically fascinating and very much worth
a brief diversion if you're heading this way.

Alternatively, leave Zion on US 89 south
towards the Grand Canyon.

Bryce Canyon National Park.

Directory

Getting Around

ARRIVING & LEAVING

By air

Las Vegas's **McCarran International Airport** (261 5211, www.mccarran.com) is just five minutes from the south end of the Strip, which makes the trip from airport to hotel relatively painless. The airport itself is clean and modern, and takes first (and last) tilt at the tourist dollar with halls of slot machines and video poker.

There are hundreds of internal flights to Las Vegas each week. However, direct international flights are limited; from the UK, for example, only Virgin Atlantic (from London Gatwick) and BMI (from Manchester) fly direct. Most flights to and from Europe require passengers to change at an East Coast airport or at LAX.

Public bus routes 108 and 109 run north from the airport: the 108 heads up Swenson Avenue and stops at the Las Vegas Hilton, while the 109 goes along Maryland Parkway. Shuttle buses run by **Bell Trans** (739 7990, www.bell-trans.com), **Grayline** (739 5700, www.grayline.com) and **Ritz** (889 4242, www.shuttlelas vegas.com) run to the Strip and Downtown 24 hours a day. Expect to pay $7 for transport to a Strip hotel, slightly more to Downtown.

Taxis can be found outside the arrivals hall. There's a $1.80 surcharge on all fares originating at McCarran; bearing that in mind, expect to pay $15-$25 to get to most hotels on the Strip, or $20-$25 to Downtown (plus tip).

Airlines

Air Canada *1-888 247 2262, aircanada.com*

Alaska Air *1-800 426 0333, www.alaskaair.com.*

American Airlines *1-800 433 7300, www.aa.com.*

BMI *UK: 0870 607 0222, www.flybmi.com.*

Continental *domestic 1-800 523 3273, international 1-800 231 0856, www.continental.com.*

Delta *domestic 1-800 221 1212, international 1-800 241 4141, www.delta.com.*

Jet Blue *1-800 538 2583, www.jetblue.com.*

Southwest *1-800 435 9792, www.southwest.com.*

United Airlines *domestic 1-800 864 8331, international 1-800 538 2929, www.united.com.*

US Airways *domestic 1-800 428 4322, international 1-800 622 1015, www.usairways.com.*

Virgin Atlantic *UK: 0870 380 2007. US: 1-800 862 8621, www.virginatlantic.com.*

By road

The main roads leaving the city are the **I-15**, which runs south-west towards LA and north-east towards Salt Lake City, and the **US93** and **US95**, which head respecctiverly, north into Nevada and so south into Arizona and California. For details of car hire, *see p310.*

Greyhound buses (1-800 231 2222, www.greyhound.com) arrive at the bus station on 200 Main Street, just by the Plaza. The ride from LA $42 one-way, $84 round trip) takes between five and eight hours. Reservations are not required.

PUBLIC TRANSPORT

The Citizens Area Transit bus network (CAT, though the name may change), is run by the Regional Transportation Commission of Southern Nevada (RTC). The Downtown Transportation Center (DTC) is the transfer point for many routes. For a system map, *see p330.*

Bonneville Transit Center (BTC) *101 E. Bonneville Avenue, Downtown (228 7433, www.rtc southernnevada.com). Bus Deuce & all BTC-bound buses.* **Open** 7am-5.30pm daily. **Map** p334 D1.

CAT fares & tickets

Most CAT routes cost $2 or $1 for over-62s and 6-17s and the disabled, but only with a Reduced Fare Photo Identification Card (available from the DTC). The exception is the Deuce route along the Strip, which costs $5 or $7 for a 24-hour pass. $20 gets you a 3-Day All Access Pass. Use exact change. Transfers are free, if you ask for one when you pay. A 30-day system pass costs $65.

CAT routes

Buses run 24-7 on the Deuce route along Las Vegas Boulevard, and roughly 5.30am-1.30am elsewhere. The buses are safe and relatively comprehensive in their coverage of the city. Bus stops are marked by signs with the blue, white and gold RTC Transit logo; most have shelters.

The most useful bus for tourists is the **Deuce**: named as it's a double-decker bus, it travels the length of Las Vegas Boulevard from the DTC in the north to just by I-215 in the south, stopping in front of all major casinos. Deuces are often busy, especially at night.

Most bus routes run along the length of a single street, some with a quick turnaround at either end of the route. Buses with a route number beginning in '1' generally run north–south; those starting '2' run east–west. Below is a list of some key routes.

Deuce	Las Vegas Boulevard
103	Decatur Boulevard
105	Martin Luther King Boulevard/Industrial Road
106	Rancho Drive
107	Boulder Highway
108	Paradise Road
109	Maryland Parkway
110	Eastern Avenue
113	Las Vegas Boulevard (north of BTC only)

201	Tropicana Avenue
202	Flamingo Road
203	Spring Mountain Road/Twain Avenue
204	Sahara Avenue
206	Charleston Boulevard
207	Alta Drive/Stewart Avenue
208	Washington Boulevard

Many bus routes, among them the Deuce, 105, 107, 108, 109, 113 and 207, stop at the BTC. Throughout the listings in this book, we have used the shorthand 'BTC-bound buses' to refer to these buses.

Monorails & shuttle buses

After teething problems, the **Las Vegas Monorail** is now running a reliable service along Paradise Road and then behind the Strip. However, it hasn't displaced the numerous hotel buses and monorails.

Las Vegas Monorail
699 8200, www.lvmonorail.com.
The pricey and not wholly convenient Las Vegas Monorail runs from the **Sahara** to the **MGM Grand**, stopping at the **Las Vegas Hilton**, the **Las Vegas Convention Center**, **Harrah's**, the **Flamingo** and **Bally's**. The service runs 7am-2pm Mon-Thur, and 7am-3am Fri-Sun. The journey time from end to end is usually around 15 minutes. Single-ride tickets cost $5 and one-day passes go for $12; three-day passes for $28.

Other monorails
Free, 24hr monorails, separate to the Las Vegas Monorail, link the **Mirage** and **TI**; and **Excalibur**, the **Luxor** and **Mandalay Bay**. For all of them, it's often quicker to walk. A free monorail connects the **CityCenter** complex with the adjacent **Monte Carlo** and **Bellagio** resorts.

Free shuttle buses
A shuttle bus connects the **Rio** with **Harrah's** on the Strip, just south of **Planet Hollywood** (formerly the Aladdin). Nearby, the **Palms** lays on a shuttle to and from the **Fashion Show Mall** and the **Forum Shops**. The **Hard Rock** runs a shuttle that loops

around from the hotel to the **Forum Shops**, **Planet Hollywood** and **the MGM Grand**. Shuttle buses link **Sam's Town** to Downtown and the Strip, and the **South Point** and the Strip. And there are free shuttle buses linking **Green Valley Ranch**, **Red Rock**, **Palace Station** and **Sunset Station** to both the Strip and McCarran Airport.

BUS TOURS

Gray Line Tours *1-800 634 6579, www.graylinelasvegas.com.*
Gray Line offers a handful of Vegas-based bus tours, including an evening city tour (6hrs, $55), plus trips out to the Grand Canyon (12hrs, $159), and a half-day jag to Lake Mead and the Hoover Dam (8hrs, $92). Discounts are often available by booking in advance online.

TAXIS & LIMOS

There are **taxi ranks** outside most hotels; restaurants and bars will be happy to call a cab for you. Technically, you're not allowed to hail a taxi from the street and most won't stop if you try, but it's usually OK to approach an empty cab with its light on if it has stopped in traffic. Meters start at $3.30, and increase by $2.60 per mile. If you have a complaint, note the cab number and call the **Nevada Taxicab Authority** (486 6532, www.taxi.state.nv.us). For lost property, *see p314.*
Limousines are a flash and popular way of getting around. The rides vary from the basic black stretch ($50/hr) to huge SUVs with hot tubs, disco balls and the like ($115/hr). Many limos are available for hire outside hotels and the airport. Limo drivers are not allowed to solicit passengers, but you are perfectly at liberty to approach them for a ride.

Cab companies

Desert *386 9102.*

Whittlesea Blue Cab *384 6111.*

Yellow-Checker-Star (YCS)
873 2000, www.ycstrans.com.

Limousine companies

Bell Trans *739 7990, www.bell-trans.com.*

Las Vegas Limo *888 4848, www.lasvegaslimo.com.*

Presidential *731 5577, www.presidentiallimolv.com.*

DRIVING

If you're based on the Strip, a mix of buses, taxis, monorails and feet will get you to most places. However, automobile rental is affordable in Vegas; a car is recommended if you're staying away from the Strip or are keen to visit off-Strip attractions, and essential if you're planning to visit any out-of-town destinations.

The Las Vegas streets get very congested in the morning and evening rush hours (7-9am, 4-6pm), as well as at weekends, when traffic is horrific in tourist areas after 4pm. The Strip is slow-going most of the time and turns into a virtual car park when the town is busy.

The nearby parallel streets – Industrial Road and Frank Sinatra Drive to the west, Paradise Road to the east – move faster, and provide access to several casinos. For north–south journeys longer than a block or two, it's often worth taking I-15, which runs parallel to the Strip. If you're trying to get east–west across town, take the Desert Inn arterial, a mini-expressway that runs under the Strip and over I-15 (though there are no junctions at either).

I-15 intersects with the east–west US 95 north-west of Downtown. US 95 connects to the 53-mile beltway at the edges of the valley, which leads commuters around the region. Because Las Vegas is constantly tearing itself down and rebuilding itself, there's usually a great deal of road construction going on on I-15; for road conditions, call 486 3116 or see www.nevadadot.com/traveler/roads.

Speed limits vary in Nevada. In general, the speed limit on freeways is 65mph; on the highway, it's either 65mph or 70mph. Limits on main urban thoroughfares (such as Tropicana Avenue) are 45mph; elsewhere, limits are 25mph, 30mph or 35mph. Look for signs in construction zones and near schools, which often enforce a reduced limit.

Unless otherwise specified, you can turn right on a red light, after stopping, if the street is clear. U-turns are not only legal (unless specified) but often a positive necessity given the length of the blocks. In case of a car accident, call 911; do not move the cars involved in the accident until the police ask you to do so.

In Nevada, you can be arrested for driving under the influence if your blood alcohol level is 0.08 or higher (or 0.02 for under-21s. If you're pulled over, the police can give you a drink-driving test on the spot. If you refuse, you'll be taken to jail for a blood test, which will be taken by force if necessary.

Gas is far cheaper than in Europe, but pricey for the US. There are gas stations by Circus Circus and across from Mandalay Bay; stations abound in (among others) Paradise Road, Maryland Parkway, Tropicana Avenue and Flamingo Road. For mechanics and full-service gas stations, see 'Automobile repair' in the *Yellow Pages*.

The **American Automobile Association (AAA)** provides maps, guidebooks and other useful information. They're free if you're a member or belong to an affiliated organisation, such as the British AA. The main Vegas office, open 8.30am-5.30pm during the week, is at 3312 W Charleston Boulevard; call them on 415 2200 or see www.aaa.com for more details.

Car hire

Most car-hire agencies are at or near the airport. Call around for the best rate, booking well in advance if you're planning to visit over a holiday weekend or for a major convention. When business renters are scarce, though, you should get a good rate, and maybe – if you ask nicely – an upgrade.

Almost every firm requires a credit card and matching driver's licence; few will rent to under-25s. Prices won't include tax, liability insurance or collision damage waiver (CDW); US residents may be covered on their home policy, but foreign residents will need to buy extra insurance. UK travellers should note that while rental deals struck with the UK offices of the major firms include insurance, it's often cheaper to rent the car from the US office and rely for insurance on the good-value, year-long policy available from www.insurance4carhire.com.

Alamo *US: 1-800 462 5266, 263 8411, www.alamo.com. UK: 0870 400 4562, www.alamo.co.uk.*

Avis *US: 1-800 331 1212, 261 5595, www.avis.com. UK: 0870 606 0100, www.avis.co.uk.*

Budget *US: 1-800 527 0700, 736 1212, www.budget.com. UK: 0844 581 2231, www.budget.co.uk.*

Dollar *US: 1-800 800 3665, www.dollar.com. UK: 0808 234 752, www.dollar.co.uk.*

Enterprise *US: 1-800 261 7331, 365 6662, www.enterprise.com. UK: 0870 350 3000, www. enterprise.co.uk.*

Hertz *US: 1-800 654 3131, 220 9700, www.hertz.com. UK: 0870 844 8844, www.hertz.co.uk.*

National *US: 1-800 227 7368, 263 8411. UK: 0870 400 4581. Both: www.nationalcar.com.*

Thrifty *US: 1-800 847 4389, 896 7600, www.thrifty.com. UK: 0808 234 7642, www.thrifty.co.uk.*

Motorcycle rental

Eaglerider *876 8687, www.eaglerider.com.*

Harley-Davidson of Southern Nevada *431 8500, www.lvhd.com.*

Parking

Most hotel-casinos have valet parking, which is convenient, safe and free (apart from the $2-$5 tip on your way out). If you see a sign saying the valet car park is full and you're in a luxury car, stay put: chances are the valets will find a spot for you. Hotel guests also get preferential treatment; when the attendant asks to see your room key, $5-$10 will often substitute. Self-parking is free and abundant in the multilevel parking structures at every Vegas resort (Downtown casinos require a validation stamp), but the convenience of lots is variable.

CYCLING

In a word: don't. Some try and get away with cycling on the Strip on weekend nights, when traffic has slowed to a crawl. But it's dicey even then; and at other times, the drivers on the three- and four-lane roads in the city simply aren't looking for cyclists: you're taking your life in your hands.

HELICOPTER

Plane and helicopter rides over the rim of the Grand Canyon are a major cause of air and noise pollution. But if you care to disregard the concerns of Las Vegas locals and Grand Canyon environmentalists, then **Sundance** is Nevada's best regarded helicopter tour operator. City tours run from $85 $110, with trips to the Grand Canyon (the company offers quite a variety) starting at around $375. Other by-air options for the Grand Canyon include **Grand Canyon Airlines** and **Papillon Grand Canyon Helicopters** (for both, *see p292*).

Sundance Helicopters *1-800 653 1881, 736 0606, www.helicoptour.com, www.sundancehelicopters.com.*

WALKING

Pedestrians are rarely seen off the Strip in Vegas, and even there they face danger from carefree and often careless drivers. The bridges on the Strip help, but it's still tricky. Jaywalking is so potentially deadly that police often issue citations. Laws, and physics, favour the driver: never put yourself in the path of cars that have the green light.

The safest places to cross are the overhead pedestrian bridges at several key Strip locations, bridges that (of course) guide you past the entrances of the casinos on each corner. You can find them at Tropicana Avenue, at Flamingo Road, and at Spring Mountain Road near Wynn Las Vegas. Where there are no bridges, closely follow all traffic signals and check both directions twice before stepping into the street.

It's possible to take short-cuts from one Strip hotel to the next, but you're likely to get trapped in a maze of service roads. Use our maps to guide you and don't underestimate the distances between resorts: the Strip is longer than it looks, and walking it end to end will take at least 90 minutes and almost certainly longer. And always factor in plenty of time to get out of the resort in which you've been staying, dining, gambling or partying: you may be as much as a 15-minute walk from the main exit.

Resources A-Z

TRAVEL ADVICE

For up-to-date information on travel to a specific country – including the latest on safety and security, health issues, local laws and customs – contact your home country government's department of foreign affairs. Most have websites with useful advice for would-be travellers.

AUSTRALIA
www.smartraveller.gov.au

CANADA
www.voyage.gc.ca

NEW ZEALAND
www.safetravel.govt.nz

REPUBLIC OF IRELAND
foreignaffairs.gov.ie

UK
www.fco.gov.uk/travel

USA
www.state.gov/travel

ADDRESSES

Addresses follow the standard US format. The room and/or suite number usually appears after the street address (where applicable), followed by the city name and the zip code. Note that Las Vegas Boulevard South is the official name of the Strip. For more on orientation, *see p69* **Orientation in Vegas**.

AGE RESTRICTIONS

Admission to nude clubs 18 (except Palomino).
Admission to topless clubs 21.
Buying/drinking alcohol 21.
Driving 16.
Gambling 21.
Marriage 16 (with parental consent) or 18 (without).
Sex 16 (heterosexual) or 18 (homosexual).

ATTITUDE & ETIQUETTE

As a tourist city, Vegas is as formal or informal as you want it to be. During the warmer months, shorts and T-shirts are accepted wear along the Strip as well as on the gaming floors of most casinos, though dressing up to a minimum of smart-casual has become the norm. Some lounges and nightclubs have dress codes (sports shoes, T-shirts and jeans may be prohibited), and dining in some high-end restaurants can be formal.

BUSINESS

Conventions & conferences

Vegas is the convention capital of the US. The convention centre at **Mandalay Bay** is another convention popular venue.

Las Vegas Convention Center
3150 Paradise Road, at Convention Center Drive, East of Strip (892 0711, www.lvcva.com). Bus 108, 213. **Map** p335 C5.
Sands Expo & Convention Center *210 Sands Avenue, at Koval Lane, East of Strip (733 5556, www.sandsexpo.com). Bus 203, 213.* **Map** p336 B6.

Couriers & shippers

Many hotels have business centres with courier services.

DHL *1-800 225 5345, www.dhl.com.*
FedEx *1-800 463 3339, www.fedex.com.*
UPS *1-800 742 5877/www.ups.com.*

Office services

Bit by Bit *221 2255, www.bit-by-bit.com.*
Bit by Bit rents laptops, desktop computers and other technological accoutrements. Call ahead to arrange delivery.
FedEx Kinko's *395 Hughes Center Drive, at Paradise Road, East of Strip (951 2400, http://fedex.kinkos.com). Bus 108, 213.* **Open** 24hrs daily. **Map** p336 C7.
The prominent chain of copy shops has five branches in the Las Vegas area; this is one of two that are open 24hrs. Services include printing, shipping and internet access.
Other locations throughout the city.

Useful organisations

For the **Las Vegas Chamber of Commerce** and the **Las Vegas CVA**, For both, *see p316*.

CONSUMER

For complaints about casinos, contact the **Gaming Control Board** ((775) 684-7700, http://gaming.nv.gov). For general enquiries and complaints, contact the privately operated **Better Business Bureau** (320 4500, http://southernnevada.bbb.org, which receives and investigates complaints, or the Consumer Affairs Division of the **Nevada Department of Business & Industry** (486 7355, www.fyiconsumer.org).

CUSTOMS

Travellers arriving in Vegas on an indirect international flight will go through customs and immigration at the airport in which they change planes. This involves reclaiming baggage at the transfer airport, taking it through customs and then checking it in again. Connection times should take account of this.

On US flights, non-US citizens are given two forms – one for immigration, one for customs – which must be filled in and handed in at the appropriate desk on landing. Foreign visitors can import the following items duty-free: 200 cigarettes or 50 cigars (not Cuban; over-18s only) or 2kg of smoking tobacco; one litre of wine or spirits (over-21s only); and up to $100 in gifts ($800 for returning Americans). You must declare and maybe forfeit plants and foods. Check www.cbp.gov/xp/cgov/travel before travelling.

DISABLED

Vegas is a disabled-friendly city. Strip resorts are fully wheelchair-accessible, from pools, spas and

DIRECTORY

restrooms to gambling facilities; things are a little harder in the older Downtown properties. A few casinos offer games for sight- and hearing-impaired players. Disabled parking is found almost everywhere; buses and many taxis are adapted to take wheelchairs (though be sure to ask when you book).

The **Southern Nevada Center for Independent Living** (889 4216, www.sncil.org) offers advice, information, transport and equipment loans (including wheelchairs) for disabled people. The **Society of Accessible Travel and Hospitality** (1-212 447 7284, www.sath.org) can provide advice for disabled people planning trips to all corners of the US.

DRUGS

The use of illegal drugs, including clubbing drugs such as ecstasy, is quite prevalent in Sin City. Dealers will approach you all over town, but take care. And always watch your drinks: illicit, hard-to-trace drugs are sometimes slipped into unattended glasses.

The local authorities have a strict zero-tolerance policy on drug use and trafficking. If you're implicated in a drug sale or purchase, you will be arrested and subject to trial, and if convicted could receive a maximum sentence of five to ten years in prison.

ELECTRICITY

The US uses a 110-120V, 60-cycle AC voltage. Except for dual-voltage flat-pin shavers, most foreign visitors will need to run appliances through an adaptor. Most US TVs and DVDs use a different frequency from those in Europe.

EMBASSIES & CONSULATES

The nearest foreign embassies and consulates to Las Vegas are in Los Angeles.

Australia *Suite 3150, Century Plaza Towers, 2029 Century Park East, Los Angeles, CA 90067 (1-310 229 4800, www.losangeles. consulate.gov.au.* **Open** 9am-5pm Mon-Fri.
Canada *9th Floor, 550 S Hope Street, Los Angeles, CA 90071 (1-213 346 2700, www.canada international.gc.ca/los_angeles.* **Open** 8.30am-4.30pm Mon-Fri.

New Zealand *Suite 600E, 2425 Olympic Boulevard, Santa Monica, CA 90404 (1-310 566 6555, www.nzcgla.com).* **Open** 8.30am-4.30pm Mon-Fri.
Republic of Ireland *Suite 3350, 100 Pine Street, San Francisco, CA 94111 (1-415 392 4214, www.consulateofirelandsan francisco.org).* **Open** 9am-12.30pm Mon, Wed, Fri.
South Africa *Suite 600, 6300 Wilshire Boulevard, Los Angeles, CA 90048 (1-323 651 0902, www.link2southafrica.com).* **Open** 9am-noon Mon-Fri.
United Kingdom *Suite 1200, 11766 Wilshire Boulevard, Los Angeles, CA 90025 (1-310 481 0031, 24hr emergencies 1-877 514 1233).* **Open** 8am-4.30pm Mon-Fri.

EMERGENCIES

In an emergency, dial **911** (free from public phones) and state the nature of the problem.

GAY & LESBIAN

Q-Vegas (www.qvegas.com) is the leading media resource for the GLBT community. You can pick up the monthly magazine or download it from the website.

Gay and Lesbian Community Center of Southern Nevada *Commercial Center, 953 E Sahara Avenue, between S 6th Street & S Maryland Parkway, East of Strip (733 9800, www.thecenterlv.com). Bus 109, 204.* Open 11am-7pm Mon-Fri .
A nonprofit gathering place and information clearinghouse that holds meetings and support groups. If you've got a question about gay and lesbian life in Las Vegas, they've got an answer or know someone who has.

HEALTH

Doctors are available around the clock in emergency rooms and at some UMC Quick Care locations, and by appointment during regular hours. Take the prescription to a licensed pharmacist (*see p210*), who'll usually be able to provide the medication within minutes.

Most hospitals accept major insurance plans, but – unless it's an emergency – you should call ahead to check. Large hotels have access to on-call doctors, at a cost.

Accident & emergency

All the hospitals listed below have a 24-hour ER, although only **Sunrise** and **UMC** have out-and-out trauma centres. The UMC on Charleston is the only hospital that by law must treat all applicants. The ER entrance is on the corner of Hasting and Rose Streets.

Desert Springs Hospital *2075 E Flamingo Road, at Burnham Street, East Las Vegas (733 8800, www.desertspringshospital.net). Bus 202.*
North Vista Hospital *1409 E Lake Mead Boulevard, between Las Vegas Boulevard North & N Eastern Avenue, North Las Vegas (649 7711, www.northvista hospital.com). Bus 113, 210.*
St Rose Dominican Hospital *102 E Lake Mead Drive at Boulder Highway, Henderson (564 2622, www.strosehospitals.org). Bus 107, 212.*
Summerlin Hospital Medical Center *657 N Town Center Drive, at Hualapai Way, North-west Las Vegas (233 7000, www.summerlin hospital.org). No bus.*
Sunrise Hospital & Medical Center *3186 S Maryland Parkway, between E Sahara Avenue & E Desert Inn Road, East Las Vegas (731 8000, www.sunrise hospital.com). Bus 109.*
University Medical Center *1800 W Charleston Boulevard, at Shadow Lane, West Las Vegas (383 2000, www.umcsn.com). Bus 206.*
Valley Hospital Medical Center *620 Shadow Lane, off W Charleston Boulevard, West Las Vegas (388 4000, www.valley hospital.net). Bus 206.*

Complementary medicine

The city's few practitioners of complementary medicine enjoy a healthy business, as do aromatherapists and herbal healers. All of the major hotel spas include some form of aromatherapy.

Contraception & abortion

Planned Parenthood *3220 W Charleston Boulevard, between S Rancho Drive & S Valley View Boulevard, West Las Vegas (878 7776/www.pprm.org). Bus 206.* **Open** (appointment only) 9am-5pm Mon,Wed,;11am-7pm Tue, Thur.; 9am-4pm Fri; 9am-2pm Sat.; 10 am-3pm Sun.
This non-profit organisation can supply contraception (including

the morning-after pill), treat STDs, perform abortions and test for AIDS (results take a week). **Other location 3300** E Flamingo Road #25 (547 9888).

Dentists

The **Nevada Dental Association** (800- 962 6710, 255 4211, www.nvda.org) will make referrals to registered local dentists, including Medicaid and Medicare practitioners.

Hospitals

See p312 **Accident & emergency**.

Pharmacies

Both over-the-counter and prescription drugs are readily available all over town. For pharmacies, *see p210*.

STDs, HIV & AIDS

For specific information on HIV/AIDS, local resources, various support groups and free, confidential tests, contact **Aid for AIDS of Nevada**. For treatment of STDs and free AIDS tests, visit **Planned Parenthood** (*see p312*). *See also below* **Helplines**.

Aid for AIDS of Nevada (AFAN)
Suite 170, 701 Shadow Lane, West of Strip (382 2326, www.afaniv.org). Bus 206. **Open** 7am-5pm Mon-Fri.

HELPLINES

For information on what to do in an emergency, *see above*. *See also above* **Health**.

AIDS Information Line *759 0743.*
Alcoholics Anonymous *598 1888.*
Gamblers Anonymous *385 7732.*
Narcotics Anonymous *369 3362.*
Poison Control Center *732 4989.*
Rape Crisis *366 1640.*
Suicide Prevention *731 2990.*

ID

You'll need to prove your age with a photo ID (passport, driver's licence or state ID card) when buying tobacco and alcohol, gambling, and entering strip clubs and nightclubs.

INSURANCE

Non US nationals should arrange comprehensive insurance, including

medical insurance, before departure; US citizens should consider doing the same. Medical centres will ask for details of your insurance company and your policy number; keep them with you at all times.

INTERNET

Most hotels have high-speed connections wired into every room (around $10 per day); some have wireless access. Savvy laptoppers can link to free Wi-Fi at 12 branches of the **Coffee Bean & Tea Leaf**, among them in the Miracle Mile Shops (*see p195*; 696 0564), at the Venetian (*see p195*; 650 0734) and in the University District (4550 S Maryland Parkway, between E Flamingo Road & E Tropicana Avenue (944 5029). There's also free wireless in the **Fashion Show Mall** (*see p197*) near the Apple Store, and in the city's libraries (*see below*).

For those without a laptop, the pickings are slimmer. A few convenience stores have terminals, but prices are high. Public libraries (*see below*) offer free, time-limited access; **FedEx Kinko's** (*see p311*) has paid-for access; and the display computers in the Apple Store serve as an unofficial internet café.

LEFT LUGGAGE

Hotel bell desks are happy to look after bags for up to 12 hours. Lockers are available in McCarran Airport; expect to pay $2-$3/hr or $8-$12/day.

LEGAL HELP

If you're arrested, call your insurance firm, your consulate or the Lawyer Referral Service on 382 0504. If you do not have a lawyer, the court will appoint one for you.

LIBRARIES

There are public libraries thoughout the Las Vegas-Clark County Library District (www.lvccld.org). Most are open 10am-7pm, Mon-Thur; 10am-6pm Fri-Sun. Clark County Library is one of the most central.

Clark County Library *1401 E Flamingo Road, at S Maryland Parkway, University District (507 3400). Bus 109, 202.* **Map** p333 Y3.

Lied Library *4505 S Maryland Parkway, between E Flamingo Road & E Tropicana Avenue, University District (895 2255, www.library.nevada.edu). Bus 109.* **Open** 7.30am-midnight Mon-Thur; 7.30am-7pm Fri; 9am-6pm Sat; 11am-midnight Sun. **Map** p333 Y3.
This $40-million university facility houses 1.8 million volumes.

LOST PROPERTY

Casinos all have lost and found departments. If you lose an item in a cab, call the taxi firm.

McCarran International Airport
Terminal 1 (261 5134). **Open** 7am-11pm, daily .
Citizens Area Transit (CAT)
South Strip Transfer Terminal, 6675 S Gillespie Street, at I-215 (1-800 228 3911, 228 7433). Bus Deuce, 105, 109, 212. **Open** 7am-5.30pm Mon-Fri.

MEDIA

Daily newspapers

The **Las Vegas Review-Journal** (50¢, or $1 in casinos; $2.50 on Sunday; www.lvrj.com) offers toothless but serviceable coverage of local and national stories. John L Smith is the must-read columnist for local politicos, a useful counterpoint to the entertainingly awful weekly columns of publisher Sherman Frederick; Norm Clarke covers gossip with tireless enthusiasm; and Mike Weatherford writes astutely about the local entertainment scene. 'Neon', the *R-J*'s pull-out entertainment guide issued each Friday, has listings for films, shows and restaurants.

The **Las Vegas Sun** (www.lasvegassun.com) once offered a populist, left-leaning alternative to the conservative *R-J*, but it's now an eight-page shadow of its former self, folded into the *R-J* each morning; however, despite this curious arrangement, the papers are run separately. The *Sun*'s news reporting has considerably more bite than the *R-J*, with Jon Ralston's column a real draw.

As well as the city's two daily papers, the **Los Angeles Times** (50¢) is widely available, and most Strip hotels will also carry the **Wall Street Journal** (75¢) and the **New York Times** ($1). International newspapers and magazines are harder to find.

Alternative weeklies

The newest, hippest and slickest of the alt-weeklies is Seven (www.weeklyseven.com), a comprehensive city magazine with a special interest and affection for the club and pool-party scene, run by Wendoh Media, which funs luxury-conscious publications as 944 in other nightlife-oreinted cities. Nightlife writer Xania Woodman is the final word on where to go, what to wear, what to drink—and how to get in.

Established in 1992 as *Scope* and purchased in 1998 by the Greenspun family, the **Las Vegas Weekly** (free, www.lasvegas weekly.com) has gone through various editorial phases, but is now very much focused on entertainment. Ironically, then, it's at its best when it looks at the broader picture of Las Vegas life.

It's debatable whether Las Vegas really needs three alt-weeklies. Even so, until **Las Vegas CityLife** (www.lasvegas citylife.com) absorbed the *Las Vegas Mercury* into its pages in 2005, the city actually had three of 'em. A good deal less glossy and a touch more political than the *Weekly*, the relatively low-key *CityLife* retains a fanbase. The writing is solid and often excellent, but the design is right out of 1985.

Other magazines

Numerous freebie mags, such as **Today in Las Vegas**, **What's On** and **Las Vegas Magazine**, are distributed for free at hotels and other tourist spots. They're useful for show listings and discount coupons, but the editorial is little more than regurgitated press releases; don't stop here if you're after recommendations.

For gaming news, check out the monthly **Las Vegas Advisor**, focused on the city, or the weekly **Gaming Today**, which has a wider remit. Other business news is covered in the monthly **Nevada Business Journal**, and two weeklies, **In Business Las Vegas** and the **Las Vegas Business Press**. And last but not least, keep an eye out for **Las Vegas Life**, a better-than-average monthly glossy that costs $3.99 on newsstands but is often found for free in hotel rooms.

Radio

FM radio in Vegas is a bland parade of hackneyed playlists

and punchable DJs suitable only for splicing together ads for car sales and topless joints. The best station in town is **KNPR**, one of two National Public Radio affiliates.

On AM, news and sports dominate. All the big national shows are syndicated here, with **KXNT** 840AM bringing a particularly pungent triple-threat in the forms of fearsome conservative Rush Limbaugh (9am-noon), agony aunt Laura Schlessinger (noon-3pm) and serial controversialist Sean Hannity (3-6pm).

KCEP *88.1 FM*
www.power88lv.com.
Urban contemporary tunes.
KNPR *88.9 FM*
www.knpr.org.
News, talk and commentary from this National Public Radio affiliate.
KCNV *89.7 FM*
www.classical897.org.
Classical music; an NPR station.
KUNV *91.5 FM*
http://kunv.unlv.edu.
Mostly jazz, but pretty eclectic.
KOMP *92.3 FM*
http://werlv.com.
Mainstream rock.
KMXB *94.1 FM*
http://mix941fm.radio.com.
Mainstream pop.
KWNR *95.5 FM*
www.kwnr.com.
Country and western.
KXPT *97.1, http://werlv.com.*
Classic rock.
KLUC *98.5 FM*
http://kluc.radio.com.
Urban pop.
KWID *101.9 FM*
www.lapreciosaenlasvegas.com.
Spanish language pop, news and sports.
KJUL *104.7 FM*
www.kjul1047.com.
Your (grand)parents' favourite tunes.
KSNE *106.5 FM*
www.ksne.com.
Light rock and pop.
KVGS *107.9 FM*
www.1079thealternative.com.
Mainstream alternative.

Television

The Las Vegas affiliates of the four major American networks are **KSNV 3** (NBC), **KVVU 5** (Fox), **KLAS 8** (CBS) and **KTNV 13** (ABC). The city's public broadcasting affiliate is **KLVX 10**. Every hotel TV will get these stations and plenty of others; among them is **Las Vegas One**, co-run by KLAS. Most hotels will also offer subscription-based cable

networks such as **CNN** (news), **ESPN** (sport) and **HBO** (movies). Daily TV listings can be found in the *R-J* and *TV Guide*.

MONEY

The US dollar ($) is split into 100 cents (¢). Coins run from the copper penny (1¢) to the silver nickel (5¢), dime (10¢), quarter (25¢), the less common half-dollar (50¢) and the rarely seen dollar (silver and gold). Notes ('bills') are all the same green colour and size, but come in denominations of $1, $5, $10, $20, $50 and $100. Credit cards are accepted in almost every hotel, shop and restaurant, but do keep cash on hand just in case (and, of course, for tips).

Banks & ATMs

ATMs are ubiquitous in Las Vegas: you'll find them in stores, bars, casinos and even strip clubs. ATMs accept most major credit and debit cards, but almost all will charge a usage fee. You can withdraw cash on a card without a PIN at most casinos, though you'll be charged a premium. It's cheaper to visit one of the banks scattered all over town; ask staff at your hotel for details of your nearest.

Bureaux de change

Some casinos have their own bank or bureau de change; all have a 24-7 cashier's cage where you can cash most US bank and travellers' cheques, and exchange most major currencies. Indeed, the casinos tend to offer better rates on currency than **American Express**. At non-casino hotels, you should be able to cash travellers' cheques at the front desk with photo ID.

American Express *Fashion Show Mall, 3200 Las Vegas Boulevard South, at Spring Mountain Road (739 8474, www.american express.com). Bus Deuce, 205, 203.* **Open** 9am-9pm Mon-Fri; 10am-8pm Sat; 11am-6pm Sun. **Map** p335, p336 A6.

Lost/stolen credit cards

American Express *1-800 992 3404, travellers' cheques 1-800 221 7282, www.americanexpress.com.*
Diners Club *1-800 234 6377, www.dinersclub.com.*
Discover *1-800 347 2683, www.discovercard.com.*

MasterCard *1-800 622 7747, www.mastercard.com.*
Visa *1-800 847 2911, www.visa.com.*

Tax

Sales tax is 8.1%; food (groceries) purchased in stores are exempt. Room tax is 12%.

NATURAL HAZARDS

The most obvious hazards are the heat and sun, but summer visitors should be prepared for other severe weather: flash floods are not uncommon in July and August.

OPENING HOURS

The casinos, their bars and at least one of their restaurants or coffeeshops are open all day, every day. Many grocery stores, dry-cleaners and gas stations are also open 24-7. On a local level, however, Las Vegas keeps small-town hours. Many eateries close at 10pm; non-chain shops may shut at 6pm and won't open on Sundays. Office hours are 9am to 5pm or thereabouts.

POLICE

For emergencies, dial **911**. For non-emergencies, there's a police station at 400 E Stewart Avenue, just off Las Vegas Boulevard in Downtown (795 3111).

POSTAL SERVICES

US mailboxes are red, white and blue. Packages weighing more than 16 ounces must be taken to a post office (*see below*). For couriers and shippers, *see p311*.

Stamps are sold in shops and from machines. For most transactions, contract stations in Albertsons stores should suffice. For your nearest post office, call 1-800 275 8777 and quote the zip code.

Main post office *1001 E Sunset Road, at Paradise Road, East of Strip (1-800 275 8777). Bus 212.* **Open** 8am-9pm Mon-Fri; 8am-4pm Sat. **Map** p333 Y4.
Downtown station *201 Las Vegas Boulevard South, between E Fremont Street & E Bonneville Avenue (1-800 275 8777). Bus Deuce & all DTC-bound buses.* **Open** 8.30am-5pm Mon-Fri. **Map** p334 D1.
Strip station *3100 Industrial Road, at Stardust Way, West of*

Strip *(1-800 275 8777). Bus Deuce, 105.* **Open** 8.30am-5pm Mon-Fri. **Map** p335 A5.

Poste restante

General delivery mail (*poste restante*) can be collected from the Downtown station (to: General Delivery, Las Vegas, NV 89101). You'll need to show photo ID when you collect it.

RELIGION

For your nearest **Episcopal** church, call 737 9190; and for **Methodist**, 369 7055. For others, consult the phone book.

Congregation Ner Tamid *55 Valley Verde Drive, Henderson (733 6292). Bus 112.* Jewish Reform.
First Baptist Church *4400 W Oakey Boulevard, West Las Vegas (821 1234). Bus 104.*
First Presbyterian Church *1515 W Charleston Boulevard, West of Strip (384 4554). Bus 206.* **Map** p335 B3.
Guardian Angel Cathedral *302 Cathedral Way, at E Desert Inn Road (735 5241). Bus Deuce.* **Map** p335 B5. The Catholic diocese of Reno-Las Vegas.
Islamic Center of Las Vegas *3799 Edwards Avenue, North-west Las Vegas (395 7013). Bus 106.*
Latter-Day Saints Las Vegas Temple *827 N Temple View Drive, East, Las Vegas (452 5011). Bus 208.*
The Church of Jesus Christ of Latter-day Saints (Mormons) only.
Temple Beth Sholom *10700 Havenwood Lane, Las Vegas (804 1333). Bus 211.* The city's oldest Jewish congregation.

SAFETY & SECURITY

There's less crime than you might expect in Las Vegas. Casinos have such elaborate security systems that few serious offences take place within them, and those that do occur are hurriedly swept under the carpet for the sake of reputation. However, on the streets, pickpockets and muggers strike more often than the city would like. Be careful, especially in the seedier areas of Downtown, and follow a few simple precautions.

● Only take out what you need: leave the bulk of your money in a room safe or in a safety deposit box at the hotel.

● Keep a note of the numbers and details of your passport, driving licence, travellers' cheques, cards and insurance policies, along with the phone numbers you'll need to report their loss (*see p314*).

● Take the usual precautions with your wallet or handbag, especially on buses.

● If you're threatened with a weapon, give your assailants what they want. Then immediately find a phone and call the police (**911**).

SMOKING

In 2007, smoking was banned in most establishments that serve prepared food (casinos and strip clubs were exempt). However, many businesses flouted the law, and it remains a matter for debate whether continued enforcement is possible. Smoking is ubiquitous on casino floors, though a couple have non-smoking areas. A few hotels (such as the Four Seasons) are entirely smoke-free; most others offer non-smoking rooms.

STUDY

Many local colleges feed the service and gaming industry. Those looking to learn how to become a dealer or croupier must attend one of the city's specialist dealer schools.

PCI Dealers School *90 Coronado Center Drive, Suite 140, Henderson, NV 89052 (877 4724, www.pcidealerschool.com).*

TELEPHONES

Dialling & codes

There are two area codes for Nevada: 702 for Clark County (including Las Vegas) and 775 for the rest of the state. Within Vegas, there's no need to use 702: just dial the seven-digit number. Outside the city, calls are long distance: dial 1, then the area code, then the number. The 1-800, 1-866, 1-877 and 1-888 codes denote toll-free numbers; many are accessible from outside the US, but you'll be charged for your call. Calls to 1-900 numbers will be charged at premium rates.

Most hotels charge a flat fee of between 50¢ and $1 for calls to local and toll-free numbers. You can get around this at some hotels by using a house phone and asking the operator to connect you. Long-

DIRECTORY

distance and international calls can be pricey if direct-dialled from a hotel. You're better off using a US phonecard, whether tied to a domestic account or bought as a one-off. Drugstores and convenience stores sell them in various denominations.

Mobile phones

Vegas operates on the 1900 GSM frequency.Travellers with modern tri-band phones will have no trouble using them.

Operator services

Collect calls (reverse-charge) 0. **Local directory enquiries** 411. **National directory enquiries** 1 + [area code] + 555 1212 (if you don't know the area code, dial 0 for the operator). **International calls** 011 + [country code] + [area code] + [number]. **International country codes** UK 44; New Zealand 64; Australia 61; Germany 49; Japan 81.

TIME

Nevada operates on Pacific Standard Time, eight hours behind GMT (London). Clocks go forward by an hour in late April, and back in late October. (Note: neighbouring Arizona has no daylight saving time.)

TIPPING

Tipping is a way of life in Vegas. Limo drivers ($10-$25 per ride), valet parking attendants ($2-$5), cocktail waitresses ($1-$2), housekeepers ($2-$4 a night) and even desk clerks ($10-$20 if you're looking for a better room) all ride the tip gravy train. For more

detailed information on tipping in casinos, *see p51*.

TOURIST INFORMATION

There are many self-styled tourist offices on the Strip, but only those listed below are official..

Las Vegas Chamber of Commerce *6671 Las Vegas Boulevard. South, Suite 300 Las Vegas, NV 89119 (735 1616, www.lvchamber.com). Bus 104, 408.* **Open** 8am-5pm Mon-Fri. **Map** p336 C6.
Advice, brochures, maps and a few coupons are available if you visit in person; there's also a good phone information service, and you can write in advance for a visitor pack.

Las Vegas Convention & Visitors Authority *3150 Paradise Road, opposite Convention Center Drive, East of Strip, Las Vegas, NV 89109 (892 0711, www.visit lasvegas.com). Bus 108, 213.* **Open** 8am-5pm Mon-Fri. **Map** p335 C5.
Write to the very excellent LVCVA for a visitor pack that includes lists of hotels, a brochure, a map and the regularly updated *Showguide*. In the UK, contact Cellet Travel Services for details on Vegas (01564 794999, www.visitlasvegas.co.uk).

VISAS & IMMIGRATION

Under the **Visa Waiver Program**, citizens of 27 countries, including the UK, Ireland, Australia and New Zealand, do not need a visa for stays in the US of less than 90 days (business or pleasure) if they have a passport valid for six months beyond the return date, a return (or open standby) ticket and

permission to travel through thElectronic System for Travel Authorization (ESTA) system (see www.cbp.gov/esta). Visitors must fill in the ESTA form and (and pay $14) at least 72 hours before travelling. Once granted, permission is valid for two years or until your passport expires.
Canadians and Mexicans do not need visas. All other travellers must have visas. Application forms can be obtained from your nearest US embassy or consulate.
UK travellers should check the US Embassy's website at http://london.usembassy.gov or call its helpline on 09042 450100.

WHEN TO GO

Though there's no off-season in Las Vegas, it's slightly quieter (and cheaper) between the Thanksgiving and Christmas holidays, and during the heat of July and August. Public holidays are always busy. If you're planning a short visit, try to avoid busy, pricey weekends. The convention schedule has a major effect on hotel prices and availability.

Climate

Las Vegas has blue skies and little rain all year round. In July and August, it can get absurdly hot during the day, with temperatures soaring to more than 110°F (43°C). Drink lots of water and wear a hat, sunglasses and sunscreen. Conversely, winter nights can dip below freezing.

Public holidays

1 Jan New Year's Day
3rd Mon in Jan Martin Luther King Jr Holiday
3rd Mon in Feb Presidents' Day
Mar/Apr Easter Sunday
last Mon in May Memorial Day
4 July Independence Day
1st Mon in Sept Labor Day
last Fri in Oct Nevada Day
2nd Mon in Nov Veterans' Day
4th Thur in Nov Thanksgiving
25 Dec Christmas Day.

WORK

To work, non-nationals must be sponsored by a US company and get an H-1 visa. They also have to convince immigration that no American is qualified to do the job. Contact your US embassy for details.

THE LOCAL CLIMATE

Average temperatures and monthly rainfall in Las Vegas.

	High (°C/°F)	Low (°C/°F)	Rainfall (mm/in)
Jan	14 / 57	3 / 37	15 / 0.59
Feb	17 / 63	5 / 41	18 / 0.69
Mar	21 / 69	8 / 47	15 / 0.59
Apr	26 / 78	12 / 54	4 / 0.15
May	31 / 88	17 / 63	6 / 0.24
June	37 / 99	22 / 72	2 / 0.08
July	40 / 104	26 / 78	11 / 0.44
Aug	39 / 102	25 / 77	11 / 0.45
Sept	34 / 94	21 / 69	8 / 0.31
Oct	27 / 81	14 / 57	6 / 0.24
Nov	19 / 66	7 / 44	8 / 0.31
Dec	14 / 57	3 / 37	10 / 0.40

Further Reference

BOOKS

Non-fiction

Al Alvarez *The Biggest Game in Town*
It's more than two decades old, but Alvarez's account of the World Series of Poker still fascinates.

Fred E Basten & Charles Phoenix *Fabulous Las Vegas in the 50s: Glitz, Glamor & Games*
A nostalgic full-colour collection of photographs, menus and postcards from the lost glory days of Vegas.

Susan Berman *Easy Street; Lady Las Vegas: The Inside Story Behind America's Neon Oasis*
Written by the daughter of a Mob insider, and made all the more creepy by her murder in 1999.

Christina Binkley
Winner Takes All: Steve Wynn, Kirk Kerkorian, Gary Loveman and the Race to Own Las Vegas
Wall Street Journal reporter takes you behind the back rooms and the eye in the sky to meet the moguls who created contemporary Las Vegas.

Bjourstad *Desert Rock: Rock Climbs in the National Parks*
A useful desert companion.

Jeff Burbank *License to Steal*
A detailed exposition of the legal side of Nevada gaming control and how it participated in building Las Vegas.

Norm Clarke *Norm Clarke's Vegas Confidential: Sinsational Celebrity Tales*
The dirt behind the dirt, by Vegas' premier newspaper gossip columnist.

Deke Castleman *Whale Hunt in the Desert: The Secret Las Vegas of Superhost Steve Cyr*
A fascinating glimpse into the world of the high roller, via one of the town's most powerful casino hosts.

Su Kim Chung *Las Vegas Then and Now*
Vintage photographs of Las Vegas, printed alongside images of the same locations in the 21st century. A nice idea, executed well.

John D'Agata *About a Mountain*
A dual meditation on the US government's plan to store nuclear waste in nearby Yucca Mountain – and on the toxic darkness of Vegas itself.

Sally Denton & Roger Morris *The Money and the Power: The Making of Las Vegas and Its Hold on America*
This investigative history of how Vegas was shaped and corrupted is perhaps the best single-volume history of the city.

Pete Early *Super Casino: Inside the 'New' Las Vegas*
A fizzing journalistic account of the 1990s revolution in resort-building.

William L Fox *In the Desert of Desire*
The nature of culture and the culture of nature in Las Vegas.

Steve Friess *Gay Vegas: A Guide to the Other Side of Sin City*
Comprensive exploration of the flip side of Las Vegas.

Jeff German *Murder in Sin City: The Death of a Las Vegas Casino Boss*
Reporter German explores the 1998 death of Ted Binion.

Mark Gottdiener, Claudia C Collins & David R Dickens *Las Vegas: The Social Production of an All-American City*
A fascinating look at the social phenomenon of Vegas, from how a city grows in the desert to what it means to live off the tourist dollar.

Rick Harrison *License to Pawn: Deals, Steals and My Life at the Gold & Silver*
True tales from the patriarch of the hit History Channel series Pawn Stars.

AD Hopkins & KJ Evans (eds) *The First 100: Portraits of the Men and Women Who Shaped Las Vegas*
A thought-provoking, well-written encyclopaedia.

Joan Burkhart Whitely *Young Las Vegas 1905-1931: Before the Future Found Us*
A photographic essay on the city's early years.

Paul McGuire *Lost Vegas: The Redneck Riviera, Existentialist Conversations With Strippers, and the World Series of Poker*
A vividly funny behind-the-curtain take on the adult playground.

Rick Lax *Fool Me Once: Hustlers, Hookers, Headliners, and How Not to Get Screwed in Vegas*
Clever and illuminating first-person study of deception, as personified by showgirls, call girls, card counters, magicians and pickup artists.

Shaun Levy *Rat Pack Confidential*
A modern, funky appraisal of the Rat Pack years and beyond.

David Littlejohn, Eric Gran *The Real Las Vegas: Life Beyond the Strip*
A writing team of UC Berkeley journalism graduate students look at how real life is lived in this 24/7 service economy and shed light on its implications and repercussions.

Eric Andrès Martinez *24/7: Living It Up and Doubling Down in the New Las Vegas*
An attorney and journalist spends his $50,000 advance in this modern-day *Fear and Loathing*.

Robert D McCracken *Las Vegas: The Great American Playground*
A mix of history and commentary, and a great read to boot.

James McManus *Positively Fifth Street: Murders, Cheetahs, and Binion's World Series of Poker*
McManus was sent on assignment to cover the 2000 World Series of Poker, but ended up taking part. Great fun.

Ben Mezrich *Busting Vegas: A True Story of Monumental Excess, Sex, Love, Violence and Beating the Odds*
Another gripping tale of card counters beating the house, by the author of *Bringing Down the House*, which inspired the movie *21*.

Eugene P Moehring & Michael S Green *Las Vegas: A Centennial History*
The best of the centennial books.

Matthew O'Brien *Beneath the Neon: Life and Death in the Tunnels of Las Vegas*
Vegas's subterranean homeless encampments.

Dick Odessky *Fly on the Wall: Recollections of Las Vegas' Good Old, Bad Old Days*
Very readable first-person tales of 1950s and '60s Vegas.

William F Roemer *The Enforcer: Spilotro – The Chicago Mob's Man over Las Vegas*
Vegas attorney Oscar Goodman kept Tony 'The Ant' Spilotro out of jail. Now Goodman is mayor and Spilotro is dead, beaten to death and buried in an Indiana cornfield.

Hal Rothman *Neon Metropolis: How Las Vegas Started the 21st Century*
Late UNLV history professor deconstructs Las Vegas's myth.

Hal Rothman & Mike Davis (eds) *The Grit Beneath the Glitter: Tales from the Real Las Vegas*
A spotty but often fascinating collection of essays about the city.
Geoff Schumacher *Sun, Sin and Suburbia: An Essential History of Modern Las Vegas*
The former editor of *Las Vegas CityLife* surveys the last few decades in readable fashion.
Cathy Scott *Murder of a Mafia Daughter: The Life and Tragic Death of Susan Berman*
Journo investigates the murder of the mafia daughter-turned-author.
John L Smith *No Limit: The Rise and Fall of Bob Stupak & Las Vegas' Stratosphere Tower; Running Scared: The Life and Treacherous Times of Las Vegas Casino King Steve Wynn; Of Rats and Men: Oscar Goodman's Life from Mob Mouthpiece to Mayor of Las Vegas; Sharks in the Desert: The Founding Fathers and Current Kings of Las Vegas*
Preposterously prolific *R-J* columnist dishes the dirt on two major casino players, the current mayor and the men who shaped the town.
Lyle Stuart *Howard Hughes in Las Vegas*
This history of a Vegas maverick gets behind the legend.
David Thomson *Into Nevada*
Musings on Nevada – its mining, nuclear and gambling history – by an expat Brit-Californian.
Nick Tosches *Dino*
Scorching biog of the Rat Packer.
Mike Tronnes (ed) *Literary Las Vegas*
A great anthology of journalism from 1952 to the late 1990s.
Robert Venturi, Steven Izenour & Denise Scott Brown *Learning from Las Vegas: The Forgotten Symbolism of Architectural Form*
Fascinating study of the auto-driven architecture of the Strip.
Mike Weatherford *Cult Vegas: The Weirdest! The Wildest! The Swingin'est Town on Earth*
Offbeat movies, ornery characters, unforgettable trivia, all explained in gossipy detail by an *R-J* columnist.

Fiction

Larry McMurtry *Desert Rose*
The *Terms of Endearment* writer turns his attention to the portrayal of a washed-up showgirl.
P Moss *Blue Vegas*
Characterful short stories by P Moss, owner of Downtown's character-filled Double Down saloon.

John O'Brien *Leaving Las Vegas*
Love, loneliness and alcoholism in the city of fun. Better than the film.
Wendy Perriam *Sin City*
Personal drama played out against an impersonal city.
Nicholas Pileggi *Casino: Love and Honour in Las Vegas*
Book of the film: a cracking read.
Tim Powers *Last Call*
A fantasia on the Las Vegas myth, in which Bugsy Siegel is the Fisher King and tarot cards the deck of choice at the Flamingo's poker tables.
Mario Puzo *Fools Die*
The *Godfather* author returns with another 'sweeping epic'.
Hunter S Thompson *Fear and Loathing in Las Vegas*
The drug-crazed classic is always worth re-reading.
Michael Ventura *The Death of Frank Sinatra*
Cracking private-eye story set among the implosions of the early 1990s.

Gambling

Gambling guides are many and varied, but a sizeable number are poorly researched and dangerously misleading. We recommend ordering material direct from renowned gambling experts **Huntington Press** (1-800 244 2224, www.huntingtonpress.com), which publishes all the books listed below.

Ian Andersen *Burning the Tables in Las Vegas: Keys to Success in Blackjack and in Life*
A high-stakes blackjack player reveals how he gets away with it.
Rick Garman *Las Vegas for Dummies*
Insider tips on game rules, jargon and how not to make a fool of yourself.
Bob Dancer *Video Poker for Winners*
Software tutor (download, PC only) on proper strategies for video poker. A must for players.
Max Rubin *Comp City: A Guide to Free Gambling Vacations*
Classic text on casino comps, now in its second edition. A hilarious read.
Jean Scott *The Frugal Gambler*
How to get the most from the least. A classic text.
Olaf Vancura & Ken Fuchs *Knock-Out Blackjack: The Easiest Card-Counting System Ever Devised*
This former astrophysicist's 'unbalanced' count eliminates most of the mental gymnastics of other systems. Not easy, but doable.

FILM

In addition to these movies, recent TV shows worth catching (either on TV or on tape) include **American Casino, Casino, CSI: Las Vegas** and **The Real World: Las Vegas**.

America's Sweethearts (2001)
Filmed in Lake Las Vegas. Stars Billy Crystal. Abysmal.
Bugsy (1991)
Witty script (James Toback), classy direction (Barry Levinson) and great performances (Beatty, Bening).
Casino (1995)
Martin Scorsese's three-hour mishmash of gambling and the Mob, voiceovered to death.
The Cooler (2003)
Set in Vegas (but filmed mostly in Reno). William H Macy stars.
Diamonds Are Forever (1971)
Bond (Connery, this time) in Vegas. Silly gadgets abound.
Fear and Loathing in Las Vegas (1998)
This relentless adaptation of the Thompson classic was a cult movie before it was even released.
Go (1999)
Doug Liman's follow-up to *Swingers* seems a little forced, but there are some good bits of business.
The Grand (2008)
Comedy with Woody Harrelson as an unlucky casino owner in the midst of a poker tournament.
Honeymoon in Vegas (1992)
Nicolas Cage in engagingly oddball comedy mode.
Leaving Las Vegas (1995)
This Mike Figgis masterpiece stars Cage as a self-destructive alcoholic.
Meet Me in Las Vegas (1956)
Problem gambler hooks up with Strip dancer in a familiar plot, brightened by Cyd Charisse as the dancer.
Ocean's 11 (1960)
With all the Rat Pack present, this kitschy, corny film has become the de facto video history of a romantic Vegas era. Soderbergh's 2001 *Ocean's Eleven* deploys George Clooney and chums in a surprisingly vigorous high-tech remake.
Ocean's Thirteen (2007)
The sequel to Eleven and Twelve, with the usual suspects in Vegas one more time.
One From the Heart (1980)
Coppola's Vegas love story, flawed but still somehow winning. Tom Waits and Crystal Gayle (duetting!) provide the beautiful soundtrack.

Rain Man (1988)
Dustin Hoffman's autistic
Raymond – and brother Charlie
(Tom Cruise) – finds his ability
to remember numbers comes in
handy in Vegas.
Showgirls (1995)
Some films that are universally
panned on release benefit from a
later reappraisal. Paul Verhoeven's
Vegas misadventure still isn't one
of them.
Swingers (1996)
First feature by Doug Liman: 90
minutes learning how not to pick
up girls. Vince Vaughn is still
trading off the kudos.
21 (2008)
Kevin Spacey leads a crew of
card-counting MIT students in
this thriller based on the book
Bringing Down the House.
Viva Las Vegas (1963)
Fun film for those nostalgic for the
old, swanky Vegas and the young,
svelte Elvis. Ann-Margret co-stars.
What Happens in Vegas (2008)
Ashton Kutcher and Cameron
Diaz: What the 21st century has
to settle for in lieu of Elvis and
Ann-Margret.
The Hangover (2009)
Gross-out buddy comedy with
Bradley Cooper, Ed Helms and
Zachgalifianakis piecing together
an epic blackout.

MUSIC

Beyonce *I Am … Yours:
An Intimate Performance
at Wynn Las Vegas*
The new-era diva as up-close as
you're ever going to get.
Noel Coward *Live at Las Vegas*
Astonishingly racy for its time, Sir
Noel's dry wit captured during his
1955 stand at the Desert Inn.
Crystal Method *Vegas*
This techno duo studied at UNLV.
Celine Dion *A New Day: Live in
Las Vegas*
The audio and visual record of
Queen Celine's history making
five-year stand at the Colosseum
at Caesars Palace. Elvis who?
David Holmes *Ocean's Eleven*
Funky, spunky soundtrack to the
Steven Soderbergh remake of the
Rat Pack classic.
The Killers *Hot Fuss*
Indie-rock from Vegas; the first
band from the town to make it
big in aeons.
Barry Manilow *Live From
Las Vegas*
Documentary DVD about
Manilow's long-running stint
as Elvis' successor at the Las
Vegas Hilton.

Wayne Newton *Wild, Cool
and Swingin'*
Back when he still had a voice.
Panic! At the Disco
A Fever You Can't Sweat Out
Theatrical indie rockers straight
out of Summerlin.
Elvis Presley *Live in Las Vegas*
As Elvis got fatter, his shows
got glammier. This box set is
all the fat Elvis you'll ever need,
and then some.
Louis Prima *Collectors Series*
Glorious, hard-swingin' lounge
stuff from the 1950s.
Frank Sinatra *Sinatra
at the Sands*
Classic recording of Frank backed
by the Count Basie Orchestra.
Various Artists *The Rat Pack:
Live at the Sands*
The definitive audio record of
Dino (on top form), Sammy and
the Chairman of the Board.

BLOGS & PODCASTS

**www.lasvegasadvisor.com/
whatsnews.cfm**
Anthony Curtis offers news
and tips on the Las Vegas
Advisor blog.
**www.lasvegassun.com/
blogs/kats-report**
In The Kats Report, personable
journalist John Kasilometes
interviews the citizens of the Strip.
http://dmckee.lvablog.com
The inside info from Dave
McKee's Stiffs & Georges
blog/podcast will make you
feel like a Vegas local.
**http://thestrippodcast.
blogspot.com**
Tireless journalist Steve
Friess provides big scoops and
Top Tourist Tips of the Week
on his blog and its companion
weekly podcast.
www.vegasdeluxe.com
Wondering where Robin
Leach went? He's here in Vegas,
schmoozing and boozing with
Vegas stars and starlets on this
blog and video podcast.

WEBSITES

www.bj21.com
Head here for the invaluable
monthly *Current Blackjack
News*, which details current
playing conditions at every
casino in the city.
www.cheapovegas.com
An excellent guide to Vegas
casinos, slanted towards
cash-poor travellers but with
enough useful information (and
fine writing) for all. Run by Big

Empire, which supplements it
with a guide to Vegas on 25¢ a
day (www.bigempire.com/vegas).
http://crecon.com/vintagevegas
Nothing here but images of classic
Vegas matchbooks, postcards and
gambling chips. Isn't that enough?
www.firstfriday-lasvegas.org
Information on Vegas's highly
successful monthly cultural event.
www.intercomm.com/koala
The Nevada Movie Page is a wide-
ranging look at the more than 500
movies made in or about the state.
www.knpr.org
Run by the local NPR affiliate,
this site has a great programming
archive with transcripts and
audio files.
www.lasvegas.com
Links to local news, event listings
and other resources.
www.lasvegasadvisor.com
The online version of the
gambling bible has all the latest
gambling tips, advice on how to
make the most of your cash, and
an always-interesting 'Question
of the Day' section.
www.lvrj.com
Your first stop for Vegas news.
The weekly eNeon newsletter is
a useful entertainment resource.
www.lasvegassun.com
Award-winning website of the
daily newspaper, with cool
interactive history features.
www.nextshooter.com/vegas
The latest news on craps in Vegas:
where to play and where to avoid.
www.vegas.com
This portal includes reviews of
bars and restaurants, and listings
of shows, films and nightlife.
A useful resource, even if the
reviews sometimes read a little
like PR copy.
**www.vegastodayand
tomorrow.com**
The design is a little loud and
rather 1999, but don't be fooled:
Mark Adams' labour of love,
documenting the extraordinary
wave of construction in the city
with maps, features and hearsay,
is perhaps the city's most vital
website right now.
www.visitlasvegas.com
The official consumer website
of the Las Vegas Convention &
Visitors Authority has all sorts
of information.
www.weddinginvegas.com
Planning to get hitched in Vegas?
Find information and ideas here.
http://wizardofodds.comA
phenomenally detailed survey of
casino games, including incisive
tips on where to find the best odds
in Vegas. An excellent site.

DIRECTORY

Content Index

INDEX

Venue Index

INDEX

INDEX

INDEX

INDEX

Maps

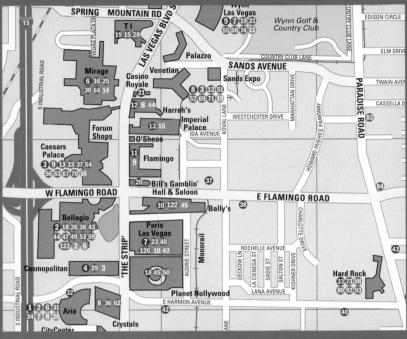

Major sight or landmark	
Major casino & hotel	
Park or forest	
Pedestrianised street	
One-way street	→
Interstate highway	80
US highway	95
State or provincial highway	75

Escapes and Excursions

50

Austin

93

6

50

15

6

A D A

Great Basin
National Park

70

Warm
Springs

U T A H

Extraterrestrial
Highway
(p303)

89

Nellis

Air Force

Base

Rachel

93

Zion
National Park
(p304)

Bryce Canyon
National Park

375

Caliente

*Lake
Powell*

Nevada

Test

Site

Nellis

Air Force

Base

93

St George

15

9

Springdale

89

Beatty

Amargosa
Valley

95

See p284

Grand Canyon
National Park
(p285)

67

89

160

*Spring Mtns
Recreation
Area*

Lake

North Rim
Village

Death Valley
Junction

Pahrump

Mead

Supai

Grand Canyon
Village

**Death
Valley
National
Park
(p295)**

127

**LAS
VEGAS**

National

Tusayan

180

Recreation

Jean

95

Area

64

180

Primm

93

66

Seligman

Williams

Baker

15

Nipton

160

40

Flagstaff

D E S E R T

Zzyzx

**Mojave
National Preserve
(p293)**

Laughlin
(p300)

Kingman

Kelso

*Providence
Mtns State
Rec Area*

89

Amboy

40

93

Twentynine
Palms

Colorado River

60

PHOENIX

Palm
Springs

*Joshua Tree
National Park*

10

*Salton
Sea*

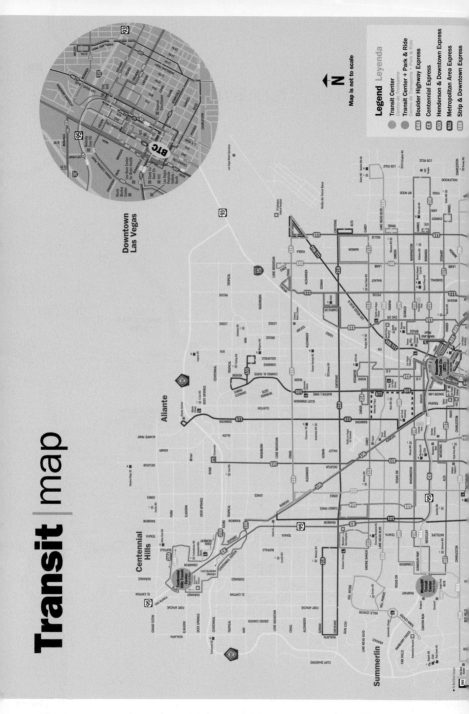

Transit | map

Downtown Las Vegas

Aliante

Summerlin

Centennial Hills

Legend Leyenda

Transit Center

Transit Center + Park & Ride

BHX Boulder Highway Express

CX Centennial Express

HDX Henderson & Downtown Express

MAX Metropolitan Area Express

SDX Strip & Downtown Express

N

Map is not to scale

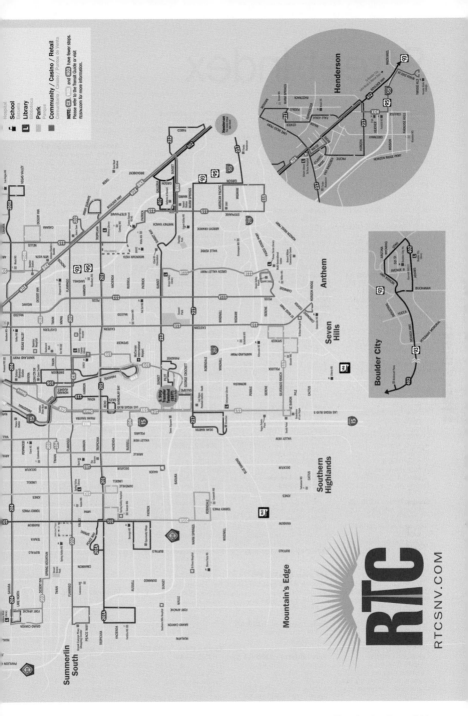

Street Index

STREET INDEX

Central
Las Vegas

X   Y   Z

W LAKE MEAD BOULEVARD

61 Texas Station

VEGAS DRIVE

W WASHINGTON AVENUE

W BONANZA ROAD

113

Lorenzi Park

Nevada State Museum

Las Vegas Springs Preserve

ALTA DRIVE

Las Vegas Premium Outlets

See p335

To Arizona Charlie's
W CHARLESTON BOULEVARD

W OAKEY BOULEVARD

Las Vegas Motor Speedway

604

W OWENS AVENUE

15

Moulin Rouge

Lied Discovery Children's Museum

Old LV Mormon Fort Historic Park

Cashman Field

LV Natural History Museum

95

515

GRAND CENTRAL PKWY

MAIN STREET

LAS VEGAS BOULEVARD

FREMONT STREET

DOWNTOWN

Arts Factory

See p334

159

E WASHINGTON AVENUE

S PECOS ROAD

1

Desert Pines Golf Course

E WYOMING AVENUE

E OAKEY BOULEVARD

MAIN ST

S MARYLAND PARKWAY

FREMONT STREET

BOULDER HWY

93

2

515

Stratosphere

589

Palace Station

41 **116**

Circus Circus

Las Vegas Hilton

THE STRIP

Riviera

Las Vegas Country Club

E SAHARA AVENUE

86 **87** Commercial Center

Las Vegas ConventionCenter

S EASTERN AVENUE

To Sam's Town & Boulder Station

95

SANDHILL ROAD

Fashion Show Mall

119 **118**

SPRING MOUNTAIN ROAD

TI

Wynn Las Vegas

Palazzo
Venetian

SANDS AVENUE

Monorail

TWAIN AVENUE

94

E DESERT INN ROAD

38

36

115

Las Vegas Hilton Country Club

To Henderson, Lake Mead, Boulder City & Laughlin

3

36 **96**
122

Mirage

59
Rio

Caesars Palace

Harrah's
Imperial Palace
Flamingo

E FLAMINGO ROAD

120

d
st

95 **98** **99**
0 **23** **24**

Palms

Bellagio

Cosmopolitan

Bally's
Paris LV

Planet Hollywood

PARADISE ROAD

117

UNLV

E HARMON AVENUE

114

CityCenter
Monte Carlo
New York
New York

Orleans

17

593
46

Excalibur

Tropicana

Luxor

Mandalay Bay

15

HARMON AVE

Showcase Mall
MGM Grand

Hooters

Hard Rock

SWENSON ST

Thomas & Mack Center

40

37

S MARYLAND PARKWAY

E TROPICANA AVENUE

39

40

S EASTERN AVENUE

MCLEOD DRIVE

S PECOS ROAD

McCarran International Airport

See p336

604

46

E SUNSET ROAD

562

S VALLEY VIEW BOULEVARD

LAS VEGAS BOULEVARD SOUTH

4

To Sunset Station

1 Casinos & Hotels pp98–152
1 Restaurants & Buffets pp153–178
1 Bars & Lounges pp179–189

0   1 mile

0   1 km

© Copyright Time Out Group 2012

Sunset Park

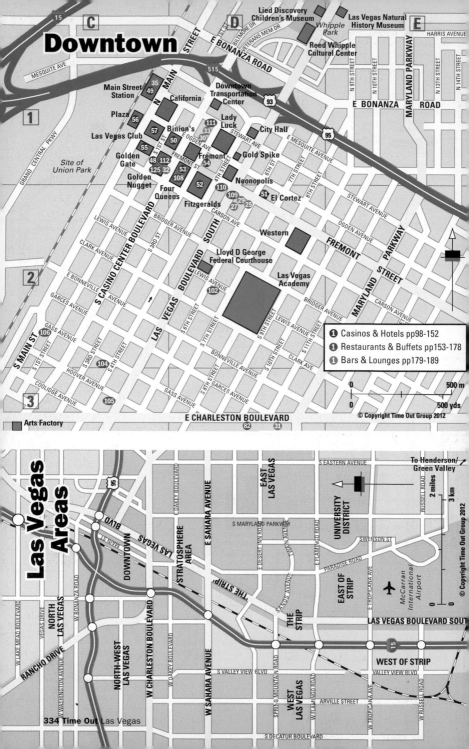